# Three Years Aboard A Navy Destroyer

3/24 to 4/9/23

# Three Years Aboard A Navy Destroyer

## USS BRUSH(DD745)

### Pacific Fleet
### (1952 – 1955)

OTIS TED HOLLY

Order this book online at www.trafford.com
or email orders@trafford.com

Most Trafford titles are also available at major online book retailers.



Printed in the United States of America.

ISBN: 978-1-4269-4181-8 (sc)
ISBN: 978-1-4269-4794-0 (e)

*Trafford rev. 04/18/2011*

www.trafford.com

**North America & international**
toll-free: 1 888 232 4444 (USA & Canada)
phone: 250 383 6864 • fax: 812 355 4082

As the son of one of the USS Brush's skippers identified in Ted Holly's book I was particularly fascinated to read of his and his shipmates' many and varied experiences during their three Far East cruises. His folksy stories of a young man's explorations of the vastness of the oceans, the wonders of the orient, and the uncertainties of combat are told in a detailed and entertaining style offering multiple layers of insight to life aboard a "tin can" in the 1950's. In addition to his prose, Mr. Holly has included many photographs and maps which enhance and elucidate the storytelling. It is a terrific read for anyone interested in the naval service in general and the "unforgotten" Korean War in particular.

Dennis Quigley

It was interesting as well as enlightening to finally learn of the experiences my brother had while he was in the navy during the time of the Korean "conflict". Very well written and enjoyable.

Fay Rogers

...the straightforward and unglossed memories of a young sailor, out of high school and soon into a U.S. destroyer, "greyhound of the seas". Ted Holly was everybody's favorite sailor, squared away with a great attitude in a key job around the nerve center of a 2200 tonner loaded for whatever kind of scrap. This book is an honest snapshot of the times, the people, and the ships that sailed to the Korean Conflict.

Ted Brown, LT USNR Ret

**This book is dedicated to my late wife, Carolyn, the love of my life.**

**And to all old U.S. Navy Destroyer sailors.**

# PREFACE

I reported aboard the USS Brush(DD745) for duty in late August, 1952, and served on her until late October, 1955. I've always thought that the men, and boys, who served on the Brush during that period of time had a memorable experience, and a story that was worth telling and should be told. At long last, I took it upon myself to write that story.

For many years I have thought about writing this book – some day – about my seafaring years aboard the Brush, but I always seemed to be too busy with life to commence such a task. You know, I was busy with such time consuming things as going to college, working and earning a living, raising a family, and being involved in a number of organizational activities. But finally events in my life, in 2005, forced me to stop thinking about it and start writing it. I realized that time was running out for me, that there is no certainty of tomorrow, and that I had to start writing the book now or it might never get done.

I started writing this book in October 2005 and it took 5 years and over 4000 hours to complete it. So, it wasn't exactly a small task, and I suppose that is the main reason it took so long for me to get around to doing it. Although, I rather enjoyed writing it once I got started, because I was finally putting into written words many of the things that I had thought about for many years from time to time – since leaving the ship and the navy. In fact, I've thought about some of the things that took place back then almost every day of my life for the last 50 years. Some things you don't forget, you know. I deeply regret, though, that it took over 50 years for me to get around to writing this book. I should have written it 20, 30, or 40 years ago. If I had, maybe I would have remembered more things to write about. And maybe more of my old shipmates would be alive to read about that period of time in their lives. I know some of them have died in recent years. Maybe some of the descendents of these men would like to read about what their father or grandfather did in his youth.

I would also think that the crew members, and their descendents, of the other ships of Destroyer Division 92 – the Maddox, Moore, and the Thomas – would have a special interest in reading this book. Because these ships operated together much of the time, went to the same places, and engaged in similar duties and activities.

In addition, there were a rather large number of other destroyers that operated in the Pacific during the Korean War era and for years afterwards, too. I believe the sailors on all these ships could relate to this story also since we all had similar duties, experiences, and went to the same liberty ports.

Furthermore, if I had written this book sooner, maybe I would have remembered more names of my old shipmates. Unfortunately, and regrettably, I've forgotten the names of many of them, probably most of them. However, I do remember the names of the bridge gang, the quartermasters, because I worked with them almost every day, and for years in most cases. Forgetting their names would be about like forgetting my own. I also still remember the Morse code even though I haven't used it for over 50 years.

I obtained the information to write this book largely from 3 sources – my memory, the ship's logs, and old letters that I wrote to my mother and that she kept. But, unfortunately, she didn't keep all of them, or if she did, they haven't been found. I also got some information, stories or pictures from a few of my old shipmates.

As a quartermaster on the Brush, I spent much of my time on the bridge. And one of the duties of a quartermaster at that time was to keep a log of all the things that took place on and around the ship when it was underway. This record of events was jotted down in the quartermaster's notebook from which the official ship's log was written by the officers – the OOD on duty during each watch. Consequently, I probably wrote this book from a quartermaster's perspective and put a lot of emphasis on the times and places that events took place – like I did as a quartermaster.

All of us on the ship experienced many of the same things, particularly in regards to the places that the Brush went and the activities that she was engaged in. We all have those experiences in common. We all had our own personal experiences also and thus have our own individual stories. I am primarily telling my story in this book and actually that is the only one I know. All my old shipmates would have somewhat of a different story to tell because they had different experiences than I had. If another shipmate would like to have his story told, then he is going to have to write it himself because he is the only one that knows it.

As I previously mentioned, I went aboard the Brush in August, 1952, and left it in late October, 1955 – a period of 3 years and 2 months. During that period of time the Brush made 3 seven month cruises to the Far East. The first cruise was in early 1953 and during the latter months of the Korean War. The Brush played her part in that conflict and actually had a total of 3 tours of duty to Korea during the war. We were there when the war ended. And I would say that we had a very interesting tour of duty off the coast of North Korea in 1953, which I have written about in considerable detail in this book. I know the crew of the Brush returned to the States with a lot of memories of the things that we experienced. And I'm sure they still often think about some of the things that happened during that cruise over 50 years ago, that is, if they are still living.

Our other 2 cruises to the Far East were also quite interesting, looking back on them, especially from my personal experiences aspect. Although, on the second cruise, we did go into harm's way a couple of times and maybe even a third time. The third cruise was more of a peace time cruise and I don't remember us doing anything especially dangerous. However, we did have to dodge a number of bad typhoons and were in a lot of rough water. And I had a number of interesting personal experiences.

Sailors in the U.S. Navy serve on many different types of ships and vessels – those not on shore duty. All of these ships have an important job to do in the navy otherwise they wouldn't exist. But it is my conviction that serving on an older type destroyer, especially during war time, is the ultimate sea-going experience for a navy man, because of all the different types of activities that those ships engage in, the Spartan living conditions on that type of ship, and living closely with the elements – such as the wind, waves, storms, cold weather, hot weather, and the fact that they stayed at sea so much. And they are considered by many to be the roughest riding ships in the navy. Destroyers were also sometimes referred to as "tin cans" because of their thin hulls. The hull was only ¼ inch thick.

I have attempted to inform the readers of this book what our lives were like on these ships. In addition, I have included in considerable detail all the activities and actions the ship was involved in over the 3 years and 2 months that I was aboard her. I also have written a great deal about my personal experiences – the things that I saw, and did, and my biased opinion on a number of issues.

# Acknowledgements

I would like to acknowledge Mildred Van Fleet and Brenda Dasef for the many hours they spent on a computer putting this book in a printed form for me. I greatly appreciate their efforts. Another person, Kay Holton, also helped some in this respect. I appreciate her efforts, too.

In addition, there were a number of people that contributed something to this book in the way of either pictures, stories, or both, and in one case, a poem. The contributors were mostly old shipmates, but not entirely. These people include Willie and Jeanie Nash, Joseph and Dixie Valentine, Lloyd and Jean McCord, Henry Gardner, Sammie Baker, William (Robbie) Robbins, Russell Maxwell, Dennis Quigley, Robert Bodoh, Theodore S. (Ted) Brown, George T. Bailey, A.O. (Jack) Easterling, Tom and Marci Barth, Beuford and Elouise Randall, and Frank L. Johnson.

I obtained copies of the ship's logs from the National Archives – logs for all the 38 months that I was aboard her.

I would also like to thank Terry Miller, Editor of The Tin Can Sailors Newspaper, for permitting me to use two maps that appeared in that newspaper.

And lastly, I would like to give credit to the company, Real War Photos, Ann Arbor, Michigan for providing me with several great ship photos that are identified in my book as U.S. Navy Photographs. The picture shown on the front of the book is also a U.S. Navy Photograph. The National Archives and Records Administration (NARA), however, is the original source of these pictures.

# CONTENTS

# LIST OF MAPS

## DESTROYER DUTIES IN THE FLEET

The U.S. Navy has many different types of ships and they all have important roles to play in the navy's scheme of things. But it is the carriers, battleships, cruisers, and destroyers that are regarded in the navy as the major combatant ships, or were. The battleships are now considered obsolete and are no longer in service. The submarines fit into the picture somewhere, but they are sort of in a category by themselves. However, it is the lowly destroyer that is considered the navy's most versatile warship. They are capable of performing a number of different tasks, and they have a lot of firepower for ships their size. They are actually the navy's close-in fighting ships even though they are the smallest.

The destroyers engage in close-in shore bombardments; they attack other ships with shells and torpedoes; they attack submarines with depth charges, hedgehogs, and gunfire; they shoot planes out of the sky with their 5 inch guns and rapid fire 40mm, 20mm, and 3 inch guns; they escort larger ships and try to protect them from submarine and airplane attacks. One of the main duties of a destroyer is to protect the heavier ships from harm if they can, and in anyway they can, even if it means sacrificing themselves to do it. That duty was gallantly carried out a number of times during World War II in the Pacific theatre with great loss of life of the destroyer sailors involved. The destroyers are called upon to do a lot of patrolling at times. They also sometimes participate in covert operations where they put troops ashore behind enemy lines and give them gunfire support if they need it. In addition, destroyers escort minesweepers while they conduct minesweeping operations in coastal waters. The destroyers also go on search and rescue missions when that need arises. Actually, they are called on to do just about whatever comes up.

The old United States Navy destroyers were very sensitive to the motion of the ocean and tended to roll constantly unless they were tied up to a pier or a buoy in a protected and calm harbor. Of course, in rough seas they tended to do a lot of pitching, too. So, when the seas were rough, they did a lot of pitching and rolling at the same time. Consequently, learning to walk on the swaying and pitching deck of a destroyer was quite a different experience for a new seaman. In fact, sometimes walking on the deck of a destroyer could be a rather difficult undertaking for an experienced seaman; because one second you were walking uphill, so to speak, and the next second you were going downhill, and at the same time the roll of the ship was pitching you from side to side. After awhile, though, it just became a way of life. These old destroyers had the reputation of being the roughest riding ships in the navy and from what I experienced, they have rightfully earned that reputation.

In addition, the crews of old destroyers had very Spartan living conditions. In my opinion, the welfare of the crew wasn't given too much consideration when these ships were being designed and built. They were primarily built to fight on, not to live on.

Of course, I have been writing about how things were in the old navy. I'm sure many things are done very differently in the modern navy. I know destroyers in the modern navy have totally different types of weapons than were used during the period of time that I was in the navy. In addition, modern-day destroyers are much larger than the old World War II type destroyers. I hope they have a lot better living accommodations for their crews.

## To the Men who Sail Destroyers

Anonymous

There's a roll and a pitch
And a heave and a hitch
To the nautical gait they take.
For they're used to the cant
Of decks aslant
As the white toothed combers break.

On the plates that thrum
Like a beaten drum
To the thrill of the turbine's might,
And the knife bow leaps
Through the mighty deep
With the speed of a shell in flight.

Oh! Their scorn is quick,
For the crews that stick
To the battleship's steady floor.
For they love the lurch
Of their own frail porch,
At thirty knots or more.

They don't get much
Of the drill and such
That the battleship jockeys do.
But they sail the seas in their dungarees,
A grimy destroyer crew.

They don't climb,
At their sleeping time,
To a hammock that sways and bumps.
But leap "kerplunk' to a cozy bunk,
That quivers and bucks and jumps.

They hear the sound of the waves that pound
On the quarter inch plates of steel.
And they close their eyes to the lullabies
Of the creaking sides and keel.

They're a lusty crowd
That's vastly proud
Of the slim grey craft they drive.
Of the roaring screws and the humming flues
That make her a thing alive.

They love the lunge of her surging plunge,
And the murk of her smoke screen, too.
As they sail the seas in their dungarees.
A grimy destroyer crew.

# 1

# BEATING AROUND AFTER HIGH SCHOOL

I graduated from Haines City High School, Haines City, Florida on June 7, 1951. The Korean War was in full swing and I knew I was faced with the draft, military service, and probably going to Korea. That really didn't bother me too much, however, because I recognized the fact that I didn't have anything especially going for me and a hitch in the military might be a good move. As far as I could tell, I didn't have anything better to do. There were several things I realized about my situation. I fully realized I didn't know a thing about how to make a living for myself. I knew I didn't have a skill of any kind that could be converted to any significant dollars and I didn't see any opportunity to learn one. Essentially, all I knew how to do at 18 years old, fresh out of high school, was to hunt, fish, play basketball, and hoe orange groves. None of those things paid very well.

I suppose I could have gone to college, maybe, but I wasn't interested in going to college at that time in my life because I was sick of school. In fact, I never liked going to school in the first place. I went because I had to; although, I was wise enough to understand that going to school was something every one had to do if they wanted to get very far in life. Unfortunately, because of my dislike for school, I spent much of my time in the classroom looking out the window and wishing I was out there. I hated being cooped up inside on a beautiful day. I wanted to be outside doing something interesting like hunting, fishing, roaming the woods, going to the beach, just loafing around, and such things. To me, being inside on a beautiful day was a wasted day. I knew what my long term goal in life was, however; I wanted to own lots of land, cattle, and orange groves, but that dream was way down the road somewhere.

So, really, the biggest decision I had to make upon graduating from high school was which branch of the U.S. armed services I wanted to join – the U.S. Army, Navy, Marine Corps, Coast Guard, or Air Force. In an attempt to help me decide which branch of service to enter, an army recruiter came to my home twice during the latter months of my senior year to explain to me the advantages of joining the army. I listened to what he had to say with somewhat of an open mind and saw the advantages of what he was offering me. One of the things he told me was that I would only have to join the army for 3 years instead of 4 years like some of the other branches. He also guaranteed me that the army would assign me to the tank corps, and I would get to spend my entire time in the army at Fort Benning, Georgia after basic training. He thought that was a strong enticement for me to join the army, because Fort Benning was a much safer place to be than Korea. It would have been a smart thing to do – to accept his offer of a safe hitch at Fort Benning; although, I'm not sure he could actually guarantee me being assigned to the tank corps, or spending my entire time at Fort Benning. The army, as well as the other services, has a practice of sending troops to wherever they are needed, whenever they are needed, regardless of promises.

I never accepted his offer and I never told him why. I didn't accept his offer, or join his army, because, to me, spending 3 years in the army at Fort Benning didn't seem like an exciting thing to do. I had the notion that if I went into the military, I wanted to go places and do things and not stay in one place and be bored to death even if it was safer.

Frankly, deciding which branch of the military service I wanted to join wasn't that big of a decision to make. I had already given it a lot of thought during my senior year of school and had pretty much made up my mind that I wanted to go to sea. Consequently, the navy was the branch of service I was probably going to join; although, the coast guard and merchant marine were also considerations. I wasn't interested in being a seaman forever, just for a few years during my younger years.

I had read a number of seafaring books during my young life and going to sea on big ships seemed to me like an interesting and adventurous thing to do. I liked the idea of going to faraway places with strange sounding names. Besides, ships always fascinated me and still do. One of the books that influenced my thinking the most, I believe, was entitled "Two Years before the Mast". However, I really wasn't quite ready to do that either, to go to sea, immediately after graduating from high school. Actually, all I really wanted to do after graduating from high school was just loaf around for a few months and enjoy myself before joining the navy or whatever else I might get involved with. I especially wanted to spend some time around the Ocala National Forest area where I had spent all my life prior to my family moving to the Haines City area, or Dundee, to be exact. I wanted to roam the woods again and fish in some of the old familiar lakes one more time before heading off into military service and who knows what. In addition, I wanted to spend some time in the mountains of western North Carolina where my mother grew up and where I had spent the previous summer getting acquainted with my relatives, enjoying the mountains, and learning about my mountaineer heritage. I like to tell people that I am half redneck and half hillbilly. I greatly enjoyed my visit there the previous summer and wanted to experience it again.

In order to finance this venture, I needed some money so I got a job at the Dundee Citrus Packinghouse, which was just a few blocks down the street from my home. It was the only job available to me that I knew about and I could even walk to work. At the packing house I was given a job that was called "trucking fruit". Trucking fruit involved loading semi-trailers and railroad boxcars with boxes of packed citrus fruit. The job consisted of operating an upright handcart on wheels, or a "truck", as they were called. The "truckers" would pick up boxes of packed fruit at the packing lines that were stacked 4 to 5 boxes high and weighed 400 to 500 pounds. I was 18 years old and weighed 130 pounds at the time. I, or we, would take, or "truck", these boxes of fruit from the packing lines to the semi-trailers and boxcars. Sometimes we would have to push these boxes of fruit up a steep ramp, which was several feet long, up into the trailers or boxcars. We would have to get a running start to accomplish this and hoped we had enough momentum to get up to the top of the ramp. Sometimes we didn't, which always created a little problem like the boxes falling off the trucks onto the ramp or floor. It certainly didn't do the fruit any good and created extra work, too.

Most of time the truckers would have to "truck" boxes of fruit all day long without much slack time or rest. We worked at a run much of the time. Trucking fruit was a hard, hot job and we stayed soaking wet with sweat most of the time, but I was thankful for the job because it gave me the opportunity to make some money and that certainly was more than I had. My career at the Dundee Packinghouse was short, however, because in a month or so I was able to save a couple hundred dollars and I hit the road. Of course, back then you could buy a coke for 5 cents and a hamburger for a quarter. So a little money went a long ways and I had enough to last me for several weeks.

## OCALA AREA

I first spent a couple of weeks around the Ocala area staying with one relative and another. I hadn't seen any of them very much for 2 years. I spent a few days with my aunt Agnes Fort in Ocala and that was somewhat my headquarters while I was in Marion County. I also spent a couple nights with my cousin Billy Holly out in the Ocala National Forest. He lived at the old James Preston Holly place, my grandfather's homesite, and where my father was born and spent the first 34 years of his life. My uncle Pat Holly now owned the old estate of around 700 acres. I spent some time exploring the "Old Place" as we called it. I was always fascinated by the "Old Place" because there was so much family history associated with it. Billy hadn't been married too long during this summer. His wife's name was `Helen. She was a little on the mannish side. She treated me just fine and I liked her. However, that marriage didn't last because of irreconcilable differences and ended in divorce while I was in the navy. I also spent a day or two with my aunt Essie Randall and her family who also lived in the forest at Lacota.

My aunt Agnes and her husband, Chester Fort, owned a little house on North Lake in the forest, which they called the "Camp" and spent all the time they could there to get away and do some fishing. They actually owned the entire east side of North Lake and all the way back to Highway 40, plus another couple hundred acres on the north side of Highway 40 – an estate of around 650 to 700 acres. The properties were originally owned by his father, Norman Fort, and his uncle, Tobe Fort. So, my aunt and uncle had a very private little fish camp. It was also kind of a family gathering place, too.

### Catching a Big Fish – Almost

Agnes and Chester decided to spend a few days at the camp while I was in the area and invited me to go with them, which I did. So, for the next 4 to 5 days we rested and fished. We caught some fish, bass, off the dock and out in the lake around the grass but not enough to get too excited about. One afternoon my uncle Chester decided he wanted to fish in a little clear lake he owned on the north side of State Road 40 near the Levy Hammock Road. It didn't have a name as far as I know. There was a rowboat in the little lake that was owned by his cousin who fished in the little lake occasionally. Uncle Chester normally didn't fish in this lake at all.

We got to the little lake and all three of us started fishing with fishing poles and shiners. I hadn't fished too long before I got hung on the bottom – I thought. I started pulling on the line to either break loose or break the line. I was pretty disgusted with the situation. Finally, whatever I was hung on to started coming to the surface. The object surfaced and it turned out to be the biggest bass's back that I had ever seen, certainly the biggest one that had ever been on one of my hooks. The big fish looked the situation over on the surface for 3 or 4 seconds, made a roll, broke the line, and went on his way. I think all 3 of us were amazed at the size of it when we saw it and totally sick a few seconds later when it got away. It must have weighed 12 – 15 pounds. We fished a little while longer but didn't have any more action. We were so disgusted about losing that big fish that we just quit and went back to the Camp.

## Fish Feasting on Mayflies

Something happened while we were staying at the camp on this occasion that I had never seen before and have never seen since after all these years. I got up one morning, walked down to the lake, and discovered that hordes of mayflies were flying across the lake from west to east and we were on the east side. There must have been millions of them. Mayflies look somewhat like dragonflies, or mosquito hawks, but don't have as big a head. They have similar looking wings and long slender bodies. I never knew where these mayflies were coming from and I didn't know where they thought they were going. I did observe right off, though, that thousands of them weren't going to make it to their destination.

I was standing on the dock and as I looked out across the lake, I saw just hundreds of splashes in the water all over the lake, as far as I could see. Every time a mayfly would hit the water, a fish would get him almost immediately. I noticed that the mayflies that landed in the water near the dock on which I was standing were eaten within 3 or 4 seconds of hitting the water. The fish were literally having a feeding frenzy all over the lake. As I began to realize what was going on with all this feeding activity, I thought to myself, "Man, this is a tremendous opportunity to catch some fish."

I went into the house and told Uncle Chester what was going on down at the lake with all the mayflies flying about, that it looked to me like an excellent time to catch some fish. Uncle Chester told me that he had seen this situation before and had tried to fish with the mayflies, but they were too little to put on a hook and you couldn't catch any fish with them. He was so convinced that you couldn't catch any fish with the mayflies that I didn't try to. After all, he had already tried it and it couldn't be done.

I watched fish eating mayflies all day long. They weren't interested in eating anything else either. The mayflies flew all night and were still flying across the lake by the thousands the next morning. It didn't look like there was ever going to be an end to them. About 10:00 o'clock in the morning I decided I had to at least make an attempt at catching some fish while these mayflies were flying. I found me a small hook – a bait-catching size hook. I gathered me up some mayflies that had gotten caught on some spider webs and went out in the lake a little ways in the boat. I put a mayfly on this very small hook and threw it on the water. A fish got it immediately. I started catching fish. At least half the fish that took the mayfly bait got off the hook. In just a few minutes, however, I caught and put in the boat 3 huge bluegill bream and 1 small bass. All of a sudden, I realized that something had changed. I looked around me and noticed that there was no more splashing taking place. Furthermore, I noticed that there weren't any more mayflies to be seen. It was over. I only took advantage of the last 20 to 30 minutes of that tremendous opportunity to catch a boatload of fish. At least I now knew I could catch fish with mayflies, and if I ever encountered this opportunity again I knew what to do. Unfortunately, I have never seen mayflies flying in those numbers again, so I've never had the opportunity to fish with them.

## I Register for the Draft

Somewhere along the line, I finally got around to registering for the draft in Ocala, Marion County. I was only a few weeks late doing so and the woman registering me quizzed me kind of close on that fact. I told her that I was going to join the navy right away, in a few weeks, so she let it go and didn't ask me any more questions about it. However, from her attitude, I'm sure she would have seen to it that I was put at the top of the draft list if I hadn't told her that I was joining the navy right away.

## A Disappointing Detour

I left the Ocala area after a stay of a couple of weeks and headed in the direction of western North Carolina. However, on the way out of the state I made a little detour to Baker County to visit a family I knew that once were our neighbors in the forest at Lynne. They were our neighbors for a year or two; I don't remember exactly how long, but they had moved back to their home in Baker County 9 years prior to the summer of 1951. We hadn't seen any of them since they moved away. However, my mother had kept in touch with this family through the years by means of the mail. There wasn't any phone service in rural areas back then, so there wasn't any opportunity to do any visiting by phone.

At the time we were neighbors this family had 3 little girls, the oldest one being 7 years old when they first moved to Lynne. I was 8 years old, a year older than her. I liked the 7 year old girl very much. She was blond-headed and quite pretty, I thought. We played together a lot and spent a great deal of time just hanging around together. We were big buddies as kids and neighbors and I was very sad when she moved away. We did write each other occasionally for a few years, but not after I was 12 or 13 years old. So, by the summer of 1951 I hadn't seen my special childhood friend for 9 years. I had often thought about her over the years but had never had the opportunity to go see her. In addition, I was involved with growing up and teenage things and I suppose she was, too. Anyway, I thought it would be nice to see my childhood pal again and that is the main reason I wanted to visit this particular family.

I hitchhiked to Baker County to a little place, a little spot in the road, called Sanderson where I got on the road that led to the little out-of-the-way community where they lived. The road to their community was paved but not much traveled. I hadn't been standing by the side of the road very long when this half-ton truck came along and stopped to pick me up. The truck had high sideboards and was fully loaded with stuff. I believe it was the first vehicle to come along since I had been standing there. The truck stopped right beside me; I looked into the truck and on the passenger side, lo and behold, if it wasn't the fellow I was going to visit. I recognized him immediately, but I had to introduce myself to him because he hadn't seen me since I was 8 or 9 years old. Besides that, he wasn't expecting to see me standing by the side of the road near where he lived. So, we had a little reunion by the side of the road for a few minutes. I told him I was coming to pay him a visit, which was fine with him. He was always a very friendly and likeable fellow and everybody who knew him liked him. There had also been an amiable relationship with him and members of my mother's family for many years. So, I didn't have any reservations about visiting this family, unexpectedly, because I felt like I would be accepted somewhat like a close relative.

The only place for me to ride, however, was on top of his load and that is where I rode the 15 miles or so to the community where he lived. You could certainly say it was off the beaten path. The ride on top of the load was kind of windy, but it was better than walking. As I was riding down the road, I began to look around to see what my friend was hauling. I noticed that the load consisted of 100 pound sacks of sugar and corn, some wire, and some big 5 gallon jugs. There might have been other things, but those are the things that I remember. I didn't know too much about the moonshine trade, but the load looked mighty suspicious to me like it could be used for that purpose.

We finally arrived at the little community where my friend lived. It developed that he owned a little country store that was located next door to his home. It soon became obvious to me that my friend had a thriving business at his store supplying moonshiners with the things they needed to operate their businesses. The whole deal was wide open and nobody was trying to hide anything. Moonshining, I learned, was the main local industry and anyone engaged in it didn't seem to worry about getting caught by the feds. There must have been a lot of "paying off" going on somewhere. I'm sure there couldn't have been too many opportunities available to make money back in those piney woods and swamps near the St. Mary's River and the Georgia line.

I stayed with the family for a day or so and part of the time I hung out in and around the store. There was a lot of coming and going at the store and I overheard a lot of conversations. People talked about their moonshine operations like people in other places talk about growing corn or peanuts. I couldn't believe my ears at some of the discussions I heard. I learned later on that Baker County was considered to be the moonshining capital of Florida at the time and was for a good many years afterwards. Eventually, though, the law did crackdown on the moonshiners and put some of them in jail, so I was told years later by an ex-moonshiner from that area, and who was one of the ones who went to jail.

Of course, I saw my old childhood friend and playmate while I was staying with the family. Wow! It was absolutely amazing to me how a skinny little girl could change so much over a period of a few years. That little 7 and 8 year old girl, and playmate, that I knew had developed into a beautiful young lady in those 9 years that I hadn't seen her. She was now 17 years old and essentially grown. However, seeing her again was a total disappointment. She couldn't have cared less that I came by to especially see her. I would go as far as to say she wasn't even friendly toward me. The reception was much worse than I expected it to be. I didn't necessarily think she would jump up and down with joy upon seeing me, but I did think she would at least be mildly glad to see me since we were such good pals as children. However, that was not the case. I definitely was not in her plans for the future. She already had a serious boyfriend. I met him and he seemed a nice enough fellow. He was 2 or 3 years older than her and was already a rising star in the community. Apparently, he had already found his nitch in life and was doing quite well financially. He even owned a pretty decent car for a young fellow and he also gave me a ride back out to civilization when I left. He didn't seem to be too concerned about me coming by to see his girlfriend. Come to think of it, he should have been in the army at his age. I wonder how he avoided getting drafted. Well, so much for that venture. I left Baker County and that family and continued on my way to North Carolina and the mountains. I have never seen my friend again or have ever heard of anything about her. I have no idea what her life has been like and will probably never know. I have never been back to that community nor have I ever met anybody that has been.

I traveled on to the mountains by means of hitchhiking and the Greyhound bus. When nightfall approached, I went to the nearest bus station. I didn't like hitchhiking at night even back then. However, I felt perfectly safe hitchhiking during the day. I never had to wait very long for a ride anywhere. I actually encountered some pretty nice folks among the people that gave me a ride. I rode with some of them quite a distance and the long rides usually involved a lot of conversation. Thankfully, I never had a problem of any kind when I was hitchhiking.

## A Fellow with a Guilty Conscience

One fellow I remember riding with a long way was an army veteran of World War II in Europe. He suffered from a very guilty conscience for something he did during the war that he had always deeply regretted doing, and wondered if the Lord would forgive him, or was he condemned to hell. He told me about the incident which went something like this, as I remember it.

He told me that one time he was assigned the job of escorting a captured German soldier back to the rear somewhere where the prisoners of war were held by the army. He wasn't interested in walking him back to the rear where he had to take him. So he walked the German prisoner back far enough to be out of sight of the officer who gave him the order and just shot and killed him and left him lay. He murdered him in cold blood, in other words. He then walked back to his unit and continued on with them. Nobody ever knew he murdered the German soldier except him and the Lord. Later on, he deeply regretted committing that awful, unnecessary deed, and it was weighing heavily on his heart and mind. He apparently needed someone to talk to about it and I was available, a stranger, and he probably would never see me again.

He wanted to know if I thought he was going to hell for committing that terrible deed. Personally, he didn't think he deserved to be forgiven. I told him that the Lord did forgive people of sin and the best thing for him to do was to ask the Lord for forgiveness and he probably would forgive him. I don't know if I did him any good or not. We eventually came to the fork in the road where I had to get out of his pickup truck. He went one way, I went another, and I never saw or ever heard of him again. I continued on to the mountains. My destination in North Carolina was Graham County, the westernmost county in the state.

## THE MOUNTAINS AND WEST BUFFALO CREEK

Upon arriving in Graham County, I went directly out to the West Buffalo Creek area where my mother grew up and where I had a number of aunts, uncles, and cousins. The West Buffalo Creek area is about 15 miles out in the mountains from the little town of Robbinsville, which is the county seat. My relatives lived in a very beautiful little valley that was mostly cleared with the creek running through it.

West Buffalo Creek itself is a beautiful mountain creek, as pretty as you will ever see. It's usually about 20 feet wide and, of course, full of rocks of all sizes and shapes. Tall trees grow along its banks and shade the creek in most places. The water in the creek was just about as cold as ice and not much fun to wade around in. The stream was shallow with the water usually less than knee deep in the deepest places. In earlier times the creek was full of rainbow trout, but now they were very scarce; a person would starve to death trying to catch one. The only kind of fish in West Buffalo Creek was a little fish called "knotty heads" and they weren't good for a thing, except to eat baby trout if one was to come along. The rest of the creeks in the region didn't have any trout in them either to amount to anything. It wasn't always that way, however. My cousin, Russell Stewart, who was raised near West Buffalo Creek, told me that when he was a boy in the 1930's West Buffalo Creek was full of rainbow trout and a person could usually catch all he wanted out of just one pool.

The valley land had been farmed in one way or the other for many years and by at least three generations. The story goes that my great, great grandfather, Enos Hooper, settled in the area in 1840, which was soon after most of the Indians had been removed from the region and sent to Oklahoma. He was the first white man to settle in this part of Graham County, North Carolina. Enos was a country doctor and was also the first medical doctor in that part of the state. He had a practice in both North Carolina and Tennessee and divided his time between the two places. The Tennessee line was just a few mountains over from his home in North Carolina. He did his traveling by horseback because there weren't any roads – just Indian trails.

Apparently, Enos acquired a large tract of land in Graham County before moving into the area – a total of 30,030 acres, including the little valley on West Buffalo Creek. However, he never lived there; he lived somewhere else in the area and the location of his homesite is not known for certain.

It is claimed by some of my mountaineer relatives that Enos acquired all that land in a trade with an Indian chief. The chief traded all that land to Enos for a flintlock rifle. However, if that actually happened, there may be more to the deal that what meets the eye, so to speak. It could be that the chief knew that he and his people were going to lose the land anyway, so why not swap that tract of land for that white man's rifle. I imagine that rifles were hard to come by back in those days, especially for an Indian. In addition, they were probably on friendly terms. I would suspect that the chief was happy with his trade.

Unfortunately for Enos and his descendants, most of the mountain land, which was covered in virgin timber and with miles and miles of beautiful creeks flowing through it, was lost by Enos somewhere along the way. Again, some of my mountain relatives claim that he lost most of the land soon after the "War Between the States", because the Yankee controlled reconstruction government raised the taxes on it so high that he couldn't pay them. Consequently, they took most of it from him. In other words, it was stolen by corrupt reconstruction officials like so many properties were in the South after the war.

There is a mountain in the region called Hooper's Bald that was named after Enos. He supposedly owned it at one time and it was part of the 30,030 acres tract of land. The mountain was called a bald because it didn't have any trees growing on its summit for some unexplainable reason. The Bald was a relatively large area and a number of the local folks took their cattle up there in the summer time to graze on the lush grasses that grew there. The cattle would get nice and fat and in a good healthy condition for going into the winter.

There was also an abundance of blueberries on the Bald for a period of time during the summer. Some of the local people would go up there every summer and pick buckets full of them. Some of the blueberry bushes were quite large, more like small trees, and were always loaded with berries. Bears loved the berries, too, and sometimes the berry pickers would have to compete with the bears at picking the berries. It always created an uncomfortable situation when both parties were trying to pick berries in the same area at the same time.

Until recent years, the Hooper's Bald was a very remote place and rather difficult to get to and only the healthy and strong of body attempted to go there. The dirt road up to Hooper's Bald was rocky and very steep for several miles, and it took a truck with a 4-wheel drive to reach it. Of course, a person could walk or ride a horse to get up there like people had to in earlier days – like when my mother was growing up on West Buffalo Creek, but that was even more difficult. Now, however, a highway has been built that goes close by it and it's a relatively short hike up to the top of Hooper's Bald. I'm sure many people hike up to it now.

When Enos died in 1872 he owned around 2,500 acres of land, which he willed to his 9 sons in varying amounts depending, I suppose, on the value of the land to some extent. He willed the largest tract, 930 acres, to his oldest son, William, who was supposed to take good care of his mother for as long as she lived. My great grandfather, Thomas Jefferson Hooper, was willed 200 acres on West Buffalo Creek including a large part of the little valley where my mother and her siblings were raised.

So, my great grandfather, Thomas Jefferson, or Jeff, as he was called, was the first white person to live on West Buffalo Creek, and he probably was also the person that cleared the valley land in order to farm it.

Jeff Hooper married Catherine Colvard around 1855. He went to Missouri to get her and married her there. However, the marriage records have been lost to give us the exact date. The Colvard family was originally from Graham County, North Carolina and probably neighbors of the Hooper family at one time. Catherine's grandmother was a Cherokee Indian and Catherine had the Indian name of "Piettia". Consequently, all of Jeff's and Catherine's descendents have a touch of Indian blood in them.

Anyway, Jeff built a relatively large house on West Buffalo Creek, and he and Catherine raised a family of eight children. When Jeff died in 1896, my grandmother, Ella Hooper, inherited the homesite and much of the 200 acres. My grandmother was the youngest child and she got the bulk of the inheritance with the understanding that she was to take care of her mother for as long as she lived – which she did.

Ella married Homer Martin and they had 7 children that were also raised in the old Jeff Hooper house on West Buffalo Creek. Of course, my mother was one of Ella's children that were raised at the old homestead. As the succeeding generations came along, they kept dividing up the valley land until now my relatives only own a few acres each and in a few cases even less. My mother sold her little inheritance to her brother, Oliver, in the early 1940's for whatever he wanted to give her for it. It was only 7 or 8 acres and he gave her $200 for it.

My mother and her younger sister, Essie, ended up in Florida, by chance, married, and spent the rest of their lives in Florida. But, it took most of my mother's life to get over living in that little valley on West Buffalo Creek. Eventually, though, she did adjust to living in sunny Florida and Florida became her home. She did, however, retain fond memories of her old mountain home and went back to visit it at every opportunity.

Sadly, however, when my mother was nearing the end of her life, in a nursing home, her mind going, her body gone, she would beg to be taken home. Every time I would go see her, she would beg me to take her home. At first, I thought she was talking about me taking her to her Florida home where she had lived most of her life. However, from the remarks she made, I eventually realized she was begging me to take her to her childhood home, her old mountain home, where she grew up. Apparently, the memory of her Florida home had totally slipped out of her mind, but she still remembered the old mountain home of her youth. It was a heartbreaking situation, but there wasn't anything anyone could do for her. By then, the old place only existed in her mind.

I had a great time in the mountains during the summer of 1951. I stayed up there around 2 months visiting first one relative and then another. I enjoyed staying with all of them and they seemed to enjoy having me around. I would usually stay 2 or 3 days with a relative then go to another one's house. However, later on, I would come back and stay with them another couple of days or so. I would just show up one day, unexpectedly. I spread myself around because I didn't want to offend any of them. Mountain folks seem to get offended real easy if they think they have been slighted in some way, like you spending more time with another relative than with them. I tried to keep all of them happy with me and did, I think.

## Uncle Oliver and Aunt Vesty

My uncle Oliver Martin and his wife Vesty lived in a little frame house by the side of the road – a dirt road. I might mention that all the country roads out in the mountains were dirt roads, but good dirt roads. There wasn't any danger of getting stuck on any of them. Uncle Oliver and Vesty raised a family of four girls on this site. When they first got married in the early 1920's they lived in the old Jeff Hooper house, but sometime in the early 1930's he built a new frame home on the same site and tore down the old house. All his girls were grown and gone by the time I started showing up on West Buffalo Creek in the early 1950's. They all married young. In fact, practically all my mountaineer cousins were older than I was.

Oliver and Vesty still used a woodstove and were experts at firing it up and cooking on it. They made homemade biscuits in it almost every morning, at least when I was there. Their biscuits were as good as they ever get, light and fluffy every time, and they both were equally good at making them. There was a good chance that some mighty good cornbread would also be made in that stove sometime during the day, too. I don't remember seeing any store bought bread there. I don't believe they would spend their money on that kind of bread.

Uncle Oliver's water source was a beautiful little spring in the backyard. Water flowed out of an iron pipe and spilled into a little concrete pool that someone had made years ago – nobody remembers now who did it or when. The spring had the best tasting cold water that one could possibly want. A little white dipper always stayed at the spring, and it was almost a ritual for people that visited Oliver and Vesty to go to the spring and get a drink of water with the dipper. Oliver was very proud of his spring and it pleased him very much when someone wanted to get a drink from it.

Uncle Oliver loved the mountains and West Buffalo Creek. He essentially lived his entire life in that valley and couldn't imagine living anywhere else. In fact, all my older relatives pretty much thought the same way about the mountains and didn't have any desire to live anywhere else. I believe Oliver lived to be 84 years old.

## Aunt Katy and Uncle Sam

Aunt Katy Stewart and her husband, Sam, lived right up the road from Oliver and Vesty and within 100 feet or so of the creek. The two houses were within sight of each other across some fields. They were about 200 yards apart. Sam and Katy lived in a nice block house which they built sometime in the early 1940's. Some of their older children were already grown and gone by the time they moved into this house. They raised a family of six boys and three girls. However, all the Stewart children were gone from home except the two youngest, Nell and Marcelle, before the summer of 1950 when I made my first visit to the mountains and West Buffalo Creek.

The Hooper family cemetery was located across a field and at the top of a little hill sort of behind Katy's and Sam's house. It was a pretty steep climb up there, and exhausting. However, in the summertime you could pick and eat wild blackberries all the way up to it, and picking and eating blackberries, alone, made the climb worthwhile.

There was a little A-frame shed at the cemetery that was made of wood and had a wooden shingle roof. Jeff and Catherine Hooper's graves are under this little shed. The shed is there because Jeff requested it be built over him after he died to protect his bones from the weather. He wanted it done because he was in the "War Between the States" and always remembered how the Confederate soldiers suffered in the cold winter weather, because they didn't have adequate clothing to keep them warm. The soldiers would have to huddle together real close to try and get a little body heat from each other. Consequently, he didn't want his bones exposed to the weather – so the story goes.

One day Russell Stewart and I were walking across the field between the Stewart house and the little cemetery hill toward an apple tree with the intent of picking some apples. When we were about 100 feet from the tree, something hit me in the shoulder so hard that it staggered me. For a second I thought I had been shot. Russell hollered out, "Hornets" just after one of them hit me. We ran as fast as we could away from that tree and the hornets' nest. We didn't get hit again but they were buzzing around us mighty close. I don't remember how Russell got rid of the hornets' nest. He did it one day when I wasn't around. Anyway, we didn't pick any apples from that tree that day.

On one of the occasions that I was staying with Katy and Sam, Uncle Sam wanted to know if I would like to go with him to take a couple of horses up to a mountain meadow that he knew about. He wanted to leave them there for a couple of months to graze on the good meadow grasses that grew there. I said, "Yes, I would like to go." So, early on this morning we headed out. We rode the horses bareback down the mountain road. It took 2 to 3 hours to arrive at this meadow where he turned the horses loose. Now we had the task of getting back home. We rode the horses up to the meadow the long way – by way of the road. Now Uncle Sam was going to get us back home the shorter way–down the side of a mountain. It was an overcast day and it started drizzling rain about the time we started down the mountainside. Uncle Sam knew the way back to his house by the new route, but I didn't; I was just following him. About halfway down the mountain, in the rain, up against a big tall tree, we had lunch. The lunch consisted of sardines and biscuit which Uncle Sam had carried with him in his coat and I didn't even know he had it. The lunch was mighty good and I was glad, but surprised, to get it.

We went on down the mountain and eventually came to a road. We started walking down this road, in the rain, toward his house, which was still several miles away. We were soaking wet from the rain. Luckily for us, a fellow in a pickup truck came along, picked us up, and took us to Sam's house. We were glad to see that fellow because he saved us a lot of walking in the rain.

When we got back to the house, Aunt Katy gave me some dry clothes to put on. I lay down on the couch by the fireplace and fell asleep for an hour or so. I had had a tiring experience and I will always remember it.

## Aunt May and Uncle Albert

Aunt May Huffman and her husband, Albert, lived a little further down the road from Sam and Katy and across the creek down another road called Huffman Creek Road. To get to May's house, you crossed West Buffalo Creek on a low-water bridge, as it was called. This low-water bridge was made out of logs and heavy boards and was built just above the rocks and water when the creek was at its normal stage of flow. At flood stage, after heavy rains and melting snow, the bridge might be covered in 1 or

2 feet of water with the stream flowing swiftly. The bridge was cheaply built, as far as bridges go, and served the purpose of a bridge most of the time quite well. However, when the creek was at a high water stage, with a swift current, crossing it was kind of scary.

Huffman Creek Road was very little traveled and May and Albert were the only ones that lived on it. Huffman Creek was somewhat smaller than West Buffalo Creek and flowed into that creek just above the low-water bridge. It was about half a mile up the road from the bridge to May's house. The house was located on a level area that had been carved out of a side of a mountain. You had to go up a steep grade from Huffman Road to get to the house. Their house was made of wood and was a fairly good size home with 3 bedrooms. It stood 30 feet or so above Huffman Road and Huffman Creek and was within hearing distance of the creek; the sound of the creek was always present. It was a comfortable home in a quiet place and I'm sure they enjoyed living there.

Aunt May was a big woman; she was 6 feet tall and weighed around 180 pounds. She dipped snuff like many of the older mountain women did.

May and Albert raised 3 children, a boy and two girls, but they were long gone. However, during the summer of 1951, May's oldest daughter, Bertha, and her daughter, Sophia, came to stay with her for most of the summer. I had seen Bertha a few times in my life but I had never met Sophia. I had heard of Sophia all my life but had never had the opportunity to meet her. One thing we had in common was the fact that we had been born within a few days of each other. Sophia was 10 days older than I was. When we were babies, just barely crawling, a picture was made of us together. That picture was all I knew about Sophia, except the fact that I knew her father was a Greek and that she lived in Miami, Florida.

Sophia and I hit it off real well and palled around a lot during the times I stayed with Aunt May. There wasn't very much for young people to do out on West Buffalo Creek or Huffman Creek, but we talked a lot and went on long walks down mountain roads. We also had some great meals at Aunt May's table.

Uncle Albert could play the banjo some and would do it occasionally if someone would beg him to do it enough. He seemed to enjoy playing his banjo once he got started. He would have a big grin on his face all the time he was playing it. His music playing was very lively and entertaining enough, but all the songs he played sounded the same to me. Regardless, I loved to hear him play his banjo because it fit right in with the mountain scene.

Uncle Albert and Uncle Oliver were both loggers and worked for Bemis Lumber Company. They stayed at a logging camp up in the mountains on Santeetlah Creek during the week and came home on Friday evenings. Other men from the area also worked there. There were very few job opportunities in the mountains other than logging of some kind. The loggers were in the process of cutting down the last of the remaining old original timber in the mountains in that part of the country and maybe in the entire Appalachian Mountains. I wish I had paid more attention to those old, huge trees that they were cutting down. The only area of original timber remaining in the Appalachian Mountains now is in Joyce Kilmer National Park. The park is in Graham County and only a few miles from Robbinsville; it's an area of about 5,500 acres. Anyone with an interest in the mountains should visit the park at least once to see how the mountains looked in their original state before all the big timber was cut.

## Cousin Ramona

Another relative I spent considerable time with was my cousin, Ramona Martin, who lived in Robbinsville with her mother, Belle, and her mother's elderly parents. They lived in a comfortable rock house that had indoor plumbing and other modern conveniences. Ramona was a pretty girl and had a lot of class. Aunt Belle was a school teacher and Ramona was preparing herself to be one. She had just finished her first year of college and was two years older than I was. We got along real well and I greatly enjoyed staying with her. Although, I can't remember anything we did particularly that had a lasting effect on my life. We just palled around, I suppose. Aunt Belle didn't own a car for Ramona to drive, so we had to walk if we wanted to go anywhere–like downtown. They lived about a mile from downtown Robbinsville. I met a number of her girlfriends there. Ramona didn't have a boyfriend and up to that point in her life she apparently had never had one. Later on, she found her man while attending college and married him. He was a marine.

## Cousin Russell

One time I stayed at Ramona's so long, a week or so, that cousin Russell Stewart drove up one day and told me that I had stayed with Ramona long enough and that he had come to get me to take me home with him. So, I didn't argue; I packed my suitcase and went home with Russell.

Russell Stewart was a game warden for the state and lived in a house on the Cheoah River near where Barker Creek flows into it. Also, they lived just a few miles from the little town of Topoka and about 20 miles from Robbinsville in the other direction. Fontana Dam was just a few miles away, too. Russell's wife was Lorene and they had 3 children–Shirley, Larry, and Sandra. They were a close family.

Since Russell was a game warden, he could come and go pretty much as he pleased. It was almost like not having a job it appeared to me. Consequently, we roamed around over the mountains a lot – looking for poachers, of course. We fished some and we visited country stores in the area and conversed with the locals, or at least Russell did while I listened to them talk. Some of the locals talked differently than anyone I ever heard. Maybe their conversations should have been recorded because some of them had such a unique way of talking.

Russell took me trout fishing twice during the times I was staying with him. Since Russell was a game warden, and a local mountaineer besides, he knew where the best places were to fish for native mountain trout. Russell was only interested in catching native trout because they tasted much better than stocked trout.

One of the creeks we fished in was called Deep Creek and was fairly close to his house. The other creek we fished in was called Squally and it was one of the streams that contributed water to West Buffalo Creek. Both creeks were way back in the mountains, remote, wild, rocky, and had numerous small waterfalls. They were both absolutely beautiful streams of water and there were just dozens of picturesque scenes along each creek. The streams were essentially a series of small waterfalls and pools with relatively short stretches of level streambed in between them.

Mostly, we fished up the creeks jumping from rock to rock and in the pools where the deeper water was. We usually had to get out of the streambed to climb around the falls. It was hard work going up these streams and a person had to be in fairly good physical condition to do it.

The business of jumping from rock to rock was very risky and really kind of dangerous. Some of the rocks were wet and slippery and if your feet didn't land on them just right, you would find yourself on your back in a flash. I slipped and fell, hard, on these wet rocks several times. It all happened so fast. It's a wonder that I didn't break something because those rocks were so hard. It would have been quite a chore to get an injured person out of the places we were fishing in.

We used salamanders for bait, which are lizard type creatures that lived in the water under rocks. We had to turn over rocks near the edge of the streams to find them. Mountain trout loved them; however, we fished with only small pieces of them on our hooks – not the whole salamander.

In spite of all the fishing we did, and energy we expended, most of 2 days worth, I never caught a single trout. I hung several of them but they all managed to get off the hook. Russell, however, had the knack of it a little better and caught several nice-size rainbow trout each time we went fishing. He caught just about enough for a mess of fish for supper each fishing trip. Native rainbow trout are a very beautiful and colorful fish. It's a shame that there are not more of them – like a bunch of them in every pool like they used to be. Eating native mountain trout was a new and enjoyable experience for me. I thought they had a much better flavor than any other fresh water fish that I had ever eaten. Unfortunately, I've never had the opportunity to eat any of them since those times.

Russell also caught a nice brown trout in Barker Creek near his house. He knew where the trout hung out and had been trying to catch it for months and finally did while I was there. It probably weighed 3 pounds, which is pretty big for mountain trout in that part of the world.

I fished a little bit in Cheoah River one time when Russell was off on a camping trip and couldn't take me with him. I caught a few little black fish of some kind that were different than anything that I had ever seen. They weren't trout, but I think they called them some kind of bass.

One day while Russell and I were roaming around the mountains – hunting for poachers, we came upon an old abandoned homestead. It had been abandoned for many years. There wasn't a house, or barn, or any other building as I remember, but there were trees and other evidence that indicated that someone had once lived there. While looking around, we came upon a peach tree that was loaded with big, beautiful, ripe peaches. We sampled them thoroughly. They were absolutely delicious and we ate our fill. In addition to that, Russell found a big bag in his truck; we filled it with peaches and took them home with us. We felt great about our good fortune in finding them. We felt like we had hit the jackpot that day. Lorene, Russell's wife, made a big cobbler pie for supper with some of them. In addition to that, everybody ate some great tasting peaches for several days afterwards. However, it amazes me to this day how that peach tree could still be living and bearing such great fruit after so many years of neglect.

## Mountain Cooking

All my female relatives in the mountains were excellent Southern cooks. Every meal I had was an eating experience. In the summertime most of the people in the mountains had a garden and their home-cooked meals were mostly fresh vegetables out of the garden, plus either cornbread or biscuits at every meal. The women, and some of the men too, made cornbread and biscuits almost everyday and they were good at it. I'm convinced that most people today have never tasted really good cornbread and biscuits, because most people don't cook it enough to get the knack of it.

As I remember, some of the things that they always grew in their gardens were corn, beans, squash, potatoes, cabbage, cucumbers, onions, and tomatoes. The flavor of all of the vegetables were outstanding, especially the corn-on-the cob. You could hardly get enough of it. The fried corn was also just out of this world.

The mountain folks didn't eat much meat. When they did eat meat, they usually ate either chicken or pork. They ate very little beef and most of them didn't like seafood of any kind. However, later on, many of the younger crowd developed a taste for it.

They were all good gravy makers, too, and made it frequently, especially in the mornings out of bacon or pork chop grease.

Most of the mountain women around where I hung out made a lot of sauerkraut in the summertime. I think they made it and stored it in big crocks. I never saw any of it, but they claimed they ate it in the winter when there weren't any fresh vegetables in the garden.

Another thing I saw a few times was fresh green beans that were strung on strings and hung around on the front porch to dry; the end product was called "leather britches". It was another way of preserving food for the winter. I've eaten them a few times in my life and they taste just about like fresh green beans when they are cooked. Leather britches were one of my mother's favorite foods and I heard her talk about them all her life.

## I RETURN TO FLORIDA

Eventually, all good things have to come to an end. I left the mountains some time during the early part of September and went back home to Dundee. Again, I traveled by means of the Greyhound bus and hitchhiking to get home. I arrived home with less than a dollar in my pocket.

I hung around home for 2 or 3 weeks and must have worked somewhere to make a little more money, because I went back to the Ocala area and loafed around some more. I stayed with my aunt Agnes Fort in Ocala some of the time, and I stayed out in the forest some, too, but I can't remember who I stayed with this time.

### My Attempt to Join the Merchant Marine

During this time I got the idea that I should, at least, investigate the possibilities of getting into the merchant marine. I had heard that merchant mariners made a lot of money and that sounded like something I would be interested in. In fact, I knew I would much rather go to sea and make money than go to sea and fight for my country. I was just that way.

I went to three seaports to try and find out if I had any chance at all of getting into the merchant marine. I went to Tampa, Brunswick, and Mobile, but eventually I figured out that a person had to belong to a mariner's union to be considered for a seaman's job on a freighter. In order to become a member of a union, a fellow had to have some shipboard experience or know someone that was a member and could get him in. Of course, I didn't have any shipboard experience or know anybody that was in the merchant marine, so I had to forget about that idea. However, I was told that if I got some sea duty experience in the navy, they would have to let me become a member of the mariner's union. So, if I wanted to go to sea, my choice was narrowed down to the navy or coast guard.

On the way to Mobile, Alabama I rode the Greyhound bus part of the way again and hitchhiked part of the way. I rode the bus along the coastal road because I had never seen the Gulf of Mexico and I wanted to see it. I remember how beautiful the gulf water was in places. We would be up on a bridge where you could look out over the gulf and see all shades of yellow, green, and blue depending on the depth of the water. I thought it was a very beautiful sight and worth seeing.

## A Stranger Takes Me In

An interesting thing happened to me while I was hitchhiking way out in West Florida on my way to Mobile. A semi-truck stopped and picked me up. It was kind of late in the day. I rode with this driver for a couple of hours, and we had a nice conversation as we rode along. He lived around Pensacola, Florida somewhere and was on his way home for the night. He asked me if I would like to spend the night with him. He seemed like a nice fellow and I had learned that he had a wife and some kids. So, I said, "Okay." He took me home with him and introduced me to his wife and two kids and told them they had a guest for the night.

He had a very nice wife and they seemed to have a good relationship. He had great kids, too; they were well behaved, had good manners, and were respectful to their parents. All in all, they were a very good family, and as a family, they seemed to have it all together like all families should have.

They treated me just like I was one of their favorite kin that had come to visit them. They fed me a good supper with the family and when bedtime came, they gave me a comfortable couch to sleep on. They fed me a good breakfast the next morning. After breakfast, he took me to the road that went to Mobile and then went on his way. I've never seen that family again and I forgot their names long ago. But I'll always remember and appreciate the kindness and hospitality they showed me that one time our paths crossed. They didn't have to do anything for me because I was just a stranger passing through. I've thought about that family from time to time through the years and the happiness and contentment that I saw there. I was just a boy myself, but I was old enough to recognize what I saw. I saw a happy and contented woman that was happy with her role in life as a wife and mother. This was in the days before women's lib and this woman didn't know she was supposed to be discontented and unhappy. They lived in a rather modest house, nothing fancy, and I'm sure there was just a modest income. There was both a father and mother in the home and the children seemed to be model children. It's too bad there can't be more families today like that family was back then.

## My Experience with a Marine Recruiter

One day around the first of November, I decided it was time for me to go see the navy recruiter in Ocala because that is where I was hanging out. So I went to the navy recruiter's office, which was in the old federal building at the time. When I got there the navy recruiter wasn't in his office. I was standing in the doorway of the recruiter's office trying to decide what to do, wait around for him or come back later.

It just so happened that the marine recruiter across the hall saw me and wanted to know what I was there for. I told him that I had come to see the navy recruiter. He told me that the navy recruiter was going to be gone for awhile, but I could come in and visit with him till he got back. So I did. I went into the marine recruiter's office. He was a nice friendly fellow with a lot of ribbons on his chest and some stripes on his arm. We began to have a nice conversation and he asked me a few questions about myself. He was genuinely interested in me as a person it seemed and I could tell right off that he had my best interest at heart. Somewhere in our chit-chat he began to tell me how great an organization the Marine Corps was. I was impressed with what he had to say about the Marine Corps because I had never given it much thought before. I was a navy man myself and wanted to go to sea.

One thing led to another and he seemed to think it would be a good idea for me to take the Marine Corps mental examination just for fun, to see if I could pass it, and since I wasn't doing anything anyway. So I did. I passed the Marine Corps mental exam without any trouble. In fact, it really wasn't that hard. The marine recruiter then decided that, since I was there just waiting around, he might as well fingerprint me as well. So he did. I waited around some more for that navy recruiter to come back but he never did come back. When 5:00 o'clock came, I decided I might as well leave because I didn't think he would be back that day.

I didn't get to see the navy recruiter that day, but I did everything but sign my name to get into the Marine Corps. As I was leaving the marine recruiter's office, he invited me to come back and see him and consider getting into the Marine Corps instead of the navy. He thought I had all the qualifications to make a mighty fine marine. The marines were looking for good fighting men like he knew I would be. He wanted me to think about it and come back and see him. I told him I would. I would think about it. He did paint a mighty rosy picture of the Marine Corps and the advantages of being in it. Besides that, I felt pretty good about myself when I left his office. I had never thought about myself being a fighting marine before. Over the next couple of weeks I gave some serious thought about whether I wanted to be a sailor or a fighting marine. The recruiter thought I would make a mighty fine marine. I got to thinking about some war movies that I had seen of marines in combat situations, charging machinegun nests and wiping them out and such. Could I do that?

I also got to thinking about hornet and yellow jacket nests that I had, unexpectedly, encountered in the woods. I knew from experience that when I stumbled onto a hornets' nest in the woods, and they started buzzing around me, my instinct was to run as fast as I could to put some distance between me and them. I had been hit a few times by hornets and yellow jackets and I knew how it felt. I wanted to avoid getting hit if I could. Was I brave enough to go charging into a hornets' nest and wipe it out? I don't think so. I got to thinking, if bullets were as bad as hornets, I didn't think the Marine Corps could instill enough gung-ho into me to make me brave enough to go charging into a machinegun nest. I began to doubt whether that marine recruiter knew me as well as he thought. I began to think that I knew myself better than he did. After considerable thought, I decided I would have to pass on joining the Marine Corps. I decided I wasn't big enough, mean enough, or brave enough to make a good marine. The glory and the girls would just have to go to someone else. I would stick with my original plan and join the navy.

## I JOIN THE NAVY

I went back to the navy recruiter's office and joined the navy somewhere around the middle of November, 1951. A day or two later the recruiter put me on a greyhound bus that was bound for Jacksonville, Florida. In Jacksonville, I was to take my physical examination, get sworn into the navy, and continue on to San Diego, California to take boot training.

I went to the address where I was instructed to go for my physical examination. When I got to the place, there were a few dozen other young men there to take the physical examination to enter the navy, too. When the time came to examine us, they had us all strip down and proceeded to examine us from head to toe for all kinds of things like they usually do.

After a time, the examination was over with the exception of checking our hearts. I hadn't had a problem up to this point. They lined us up in single file to have our hearts checked by this doctor. I was the fifth man in line for the heart examination. The doctor listened to the first man's heart very briefly and told him to go put on his clothes. He briefly listened to the hearts of the second, third, and fourth fellows and told them all to go put on their clothes, which meant that they had failed the heart examination and they weren't going to be getting into the navy.

After watching all 4 of the boys in front of me fail the heart examination, I got real worried that I wasn't going to pass it either. It came my turn to have my heart examined. I stepped up to the doctor and he put his stethoscope to my chest for a second then told me to go lay down on that cot over there, that he pointed to. The trouble was – my heart was racing away because I got so anxious about failing the heart examination, which would have prevented me from entering the navy. I didn't have any plans other than joining the navy. It was very important to me to get into the navy, and the prospects didn't look good for me when all 4 of the guys ahead of me failed the heart examination.

I lay on the cot for 20 to 30 minutes until all the guys had been examined and had left the room. Eventually, a corpsman came over to the cot where I was lying and told me that I had passed the physical examination and would be accepted into the navy. However, he thought it was terribly funny that my heart raced away like it did because I was so worried. I never saw the doctor again. The corpsman just grinned and laughed till I left the room. He thought it was so funny. Personally, I was relieved to know that I had passed the physical so I could continue on with my plans to get into the navy.

Before going to Jacksonville, I was told that if I passed the physical, I would be sent on out to San Diego, California for recruit training. However, some of us younger fellows were sent back home for a week, because the navy could only send a certain number of enlistees from Jacksonville that week and the recruiters had exceeded that number. Some of the older enlistees, in their early 20's, were on the verge of being drafted into the army and they needed to go first. So, I went back home for a week.

My parents had moved from Haines City back to our home at Lynne in Marion County some time in November. So, I got to stay home with them for another week, which suited my mother because she wasn't in favor of me joining anything in the first place. I got in a little hunting the extra week I stayed home; however, I wasn't too successful at killing anything.

I went back to Jacksonville after the week was up and was sworn into the U.S. Navy on December 5, 1951. I don't know why I didn't wait until after Christmas to join the navy since it was so close to Christmas. That would have been the most sensible thing to do, but apparently I wasn't thinking too clearly.

After being sworn into the navy, the new enlistees were put in a big room to wait around until the time came for them to go to the train station to meet the train that was to take us to San Diego, California, or at least part of the way there. There must have been 50 or 60 of us new enlistees.

I was impressed with the chief petty officer that was in charge of us and leading us around. He treated us all like we were human beings. His service ribbons indicated he was a well traveled man and had seen much of the world. He always referred to Los Angeles as L.A., which made it sound like he was very familiar with the place. He had already seen much of the world, and we would soon be seeing some of the world, too. Maybe, in a year or two, I would be also calling Los Angeles, L.A.

Just before leaving the room to go to the train station, the chief called out my name. I identified myself. He took one glance at me and hollered out someone else's name. That fellow identified himself and the chief informed him that he was going to be in charge of us during our trip to California. He was to be in charge of us in regards to keeping order, handling the meal tickets, and any situation that might arise.

I think the chief was looking at some test scores when he called out our names. I must have had the highest score of the bunch. He looked at me and instantly decided that I looked too young for the job of being in charge of that group of troops. The fellow he chose to be in charge of us was much bigger, older, and more mature looking than I was. His decision suited me just fine because I wasn't interested in being in charge of anything at that point in my naval career anyway.

## The Train Ride to San Diego

It was late in the day of December 5, 1951, that the train we were on left Jacksonville, Florida and headed west toward California. When evening came, and supper time came, we all ate in the dining car just like important people and at the government's expense. I thought all the meals we had in the dining cars on our trip to California were surprisingly good. I was impressed with the experience of eating in a train's dining car. I thought it had a first class atmosphere. It certainly beat those greasy hamburgers that I usually ate in a restaurant.

Eventually, sleeping time came and we discovered that we were riding in a Pullman car when the porter started turning our seats into beds. This was probably the first time that any of us had ever ridden on a train. What did we know? It didn't ever occur to me, or any of us, that we would be riding in a Pullman car; that luxury was far more than we could expect from the navy. We began to get the notion that the navy was going to take good care of us on this trip, nothing but the best for us navy men. We had already gotten above our raising and we hadn't even got started yet. We crawled into our bunks and had a good night's sleep, and we had a great breakfast the next morning. I really thought that I was having a great experience riding and sleeping in a Pullman car and eating in the dining car. I loved the navy at this point in my career.

When we got up our first morning in the navy, we soon found out that we were no longer headed west. We were somewhere in northern Alabama and were headed north. We thought that was a strange turn of events. We weren't headed toward California and the thought came to my mind that they are taking us somewhere else. They had tricked us into joining the navy, but now they had other plans for us. I knew that the military didn't always live up to its promises and the thought entered my mind that the military decided overnight that they needed infantrymen more than sailors, so they were sending us to a army base somewhere and were going to make soldiers out of us instead of sailors.

We were a little apprehensive for a few minutes. However, we soon learned from the porter what the story was; we were headed to Kansas City before heading west, and we were to pick up other car loads of navy enlistees along the way. So, we continued to head north to Kansas City. Somewhere in southern Missouri the countryside became covered with snow. That was my first glimpse of snow. We traveled all day in this snow covered countryside. We were very comfortable in the train, but we could tell that it was very cold outside the train by how the people were dressed.

The train would stop for something in small towns ever so often and stay there a few minutes. The train didn't seem to be in any hurry to get anywhere because it stopped ever so often. At one of these stops, I decided I would get off the train and see how cold it was and make a snowball. I got off the train and couldn't believe how cold it was. I had never experienced such cold, and to make things worse, I had my light Florida clothes on. I didn't stay long in the snow – just a few seconds; that was all I could handle. We went on to Kansas City and got off the train. We had a layover there of a few hours. We just hung around the train station pretty much together. It was a huge train station. Eventually, the call came for us to get on a new train; we did, and the train headed southwest toward California this time. We traveled through Kansas which was also flat country, like Missouri, and was covered in snow all the way across it. We went to bed that night and woke up the next morning in northern New Mexico and were headed west. As I remember, the countryside was still covered in snow. We went through Santa Fe, Albuquerque, and Gallup. The whole trip was fascinating to me because I was seeing new things and having new experiences. We continued heading west and crossed Arizona going through Flagstaff. Somewhere in Arizona the snow petered out. We continued on to Los Angeles and then headed south to San Diego. One thing that I especially noticed going south through Southern California was the treeless hills, just miles and miles of treeless hills, so unlike the eastern hills and mountains that are always covered in trees and other vegetation. I think most of these treeless hills were covered in short grass.

# 2

# BOOT CAMP

## TRANSFORMING CIVILIANS INTO SAILORS

We finally arrived in San Diego after 3 days and nights on the tracks, and we had a regular troop train by the time we got there; several hundred recruits got off the train. I believe it was in the late afternoon that we arrived at the train station. There were some navy personnel there to meet us, and they loaded us onto buses that took us to the San Diego Naval Training Center.

Our recruit training commenced on December 9, 1951. However, the first 2 or 3 days at boot camp was mainly spent getting organized and getting ready to train. My memory gets a little fuzzy here as to the exact sequence of events that took place our first 2 or 3 days in boot camp, but probably the first thing that took place was that we were organized into companies of 80 men each. The group of 80 men that I was put with was assigned the number 236. So, we were going to be Company 51-236, or just Company 236. The men in Company 236 were from a number of different states. A dozen or so of the Jacksonville group were put in Company 236. A lot of the recruits in Company 236 came from western states, especially Washington and Oregon, as I remember. They all had very pale complexions and it was quite noticeable to us Southern boys.

The next thing that took place was that the companies were assigned company commanders, which were all chief petty officers. It so happened that the chief that was assigned to Company 236 was named Stevenson. Chief Stevenson was a machinist mate, an old salt, with 15 or more years of sea duty. This was probably his first shore duty, and I'm sure his first experience at training recruits. However, he proved himself to be an excellent company commander and I think everybody liked him. He treated everybody fairly as far as I know. I never saw him verbally abuse anybody like you see in the movies. Chief Stevenson was a relatively small man with black hair, brown eyes, and a mustache. He was married and lived off base at night.

The next thing that took place was that we were issued our navy clothes and other gear, including such stuff as our bedding, towels, sea bag, and a ditty bag full of personal stuff. Immediately after receiving our pile of gear, we were herded out to an open space on a concrete court and instructed by the chief on how and when to wear our various items of clothing. For instance, we only wore dungarees our first few weeks at boot camp. In addition, we were issued tan-colored leggings and had to wear them everywhere we went in boot camp. Those leggings were a distinguishing feature of a recruit. Only recruits wore leggings in the navy. Therefore, a recruit could be recognized as a recruit as far away as you could see him because of his leggings. Of course, we didn't have any more need for our civilian clothes so they were boxed up and sent back home.

In the first day or so at boot camp, we also were given our short haircuts and our shots. Getting our shots was something of an experience, too. We were lined up single file and passed between 2 pair of corpsmen. Therefore, each recruit was jabbed twice in each arm by the 4 corpsmen. Of course, the same pair of corpsmen would try to time it so that they would jab the needles into the arms of the recruits at the same time – for affect. The corpsmen seemed to be enjoying their work, but the recruits weren't enjoying it as much. In fact, several of the recruits keeled over upon receiving their shots. The sounds of the "thuds" were always behind me, so I never actually got to see them keel over. Of course, it was always the big, macho-type fellows that passed out. Those shots did hurt, I admit.

All the companies were assigned a barrack to live in; and then, everyone was assigned a specific bunk to sleep in and mine was a top bunk. We were instructed how to make our beds the navy way and which had better be done that way, too.

In addition to the company commander, Chief Stevenson, we also had a recruit company commander and several recruit petty officers. I've forgotten now how they were selected. They were all good fellows, though. The recruit company commander was in charge of us when Chief Stevenson wasn't around. Our recruit company commander was somewhat older than most of the other recruits. He must have been 24 or 25 years old and had been in the army during the latter months of World War II. I think he was about to be drafted back into the army when he enlisted into the navy. He was a good fellow and the best choice in our company for that position. I think his last name was Underhill.

After 2 or 3 days at the San Diego NTC, I've forgotten exactly how long, we were put on buses again and hauled a few miles out into the desert to another training facility called Camp Elliot. We were told that it was a marine training camp during World War II. Here at Camp Elliot is where we would stay 6 weeks or so and receive our initial boot camp training.

One of the first things that is taught new recruits in the navy is how to take care of their clothes. We were given specific instructions about how to fold, roll, and store our clothes, and it better be done that way, too, come inspection time, which was quite frequent. Space aboard ship is very limited and sailors have to learn how to live in a small space. So, knowing how to store his clothes, and other belongings, in a small space is a part of the sailor's way of life.

Then, there was the chore of keeping the barrack and bathroom clean. Everyone was assigned a job to do, or an area to clean, so it wasn't a big job for any one person. The cleaning assignments rotated around, too, so that nobody would be stuck doing the same dirty job.

There wasn't any such thing as privacy in boot camp or aboard ship either as far as that goes. In the boot camp bathrooms, the dozen or so commodes per bathroom didn't have any partitions between them, or doors. They were just sitting there in the middle of the floor, or deck, as they call it in the navy. Any time a person had to answer the call of nature, he usually had plenty of witnesses and probably some company, too. However, we quickly adapted to the lack of privacy situation and didn't think much about it.

I think the chore that everyone in boot camp hated the most was having to wash their clothes by hand, every night, in a bucket, rain or shine. It would take an hour and a half each and every night to accomplish this task. Every night we would hurry back from evening chow, grab our buckets, and start scrubbing our dirty clothes by hand. The clothes had better be clean, too. We washed them outside in the open, and a few times we had to wash them in a drizzling rain – that is the only kind of rain I ever saw in California. We had a drying room we hung our clothes in to dry, but a few times they didn't get dry for some reason and we had to put wet clothes on. We only had 2 sets of dungarees and it was required that we put a clean set of clothes on everyday, wet or dry. That washing clothes chore, alone, was enough to make a fellow want to get out of boot camp as quickly as he could.

We had to stand a number of inspections on Saturday mornings, but I don't think it was every Saturday morning. Anyway, a clean uniform was one of the main things they looked at when they did inspect us, particularly T-shirts.

We were required to shower every night whether we thought we needed to or not. Sailors lived in close quarters and the navy didn't tolerate smelly sailors.

At boot camp the lights were turned off every night at 10:00 o'clock, and everyone was required to go to bed unless they were on watch. Standing watches was another thing we got acquainted with. The watches were 2 hour watches and everybody had to stand them from time to time. There were 2 recruits per watch; one was inside the barracks walking around, and the other one was outside the barracks walking around. Each one of them was walking around with a night stick. Sometimes officers were walking around checking on the outside watch standers. If an officer showed up you were supposed to holler out, "Halt, who goes there?" When the officer identified himself, you were then supposed to say, "Advance and be recognized." The officer would then walk up to you. Then, if the officer chose to, he could quiz you about some standing order things that all recruits were supposed to know. Luckily, I never saw an officer when I was standing my watches. Standing watches was something that everybody hated to do because it cut into their sleeping time. Our nights were short and we never got enough sleep. So, it was usually a tough day following the nights you had to stand a watch.

Soon after arriving at Camp Elliot we were issued a rifle – an old World War I Springfield, bolt action rifle. We weren't issued them to shoot or learn how to fight with. We only used them to march with, and we marched with them everywhere we went except to breakfast early in the morning. The rifles all had a number burnt in the stock so that each recruit could easily identify his rifle. We were told that if a recruit dropped and broke his rifle, he would automatically be set back 2 weeks in recruit training. In my experience, the rifles were dropped very few times and I never heard of one ever breaking.

We started learning how to march with the rifles immediately after arriving at Camp Elliot. We had to carry them just so; our elbows had to be tucked in close to our side so that all the rifles down a line of recruits would be all lined up and at the same angle. The manner in which a company carried its rifles determined to a large extent how sharp they looked.

The recruits also had to learn how to "stack" their rifles correctly. We attended a lot of classes during our recruit training, and when we went inside a building, or class room, we had to "stack" our rifles. Five or six of the same guys would always stack their rifles together. When stacked, the rifles would be leaning against each other in a teepee type fashion. There was a little hook on the barrel of each rifle that made it possible to hook them together.

We had to start learning the nautical term for things as soon as we got to boot camp. For instance, the floor was called the deck, the bathroom was called the head, the ceiling was called the overhead, the stairs were called a ladder, etc. A rifle was always called a rifle, never a gun. The navy was very particular that you called your rifle, a rifle. If the chief ever heard a recruit calling his rifle a gun, they were given some special, individualized instructions by the chief as to the difference between the two things. The chief would take the recruit that erred aside and explain to him in great detail the difference between a rifle and a gun. The chief had a little phrase that he used to teach him and made him repeat it 3 or 4 times, as well as point to the appropriate objects. The little phrase went like this – "this is my rifle, and this is my gun; this is for fighting, and this is for fun." Of course, the recruit had to point toward the appropriate objects as he was saying this little phrase. The difference between a rifle and a gun was learned very quickly by the rest of the recruits, too, using this teaching method.

In addition to learning the nautical terms for various things, we were also introduced to some salty terms and phrases. However, I won't discuss those in this book. It would be a little too much for polite society.

## I Develop a Serious Problem

I had a little problem the first week at boot camp that got to concerning me very much. About the 4th day of boot camp, I approached the chief and told him my problem. I was constipated. I hadn't had a bowel movement since I left home and that had been 7 days. It had gotten where I didn't want to eat anything more. The chief told me to go to the infirmary and tell them about my situation and they would take care of me. Also, he told me to just hang around the barracks that day. I went to the infirmary and saw a corpsman. A corpsman is usually all a sailor ever saw in the navy when he had a medical problem. I told the corpsman that I was constipated and had been for several days. No problem; he knew exactly what to do. He gave me a capsule of something and told me to hurry back to the barracks because things would be happening right away. It was a relief to know that because I was getting very concerned about myself. I went back to the barracks and waited for great things to happen. I waited, and I waited, and I waited all day and absolutely nothing ever happened.

The next morning I told the chief what had transpired and he told me to go back to the infirmary and hang around the barracks again another day. I went back to the infirmary and saw the same corpsman. I told him that his pill didn't give me any relief. He gave me 2 of the same pills this time and told me to run back to the barracks, don't walk, if you do, you will be in trouble. I ran back to the barracks hoping all the way that I would make it in time. I got back to the barracks okay and waited, and waited, and waited all day. The whole day passed and still nothing happened. The next day I had a tiny, little, normal bowel movement and was regular after that. I don't know what happened to all the food I ate for 7 days. It never showed up, ever. I suppose it could be argued that it is still in me.

## Swimming Test

Soon after we arrived at Camp Elliot, probably in the second week, our company had to undergo a swimming test to determine who could swim and who couldn't. So, early on this cold morning, it was now the middle of December, we walked down to this long, outdoor, heated swimming pool that was only a block or so away from our barracks. We only had our swimming trunks on in the cold air. When we got to the pool, we were instructed to jump in and swim to the other end, if we could, and then get our names checked off as a swimmer. I jumped in and swam to the other end with comparative ease. The warm water felt good. I climbed out of the pool and waited in line, in the cold air, for a few minutes to get my name checked off as a swimmer. Some of the men in Company 236 couldn't swim, but they had to learn how before they left boot camp. The navy believed that anybody that goes to sea needs to know how to swim, at least a little, because it could make the difference whether a person lived or died at sea.

As a consequence of being in that warm water and standing around in that cold air, within hours, I had one of the worst colds I've ever had in my life. I was absolutely miserable for the next several days, because I was in a situation where I couldn't take care of myself the way I needed to – like being able to blow my nose when I needed to, or do anything about a stopped up nose, and having to breathe through my mouth while I marched along. I just had to suffer through it until it was over. There really wasn't much you could do to help yourself get over a cold back then anyway. You just had to wear it out and suffer through it.

## Christmas Leave for the Instructors

Normally, navy boot camp was 12 weeks but we had to stay 14 weeks. We had just got started good with our training when the whole operation shut down 2 weeks for Christmas. All the company commanders and instructors went on Christmas leave. This was part of their duty arrangement somehow. Some of the recruits that were nearing finishing their recruit training took their boot leave at this time, too. So, the newer recruits had an extra 2 weeks of boot camp that didn't count towards their training time. I don't remember what we did to pass the time away for those 2 weeks, but we were kept busy doing something. As I remember, we always had Saturday afternoons and Sundays off at boot camp, though.

For the first 8 weeks or so that we were in boot camp, we were out of touch with the rest of the world. We didn't know anything about what was going on in the rest of the world unless someone got some news in a letter from home. We didn't have access to TV's, radios, newspapers, or magazines. There wasn't any time for those things anyway. In fact, I guess we were too busy trying to survive in our own little world that we couldn't get too concerned about what was happening in the rest of it.

The food at boot camp was reasonably good. Most of the recruits were served enough food at every meal to satisfy them, I'm sure. Of course, our food was called "chow". There was morning chow, noon chow, and evening chow. With all the good food and exercise, mostly walking, the skinny boys gained weight and the fatter boys usually lost weight. Some boys even grew an inch or so in boot camp. My weight went from 130 to 145 pounds, and I stayed at that weight, pretty much, throughout my navy years. In addition, I believe I grew an inch.

Furthermore, at boot camp, new recruits only got navy chow to eat and at the normal meal times. There wasn't any place to get junk food or drinks. There weren't any vending machines at the Naval Training Centers that I ever saw. However, my boot training might have been in days before there was such a thing as vending machines. There was a PX on base but new recruits weren't allowed to go in them. So, new recruits ate at chow time and that was it. But I don't remember ever being hungry or ever remember hearing anyone else complain about being hungry. We were probably too busy to think about it anyway. However, in the last few weeks of boot training, we were allowed to go into the PX at the San Diego NTC. I did but I don't remember buying anything. I think I went into the PX just because I could, as an advanced recruit, and to satisfy my curiosity as to what was in them. I must have bought a candy bar or something.

## A Recruit Shares His Cake – In a Fashion

One Saturday afternoon around Christmas time, one of the fellows in Company 236 received a chocolate cake from home, a homemade chocolate cake with chocolate icing on it. It must have been delivered to him at the gate because it was in good condition – all in one piece and it looked like a cake. If it had been sent through the mail, it probably wouldn't have arrived in very good condition. I think the boy was from Southern California so he had an advantage over most of us in that respect. A dozen or so of his fellow recruits seemed as pleased as he was that he got this cake.

The recruit that received the cake set it out on a table with the intention of cutting himself a piece of it. A dozen or so of his buddies gathered around the table also and showed every indication that they wanted some of it. In fact, they looked and acted like they were very eager to have some of it.

Several of us other recruits were sitting back and taking all this in. The question that came to my mind was – was the receiver of the cake going to get to eat any of it himself. His buddies were acting mighty restless and anxious looking as they milled around this table. The recipient of the cake sized up the situation and realized that he wasn't going to get to eat all of his cake himself. He was going to have to share it with his buddies. So, he told his recruit mates that if they would let him cut himself a piece of cake, they could have the rest. Those words seemed to settle them down a little bit. The boy cut himself a nice size wedge of cake, backed off, and told them that they could have the rest. There was not any thought given to cutting up the balance of the cake into neat little pieces so everybody could have a little wedge. Instead, it was every man for himself; they all grabbed for the cake with their hands at the same time to get what they could. It was the darndest sight you ever saw. Those of us that were looking on were just beside ourselves with laughter. It was one of the funniest sights that we had ever seen. That cake was reduced to crumbs in about 5 seconds. Those guys' fingers were just aworking and crumbs were flying all over the place. It reminded me of fish in a feeding frenzy. Crumbs were litterly being tossed up into the air above all these grabbing hands. Consequently, due to their unorganized efforts, all any of them got of the cake was a few crumbs. Half of the cake ended up on the floor. I still laugh about that sight to this day.

When the company commanders and instructors got back to camp after Christmas leave, boot camp training started in earnest. Life consisted mostly of marching and attending classes. I've forgotten what was taught in most of the classes, but I do remember some of the things. We learned how to tie knots; we learned about how to put out shipboard fires; we learned how to use our dungarees as a makeshift life preserver; we learned how to use gas masks and go through a room full of tear gas; and we spent one day on the firing range where we learned how to use an M-1 rifle. We were issued an M-1 rifle for that day, along with a certain number of rounds of ammunition. We learned to fire in different positions – sitting, standing, and lying down. We fired at a target about 100 yards away. I qualified as a marksman.

I found that loading an M-1 rifle was kind of tricky in a way. I know because I got my thumb in the way of the bolt that was inside the rifle mechanism and that was involved with putting a round into the chamber. When the bolt slid forward, I didn't get my thumb out of the way fast enough and it split it open. I bled all over the rifle. But, I just had to keep shooting with my thumb bleeding. I'm sure some poor seaman had to clean it up when it got back to the armory.

## I Develop Another Health Problem

I developed another health problem while I was in boot camp. I developed Carpal Tunnel Syndrome in my right arm – my rifle carrying arm. My arm became numb when I was marching with my rifle. I couldn't feel a thing with my hand except pain. My whole right arm ached something awful at night, too, and would always wake me up.

Anyway, I reported my problem to the chief and he allowed me to march without my rifle. Gripping the stock of my rifle tightly was the thing that seemed to be causing the problem. After a few days of not carrying my rifle, my arm quit hurting, I regained the feeling in it and I was able to resume marching with my rifle. I don't remember my arm bothering me after I left boot camp. However, I've been bothered by the same problem all my life since when I use my hands a lot for two or three days straight.

## Hershey Bars for Sale

One evening after we had been at boot camp for 8 or 9 weeks, a more advanced recruit walked up to our barracks where we were washing clothes. He had a box of Hershey chocolate bars in his hand and asked the question, "Would anybody like to buy a Hershey bar?" Nobody said anything for a few seconds. We just looked at him in a state of disbelief. We couldn't quite grasp what he said somehow. Finally, somebody came to their senses and said, "Sure, I would like to buy one." Then, others told him that they would like to buy one, too, including myself. In fact, I bought 2 of them. Some of the other guys did also. This business minded young recruit was selling 5 cent Hershey bars for 25 cents just as fast as he could hand them out and collect his money. He sold his entire box of Hershey bars to us in just a few minutes. Those 5 cent Hershey bars were twice the size of what 70 cent ones are today. I got my candy bars, tore the paper off one of them as fast as I could, and crammed the whole thing into my mouth at one time. I had never had the need to eat one in that manner before in my life and have never eaten another one that way again. I don't know why I was so desperate for a chocolate bar. I wasn't even thinking about candy bars before they showed up. Anyway, I ate the second one later and slower in the normal manner.

We stayed at Camp Elliot 6 weeks or so; I don't remember exactly how long now. Then we went back to the San Diego Naval training Center for the remainder of our recruit training. When we got back to the NTC in San Diego, we spent some time on the USS Neversail and on the bay rowing around and learning how to use a lifeboat. I think this was called a boat drill.

## Mess Cooking or Hell Week

Toward the latter part of our recruit training we had to spend a week on mess duty. It was also sometimes referred to as "Hell Week", and after going through it, a person could easily understand why it was called that. It certainly was one of the worst weeks of my life, if not the worst. All companies had a week of either mess duty or garbage duty at boot camp. We were assigned mess duty. Our days started around 4:00 o'clock in the morning during mess duty week and ended about 11:00 o'clock at night. We got up, cleaned our barracks, and were marched down to the mess hall where we started working in preparation for the breakfast chow. Some low rated cooks were in charge of us. They didn't make life easy for us or have any sympathy for us in regards to our long days. They lorded it over us at every opportunity. We didn't dare say a word of protest about anything.

We were all assigned various jobs involved with getting ready for chow and serving chow. After breakfast chow was served to the other recruits, we were allowed to quickly eat our breakfast and then start cleaning up the mess hall. When we got through cleaning up the mess hall, it was time to start preparing for noon chow. The noon chow was served; we hurriedly ate our noon meal and totally cleaned up the mess hall again. When we got through cleaning up the mess hall, it was time to get ready for the evening chow. We served the evening meal, hurriedly ate our meal, and started cleaning up the mess hall again. We finished cleaning the mess hall about 8:30 o'clock at night. We were marched back to the barrack, grabbed a bucket, and started washing our clothes. The lights went out at 10:00 o'clock, and some nights, some of the recruits wouldn't get through washing their clothes and get to bed till around 11:00 o'clock. Those recruits that hadn't finished washing their clothes when the lights went out just had to wash them in the dark.

We had to wear our white uniform during mess duty week. We only had one pair of whites, and we had to wash them every night so they would be clean for the next morning. Sometimes our clothes were dry when we put them on in the early morning and sometimes they weren't. Regardless, wet or dry, we had to put them on.

It was short nights for everybody during mess duty week. However, it was even shorter nights for the recruits that had to stand the nightly watches. The sleeping time available for recruits during mess duty week was about 5 hours a night at best. The poor recruits that had to stand watches during the night got only about 3 hours of sleep, which wasn't nearly enough for an over-worked person. It made for a very tough next day.

The second morning we got up at 4:00 o'clock, cleaned up our barracks, and were marched down to the mess hall in the dark to commence work about 5:00 o'clock. We made preparations to serve breakfast chow and then served chow to the recruits. After the rest of the recruits were served their morning chow, we were allowed to hurriedly eat our breakfast and then start cleaning up the mess hall. When we got through cleaning up the mess hall, it was time to start getting ready for the noon chow. We served the noon chow, hurriedly ate our noon meal, and started cleaning up the mess hall, etc. I think you get the picture what the routine was like for 7 days with but very little sleep.

After several days of this routine our bodies were desperate for sleep. It was a major effort for everyone to just stay awake – even when working. On Saturday afternoon, the 6th day of mess duty, one of the fellows in Company 236 broke down and cried like a child and wanted his mother. He just lost it for awhile. I think all of us were in about the same mental state and about at the end of our mental and physical endurance. We could relate to him and sympathize with him, but there was nothing we could do for him. We all had to endure this mental-breaking routine just one more day and it would be over.

I firmly believe that, if prospective navy recruits knew about this "Hell Week" before enlisting in the navy, they would never enlist. However, I suspect that the navy has by now either done away with this mess duty week entirely, or has at least greatly modified it. In my opinion, no recruit should have to endure what we went through. That "Hell Week" served no useful purpose and was just a waste of time. I don't think the modern navy could get by with such a torturous practice.

## Saturday Morning Parades

Every Saturday morning at the San Diego Naval Training Center the more advanced recruit companies had to participate in a parade – this was probably during the last 6 weeks or so of training. The companies would have to assemble on a big parade court in preparation for marching past a reviewing stand where the camp commander, other officers, and civilian guests were sitting. The participating companies were real sharp in their marching skills by this time in their training, and all of them looked sharp when they passed in review. Everybody was in step. All the rows of men were straight, and all the elbows were tucked in with all the rifle barrels at the same angle. The company commanders could be real proud of their companies, and the camp commander could be real proud of the quality of training the men were receiving.

Marching music was always played during our Saturday morning parades, of course. It was the same marching music every time and was a famous marching song composed by John Philip Sousa, but I can no longer remember the name of it. However, whenever I hear it, even to this day, my legs have the urge to march to that music.

As each company got abreast of the reviewing stand, the company commander would give the command, "Eyes right" and all the recruits would turn their heads sharply toward the reviewing stand and the training center commander. In a few seconds, after the company had passed the reviewing stand, the company commander would give the command, "Eyes front" and everybody would sharply turn their heads toward the front again.

Sometimes on the parade field, prior to marching in review, we had to stand at attention, or at parade rest, for a considerable length of time. Invariably, if we stood there very long, a recruit or two would always pass out. You could tell when it happened because you would first hear a rifle hit the concrete, followed by the thud. You didn't dare turn your head to see what was going on. Nobody ever made a move to help the poor fellow in any way. I guess they just laid there on the concrete until the parade was over, eventually woke up, and walked back to the barracks on their own. I never saw anybody keel over myself. They were never in front of me where I could cut my eyes around a little bit, if I had to, to see what was going on. No one in Company 236 ever passed out.

## Liberty in San Diego

In the latter weeks of recruit training we were allowed to go on liberty in San Diego for half-a-day, either Saturday or Sunday afternoons. Of course, we got to wear our dress blue uniforms, finally. However, anybody with any experience being around sailors could spot a recruit as far as they could see him by the way he wore his uniform. Recruits wore their uniforms in a strictly regulation manner. Whereas, naval personnel with more time in service tended to wear their uniforms in a more salty manner – like tying their neckerchief up closer to their chin, and like putting wings in their white hats and wearing them lower down on their foreheads. A white hat just sort of sets on top of a recruit's head. In addition, the older sailors only wore trousers with the old traditional 13 buttons. Whereas, the recruits were issued, and wore, sloppy looking zipper trousers which looked very unseaman like, we thought. Anyway, new sailors got rid of their zipper pants as soon as they could after leaving boot camp. However, they had to buy them with their own money at navy surplus stores, because the navy didn't make the 13 button pants anymore. The navy surplus stores were plentiful, though, around navy towns like San Diego, Long Beach, and San Francisco.

Liberty in San Diego was a wonderful break from the boot camp routine. However, I don't remember doing anything too exciting when I was on liberty. Most of us were too young to drink even if we had wanted to. So, the bars were out as a recreational possibility. We had plenty of money to spend, but there wasn't too much in San Diego that we wanted to spend it on, except eating in good restaurants and going to movies. I hung around the YMCA some because it was a good place for sailors to hang out in navy towns. They were mainly located there for that purpose. It was an effort on somebody's part to provide a place for servicemen to go and keep some of them out of the bars. It must have worked to some extent because a lot of military personnel visited the YMCA's.

On one of my recruit liberties in San Diego, and I believe it was my first one, I ran into an acquaintance of mine from Marion County, Florida. This was Muriel Perry from Summerfield. He was a navy recruit also, but he was a little more advanced in training than I was. We used to play basketball against each other in high school. He played for Summerfield High School and I played for East Marion High School. We were sophomores at the time. It just so happened that East Marion won the county championship that year. Muriel and I kept crossing paths after we got out of the navy and essentially became lifelong friends.

## The End of Boot Camp

Finally, graduation day came and we marched past the reviewing stand on Saturday morning for the last time. What a great feeling that was to know that boot camp was over. And now, we would become part of the real navy.

After the parade was over, we checked in our rifles, went to see the paymaster, and then assembled back at the barracks. Chief Stevenson spoke to us for the last time and told us what a great company of recruits we had been and wished all of us well in our navy careers. He had tears in his eyes when he finished speaking to us. He wasn't so tough after all. I never saw the chief again after his farewell address in the barracks.

Looking back on the boot camp experience, I believe Chief Stevenson had a relatively easy time with us as recruits. I think everybody in Company 236 tried to do their best and stay out of trouble. He didn't have any problem recruits or experience any problems with us of any kind that I know about. In addition to that, he molded us into a sharp company that looked good on the parade field. We were his first company of recruits, I believe, and I know he was proud of what he had accomplished with us.

Furthermore, I would like to say that I never once experienced, or witnessed, any of the in-your-face verbal abuse in navy boot camp like you see shown in the movies of marine and army basic training camps. The chiefs were totally in charge, but they never tried to make life miserable for anyone. However, you better not mess up too much or they would call it to your attention. You couldn't fault them for that.

In fact, during all my time in the navy, I never had anybody, officers or petty officers, try to give me a hard time about anything. And, as far as I know, no one else on my ship was given a hard time for no reason either. However, if a sailor did screw up too much, like shirking his duties, going AWOL, or insubordination, life would get harder for him. The sailors that messed up too much would usually have to go to captain's mast and be given punishment of some kind. There seems to be some goof-ups in every crowd; although, that is not exactly the terminology that sailors would use to describe such people.

## Duty Assignment

We packed our seabags and cleared out of the barracks. The big question remaining for the men of Company 236 was – where will we be going now? To answer that question, our recruit company commander marched us down the street a few blocks to a certain building. In this building we were to be interviewed by some personnel men. It was their job to determine our main interest in the navy, if we had any, and decide where would be the best place to assign us, taking our desires, abilities, and the navy's needs into consideration. Probably, most of the men in Company 236 would be assigned to various ships, a few would probably go to shore duty somewhere, and a few would probably go to a navy school of some kind. My desire was to be assigned to a ship and go to sea, because that is why I joined the navy in the first place.

After arriving at the building, it soon became my turn to be interviewed. My interview with the personnel man was very brief. It only lasted a few seconds. He called me into his office, told me to sit down, and immediately asked me if I knew what I would like to do in the navy, or what job I would like to have. I told him that I thought I would like to be a quartermaster. He then asked me, "How would you like to go to quartermaster school?" That question caught me totally by surprise. I hadn't even thought about going to a school. In fact, I didn't even know there was one. I just assumed that I would be going aboard some ship. However, I quickly decided that going to quartermaster school might be a good idea since I didn't know anything about the job, so I said, "Okay." He seemed pleased that I made that positive decision. The interview was over. He jumped up, went to another desk, and started typing up my orders. About 10 minutes later, I was issued my orders and told that I was going to quartermaster school at the Bainbridge Naval Training Center at Bainbridge, Maryland. It turned out that the NTC was located at the north end of Chesapeake Bay and near the little town of Elkton, Maryland. I was going all the way across country to the east coast. I walked out of the building with my orders, train tickets, meal vouchers, and about $250 in my pocket. But remember, $250 was a nice sum of money for that day and time when cokes were 5 cents, hamburgers were 25 cents, movies were 25 to 50 cents, and you didn't have any living expenses.

When I left that building, I was finished with recruit training and the San Diego Naval Training Center. I was now a seaman apprentice. Navy recruits are automatically promoted to seaman apprentice upon completion of recruit training. We also got a pay raise. My pay was increased from $75 per month to $100 per month.

At the time I walked out of the building where I was interviewed, there wasn't anybody from Company 236 in sight, anywhere. I don't know what happened to them. They had just vanished. My association with the men of Company 236 was abruptly over. I never got to compare duty assignments with anybody, or say goodbye, or anything. I'm sure most of them went home on boot leave because that was the standard practice, but I don't know what happened to any of them after that.

## THE TRAIN TRIP ACROSS COUNTRY

I left the Naval Training Center and went straight to the train station. Rather late in the day, I boarded a train bound for Chicago. Again, I was in a Pullman car and ate my meals in the dining car. I soon went to bed and slept all night without waking up. The train traveled all night through the state of Nevada, but I didn't see a thing because it was dark, and I was fast asleep in my berth without any watches to stand. I think we went through Salt Lake City, Utah. When I got up Sunday morning the train was in southern Wyoming and was traveling northeast. From what I could see through my Pullman window, the state of Wyoming was a very pretty state. Snow was still on the ground in patches and there were a lot of hills, rocks, and trees in beautiful combinations.

The train ride across country was very enjoyable and quite a change from the daily rigors of boot camp. It was going to take 3 days and 3 nights to reach my destination in Maryland. For me, the train ride across country was a mini vacation. Compared to boot camp, I was in the lap of luxury. All I had to do for 3 days was rest, eat my meals, and look out the train window at the passing scenery – places and things I had never seen before. After two nights and one and a half days on the track, we arrived in Chicago and there I had a lay-over of several hours. I spent much of my waiting time walking around town looking at all the strange sights. One of the things I saw that especially caught my attention was the overhead trolley cars traveling around on tracks 30 feet off the ground. I decided that Chicago was a big and interesting place, and a great place to visit, but I would never want to live there.

Late in the afternoon, I boarded another train that would go through Elkton, Maryland where I would get off. We were traveling at night so I didn't get to see much of the countryside between Chicago and Elkton. I got off the train at Elkton about 9:30 in the morning and reported in to the Bainbridge Naval Training Center at about 10:00 o'clock on a Tuesday morning. The sailor at the front desk where I reported in to checked my orders and told me that my class didn't start for another 2 weeks, so I might as well go home on boot leave. That was good news to me, otherwise, it would be another 4 months before I could go home on leave.

## BOOT LEAVE

The sailor at the front desk typed up my leave papers, gave them to me, and sent me on my way. I went back to the train station at Elkton, and, after a wait, caught a train going to Washington, D.C. In Washington, I boarded a train late in the afternoon that was going through Ocala, Florida on the way to Miami. I traveled all night on this south bound train, but I wasn't in a Pullman car this time. I was paying my own way, and I was too cheap to pay the extra cost for a Pullman car and a bed. That was very foolish on my part because I had a pocket full of money. Poverty thinking, I guess. I wasn't accustomed to having a pocket full of money and with more coming in soon. Believe me, spending the night sleeping in a Pullman car bed is a much better way to travel than sitting in a regular passenger car seat all night trying to doze.

I got to the train station in Ocala about mid-morning the next day. Nobody was there to meet me because nobody knew when, or if, I was coming home on leave. However, it just so happened that my brother, Sid, was working at the train station at this time. He was in between enlistments in the air force. I knew he was working at the train station, but he was nowhere to be seen when I got there. There wasn't anybody else there either. However, in 30 minutes or so, he showed up. He was surprised to see me and kept staring at me. I think he was somewhat fascinated by the sight of seeing his younger brother in navy blues. I'm not sure what he was thinking, but it could have been that he wished he had joined the navy instead of the air force so he could have worn navy blues himself – just a guess. Sid took me home around noon when he got off work.

Boot leave for a new sailor should be one of his most memorable leaves, because he has just completed all the mental and physical rigors of boot camp. Furthermore, he is home for the first time for his family and friends to see him in uniform. However, for the life of me, I can't think of much I did on boot leave. I know I must have enjoyed just being home, seeing the folks, and getting plenty of sleep, rest, and home cooking. I know I must have done a little visiting with friends and relatives, too, but I'm blank when it comes to many specific experiences. I'm quite sure I didn't engage in any romancing, like all good sailors are supposed to do, because I didn't have access to a car to drive. The local girls I knew didn't like to walk or hitch-hike, especially at night. They were funny that way.

## Smitten on the Shores of Church Lake

However, the one thing that I remember very clearly on this leave, though, is the Saturday afternoon that my brother, Sid, and I went over to Church Lake, behind the church, to just see what we could see. The Ocklawaha Bridge Baptist Church is located on the lake and that is why they call it Church Lake. It is about one-half mile from home. Church Lake was a big part of my young life, and I spent considerable time during my younger years hunting, fishing, swimming, and just messing around this lake. The church is the one I attended all my young life and in later years, too.

Anyway, we decided we would go to the landing on the lake that was behind the church. I had just gotten out of the car and was looking out over the lake. Suddenly, this pretty young girl appeared. She was quite close to me before I realized she was there. I was concentrating on the lake so intensely that I didn't see or hear her approaching us. She didn't make a sound. Sid seemed to know her and introduced me to her. Her name was Bobbie Nann Lampp, the preacher's daughter, who lived in the parsonage at the church. I got so interested in meeting her, and getting to know her, that I totally forgot about the lake – the reason I came there. It seems that young boys are usually easily distracted by pretty young girls.

# 3

# QUARTERMASTER SCHOOL

When boot leave was over, I boarded a train back to the Bainbridge Naval Training Center to start quartermaster school. The school started around the first of April and lasted for four months – until the first of August, 1952. There were 28 sailors in my class. Most of them came from various ships in the Atlantic fleet with home ports on the east coast. Only myself and one other fellow was fresh out of boot camp and had never been to sea or even been aboard a ship. The other fellow's name was Jack, and he had just completed his recruit training at the Great Lakes Naval Training Center. As I remember, Jack was a Jewish boy from New York City. The way things worked out, we would be associated the rest of our navy careers and would see each other occasionally.

Going to service school was a big step up from boot camp, although, we still had to assemble in formation and march together to our classes. We attended classes of some kind all day long and were marched from one class to another by a chief petty officer. However, we didn't have to wash our clothes in a bucket every night like we did in boot camp. That was a big relief. We didn't have to stand watches at night either. In fact, we didn't have to perform any kind of duty while we were at the NTC. We were there to go to school and that was all. We would get plenty of duty later.

The subject matter taught in quartermaster school consisted of things pertaining to visual communication and ship navigation. We started learning the Morse code right away, because the use of the Morse code is a big part of visual communication. Some of the ship sailors already knew the Morse code, however, and that part of our training was no big deal for them. Quartermasters send and receive messages by flashing light utilizing the Morse code system of dots and dashes. Radiomen, on the other hand, send and receive Morse code messages by sound, which is much faster and inside out of the weather, too. In addition, we had to learn how to communicate with flaghoist and semaphore. Flaghoist is a nautical system of communicating by means of brightly colored flags with different flags representing different letters of the alphabet and numbers from zero to nine. The flags are hoisted into the air by means of a halyard that is connected to the yardarm of the mast. The flags are thus flying in the breeze so that the quartermasters on other ships and shore stations can see and read them. The flags could be hoisted in many combinations which meant something, or created a "signal", which would convey a message. Although, to understand what the signal meant, the quartermaster, or officer-of-the-deck, would usually have to consult a signal book. However, over time and experience a good quartermaster/signalman would know what many displays of the flags meant without having to consult the signal book.

With semaphore, the position of the arms indicates a letter of the alphabet, and, consequently, it was possible to spell words by extending the arms in different positions. We had to practice sending and receiving messages by both flashing light and semaphore once we had mastered the Morse code and the arm positions. In addition to actually doing it, there was a proper procedure for sending messages by flashing light and semaphore and that had to be learned, too.

In the navigational part of our training, we were taught about the concept of latitude and longitude, Greenwich time, navigational charts and symbols, navigational aids – like buoys and lighthouses, rules of the road for ships, and the 3 methods of navigating – piloting, dead reckoning, and celestial. When I got aboard ship, I also had to learn to navigate with radar and the loran gear, which was very primitive in those days compared to today's equipment.

I would say we had a lot of information to learn in a relatively short period of time. I would also say that most of the guys from the ships had a definite learning advantage over us landlubbers, Jack and myself, because they had already been exposed to much, or at least some of the things that quartermasters do on ships. Consequently, they already had some knowledge of the information being taught. On the other hand, Jack and I had no knowledge of quartermastering or anything else along the nautical line. Everything taught was totally new information for us. Sometimes, I didn't have a clue about what the instructor was talking about. I just memorized stuff without fully understanding it. However, after I got aboard ship and started working as a quartermaster, I found that I could learn things rather quickly because of the training I got at Bainbridge.

## LIBERTY IN THE AREA

As I remember it, we weren't given liberty during the week. We pretty much stayed in the barracks at night and studied something, practiced something, or just made conversation, or a little of all three.

However, we had every week-end off to do whatever we wanted to do and everybody scattered. I went somewhere every week-end; at least, I was off the base. I spent a couple of weekends around Elkton, but there really wasn't much to do around there that I saw, so that is the reason we all left the area on weekends.

Elkton was a relatively quiet, pretty little town with lots of trees and older homes, and I'm sure it was a pleasant place to live. It was located at the upper end of Chesapeake Bay but it wasn't on the bay. It was inland a little ways. The little train station in Elkton was greatly used by the sailors and soldiers that were attached to the NTC in some way. There was a lot of coming and going by the military men. It seemed strange to me, but there were quite a few army personnel at the training center that were there learning something.

### Dinner on the Terrace

I don't remember too much about my entertainment activities in Elkton, but I do remember having a couple of very pleasant evening meals at a restaurant that was there. The restaurant served Southern style cooking and was located in an old colonial style building that had a terrace. I ate both meals out on the terrace under the open sky, all by myself, just at dusk. It seems like the terrace was in a garden setting, too. Anyway, the temperature was very pleasant at that time of day, especially after a hot and muggy summer day. I had a supper of pan fried chicken both times, which I thought was very good. It reminded me of the way my mother fried chicken at home. I don't remember what else I had to eat with the chicken. However, I do remember that they were very pleasant eating experiences both times I ate there, especially for an old country boy that wasn't used to much. It was a new experience for me and in a different type setting than what I was accustomed to, which made it kind of special for me.

I've wished many times that I could eat out on that terrace again at dusk, but it has never happened and probably never will. Fate saw to it that I only went that way once. Also, I'm sure that the restaurant has been long gone and probably the building, too, by now.

## Mother's Day 1952

On Mother's Day, May 10, 1952, I happened to be in Elkton. I had spent the day in Baltimore the day before, but I had come back to Elkton to spend the night to experience a little peace and quiet. I got up, had breakfast, and then decided I would like to go to church. It was a very pleasant spring morning. I didn't know where a church was in town, however, so I asked a young boy that I encountered where a church was. He told me about a Baptist church that was on the other side of town and a Presbyterian church that was only a block away. I decided I would go to the nearest one since I wasn't too concerned about the denomination at the moment.

The church I attended was a small church on a street corner in the middle of the town. It was an old church, quite pretty, and made out of stone, I believe. Anyway, I walked into the church and took a seat about halfway down the aisle on the right hand side of the church. The service wasn't too well attended on this morning because there were a lot of empty seats. I was the only sailor in the church which made me a little conspicuous. They had a very good service – choir, organ music, and everything else that churches have. Anyway, I enjoyed the service and being in the House of the Lord on that Sunday morning.

It turned out that this was a very friendly church. As soon as the service was over, people just flocked around me, asking me all kinds of questions, inviting me back to church, telling me how glad they were to see me in church, and all those kind of remarks. I came to the conclusion that this was the friendliest church that I had ever been in.

It turned out that this was going to be my lucky day. A Patterson family invited me home with them to spend the afternoon. After the service was over and everybody was in the process of filing out, this nice, pleasant lady approached me and engaged me in a little conversation like a goodly number of the other people had done. She seemed genuinely interested in me. In a couple of minutes her husband and young son joined us and took part in the conversation, too. We talked three or four minutes, standing there in the aisle of the church, and this chance meeting ended up with her inviting me home with them for Sunday dinner and to spend the afternoon with them. It sounded like a good offer to me, and I accepted the invitation without having to give it much thought. It's strange how things happen sometimes. When I walked into that church that Sunday morning, I didn't dream I would be going home with some wonderful couple for Sunday dinner and a very pleasant afternoon. And, she didn't dream that she would be taking a young sailor home with her for Sunday dinner. They didn't have to do that because I was a total stranger to them – just passing through. Why did they invite me home with them? Later in the day, Mrs. Patterson told me that when she saw me come in the church, she figured I was some mother's boy, a long way from home on Mother's Day, and that she was going to take me home with her.

I went home with them and they couldn't have treated me any better than if I had been their own son. First, they treated me to a wonderful, home cooked, old fashion, Sunday dinner. They also had a really nice home, too. I've forgotten what Mr. Patterson did for a living, but it must have paid well.

After dinner, they took me out to their summer camp on Elk River, which is part of Chesapeake Bay. We spent most of the afternoon out there. We rode around in their boat some on the bay. Also, we walked along the bayshore for awhile and looked at the activities out on the bay. There were a number of fishing boats out in the bay relatively close to shore. One of the boats was very close to shore and within hollering distance of us. The two fishermen in the boat were trying to catch herring, so they said, with a net – a gill net it looked to me like. However, they didn't seem to be having too much luck because their net was giving them a lot of trouble somehow.

When we were on the shore of the bay, the Patterson's oldest son, Dewey, and his wife, Sue, joined us for awhile. They were a very nice young couple; they were in their early 20's. I couldn't help noticing that Sue was a very lovely person in every respect. I thought Dewey had done real well for himself when he got her. She fit right in with that family. The younger son, Bill, was 15 years old. I think Mr. and Mrs. Patterson were in their mid 40's. Of course, that's pretty old from an 18 year old's point of view.

Sunday night we went back to the Patterson's home in town and watched television for awhile. Then I took my departure and went back to the Naval Training Center. I had a most enjoyable day with them and told them so. I told them how much I enjoyed spending the afternoon with them and how much I appreciated them taking me in for the day. They invited me to come back and see them. I thanked them for the invitation and had every intention of going back and visit with them some more and to keep in touch with them. However, I never saw them again. Why? I think that seems to be a flaw in my character – to just walk away from a friendship and never get in touch with people again. I regret to say, I have done that same thing a number of times in my life, all of which I regret.

So, one of my life's regrets is that I didn't keep in contact with the Patterson family, because they gave of themselves so much that one day I was with them. They gave me one of life's most precious memories. However, I don't know when I would have gotten the time to go back to Elkton, Maryland to visit them. It's hard to do many of the things you want to do in life when you only have a week or two a year that you can do them, even if you've got the money. Life just shouldn't be that way. I will always cherish the memory of that day with the D.F. Patterson Family.

## My Visits to Washington, D.C.

I went to Washington, D.C. 3 or 4 times and stayed with my cousin, Elinor Randall Nicholson, and her husband, Glen, who lived there. Glen was a native of Washington, D.C. and knew D.C. and the surrounding area very well. He did a great job of entertaining me and taking me to interesting places around the D.C. area. I remember him taking me to see the White House, other government buildings, and the Washington and Lincoln monuments. He took me to the Smithsonian Museum a couple of times. We also went to see Mount Vernon, the Arlington Cemetery, and General Robert E. Lee's home. I'm sure he must have taken me to other places, too, that I now can't remember. Elinor didn't go with us on any of our excursions, because she had a small baby at the time and it would have been just too much to lug a small baby around in the summer heat. I've always felt the summer I spent around Maryland and the Washington, D.C. area was some of the hottest and steamiest weather I've ever experienced. The humidity was horrendous and I was wet with sweat all the time I was outside. I felt that Florida weather was much better, mainly, by being less humid.

## My First Chinese Restaurant

On one of my first trips to Washington, D.C., I experienced my first Chinese food. I don't remember ever seeing a Chinese restaurant before then. There weren't too many Chinese restaurants around Ocala, Haines City, or Dundee back in the early 1950's. In fact, there weren't any that I knew about. I was just curious about what Chinese food was like, and since I was going to be a world traveler, I needed to find out. Anyway, I walked into this Chinese restaurant as ignorant as I can be about Chinese food. I sat down at a table and the Chinese waiter brought me a menu. I'm the only customer in the place because it was about 2:00 P.M. and a little after the noon hour. I looked at that menu and didn't have a clue about what anything was. The waiter came over to take my order. I looked at the menu some more. The waiter kept standing beside the table waiting for me to make up my mind. Finally, I handed the menu back to the waiter and told him to bring me something. He didn't say a word to me; he just looked at me with an expression on his face that said, "Okay, you asked for it." In a few minutes he started bringing me stuff and kept bringing it, something every few minutes. I didn't know what any of it was or what it was called, but it looked good and tasted good. He quit bringing me stuff after the table was full of dishes and there wasn't any room left to put any more. He must have brought me eight to ten courses. I ate until I simply couldn't eat any more and had to leave a lot of it. The waiter hadn't said a word yet. He just looked at me eat and sat down at an adjoining table to do it. I think he thought he was sticking it to me and maybe he was. I didn't care. I had plenty of money and more coming. I believe that meal was the most expensive one I had ever eaten in a restaurant up to that point in my life. It must have cost me all of five to six dollars. Oh well, easy come, easy go. I've eaten in many Chinese restaurants since then, but I still believe that was the best Chinese food that I've ever had. For one thing, I remember having sliced pork loin that was red around the edges. I wondered how they did that. It was very good.

## A Soldier's Holiday

On another Saturday I was riding the train to Washington to visit Elinor and Glen. My seating partner was a soldier and we talked as we rode along. He was a career soldier in his late twenties and had been in the army for several years. He was stationed in Maryland somewhere, I believe, and some distance from D.C. During the latter part of our journey together, he told me why he was going to Washington. It seems he had met this woman a few weeks previously, somewhere, and she really appealed to him in some respects. She lived in Washington and he was going to see her. He had had a recent telephone conversation with her and she had agreed to go out with him. It seems he was looking forward to seeing her. I gathered from the remarks he made that he was expecting an interesting weekend. I was impressed that he knew so much about how to have a good time on liberty. I envied him for it had been a year since I had been on a date – not since the night I graduated from high school.

We got to the Washington D.C. train station, said our goodbyes, it was good to know you, etc. I never expected to ever see him again.

That afternoon, Glen decided it would be a good idea to take me to the Smithsonian Museum again, or to another part of it. So, we went to the museum and were looking around at – whatever it was, I've forgotten. We hadn't been there but just a few minutes when I saw my soldier friend with his new lady friend. She was a rather nice-looking woman and was well dressed. I could see why he was attracted to her. She was leading him around and showing him all these interesting exhibits with great enthusiasm. However, I could tell from his facial expressions and body language that he wasn't as thrilled to view all these museum exhibits as she was. I could tell that wandering around in a museum on a Saturday afternoon wasn't his idea of a good time – certainly not what he had in mind doing when coming to Washington. In fact, I don't recall him mentioning the word "museum" even one time.

We were very close together when I first saw him – almost within touching distance. I never approached him. I'm sure he saw me but he let on that he didn't. I'm also sure he didn't want me to see him in his embarrassing situation. So, I didn't. Maybe things worked out more to his liking later on in the day, or night, but he was certainly suffering through the afternoon. I will never know what developed with their relationship for I never saw him again.

## A Pleasant Time with a Girl from Back Home

On one of my trips to D.C., I accidently ran into one of my Haines City School mates at a carnival, or fair, or something like that. This was Elizabeth Jones. She was one year behind me in school. I remember having a very pleasant time this one afternoon and evening running around with her. Then, I saw her very briefly again one Saturday afternoon after that. However, I've never seen her since or have ever heard anything about her. But I still have very pleasant memories of that one occasion we spent together. In addition, I've always thought it was quite a coincidence to accidently meet someone from home in a big city like Washington, D.C.

I spent one Saturday in Baltimore and passed through it several times. The thing that intrigued me about Baltimore was the row houses–blocks and blocks of row houses where there were not any space at all between houses. All the houses were just jammed up against one another. Having lived most of my life in the country where there was always plenty of open space, I found it difficult to understand how people could live under those conditions. I came to the conclusion that the people that lived under such crowded conditions just didn't know any better. The row houses are all I remember about Baltimore.

**Ted Holly – Practicing Semaphore at the NTC**

## Gettysburg Battlefield Excursion

One Saturday morning I decided I wanted to go to Gettysburg, Pennsylvania and visit the great battlefield that was there. So I caught the train to Washington D.C. and then a Greyhound bus on over to Gettysburg. I wanted to visit the battlefield because the "War Between the States" was a period of time in American history that I was greatly interested in, and I knew that Gettysburg was the place that the Southern effort toward becoming un-united with the Northern states bogged down.

I first learned that there was a big war between the Northern and Southern states when I was eight or nine years old. A playmate revealed that fact to me one winter day when we were playing in a barn. He also informed me that the South had lost the war, which bothered me very much even at that young age. Those things were all he could tell me about the subject. However, as I grew up, I gradually learned more about this event in American history. I gained my knowledge of the war from reading books, listening to older people discuss the subject, and studying about the war in American history classes in school. As radical as it may seem to some people in our society today, correct Southern history and the real causes of the "War Between the States" were even taught in public schools when I was growing up, at least in the South. Consequently, myself, and most of the people in the South were proud to be Southerners, were proud of their Southern heritage, and were proud of their ancestors that fought for Southern rights and Southern independence, even if it was a losing cause. Even though they lost the war in the end, I'm sure most of the Southern soldiers fought the best they could with what little they had to fight with, and at the same time endured extreme hardships of all kinds including hunger, exposure to the weather, and being away from their homes and families for years. They were fighting for a cause that was dear to them, and I am proud of their efforts and sacrifices as most Southerners are that know anything about that time in our history.

Also, as Southerners, we had, and still have great love and respect for the Confederate flag, the stars and bars, which we considered to be a regional flag, the flag of the Southern states and has absolutely nothing to do with slavery, which some misinformed people like to claim today that it represents. Furthermore, most of the people from the South that I have known loved the song "Dixie", which stirs a Southerner's heart more than any other song. "Dixie" is simply the song of the South. In addition, great men like Jefferson Davis, Robert E. Lee, and Stonewall Jackson were our heroes and still are.

Along the way, I also learned the part that some of my relatives played in the war. I learned that six Holly brothers from Marion County, Florida joined the Confederate Army and fought for the South in its effort to repel the Yankee invaders. They were my great uncles. Four of these brothers left for the army the same day – in April, 1862. Of the six brothers that went into the army, two of them never returned home, and three of them were badly wounded in battles over the course of the war. The youngest and the last brother to go into the army only served during the last year of the war and came out of it unscathed as far as we know. He was just a teenager. My grandfather didn't serve in the army because he was too young to go. He was still a young teenager when the fighting stopped.

In addition to the six Holly brothers from Florida, I also had a bunch of mountaineer relatives from North Carolina that served in the Confederate army. The Confederate soldiers from North Carolina included my great grandfather Hooper and five of his brothers. They all survived the war.

Anyway, by the time I got to Gettysburg, I considered myself fairly well informed about that conflict – the "War Between the States", or the "War of Northern Aggression", whichever term describes it best. It was not a Civil War in any sense.

At Gettysburg I took a guided tour of the battlefield and found it very interesting and informative but not necessarily enjoyable. I couldn't find it enjoyable because of thinking about all those young men that died there way before their time, or got badly maimed for life. As far as I'm concerned, all those deaths were such a waste of young lives, because the war shouldn't have been fought in the first place. In my opinion, the Northern politicians should have allowed the South to just go its own way when the Southern States seceded from the Union – because they had every right to do so.

A big question that could be asked is – what would have happened if the North had said, "We've had enough of Southern domination, and we're seceding from the Union and forming a Northern nation?" I know what would have happened without a doubt. The South would have said, "That's great. We don't agree on much anyway, and it would probably be best for both of us if you did. Good luck." The South would have never tried to force the North to stay in the Union against their will, and there certainly would not have been a big war that would cause the deaths of over 600,000 young men in order to "preserve the Union".

The war was fought mainly over States Rights, Constitutional Government, a limited Federal Government, and economic reasons – not slavery, like so many misinformed, politically correct people like to claim today. Slavery would have just simply died a natural death in a few more years anyway, mechanization of farming would have ensured that. It wasn't just the South that lost the war; it was the entire nation. If you doubt these words, just look at the size and power of the Federal Government today, how the constitution has been essentially trashed, how little control the states have over their own affairs, and the out of control federal judges who interpret the constitution to suit themselves and their liberal agenda. The nation has strayed a long ways from the system of government that our wise founding fathers intended for us to have. And, I believe, because so many of our politicians and citizens have abandoned the principles that have made our country such a great nation, it will soon cease to be a great nation.

In addition, I believe the Lord has blessed America far more than any other nation in history, because it was founded on Christian principles by Christian men. And the country was considered to be a Christian nation for many years. However, now, many evil and godless people are doing everything in their power to tear us away from those Christian roots. And I imagine when we abandon God far enough, he will abandon us as a nation and there will be dire consequences for us, as a nation, for doing so. That is something the people of America need to think about.

In addition to the battlefield tour, I went into a big room where a man gave a review of the battle on a large board with colored lights that represented the movement of the different army units that took part in the battle. That presentation was very informative in regards to how the battle developed over the three days that it was fought. I greatly appreciated the fact that the people involved in the battlefield tour and the battle review were totally impartial about what they were showing and explaining. They didn't try to put a Northern slant to anything they said, or get politically correct as they would say today. They just told the facts as they happened. I greatly appreciated that.

## HEATED DISCUSSIONS

The following Monday night in the barracks after my Gettysburg trip there was the usual discussion about what everyone did over the weekend. Like I said previously, on the weekends everyone scattered in many different directions. It was learned by the group that I had gone to Gettysburg to visit the battlefield. That revelation brought on some comments from a few of the Northern boys about the "War between the States". The comments led to some verbal exchanges about the subject between the three Southern boys present and six or seven Northern boys. One remark led to another and the first thing I knew there developed a heated debate about the "War Between the States". I didn't dream at the time of that first verbal exchange about the war that the debate would continue off and on at night for several weeks – until the end of school. If I had known that this was going to be such a controversial subject, I would have never revealed the fact that I had gone to Gettysburg in the first place. The whole thing got tiresome and was such a waste of time.

Actually, everybody in the barracks didn't participate in these discussions. Most of the guys just listened or went on about their business. It simply wasn't that important of a subject to them. It was just the six or seven Northern boys that thought it was an important enough subject to bring up for debate frequently, like just about every night. The South was outnumbered as usual because there wasn't but three of us Southern boys in the barracks. However, I only joined in on a couple of the debates myself because I saw very soon that it was futile to discuss it with them. Right off, I realized that these few Northern boys were totally ignorant about the "War Between the States" or the "Civil War" as they liked to call it. At first, I joined in on the discussions in an effort to give them the benefit of what I knew about the subject. However, I soon learned that they weren't too interested in being educated either. They intended to believe what they wanted to and the facts and the truth didn't play a part in it. I came to the conclusion after a couple of debates that they were determined to remain ignorant about the subject, and it was pointless to discuss it with them anymore. The other two Southern boys continued to argue with them, however. One of the boys was from North Carolina and the other one was from Texas.

## General Lee Steps Forward

However, after a couple of weeks of just listening to this on-going verbal exchange about the war and negative remarks about the South in general, another boy steps forward and takes up the Southern cause. I guess he saw we needed help and got tired of listening to all the unfactual comments from the Northern side. This boy's name was Frank and he claimed to be from Miami, Florida. However, the interesting thing about Frank was that he was largely raised in New York City. His family only moved to Miami when he was 14 years old. Everybody, including myself, thought that this was a strange turn of events. Here this Yankee boy by birth was vigorously defending the South and I mean vigorously. He would argue with the Yankee boys just as long as they wanted to argue and face to face if that is what they wanted to do. He never gave any ground to them.

One day I asked Frank why he had such strong Southern leaning when he was actually from the North. Frank told me that when he left New York City at 14 years old, he thought the same way the Yankee boys did about the "War Between the States," plus being biased against the South in general. He thought that way because that is what he had been taught. However, as he finished growing up in Miami, the least Southern city in the South, he gradually and reluctantly came to realize that there was another side to the North/South issue that differed greatly from what he had been taught in school and on the street. Consequently, over time, as he learned the truth about the real causes of the "War Between the States", he realized the South had gotten a bad deal from the North all the way around. So, he became a Southern by choice. Some of us are born Southern by the grace of God. Others become Southerners by choice, which mainly involves abandoning their unfounded biases against the South and adopting Southern values.

Personally, I've always appreciated the Northern born Southerners. Many times they make some of the best Southerners. However, this transition from a Northerner to a Southerner usually, but not always, takes place over a period of years, and the people making the change often aren't even aware that it's happening.

Anyway, Frank became our honorary General Robert E. Lee, and we greatly appreciated him standing up for the Southern cause like he did. I doubt if Frank ever changed anybody's mind about anything, but they certainly didn't change his either. Who knows, maybe some of the Northern boys changed their thinking about things further on in life as they got older and wiser because of something that Frank said to them in one of their heated discussions.

## V.D. INSPECTION

One morning toward the end of our stay at the Bainbridge NTC, our class was informed that we were going to have an inspection that day for venereal disease. So, at the appointed time for it, in the early afternoon, we were marched down to the infirmary. At the infirmary, we were herded into this big empty room and instructed to strip down to our shorts. We did. We were then lined up in two rows for inspection. Some lowly corpsman was giving us our instructions. There weren't any doctors to be seen. After we got lined up for inspection, another corpsman, a 2nd class petty officer, walks out of an office and strolls over to where we're standing all lined up in rows. He stands in front of us and gives us specific instructions about what he wanted each one of us to do as he walks by us. I won't comment on what those instructions were, because I believe it would be a little bit too much information for the female readers of this book. Any male that has been in any branch of the military services will have a pretty good idea what those instructions were, however.

Anyway, the corpsman puts on his most concerned look and starts his inspection of us. He slowly walks down the row of sailors and inspects each one of us very carefully. He was taking his job very seriously; you could tell by the look on his face. After all, he did have a great responsibility involved with checking all of us young virgin boys for V.D. That was his contribution toward the war effort. I'm sure he was very concerned about the health and welfare of all the young sailors at the training center and didn't want them to have any dreaded social diseases.

After the corpsman completed his inspection, he walked over to one side of the room and tells everybody to gather around him. We did as we were told. However, we didn't have any idea what he had on his mind. By now, he had on his most disgusted look. He says, "You people have undoubtedly got the scrongiest peckers that I have ever seen. When we get through here, I want every one of you to go back to the barracks and get those things washed up." With that said, he turned around, stalks off, and goes back into his office.

We were kind of stunned for few seconds because we weren't expecting any comment like that. After we came to our senses, it dawned on us that we had just been had. We all knew that there wasn't a word of truth to what he said, because everybody showered every night and those "things" were washed every night along with the rest of us.

I'm convinced that the inspection was conducted for the sole purpose of that corpsman being able to make his remark at the end of his inspection. In other words, the whole thing was basically a big joke for the amusement of the corpsmen. I'm sure those corpsmen would go back into their office and laugh hysterically every time they had one of those V.D. inspections. I'm sure they arranged that kind of inspection frequently just for the purpose of having a big laugh. The V.D. inspection was certainly one of my most memorable events at Bainbridge.

I never had another V.D. inspection the rest of the time I was in the navy. The question in my mind is – are V.D. inspections ever necessary anyway? Later on during my naval career, a few of my shipmates did catch a dose of clap from time to time, but I noticed when it happened the affected person was looking for the corpsman, the corpsman didn't have to look for him. The sailors that caught the disease wanted some relief as quickly as they could get it. They claimed the pain was almost unbearable when they tried to pee. It burned like fire, so they said. When they caught something, I think it was always a case of getting drunk and getting careless.

## GRADUATION AND DUTY ASSIGNMENT

I graduated from quartermaster school on August 2, 1952. With our schooling over, all the class members departed the Bainbridge Naval Training Center for their various duty stations. Most of them, of course, went back to their ships that were based on the East Coast and that were part of the Atlantic fleet. Consequently, when their ships were deployed overseas they got to visit choice liberty ports in many of the countries in Europe that were located on the Atlantic coast and in the Mediterranean Sea area. They also sometimes went on voyages down into the Caribbean and to some of the South American countries. In addition to that, most of them were just a few hours from home when they got the opportunity to go home on leave, which they probably did two or three times per year.

Jack and I, however, went in the opposite direction. We were the only two in the class that weren't already assigned to a ship. When it came time to assign us to a ship, the navy gave us the choice of three destroyers, all of them based on the West Coast and part of the Pacific Fleet. Two of the destroyers were the USS Brush(DD745) and the Samuel N. Moore(DD747). I don't remember the name of the other ship. We didn't know anything about any of them. Anyway, Jack chose the Moore and I chose the Brush. We both learned later on when we got to our respective ships that they were in the same destroyer division and usually operated together. Consequently, we saw each other occasionally when we were in port. We never saw any of our East Coast classmates again. I also learned that Long Beach, California was my ship's home port and that is where I would be going to meet it.

When I graduated from quartermaster school, I was given the rating of quartermaster seaman apprentice. I wasn't paid any more money than a seaman apprentice, but it probably kept me out of some of the dirty jobs that seaman apprentice are usually assigned to when they first go aboard ship. I think most of them are assigned to the deck force when they first go aboard. In my case, I went straight to the bridge as a quartermaster.

## AFTER SERVICE SCHOOL LEAVE

However, before going back to California to meet my ship, I was given the opportunity to take another 10 day leave if I wanted to, which I did. Besides, it was sort of on the way to the West Coast anyway. It was just a little detour south to go by home for a few days. So, I boarded a train at the Elkton train station and headed home. This time on the trip across country the navy just gave me the money to pay for my transportation back to California, and I could travel by any means I wanted to. So, I rode the train to Ocala, Florida and then took a Greyhound bus from Ocala on to Long Beach. Big mistake! The bus fare to Long Beach was somewhat cheaper than the train fare, but if I had used good judgment, I would have traveled by train because it would have been a much easier trip. I found out that sitting cramped up in the seat of a Greyhound bus for 3 days and 3 nights was not a pleasant way to travel. The navy gave me enough money to ride in a Pullman car, but I chose the cheaper way to go. I don't remember now why I made that decision, but I guess I was just a cheap person by nature, or I was afflicted with poverty thinking.

## A Concerned Lady

An incident happened on the train ride home that I've always remembered. This nice lady and her young son, 7 or 8 years old, were sitting across the aisle from me. We were facing each other so we must have been in the lounge car for this seating arrangement to have happened. I noticed that she kept staring at me with kind of a puzzled look on her face. Finally, she said to me, "I would like to ask you a question." I said, "Sure, go ahead." I didn't have any idea what she had on her mind. Anyway, she asked me the question, "Are you in the real navy or are you in the sea scouts?" She was dead serious and seemed very interested in knowing the answer to that question. I informed her that I was in the real navy, but I thought to myself, why did she ask me such a dumb question? It should be obvious to anyone that I'm in the real navy. She didn't say anything else to me, but I could tell something was still bothering her. She got off the train not too long after our brief exchange of words and I never saw her again. However, the last time I saw her she still had a very concerned look on her face.

Later on, I figured out what was actually on the lady's mind and what was troubling her so much. She was thinking that I looked much too young to be in the military service. She was right, even though I was 19 years old by then. She might have been thinking, too, that the country was in big trouble if the armed services were having to resort to such young boys to fight their battles. Also, she might have been thinking that her own son might have to go into military service one day. She didn't know it then, on that train, but her son would grow up just in time for the Vietnam War. I wonder what happened to him and if he was involved in that conflict. If he was, then she really had something to be concerned about.

So, I went by home for 10 days on my way to Long Beach, California to meet my ship. Again, I don't remember much about what I did at home during this leave; it has been too long ago. Although, I do remember leaving home this time with some very special memories.

## A Layover in New Orleans

When my leave was up, I boarded a Greyhound bus in Ocala and three days and three nights later I was in Long Beach, California. The only thing I remember about the trip to California was a layover of a few hours in New Orleans. To pass the time away, another sailor and I took a walk down one of the streets in downtown New Orleans. It must have been a slow season because there were few people on the street, and all the bars we passed were essentially empty. As we walked by some of the bars, pretty women would come to the entrance and try to entice us to come inside. Some of them would get a hold of our arms and try to pull us into their lair. All the bars were real dark and nearly empty of customers it appeared to me. The ladies we saw needed some customers, I'm sure, but we weren't going to be one of them. Besides, the ladies looked a little advanced for me, and I believed they were a little more woman than I could handle at my tender age. I don't remember hearing any New Orleans type music that night either.

I also got introduced to chicory coffee in New Orleans. Every time I ordered coffee from a café, I would get chicory coffee. Apparently, that's the kind they drank in Louisiana, or at least in New Orleans back then. I didn't like it and didn't drink much of it.

Upon arriving in Long Beach, I had a taxi take me to a place on the harbor called Fleet Landing. There were usually a number of ships moored out in the harbor, and the Fleet Landing is where the ships' boats and water taxis came to pick-up and deposit sailors that were either going out to their ships in the harbor or coming ashore. There was a little shore patrol office and a little café at the fleet landing. I went into the shore patrol office and told them that I needed to report aboard the USS Brush for duty and needed a ride out to it. Somehow, they notified the ship that they had a new crew member at the Fleet Landing that needed transportation out to the ship. The shore patrol told me the ship would be sending a boat to pick me up shortly and they did. It was rather late in the day by now.

## My Unforgettable Ride Out to the Ship

In about 30 minutes the Brush's motor whaleboat arrived and took me aboard. The ride out to the ship in the motor whaleboat is also an event that I will never forget. The weather that day was rather blustery and the waters of the harbor was rather choppy, so the boat crew had put up a little canopy for me to sit under so I wouldn't get wet from the spray that was stirred up by the boat as it went through the water. There were 3 men in the boat crew – the coxswain, the engineman, and the bow-hook man. The coxswain was a machinist mate 3$^{rd}$ class by the name of Andy Anderson. He just happened to have the boat duty that day. Andy was a rather small, dark-haired fellow from Pennsylvania. We became acquainted that day and became friends later on after that day. I served with him for probably 2 years until he was released from active duty. He reminded me several times during our time together as shipmates that he was the one that took me out to the ship for the first time. I think taking me out to the ship that day was the highlight of his naval career for some reason.

The ride out to the ship was the thing that made the day so unforgettable. All the way out to the ship, a ride of about 15 minutes, Andy stared at me and giggled like an imbecile and looked like one. He apparently thought that taking this new man out to the ship was the most amusing thing that he had ever experienced. I was new meat, so to speak. I thought to myself, this fellow knows something that I don't know, and I knew I would soon be finding out what it was. I did, over time.

The motor whaleboat soon pulled alongside the Brush. I came out from under the canopy and looked at the ship for the first time. This was going to be my home for the next 3 years and 2 months and most of that time would actually be spent at sea. I threw my seabag over my shoulder and started climbing up the ladder that led up to the main deck at the quarterdeck where I was to report in. As I climbed up the ladder to the main deck, I had the thought – the adventure begins.

# USS Brush(DD745)

4

# REPORTING ABOARD

I reported aboard the Brush for duty on Thursday, August 21, 1952, at 2000 hours (8:00pm). I checked in at the quarterdeck as it was the customary thing to do when a ship was in port. Although, I don't know how I knew that; maybe I asked somebody. Anyway, the petty-officer-of-the-watch passed the word over the P.A. system for a certain petty officer from the operations department to "lay down" (report) to the quarterdeck, and he soon showed up. The petty officer that came down to the quarterdeck was Tommy Tomlinson QM2/C. The petty-officer-of-the-watch informed him that I had just reported aboard and needed to be shown my sleeping quarters. So, Tommy led me to the operations department's sleeping compartment where he assigned me a rack (bunk) and a locker.

It developed that the operations department's sleeping compartment was somewhat forward on the ship and two decks down from the main deck. It was also directly beneath the bridge but four decks down. In order to get to the compartment you had to go from the main deck, port side, down a ladder (stairs) into and through the chow serving compartment, into the mess deck, and down another ladder in the middle of the mess deck to the compartment.

After assigning me a rack and locker, Tommy showed me where the forward head (bathroom) was – the one that "O" department used as well as part of the deck force that was in a compartment just forward of us and in which about another 40 sailors were berthed. To get to the head, we climbed the ladder into the mess deck and went forward a few paces through a hatch out of the mess deck. The head was located just forward of the mess deck on the port side. In all, about 80 sailors used this head. I'll say more about the head later.

It was kind of late in the day when I reported aboard the Brush, so I didn't get to see much of the ship on that first day since it got dark so quickly. However, I was introduced to the chow serving compartment, the mess deck, the forward head, and the bridge area just at dusk. There wasn't anyone on the bridge at the time and we didn't linger up there very long.

Tommy went to a movie on the fantail, I believe, and I went back down to the compartment, stored my gear away in my locker, and made up my rack by putting a cover on my mattress and on my small pillow. I still hadn't seen anybody much because most of the crew was either on liberty, leave, or at the movie.

After taking care of things in the compartment, I went up to the main deck, stood at the port rail and looked at the harbor lights for awhile and wondered. I wondered what my new seafaring and shipboard life was going to be like. I wondered what had I really gotten myself into. I wondered what that coxswain knew that I didn't know yet.

The sleeping compartment lights were always turned out at 2200 (10:00 p.m.). So, just before 2200 I went back down to the compartment and crawled into my rack. I think I was the only one in the compartment at 2200, but I heard the rest of my compartment mates stagger in, one or two at a time, throughout the night. I didn't get much sleep my first night aboard ship.

The next morning after breakfast I went up to the bridge and met the bridge gang – the quartermasters. The members of the bridge gang at the time that I came aboard were Amos Phillips

QM1/C, Tommy Tomlinson QM2/C, Charles Layton QM3/C, Poncho Arredondo QM3/C, Edwin (Ed) Geffert QMSN, Billy Tomlinson QMSN, Charlie Beason QMSN, Sam Smith QMSN, Norman Jackson QMSN, Robert Kreider QMSN, and Lawrence Barth QMSN. Most of these guys I got to know real well over the next two and a half to three years that we were shipmates. However, Phillips and Arredondo left the ship for discharge soon after I came aboard and I never got to know them very well. Also, Layton and Barth both left the ship in April 1953 for shore duty. Layton went to Norfolk, Virginia and Barth went to Guam. However, I got to know them quite well during the 8 months or so we served together on the ship. In fact, I worked with Layton a great deal in the charthouse; he was my instructor there.

## GETTING AQUAINTED WITH THE SHIP

After I had met everybody and visited a little bit, Tommy took it on himself to give me a tour of the ship starting with the bridge and pilothouse. After showing me those places to his satisfaction, Tommy took me down to the main deck and showed me many other features and spaces of the ship. We started our tour at the bow, with the anchors, and walked aft. Tommy showed me the guns, torpedoes, depth charge racks, the galley, sickbay, the officer's wardroom, the radar room, the commodore's cabin, the radio shack, the charthouse, and the after crew's sleeping quarters. The after crew's quarters was near the fantail, and the firemen and some of the deck force were berthed at this location. I liked the location of my sleeping quarters better; it was somewhat amidships and not in motion as much as the fantail.

The ship was going to be in port for the next three days so I spent that time getting acquainted with the bridge gang and learning more about the bridge and the rest of the ship to some extent. However, all the members of the bridge gang spent some of the weekend on the beach on liberty. But I didn't go ashore. I was more interested in getting acquainted with the ship and learning to live on it.

Of course, I heard a lot of sea stories from the bridge gang and some of the ship's history and involvements, too. All of them had made at least one trip overseas so they were old salts compared to me. However, I was somewhat of a novelty to them because I had been to quartermaster school. They accepted me as one of them, I felt, even though I was totally inexperienced as a seafarer. Besides, I was someone new who they could tell their sea stories to for the first time. I learned a lot of things those first three days on board.

I learned that the Brush was part of Destroyer Division 92 that consisted of four ships – the Maddox (DD731), the Herbert J. Thomas (DDR833), the Samuel N. Moore (DD747), and the Brush (DD745). These four ships operated together most of the time. The commodore, with the rank of captain, was the commander of Destroyer Division 92 and he was usually aboard the Maddox. The name of the commodore at this time was Bowen.

The captain of destroyers usually, if not always, had the rank of commander and the executive officer, who was second in command, had the rank of either lt. commander or lieutenant.

I learned that the Brush had just returned from the Far East around the first part of July and so wouldn't be going back for several months. So, that gave me a few months to learn something about being a quartermaster. I also learned that our captain, Commander Donald F. Quigley, had just taken command and was a new man on board, too, just like me.

**Commander Quigley Assuming Command of the Brush – Relieving Commander Watkins**

I also learned that the Brush was a Sumner class destroyer that was 376 feet long and 41 feet wide amidships – the widest point. Consequently, the ship was long and narrow and sat rather low in the water with a draft of about 14 feet. The main deck was about 20 feet above the water at the bow and about 8 feet at the fantail. The ship operated on steam and had four boilers, two engines, two screws (propellers) and two smokestacks. The ship had a single mast that stood right behind the signal bridge, as did the forward smokestack. She had a cruising speed of 16 knots and a top speed of 33 knots, or about 40 miles per hour, which is pretty fast for a ship. The Sumner class destroyers carried a crew of from 275 to 300 men, including the chief petty officers and 18 or so officers. The crew, as on all navy ships, was constantly changing as some of the old hands were leaving the ship for some reason and new, untrained personnel were coming aboard. However, just by chance, I served with a large percentage of the same men in the operations department most of my navy career – all but the last four to six months when they all left the ship one by one before I did. This exodus from the ship happened this way because most of them joined the navy soon after graduating from high school; whereas, I didn't join the navy until five months after graduating from high school.

I learned that destroyers carried a lot of firepower for ships their size. The Brush had three 5 inch twin mounts or a total of six big guns. Two of the mounts were forward of the bridge and were designated Mounts 51 and 52. Mount 51 was on the main deck near the bow and forward of Mount 52, which was on the next deck up, 01 deck, and just forward of the bridge. There was also a Mount 53 which was on the main deck in the stern near the fantail. These five inch guns fired a shell that weighed approximately 54 pounds and that had a range of around seven miles if enough powder was put behind them, so I was told. In addition to the five inch guns, the Brush had four 40mm rapid fire guns. Two of these gun tubs were right behind the bridge, one on the starboard side and one on the port side. The other two 40mm guns were back toward the fantail but forward of Mount 53. They had a distinctive rhythmic sound when they were firing. The 40mm's were good for close range targets and, I believe, were our best defense against airplanes.

The antisubmarine weaponry the Brush carried included depth charges and hedgehogs. There were two depth charge racks on the fantail – one on each side of the ship. During an attack on a submarine, the depth charges were just simply rolled off the fantail, or could be. Of course, before they were rolled off, the torpedomen had to set the depth charges to explode at a certain depth depending on how deep the submarine was. In addition to rolling the depth charges off the fantail, the depth charges could be fired over the side by means of something called K guns. As I remember, the K guns could fire them over the side for a distance of 30 to 40 yards. It was possible to roll the depth charges off the fantail and shoot them over the side at the same time. It was very difficult for a submarine to evade all of them. The depth charges were rather heavy things. They were about the size of a 30 gallon drum and were packed with explosives. They must have weighed 200 to 300 pounds.

The hedgehogs were stored in hedgehog launchers that were located forward on the ship, on the 01 deck at the bottom of the ship's superstructure. They looked like small, narrow bombs with a round fin at the back end of them. They were shot out from the side of the ship for a distance of 40 to 50 yards. Several Hedgehogs were shot off at the same time and fell into the ocean in a circular pattern. I believe they only exploded on contact with a submarine.

**USS Maddox**
**Official U.S. Navy Photograph,**
**From the collection of the Naval Historical Center**

## THE BRIDGE GANG – FALL 1952

### T.A. (Tommy) Tomlinson QM2/C

Tommy was a tall, lanky fellow about 6 feet and 2 inches and had black hair and rugged features. He was from Norman, Oklahoma. However, to me, he looked more like an Oklahoma cowboy than a seaman, but he was a career sailor. I don't imagine that there were too many opportunities for a young fellow back in Norman and that is probably the main reason he made the decision to stay in the navy. I believe he had a widowed mother back in Oklahoma, but he seldom went back there after joining the navy, at least after I knew him. Tommy was around 26 years old at the time I met him and was married. His wife lived in Long Beach and he went ashore there at every opportunity.

Tommy was the lead signalman on the bridge the entire time I was on the Brush. Of course, the chiefs outranked him, but Tommy was the one that ran things on the bridge. He had been in the navy around 8 years when I came aboard ship. Thus, he was an old salt with a lot of sea time under his belt. Tommy had been on the Brush 3 years or more by the time I went aboard her and had already been on 2 tours to the Korean War theatre, including one in 1950 soon after the war started. However, his first cruise was cut short when the Brush hit an enemy mine and suffered extensive damage and numerous casualties. Tommy didn't lose any blood at the time of the incident, but he was knocked out for awhile, so I was told.

Like a lot of sailors, Tommy liked to indulge in strong drink with his shipmates, but, I believe, he engaged in that activity mostly when he was away from Long Beach and his wife – but not always.

Tommy was a good petty officer and a good fellow. As far as I know, he treated everybody fairly and everybody liked and respected him. I know he always treated me as good as I could expect to be treated.

Tommy was also as good a signalman as the navy had, but he apparently didn't care anything about the navigational part of the quartermaster rate and never made any effort to learn anything about it, as far as I knew. Consequently, it kept him from advancing any further as a petty officer in the quartermaster rate. I hoped he changed his ways and became first class and chief somewhere in his career, but I don't know what happened to him after I left the navy. Although, I do know that he was scheduled for shore duty after 10 years or so of sea duty, which I felt like was long overdue for him.

### W.A. (Billy) Tomlinson QMSN

Billy was the younger brother of Tommy and was about 7 years younger than him. Billy joined the navy right after graduating from high school in June, 1951, and requested that the navy allow him to serve with his brother on the Brush. The navy agreed to it and he came aboard the Brush right after boot camp. I believe he served on the deck force for awhile, because I remember him telling me he had to chip a lot of ice off the ship during the winter of 1951 and 1952 when the ship was operating off the coast of North Korea. So, he also had had 1 tour of duty off the coast of North Korea. Somewhere along the line, early in his navy career, he decided he wanted to be a quartermaster, too, like his older brother and became a QM striker. He made 3rd class petty officer in the summer of 1953. He was an all around good fellow, a good signalman, and a good helmsman. I believe he must have been at least one of the special sea detail helmsmen before I took over the job, because, as I remember, he was the only one that ever relieved me at the wheel when I had to stay on it too long – like over an hour or so. This was always when we were alongside other ships at sea.

Billy wasn't as tall as his brother; he was about 5 feet and 10 inches tall. Billy also had a slim build, dark hair, and rugged features; although, he and his brother really didn't look alike. Billy was a good natured fellow and got along well with everybody. Billy liked to drink with his buddies, too, but it usually made him happy. He didn't over do it too much, as I remember. Billy left the navy when his time was up in June, 1955, and that was the last I ever saw of him. But I heard years later that he had got out of the navy and joined the air force. Apparently, he had had all the sea duty he wanted. The navy lost a mighty good signalman – one more time.

### Charles Layton QM3/C

Layton was a career sailor and had been in the navy 4 or 5 years or more when I met him on the Brush. I believe he had served on several other small ships other than the Brush. I remember hearing him talk about serving on a frigate off Korea. He had had several tours of duty in North Korean waters starting at or near the beginning of the Korean War.

Layton tended to be a rather nervous, high strung type fellow it seemed to me. Although, I liked him and we worked well together in the charthouse. He was my mentor there, and he taught me everything I needed to know about that part of being a quartermaster.

Layton was a medium size fellow in height and had dark, somewhat curly hair. He liked to indulge in strong drink – maybe a little too much for his own good. I believe he was raised in Oregon, but I'm not positive about that.

I only served with Layton 8 months. In April, 1953, he was transferred to shore duty at the Norfolk Naval Base in Virginia. He spent the rest of his life around Norfolk either on shore duty, on ships operating out of there, or as a navy retiree. He must have liked it around Norfolk. Eventually he became a chief signalman.

### Edwin (Ed) Geffert QMSN

Ed was about 6 feet tall and of muscular build; in fact, he was a well-built fellow. He had sandy blonde hair and pale blue eyes. He was of German descent and it showed. He had a couple of tattoos on his arms. He had a tattoo of a panther on one of his arms, but I can't remember what the other tattoo was.

Ed was a big city boy from Chicago, Illinois. He joined the navy right out of high school but when he was still 17 years old. His enlistment was called a "Kiddy Cruise", which, I think, meant that he didn't have to stay in the navy for a full 4 years. However, he spent the last few months of his enlistment aboard the Maddox, because they were short of quartermaster petty officers and the Brush had several more than they needed. The Brush was where he felt at home, though.

Ed and I were always good buddies, although, we didn't have that much in common and never went on liberty together. Ed liked to drink beer with the boys and I didn't fit in with that activity too well. Ed made 3rd class petty officer in the summer of 1953.

Ed also came aboard the Brush right after boot camp and already had one tour of duty off North Korea – during the winter and spring of 1951 and 1952.

## Paul Haney QMSN

Paul Haney came aboard ship a little after I did and joined the signal gang a exactly remember when he joined us, but he was one of us when we were operat

Haney was a big fellow. He was around 6 foot and 4 inches tall and weighed I imagine. And he was from the great state of Texas. He never became a petty aboard the ship. That's all I can remember about Haney.

## Charlie Beason QMSN

Charlie was a farm boy from Ohio. His father owned and operated a relatively large Xenia, Ohio. I don't remember him saying so, but I suspect Charlie was his father's number o hand when he was growing up. Charlie joined the navy right after graduating from high school. H one married sister whose husband was in the army and on the front line in Korea at the same time were there during the spring of 1953.

Charlie was around 5 feet, 8 inches tall, had dark hair, and carried no excess weight like the rest of us.

Beason was an exceptionally good signalman and made 3rd class petty officer sometime in the summer of 1953.

Like the rest of us, Charlie did not enjoy his life on the Brush, and it would sometimes get to him in a big way. Occasionally, he would feel the need to strongly vent his frustrations to the point that his shipmates would get concerned about what he might do. But he would eventually calm down and adjust his mind to endure a little longer.

Charlie apparently inherited the tendency to go bald, and during the 1954 cruise to the Far East, he lost most of his hair, which I am sure was largely due to stress and the lack of proper nourishment.

Taking everything into consideration, Charlie was a good shipmate and an all around good fellow.

## Lawrence Barth QMSN

Barth was of medium height and tended to be on the skinny side. He had dark hair and sharp facial features. He was from the state of Wisconsin.

I only served with Barth for 8 months. He was sent to shore duty in Guam in April, 1953. I think he requested shore duty in Guam to get off the ship. He knew he stood a good chance of getting it because not very many sailors wanted shore duty in Guam. It was a long way from anywhere and there wasn't anything exciting to do there. I suppose he thought it was preferable to sea duty on the Brush. I believe Barth made 3rd class petty officer a few months after he left the Brush. That is all I remember about Barth. Although, I learned years later that he went back to Wisconsin when he got out of the navy.

## Norman Jackson QMSN

Jackson was about 5 feet and 9 inches tall and had dark hair which tended to be a little curly. Jackson was a rather good-looking fellow and loved to drink, party, and have a good time, especially with the girls. He frequently came back from liberty and told the bridge gang about his adventures on the beach. They sounded like tall tales to me, but I'm sure they were true if he said they were. Jackson was also sometimes called Norm by his buddies.

ofessed to be a Mormon like so many people are that are from own near Salt Lake City called Murray. I would say that Jackson his hitch in the navy, but I imagine he straightened up after he re Mormons and other normal people.

manned the engine-order-telegraph during special sea was the special sea detail helmsman. So we had a lot of Norm was a good man on the engine-order-telegraph. d always responded correctly to the speed change

ut he apparently wasn't interested in becoming a ss exam to become one. I suppose he was just interested g out.

was a westerner from the state of Colorado – Pueblo, Colorado to be exact. He the Rocky Mountains was the only place on this earth to live, and after he got out of the nd back home, that is where he spent the rest of his life.

Sam was about 5 feet, 8 inches tall and had red wavy hair. He was a good, likeable fellow and everybody on the ship liked him that knew him. He joined the navy soon after leaving high school. For some reason, Sam never wanted to be a petty officer either because, as far as I know, he never took the exam for 3rd class petty officer. In spite of the fact he stayed a seaman, he was a good signalman and a good helmsman and was a special sea detail helmsman for a time.

Sam was the one that made the signal flags. He had a little space below deck, forward on the ship, where the cloth (bunting, as they called it) was stored and everything else that was needed to make the flags. The space where he worked was called the "bunting locker". He used a sewing machine to sew the pieces of cloth together to make the flags.

Sam also had a little side business. He could work with leather and make people belts and billfolds. He made me a small billfold that would fit into the small pocket of my dress blues. I still have it. He may have made other leather things, too.

## Robert Kreider QMSN

Robert Kreider was a sandy blonde fellow about 5 feet 9 inches tall. He was from the state of Ohio, but I don't remember which town or city he was from. Kreider made 3rd class petty officer in the summer of 1953.

Kreider didn't drink alcohol as I remember, and he usually went on liberty by himself and did his own thing. He was into body-building to some extent and spent some time around gyms. He had aspirations to become a lawyer when he got out of the navy, but I don't know whether he ever was or not. Kreider also tended to be rather "progressive" in his thinking for that day and age and which didn't set too well with the rest of the signal gang. I think he performed his signal duties well enough, but I don't think he was on the same page with the other signalmen as far as basic beliefs went. But everyone got along together pretty well.

_____ Sharpe QMSN

Sharpe was on the bridge for a few months after I came aboard, but he the navy, I believe. He was a very likeable fellow and everyone seemed to like too much about him except he was about medium size, 5 feet, 8 inches tall or blonde, wavy hair. He also liked tattoos and had a number of them on him. One liberty with a new one, a big one, which was an old sailing ship across his chest. It w tattoo at one time and it made him sick for several days.

## THE QUARTERMASTER RATE

The term "quartermaster" in the modern navy is a holdover from the days of the old saili As I understand it, these old sailing ships had an area, or short deck, in the after part of the ship a quarterdeck. On this quarterdeck is where the activities of the ship were directed by the captai other officers, and where the ship's wheel was located. The seamen that steered the ship and perform other duties on the quarterdeck eventually became known as quartermasters. Some of the other dutie that these early quartermasters performed undoubtedly included signaling or communicating with other ships. This was probably done by means of flags of some kind during the day and some kind of light signals at night by using lanterns, probably.

These early quartermasters also determined the depth of the ocean in shallow water by the use of the lead line. The lead line was a small rope that had a heavy lead weight tied on the end of it and that was marked, probably by knots, at various intervals on the line. The seaman using the lead line would stand near the bow of the ship and throw it forward as far as he could. The lead line would sink to the bottom very quickly because of the heavy weight at the end of it. The seaman could feel when the lead hit bottom, and by looking at the markers on the line could tell the captain the depth of the water.

In addition, the early quartermasters could roughly determine the speed of the ship with another line that had a flat piece of wood attached to it that offered a maximum resistance to passage through the water. This line also had knots in it. This flat piece of wood was called a "chip log." In the early days, a quartermaster would throw the "chip log" off the stern and let the line reel out for two to three minutes. The speed was calculated by the number of knots that was reeled out in the two to three minutes. Thus the seagoing term "knots" got established. The word knots means "nautical miles per hour" – never knots per hour. A nautical mile is 6,080 feet instead of 5,280 feet as in a land mile.

### Bridgemasters

Modern ships have an area called the bridge which is usually, if not always, the highest deck on the ship. On the bridge, at sea, is where the operation of the ship takes place and where the activities of the ship are directed by the captain or the officer-of-the-deck. The ship's wheel is located on the bridge, in the pilothouse, along with the engine-order-telegraph, which informs the engine room of the speed wanted or speed changes desired.

Modern day quartermasters perform most of their duties on the bridge which includes the pilothouse. The term "bridgemasters" would probably more accurately described the seamen that work on the bridge of modern day ships than the term "quartermasters," because there isn't an actual quarterdeck on modern ships for seamen to work on. However, there is a place on the main deck, about amidships, where the OOD stays when the ship is in port, which is called the quarterdeck. But old sailing ship sense. I suppose the navy uses that terminology tivities of the ship are directed in port.

ked on the bridge were separated into two different rates. communications were called signalmen. The sailors that ise duties such as steering, keeping the quartermaster termasters. I suppose the navy needed men to get artermaster duties and visual signaling duties were obably take the sailors twice as long, perhaps, for had to learn both sets of information.

ar II and before I joined the navy in 1951, somebody, somewhere, o combine the rates and call them all quartermasters. Consequently, ir duties on the bridge had to learn both navigation and visual signaling. It a, but it just didn't work that well in actual practice. The reason that it didn't work cause some men liked the visual signaling but weren't interested in the navigational part and didn't put much effort into learning it. On the other hand, some of the men liked the termaster side of the rate but didn't like the signaling. The result was that they would learn the part they liked real well but wouldn't attempt to learn too much about the part they didn't like. It probably didn't make too much difference if a quartermaster just planned to do his four years in the navy and get out, but if he planned to make the navy a career he had to know both if he wanted to advance in rate. I didn't plan to stay in the navy longer than my four year hitch, but I was interested in getting good at both areas of the quartermaster rate and did. Years later, the rate was divided again back into a signalman rate and a quartermaster rate, so I was informed by a modern day sailor.

## Why Quartermaster?

The question could be asked – why was I interested in being a quartermaster in the navy in the first place? There were essentially three reasons why I thought I wanted to be a quartermaster. First, it was one of the most nautical occupations in the navy and the things that quartermasters did intrigued me somehow. I felt it was on par with the boatswain's mates that are involved with all the duties on the deck such as line handling, mooring, and anchoring. Second, I thought it would be interesting work and it was most of the time. However, there were times that I questioned my decision to be one. Third, I felt that I would have a better chance of getting off the ship in case it went down fast like so many destroyers did during World War II. In addition, I really didn't realize what I was getting myself into. In time, I began to understand why most people didn't want to be one; there were too many other less stressful things to do. Besides that, the QM's had to work closely with the officers and a lot of the guys simply weren't comfortable doing that. The QM's got accustomed to that association real quick and didn't think much about it. Then, after working on the bridge as a quartermaster for awhile, I learned that the bridge was the best place on the ship to be to know and to see what was going on. That kind of situation kind of suited my personality. I always liked to know what was going on and I can't imagine being any place on the ship other than the bridge.

# 5

# FIRST STATESIDE DUTY – FALL 1952

## MY SEAFARING LIFE BEGINS

My first 5 months aboard the Brush was a time of pretty intense training involvi a ship does at sea, or might do, in regards to combat readiness, emergencies aboard ship, operations like replenishment at sea of fuel oil, ammunition, and provisions. The Brush, our sister ships, trained a lot in antisubmarine warfare (ASW), screening large ships, gunn operating with carriers during flight operations. In addition, the captain would conduct drills a ship such as general quarters (battle stations), abandon ship drills, man overboard drills, enginee casualty drills, steering casualty drills, and signal drills. The captain wanted his ship to be ready handle anything that might come up when we went overseas, and I think the crew was – based on what I saw of its performance. The navy ships constantly had to train, I suppose, because of the turnover of personnel, both enlisted men and officers. Highly trained men were constantly leaving the ship and new, inexperienced men were coming aboard, including the officers. Most of the new ensigns coming aboard were just as ignorant about seamanship as new seaman apprentices and had to be trained, too.

Generally speaking, the petty officers ran the ship because they were experienced and very knowledgeable about their particular trade. The chief petty officers were especially valuable to the navy. I'm convinced the Brush had some of the best petty officers in the navy, including those that worked on the bridge – the quartermasters. Unfortunately, we also had our share of sailors that weren't so great to put it nicely. Consequently, the captain had to spend a lot of his time holding captain's mast to deal out punishment to wayward sailors. A lot of court-martials were convened, too, and sometimes wayward sailors were sent to the brig for few days to have their attitudes adjusted.

I also felt like the Brush had some of the most competent officers in the navy, that is, the ones that had been aboard ship long enough to learn something. The conning officers, especially, had a very difficult job on a destroyer, and an officer had to be pretty sharp to be given that responsibility. In my opinion, Captain Quigley was a great captain and was always cool and collected under pressure. I never knew of him making a mistake or exercising poor judgment about anything. Although, he was a rather quiet man and really didn't fit the image that Hollywood likes to portray of ship captains barking orders at everybody. He got the job done in his own way. Captain Quigley was a man of medium height and reddish hair. I believe he also had faint freckles on his face. He was a WWII destroyer veteran, a Pearl Harbor survivor, and in his late 30's at the time he was captain of the Brush, which was quite old to us 18 to 20 year old fellows.

**Captain Donald F. Quigley**
**(This picture was actually taken a few years after he was captain of the Brush.)**

n weekends, somewhere, but it could be San Diego, Long Beach, ek or so, the ship would stay in port for a week.

a big problem for navy ships during the fall of 1952. Very cean and hang around all day. It was always a rather tense had to leave port in a dense fog. Of course, the ship would ddition, sometimes the planned training exercises would visibility was so poor.

nday morning, 25 August, 1952. At 0400 reveille everybody to heave out of their racks, trice up, and start way. This procedure probably started with the firemen lighting the "special sea detail" was set, and at 0605 the ship's anchor chain o which the ship was moored. Also, the lines (ropes) were cast off from ) to which the Brush was secured on the starboard side. The handling of the of the boatswain's mates and members of the deck force. Anyway, at 0605 the ship way and commenced maneuvering at various courses and speeds to stand out of the harbor. wever, just as we got underway, a thick fog rolled in off the ocean and the ship had to start making fog signals with the ship's bell. The ship was barely making headway because the visibility was so poor. At 0640 we passed through the inner breakwater with the breakwater light abeam to port at a distance of 150 yards. At 0709 we passed through the outer breakwater with the breakwater light abeam to starboard at 100 yards. As we passed through the outer breakwater and into the open ocean, I began to feel the ocean swells under the ship for the first time. It seems that the Pacific Ocean is always restless. Even if the surface of the water is as smooth as glass, the swells are always present and rocking the ship. As I remember, when fog was present there wasn't any wind or waves, like the conditions were during my first venture out to sea.

Upon passing through the outer breakwater, the Brush set a course of 158°(t) and increased speed to 7 knots to proceed to an operating area off the coast of Baja, California to rendezvous with the aircraft carrier, USS Valley Forge(CV45), to conduct flight operations. The fog was still rather thick and the ship still had to make fog signals at this point. At 0710 the ship secured the special sea detail and set the regular steaming watch. The foggy conditions gradually got better the further out to sea we got, and the ship gradually increased its speed, too. At 0906 the visibility increased to 10 miles and the ship increased its speed to 20 knots. At the same time, the fog signals were discontinued and the forecastle lookout was secured. The sky was blue and cloudless as it is so much of the time in the Southern California area. The ship soon increased its speed to 25 knots and a little later to 26 knots. The ship was churning right along at that speed and was leaving a long, straight ribbon of foam behind it. The dense fog had put the ship behind schedule and the captain was trying to make up for lost time.

At 1130 the Valley Forge was sighted bearing 126°(t) at a distance of 13 miles. At 1205 we rendezvoused with the carrier and started steering various courses and speeds to take station 1500 yards astern of her, and a little to starboard, which was the usual plane guard station. The Brush's job was to try to rescue the pilot in case a plane fell into the ocean when it was either taking off from the carrier or attempting to land on it. Fortunately, there weren't any problems on this trip out, and we didn't have to perform that kind of service. There was usually a helicopter hovering around behind the carrier, too, for the same purpose as ours. The presence of a helico operations was for the purpose of increasing the chances of the pilot being crashed into the water.

At 1443 the Valley Forge commenced air operations by launching aircraft head into the wind at a speed of around 25 knots when conducting flight operat rather breezy on the bridge of a destroyer when she was steaming at that speed the wind, too, regardless of the occasion. The carrier either launched aircraft or la afternoon and until nightfall. At 1930, after the last plane landed, the captain of the decided to call it a day and ceased air operations. When the flight operations were over Brush took position ahead of the carrier about 1500 yards, and a little to starboard, and this position during the night. The 2 ships steamed along off the coast of Baja, California al a speed of 10 knots. They were mainly just killing time until morning when flight operations commence again. According to the ship's log, the Brush was on regular steaming watches with ma condition baker set. The engineering plant was in condition of readiness 3 and with boilers 2 an and generators 1 and 2 in use.

At 0745 the Brush started maneuvering at various courses and speed to assume plane guard station on the Valley Forge. At 0758 the Brush arrived on station. At 0800 the carrier commenced launching planes. So, planes took off and landed on the carrier off and on all morning, all afternoon, and way into the night. She ceased flight operations around midnight. And again, we steamed around the rest of the night on various courses at a speed of 10 knots waiting for the new day to arrive. So, following the Valley Forge around off the coast of Baja, California while she conducted flight operations is what we did during my first week at sea. It was mighty breezy on the bridge, because we were steaming at a speed of 25 knots much of the time and were headed into a wind of 15 to 20 knots, too.

What did I do, personally, during my first week at sea? I assumed the duties of the quartermaster-of-the-watch and kept the quartermaster notebook when I was on watch. I hung around on the signal bridge when I wasn't on watch. I wasn't given too much responsibility of any kind, because I was a new man on board and as green as grass about being a seaman so not too much was expected of me.

The thing that I remember the best about my first days at sea was carrying a bucket around with me everywhere I went. I carried the bucket around with me to heave into. I was seasick some of the time like most people are when they first go to sea. I had what was called the dry heaves. I never threw up anything but green stuff. But the urge to do that came frequently, so I had to carry the bucket around with me to keep from throwing up on the deck. I had to carry the bucket around with me for 2 weeks, and after that, I was alright and didn't get seasick any more. I ate very little during my first 2 trips at sea as a result of being seasick. I wasn't hungry in the least. However, when I was lying down in my rack, I didn't experience any seasickness at all. Consequently, I was always glad to see night come so I could get some relief from the nausea feeling.

On Friday morning, August 29, at 1010, the Brush was detached from plane guard duty by the Valley Forge and proceeded independently back to Long Beach. At 1414 the ship set the special sea detail and commenced steering various courses and speeds to enter Long Beach Harbor. The captain was at the conn and the navigator was on the bridge. At 1455 the Brush commenced making approach to buoy 6 in the harbor. At 1503 she was moored alongside the USS DeHaven(DD727) with 6 standard destroyer mooring lines and with 30 fathoms of starboard anchor chain secured to buoy 6 and wire rope to buoy 7. At 1510 the special sea detail was secured and the regular inport watch

Moore(DD747) moored alongside to port, and at 1843 the USS ...ide of the nest alongside the Moore.

...rted aboard for duty. Cote would be our chief quartermaster ... He came aboard to replace Amos Phillips whose time had ...y good and competent chief. He was a career sailor and ...navy when WWII started. One day he made the remark ...t foot on land for 2 years. So he had been around and ...ond week that I was aboard her.

...ongside the DeHaven was that a Haines City High School ...at ship. The Brush and the DeHaven were in the same destroyer ...ere on opposite sides of the Pacific Ocean most of the time. However, ... be on the same side of the ocean on this particular day. Long Beach was ...ships. Somehow, I knew Billy was on the DeHaven; I can't imagine how I knew ... I went aboard the DeHaven and paid Billy a visit. It ended up we went on liberty ...that afternoon and into the night. We also rendezvoused with another classmate of ours, ...ward O'Neal, who had just returned from the Far East. Billy must have known about Edward's whereabouts; I'm sure I didn't. Anyway, we had a mini high school reunion in California that afternoon and an enjoyable liberty together.

This day, Friday afternoon, 29 August, 1952, was my first liberty in Long Beach, and it turned out to be one of the best ones that I ever had there. Billy and I took a water taxi to Fleet Landing where we went ashore. We proceeded to walk the mile or so to downtown. I had the most peculiar feeling as we walked along the sidewalk. The sidewalk felt like it was in motion just like the ship was when we were at sea. I know I must have had a strange looking gait if anyone happened to be watching me. The same thing happened after my second week at sea, but after that, the sidewalks weren't in motion anymore.

Of course, I spent the afternoon and evening with Billy and Edward, but I don't remember anything about what we did. Around 11:30 P.M., though, I decided it was time for me to go back to the ship and get a little sleep since I hadn't had much for several days. Anyway, I was going back to the ship alone.

As I was walking along on the way back to Fleet Landing, I noticed another sailor that was walking by himself, too, just like I was. Somehow, he looked familiar to me and I felt like I should know the fellow. I observed him for a few minutes and could tell he was just killing time. There was a permanent carnival at the edge of town and this fellow decided to check it out. I followed him. Finally, I figured out who he looked like and why I felt like I should know him. He looked like a mountaineer cousin of mine from West Buffalo Creek, North Carolina. I knew he was in the navy, but I had never actually seen him in person, although, I had seen pictures of him. This cousin was a year older than I was and had joined the navy right after graduating from high school in 1950. The last I knew about him he was on the carrier, the USS Roosevelt, in the Atlantic.

This sailor came to a board fence of some kind, stopped, and started leaning on it to look at something concerning the carnival. I walked up beside him and started leaning on the fence, too, where I could get a closer look at his face. Finally, I decided this fellow had to be my cousin or his father hadn't told his family everything about himself. So, I asked him, "Are you Ross Stewart?" He hadn't even noticed me up to this point. He looked me over real good for a few seconds without saying anything and without any kind of expression crossing his face. I saw that he didn't have a clue as to who I was. In a few seconds I said, "I'm Ted Holly." His face lit up and he broke into a big smile. I knew right then that this fellow was Ross. So, we walked around for the next couple of hours talking and getting acquainted. I forgot about needing sleep. It so happened that he was a fireman aboard the aircraft carrier, USS Kearsarge(CVA33), and it was leaving early the next morning for the Far East. His ship was an Atlantic Fleet ship and was on an "around the world" cruise. Finally, we had to go back to our ships, but I'll always remember that first liberty in Long Beach as probably being my best one.

## 13 Button Pants

On one of my first liberties in Long Beach, and I believe it was during this week in port, I went into an army-navy surplus store and bought myself a pair of second-hand dress blue pants that had the old traditional 13 buttons on them, and I got rid of my sloppy-looking navy issue zipper pants. I must have left them there at the store. Anyway, I never knew of any sailor in the fleet that kept and wore his navy issue zipper pants any longer than he had to after getting out of boot camp. We all hated them. If the navy had used a different type of cloth, the pants might have been acceptable to the sailors that had to wear them, but they didn't do that. They used the same kind of cloth which the sailors thought made them sloppy-looking and un-seamanlike. It was a dumb idea on somebody's part. I can assure you that the sailors in the fleet weren't consulted about that change in dress. It was probably some admiral's wife that made the decision to do that. All the sailors I ever knew loved their 13 button pants, and they weren't any problem at all to unbutton like people might think who aren't familiar with them. The flap on the front of the pants, fastened by the 13 buttons, could be opened in a second, for whatever purpose, by just a flip of your hand. There never was any fumbling around with the buttons to open the flap, even by a drunk sailor. A little more effort had to be expended when it came time to button the flap but not much.

## Shower Shoes

In an interesting way, I soon learned which ones of my shipmates had already made at least one trip to the Far East by the footwear they wore to the head when they intended to take a shower. They wore "shower shoes" as they were called by the sailors. They are known by everybody today as "flip flops". However, back in the early 1950's the only people that knew about flip flops were servicemen that had been to Japan, especially the sailors. Nowadays, however, it seems that essentially everyone in the U. S. has a pair of them. These flip flops were very practical for the sailors to wear to the shower. Otherwise, if they didn't have any, they had to wear their black leather shoes to the head because that is the only kind of shoe they had. I never saw anybody walking around on the ship barefooted because metal can be very hard on toes. Besides that, it was probably against regulations.

The usual price for a pair of flip flops in the early 1950's in Japan was $1.00.It stayed at that price the entire time I was around that part of the world. Flip flops are very similar to a kind of shoe that the Japanese people had been wearing for centuries called getas. I will say more about getas later.

## Personnel Inspection

I stood my first personnel inspection aboard ship on Saturday morning, 6 September, 1952. It may have been Captain Quigley's first inspection as captain, too, certainly one of the first. Inspections were something that the ship had every month or so throughout the time that I was aboard her. I'm sure all navy ships have inspections from time to time. That is just part of navy life.

In addition to personnel inspections, there were also inspections of berthing spaces and work spaces. My work space was the charthouse, but all my different captains ever did during inspections was to just walk in and walk back out without saying anything. The inspections of the charthouse never lasted over 5 seconds.

The members of the various departments aboard ship had specific locations to stand personnel inspections. The place the communications division went to was on the main deck, port side, just forward of amidships. There were about 20 of us in our group, which included the quartermasters and the radiomen. We would form up into 2 rows with about 10 men in each row. We would face outward. The chief quartermaster was in charge of us. When the time came for the inspection, the men would fall in and stand at parade rest. When the captain approached the group, the chief would give the order to come to attention and that is what we would do. Everybody would look straight ahead without any expression on their faces. The captain would take a quick glance at everybody and move on to the next group. The captain usually didn't say anything unless there was something about somebody that he didn't like. There were usually 2 or 3 officers accompanying the captain during his inspections, and one of them would be taking notes of things if the captain told him to.

The men in the communications division always passed inspection, the best I can remember, and the captain never had any negative comments to make about any of us. When the captain inspected us and moved on, the chief would give the order "parade rest" again, and we would stay in that position until the word was passed over the P.A. system to secure from personnel inspection. I think that everybody tried to look their best at the personnel inspections to make life easier for themselves. At the inspection, the captain looked for neatness in dress which included clean, pressed dress uniforms and shined shoes. It helped to have a clean white hat on, too. Plus, a fellow needed to have a recent haircut and be clean shaven.

## My Second Week at Sea

Monday, 8 September, the Brush went to sea again with the other ships of Destroyer Division 92 – the Maddox, the Samuel N. Moore, and the Herbert J. Thomas. This would be my second week at sea. At 0502 the boiler tenders lighted fires under boiler no. 2. The no. 4 boiler was already on line. At 0600 the ship began to make preparations for getting underway. At 0630 the Brush stationed the special sea detail. At 0647 the no. 2 boiler was cut in on the main line. At 0700 the Thomas got underway and stood out of the harbor. At 0706 the Moore got underway and stood out of the harbor. At 0712 the Maddox got underway and stood out of the harbor. At 0722 the Brush got underway from buoy 6 and 7 and commenced maneuvering at various courses and speeds to stand out of the harbor. The captain was at the conn and the navigator was on the bridge. At 0750 the Brush passed through the outer breakwater into the open ocean. Upon the Brush reaching the open water, the ships of Destroyer Division 92 formed up into a column formation with the Maddox in the lead and the Brush in the number 4 position. The ships assumed a southerly course at a speed of 20 knots to proceed to Operating Area No. 2 off the coast of Southern California to rendezvous with a number of other ships of Destroyer Division 72 and Cort Division 91 to conduct antisubmarine warfare (ASW). In Operating Area No. 2 the ships would conduct very intensive antisubmarine warfare (ASW) exercises for the next 4 days, both day and night. It wasn't exactly a fun trip or a fun thing. It was all work.

However, early in the afternoon of Thursday, 11 September, the formation of ships ended up a few miles off the coast of San Diego. At 1310 Point Loma was sighted bearing 074°(t) at a distance of 16 miles. At 1346 the destroyers were detached from the formation to proceed independently into the port of San Diego. At 1358 the Brush set the special sea detail. The captain was at the conn and the navigator was on the bridge. At 1405 the ship commenced maneuvering at various courses and speeds to conform to the channel. At 1312 we passed buoy 1SD abeam to port. At 1435 we passed Ballast Point abeam to port. At 1537 the Brush was moored to the port side of the Thomas at buoy 18 in a nest of 4 ships. At 1543 the ship secured the special sea detail and set the inport watch. Liberty was granted, but I didn't go ashore and I don't think too many people did – that assumption was based on the number of people that were AWOL the next morning – none.

Late Friday morning, 12 September, the ships of DesDiv 92 got underway and proceeded out of San Diego Harbor en route to Long Beach. The ships of DesDiv 92 arrived at the entrance to Long Beach Harbor around 1700 and at 1750 the Brush was moored to buoy 3. Here is where we spent the weekend.

I went on liberty Saturday morning. I took a boat to fleet landing and walked downtown from there. Again, the sidewalk was in motion just like the ship was doing during the week and the way it was after my first week at sea. It was an extremely unusual sensation. However, I never was seasick after my second week at sea, and, consequently, I never had to carry the bucket around with me anymore. The sidewalks never swayed anymore either, thank goodness. I really wasn't a sailor yet by a long ways but I was working on it.

## My Third Week at Sea

Early Monday morning, 15 September, 1952, the Brush got underway again to rendezvous with the aircraft carrier, USS Valley Forge(CV45). This would be my third week at sea and a rather interesting one in some respects. At the early hour of 0230 the ship began to make preparations for getting underway. At 0330 the ship stationed the special sea detail, and at 0400 we were underway from alongside the Thomas at buoy 3. The captain was at the conn and the navigator was on the bridge. The ship began to maneuver at various courses and speeds to stand out of the harbor. At 0435 the ship was in the open sea, secured the special sea detail, and set the regular steaming watch. The Brush assumed a southerly course to rendezvous with the carrier that was steaming up from the south, probably from San Diego.

Around 1030 we rendezvoused with the Valley Forge and proceeded to take screening station 1500 yards ahead of her. The 2 ships steamed around together on various courses and speeds for several hours without any planes being launched. The Brush conducted some onboard drills for something to do. I don't know what the carrier was doing. And I don't know why it was so necessary to get underway during the middle of the night, because the carrier didn't conduct any air operations until late in the day. But, who was I, a lowly seaman apprentice, to question anything that the navy did? Finally, at 1607 we assumed our plane guard station 1500 yards astern of the carrier and she commenced launching aircraft. The Valley Forge conducted air operations off and on until 1846 at which time she called it quits for the day. Upon completion of air operations, the Brush returned to her screening station 1500 yards ahead of the carrier. Now the carrier steamed more on a northerly course toward our destination – San Francisco. The carrier did conduct some air operations the next day on our way to San Francisco.

## San Francisco

Wednesday, 17 September, at 1040 we sighted the San Francisco light ship at a distance of 5000 yards. There was a slight fog that prevented us from seeing her any sooner. At 1134 the Brush began maneuvering at various courses and speeds to stand into San Francisco Bay. At 1146 we passed under the Golden Gate Bridge. Seeing the Golden Gate Bridge from seaward, and steaming under it, is somewhat of a thrill itself. The bridge is an awesome thing and it doesn't seem possible that it could have ever been built, especially where it is. There are some smart people in this world.

At 1159 we passed Alcatraz Island abeam to port at a distance of 2000 yards. At 1306 the Brush was moored portside to pier 15, Treasure Island, San Francisco, using 6 standard mooring lines. At 1340 the ship secured the special sea detail and set the regular inport watch. At 1342 fires were let die out under no. 4 boiler. At 1435 the ship commenced receiving steam, electricity, and telephone service from the dock. At 1515 the ship let the fires die out under no.1 boiler. At 1520 the ship commenced receiving fresh water from the dock, and at 1625 the ship secured from taking on fresh water having received 7,200 gallons. At 1600 two petty officers from the Brush left the ship to go on shore patrol duty.

The Brush and the Valley Forge only stayed in port one and one-half days and two nights. Early Friday morning, 19 September, the two ships got underway and departed San Francisco Bay independently. We passed under the Golden Gate Bridge at 0818 on the way out of the bay and into the open ocean. At 0919 we joined back up with the Valley Forge and took our normal screening station 1500 yards ahead of her. The two ships steamed south toward Long Beach and San Diego – thus ended our brief visit to San Francisco.

Regrettably, I don't remember a thing about what I did on liberty in San Francisco my first time there. I know I must have gone ashore Thursday morning, but I don't have any recollection of what I did or what I saw. The only things I remember are passing under the Golden Gate Bridge and passing Alcatraz Island where the prison was. At least three of my shipmates probably have more memories of San Francisco on this visit than I have, because they were brought back to the ship under arrest by the armed services police. They must have been having a great time – if only they can remember it. One of the offenders was Norm Jackson, one of the quartermasters. I'm sure he had an interesting story to tell because he usually did after coming in off liberty. I'm sure he told us all about his adventure in San Francisco, but I've forgotten what he told us happened to him on this liberty. Even if I remembered his tale, my sense of honor and loyalty to a fellow shipmate would probably prevent me from revealing his experience on this particular occasion.

The two ships just steamed south Friday, 19 September, and didn't do anything worth recording in the ship's log. There weren't even any air operations. I think the purpose of this whole trip was to give somebody the opportunity to go on liberty in San Francisco.

There were a lot of navigational aids to be seen at night as we steamed down the coast, and it was easy to keep ourselves located on the chart. I found that experience interesting from the navigational aspect and did a lot of practicing of coastal navigation. At 2305 we passed Santa Rosa light abeam to port bearing 076°(t) at 10 miles. At 0039 we sighted San Nicholas Island north light bearing 151°(t) at a distance of 14 miles. At 0057 Saturday, 20 September, we were detached from the Valley Forge to proceed independently to Long Beach. At 0114 we passed San Nicholas Island north light abeam to starboard at a distance of 13 miles. At 0314 we passed Santa Barbara Island light abeam to starboard at a distance of 7 miles. At 0652 the Brush set the special sea detail to enter Long Beach Harbor, and at 0752 we were moored starboard side to the Thomas at buoy 9 in a nest of 4 ships. We would stay in port for the next 9 days.

On Friday, 26 September, one of the quartermasters, M. (Pancho) Arredondo QM3/C, left the ship to be released from the navy. He was a Mexican-American and seemed to be well-liked by the other quartermasters. However, I really never got to know him very well during the short time we were shipmates.

## OCTOBER 1952

Monday morning, 29 September, 1952, the Brush, Maddox, and the Thomas got underway, went to sea, and conducted battle problem drills all day. But late in the day they came back into port at Long Beach and anchored in berth Q-9 in the outer harbor. Here, the ships spent the night without granting liberty.

Early Tuesday morning the ships commenced making preparations for getting underway, but a very heavy fog moved into the harbor and the visibility became very poor. Consequently, the ships just stayed at anchor where they were. I suppose it was the commodore that made the decision to do that. The fog hung around all day. The captain took advantage of the idle time by holding one of his frequent non-judicial punishment sessions and awarded varying amounts of punishment to five crew members for their indiscretions. Liberty was granted to the crew late in the day.

Wednesday, 1 October, the ships got underway and departed the harbor even though the fog was still present and the visibility was poor. The Brush made underway fog signals on the way out of the harbor. However, out at sea a few miles the visibility increased to three miles and the ship ceased making fog signals. The ships headed for San Clemente Island to conduct gunnery practice.

The crew didn't know it at the time, but they wouldn't be seeing much of Long Beach for several weeks. Although, I don't imagine anybody much cared unless it was the few married men that were aboard. The Brush was involved in intensive training of various kinds for most of that time, and we also operated with other ships most of the time, which always kept the signalmen busy.

We operated out of San Diego much of the time, too. Some of those days we took a bunch of personnel out with us to either observe how the ship did things or to test the ship's crew for readiness. Fog remained a problem for the ships and sometimes they would just have to wait until it lifted before they could conduct some of the planned exercises.

The Brush arrived at San Clemente Island Wednesday afternoon, 1 October, to conduct some gunnery practice, but the exercise had to be cancelled due to poor visibility. Late in the day the ship dropped anchor in Pyramid Cove and we spent the night there.

Early Thursday morning, 2 October, the Brush got underway and went to San Diego to pick up several men from the Naval Electric Laboratory that came aboard to conduct some sonar exercises. We took them to sea around 1000 and they conducted their sonar exercises for several hours. We went back in port around 1600 and spent the night there. Our passengers, of course, disembarked.

While we were in port this time another one of the quartermasters, Amos W. Phillips QMS1/C, left the ship for discharge. I know he was glad to be going home. He was a World War II veteran and had been recalled to active duty when the Korean War started.

Friday morning, 3 October, the Brush left San Diego Harbor with a number of other ships. This group of ships was designated Task Group 16.1. Fog was a problem for much of the day. The Brush and the other destroyers engaged in ASW exercises and formation screening exercises all day and all night, too.

Saturday morning the Brush went back to San Clemente Island and dropped anchor in preparation for a shore bombardment exercise. At 1330 the ship commenced firing at targets on the island. She ceased firing at 1428 having expended 85 rounds of 5″/38 common shells during the shoot. Upon completion of the gunnery practice the Brush returned to the task group.

Around 0700 Wednesday, 8 October, the ships of TG 16.1 arrived in the vicinity of Aliso Canyon off Camp Pendleton and the ships dropped anchor. I believe the ships went there to conduct some shore bombardment exercises. We stayed at anchor there for several days, but we never did do any firing because of poor visibility due to fog. Dense fog kept rolling in on us and the ships had to sound fog signals from time to time to let other ships know that we were lying in there in the dense fog.

We actually stayed off Camp Pendleton for five days and never did do anything of any significance. Apparently, the TG commander finally decided that the ships weren't going to be able to conduct the gunnery exercises that they came there to do , so DesDiv 92 was given the order to weigh anchor and proceed to Long Beach, and that is what we did around 1600 Sunday afternoon, 12 October. It didn't take very long to get there. The ships arrived at the harbor entrance around 1900 and were all moored to buoys 6 and 7 by 1948. Liberty was granted, but I don't think many men went ashore because of the lateness of the hour and the fact that we were getting underway again early the next morning.

DesDiv 92 departed Long Beach Monday morning, 13 October, and headed back to San Diego. The Brush operated out of there for the next 4 days. She took a group of men out to sea each day for some purpose or other. The first day, Tuesday, 14 October, several navy personnel, both officers and enlisted men, came aboard the Brush to conduct an Operational Readiness Inspection. So we went to sea and performed all kinds of battle drills and exercises for them, which included some ASW and gunnery practice. The ship fired 22 rounds of 5 inch shells and 73 rounds of 40mm shells during the day. We went back into San Diego Bay about 2000.

The next day, Wednesday, 15 October, 42 more navy personnel, both officers and chief petty officers, came aboard to conduct an Operational Readiness Inspection battle problem. We went to sea for approximately 3 hours during which time the ship conducted their battle problem. We went back in port around 1530. I'm sure the ship passed inspection to their satisfaction, because the Brush had some of the best officers and petty officers in the navy, in my opinion.

The next two days, Thursday and Friday, a group of men from the Fleet Gunnery School in

San Diego came aboard for some underway training. There were 287 of them, which were mostly seamen and seamen apprentice, but there were also a few ensigns, chiefs, and other rates among them. I suppose the chiefs were instructors from the school and were in charge of the trainees. We brought them back in port during the afternoon. The second day, Friday, 17 October, the ship put on quite a show for them by firing our 40mm guns at balloons in the water. The ship fired a total of 1,056 rounds of 40mm shells at the balloons. The Brush took the observers back in port around 1300. The ship then immediately departed the harbor and headed for Long Beach at a speed of 25 knots. We arrived in Long Beach around 1800 and spent the weekend there.

Monday morning, 20 October, the ships of DesDiv 92 went to sea and became part of a group of ships designated Task Group 11.7. The destroyers took screening stations around the USS Rochester(CA124) and the other larger ships in the task group. The formation conducted a lot of tactical maneuvers. The destroyers practiced changing screening stations around the formation both day and night for 4 days. I imagine those 4 days were a very challenging time for the OOD's and the people in C1C – to get the ships from one station to another without having a collision, especially at night. The destroyers also conducted a lot of ASW exercises during the week. I would say it was a rather intensive week of training for some of the crew. DesDiv 92 went back into port at Long Beach late Thursday afternoon, 23 October, and stayed in port there for 10 days.

## Portuguese Man-of-War

During the fall of 1952 the Pacific Ocean off Southern California was covered in Portuguese man-of-war. There must have been millions of them. Their vast numbers were a subject of conversation in the area at the time. In case you don't know, these Portuguese man-of-war are rather small ocean creatures that float on the surface of the water and look like small plastic bags that are filled with air. They are oblong in shape and are about 2 to 3 inches long. There is always a blue tint to part of the little bag. In addition, they have long narrow tentacles that hang down a foot or so beneath the body. These tentacles are loaded with little needles, and, as I understand it, they can give a person a severe sting if they are touched. Many of them washed up on the beaches of Southern California, and it was a bad time to be swimming or wading around in the water when the ocean was full of these things. When we were steaming off the coast of California, we would be traveling through them for miles and miles. After the fall of 1952, however, we never saw that many again; although, we frequently saw a few from time to time.

## Flying Fish

I saw an abundance of flying fish in the Pacific Ocean. They seem to be everywhere in that body of water, especially off the coast of California. They always fascinated me for some reason. Many times as the ship proceeded through the ocean, the flying fish would be continuously taking off in front of us. Flying fish were a relatively small, tubular shaped fish; a large one looked to be about 12 to 15 inches long and had a "wing" span of 15 to 18 inches, depending on the size of the fish. The wings were clear and looked very similar to those of a mosquito hawk (or dragon fly). Actually, their wings were oversized and elongated pectoral fins.

When flying fish would leap out of the water ahead of the ship, they would usually fly along just above the surface of the water and would be rapidly fanning their wings (pectoral fins). The wing tips would be flapping the surface of the water most of the time. However, they could do some soaring, too, if there happened to be a pretty strong wind blowing. The flying fish would usually take off in front of the ship and fly, or soar, out away from the ship 100 to 150 feet and then set back down. I never saw any flying fish except when a ship was passing through the water and disturbing them. I never saw any larger fish chasing them and I have no idea what they ate, because I never saw them act like they were chasing anything either.

Out in the mid-Pacific one time, during relatively rough weather, a large flying fish was found dead on the fantail one morning by one of the crewmembers. He brought it up to the bridge and was showing it around. The fantail was 8 to10 feet off the water. The fish flew up there somehow. My guess is it took off from the crest of a sizeable wave and soared accidentally onto the fantail. That fish was the only one that I ever saw up close.

## NOVEMBER 1952

At 0600 Monday, 3 November, the Brush and Thomas got underway and stood out of the harbor. The Moore had left our nest of ships at 0058 to go somewhere, and the Maddox wasn't with us, so it was just the Brush and the Thomas that were operating together on this Monday morning. We went out to sea and around 1000 rendezvoused with the submarine, USS Hammerhead(SS364). The Brush put her small boat in the water in order to transfer an observer from the submarine to the USS Electra(AKA4), which was also in the vicinity and was going to be operating with us for a few hours. After transferring the observer to the Electra, the surface ships got into a formation with the destroyers in their screening stations. The submarine submerged. So for the next several hours the surface ships steamed along in accordance with various zigzagging plans in an effort to evade the submarine. I suppose the submarine was trying to intercept the ships and simulate attacking the AKA. Of course, we couldn't see what she was doing since she was submerged.

At 1430 the Thomas was detached and left the formation. At 1606 the Brush got a submarine contact at 1100 yards distance and simulated an attack on it. That was the end of the operation. At 1614 the Brush was also detached from the Electra to proceed independently elsewhere.

At 1645 the Brush commenced a six hour, fifteen knot, economy run. She first assumed a course of 270°(t). The ship would steam for an hour or so on course 270°(t) and then reverse course to 090°(t) and steer that course for an hour or so. I believe it was on this afternoon, on this economy run, that an event took place that I've always remembered and regretted that it happened.

## An Unlucky Whale

On this afternoon, we were steaming probably 40 to 50 miles off the coast of Southern California. It was a clear day like so many of them are in that part of the world, and the ocean was quite calm with barely a riffle on it. Conditions on the bridge were unusually quiet, because we were just steaming along all by ourselves at 15 knots on this economy run. The ship was on a westward course of 270°(t).

I was the quartermaster-of-the-watch during this quiet afternoon. I didn't have anything to do so I was just standing up looking out one of the forward portholes. I noticed the OOD and JOOD didn't have anything to do either. I could tell that they were just engaged in idle chatter and not paying much attention to the ocean in front of them. Although, I could see for myself that there wasn't anything to be seen on the ocean in front of us as far as the eye could see. The ocean was empty clear to the horizon, so there really wasn't any reason for them to be too attentive. I also noticed that the lookouts seemed to be bored and weren't looking out too much either.

After awhile, I noticed a pod of whales cruising along some yards off our port bow. There must have been 5 or 6 of them. They were headed due north. They were interesting to watch because of the way they made forward progress. They would swim a little ways, barely beneath the surface of the water, then come up and blow, then go barely underneath the water again. They just kept repeating these motions as they swam along. They never were overly visible. I kind of noticed that nobody else had spotted them, and I knew that if they had seen them, they would be pointing and commenting about them, because we didn't see whales very often. The OOD looked in their direction a couple of times but apparently didn't see them. After watching the whales for a minute or so, I realized that the ship and the whales were on a collision course, and if one of them didn't change course, or do something, we were going to run together.

I noticed that the officers were still unaware of their presence. Then, I thought to myself, "Surely the whales are smart enough to stop, dive, change course, or do something to avoid the ship." After all, the ship was a lot bigger than they were. However, that was not to be; the whales kept plodding along in the same manner, and we had an unplanned and unpleasant rendezvous. When the whales got real close to the ship, I walked out onto the open bridge and looked over the rail to see what the whales were going to do. The lead whale did appear to dive along with the rest of the pod when she got within 30 feet or so of the ship's port bow; nobody, except me, had seen them yet. I thought to myself, "I hope she dives deep enough to clear the bottom of the ship and those propellers," but I doubted if she would. I went back into the pilothouse and stood by my desk and waited to see if I could determine in some way if she did or didn't. In 5 or 6 seconds the ship shuddered to the extent that it was easily felt by everyone on the bridge and probably the entire ship. Someone said, and I think it was the OOD, "What was that?" I went out the starboard hatch onto the open bridge and looked aft. I saw what I didn't want to see. There was a dark cloud beneath the surface of the water that looked red to me, and it told me the fate of the whale.

We had just run over and killed a whale. There is absolutely no way it could have survived those big screws. They hacked her to pieces, I'm sure. I've always regretted that incident and have felt that I should have done something to prevent it. I should have opened my mouth and told the OOD about us being on a collision course with the whales, but I didn't. However, the OOD should have noticed them himself and changed course slightly to avoid them, but he didn't. The port lookout should have seen them and reported them to the OOD, but he didn't. Since I saw them and nobody else did, apparently, I should have reported their presence to the OOD, although it wasn't my job to do so. I was a relatively new man on the bridge, and somehow I didn't feel comfortable about telling the officer-of-the-deck (OOD) or the lookouts how to perform their duties. So I kept my mouth shut; big mistake – especially for the whale. The whale's death just seemed so unnecessary. Consequently, because of my inaction, I have to share some of the blame for her death. However, I'm probably the only one on the ship that ever knew that we ran over and killed a whale, and I never bothered to tell anyone. What was the use? The deed had been done. Besides that, most of the crew probably wouldn't have cared anyway. I can excuse my inaction to some extent, however, because I didn't have too much time to think things out; because it was probably only a minute from the time I realized we were on a collision course with the whale and when we ran over it. I would do things differently if a situation like that ever occurred again, but it never did.

The Brush completed the fuel economy run at 2245 and decreased speed to 8 knots. However, she continued on the same courses for the rest of the night and most of the next morning, Tuesday, 4 November.

At 1206, Tuesday, the Brush went to general quarters in preparation for an anti-aircraft firing exercise. At 1220 an airplane came over towing a sleeve and the gunners commenced firing at the sleeve. The gunnery practice lasted until 1349, and during that practice session the ship expended 130 rounds of 5″/38AA common shells and 585 rounds of 40mm shells. When the gunnery exercise was completed, the Brush secured from GQ and set a course to rendezvous with the USS Philippine Sea(CA47) that was some miles south of us. The Brush reported to the carrier at 1800 as a plane guard ship. The Moore was already steaming with her in plane guard station number one, so the ship took plane guard station number two.

However, the formation just steamed around most of the night without doing anything. At 0400 the carrier finally commenced flight operations. They continued off and on until 0615 at which time the Brush was detached to go her own way. She went back north and rendezvoused with the Maddox around 1230, Wednesday, 5 November, and fell in astern of her 1000 yards. The Brush went to general quarters again in preparation for another anti-aircraft gunnery exercise. A plane came over towing a sleeve at 1238 and the Brush and the Maddox commenced firing at the sleeve. The gunnery practice was completed at 1345 and the ship expended 71 rounds of 5″/38 AA common shells and 786 rounds of 40mm shells.

Upon completion of the gunnery exercise, the Brush went back south to rendezvous with the Philippine Sea. Around 1700 the Brush took screening station 2000 yards in front of the carrier. At 1820 the Brush took plane guard station 1500 feet astern of the carrier. The Philippine Sea commenced flight operations at 1827. However, before the flight operations were completed, the Brush was detached from the carrier to proceed to San Diego. She was detached at 2110 and arrived at the entrance to the harbor at about 2230. The ship stationed the special sea detail at 2237 and at 2330 the Brush was moored to buoy 18.

Early the next morning, Thursday, 6 November, a whole bunch of gunnery students from the San Diego Naval Gunnery and Torpedo School came aboard to observe gunnery practice aboard ship. The Brush got underway at 0645 and proceeded to operating area KK 34 to conduct gunnery exercises for the benefit of the students. At 0858 the crew went to general quarters. At 0950 an airplane came over towing a sleeve and the ship's gunners commenced firing. The gunnery exercises were completed at 1124. The crew secured from general quarters and the ship set a course of 093°(t) to return to San Diego. The ship expended 109 rounds of 5″/38 AAC shells and 1104 rounds of 40mm shells.

The gunnery students disembarked upon arriving back at San Diego; that task was completed at 1400. The ship immediately got underway again and proceeded out of the harbor. The Brush assumed a course of 325°(t) and a speed of 27 knots to proceed to Long Beach. The Brush arrived at the Long Beach Harbor entrance at 1748. At 1845 the Brush was moored alongside the Thomas at buoy 9. The Brush stayed in port for four days.

Early Friday morning, 7 November, a seaman was caught coming aboard ship with two cans of beer in an overnight bag. At 1115 this same seaman had to appear at captain's mast and was awarded a summary court martial for his indiscretion. At his court martial a few days later he was awarded a few days in the brig. That was a big price to pay for the doubtful enjoyment of two cans of warm beer.

Tuesday night at 2030, 11 November, the Brush commenced making all preparations for getting underway. At 2230 the ship stationed the special sea detail, and at 2257 the ship was underway from buoy 9 and commenced maneuvering at various courses and speeds to proceed out of Long Beach Harbor. At 2334 the ship took departure from the harbor and set course 165°(t) and a speed of 10 knots en route to operating area MM 18 to rendezvous with the USS Philippine Sea(CV47). The Brush rendezvoused with the carrier Wednesday morning around 0900. We operated with the Philippine Sea for the next three days while she conducted flight operations. Nothing unusual happened during these three days. It was just breezy duty on the bridge much of the time. At 1100 on Saturday morning, 15 November, the Brush was detached from the carrier to proceed back to Long Beach. At 1552 the Brush was moored alongside the USS Hooper Island(ARG17) at buoy 6 and 7. Here we spent the rest of the weekend.

Monday morning at 0630, 17 November, the Brush got underway and proceeded out of the inner harbor into the outer harbor and dropped anchor in berth L5. At 0915 we received YFN-656 alongside to starboard to receive all of our ammunition. At 0940 the ship commenced unloading ammunition onto the YFN. The ship completed the unloading of ammunition at 1215 and a tug came alongside the YFN and towed it away. The ship weighed anchor at 1235 and departed Long Beach Harbor en route to San Diego to go into dry-dock. En route to San Diego, the ship conducted exercise Y-17-AW and dropped 11 depth charges over the side to test for weaknesses in the hull. At 1640 we entered San Diego Harbor, and with the help of a pilot and tugboat, the Brush moored starboard side to pier 4 in berth 43 at the naval station.

## In Port at the San Diego Destroyer Base for Maintenance

Tuesday morning, 18 November, some yard tugs and a harbor pilot moved the ship into dry dock 1. At 1030 the ship was moored in the center of the dry dock. The Maddox and Moore also entered the dry dock. The Brush stayed in dry dock for fifteen days. Wednesday afternoon, 3 December, the ship was moved out of the dry dock by tugs and moved to pier 4, berth 43. The ship would stay at berth 43 for another two weeks or so. A lot of maintenance was being done to the ship is the reason she stayed at the naval station so long. However, before Christmas the ship went back to Long Beach, but I didn't make the trip with her because I was on leave.

## Sea Planes

There was a seaplane base at San Diego and seaplanes were continuously taking off and landing in the harbor. I thought they were interesting to watch, and that is what I did some when we were moored there and I didn't have much of anything else to do. I believe they were the old PBM's and maybe some PBY's, too. But, they have both been long gone from naval service.

## A Minor Operation

All through my high school years I had a lump under the skin of my left cheek. I noticed it everyday, but I don't know if anybody else did or not. Anyway, it bothered me, so one day when the Brush was in dry dock in San Diego, I decided I would go to the base infirmary and see if I could have it removed. I walked into the base infirmary early one morning at sick call. There were a couple of dozen or so other sailors there, too, with various ailments. We were all lined up in a row in the middle of the room. A couple of corpsmen started walking down the row of patients, one from each end, and asking each one what their problem was. The corpsmen were the doctors. I wonder if they had a license to practice medicine. Anyway, when one of the corpsmen got to me, I showed him my facial lump, a cyst, actually, and told him I would like to have it removed. He looked at it, felt it, and said, "I think I can take care of that right now." He looked and acted pleased to have the opportunity to practice his surgical skills. I'm sure that was more interesting to him than just handing out pills, mostly APC's. He walked off and got an ointment of some kind to deaden the pain. He rubbed the ointment on my cheek, on the lump, waited a few minutes, and came back with a scalpel; all the while I am still standing in line. The corpsman took the scalpel and made a little half inch cut on my face over the lump. He squeezed and pops that cyst out from under the skin. He showed it to me. He looked pleased with himself and so was I. I was pleased to get that thing off my face, and I was pleased that he had done the job so easily and painlessly. As far as I was concerned, he did as good a job as any high priced surgeon could have done. Of course, he put 2 or 3 stitches in my cheek to close up the cut. Two or three days later I had them taken out by one of our ship's corpsmen. The cut on my face never left a scar either. Anyway, I thought it was kind of interesting to have a little operation performed on me by a lowly corpsman while standing in a line of men.

## Tijuana, Mexico

One Saturday, when the Brush was in dry dock at San Diego, I decided I would pay a visit to Tijuana, Mexico. It was a short distance south of San Diego and just over the border into Mexico. I had heard some of the sailors talking about their adventures in Tijuana. Apparently, it was a place to obtain cheap whiskey and willing senoritas. Also, it was a quite dangerous place, so the stories went, because some of the senoritas made the practice of luring naive young sailors to her place for a good time, but when he would go to her place, he would be jumped by one or more thugs that would beat him up and rob him of his money. Or, sometimes, these nice senoritas would get a fellow real drunk and then steal his money, or "roll him", as the term was. In addition, in some of the bars there were senores present that were real handy with a big knife and were always looking for an excuse to use it, especially on American sailors who they didn't like anyway.

I didn't go down to Tijuana to have a "good time". I just went to see what it was like, and I didn't like what I saw and didn't stay down there very long. I walked around the town a little bit and figured it was certainly one of the poorest looking places that I had ever seen. The buildings were all very shabby looking, and I don't think any of the streets were paved. It reminded me of the worst, poorest section of towns in the States. There were just dozen of vendors on the street trying to sell you something. They were always friendly enough when they were trying to sell you their wares, but when they saw that you weren't going to buy what they were selling, they would say something in Spanish. I couldn't understand what they were saying, but I knew it wasn't something nice or complimentary.

I believe the only thing I bought in Tijuana was one of those brightly colored throw rugs which I gave to my mother the next time I was home. My curiosity about Tijuana was satisfied and I didn't go back while I was in the navy.

In a letter to my mother I wrote about my visit into Mexico. "My short visit into Mexico wasn't very pleasant. It was nothing like the romantic Mexico I've heard so much about. All the stores were either a bar or a curio shop. There were gobs of sidewalk fiddlers, too. Everybody was trying to sell me something, and if I wouldn't buy, they usually looked like they wanted to cut my throat. The dwelling houses were mostly one room shacks, about to fall in, I might add. In fact, the town was a lot worse looking than the worst part of Ocala. Maybe someday I will go inland and find conditions better."

I did go back to Tijuana, Mexico around 1990 for a few hours. I was in San Diego for a Brush reunion and some of my old shipmates wanted to go down there so I went with them. In 1990 I found that the little nothing town of Tijuana had grown into a big, modern city and it wasn't the same place.

## CHRISTMAS LEAVE 1952

Around the first of December, 1952, I was told that I could go home on Christmas leave if I wanted to. I did. Although, I didn't think I had any leave time left for the year 1952. I didn't try to figure it out or call it to their attention that I may not have any leave left. They said I could go so I started making plans to go. The ship was going to be in port till after Christmas anyway so my services weren't urgently needed. So I took a 21 day leave to go home starting, 15 December, and lasting until, 5 January. However, 6 days of that time was going to be spent in traveling since I was going to be riding the bus. Enlisted servicemen didn't do much commercial flying back in the 1950's because they usually couldn't afford it. The Greyhound bus was usually the mode of transportation for sailors. Very few of the ship sailors had cars, unless they were married, because they didn't have much opportunity to drive them.

I arrived in Ocala around 9:00 pm, December 18, 1952. I decided the best thing to do was to go to my uncle Flint Holly's home and spend the night. I had a taxi take me to his house on 4th Street. They didn't know I was coming, of course. I just showed up at their door – that was my normal way of doing things. They were glad to see me and took me in, as I knew they would. Uncle Flint volunteered to take me home the next morning and did.

It was a rather cold December night and my aunt Lois gave me a bed with an electric blanket on it when we went to bed. Electric blankets were a new thing at the time and I didn't know there was such a thing until I found myself sleeping under one. I fought with that thing all night. I didn't receive any instructions about how to adjust the temperature, and she had set it on high, I guess, to warm the bed. When the blanket was on me, I was too hot, and when I threw it off of me, I was too cold. I felt like there should be some way to adjust the thing, but I couldn't locate the controls. I discovered the next morning that they were way back under the bed and out of reach. So my first encounter with an electric blanket was not a good experience. I didn't get much sleep that night.

Uncle Flint took me home the next morning like he said he would. Again, I can't remember much about what I did on this leave. I do remember going to Ocala a few times just before Christmas to do a little shopping, to see the Christmas sights, to feel the spirit of Christmas, and to look at the mob of people on the sidewalks around the square. The sidewalks around the square were usually crowded with people around Christmas time back in the 1950's and even later – until the city fathers saw fit to tear down the courthouse –big mistake.

One day just before Christmas, I met up with my cousin, Billy Holly, on the square in Ocala. We were having a little chat on the sidewalk when I noticed something in a store window that caught my eye. I believe it was a pipe and tobacco holder, and it had an old fashion ship's wheel on the front of it.

I thought it looked quite nautical, and I told Billy that I wanted to give it to him as a Christmas present and I did.

Several months later, Billy and his first wife, Helen, were having a pretty serious disagreement about something, and Helen picked up the gadget and reared back to throw it at him. But Billy told her that I had given that to him as a Christmas present and that she had better not break it. She immediately set it back down and started looking for something else to throw at him. Billy told me that tale many years later. I don't know if the gadget is still around or not.

As I said, I'm rather vague on most of the things that I did on this Christmas leave, but I do remember going on a hayride just before Christmas that I especially enjoyed. I met the Brush back in Long Beach after my leave was over.

## JANUARY 1953

Early Monday morning, 5 January, 1953, the ships of DesDiv 92 got underway and proceeded out of the harbor. The cruisers, USS St. Paul(CA73) and the USS Manchester(CL83), also departed the harbor, as did the tanker, USS Navasota(AO106). When all of the ships reached the open ocean, the destroyers formed a protective screen around the larger ships as usual. Fog was a problem during the day and all week, too. The ships had to occasionally resort to making fog signals. Around 1100 two other destroyer divisions from San Diego joined the formation and Task Force 13 was formed. The officer in tactical command (OTC) was ComCruDiv 1 embarked in the Manchester. This was going to be another week of intense training during the day and at night, too, sometimes.

Some of the exercises and drills the destroyers were engaged in included changing screening stations around the formation, air defense exercises, antisubmarine warfare (ASW), torpedo attacks, engineering casualties drills, refueling at sea, transfers at sea exercises, radar calibration exercises, sonar communications, and general quarters drills. Of course, the signalmen stayed very busy, too, because there was always a lot of visual signaling going on when we were in a formation of ships.

Task Force 13 started operating off the coast of Southern California, but during the week it drifted north. The OTC probably had a certain destination in mind all the time, but he didn't reveal it to anybody. Anyway, at 1040 Friday, 9 January, DesDiv 92 got orders from the OTC to proceed into San Francisco Bay, so that is what the ships did. In fact, all the ships in the TF got the same order and that is where all the ships of TF 13 spent the weekend. The ships proceeded independently into the bay, however. At 1259 the Brush passed under the Golden Gate Bridge. At 1309 a harbor pilot came aboard from a harbor boat and took the conn. We passed beneath the Oakland Bay Bridge at 1328. At 1350 a navy tug came alongside and assisted the pilot at docking the Brush at pier 2, berth 9, at the Alameda Naval Air Station. At 1410 the ship secured from special sea detail and set the inport watch. Liberty commenced at 1700. There were a lot of sailors from the task force ships roaming the streets of San Francisco that weekend.

## My Visit with the Snider Family

While we were in port in San Francisco, I took this time to visit a family I knew in San Jose, California. It was some people I knew from back home in Florida. They were the Dent and Vera Snider family. They had 4 children with the oldest one around 9 years old at the time.

Vera was a daughter of one of my neighbors back home, Doretha Pool, and I had known her for most of my life. Doretha lived on Church Lake, near home, and I used to cut her grass with an old fashion push mower when I was a young boy; this was during World War II. Dent was a navy pilot and was serving on various aircraft carriers in the Pacific. Vera lived with her mother much of the time while Dent was away helping to fight the war in the Pacific. Dent got out of the navy after the war and became a lawyer.

When Vera lived with her mother during the war, she had a pretty little dark-haired daughter named Vera Marie that was about 2 to 3 years old. I was around 11 to 12 years old. Vera Marie and I got to be big buddies, and she was always making me forsake my lawn care duties to play with her. I suppose we developed a bond with each other that has lasted to this day. How can a fellow say no to a pretty little girl that wants some of his attention? Vera Marie could barely talk but she would let everybody know that showed up that I was her "fwiend". She couldn't say friend. The word "fwiend" has been in my vocabulary ever since.

Anyway, I went to San Jose to visit my friends, the Sniders. We had been in touch with each other and they knew I was coming or they had invited me to come over. I can't remember exactly how all that came about. It just so happened that the day I got to their house, they were in the process of moving to a new home near Santa Cruz, California. So I got to help them move and rode in a big truck with Dent to their new home. That's all I remember about the occasion. Although, I did visit them a couple more times a year or so later at their new home in Scotts Valley near Santa Cruz.

The ships of Task Force 13 departed San Francisco early Monday morning, 12 January, 1953. They proceeded independently out of the bay, but upon reaching the open ocean, the ships joined back up and went into a formation with the destroyers taking their screening stations around the larger ships. Task Force 13 would be engaged in another 4 days of intense training exercises similar to those of the previous week. The TF was generally headed in a southerly direction.

At 2100 Wednesday, 14 January, the St Paul departed the formation to proceed to San Diego. At 2200 Thursday night, 15 January, the destroyers that came up from San Diego were detached from the formation to proceed to San Diego also. At 0627 Friday, 16 January, the remaining ships sighted Long Beach Harbor entrance light at a distance of 11 miles. At 0640 the Brush was directed by the OTC to proceed into port – which she did. At 0754 the ship was moored at buoy 9 in Long Beach Harbor in a nest with the Moore and the Thomas. Here is where we would spend the weekend. The Maddox had gone elsewhere.

## The Randall Family

When I was home on Christmas leave, my aunt Essie Randall gave me the address of her husband's brother and his wife that lived in the Los Angeles area. They had just recently moved out there from Atlanta, Georgia. They were Merwin and Lucy Neal Randall. Their younger son, Jerry, about 21 years old, also lived with them.

I had known of this family all my life but had only seen them a time or two when I was real small. We were raised in the same community but at different times. They had moved to Atlanta when I was still quite young. We actually weren't blood related, but we did have a family connection which made us feel somewhat related.

Saturday morning, 17 January, 1953, I just showed up at their door, unexpectedly. They lived in an apartment house in the city of Hawthorne at the time. When they opened their door, I had to introduce myself because they hadn't seen me for several years – since I was a young boy. They invited me in and we had a great reunion. We were all homefolks, far from home. I visited this family a number of times over the next 3 years when I was in the States, and we had a lot of good times together. However, I was going overseas the first of February for 7 months so my visiting with them had to wait for awhile. But I did visit with them one more time before I left.

## San Clemente Island Gunnery Practice

Early Monday morning, 19 January, the ships of DesDiv 92, less the Maddox, went to sea again to engage in gunnery practice around San Clemente Island. This was our last week at sea and our last week of training before going overseas.

Monday afternoon on the way there, a plane came over towing a sleeve and the ship got in some antiaircraft gunnery practice with her 40mm guns. The gunners fired at the sleeve off and on for about 20 minutes and expended 458 rounds of 40mm shells during that time. The Brush then proceeded on to Pyramid Cove, Clemente Island to conduct a shore bombardment rehearsal exercise, but actually she didn't do any firing at this time. Upon completion of the rehearsal exercise, the Brush proceeded to rendezvous with the Thomas and the two ships steamed around together all night south of San Clemente Island.

At 0600 Tuesday morning the Brush was detached from the Thomas to proceed back to Pyramid Cove to conduct gunnery practice. At 0857 the Brush commenced firing at targets on the island. She ceased firing at 1254 after expending 44 rounds of 5″/38 AA common shells.

Early Tuesday evening, after dark, the Brush fired her 5″ guns some more off San Clemente. This session, she fired 38 rounds of illumination shells, or star shells, as they were commonly called, and 8 rounds of 5 inch AA common shells. At 2136 Tuesday night the Brush dropped anchor in Pyramid Cove and spent the night there.

The next day, Wednesday, the Brush was involved in some more gunnery practice. In the early afternoon a plane came over again towing a sleeve and the ship's gunners got in some more anti-aircraft practice. They shot at the sleeve for an hour or so and expended 92 rounds of 5″/38 AA common shells and 1008 rounds of 40 mm shells. Then, late in the afternoon on Wednesday, the Brush went back to the vicinity of Pyramid Cove and conducted some more shore bombardment exercises. On this occasion, she expended 32 rounds of 5″/38 AA common shells. Wednesday night the Brush again dropped anchor in Pyramid Cove and spent the night there.

Thursday, 22 January, the Brush conducted various exercises associated with gunnery, but she didn't actually fire her guns. Late Thursday afternoon the Brush went back into Long Beach Harbor and dropped anchor in explosive anchorage L7 in the outer harbor. She went there to take on ammunition. At 1650 an ammunition barge came alongside, moored to the ship, and the ship commenced loading ammunition. The task was completed at 1730 and the barge left. At 1745 the Brush weighed anchor and proceeded to Net Pier. At 1818 the Brush was moored to Net Pier at the Long Beach Naval Base. The Brush stayed moored here until the ships of DesDiv 92 left to go overseas, 2 February, 1953, a period of 11 days.

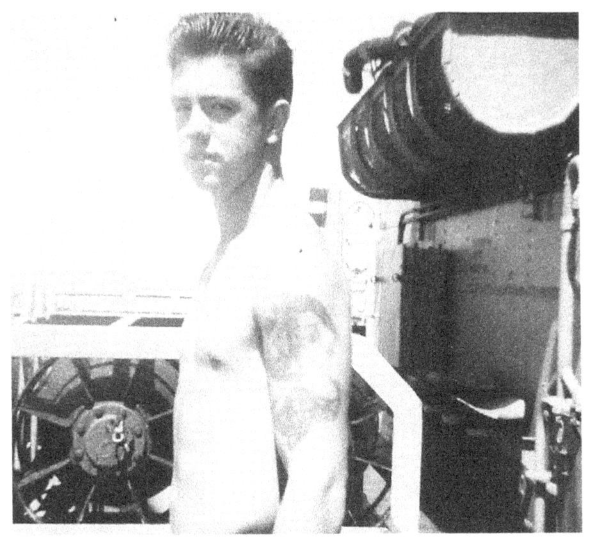

Pat Ryan, Torpedoman

Hank Chaulker & Dave Tautolo GM3

Lloyd McCord GMSN, ________,
Leroy Rupp & Dave Tautolo GM3

Lloyd (Mac) McCord GMSN

**Unknowns**

**Hank Chalker, Torpedoman**

**Sammie Baker GM3**

**______, ______, Raymond Ward GMSN, Sammie Baker GM3**

John Duggan, Russell Maxwell, Rex Arnold

Rex Arnold, Frank Adamson MMC, Ted Wilson, ______Adamson

## LONG BEACH

As I remember, Long Beach had about the same kind of businesses that you would find in any other town. There was an assortment of clothing stores, drugstores, a few restaurants, a few bars, a couple of small hotels, a movie theatre, a permanent carnival, and 2 or 3 army-navy surplus stores, which was a little out of the ordinary. The army-navy surplus stores were there because of all the servicemen in the area, especially the sailors. There was also a YMCA, which catered to the sailors and tried to provide them with a little wholesome entertainment, if they were interested in that sort of thing.

In my opinion, Long Beach wasn't much of a liberty town, especially if you didn't drink, because there wasn't very much to see or do. Of course, if a person was a drinker, he could spend most of his time ashore hanging out in the bars, that is, if he was old enough to go in bars and drink. However, I would say that most of the sailors in the fleet were less than 21 years old, the legal drinking age at the time.

So what did I do when I was on liberty? I always went to a restaurant and had myself a good meal. Then, if there was a good movie playing at the theatre, I would go to the movies. I hung around the YMCA some, too, but there usually wasn't much going on there during the day, but it was a place I could go and hang out.

The YMCA had dances sometimes on Saturday nights that were held especially for the benefit of the sailors. I went to a few of them. Of course, I couldn't dance a lick when I first arrived in Long Beach. However, I did trouble myself by going to a local Arthur Murray dancing studio and learn how to dance for lack of anything better to do. So, I attended a few of the dances during the fall of 1952 and did a little ballroom dancing. In fact, that is the only kind of dancing they ever did and I wasn't too good at that. However, I was able to wander around on the dance floor without stepping on too many toes. Also, I couldn't help noticing that most of the sailors on the dance floor weren't very good dancers either. Most of them didn't have a clue about how to dance it appeared to me. The girls on the other hand were usually very good dancers and tolerated whoever they were dancing with.

I don't know if any serious romances ever developed from those Saturday night dances, but I believe it was a good possibility for some of the sailors, if they were looking. I wasn't looking myself. I was just bored and needed something to do to entertain myself. However, I observed that a lot of nice girls and good-looking girls attended those dances.

Personally, I found that just dancing with a girl really wasn't all that satisfying anyway, because it didn't take the place of a meaningful relationship with a special girl that you really cared about. I didn't do any dancing at the YMCA after the fall of 1952, because I found more interesting things to do – like visit a hometown family I knew that moved to the area.

Another thing I did during the fall of 1952 was to take the Greyhound bus to nearby towns on the ocean that had the reputation of having good beaches. I've forgotten the names of these towns now. But I found that the beaches weren't all that great compared to most Florida beaches. The ocean water was much too cold to enjoy swimming in or even wading in it. I think the water must have come from melting glaciers around Alaska. I really didn't see too many people venturing into the water, at least, not for long. The beaches tended to be a little trashy, too, as I remember. I didn't see anybody surfing in the waves back then either.

I did see people surf fishing some and they were sometimes successful at catching fish off the beach. In fact, I did some surf fishing myself later on and caught some fish and I also got sunburned.

On 2 or 3 occasions I remember checking-in at one of the local hotels and spending the afternoon sleeping, because I needed sleep so badly and I knew I couldn't get any on the ship. As I remember, I could rent a pretty nice room at the hotels for 5 or 6 dollars. The hotels weren't anything elaborate but I didn't care. All I wanted was a clean bed for a few hours.

One thing I especially noticed as I traveled around Southern California was all the beautiful flowers that were growing around many of the homes there. The houses themselves tended to be small and on small lots, and, consequently, the brightly colored flowers were grown up around the sides of the houses. It was a very beautiful sight.

## Bars and Barmaids

Many of the sailors that were 21 years old and older, and of legal drinking age, hung out in the bars for their entertainment. Sailors seem to have a reputation for doing such things. Their main objective most of the time, of course, was to try and make out with the barmaids and the barfly girls. Sometimes they were successful according to some of the tales that I heard from some of my shipmates. I could understand why the young sailors needed some female companionship, but I'm sure most of the girls they were associating with in the bars weren't the type of girls that a fellow wanted to take back home to meet the folks. However, most of the time the sailors weren't interested in taking the girls back home to meet the folks anyway, regardless of what they might be telling them in an attempt to achieve their objective.

I'm sure some of the barroom women must have been halfway decent and would have made a good companion for a fellow, but I would guess that it was a pretty poor bet, generally speaking. Of course, I didn't have any first hand knowledge about the barroom activities myself. I only knew what I was told by some of my shipmates, and some of them were well informed and highly qualified to talk about it.

## California Foods

One thing I did do in Long Beach that I found interesting was to try foods that were new to me or that were grown in California. One of the things that I ate occasionally was Pacific Ocean prawns. They looked like shrimp and tasted like shrimp to me. I don't know what the difference is between shrimp and prawns. Maybe the people on the West Coast just didn't know what shrimp are. Nevertheless, I played their game and called shrimp, prawns, while I was on the West Coast.

Another seafood I ate a few times was abalone. Abalone is a shell fish that was indigenous to the Pacific Ocean. It was a delicacy on the Pacific Coast and rather pricey. I would have eaten more of it if it hadn't been so expensive. The flesh of the abalone was very tough and was usually pounded, or tenderized in some way, before being cooked – usually fried. The abalone had a very beautiful mother-of-pearl shell, too, from which jewelry and other objects were made. I bought a few ornaments that were made from the abalone shell. I also brought a big abalone shell home with me; they are about as pretty as a seashell can get.

Some of the other things that I ate when I had the opportunity were Californian grown watermelons, cantaloupes, strawberries, peaches and plums. I thought all of these Californian grown fruits were quite delicious. However, I didn't like the oranges that much. They were just so-so, because they had a thick rind and the good orange flavor simply wasn't there as compared to a good Florida orange. But I ate them and was glad to see them come aboard ship occasionally.

We also got apples aboard ship occasionally but I don't know where they were grown. They could have been grown in Northern California, Washington, or Oregon, but they were always delicious regardless of where they were grown.

## Oil Wells

One thing I thought was interesting about Long Beach was the oil wells. There were, I suppose, hundreds of oil wells in the city of Long Beach that were pumping away both day and night for 365 days a year. They were located in people's yards all over the place. I always thought I would love to have an oil well in my back yard. They were kind of unsightly, but who cares if it is bringing in easy money 365 days a year. At one time there was a tremendous amount of oil under the Long Beach area, but I imagine it has all been pumped out of the ground a long time ago. But I am sure it was a good thing for the people who benefited from it for as long as it lasted.

## Weather

The weather around Long Beach was usually rather pleasant but tended to be rather hazy most of the time. The Sierra Madre Mountains were some miles to the east of us, but we rarely ever got to see them clearly. Most of the time, we could only see an outline of them against the sky. I believe the tops of them were usually covered in snow. I know they were a beautiful sight from a distance before the days of automobiles and smoke stacks that created the haze and smog around Long Beach. I've seen pictures of the mountains that were made years earlier when the atmosphere was clear. They were a beautiful sight to see.

In addition to the haze, the area had a lot of foggy mornings, fog that rolled in off the ocean. Sometimes it would hang around all day, too, and occasionally, under certain atmospheric conditions, the fog would mix with the smoke and reduce visibility to a few feet. The city would have to turn the street lights on in the middle of the day and it was still rather dark. Everything tended to look different in town, you could barely see across the street, and you couldn't tell where you were and stayed lost most of the time. Of course, it wasn't worthwhile, or safe, for ships to get underway under such conditions either.

It didn't rain very much in Southern California. It was rather amusing to me what people in that part of the country called a heavy rain. A heavy rain in Southern California would have been called a drizzle in Florida. I never saw a heavy rain, or a downpour, in California like we frequently have in Florida.

My opinion of the weather around San Diego was that it was about as good as it gets. They had a Mediterranean type climate with clear, deep blue skies most of the time. It was very similar to Florida skies in the fall of the year. All of Southern California could have benefited from more rain, however.

## My Queer Encounter

On one of my liberties in Long Beach, I decided to go to the movies, although, the movie didn't appear to be that great according to the posters that I saw in front of the theatre. However, I didn't have anything better to do. I had already had my usual dinner, and I wasn't interested in going back to the ship yet because I had just come ashore. So, it was still rather early on this Saturday afternoon that I went into this theatre. There were relatively few people in the theatre and I had a big choice of seats. I took a seat in the middle section of the movie house. There wasn't anybody sitting within 10 seats of me in any direction. After the movie had been playing for 20 minutes or so, a fellow came in and took a seat right beside me. I was barely aware of his presence, but I do remember thinking, "why did he select a seat right beside me when there are so many empty seats in the house?" However, I was concentrating on watching the movie and didn't give it anymore thought. After a few minutes, I suddenly became aware that this fellow had put his hand on my leg. Then it hit me what this fellow had on his mind, and I think my hair stood straight up on top of my head. I quickly got up and went to the restroom, mainly to get away from him and to try to decide what I wanted to do – go back in and find myself another seat or leave the theatre. I was actually in somewhat of a state of shock – the innocent country boy that I was. I had heard about such fellows, but I had never encountered one before. Anyway, I didn't have long to think about it because he came into the restroom. He was a rather tall, slim, good-looking young man with black hair. I knew he was after me and his intentions weren't honorable. The time for a decision had arrived. I said, "Fellow, you have the wrong person." I walked past him out of the restroom and left the theatre. He hadn't said a word yet, although, he did have a rather disappointed look on his face when I walked past him. That was my first encounter with a queer and I never saw that one again.

Society uses the word "gay" nowadays instead of the old fashion word "queer", but I believe the word queer more accurately describes such people. In my opinion, as well as the opinion of most normal people, any man that would prefer another boney, shapeless, hairy man over a beautiful, curvaceous, soft, loving woman, who has been perfectly constructed by our creator for a man to have sex with, is queer, weird, and mentally sick. In addition, any straight person that thinks homosexuality is just fine, normal, and just an alternative lifestyle has got a mental problem, too. They might as well go ahead and be one themselves.

According to the Christian Bible, God thinks the act of sex between men is despicable and a sin. And if that is the case, then maybe us mortals should, too; the quality of your future life may depend on it. If anyone thinks that what I have said is unreasonable, and you don't agree with it, don't argue with me about it. Instead, you can tell God that you think that he is wrong and unreasonable on the homosexual issue when you stand before him on judgment day. Furthermore, there are probably a few other issues that you don't agree with him on either, and that would be your opportunity to tell him so – and see where it takes you. It would probably be best for you to make a list of all the things you disagree with God on so that you don't forget anything. Maybe you can impress him with your vast intellect.

## SOME OF THE SHIP'S OFFICERS

**Lt. Addison Beaty**

**Lt. Herbert Childers**

**Lt. Robert Walters**

**Ens. William (Robbie) Robbins**

**Lt. Addison Beaty, Lt(jg) Cecil Barlay**
**Ens. Theodore (Ted) Brown**

# Other Officers Aboard the Brush that made the 1953 Cruise to the Far East

1. Ens. George T. Bailey
2. Lt(jg) Herbert O. Burton
3. Ens. T. L. Clabeaux
4. Lt. O. A. (Jack) Easterling, Jr.
5. Lt.(jg) W. F. Mitchell
6. Lt.(jg) W. J. McCaine, Jr.
7. Ens. Patrick M. O'Meara
8. Lt. M. A. Ricker
9. Lt. I. J. Rudick
10. Ens. C. E. Sloan
11. Lt. W. A. Sperry
12. Ens. R. S. Tuszynski

# 6

# FIRST CRUISE TO THE FAR EAST – 1953

## LONG BEACH TO HAWAII

My long anticipated trip to the Far East finally took place early on Monday morning, 2 February, 1953, as the ships of Destroyer Division 92 got underway for Pearl Harbor, Hawaiian Islands on their way to Japan and North Korea. At 0510 word was passed over the P.A. system for the ship's crew to make all preparations for getting underway. At 0700 the special sea detail was stationed, and at 0718 all mooring lines were cast off and the Brush was underway from Net Pier, U.S. Naval Station, Long Beach, California. The ships steered at various courses and speeds to proceed out of the harbor. The captain was at the conn and the navigator was on the bridge. The ships of DesDiv 92 steamed out of the harbor in a column formation, as was their normal practice, with the Maddox at the head of the column and the Brush at the rear of the column. At 0732 we passed through the Long Beach inner breakwater, and at 0754 the Brush secured the anchor detail and set the regular steaming watch.

Upon reaching the open ocean, the ships of DesDiv 92 joined up with 3 larger ships that were to accompany us to Pearl Harbor. The destroyers disbursed from their column formation and proceeded to form a screen around the larger ships. The 3 ships that we joined up with were the USS Navasota(A0106) – an oil tanker, the SS Marshfield Victory, and the SS East Point Victory – 2 cargo ships. The officer in tactical command, or OTC, was DesDiv 92's commodore, Captain Bowen, who was embarked in the Maddox. The guide of the convoy was the USS Navasota.

During the afternoon some more ships joined up with us – the USS Vammen(DE644), the USS Lewis(DE535), the USS Marsh(DE699), and the USS Naifeh(DE352). And, after nightfall, a couple more ships joined up with us – the USS Sitkoh Bay(T-CVE-86) and the Pvt. Joseph F. Merrill (T-AKV-4). So, we had a pretty nice little convoy after all the ships got together. The convoy's course was generally in a southwest direction, something in the order of 220° to 240°. However, the destroyer escorts, DE's, didn't stay with us too long. During the night they were detached from the convoy to proceed independently on their way to somewhere.

Anyway, our trip over to Hawaii wasn't just a leisurely little cruise to paradise. It was one continuous drill or ship exercise of some kind all day long and half the night. The destroyers were continuously changing courses and speeds, on zigzag courses, and changing screening stations in formation. I think much of our time was spent playing with friendly submarines. They were trying to "attack" the convoy, and the destroyers were trying to prevent them from doing it.

On Friday, 6 February, at 0742 the Brush went alongside the Navasota to take on fuel. The ship secured from receiving fuel at 0842 and during the refueling operation received 67,408 gallons of fuel oil.

On Saturday, 7 February, 1953, Captain Quigley held non-judicial punishment, or captain's mast, for a group of 13 sailors, mostly for being AWOL for varying amounts of time from a few hours to several days. The severity of the punishment to the sailors varied according to how long they were AWOL or how many times they had previously been AWOL. Some of the sailors got 2 weeks restriction, some of them got summary court-martials, and some of them got special court-martials. However, one fellow was awarded 10 hours extra duty for being a "late sleeper". In other words, he didn't bother to get up at reveille one morning.

## HAWAII

Right after midnight on Monday, 9 February, 1953, the first sign of Hawaii was observed at 0006; the Molokai light was sighted bearing 156°(t) at a distance of 19.5 miles, and the Makapun Point light was sighted at 248°(t) at a distance of 26 miles. Then we began to sight other navigational lights as we proceeded toward the islands. At 0226 the Diamond Head light was sighted, and at 0329 we passed the Diamond Head light abeam to starboard at a distance of 11 mile.

At 0747 the special sea detail was set and the ship commenced steering various courses and speeds to enter Pearl Harbor, T.H. The captain was at the conn and the navigator was on the bridge. At 0856 we moored starboard side to the Thomas at fuel pier 3 at the U.S. Naval Base at Pearl Harbor. At 0906 the special sea detail was secured. After refueling, the ship got underway and proceeded to berth B-3 and moored port side to it.

### Waikiki Beach

We spent the afternoon and night in port. Liberty was granted and some of the crew went ashore, including me. Liberty started fairly early in the day. I went ashore to specifically check out the town of Honolulu and Waikiki Beach. There really wasn't too much to see in Honolulu, I thought, but I got my curiosity about it satisfied. Also, I found Waikiki Beach to be rather disappointing as far as beaches go. It was a relatively small beach and really not all that great when you compare it to Daytona Beach and dozens of other Florida beaches. However, there was a beautiful view of Diamond Head at Waikiki and I suppose that is worth something. Nevertheless, I enjoyed just being there. Waikiki Beach has its own special charm, and I probably shouldn't compare it to Florida beaches anyway. I know I went to an exotic restaurant while I was there, but I don't have any recollection of that now.

### Operating Around Hawaii

Early the next morning, Tuesday morning, the Brush got underway and proceeded out of the harbor along with the rest of DesDiv 92. We soon rendezvoused with a submarine, the USS Bugara(SS331), and played around with it for a couple of hours. We left the sub and that area of operation in the early afternoon and rendezvoused with a tug, USS Apache(YTF67), with the purpose of target practicing with the 5 inch guns. The tug was towing a sled. The Brush conducted gunnery practice for about 1 ½ hours and expended 72 rounds of 5 inch shells during that time. We then operated with the cruiser, USS Manchester(CL83), and 4 other destroyers for the rest of the afternoon. The destroyers were the Maddox, Thomas, USS Sproston(DDE577), and the USS Jenkins(DDE447). However during the time that those ships were operating together, they were steering a course that was generally in the direction of Maalaea Bay, Maui, T.H. I think all the ships were going there to conduct gunnery practice. At 0316 the Brush was detached from the formation to proceed independently to her fire support area. At 0420 the Brush set the anchor detail and commenced maneuvering at various courses and speeds to proceed to her anchorage in Maalaea Bay, Maui. At 0430 the Brush anchored in 10 fathoms of water over sandy and coral bottom with 45 fathoms of chain to the port anchor. Here we stayed anchored the rest of the night, all the next day, and the next night. We didn't do much of anything during this time except enjoy the Hawaiian weather.

Wednesday night at 2110 the deck crew had to let out 45 fathoms more of anchor chain to keep the ship from drifting due to strong winds.

Thursday, 12 February, the Brush conducted gunnery practice off Kealikahiki point, Kahoolawe Island most of the day. She was firing at targets on Kealikahiki Point as directed by somebody.

# THE BRIDGE GANG IN HAWAII

**Sam Smith & Eugene Cote QMC**

**Ed Geffert & Norman Jackson**

**Lawrence Barth**

**Ted Holly**

**Eugene Cote QMC**

**Sam Smith & Norman Jackson**

We stayed at general quarters most of the day. The ship fired 52 rounds of 5 inch shells during the day's shore bombardment practice.

Friday morning the Brush returned to the submarine operating area and conducted some ASW exercises with the USS Cabezon(SS334) for a couple of hours. However, at 1138 the ship secured from ASW exercises and set a course for Pearl Harbor. At 1233 the Brush stationed the special sea detail in preparation for entering the harbor. At 1327 we moored starboard side to the Moore at berth B-25. Liberty call was announced soon after the ship was moored. We were to be in port for 3 ½ days, until Tuesday morning, 17 February.

## A Hawaiian Luau on Waikiki Beach

I went on liberty 2 of the 4 days we were in port, Saturday and Sunday. I can't remember everything that I did on liberty those 2 days ashore, but I do remember some. I spent most of the day Saturday ashore. Saturday evening I went to a luau on the grounds of some big hotel on Waikiki Beach and had a very exotic meal, Hawaiian style, including poi. However, I didn't get too excited about the taste of poi. I thought it looked and tasted like paste. They had a lot of food at this luau, but I believe the main item was a pig that was cooked in a pit in the ground. I can't remember everything that was served at this dinner, but I do remember there was plenty of fresh pineapple that was as good as it gets. I've always remembered that evening as a very special evening, because it was such a different experience than what I had ever had before. I was in Hawaii, live Hawaiian music was playing in the background, I had a wonderful Hawaiian dinner, the temperature was very pleasant, the trade winds were rustling the coconut palms, and the scent of plumeria flowers was in the night air. Taking everything in consideration, it was a very pleasant, special evening. The only thing I lacked was a special someone to enjoy it with.

On Sunday, there seemed to be a lot of entertainment everywhere on Waikiki Beach in the way of Hawaiian music and hula dancing. I wandered around and watched and listened to a lot of it. I took in all I could and enjoyed the day very much. Liberty in Hawaii was sort of what I had in mind when I joined the navy. I found the weather in Hawaii to be rather hot and humid during the day, but the nights were very pleasant. I especially enjoyed the early evenings and nights because the temperature was just right, a gentle breeze was usually blowing, and the scent of plumeria flowers was always present in the night air. I don't remember smelling the scent of this flower during the day.

Being the country boy that I was, I noticed a lot of things that maybe other people wouldn't give any thought to. I thought the color of the Hawaiian sky was very beautiful. It was a deep blue, similar to Florida skies in the fall, with an abundance of fluffy white clouds floating about much of the time. A lot of little rain showers seemed to fall out of little nothing-type clouds and would get you wet if you weren't careful. But I never saw a downpour of any length like we frequently have in Florida. I don't remember seeing any lightning either or hearing any thunder.

I thought the color of the ocean around Hawaii was very beautiful also – just like the advertisement pictures showed. I think the color of the water went beyond a blue to maybe a purple, at least sometimes. It certainly was a deep color and different from any other place in the ocean that I have ever seen.

One of the things I saw in Hawaii that fascinated me was jewelry that was made from butterfly wings. I thought it was very pretty and so unusual. I bought a necklace, I believe, made from a blue butterfly wing and sent it to a very special person back home. If I bought any other trinkets in Hawaii on that visit, I don't remember what they were. After all, it has been over 55 years ago since I made that first visit there. I actually made 6 visits to the island of Oahu while I was in the navy.

## HAWAII TO JAPAN

On Tuesday morning, 17 February, 1953, Destroyer Division 92 got underway from Pearl Harbor en route to Yokosuka, Japan. The ships of DesDiv 92 had to steer some southerly courses for a few hours to clear the islands before heading west. However, at 1740 the formation changed to the westwardly course of 270°(t). The ships were cruising at a speed of 16 knots.

At 1747 the USS Manchester(CL83) and the USS Princeton(CVA37) rendezvoused with the ships of DesDiv 92. Of course, the destroyers immediately formed a protective screen around these two bigger ships – a cruiser and a carrier. So, all together, we headed west toward Japan. It was going to take 10 days to make the voyage from Pearl Harbor to Yokosuka.

The Pacific is a mighty big ocean and it was overcast the entire trip across except around Hawaii. It was wonderful weather there. The only way we had to keep track of our position was by means of dead reckoning and our loran gear, which was very primitive compared to what is available today.

Early one morning out in the mid Pacific, the navigator, Lt Childers, burst into the charthouse where I was and said, "Holly, where are we? What's our position?" I think he was late in sending in his morning position report. Of course, it really wasn't my responsibility to determine our position. However, I had been operating the loran gear for my own pleasure and had determined our position the best I could with the poor signals that I was able to get. I was able to receive 3 poor quality signals and had plotted them on a small scale navigational chart that was spread out on the charthouse desk. I told Lt Childers that I could only show him our position within 15 miles, because the loran signals were so poor that morning; we were several thousand miles from the nearest loran stations. He looked at the triangle I had plotted on the chart and said, "That's close enough." He set the point of a pair of dividers in the center of the triangle that the 3 loran signals had made, determined the latitude and longitude, and went dashing back out. I was surprised that he didn't question or check what I had done. After all, I was just a lowly seaman at the time and he was a lieutenant and the navigator. Apparently he had confidence in me and I didn't realize he even knew my name.

For the first 6 days on the trip across the central Pacific the ships were continuously engaged in some sort of exercise or tactical maneuvers of some kind. I learned early on in my naval experience that destroyers seldom just steam from one point to another. Most of the time there was some kind of drill or exercise going on, except maybe on the mid-watch (0000–0400) when the commodore was asleep. It all got kind of tiresome. In fact, it was almost a pleasure to just go steaming along like most ships do. However, the last 4 days before arriving in Japan, the ships just cruised along at 16 knots without doing much of anything in the way of ship maneuvering. That was more like my kind of ocean traveling. A day or two out of Japan we began to get Japanese music over the shortwave radio; it sounded mighty strange to me. We also began to see a few strange looking Japanese fishing boats, too. I was soon going to be in a different world for my first time.

DOMAIN of the GOLDEN DRAGON

INTERNATIONAL DATE LINE

U. S. S. BRUSH DD 745

Ruler of the 180th Meridian

To all Sailors, Soldiers, Marines, Wherever ye may be and to all mermaids, flying dragons, spirits of the deep, devil chasers, and all other living creatures of the yellow seas, Greetings: Know ye that on this 20 day of February 1953, in latitude 25-00N longitude 180-00 there appeared within the limits of my august dwelling the

(U. S. S. BRUSH DD-745)

Hearken Ye: The said vessel, officers and crew have been inspected and passed on by my august body and staff. And know ye: Ye that are chit signers, squaw men, opium smokers, ice men, and all-round landlubbers that Otis T. HOLLY having been found sane and worthy to be numbered a dweller of the Far East has been gathered in my fold and duly initiated into the

Silent Mysteries of the Far East

Be it further understood: That by virtue of the power vested in me I do hereby command all moneylenders, wine sellers, cabaret owners, ______ manager s and all my other subjects to show honor and respect to all his wishes whenever he may enter my realm. Disobey this command under penalty of my august displeasure.

H.E. Childers Golden Dragon
Ruler of the 180th Meridian

## A Rogue Wave

The ocean in the western Pacific was a little on the rough side but not too bad. However, two nights out of Japan during the mid-watch around 0200, the watch standers on the bridge had quite a fright for a few seconds, including myself. The ship must have encountered a rogue wave of some kind, because the ship rolled over a terrific amount of degrees for a few seconds. Everything that wasn't tied down, and everybody that wasn't holding onto something, went flying across the pilothouse. It was a very critical time because the ship felt like it was going to capsize. The inclinometer on the bulkhead at the rear of the pilothouse read 54°, and the ship may have gone on over if it had keeled over just a few more degrees. It was a strange and unexpected occurrence and very scary. It was a very dark night and you couldn't see much of anything outside the pilothouse. I know that roll must have thrown just about everybody out of their racks in the sleeping compartments.

I call it a rogue wave for lack of a better term to call it. The encounter with this unusual wave occurred during the middle of the mid-watch when nothing was going on in the formation. There was not any maneuvering of any kind taking place. The ship was steering a course of around 272°(t) at the speed of 17 knots. So the ship wasn't doing a thing in the way of turning or maneuvering that would have caused this roll to occur. It took everybody by surprise. Maybe if it hadn't been such a dark night we might have seen it coming and been prepared for it to some extent. But it was a very dark night and we didn't see a thing.

**USS Herbert J. Thomas DD833**
**(U.S.Navy Photograph)**

## YOKOSUKA

On Friday, 27 February, 1953, Destroyer Division 92 arrived in Japan. At 0436 in the early morning hours, we had our first sight of land. We sighted Nojima Saki light bearing 346°(t) at a distance of 18 miles. After that, more lights came into view as we got nearer to land.

At 0925 DesDiv 92 passed through the submarine net at the entrance to Tokyo Bay. The ships were steaming in their normal column formation to enter port. At 0928 the Yokosuka Harbor breakwater light was sighted bearing 290°(t) at a distance of 3.2 miles. The Brush and the other ships steered various courses at various speeds to conform to the channel to enter Yokosuka Harbor and to proceed to buoy 3. At 1027 the Brush was moored port side to the USS Samuel N. Moore at buoy 3. We were moored in a nest of 4 destroyers including the other 3 ships of DesDiv 92. At 1038 the Brush set the regular inport watch. At 1125 a LCT came alongside to starboard to deliver us mail.

### My First Liberty in Japan

Liberty call was announced at 1700 and those that had liberty went ashore, including me. We rode ashore in a landing craft provided by the naval station. At 1710 two of the Brush's crew reported aboard under technical arrest having been AWOL since 0530, 12 January, 1953.

When we came into Yokosuka Harbor, I noticed the aircraft carrier, USS Kearsarge(CVA33), was in port and tied up alongside a pier. Since my cousin, Ross Stewart, was aboard the Kearsarge, I decided it would be a good idea to visit him and go ashore with him if he was aboard and could go on liberty. So I went aboard the Kearsarge and asked the petty-officer-of-the-watch to pass the word over the P.A. system for Ross Stewart to lay down to the quarterdeck. Word was passed for him to report to the quarterdeck, but he didn't show up. The petty officer knew he was aboard, somehow; maybe he was looking at a roster of names he had. Anyway, after about 20 minutes, he passed the word again for Ross to report to the quarterdeck and soon he did. Of course, he was surprised to see me. He said he was at the ship's movie and didn't hear his name called the first time. Anyway, Ross could go on liberty, and he decided it would be a good idea for him to take me on my first liberty in Japan since he was an old hand at it. He was just completing his first tour of duty to the Far East, and his ship was to continue on with her cruise around the world and back to the States. I never saw his ship again after that time in port or him either. In fact, that was only the second time in my life that I had ever seen him. The first time had been that chance meeting back in Long Beach at the end of August. Then, it was over 25 years before I ever saw him again.

Anyway, we went on liberty together. I can't remember too much about what we did on my first liberty in Japan. I'm sure we must have gotten something to eat in a Japanese restaurant, visited some of the souvenir shops, visited a cabaret or two and had a beer, because those are some of the things that sailors did on liberty in Japan. However, I'm sure some of my more experienced shipmates found more exciting things to do than what we did. The thing that I remember most clearly about our night on the town was the time we spent gazing up at the stars together. It happened this way as I remember it. It was late in the evening and we were walking along on a side street that wasn't too well lit. I made the comment to Ross that I had to find a restroom because my bladder was pleading with me. He looked around and said, "This looks like just as good a place as any." I got the message how things were done in Japan. So, we whipped down our flaps from the 13 buttons and proceeded to relieve ourselves in a vacant lot gazing up at the stars all the while. Sometimes a man can get a great deal of pleasure out of relieving himself out under the stars. A man has to experience it to understand what I am talking about.

City dwelling men probably never get to experience that simple pleasure. In this particular case, on this night, there were plenty of both Japanese men and women walking by, but nobody seemed to have paid us any mind. After all, what can you expect out of a couple of American sailors? Besides, you saw Japanese men doing the same thing from time to time in the day time. Nobody thought anything about it. So that is the way things were done in Japan in those days but maybe not today in modern Japan.

For months I had been hearing how great the Japanese women were and how pretty they were. However, on my first liberty in Japan I was somewhat disappointed in their looks. They didn't seem all that pretty to me. I found out, though, as time went by, as the years went by, that they got better looking all the time. I guess it was just a matter of getting used to looking at them.

## Loading Ammunition

We stayed in port 2 days and 3 nights. Saturday night at 0112 a LSU came alongside to deliver ammunition to DesDiv 92. So in the middle of the night there was an all hands working party to bring the ammunition aboard. I don't know why the navy couldn't have waited to do that during the day and not disturb everybody's sleep but they didn't. So, for the next hour and twenty minutes we took on ammunition and received 228 rounds of 5″/38 shells, 449 canisters of powder, and 704 rounds of 40mm shells. Loading ammunition was a chore and one that everyone dreaded. The 5 inch shells weighed approximately 54 pounds and had to be stored in one of the magazines way below the main deck. The only way it could be done was for the sailors to form a line from the main deck, down 2 or 3 flights of ladders (stairs) to the magazines. Every 54 pound shell had to be passed from man to man, across the decks, down the ladders into the magazines, and stored in their proper places, hopefully, without anybody dropping one. If a shell was dropped on the main deck, the instructions were to kick it over the side. However, I never heard what a fellow was supposed to do if one was dropped below deck somewhere. Maybe it wasn't necessary to consider it; the situation just took care of itself. Twice, I heard a seaman ask a ranking petty officer the question, "What do you do with a shell that is dropped below deck where you can't kick it over the side?" Both times the petty officer just gave the seaman a blank look and walked off. I took that to mean – he didn't know what to do with it. Luckily, nobody ever dropped one, and I could tell by the way the sailors handled those shells that it wasn't necessary to tell them to be careful.

## Mr. Lee – Our ROK Interpreter

Sunday afternoon, 1 March, Ensign Lee Oun Su, of the ROK Navy reported aboard for duty. As far as I know, all the destroyers that were going to be part of the North Korean blockade had a ROK Naval officer assigned to them as an interpreter. I'm not sure whether the other type ships, like the cruisers and carriers, carried a ROK Naval officer or not. I wouldn't think they would have any particular need for them, but I don't know. Anyway, I got to know the ROK officer quite well, and we spent quite a bit of time together in the charthouse. I called him Mr. Lee. I think half the people in Korea must have the name Lee. Mr. Lee could speak English fairly well, and my job was to teach him all I could about navigation and especially how to read and use the navigational charts. I don't know whose idea it was for him to learn about navigation, his or the captain's; however, he did need something to do to pass the time away. He didn't have any shipboard duties that I knew about. His only duty was to be an interpreter if we needed one and that wasn't too often. He was a very likeable fellow, though, and I enjoyed my association with him.

The men in the forward boiler room shaved their heads while in Hawaii. When they got to Japan they found out that a shaved head meant that one had been in prison. This caused them to have to do a lot of explaining to the Japanese they encountered.

## The Pilothouse Weapons

Just before we left port in Yokosuka to go to Korea, a gunner's mate brought 2 loaded weapons up to the bridge and hung them on a gun rack that was located inside the pilothouse just forward of the port hatch. One of these guns was a 30 caliber carbine and the other one was a Thompson submachine gun. The purpose of bringing these guns up to the bridge was to have some weapons handy just in case they were needed. After all, we were going to be in a combat zone off the coast of North Korea and anything could happen and happen quickly. The instructions to the pilothouse watch standers were, when one was needed, the person nearest to the guns was to grab one and do what was necessary; the circumstances at the moment was to determine which gun he would grab. I suppose we all received instructions about how to use them; I know I did.

The weapons were in the pilothouse all the time we were operating off North Korea. Every time we left port to go to Korea, a gunner's mate would bring them up to the bridge. And every time we would go back in port, the same gunner's mate would come get them and put them back in the armory. It wasn't too good of an idea for drunken sailors to have access to loaded weapons; otherwise, they could have stayed in the pilothouse.

The carbine was used a number of times while I was on watch. It was always used at night when challenging small boats. That seemed to be the time that they were stirring about. The operators of these small boats were supposed to know and give us the proper reply when we challenged them. However, they were sometimes slow about giving us a reply. They usually did give us the proper reply, but sometimes they had to be encouraged to do so by a couple of rifle shots near their bow. I'm sure we were dealing with mostly peasant type people on these occasions and they couldn't remember what the reply to a challenge was and couldn't readily find the note they had written it on.

I confess I never grabbed one of the guns myself. I always let someone else beat me to them, intentionally. I really wasn't too anxious to shoot anybody and I was going to avoid it if I could. However, I believe I could have shot a communist without hesitation and not thought too much about it if I saw we were being threatened in any way. I put a hard core communist in about the same category as a cockroach.

I remember that there was a JOOD, an ensign, that was always anxious to use the carbine if the occasion arose to do so. The pilothouse crew always hesitated and let him be the one that reached the guns first. He seemed to be more anxious to use them than the rest of us so we let him.

## JAPAN TO NORTH KOREA

Early Monday morning, 2 March, 1953, Destroyer Division 92 got underway for the east coast of North Korea. But the Brush didn't accompany the other ships of the division. Instead, the Brush accompanied the cruiser, USS Manchester(CL83), out of the harbor and was her escort on the way to Korea and also for the next 2 weeks that we operated off the coast of North Korea. The Brush took a screening station 2000 yards in front of the cruiser and remained in that position most of the time that we were with her. On the way to Korea the 2 ships steamed along at 16 to 18 knots and steered various courses to navigate around the Japanese main islands. There were many navigational aids to take bearings on, so we were able to keep ourselves accurately located on the charts. Of course, all these navigational objects – lights, buoys, lighthouses, islands, etc. – had strange looking names on the charts. In addition, there was a tremendous amount of beautiful coastal scenery along the coast of Japan. The coastal waters had an abundance of little islands with little scrubby, bonsai-looking trees growing on the tops of them. Most of these islands were too small for people to inhabit, but a few of them had quaint little houses on them with small boats pulled upon the shore. I thought coastal Japan had some of the most exotic, picturesque scenery that I had ever seen.

The coastal waters also had a multitude of weird looking little boats cruising up and down the coast. Some of them were fishing boats, but some of them seemed to be hauling something. I called them putt-putt boats because that is how their engines sounded. They would just go putt-putting along at a relatively slow speed. These boats were about 25 feet long, made of wood, and had a funny looking little square shaped cabin on them that had a hole in the front and on both sides to look out of, but they didn't have any glass in these holes. It looked like that there was room for about 2 small people in the little cabins. There were usually 2 men in the boats with one of them in the cabin steering. I thought they were very unique looking and seemed to be part of the latter day old Japan. Cruising along in Japan's coastal waters made me realize that I was in a totally different world than what I was accustomed to.

## Abandon Ship Drill

On Wednesday afternoon, 4 March, the ship had an abandon ship drill. After all, you never know what's going to happen in a combat zone. The "0" division's abandon ship station was on the 01 deck just beneath the bridge, portside. The first thing we did was to put on life preservers, then go to our station and stand there until the drill was over. We didn't have a life boat or raft. The only boat aboard ship belonged to the captain. Our, supposedly, life-saving device was a big net-type thing with floats around it to make it float in the water. The net and floats would go sliding into the ocean when some lines (ropes) were pulled that released the net from its storage space. When the need arose, when the ship was abandoned, the sailors were to hang onto the net if they were able to and the sharks didn't get them. It was a long ways from being shark proof. Fortunately, we never had to put the net and floats to the test to find out how well it would actually work to keep us from drowning. All the rest of the crew had the same life-saving device but were located in different places about the ship.

## ARRIVING OFF KOREA

On Thursday morning, 5 March, 1953, I saw the mountains of Korea for the first time. I went up to the bridge around 0750 for the morning watch as the quartermaster-of-the-watch. I knew we were supposed to arrive off the east coast of North Korea on this particular morning, and I knew that as soon as I went up to the bridge, I would see it. Anyway, I climbed the ladder up to the pilothouse and stepped out of the port hatch onto the open bridge. And there it was, the place that I had heard so much about for the past two and a half years. We were fairly close into shore, about 6000 yards or so, and I had a good view of the snow covered mountains. It was rather cold on the bridge, but not frigid, maybe 40 to 45° or so. I looked at the snow covered mountains for a few minutes before going in and relieving the watch. I couldn't help but wonder what kind of situations we would be encountering in the next few weeks and months ahead. It turned out we didn't have long to wait and wonder before things started to happen.

Upon arriving off the east coast of Korea, the Manchester and the Brush became designated as Task Unit 77.1.7. Later in the morning Task Unit 77.1.7 rendezvoused with the USS Guadalupe(A032) and the USS Virgo(AKA20). The Brush took on 65,614 gallons of fuel from the tanker, and the Manchester took on both fuel from the Guadalupe and ammunition from the Virgo. The replenishment for both ships was completed around 1100. At 1117 the Brush commenced lying to in the vicinity of the Manchester. At 1123 the Manchester's motor whaleboat came and picked up Lt. Childers and took him over to the cruiser for a conference. At 1226 Lt. Childers was returned to the Brush. We then assumed our screening station in front of the Manchester.

The ship was in a war zone all the time we were operating off the coast of North Korea. The ship could have stayed at general quarters much of the time, but men can't stay awake indefinitely; they have got to get a little sleep occasionally; that is just the way the body works – it has to have sleep. Consequently, the ships went to the next best thing. They went to what was called "condition of readiness II". At this condition of readiness, at least some of the guns were manned at all times, both the 5″ guns and the 40mm guns. Consequently, some of the guns could be fired at a moment's notice.

## JAPAN, KOREA & THE SEA OF JAPAN

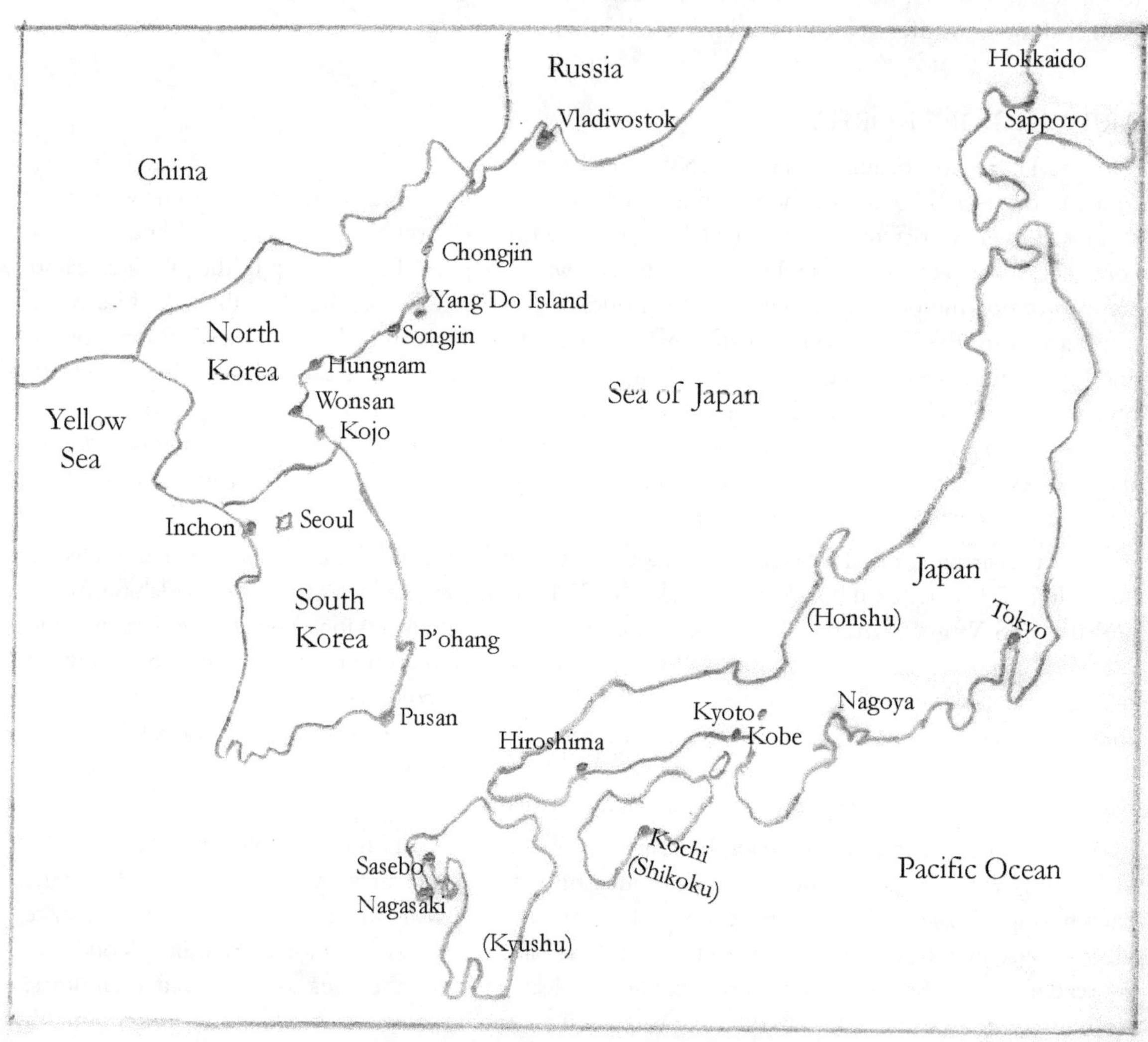

## THE BOMBLINE PATROL

We cruised up and down the coast the rest of the day. The Brush remained in her screening station 2000 yards ahead of the cruiser and changed courses and speeds as she was directed to do so. The ships steamed along at the relatively slow speed of 10 knots much of the time. Late in the day Task Unit 77.1.7 arrived at the frontline, which was somewhere north of the 38th parallel. It was also called the Bombline. Here around the Bombline is where Task Unit 77.1.7 would spend much of its time for the next two weeks. And, as it turned out, it was an interesting 2 weeks. Our assignment was called the Bombline Patrol. We stayed in our screening station 2000 yards ahead of the Manchester much of the time, but we also operated some independently away from the Manchester and the Bombline. However, the Manchester was usually close by.

We saw our first action Friday afternoon, 6 March. Although, it was more as a spectator rather than as a participant. In fact, we saw action taking place against the enemy a number of times over the next several months that we didn't take part in; we just had a ringside seat, so to speak. However, what I witnessed at the Bombline on this Friday afternoon was jet planes coming in low and firing their rockets at something on the ground that was out of sight of us, so we couldn't see what they were attacking. But it was interesting watching the planes fire their rockets. I'm sure they were putting a hurting on somebody. At least one plane came roaring in real low and dropped a napalm bomb on a mountainside that created quite a fiery show. A long streak of fire just went flowing down the mountainside, burning up everything and everybody that was in its path, I'm sure. Watching the napalms made me feel glad that I wasn't on the receiving end of that stuff. We saw a number of napalms dropped while we were at the Bombline, but I can't remember exactly when they were, except on that first day.

At 1525 a ROK F-51 plane was observed by some of the men on the bridge to crash about 1500 yards inland in the vicinity of friendly frontlines at the Bombline. However, for some reason, I didn't witness that event myself. I must have been looking in another direction at that moment. The incident was reported to the commander of Task Force 77. Thus, part of the activity around the Bombline that afternoon after the plane crash might have been directed toward rescuing the pilot.

In addition that Friday afternoon, the cruiser's helicopter crashed into the sea close aboard her port quarter while attempting to land. The Brush quickly began maneuvering to assist in rescuing the crew, but our efforts weren't necessary because the pilot and the others aboard were quickly picked up by the Manchester's motor whaleboat.

We fired our first shots at communist troops at 2200 Friday night. I don't know how it was determined in what direction to fire, but I imagine there was a spotter on a mountain somewhere that was telling our fire control officer where to place the shells. Anyway, at 2200 the Brush commenced harassing and interdiction firing from one of the main batteries against enemy frontline troops and installations, according to the ship's log. Over the next hour or so the Brush fired 15 rounds of 5″/38 shells. Then, off and on throughout the rest of the night the Brush fired 30 more rounds of 5″ shells at the enemy troops. The Manchester might have been doing some firing, too – I can't remember. Unfortunately, we had no way of knowing what kind of damage we were inflicting on the enemy.

On Saturday, 7 March, we just steamed up and down the coast in the general vicinity of the Bombline and didn't do any more firing until late in the evening. Then, from around 2200 to 2330 the Brush fired a total of 8 rounds of 5″ high capacity shells at targets 5 to 7 ½ miles inland. It would have been interesting to know what we were shooting at and if we hit it. The ship's 5″ guns continued to fire occasionally throughout the night until 0500, and by that time we had fired a total of 28 more rounds of 5″ HC shells at targets around the Bombline.

At 0751 Sunday morning, 8 March, the Brush was detached from the cruiser to proceed independently to conduct some shore bombardment in Wonsan Harbor, which was a few miles up the coast and was considered to be one of the hotter spots on the east coast of North Korea. A ship was always subject to being fired upon by shore batteries when operating in Wonsan Harbor. Consequently, everyone that had to be topside had to wear a flack jacket. At 0807 the Brush sounded general quarters and everybody rushed to their battle stations. At 0812 the Brush commenced steering various courses and speeds to enter the harbor and proceed to her assigned shore bombardment station.

The weather was rather cold on this morning that we went into Wonsan Harbor – something on the order of 35 to 40°. To stay warm, we were given some cold weather overalls before going in. In addition, there wasn't any noon meal that day. However, the cooks brought us up a cup of hot chicken soup that was good and was greatly appreciated. At 0845 the Brush arrived on station and commenced firing on enemy installations and gun positions. We stayed in Wonsan Harbor for 6 hours and during that time fired a total of 76 rounds of 5 inch HC shells. This was the first time that we had done any firing during the day. Some of the time we were shooting toward the snow covered mountainsides, and I noticed that a few seconds after our 5 inch guns would fire, black dots would appear on the white mountainsides; for some reason, I thought that was fascinating.

At 1440 the Brush secured from firing and proceeded out of the harbor. Fortunately, we didn't receive any return fire while we were firing. The Chinese in the gun positions on the mountainsides must have been taking the day off since it was Sunday. That's probably what we should have done. However, that was a different way to spend a Sunday.

After the Wonsan venture, we joined back up with the Manchester and, together, we resumed the Bombline patrol. During the night we did some more shelling and expended a total of 32 more rounds of 5 inch HC shells at targets around the Bombline. So, that made a total of 108 rounds of 5″ shells that we fired that day. That is quite a bit of noise, smoke, and the smell of burnt powder for one day.

The following day, Monday, 9 March, proved to be a most interesting day and produced a lot of memories for the Brush crew. At 0650 the Manchester and the Brush departed from the Bombline to rendezvous with a couple of replenishment ships, the USS Manatee(AO58) and the USS Firedrake(AE14), to take on fuel and ammunition. We rendezvoused with the ships at 0730 and proceeded to go alongside the USS Manatee for fuel. We commenced taking on fuel at 0754 and completed it at 0914. The Brush received 49,277 gallons of fuel over the hour and twenty minutes it took to complete that job. The ships were cruising along side by side at 10 knots with only 50 or 60 feet between them for that entire time period. A highline was also rigged between the two ships in order to transfer mail, movies, and empty brass.

At 1000 we went alongside the USS Firedrake to take on ammunition by highline. These replenishment projects were always a big job for the boatswain's mates and members of the deck force. The ammo was sent over to the Brush in big cargo nets and laid on the deck as gently as possible; and during rough seas, that wasn't easy to do. The hard part started as soon as the ammo was received aboard, because it had to be man-handled down to the magazines several decks down, which wasn't easy to do on a rolling and pitching ship. But it always got done and was done by somebody; it was a bad job, though. On this day the Brush received 250 rounds of 5″/38 HC shells, 250 rounds of powder and 200 steel-nosed plugs. The replenishing task was completed at 1050, and the Manchester and the Brush set a course to return to the Bombline to resume patrolling.

## Submarine Contact

At 1121 the sonarmen reported a sonar contact bearing 085° relative and at a distance of 1500 yards. The Brush changed course to investigate the contact. The sonarmen positively identified the contact as being a submarine. Upon the sonarmen positively identifying the underwater contact as a submarine, they repeatedly made an effort to get the submarine to identify itself but to no avail. Consequently, the conclusion was reached that it wasn't ours, or friendly. At 1125 the ship set condition of readiness I in sonar, C1C, and underwater battery. Most of the crew was unaware of what was going on at this point. However, at 1139 the ship sounded general quarters and everybody rushed to their battle stations not knowing what to expect. I think we all knew that this wasn't a drill; this was the real thing. My thought was, as I ran to the bridge, was that we were going to be attacked by airplanes because there wasn't anything hostile in sight on the ocean. It didn't even occur to me that we were going to general quarters because of a submarine.

I'm sure the captain was in touch with someone of higher authority than himself to inform them of finding this submarine in a combat zone, somewhat near the carrier task force, and to receive instruction as to what action to take, if any.

I personally suspect the sub was snooping around the carrier task force and was probably notifying the North Korean Air Force when American Navy planes were headed their way. The submarine we had discovered was undoubtedly Russian. Russia had a big interest in knowing when American planes were headed into North Korea, because most of the pilots in the North Korean Air Force were Russian – it was later learned, or at least acknowledged. However, it turned out that the Russians in their Migs weren't any match for the American planes and pilots, because, according to my understanding, the North Korean Air Force lost 20 planes for every one that the U.S. lost. That's a pretty lop-sided ratio, 20:1.

In addition, I imagine the submarine captain was between a rock and hard place, because his naval career in the Russian Navy was at stake. If he identified himself, the American Navy would probably demand that he surface and he would be in trouble with his Russian Naval superiors. And, if he didn't identify himself, the American Navy would probably try to sink him. Consequently, his only chance of staying in good standing with the Russian Navy was to take the risk of surviving an American Navy depth charge attack, and that is what he chose to do. Who knows, if he was to embarrass his communist bosses, they might shoot him and his family. That is just the way they handled things.

Anyway, somebody, somewhere, made the decision for us to attack the submarine. So at 1205 the Brush proceeded to attack the submarine with the intent of sinking it. I was in the pilothouse as the quartermaster and was in an excellent position to witness all the attacking efforts that took place. I was also recording all the events that took place in the quartermaster notebook. As I remember it, the sonar scope in the pilothouse was on and we all could hear the sound waves pinging against the submarine's hull when we had contact with it. An officer, I think it was the gunnery officer, Lt. Beaty, was standing in back of the pilothouse with a sound powered headphone on and was in communication with the sonar shack, C1C, the torpedomen, and some of the gunner's mates. He seemed to be directing the operation, or at least a big part of it. He would repeat much of the information he was receiving for the benefit of the captain. This officer would repeat the information he was receiving in the way of distance to the submarine and the depth of it. It was a very hectic time on the bridge and there was a lot going on. Sometimes sonar would have the conn, sometimes C1C would have the conn, and sometimes the captain would have the conn. It was always switching back and forth. Sometimes we would have contact with the submarine and sometimes we wouldn't. Then we would have it again, etc. In my observation of the attack on the submarine that afternoon, I thought it was carried out with the greatest of professionalism, probably as a result of all the ASW training that everyone involved had received during their naval careers. As far as I could tell, everyone involved in the operation, both officers and enlisted men, performed their duties with perfection. I was mainly a spectator myself.

I'm sure the submarine captain was a very sharp skipper, too, because he did a great job at doing something that made us lose contact with him so much and evade at least some of the depth charges and hedgehogs that were dropped on him. He was probably able to evade most of them.

At 1213 the Brush made her first attack on the submarine. When the ship was in the process of making an attack, it would be traveling at a speed of 25 knots or so. The reason for moving so fast was to get as far away from that underwater blast as they could, because, even at best, the ship was going to experience a terrific jolt. When the depth charges would explode 100, 200 or 300 feet underwater, or whatever the depth was, it would shoot a huge column of water 20 to 30 feet up into the air. In addition, when we were in the process of attacking, the sonarmen would be telling the gunnery officer the distance to the submarine. The gunnery officer would repeat those distances like – 1000 yards to the submarine, 900 yards, 800 yards, 700 yards, 600 yards, and 500 yards, and as I understood it, the sonarmen would lose contact with the submarine when it was within 500 yards. Consequently, somebody had to calculate the time required to reach the point that the submarine was directly beneath the ship. I'm not sure who did that now – the gunnery officer, the sonarmen, or CIC.

However, the submarine captain knew this shortcoming of the sonar system and this was the time he would make his evasive move. He could turn the submarine sharply to starboard, or to port, or maintain his course. In addition, he could dive deeper, or decrease his depth, or a combination of things. It would take several seconds for the underwater projectiles to reach him. So that is why it was so difficult to put them exactly on the submarine. We knew exactly where the submarine was on every attack, and it seemed impossible that he could dodge all the depth charges dropped on him.

When the point was reached where the sub was directly beneath us, the captain would give the order to fire so many depth charges off the fantail, using the K guns to shoot them over the side, or fire a spread of hedgehogs from the hedgehog launchers on either the starboard or port side, or from both sides. The gunner's mates manned the K guns and hedgehog launchers. So, at 1213 the ship made her first attack and fired 24 hedgehogs from the starboard launcher. Then the ship lost contact with the submarine, regained it for few minutes, lost it again, regained it, and at 1249 totally lost it for a time.

At 1318 the USS Black(DD666) joined us in the search and attack. At 1336 we regained contact. Upon regaining contact this time, the Brush proceeded to make another attack. At 1340 the Brush fired 10 Mark 14 depth charges over the side. The Brush made another attack and at 1358 fired 11 more depth charges over the side. Of course, when these depth charges exploded down below, it caused a huge column of water to shoot up into the air just like in the movies. Plus, the tremendous jolts on the bottom of the ship followed the explosions. We thought that every pass we made on the submarine would be the fatal one because we knew exactly where it was when we dropped the charges. Myself and a couple of others would step out on the open bridge and look aft to watch the column of water shoot up – the purpose of which was to see if we could see any kind of debris or bodies, which would be a sure sign that we had busted her open. However, we never saw any bodies or debris.

This was a very serious game we were playing. The American destroyers were doing everything they could to sink the submarine, and the sub's captain was doing everything he could to prevent his boat from being sunk and thus losing his life and the lives of all his crew.

At 1408 the USS Black made a depth charge attack on the submarine. At 1442 the Black made another depth charge attack. Then, again at 1450, the Black made another depth charge attack.

At 1453 the Brush made an attack and fired 48 hedgehogs on the submarine. At 1506 the Brush fired another 48 hedgehogs. Then at 1516 the Brush fired 11 more depth charges over the side on the submarine. When the depth charges were fired over the side, they were fired off both sides of the ship at the same time in an effort to have some of them explode close to the sub, regardless of which way she may have turned. The depth charges were shot about 30 to 40 yards out when they were fired over the side.

At 1523 the USS Black made another depth charge attack. Then, both ships totally lost contact with the submarine for some reason. I can't imagine how that can happen because it was still down there somewhere. The two ships continued to search for the submarine for several more hours, however, but couldn't locate her.

At 1700 we investigated a possible oil slick at the location of our last attack. Then at 1800 another small oil slick was sighted. However, in my opinion, the oil slicks weren't enough to get too excited about. Both destroyers continued to search for the sub into the night.

That submarine had a tremendous amount of stuff dumped on her. I can't imagine how she avoided being sunk. I can only say that the captain was either mighty good, or mighty lucky, or maybe some of both. However, the affair wasn't over yet.

After the attack on the submarine by the two ships without definite results, there was a question in some people's minds on the other ship whether we were attacking a submarine or a big school of fish. Personally, I have to believe our sonarmen. They said that there was a submarine down there and I have to believe them because they were highly trained and experienced men. Apparently, Captain Quigley had confidence in them, too, because he was very aggressive in all of his attacks. I don't believe there was a doubt in his mind about a submarine being down there. The pings that were heard on the pilothouse sonar scope sure sounded metallic to me and to everyone else that heard them. Furthermore, if there had been a big school of fish down there, they would have all been killed by the first depth charge blast, and they would have all either sunk to the bottom or have floated to the surface. Thus, there would have not been any more contacts made. I was looking and I did not see a single dead fish floating on the surface. So, I personally don't think that the fish notion has any merit. Furthermore, maybe it was possible for the sonarmen to make a mistake one time but not the same mistake over and over all afternoon. It would be highly unlikely for them to do that.

## The Midnight Contact

Something happened on the mid-watch (0000–0400) on Tuesday, 10 March, 1953, that I will always remember. Again, I was the quartermaster-of-the-watch and was making entries in the quartermaster notebook as events happened. I was briefed on our situation when I relieved the watch at 2355. The quartermaster that I relieved, and I think it was Jackson, informed me that the ship had just regained contact with the submarine and was hovering over it, or close to it, and was essentially dead in the water. I noticed the captain was at the forward part of the bridge conferring with the OOD's-the officer being relieved of the watch and the officer relieving the watch.

As I remember the situation on this night, the submarine was about as deep as it could safely go–200 feet, 300 feet, or whatever it was. I've forgotten exactly how deep it was. In addition, the sub was making very little headway–around 1 knot, according to the sonarmen. There was also another sub traveling along with it. Apparently, the submarine was damaged to the extent that it could barely make headway. The sub didn't make any attempt to evade us and probably couldn't. She was on a course that would take her to Vladivostok, Russia, undoubtedly her homeport.

The sonar scope was on in the pilothouse, and we could clearly hear the steady pinging of the sound waves as they bounced off the metal hull of the submarine. There was no question about something being down there, and the sonarmen claimed it was the same sub that we had attacked the previously afternoon. They are supposed to know about these things and I'm sure they did. Therefore, I have to believe them.

It appeared that the sub was a sitting duck, so to speak, and could be easily finished off. Because we knew the depth of the submarine, its course, its speed (barely moving), and that it was apparently damaged to the extent that she wasn't able to do much in the way of dodging depth charges. So, essentially all we had to do was just drop some depth charges on her to finish her off. The depth charges would simply burst open the hull of the sub and sink it.

It seemed that I was just about to witness the deaths of 75 to 80 young submariners, and I'm sure that the rest of the pilothouse crew had that same thought, too. It was a very tense time and a very sobering situation to be in. I began to think about all those young sailors down there in that crippled sub–in that cold, dark, and wet depth. I thought about what a horrible, cold, and wet death they were going to experience down there in that total darkness when the water came rushing in on them. Maybe death would be quick for most of them because of the pressure at the depth they were. I couldn't help but feel sorry for those young men down there in that sub, because they were going to be dying in the next few minutes. They were going to be dying so young–too young. I knew they wanted to live just like I did and go back home, marry, raise a family, and live to be a ripe old age like most men wanted to. But the chances of them doing that seemed mighty slim at that moment. I imagine, too, that some of them were trying to get on good terms with their god, even though they may not have had one the day before since they were communist, or at least came from an ungodly communist country.

In a few minutes the captain came into the pilothouse and sat down in his chair that was located on the port side of the pilothouse up against the bulkhead. I thought that was a rather strange thing for him to do under the circumstances. I expected him to be on his feet, at the forward part of the bridge, directing the attack on the submarine and also to bring the crew to general quarters, or at least the men that would be involved in the attack. Instead of that, he was sitting in his chair in the pilothouse. The pilothouse was rather dark and I couldn't see his face. The only light in the pilothouse came from the compasses, the engine-order-telegraph, and the glow from the sonar and radar scopes.

I was standing by the sonar scope and it was steadily pinging away. I would look at the sonar scope and then glance at the captain sitting there in his chair. I assumed he was listening to the pinging of the sonar, too. I wondered what he was doing just sitting there in his chair in the semi-darkness. I thought all kinds of attacking activities should be going on at this point to deal the final blow to the sub. I couldn't understand what was going on or why it wasn't going on. It wasn't that I wanted us to sink the submarine; I just assumed that we would since we had found it again and because the captain had made such an aggressive effort to sink it the previous afternoon.

I looked at the scope and glanced at the captain a few more times. I know he had to have noticed me glancing at him in a rather puzzled manner. However, he didn't volunteer to give me any information concerning his thoughts or his intentions. After all, he was the captain and he could do as he pleased, and it didn't make any difference whether anybody understood him or not. At this point in the drama, the sonarmen and the bridge crew were probably the only ones on the ship that knew what was going on. Also, I am pretty sure the captain never sent a message off the ship to anybody to notify them that we had regained contact with the submarine. He and he alone was the one who was going to make the decision about what to do about the submarine.

There was dead silence in the pilothouse; there was no idle chatter on this mid-watch. The OOD may have given a brief order or two to the helmsman, or lee helmsmen, to keep the ship in a position over the submarine, or near it, but that was all.

After 10 minutes or so of inaction by the captain, it dawned on me that he wasn't going to attack the submarine and drop depth charges on it. The captain just sat there in his chair, in the semi-darkness, without uttering a sound for over 2 hours, but I'm sure he was thinking the whole time. However, when he came in and sat in his chair, that was a clue as to what he was going to do about the sub – nothing. Basically, he wasn't going to report finding it or attack it. That decision of his didn't occur to me at the time, however.

After a couple of hours the captain stirred in his chair and called for the OOD. The OOD came to the forward open porthole and the captain told him to instruct the sonarmen to send the submarine a message. The brief message that he instructed sonar to send to the submarine was, "Bon Voyage." In a few seconds the OOD informed the captain that the message had been sent. Upon learning that, the captain got up, gave the OOD some instructions, and walked out of the pilothouse. He seemed pleased that he had made the decision he did. I also thought that the message he sent to the sub was rather clever, too. It meant, without saying it, I'm not going to attack you so continue on your way. I'm sure that the submarine crew was relieved to receive that little message.

When the captain left the pilothouse, the OOD kicked the ship in gear and we departed the area and headed back south. The time was 0213. The OOD set a course of 180°(t) and a speed of 10 knots. In effect, we resumed the "search" for the submarine but way south of the position that we had last had contact with it for more than two hours. The Brush continued to "search" for the submarine until around 1530 that afternoon; at that time the search was discontinued and the Brush proceeded to rejoin the Manchester at the Bombline. We joined back up with the cruiser at 1600 and assumed our screening station 2000 yards in front of her. Officially, the midnight contact with the sub never happened.

Personally, I think the captain made the right decision that night to spare the lives of those young Russian sailors and should be praised for doing the humane thing. In addition, he probably deserves a medal for doing it. Of course, I'm sure he was never praised or condemned for his actions because nobody off the ship ever knew what he had done. I'm sure naval officers of lesser character than our captain would have sunk the submarine simply to promote their careers and enhance their standing in the officer's club. But the Brush had a captain of higher character than that. He did the right thing because the sub wasn't posing a threat to us in any way. Those men were just trying to get home.

The big question that remains is – was the submarine able to make it back to port? It still had to travel around 200 miles to reach port when we last had contact with it. It's something that I've always wondered about, but I'll probably never know whether it did or didn't make it. I hope she did because I'm sure most of the young sailors aboard her really weren't communist; they were just young boys fulfilling their military obligation to their government.

I'm quite sure that relatively few people on the ship ever knew what took place that night with the submarine. The captain, the OOD, the JOOD, the 5 men in the pilothouse, the couple of men in sonar, and maybe the 2 signalmen may have been the only people that knew that the ship had regained contact with the sub and had hovered over it for over 2 hours. I can't imagine that the ones that did know ever talked about it. I know I didn't. Actually, things of that nature were never talked about by the crew very much for some reason. Young sailors were more interested in talking about girls or things related to girls.

The next 3 days, Wednesday, 11 March, through Friday, 13 March, weren't too eventful. We mainly just steamed up and down the coast about 6000 yards offshore at a leisurely speed of 10 knots. We did challenge a couple of unidentified small boats, but the occupants were able to give us the proper signal that identified them as friendly. We also rendezvoused with the Navasota(A0106) on Thursday afternoon to take on fuel. And on Friday morning, we rendezvoused with the supply ship, USS Chara(AKA58), to take on a little ammunition, but we didn't take on very much because we hadn't been doing any firing for the last several days.

## Ducks, Ducks Everywhere

One thing I noticed as we steamed up and down the coast was the number of ducks floating around on the ocean. There were literally thousands of them. As we steamed along, the ducks were continuously taking off in front of us, and as I looked out over the water, I saw thousands of them as far as I could see in every direction. However, the ducks were a different kind of duck than any that I had ever seen. I would especially notice these ducks because I was a big duck hunter when I was growing up in the Ocala National Forest. I would love to have seen that many ducks when I was out hunting them. However, the ducks must have been migrating because I didn't see them for too long, maybe 2 or 3 weeks. The sea was relatively smooth during these days and it made for rather pleasant steaming weather. Although, the weather was still rather cool and the mountains were still covered in snow.

Friday night, 13 March, the Brush commenced firing at enemy troops and installations around the Bombline again. During the night the Brush fired a total of 57 rounds of 5 inch shells, including 41 rounds of high capacity shells and 16 rounds of illumination shells, or star shells as they were commonly called. These star shells were fired during the early part of the night and the reason for firing these types of shells was to light up the sky. The troops on the beach needed some light for some reason. Either our troops were sneaking around doing something and needed some light, or the Chinese troops were sneaking around trying to do some mischief and the American troops were trying to prevent it.

The star shells were shot up in the sky and exploded over the land. A small parachute would open up and this very bright light would slowly float down to the ground lighting up the surrounding countryside. About the time a star shell would start fizzling out near the ground, another one would be shot up in the sky and the whole process would start over. It was a very eerie type of light, a ghostly thing, and I imagine it was even more eerie over the land. I suppose it took from 2 to 3 minutes for these star shells to float down to the earth.

We could only imagine what was going on on the beach that necessitated the need for them. I know that there was a fire-fight going on some of the time, because I could see the tracer bullets streaking through the night darkness when I was looking through the big binoculars.

Early Saturday morning, 14 March, around 0630, the Brush and the Manchester rendezvoused with the USS Aludra(AF55) to take on provisions. The USS James E. Kyes(DD787) was also there for the same purpose. The Brush and the Manchester completed taking on provisions at 0750 and returned to their patrolling station around the Bombline.

Saturday night the Brush again fired her 5″ guns at enemy frontline troops. She fired her 5″ guns occasionally throughout the night until around 0500 and expended a total of 30 rounds of high capacity shells. I don't know what kind of damage we did, but I suppose, if nothing else, that the exploding shells kept the enemy troops from sleeping.

## A Busy Day

Sunday, 15 March, was an action filled day for us. We didn't observe the Sabbath in any stretch of the imagination. We were detached from the Manchester at 0800 to proceed independently into Wonsan Harbor to do some shelling of shore installations and shore batteries. The cruiser steamed around in the Sea of Japan near the entrance to the harbor while we went in to engage the Communist Chinese and North Koreans, if they were willing. At 0804 the general quarters alarm was sounded and everybody rushed to their battle stations. When a ship, a destroyer, usually, was in Wonsan Harbor, it was always subject to being shot at. Consequently, the sailors topside had to don flack jackets and steel helmets. In addition, nobody was allowed to be topside unless they had something important to do – like man a battle station of some kind or repair something.

There was a relatively small island inside Wonsan Harbor called Yo Do on which a small detachment of marines and a few naval personnel were entrenched. It was easily in shooting range of the communist guns on the surrounding mountainsides. The island dwellers must have lived underground mostly because the word was that they got shelled frequently. As we neared the island, a small boat came out to meet us and a naval officer came aboard. His name was Manigau, Lt(jg), USNR. I'm not sure what his purpose was for coming aboard unless it was to advise the captain and fire control officer about what to shoot at. Anyway, we proceeded at various courses and speeds to reach a location in the harbor known as FSA Gridiron. From this position we were to do our firing and we steamed at various courses and speeds to remain in this area. The ship didn't dare stop to do its firing, because we might have been too tempting a target for the communist gunners to resist and too easy a target for them to hit.

At 0843 the ship commenced firing on various targets – some of which were installations and some were gun positions on the mountainside. So, we fired our 5 inch guns pretty steady for the next 5 ½ hours, and during that time the Brush expended 119 rounds of 5″ HC shells. I'm sure all 3 of the 5 inch mounts participated in this shoot. The Brush ceased fire at 1410 and immediately commenced maneuvering at various courses and speeds to proceed out of the harbor. Fortunately, we didn't receive any return fire on that day. Apparently, the enemy gunners were taking the day off being it was Sunday and all. As we passed Yo Do Island on the way out of the harbor, a small boat came out to meet us and picked up our passenger, Lt(jg) Manigau, and took him back to the island.

At 1434 the Brush joined back up with the Manchester, who was waiting for us outside the harbor, more or less, and we resumed our normal screening station 2000 yards ahead of her on a course of 050°(t) and at a speed of 10 knots. A little later the two ships changed to a southerly course and went down the coast a few miles to Kojo Harbor. This was a much smaller harbor than Wonsan. Here, the Brush entered this harbor and commenced firing on assigned targets at 1613. At 1650 the Brush ceased firing having expended 32 rounds of 5″ HC shells.

At 1700 a mine was spotted in the water off the starboard quarter and the ship went to investigate it. It was identified as a R-MYAM type mine – whatever that is. The mine was sunk with rifle fire. At 1740 the Brush started proceeding out of Kojo Harbor and in a few minutes joined up with the cruiser. The two ships headed back to the Bombline. However, at 1755 the starboard lookout on the bridge spotted an object in the water that appeared to be another mine. The Brush departed the formation to investigate it. Sure enough, the floating object was a mine, and this second mine was also sunk with rifle fire. After taking care of that little task, the Brush went back to her screening station 2000 yards ahead of the cruiser, and the two ships continued on down the coast toward the Bombline. The ships arrived at the Bombline around 2000 and commenced patrolling along the coast around the Bombline at a leisurely speed of 10 knots. Just slowly patrolling up and down the coast for the rest of the night was the ships' plan of action. However, at 2034 the Brush had a radar contact which changed the whole night's plans.

## Radar Contact: Two Fast Small Boats

Sunday night at 2034 the Brush had a radar contact bearing 245°(t) at a distance of 2000 yards. The radarmen could tell that there was something out there in the dark that was moving along across the water at a fast clip. Of course, the cruiser and the destroyer were patrolling along in the dark without their running lights on, so whatever it was out there couldn't see them and know that they were there. The object on the radar scope didn't have its running lights on either. The Brush was detached from the formation to investigate the contact and commenced steering various courses and speeds to intercept it. Upon closing the radar contact, the contact was identified as two small power boats running close together and were loaded with men. The Brush challenged them with a light signal and received an improper reply to the challenge. The small boats were instructed to come alongside our starboard quarter near the fantail. The instructions to the small boats were given from the bridge by our Korean interpreter, Ensign Lee Eun Su, by means of a megaphone. The men in the small boats had to follow Mr. Lee's instructions or get blown out of the water by one of our 40mm guns.

A few minutes prior to the boats coming alongside, Lt. Childers burst into the wardroom where the officers were watching a movie – a cowboy movie of some kind, and hollered out in a very excited voice, "Mr. Brown, call away the boarding party and have them muster on the starboard quarter." Mr. Childers tended to stutter when he got excited and he was stuttering badly on this occasion. He wasn't too interested in having a bunch of heavily armed enemy troops boarding the ship unopposed and he

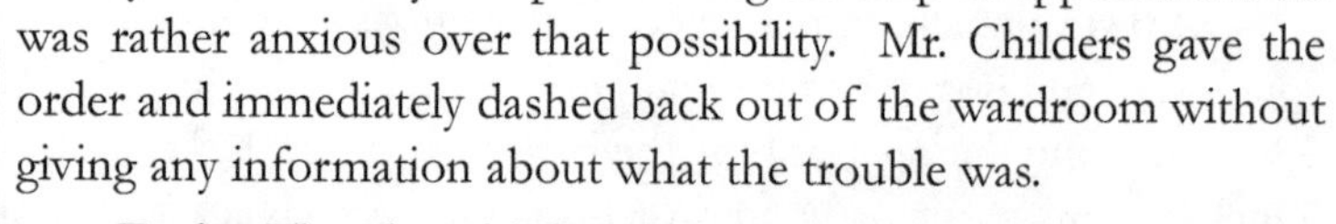

was rather anxious over that possibility. Mr. Childers gave the order and immediately dashed back out of the wardroom without giving any information about what the trouble was.

Ensign Theodore (Ted) Brown was the boarding party officer, but he had never performed that particular duty up to this point in his young navy career and naturally wasn't too sure about what to do; but he had to quickly get some on the job training. First of all, he had to find the gunner's mate that had the keys to the armory where all the small arms were stored, which he did. Then, Ensign Brown quickly rounded up a few members of the boarding party, got them armed, and they proceeded to the fantail to the starboard quarter. At this point, Mr. Brown still didn't know what he was supposed to do or why he was on the fantail with the armed boarding party. Although, he could see that the captain and other people were at the rear of the bridge and were looking back toward the fantail – at something. A signal light had been turned on to light up the fantail area. Willie Nash is the only member of the boarding party that he remembers being with him, although, there were several others, too.

In a few minutes the 2 small boats, loaded with soldiers, came alongside and the boarding party assumed they were there to cover them and they did. After the small boats were alongside the ship, they tied up to it. At this point, Mr. Lee directed 2 of the boat's officers to come aboard for questioning; one of them claimed to be the leader of the group.

There were 16 soldiers aboard the two boats and they were all dressed in Chinese army uniforms. The two officers that were brought aboard were interrogated in the officer's wardroom. However, the two officers that were questioned claimed that they were South Korean soldiers on a mission behind enemy lines and were just wearing Chinese army uniforms as part of that mission. Maybe so, but they didn't have any evidence of any kind to back up that story. Ensign Lee was unable to determine with any certainty whether the detained men were friend or foe. Consequently, this information was passed on to CTU 77.1.7 who was aboard the Manchester. He decided the best thing to do was to detain them and let somebody else determine who they were. So, he arranged for the minesweeper, USS Ruddy(AM380), to pick them up and take them to Yo Do Island in Wonsan Harbor for interrogation. Consequently, at 2313 all the soldiers on the small boats were brought on board and placed under guard awaiting the arrival of the Ruddy.

Mr. Brown said the soldiers seemed to be a friendly bunch and they were happy to come aboard and be detained, because that prevented them from having to take part in a dangerous raid up the coast somewhere. Some of them were already bandaged up from previous raids. The soldiers gave up their guns as they came aboard the ship. After they were brought aboard, they all sat round Mount 53. One of the soldiers even wanted Mr. Brown to meet his sister. He must have thought Mr. Brown was a nice–looking fellow and needed a girlfriend. Besides, he was one of those rich Americans. However, I don't think anything ever developed in that respect.

Anyway, the boarding party and the soldiers had a nice visit on the fantail while they were waiting for the Ruddy to show up. The soldiers were all given a cup of coffee and a piece of freshly made bread, which they all seemed to enjoy and appreciate. Around 2400 Ensign Brown was relieved of his guard duty, went to his quarters and went to bed.

At 0100 the USS Ruddy arrived on the scene and commenced lying to 200 yards off our starboard side. The soldiers were ordered back into their boats and told to go over to the Ruddy, which they did. However, they left their weapons on the Brush. In just a few minutes the minesweeper had taken custody of the soldiers and their boats and it was all out of our hands. We never learned for sure whether they were Chinese or South Korean, but I've always felt that they were probably ROK troops because they seemed to be so friendly and never acted hostile toward us. Besides, to me, they just didn't look mean enough to be communist soldiers. Although, we never did learn for sure whether they were friend or foe. A little after 0100 the Brush proceeded back to the Bombline to rejoin the Manchester. All in all, it was a long "fun" filled day.

On Monday, 16 March, Task Unit 77.1.7 just steamed up and down the coast and didn't do anything too exciting. Around 1400 in the afternoon, though, we did rendezvous with the famous ship, USS Missouri(BB63), and her escort, USS Halsey Powell(DD686), for some reason. However, we only stayed with them a short time and both formations went their separate ways. We went back to our

Bombline patrol. After dark we fired on communist troops off and on throughout the night. During the night the Brush expended a total of 50 rounds of 5 inch high capacity shells.

## My Talk with an Old Classmate

Early Tuesday morning, 17 March, the formation left the Bombline to rendezvous with some replenishment ships, the USS Kaskaskia(A027) and the USS Mount Baker(AE4). At 0730 the Brush went alongside the starboard side of the Kaskaskia for refueling, stayed alongside her for an hour, and during that time received 58,481 gallons of fuel oil. In addition to the fuel, the Brush also received two new crewmembers by highline. The most interesting thing for me that took place during our refueling from the tanker was that I was able to talk to a high school classmate from Haines City, Florida.

I was on the bridge during the refueling and somehow was notified to lay down to the main deck where the refueling was taking place, because somebody on the Kaskaskia wanted to talk to me. I was totally surprised that someone on the tanker wanted to talk to me, and I couldn't imagine who it was. Anyway, I went down to the main deck and someone handed me a set of headphones that was sent over from the tanker. I spoke to the person on the other end of the line and it turned out to be Edward O'Neal. And then, I saw him standing on the deck of the tanker 50 to 60 feet away. We waved to each other. So we had a nice conversation for a few minutes out in the Sea of Japan and thousands of miles from home for both of us. I thought it was quite a coincidence for both of us. I was also surprised that either ship would have allowed two seamen to have just a casual conversation on the ships' phone. I actual don't know if the phone was sent over to just accommodate us or whether a phone was always sent over during regular fueling operations, but in either case, it was great that the refueling personnel allowed us to have our short visit by phone. Our ships were to be in port, in Sasebo, at the same time in a few days, and we agreed to go on liberty together; and if we did, I no longer have any recollection of it. Some things I remember clearly after 50 years and some things I don't.

After refueling from the tanker, the Brush went alongside the Mount Baker to take on ammunition. This time we received 325 rounds of 5″ shells, 325 canisters of powder, and 50 rounds of steel nose plugs.

Upon completing the replenishment operation, the formation returned to the Bombline. We arrived back at the Bombline at 1050 and at 1104 the Brush received a fire mission. Mount 53 commenced firing on targets as directed by a spotter. Over the next three hours the ship was assigned four different fire missions. A spotter on a mountainside somewhere was telling the fire control officer where to shoot and probably how well we were doing. At 1349 the Brush ceased all firing after expending a total of 48 rounds of 5″ shells. The formation just steamed up and down the coast the rest of the afternoon, that night, and all the next day, Wednesday, without doing any firing. However, around 2000 on Wednesday night, 18 March, we commenced firing on enemy targets north of the frontlines. The Brush fired sporadically throughout the night and expended a total of 50 rounds of 5″ high capacity shells.

On Thursday, 19 March, we didn't do any firing at the frontline or do anything else of much significance. However, we stayed on the move all the time steaming up and down the coast. Although, early in the morning at 0625 the formation did rendezvous with the USS Ulvert M. Moore(DE442) for a personnel transfer to the Manchester. The transfer was made by small boat. We just stayed clear of the two ships while the transfer was being made.

Then, late in the afternoon, another destroyer, the USS Eversole(DD789), came to where we were patrolling and another personnel transfer was made between it and the cruiser, and this time it was by highline. The Brush took lifeguard station 500 yards astern of the two ships while they were making the transfer. We went back to our regular patrolling after the transfer was completed and the Eversole went on her way.

After dark, at 1947, the Brush had a surface radar contact bearing 308°(t) at a distance of 4000 yards. The Brush left her screening station and went to investigate it. When we approached the contact, it was observed to be a small, motorized sampan. The Brush challenged the sampan with a signal light and didn't get any reply. Someone on the bridge fired four shots from the carbine into the water just forward of their bow to get their attention. The sampan then came up with the correct reply to the challenge and was thus identified as friendly. We left the sampan to go on its way, and we went back to our screening station. We steamed back and forth off the Bombline the rest of the night at 10 knots without experiencing any incidents or doing any firing. In other words, it was a quiet night on the bridge.

## Relieved of the Bombline Patrol

On Friday morning, 20 March, at 0644 the formation departed the Bombline to rendezvous with the USS Los Angeles(CA135) and the USS Hamner(DD718) who were to relieve us of the Bombline Patrol. At 0718 we rendezvoused with our relief ships, and the Brush took lifeguard station astern of the Manchester and the Los Angeles while they made a personnel transfer by highline. At 0840 the Hamner came alongside the Brush's starboard quarter for a guard mail transfer. The 4 ships steamed along together for awhile, and then at 1003 the Manchester and the Brush (Task Unit 77.1.7) was officially relieved by the Los Angeles and the Hamner (Task Unit 77.1.9), and we departed for Sasebo, Japan by way of the Shimonoseki Strait, which is a narrow channel between the Japanese Islands of Honshu and Kyushu. This was going to be a trip of about 350 miles. At 1545 the Brush secured from condition III watch and set the regular steaming watch – thus ended our first tour of duty in North Korean coastal waters. It was an interesting two weeks.

At 0530 the next morning, Saturday, 21 March, task unit 77.1.7 was dissolved and the Brush was detached from the Manchester to proceed independently to Sasebo. Sometime during the morning we passed through the strait.

## SASEBO - MARCH

At 1320 on Saturday afternoon, 21 March, the Brush arrived at the entrance to Sasebo Harbor and set the special sea detail. A few minutes later we entered the channel that took us into the harbor. At 1337 we passed through the submarine nets and entered Sasebo Harbor – for the first time. However, we didn't go directly to our berth. We first went alongside YFNB-2, a harbor craft, at buoy 29 to take on ammunition, which was mostly antisubmarine ordnance such as depth charges and hedgehogs. The ship had just about depleted herself of both these things on the submarine.

After taking on ammunition at buoy 29, the Brush proceeded to buoy 3 and was moored to it at 1619 with 15 fathoms of starboard anchor chain. At 1634 the ship secured from the special sea detail and set the regular inport watch. Liberty commenced at 1700 for those of the crew that didn't have the duty. Of course, the ship sent over several men for shore patrol duty with the liberty party to keep the peace. I had liberty so I went ashore, too, for my first liberty in Sasebo. I found that the town was a mile or so from the landing where we came ashore and the newer sailors got introduced to the local mode of getting to town – the pedicab, or bicycle rickshaw, as the sailors called them. The pedicab was a 3 wheeled, hooded vehicle that could seat one or two people depending on their size. It was a relatively cheap ride into town, but I've forgotten the exact cost. Of course, the pedicab was pedaled by a small Japanese man that I noticed had strong highly developed leg muscles.

The ship stayed in port for 10 days and we had plenty of opportunity to go on liberty. In fact, most of the crew probably had more opportunity to go on liberty than they had money. I'm sure most of the crew left port after 10 days totally broke. However, everybody was able to get some recreation in and was able to catch up on their sleep, too, which itself was great.

## My First Experience in a Japanese Restroom

I found that the public restroom accommodations in Japan were somewhat different than what we are accustomed to in the States. I was in a cabaret one day during our first visit to Sasebo and needed to go to the restroom. Someone pointed me the way to it. I soon discovered that there was only one restroom in the place, and it was for both men and women; and there weren't any locks on the door.

Upon entering the restroom, I immediately noticed that the facilities were vastly different than anything that I had ever seen before. I noticed at a glance that there weren't any commodes in the place. Instead, there were 5 or 6 holes in the floor, all in a row, a couple of feet apart, and with a white porcelain fixture around each one. The only purpose for the fixtures that I could see was to dress them up a little. Furthermore, there weren't any partitions between the holes. They were just out there in the open. In other words, there wasn't any privacy at all. A person had to squat over the holes if there was a need to do so and in front of anybody that happened to be in the restroom at the time – man or woman. I don't know what a heavy, female, American tourist would have done if she had been confronted with such a thing and feeling a sense of urgency, too. Fortunately, I never had to use one and never saw anybody using one–not that I wanted to.

There were urinals in the restroom, though, that were similar to those found in the States, and I went in the restroom on this occasion to use one. Consequently, there was no problem in using one of them. I had just got things flowing good when in walks this Japanese woman who walked right past me. She actually didn't pay me any mind that I could tell, but my first reaction to her walking in on me was that of mild panic. I felt an adrenaline rush go through my body, and my hair felt like it stood up on my head. I leaned into the urinal and I tried to shut things off during full flow. And for an instant, I thought I must be in the wrong restroom. However, my over reaction to the situation only lasted for a second or two, because I quickly remembered that I was in Japan and this is the way that things are done here. So my hair fell back in place, I relaxed and let the good times flow. However, I really wasn't that comfortable with the situation, so I finished up as quickly as I could, buttoned up, washed up, and left the restroom. I never bothered to look back to see what the woman was doing or how she was doing it. I felt like it was more than I wanted to know.

# STREET SCENES OF SASEBO

**The Walk into Town**

**The Ride into Town**

## FIRST YANG DO ISLAND PATROL

Thursday, 2 April, 1953, the ships of Destroyer Division 92, less the Thomas, got underway from Sasebo Harbor to return to the east coast of North Korea. At 0500 word was passed over the P.A. system for the ship to commence making all preparations for getting underway. At 0515 the crew was mustered on station to find out if anyone was absent; one was, but he reported aboard at 0610 – a period of 7 hours AWOL; but luckily he did get back before the ship left.

At 0630 the special sea detail was stationed, and at 0700 the Brush was underway and began maneuvering at various courses and speeds to stand out of the harbor. At 0755 the ship passed through the submarine net and the regular steaming watch was set. Upon reaching the open ocean, the three ships formed up into a column formation with the Maddox in the lead and the Brush bringing up the rear as was usually the case.

Our destination this trip out was an island off North Korea called Yang Do. It was way north on the peninsula. Around midnight the Brush and the Moore were detached from the Maddox to proceed independently to Yang Do. We didn't see the Maddox anymore this trip out. In addition, a few hours later the Moore also departed from us and proceeded on its own way. Consequently, as a result of these departures, the Brush arrived at Yang Do all by herself at 1300 on Friday afternoon, 3 April. We were there to relieve the destroyer, USS Owen(DD536). At 1325 we commenced lying to with the engines stopped about 2000 yards southwest of the island. In a few minutes the Owen's motor whaleboat came alongside to transport Captain Quigley over to the Owen for a conference of some kind, probably to brief him on the present situation in that patrol area, and maybe to have a social drink, too – who knows? Around 1600 the captain was brought back to the ship, and we immediately got underway for a short time to close another ship that was lying to off the island. This other ship was the HMS Consort(D76), a British ship. At 1645 the Brush arrived near the Consort and commenced lying to again. Captain Quigley left the ship in our motor whaleboat to visit the captain of the Consort. At 1830 the captain returned to the ship. They must have had a lot to talk about for him to stay that long, and he must have had evening chow with them, too.

We were now part of Task Unit 95.2.2, which then consisted of the HMS Consort(OTC), USS Brush, USS Chatterer(AM40), and the Moore. Although, we saw very little of the Moore this trip out, and I don't have any idea where she was or what she was doing most of the time.

Yang Do was a relatively small island that, I believe, was a hundred miles or so north of the Bombline. So it was deep in enemy territory. However, I believe it was far enough out in the Sea of Japan to be out of range of the communist shore batteries on the mainland. At least it was never shelled while we were around it. There was a military presence on the island, which consisted of a few marines, some navy personnel of some kind, and some ROK soldiers. I suppose the island served as a far northern outpost to observe any enemy activity that might develop. And, I suppose, our purpose for hanging around the island was to provide some protection for it just in case the North Koreans decided to make a move on it.

There were 4 different areas around Yang Do Island that we patrolled in. These patrol areas were called Cadillac 1, Cadillac 2, Sweet Adeline, and Christine. Cadillac 1 was northeast of the island; Cadillac 2 was southwest of the island; Sweet Adeline was between the island and the mainland; and Christine was east of the island. In addition to the areas around the island, there were 2 other patrol areas farther away that we patrolled in also. One of these distant patrol areas was called Windshield and it had 5 patrolling areas within it – Package 1, 2, 3, 4 and 5. It was about 25 mile down the coast from the island. The other area was called the Northern Patrol area, and it was about 75 miles north of the island, up around Chongjin, which was relatively close to the Manchurian border. The destroyers of Task Unit

95.2.2 took turns at patrolling in these different areas. I imagine the OTC, which was embarked in the Consort, made the decision on a daily basis which areas the different ships would patrol in.

I feel that the time the ship was attached to Task Unit 95.2.2 was relatively pleasant duty in some respects. For one thing, we usually operated alone. But, when we did operate with another ship, we never engaged in any kind of training exercise. I thought it was great for the ship to steam from point A to point B without a lot of exercises thrown in. In addition, the weather was very pleasant; the seas were usually calm and as smooth as glass much of the time. We did have some foggy days but that wasn't all bad. We did much of our patrolling at night under darkened ship conditions so the enemy gunners on shore couldn't see us. We also stayed 4000 to 6000 yards offshore so that we wouldn't be too tempting of a target for the communist shore batteries. However, at times the ship did get closer to shore when the occasion called for it. The ship would close the beach to 2500 to 3000 yards on the nights that she was trying to ambush a train, but that was on our second tour of duty at Yang Do. We did do some firing at enemy targets on some of our patrols, but we didn't do nearly as much as we did on the Bombline Patrol. We fired some illumination shells on several of our night patrols, too.

We spent a lot of time just lying to off the island, especially in the afternoons with the sea calm. We would usually patrol around all night in an area, but during the day we would go back to the island and just lie to. We never dropped anchor but used our engines to maintain our position 1000 to 2000 yards off the island. We were able to do this because there didn't seem to be any ocean currents and there was so little wind that the sea was very calm much of the time.

## Mines

When the Korean War started in 1950 the communist forces released a lot of floating mines in the coastal waters of Korea in an attempt to sink or damage ships of the United Nations forces that might venture into these waters. These floating mines laid low in the water and drifted along with the tides and currents. Consequently, they could be anywhere in the coastal waters. These floating mines are barely visible on the surface of the water, thus, are not easily seen, especially at night and during rough seas. These mines could wreak severe damage to ships if they happened to hit one and even sink them. Several American ships, including the Brush, struck mines during the early weeks of the Korean War. The Brush suffered 37 casualties and came close to breaking in two, so the story goes. A few of my shipmates were on the Brush at the time that she hit the mine and related their experiences to me on that fateful day. It was not a good experience, according to their stories.

As previously written about, the Brush happened to spot 2 floating mines one day while operating in the Kojo area and that was during the latter months of the war. Luckily, we didn't hit one of them. But how many more of them were in that same area? Hopefully, the minesweepers swept the area and found any remaining ones.

## Minesweepers

There was always a minesweeper parked around Yang Do. It was the Chatterer when we first arrived at the island. However, they changed from time to time. Minesweepers were relatively small ships that had the job of clearing harbors and coastal waters of mines. That was their sole purpose for existing, as far as I know. I believe they had wooden hulls instead of metal hulls like most modern ships. Wooden hulls helped them to evade magnetic mines, according to what I was told. The minesweepers always had bird names like Firecrest, Chatterer, Pelican, Curlew, and Ruddy. We operated with all of the above named ships at different times while we were operating off North Korea.

The minesweepers always did their sweeping at night when we operated with them, because they were usually close into shore and, hopefully, the darkness would conceal them from the enemy gunners on the mainland. It actually was relatively dangerous work because they were dealing with very powerful mines, and the fact that they were operating so close to shore much of the time within easy range of enemy guns. The sweeping was always done at the relatively slow speed of 4 knots. The ships would sweep a swath in one direction for a certain distance; then, they would move over a short distance and sweep in the opposite direction for some distance. They would keep doing this until they had swept the desired area. Apparently, it was pretty precise work because they didn't want to miss even a small area. I don't know how they kept themselves located, because there weren't any lights or buoys to get fixes from, unless they were able to keep themselves located by radar. Since all their work was done in the dark, the seamen must have had good night vision.

The destroyers' role in the sweeping operations was to provide the minesweepers with gunfire support in case they came under fire. The minesweepers themselves didn't have much firepower. The destroyers would always position themselves around 1500 yards to seaward of the little ships and in the swept area. They would steam along at the same speed as them and on a parallel course with them, too. The ships must have communicated by shortwave radio because they couldn't communicate by light. However, I've forgotten some of these little details. Luckily, we never experienced any incidents while we were operating with the minesweepers.

The Brush began her patrolling duties the first evening we arrived at the island, immediately after the captain came back aboard after visiting the British ship, Consort. At 1830 the Brush got underway and proceeded to the Cadillac 2 patrol area, which was southwest of the island. We steamed around in this area all night until 0800 the next morning – Saturday, 4 April. It was a very uneventful night. We didn't see anything or hear anything. At 0810 the Brush ceased patrolling and returned to the island. However, on this occasion we didn't lie to. Instead, we joined up with the HMS Consort to accompany her on the Northern Patrol. Together, the Brush and the Consort made a fast run up the coast for about 75 miles to the Northern Patrol area, but we didn't see anything that needed our attention. So, at 1330 we reversed course and returned to Yang Do Island. We arrived there about 1700.

The Brush patrolled in the Cadillac 1 area Saturday night, which was northeast of the island. We patrolled there most of the night, but at 1930 we left Cadillac 1 for awhile to escort the USS Chatterer(AMS40) on a minesweeping mission. This was our first time to accompany a minesweeper. But, as usually done, the Brush took a position 1500 yards to seaward off the Chatterer's bow. The minesweeping operation lasted about 45 minutes, and after that was completed the Brush returned to patrolling Cadillac 1. During the night the Brush fired 12 illumination shells over the mainland and over the channel between the mainland and the island. At 0800 Sunday, 5 April, the Brush returned to the island, commenced lying to 1000 yards south of the island, and remained there for the rest of the day.

## A Tour of Yang Do Island

On Sunday afternoon, 5 April, seven of the Brush's officers had the pleasure of visiting the island. At 1330 the island sent a boat out to pick them up, and at 1525 the same boat brought them back. They were gone for a couple of hours which probably gave them time to make a tour of the entire island. It was something different for them to do on a lazy Sunday afternoon, and I'm sure they found it interesting. Ensign W. A. Robbins was one of the officers that visited Yang Do Island. He told me that the island was full of trenches and there were around 100 ROK soldiers on the island to man these trenches in case the need arose.

There was also a Korean family that lived on the island – a man, his wife, and their two young daughters. Mr. Robbins especially noticed that the man appeared much older than his actual age. He claimed to be 37 years old, but he looked more like 60 years old. The man's two young daughters were busy making rice powder with a special arrangement they had rigged up that pounded the rice into flour. Another thing that Ensign Robbins found interesting was the Korean man's method of drying fish. The man had sticks stuck in the ground with wire stretched between them, and he had split fish hanging on the wire to dry.

Late in the afternoon of Sunday, 5 April, the Brush got underway to proceed to the Windshield Patrol area 25 miles south of Yang Do near a place called Songjin, a town of sorts. The ship patrolled around in this area all night and all the next day. During the morning hours of Monday, 6 April, the ship fired a total of 14 rounds of 5 inch high capacity shells at targets on the mainland. During the afternoon the Brush fired another 20 rounds of 5 inch high capacity shells at targets on the mainland. Around 2000 hours the ship departed the Windshield area, returned to Yang Do, and started patrolling in Cadillac 2 southwest of the island. During the midwatch the Brush fired 9 rounds of star shells.

Tuesday, 7 April, was replenishment day and around 0700 the Brush, Consort, and the Moore rendezvoused with the USS Aludra(AF55) and the Kaskaskia(A027) to take on provisions and fuel. During the replenishment operation, we also received some new crewmembers. We received 3 new men from each ship by highline.

After the replenishment operation, the Brush returned to Yang Do. She arrived at the island at 1130, stopped all engines, and commenced lying to 2000 yards south of the island. She remained lying to for the rest of the day.

At 1741 six officers from the Consort came aboard for a wardroom visit and stayed for an hour or so. I hope they had a pleasant visit.

Tuesday night, 7 April, the Brush patrolled in Cadillac 1 northeast of the island. She steamed around all night at 7 knots and changed course every 15 minutes or so. During the night she fired 14 rounds of 5"/38 star shells. At 0600 the ship secured from patrolling Cadillac 1 and proceeded back to the island.

At 0715 Wednesday morning, 8 April, the Samuel N. Moore showed up and together the Brush and the Moore proceeded on the Northern Patrol. They steamed along at a speed of 18 knots with the Brush in station 1000 yards astern of the Moore. They steamed around on the Northern Patrol for several hours but never encountered anything that required their attention. Around 1630 the Brush and the Moore parted company, and the Brush proceeded back to Yang Do independently. She arrived back at Yang Do around 1700.

However, the Brush immediately left the island to proceed to the Windshield Patrol area to rendezvous with the Chatterer and to patrol that area. We rendezvoused with the minesweeper at 2035 and commenced giving her GFS. The minesweeping operation was completed at 2200 and the Chatterer departed the area and returned to the island. The Brush spent the rest of the night patrolling in the Windshield area, Package 2, south of Songjin. But it was a quiet and uneventful patrol. We didn't do any firing or see anything to investigate all night. The Brush returned to Yang Do around 0930 the next morning, Thursday, 9 April.

## An Unusual Morning

Upon arriving back at Yang Do on this morning, the Brush had a different type of task to perform. We had to supply the island garrison with some fresh water – ship made. The Brush proceeded to go around to the south side of the island, stopped all engines, and commenced lying to about 1000 yards offshore. A few minutes later an island boat came alongside to starboard. The boat was actually a landing craft of some kind that was filled with twenty 55 gallon metal drums. The ship proceeded to fill those drums with fresh water and gave them a total of 1000 gallons. The water transfer was completed about 1010 and the boat returned to the island. The Brush continued to lie to for the rest of the day. I took a picture of the landing craft taking on the water and I still have the picture. There were 7 ROK soldiers in the boat.

The reason I remember this particular morning so well is because the weather and sea conditions were so unusual. There wasn't any wind at all and the sea was as smooth as glass. There was a light fog and what clouds there were were very high. What made the morning so memorable to me is that there wasn't a distinguishable horizon. The sea and sky just kind of blended in together and there was not a horizon. I never saw that kind of situation again. It also is rather unusual for the sea to be so smooth, too – without a ripple. The weather was still rather cool, however.

The captain took this day to have captain's mast and dealt out punishment to 7 bad boys. This captain's mast thing was a frequent occurrence on the ship. Somebody was always getting into trouble for something, but a lot of it was due to sailors being AWOL for varying lengths of time. Court-martials were occasionally convened, too, to deal out punishment to those sailors that had committed more serious offenses. These captain masts were easy to avoid. All a sailor had to do was behave himself and he would stay out of trouble. It was many of the same ones getting into trouble over and over. I never could understand why someone wanted to make life harder for himself. In addition, if a sailor just wouldn't behave himself, he was sent to the brig on shore somewhere and that was a bad place to be. The marine guards would get their attention and usually weren't too kind to them either. At this particular captain's mast there were some offenses other than being absent-without-leave (AWOL). One sailor got 5 hours extra duty for sleeping in. Another sailor, a 3rd class petty officer, got a reduction in rate for bringing liquor aboard ship; however, it was a reduction in rate for only 3 months. The captain probably wouldn't be as lenient with him the next time if he was caught doing it again. Another sailor got 10 hours extra duty for sleeping-in. Another fellow got 3 days restriction starting the next time we were in port for violation of a verbal order; he got caught smoking in the officer's wardroom pantry after he was told not to smoke there. He must have been a steward's mate.

Thursday evening, 9 April, at around 1800 the Brush got underway and proceeded to nearby Cadillac 2 where she steamed around all night at 7 knots. Nothing eventful happened during the night nor did we do any firing.

Friday morning, 10 April, at a little after 0600 the Brush left Cadillac 2 and proceeded to the Windshield area to patrol in Package 1 and 2. We went there to do some firing at targets on the mainland, but the action never materialized for some reason. At 1720 we departed the Package 1 and 2 areas and proceeded back to Yang Do to rendezvous with the Chatterer for a minesweeping mission. At 1945 the Brush took her usual station 1500 yards to seaward of the minesweeper. The minesweeping mission was completed at 2200 and the Brush then proceeded to the Cadillac 2 area to patrol for the rest of the night. At 0225 the ship challenged a small boat and it identified itself as a ROK navy craft.

Saturday, 11 April, was replenishment day again, and early in the morning the Brush and the Consort rendezvoused with the replenishment ships – the USS Taluga(A062) and the USS Rainier(AE56). By 0900 both ships had been replenished with fuel oil and ammunition, set a course to return to Yang Do, and arrived there at 1100. However, we didn't stay there long. The ship almost immediately got underway to rendezvous with the USS James E Kyes(DD787). We joined up with the Kyes around 1330 that was escorting 2 ROK Navy motor sampans, K-192 and K-333. The Kyes immediately departed from us to rendezvous with the replenishment ships. So, we assumed the escort duty. These ROK craft were intelligence boats of some kind. I think that meant that they put soldiers ashore at night behind enemy lines to gather intelligence. We worked with some of them later on. We were escorting these boats to Yang Do. Around 1840 the Moore rendezvoused with us to transfer guard mail. She came alongside to starboard for the transfer by highline. The Moore stayed with us for an hour and a half, and we took station 1000 yards astern of her on a course of 189°(t) and at a speed of 4 and 8 knots. At 2038 the Moore departed from us taking K-333 with her. We escorted K-192 on into Yang Do and arrived there around 0300 Sunday morning. We stayed around the island all day.

Saturday, sometime while we were gone, the British ship, HMS Consort, was relieved by the Canadian ship, HMCS Crusader(DDE228).

Sunday night we patrolled in Cadillac 1 all night at a speed of 7 knots. Nothing special happened during the night; although, we did fire a total of 10 star shells over the channel north of Yang Do. Early Monday morning the Brush returned to the island, stopped engines, and commenced lying to. We continued lying to all day Monday, 13 April.

Monday night the Brush patrolled in Cadillac 2 the first part of the night from 1845 to 2250. Then, the ship proceeded to the Sweet Adeline patrol area and steamed around in it for a couple of hours. The Brush then went back to Cadillac 2 and patrolled in it for the rest of the night. Nothing was going on in either place.

We returned to the island around 0630 Tuesday morning, 14 April, and commenced lying to until 1313 in the afternoon. At 1313 we sighted the USS Owen (DD536) that was coming to relieve us and the Moore. We were relieved of the Yang Do patrol at 1500. At that time, the Brush secured from condition III watches and set the regular steaming watch. We soon joined up with the Moore, and, together, the 2 ships headed for Sasebo, Japan. The Brush and the Moore steamed toward Japan on a base course of 175°(t) and at a speed of 19 knots. They maintained this same course and speed for 14 hours or so. I mention this because it was so rare that we just steamed along without doing anything else. I think the captain of the Moore, who was OTC, was anxious to go on liberty. Of course, we were steaming in the Sea of Japan. As we neared the Japanese islands, however, we were continuously changing course to avoid fishing boats. The fishing must have been good for so many boats to be out on the water that were engaged in that activity. It was after nightfall that we encountered so many boats. Sometimes there would be just one boat by itself, and sometimes there would be a small fleet of them.

## SASEBO – APRIL

Wednesday, 15 April, at 1530 we arrived at the entrance of Sasebo Harbor. At 1503 the Brush had been detached from the Moore to proceed independently into port. At 1713 the Brush moored port side to the Moore that was moored port side to the destroyer tender, USS Dixie(AD14), that was moored to buoy 1. The Thomas came in a little later in the day and moored alongside the Brush. The Maddox came in port Friday and moored alongside the Thomas. Thus, we were in a nest of ships that included the Dixie, Moore, Brush, Thomas, and Maddox. The ships of Destroyer Division 92 started receiving steam and electrical power from the Dixie. We stayed in port for 6 days. Our next trip out was going to be much more exciting and eventful than the one we had just completed.

On Saturday, 18 April, my charthouse mentor, Charles K. Layton QM3/C, was transferred to the USS Porterfield(DD682) for further transportation to the United States and to shore duty at the naval base at Norfolk, Virginia. Layton and I got along real good together, because I was eager to learn what he knew about navigational charts and the charthouse duties; and he seemed pleased to share his knowledge with someone that was interested in learning it. I was sorry to see him go; however, I was being trained to take his place when he left. So, when he left the ship, I assumed the charthouse duties and never experienced any difficulties of any kind. Apparently, he taught me well. However, I'm sure my training at Bainbridge made his job of training me much easier. I liked working with navigational things myself, but none of the other quartermasters had any interest in it. So, after Layton left, I had the charthouse all to myself for the rest of my naval career.

### Spies in High Places

One time during a conversation with Tommy off Korea, he gave me an interesting and shocking piece of information. He told me that the navy had learned early on in the Korean War that they couldn't reveal any of their military plans to Washington if they wanted something, maybe an attack, to be a surprise, because the North Koreans and Chinese would know about them immediately and there wouldn't be a surprise.

The reason that our enemy would be so well informed about our military plans was because there were so many communist spies in the U.S. Government in Washington – some of them in high positions. The communist agents would learn about the U.S. Military's plans and pass that information on to their Soviet Union bosses, who would pass it on to the North Koreans and Chinese.

I thought that what Tommy had to say was an interesting piece of information; although, I didn't know for sure whether it was true or not. However, I was inclined to believe him, because he was on his third tour to Korea and over that length of time a person is bound to learn things whether he is supposed to or not. Personally, I was too young and ignorant at the time to give much thought to political things. Like most young people, I had much more important things on my mind.

I got more politically minded as I got older, however, and tried to keep myself informed as to what was going on in the world and also what had happened in the past – including recent past. I never forgot Tommy's remarks about communist spies in Washington, and as time went by, I learned that what Tommy said was absolutely correct. In the 1930's, 1940's and 1950's, and probably later, too, Washington was full of Soviet spies. Many of them were in the State Department. Furthermore, there weren't too many people in Washington that were concerned about the spying even when they knew about it; mainly, because many of the politicians and governmental officials in Washington were, at least, fellow-travelers themselves. Eventually, though, a few of the spies were exposed and put in jail. Although, most of them got away with their crimes against the U.S., continued on with their spying, and probably died of old age still in business. In reality, the United States didn't have any secrets from the Soviet Union. They knew all of our secrets, both large and small, almost immediately.

## The Bridge Gang

**Ed Geffert QMSN**

**Billy Tomlinson QMSN**

**Charlie Beason QMSN**

## The Bridge Gang

**Charles Layton QM3/C**

**Ted Holly QMSN**
**(Drinking Coffee at the Quartermaster's Desk)**

# The Bridge Gang

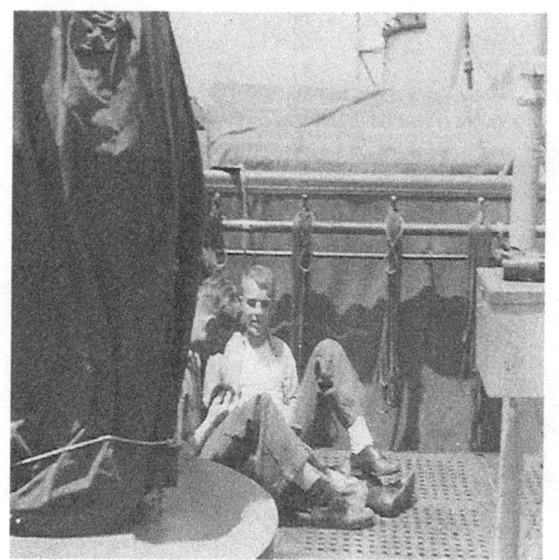

Charlie Beason QMSN & Friend

Tommy Tomlinson QM2/C

Lawrence Barth QMSN

Charlie Beason QMSN

## The Bridge Gang

Ted Holly QMSN

Ted Holly QMSN

Ed Geffert QMSN

Tommy, Chief Cote & Norm

## The Bridge Gang

Ted Holly QMSN

Returning From a Patrol & Relaxing on the Bridge

Paul Haney (on the light), Donald Gatz SO3,
Billy Tomlinson, Sam Smith, Norm Jackson,
Ed Geffert & Larry Byrd RM3 (sitting)

## SECOND YANG DO ISLAND PATROL

On Wednesday morning, 22 April, the Brush took departure from Sasebo Harbor in company with the Moore and the Thomas to return to Yang Do Island. Later in the morning, around 1030, the ship went to general quarters and we had anti-aircraft gunnery practice. At 1107 the ship commenced firing one of her main batteries at a sleeve that was being towed by an airplane. The main battery fired five rounds of 5"/38 AA shells at the sleeve. Then, the 40mm crews had their turn at firing at the sleeve. Over a period of 5 minutes the 40mm crews fired a total of 344 rounds of ammunition. I don't remember how well the gunners did on this particular occasion, but usually they did pretty well at firing at sleeves. However, the speed of the towing plane was always rather slow compared to that of a fast jet plane. I've always felt that we wouldn't have stood a chance against a fast jet if one had attacked us. Anywhere off North Korea, we would have been easy prey for a communist jet, but fortunately none ever attacked us, nor did we ever see one. I guess they were too afraid of the American jets that were flying around to attack us.

Around 1200 the Thomas left the formation to proceed independently to the west coast of North Korea. The Moore was OTC now and the Brush took station 500 yards astern of her, but late in the afternoon she took station 1000 yards astern of her. At 0100 on Thursday morning, 23 April, the Brush was detached from the Moore to proceed independently to the Bombline, which was near Suwon Dan, to rendezvous with the USS St. Paul(CA73) for a personnel transfer. At 0812 the Brush went alongside the cruiser and a Commander Hammer was sent over to the Brush by highline for further transfer to the USS New Jersey(BB62).

The Brush then proceeded toward Yang Do Island again. However, on the way there, she was instructed to rendezvous with the tanker, USS Manatee(A058), for refueling. So, at 1545 the ship was alongside the Manatee and commenced taking on fuel oil. She really didn't need much fuel, though, because she had just left Sasebo all tanked-up, but she did receive 17,500 gallons. After refueling, the Brush proceeded on to Yang Do and finally arrived there around 1800 and commenced lying to. The Brush was once again part of Task Unit 95.2.2. Other ships that were part of the task unit at that time were the USS Samuel N. Moore(DD747), USS Endicott(DMS35), HMCS Crusader(DDE228), and the USS Pelican(AMS32). We would be patrolling the same patrol areas as before but with one major difference; there would be an emphasis put on waylaying North Korean trains, or Chinese trains, whichever they were.

The Brush arrived at Yang Do rather late in the day on, 23 April, and didn't spend much time lying to at this time. At 1930 the Brush got underway and proceeded to the Cadillac 2 patrol area southwest of the island. She patrolled in this area all night at a speed of 7 knots. At 2010 the Brush commenced firing illumination shells over the channel north of Yang Do. She would fire one shell every few minutes and over a 2 hour period fired 12 rounds of 5"/38 star shells.

At 0510 Friday morning, 24 April, the Brush returned to the island and commenced lying to for a personnel transfer to the Moore for further transfer to the New Jersey. The transfer of Commander Hammer was accomplished by the ship's motor whaleboat and was completed at 0550.

At 0555 the Brush, in company with the Endicott, proceeded on the Northern Patrol up to the Chongjin area, which was 70 to 75 miles north of the island and within just a few miles of the Manchurian border. The Endicott took station 1000 yards astern of the Brush and they steamed at a speed of 18 knots to reach the area. The two ships arrived at the Chongjin area around 0930, formed a line abreast, increased their speed to 22 knots, went to general quarters, and closed the coast. At 1000 the ships increased speed to 25 knots. I believe the ships were trying to tempt the North Korean gunners on shore to fire on them so they could work them over. The ships steamed around the

Chongjin area for an hour or so, couldn't get the enemy gunners to respond, didn't see anything that needed their attention, so they called it quits for the day and headed back toward Yang Do. They arrived back at the island at 1500. The Brush stopped all engines and commenced lying to.

The Brush got underway again at 1730 and proceeded to the Windshield area, Package 2, which was 25 miles or so southwest of the island. The ship steamed around in the area for awhile, and then at 2225 she stopped all engines and commenced lying to 2300 yards off the beach. And here she stayed most of the night. Our purpose for just lying to on this night was to ambush a train. A 40mm gun mount and a 5″ gun mount were always manned when we were off the coast of North Korea. However, the 40mm mounts were usually the designated shooting mounts on our train ambushing expeditions. We didn't see a train on this occasion, though.

## Ambushing Trains

North Korea is a very mountainous country and the mountains come all the way down to the sea in many places. However, there is also considerable flat land along the coast, too, and that is where the North Koreans built their railroad tracks as much as possible. They also built a lot of railroad tunnels, too, instead of building the tracks around the side of mountains. Consequently, when a train was traveling on this coastal railroad, it was constantly going into and out of tunnels, which created a challenge when a ship was trying to hit one with its guns. However, the naval gunners were still able to destroy a number of them.

The North Koreans did a number of things in an effort to reduce their losses. The trains usually ran at night and were kept relatively short. Also, the trains were traveling fast and didn't operate on any fixed schedule. All these things, in addition to going into and out of tunnels, made it difficult for a ship to bag one.

The navy ships would usually lie 2500 to 3000 yards off the beach at night when they were attempting to ambush a train. Sometimes a train would come along and sometimes they wouldn't – you never knew when they would. You just had to wait for one to show up. When a train did come along, the gunners only had a few seconds to a minute or two to act before it would be back into a tunnel. The ships would know the locations, of course, where it would be possible to hit a train with gunfire if they acted quickly. A number of destroyers were able to destroy one or more trains, but the most successful ship at destroying trains was a British ship; she bagged 5 of them, so I read. I've forgotten the name of the ship that was so successful. However, I'm not sure that the UN Forces accomplished a whole lot when they did knock out a train, and/or destroy some railroad tracks; because the North Koreans had work crews located all up and down the tracks whose job it was to clear and repair the tracks very quickly – in a matter of a few hours. Oh well, it was great sport for the ships and it gave them something to do. In addition, when the ships were successful, the crews had something to brag about. However, the Brush's crew never achieved anything to brag about in this respect. We never were able to bag a train, although, we gave it our best effort.

## A Lost Opportunity

On one particular night, 25 April, I was standing the midwatch (0000–0400). It was a very dark night and we were just lying to out there in the dark waiting for a train to show up. There wasn't any wind at all and the sea was very calm. The ship was very quiet. Of course, everyone was asleep that could be. Essentially, the only ones awake on the ship were the men on the bridge, in the engine rooms, and in the manned gun mounts. I was the quartermaster-of-the-watch, but I didn't have much to do, so I spent a lot of my time out on the open bridge peering off into the dark toward land and wondering if a train was going to come along on this night.

All of a sudden, the forward 40mm gun on the starboard side, just a few feet from me, broke the silence with 3 quick shots – Bam, Bam, Bam. On the third Bam I observed a big splash in the water close aboard off the starboard beam. I knew the gunners were probably shooting at a train, but I didn't understand the reason for the splash, although, I knew it had to be a shell from our gun. The officer-of-the-deck didn't understand it either and sent someone to fetch the gun captain to the bridge to question him. The gunner quickly came to the bridge and had a brief talk with the OOD. It developed that the gunner saw a train alright, through his binoculars, and opened up on it, but he failed to do one little necessary thing concerning the gun. He failed to lock it in position, as I understood it, and it didn't stay aimed toward the train. The first shot went toward the train as wanted, but the second shot went straight up in the air, and the third shot hit the water close aboard. The gunner realized his error after 3 shots and quit firing. Consequently, we missed a good chance to knock out a train. It went on down the tracks and shortly into a tunnel and out of sight.

At 0400 Saturday morning, 25 April, the Brush abandoned its train watch at Package 2 and returned to the island. We arrived back at the island at 0735, stopped all engines, commenced lying to, and did so all day. On this day, two of our missing crewmen were declared "absentees from this ship and from the United States Naval Service." In other words, they were in big trouble. These same 2 guys seemed to have stayed in trouble, usually for being AWOL. They were buddies and did things together – like going AWOL. I think they hated being in the navy and hated shipboard life to the point that it was more than they could bear.

At 1838 the Brush got underway and commenced patrolling in Cadillac 1 near the island. She patrolled around in this area all night at 7 knots. It was a very uneventful night. We did fire 4 star shells over the channel during the early part of the night. The ship returned to the island around 0600. However, she didn't stay around the island very long. At 0830 she got underway and made a run down the coast to the Windshield patrol area. She steamed around in this patrol area for a few hours, saw nothing, and returned to the island at 1641.

Sunday night, 26 April, the Brush patrolled in the Cadillac 2 and the Christine Patrol areas near the island. It was a very quiet night. The ship fired 2 star shells during the midwatch. The Brush returned to the island at 0515. Thick fog enveloped the area.

During the late morning hours on Monday, 27 April, the Brush proceeded to rendezvous with the tanker, USS Navasota(AO106), for refueling. At 1154 the Brush was alongside the tanker and commenced taking on fuel. During the process of refueling, the ship transferred and received U.S. mail. Upon refueling, the Brush returned to the island, but she didn't stay too long, because at 1514 the ship got underway for the Windshield Patrol Area.

Early in the afternoon of Monday, 27 April, the HMS Cockade(D-34) arrived at Yang Do to relieve the HMCS Crusader. At 1445 the Crusader departed the island for Sasebo, Japan.

The Brush slowly steamed around in the Windshield area all night but nothing of any significance happened. The ship returned to the island at 0652 Tuesday morning, 28 April, commenced lying to, and did so all day and all night, too.

The Brush got underway at 0800 Wednesday morning, 29 April, and proceeded to the Windshield Patrol Area again. The ship patrolled around in this patrol area all morning and part of the afternoon. At 1010 the Brush commenced interdiction fire on targets on the mainland. However, she only fired 4 rounds of 5 inch high capacity shells. Around 1430 the Brush ceased patrolling in the Windshield Patrol Area, proceeded back to Yang Do and arrived there at 1700.

## Hid in the Rising Sun

The Brush conducted a little unusual, surprise attack on a communist shore battery early one morning during the latter part of April. This attack was made way north on the Korean peninsula somewhere, and the enemy guns were in a known position on a mountainside. We were operating alone. The plan was to attack out of the early morning sun so we couldn't be seen approaching the gun positions. I don't know whether it was the captain's idea to attack the guns in this way or whether he was ordered to do it in this manner. However, I am inclined to think that it was Captain Quigley's. In my opinion, it was a rather clever plan of attack regardless of whose idea it was but maybe a little on the risky side.

I saw the captain and the navigator in the charthouse the evening before looking at a chart and developing their plan of action. That was one time I stayed out of the charthouse, because I knew that there was some high level discussion taking place in there and I wasn't invited to participate in it.

A number of things had to be taken into consideration for the surprise attack to succeed. First, a clear morning was needed. The weather report had forecast a clear sky the next morning with relatively little wind, so the visibility would be good and the sea would be calm. In addition, the time of sunrise had to be determined, as well as the length of time that the early morning sun would be hanging on the horizon. The ship also had to be far enough out at sea at daybreak to be out of sight of the enemy gunners on the mountain. Then, the navigator had to calculate the amount of time it would take for the ship to reach the point near land where the ship's 5 inch guns would open up on the shore batteries at relatively close range. Hopefully, we could get quite close to shore without being seen by the enemy gunners.

At sunrise the ship was to head for the beach; at that time of day the morning sun on the horizon would be so big and bright that the enemy gunners wouldn't be able to look directly into it. Consequently, we would be hid by the rising sun during our approach to land and during our get away attempt, too, to some extent. Hopefully, of course, we would destroy the enemy guns with our salvo and not have to be concerned about them shooting back at us, but we couldn't be certain of that.

The ship went to general quarters before daybreak and waited for the sun to barely peep up over the horizon; when it did, the ship started moving toward the beach and gathered speed rapidly as she went forward through the water. Soon, the ship was traveling at flank speed (around 32 knots) and the ship was literally vibrating as she sped toward land. At 32 knots it was quite breezy on the bridge.

I imagine that we struck the enemy gun crews on this morning about the time they were having their morning bowl of rice. I can imagine them squatting around their cooking fire, eating their rice, and enjoying the view of the sun rising over a big, empty ocean or what appeared to be empty. It must have been a beautiful sight that they were observing that morning from their mountain perch. It also probably looked like it was going to be another quiet, uneventful day for them. However, danger was rapidly approaching, but they couldn't see it because it was hidden in the big, bright rising sun.

My general quarters station on this morning was on the signal bridge. As we were going in on the attack, I stood for awhile on the port side of the bridge, a little aft of the pilothouse hatch, and watched as the shore got closer and closer. I was standing by myself. The other signalmen must have been standing on the starboard side of the bridge and up forward.

There were very few people topside to witness our approach to the beach, except for the men on the bridge. Everybody had to be below deck that didn't have a battle station topside somewhere. Also, everyone topside had to wear flack jackets and helmets.

As the ship sped toward the shore at flank speed, and as I watched the beach get closer and closer, I got to thinking. What if this plan of attack doesn't work as well as they hoped it would and they see us coming. Here I am out here on this open bridge with no protection at all from an airblast, or a shell hit in the bridge area. I knew that if either one of those things happened, I would be in big trouble. Consequently, I decided that it might be wise for me to step behind the captain's cabin because I might have some protection there. And that is what I did for the rest of the ride in.

When the ship reached the desired distance from the shore, the captain gave the order, "Right full rudder" to the helmsman and then for him to steer a course that was parallel to the beach, whatever that course was. When the ship made her ninety degree turn to starboard and was broadside to the beach, the captain gave the gunners the order to, "Open fire". The port side of the ship literally exploded as all six 5 inch guns opened fire at the same moment. At least some of the guns fired a second time, but the firing of our guns was very brief because the order to "cease fire" was given after only 4 or 5 seconds. However, during that brief time 9 to 10 five inch shells were fired at the enemy shore battery on the mountainside.

Now, the challenge for the captain was to get his ship back out to sea and out of range of the enemy guns in case we hadn't done a good job of knocking them out. Immediately after firing, the captain gave the order, "Right full rudder" to the helmsman again and another 90 degree turn to starboard was made to take us back out to sea. Of course, we were still traveling at 32 knots. The ship also did some zig-zagging for a couple of minutes after we were headed seaward to make it more difficult for the enemy gunners to hit us in case we hadn't destroyed them. In addition, as we made our turn to seaward, the ship started making a smoke screen with a smoke generator on the fantail, and at the same time, the engine rooms started pouring out black smoke from our 2 smoke stacks. Therefore, we were hid behind a smoke screen in a matter of seconds and couldn't be seen by the enemy gunners to shoot at us even if they were able to.

However, we didn't receive any return fire from the enemy shore battery for whatever reason. It might have been because we knocked out the guns with our broadside; or it might have been that they were taken by surprise and things happened so fast that they weren't able to respond fast enough to do us any harm. We will never know for sure which it was, but we got away unharmed for sure; that, I do know.

## I'm A Witness at a Captain's Mast

Wednesday morning, 29 April, the captain held another one of his frequent non-judicial punishment sessions, or captain's mast, for 3 crewmembers. The offense for 2 of the men was AWOL and they got summary court-martials. However, the other sailor was charged with striking a petty officer and was awarded a special court martial. The fellow that struck the petty officer happened to be a Mexican-American boy from Texas, I believe. I was a witness to this incident.

The captain held court under the mast right behind the signal bridge and flagbags. I was on the signal bridge this morning and someone came up to me and told me the captain wanted to see me at the captain's mast. I was kind of taken by surprise and couldn't imagine what he wanted to see me about, but I hurried down to it. It so happened one day that I was in the noon chow line and my friend, Andy Anderson MM3/C, the coxswain of the boat that brought me out to the ship the day I reported aboard, was also there in line, as was this Mexican boy. Andy and I were just standing there engaged in idle conversation when all of a sudden this Mexican boy just hauls off and hits Andy and blurts out something in a very angry tone. He couldn't speak very good English. There was absolutely no reason for the attack that I could see and Andy and I were momentarily shocked because it was so unprovoked. The boy didn't attempt to strike Andy a second time, however. I think it was probably the dumbest thing I ever saw in the navy. I think the boy thought that Andy was trying to butt in ahead of him in the chow line, which he wasn't. But even if he was, you don't strike a petty officer. Anyway, Andy put him on report over the incident. Apparently, at the captain's mast Andy told the captain that I was a witness to the attack. So, I had to tell the captain what happened at the time of the incident. The captain dismissed me from the captain's mast after I told him what I had witnessed.

This particular boy had a problem somehow. I served with him 2 or 3 years on the ship and I noticed he appeared to look angry all the time. He didn't seem to have any friends or want any. He didn't seem to like anybody, even the other Mexican boys. I tried to engage him in a friendly conversation a time or two, but I could tell he wasn't the least bit interested. I always thought he must have had some very bad experiences in his past that made him hate the whole world and everybody in it. In addition, I don't think he liked being in the navy either, and he especially didn't like being aboard ship. I wonder whatever happened to the boy. Whatever it was, it probably wasn't good because of the rotten attitude he had.

Wednesday evening the Brush proceeded to rendezvous with the Moore up the coast aways and proceeded on up to the Northern Patrol area at Chongjin with her. They arrived in the area around 2300 and streamed around in it for several hours. However, the ships didn't encounter anything that required their attention. At 0406 the 2 ships headed back toward Yang Do.

Thursday night, 30 April, the Brush patrolled in Cadillac 1, but it was another very quiet night and we didn't see anything or hear anything. We mainly just watched the channel between the mainland and the island.

Friday, 1 May, was replenishment day again and around 1045 the Brush rendezvoused with the tanker, USS Cacapon(A052), for refueling. Upon completion of that task, the Brush returned to Yang Do.

Friday night the Brush rendezvoused with and provided gunfire support for the USS Pelican(AMS32) while she conducted minesweeping operations. Most of the night, though, the Brush patrolled in Cadillac 2. It was another quiet night.

Saturday morning, 2 May, the Brush went down to the Windshield area and patrolled around in Package 3 and 4. At 1035 she commenced firing at various targets on the mainland and expended 8 rounds of 5"/38 high capacity shells. A railroad tunnel was one of her targets.

## The Maddox Under Fire

Late in the morning, Saturday, 2 May, the Brush received word that the Maddox had received a direct hit by enemy shore batteries in Wonsan Harbor, but luckily there were no casualties. Later, I learned that the Maddox was patrolling in the East Muffler area when she commenced receiving enemy fire from shore batteries on Hodo Pando. She commenced maneuvering at high speed to take evasive action. In addition, the Maddox returned fire with her 5 inch guns while she was maneuvering around at 27 knots. There were 148 splashes of enemy shells that were counted by someone on the Maddox, all in a manner of a few minutes. Many of these shells came close to hitting the Maddox, but only one shell actually hit the ship. One shell hit around frame 85 on the port side and did extensive damage to one of her 3"/50 gun mounts. The Maddox fired 40 rounds of 5"/38 high capacity projectiles from Mounts 51 and 53 during the skirmish. The Maddox continued patrolling in the harbor after the encounter with the enemy guns. The Maddox divided her time between Wonsan and the Hungnam area. Two days later, the Maddox came under fire again in the Hungnam area but was able to avoid getting hit.

## Train Hunting

Saturday night the Brush proceeded to Package 2 and arrived there at 2200. She stopped all engines and commenced lying to 3000 yards off the beach. On this night the Brush had specifically gone train hunting. She lay there in the dark waiting for a train to show up. A 40mm mount was the gun that was going to do the shooting if a train was spotted. The mount captain was peering through a pair of binoculars at a specific area on the beach where a train could be seen if one was passing. At 0118 a train was spotted moving on the tracks and the 40mm opened up. In a matter of a few seconds 28 rounds of 40mm ammunition was fired at the train. However, the gunners failed to hit the train. It kept going. The manned 5 inch mount also fired 2 rounds at the railroad tunnel entrance at 0337 for good measure. I don't know how they were able to see the tunnel entrance in the dark. At 0403 the Brush headed back toward Yang Do.

Sunday night, 3 May, the Brush patrolled in Cadillac 1 again. During the early part of the night, the Brush fired 6 rounds of 5 inch star shells over the channel between the island and the mainland. The ship returned to Yang Do around 0630.

At 0946 Monday, 4 May, the Brush proceeded to Package 1 down the coast. She arrived there around 1030. At 1038 the Brush commenced firing at a train with her 5 inch guns. She fired 6 rounds at the train but wasn't able to hit it. A little after noon the Brush proceeded to Package 2. At 1237 she commenced interdiction fire in Package 2 and over a period of 30 minutes expended 14 rounds of 5 inch high capacity ammunition. A little after 1300 the ship returned to Yang Do. On Monday night the Brush went on the Northern Patrol with the Maddox. The 2 ships steamed around in the Chongjin area for a few hours but they didn't see anything. The Brush arrived back at the island around 0630.

Tuesday, 5 May, at 1127 the Brush got underway to rendezvous with a tanker for refueling. She went alongside the USS Mispillion(A0105) around 1300 and commenced taking on fuel oil. After refueling, the Brush proceeded to the Windshield Patrol area which was nearby. The Brush arrived at the Package 3 patrol area around 1500 and steamed around in it the rest of the afternoon, all night, and much of Wednesday morning, 6 May. The Brush arrived back at the island at 1100, stopped all engines and commenced lying to. She remained lying to south of the island all afternoon and into the night.

At 2155, Wednesday night, 6 May, the Brush got underway and commenced patrolling south of Yang Do in the Christine Patrol area. She patrolled in this area most of the night but saw nothing and did nothing that created any excitement. Around 0500 Thursday morning, 7 May, the Brush ceased the patrol and proceeded to rendezvous with a cargo ship, the USS Pictor(AF54). At 0550 the Brush went alongside of her to take on provisions by way of a highline. The replenishment was completed at 0623 and the Brush proceeded back to Yang Do, arriving there around 0830. However, she didn't stay there too long. At 0942 she got underway and proceeded to the Windshield Patrol area.

## Hunger Aboard Ship and Midnight Snacks

I experienced a number of different feelings during my tour of duty off North Korea in 1953 and one of them was hunger. We didn't get enough to eat and most of us stayed hungry much of the time. In fact, the Brush was a poor feeder all the time that I was aboard her. I know the navy has the reputation for serving great chow, and I have had some of it – on shore bases, but we didn't see much of it on the Brush, as far as I am concerned; and I think most of my shipmates would agree with me on that point. In my opinion, much of the food was poorly prepared, but worst of all we didn't get enough food to stave off hunger. The portions we were served were more like what you would normally give a small child. Consequently, most of the crew lost several pounds of weight on this cruise and the other two 7 month cruises I went on later. And most of the crew consisted of young, skinny fellows that didn't have much weight to lose, or should lose. They would come back from these cruises with their uniforms very loose on them.

In addition, we never had any food that could be considered Southern, but I could live with that, although, it would have been easier to do so if we had had something more edible. I admit that the menu looked pretty good on paper, but, in my opinion, what ended up on our trays wasn't so good much of the time.

The crew coped with the hunger problem in various ways. Personally, one thing that I did to help with the hunger problem was to eat little containers of shoestring potatoes. I got them from the ship's store, which was about the size of a large closet. The ship's store would open occasionally and sell the sailors a few items. The biggest seller at the ship's store was cigarettes. The cigarettes cost 10 cents per pack. The cigarettes were so cheap that we felt like we ought to smoke to take advantage of the low prices. And, I suppose, they had a few toiletries, too – such as hand soap, toothpaste, and shaving cream. They might have sold a little candy sometimes, but I don't remember seeing any of it. But like I said, what I did buy from the ship's store occasionally, when they had them, were these little cardboard containers of shoestring potatoes. The storekeepers would only sell 2 or 3 containers of them to any one person, but I would get what I could when I could. I would usually eat them on the midwatch (0000–0400) when there wasn't anyone else around because I wanted them all for myself. I didn't want to share them with anybody. At the time, I got as much pleasure out of eating those shoestring potatoes as most people would enjoy eating a great meal at a fine restaurant, because they satisfied my hungry feeling for awhile.

In addition, occasionally, someone would be able to steal some ship-made bread from the galley and give Tommy a little of it for the bridge gang, which amounted to about 3 or 4 slices. The quartermasters would always eat it on the midwatch when nothing was going on and when there wasn't anybody around that could get us in trouble for eating stolen food. I got in on these midnight snacks 3 or 4 times over a month or two. Tommy always shared his food that he was able to scrounge up. He could have kept it all for himself and nobody would have felt less of him for doing it.

We would toast the bread over the hot plate that we made coffee on. In order to toast the bread, we would get a piece of stiff wire from somewhere and rig us up something that would hold the bread so we could toast it over the hot plate. I think we always had butter to put on our toast. Apparently, some of the sailors were in on the-know when the bread had been stolen and these thieving sailors would sneak a piece of butter up under their shirts at the evening meal. A hunk of butter was sometimes put on the tables at meal time for us to put on our bread. These acts of stealing food were top secret stuff that was going on here and was a big deal for us at the time. When the time came to toast the bread, all 3 of the QM's on the bridge would get together around the hot plate, in the dark, and toast our slice of bread. The hot plate was always setting in a sheltered place on the signalman's desk. We would thoroughly enjoy our little midwatch snacks.

On a couple of occasions that I know about, Tommy was able to scrounge up a few ounces of beef for us. Somehow, Tommy had a buddy that had keys to the reefer where the meat and other frozen foods were kept. He was able to persuade this fellow to give him a few ounces of meat. This must have been a blackmail deal of some sort, because this fellow could have gotten in trouble if he had been caught taking food out of the reefer without authorization. Besides that, he had his own gang to provide food for. Anyway, Tommy was able to get a little bit of meat, and he always shared it with some of the bridge gang – whoever was on the midwatch with him, and I think it was usually me during that time. Tommy would divide this little hunk of meat up into equal shares and which amounted to about an ounce for each person. Again, we would get ourselves a piece of stiff wire, stick the little morsel of meat on the end of it, and hold it over the hot plate to cook. Again, 3 of us would be gathered around the hot plate in the dark cooking our little piece of meat. This was a big occasion for us. It was very similar to standing around a fire roasting wieners. We would eat those little morsels of beef very slowly to make the occasion last longer.

The scuttlebutt was that the engineers down below deck were also rigged up to make French fried potatoes on their hot plate. Apparently, they were able to steal some grease from the stores and potatoes that were stored in sacks on the main deck. They were probably less likely to get caught down there than we were on the bridge.

I will give the cooks on the Brush credit for making excellent bread and everybody loved it. They just probably didn't make enough of it. However, the cooks learned that they couldn't leave the galley for a second when they were baking bread, because, if they did, there wouldn't be any loaves there when they got back. Apparently, somebody was always lurking in the shadows just waiting for the cook to leave the galley, or even turn his back for a few seconds. The freshly made loaves of bread were usually stacked on a counter near the port hatch. I was told that there had been times the cook had gotten involved in doing something in the galley, wasn't paying attention to his stack of bread near the port hatch, and would look around just in time to see an arm reach around the open hatch and snatch a loaf of bread. Then, the cook would hear the fellow running off down the deck. However, he didn't dare go chase him, because, if he did, there probably wouldn't be any of it left when he got back. The cook figured it was better to lose one loaf than all of them.

I think the cooks eventually learned to keep the galley hatch closed when they were baking bread and to shut and lock the hatch if they had to leave the galley for any reason when they were baking bread. Consequently, the bread got harder to steal. As I remember, the cooks only baked bread when we were overseas. But our hunger wasn't as acute either when we were in the States, because we got ashore more often where we could get something to eat.

## Vitamins

One day as I was walking down the inside passageway, I looked down and saw a page out of a magazine lying on the deck (floor). It was just one page, was rather ragged and worn looking, and looked like just a piece of trash that someone had carelessly dropped – and it actually was. However, it turned out that that piece of trash had a significant influence on my life. Out of curiosity, mainly, I reached down and picked the page up and looked at it, but I didn't see anything of any interest to me except an ad for some vitamin capsules. Although, I had never given much thought to vitamins before, I knew that there was such a thing as vitamins, because I had learned a little about them in school. I knew that people needed them and they got them from the food they ate. I had never given any thought to taking vitamin supplements. In fact, I probably didn't even know that there was such a thing as vitamin supplements. I was young and had much more important things to think about. In fact, I would speculate that very few people in the early 1950's gave vitamins much thought in any respect.

The reason that the vitamin ad piqued my interest so much was because I knew that I wasn't receiving the proper nourishment, because we were so poorly fed on the ship. Consequently, I made the decision on the spot that I was going to order me some of those vitamins and did. I received the vitamins in a month or so and started taking them. They were liquid vitamins in a capsule. I soon learned, however, that I couldn't take them on an empty stomach, because, if I did, it would make me terribly nauseated. So at the tender age of 19, I started taking vitamins in a supplemental form on a daily basis and have continued to do so ever since. I ordered those same vitamins for the next 4 to 5 years; then I started buying vitamins from local stores wherever I happened to be living. However, I've always bought good vitamins – not the cheap stuff. In effect, I was forced to become health conscious at a very early age, and as the years went by, I made a special effort to learn all I could about maintaining good health through nutrition and other healthy practices. In case someone doesn't know it, I will tell you; good nutrition is the basis of good health; it is not prescription drugs like so many people are being led to believe these days.

When I reached down and picked up that piece of paper off the deck, I never dreamed it would have such a profound effect on my life. But as a consequence of my picking up that piece of paper at that point in my life, it stimulated my mind to open up and strive to learn all I could about nutrition and other ways to maintain a healthy body. I have been blessed with a very healthy life that has enabled me to be free from most of the ailments, afflictions, and the aches and pains that so many people seem to suffer from these days, especially as they get older. In addition, based on what I have observed, I have been able to significantly slow down the aging process for myself as well.

One thing that continues to amaze me, though, is how little most people seem to know about nutrition and maintaining a healthy body and how little interest they have in learning anything about the subject. I see an awful lot of people suffering in one way or another because of that attitude. In most cases they are listening to the wrong people and are suffering needlessly, but that is what they choose to do so they will just have to suffer. I have learned not to worry too much about it and just concentrate on taking care of me and mine.

## Assigned to the Wonsan Patrol

On Thursday, 7 May, 1953, the Brush was patrolling around in Package 2 and 3 of the Windshield Patrol area. Nothing of any significance was going on. Late in the day the Brush received word that she was going to relieve the Maddox and that the commodore was going to shift his flag to the Brush; that is, the commodore and his staff were going to come aboard our ship and live on it for awhile. And, in addition, the worst news of all, the Brush was going into Wonsan Harbor the next day for 10 to 12 days. The crew of the Brush realized immediately that this was not good news, because we knew that a ship was always subject to being shot at in Wonsan. But even worse, we also knew that the communist gunners around Wonsan had recently been very active against destroyers that were patrolling in the harbor. And we were going to be in there for 10 to 12 days. Consequently, we knew that the chances of our being fired upon were very high, and the chances of our ship being hit by enemy shells were also very high. Furthermore, the odds were great that the ship would suffer casualties. All of the crew knew, without question, that they were going to be in grave danger for the next few days, and that some of us probably wouldn't be coming out of the harbor in the same conditions as we went in. There could even be deaths. The big question was – who would be the unlucky ones?

I observed my shipmates closely during the evening to try to read their reaction to our new assignment. I didn't observe any expressions of fear on their faces the best I could tell, maybe apprehension. My shipmates did seem unusually quiet and thoughtful to me. The men didn't seem to be too talkative either, and when there were conversations, the participants tended to talk in very hushed tones. I doubt if they realized they were talking in this manner. I did not see any joking or horsing around. I think all of the men knew that they were going to be facing some very serious danger for the next 2 weeks, starting the next morning. I'm sure all of them were thinking, privately, that, if there are casualties, they hoped it wouldn't be them.

The Brush continued to patrol around in the Windshield area until 0200 that night. At that time, the Brush ceased patrolling and set a course of 230°(t), at a speed of 15 knots, to proceed to the Hungnam area to rendezvous with the Maddox. Somewhere en route we encountered heavy fog and the visibility was reduced to 250 to 300 yards. Consequently, we had to see our way forward by means of radar. We arrived in the vicinity of Hungnam, North Korea at 0648, just at daylight. We saw the location of the Maddox on our radar scope. We were still seeing by radar only because the fog was still very thick. We changed speed to 5 knots and slowly made our approach to the Maddox in the fog. Finally, at 0758 we sighted the Maddox at a distance of 300 yards. We stopped all engines and commenced lying to for the personnel transfer by the Maddox's motor whaleboat. The sea was very smooth. So, the commander of Destroyer Division 92 and his staff of 8 officer and men came aboard the Brush. By 0835 the transfer of personnel was completed and we got underway for Wonsan.

**USS Brush DD745 (U.S. Navy Photograph)**

## WONSAN HARBOR PATROL

We arrived at the entrance to Wonsan Harbor at 1000. We were in dense fog the entire trip down from Hungnam with the visibility at about 200 yards, which at sea is considered essentially zero visibility. Of course, we had radar which enabled us to know whether there were any ships, small craft, or large objects in our path or anywhere around us. Sea conditions are usually, if not always, very smooth when there is thick fog. We had to change course twice on the way down from Hungnam to skirt around small craft that were most likely fishing boats.

At the entrance to Wonsan Harbor there was a buoy designated "Buoy H", and it served as a rendezvous point for ships that had to meet up for some reason, and that is what the Brush was doing in this case – lying to in the vicinity of Buoy H to rendezvous with another ship. We were there to relieve the destroyer, USS Owen(DD536), of the Wonsan Harbor Patrol. The Maddox and the Owen had been operating in the harbor together for several days. Actually, these 2 destroyers had been dividing their time between Wonsan and Hungnam. The Brush and the Moore were the ships that relieved them from this duty. Although, neither the Brush nor the Moore ever went back up to Hungnam while they were patrolling in Wonsan. The Moore was already in the harbor and had been since the previous afternoon, 7 May.

Other ships that were in the immediate vicinity of Wonsan when we arrived there included the USS Molala(ATF106), LST 1138, USS Comstock(LSD19), and several minesweepers – the USS Curlew(AMS38), USS Firecrest(AMS10), USS Chatterer(AMS40), and ROKN(AMS502). The Brush gave gunfire support to at least one of the minesweepers every night in the harbor while they conducted minesweeping operations. We only saw them at night. I don't know where they stayed during the day because we never saw them then, but they must have been around Yo Do Island somewhere.

Just before noon the Owen arrived on the scene and the Brush officially relieved the Owen as part of Task Unit 95.2.1. At that time the Owen went on her way. So, we entered Wonsan Harbor around noon on Friday, 8 May, 1953. The harbor is quite large and was divided up into several different patrolling areas that were given names like Lake, Acre, Tin Pan Alley, Muffler, West Muffler, East Muffler, Muffler Annex, and Gridiron. We would patrol in one of them for awhile and then go to another one. The Moore was doing the same thing. The Brush went to patrol area "Lake" upon entering the harbor.

There was a buoy in the harbor that was designated "Buoy E" and was located about 1000 yards south of Yo Do Island. We rendezvoused there with a boat from the island at least once a day and sometimes twice for a "guard mail" transfer, usually, whatever that amounted to. I think "guard mail" were secret messages of some kind.

The Brush entered the harbor in a dense fog that hung around in the harbor most of the time for the next 6 days. When the fog was present it served the purpose of concealing us from the enemy gunners on the mainland, which, I suppose, was a lucky break for us because we weren't exposed to the enemy guns all the time. However, on that first day in the harbor, the fog cleared out some time during the middle of the afternoon, which was not a good thing for us as I will relate. The Brush steamed around in the Lake area for 3 hours or so and then went to rendezvous with a small boat from Yo Do at Buoy E; that accomplished, the ship went back to the Lake area and resumed her patrolling.

## An Awesome Skirmish

The Brush and the Moore were patrolling independently in Wonsan Harbor during the afternoon of Friday, 8 May. The Moore was patrolling in the Tin Pan Alley area, which was adjacent to the Lake area that we were patrolling in. Around 1630 the 2 ships just happened to come relatively close together during their separate patrols. At the time, the Brush was making very little headway – practically stopped. The Moore was southwest of us about 1000 yards and was also making very little headway.

I was the quartermaster-of-the-watch at this particular time. The situation was quiet so I wandered out of the pilothouse onto the open bridge, on the port side, just to see what I could see. I was just standing there looking out toward the Moore and was noticing how slow she was steaming. She was barely moving just like us. I didn't know it at that moment, but I was just before witnessing one of the most awesome sights of my life and a reflection of ourselves in a few days.

All of a sudden, I saw a geyser of water shoot up in the air a few hundred yards off the Moore's bow and then heard a noise that sounded like someone had hit the water hard with the flat side of a boat paddle – kind of a loud "splat" sound. Other people on the bridge saw the geyser and heard the "splat" sound, too. I thought to myself, "What in the world was that?" But before I had time to think it out, another geyser appeared much closer to the Moore's bow. At that moment, I didn't have to do any more wondering, because I realized that those splashes were enemy shells hitting the water. The Moore was being fired on and we probably would be, too. I dashed back into the pilothouse and put on my flack jacket and helmet. Someone verbalized what we all already knew, "The Moore is being fired on."

Captain Quigley was on the bridge, promptly took the conn, and put the ship in high gear. He began to maneuver the ship about at a relatively fast speed. In a few seconds, though, the captain realized that we weren't being shot at and slowed the ship down some. We all observed that the enemy gunners were concentrating all their shelling efforts on the Moore since all the shell splashes were occurring around her and none around us. Every time a shell would hit the water around her, a geyser of water would shoot up in the air about 15 to 20 feet.

All eyes on the bridge were focused on the Moore. We thought that at any second we would see her receive a direct hit that would inflict some serious damage to her. More than one shore battery was firing at the Moore and none at us – you figure. The part the Brush played in this skirmish was to just stay out of the way of the Moore and give her plenty of maneuvering room.

It just so happened that the Moore was at general quarters at the time the shooting commenced and consequently had all of her guns manned. So it didn't take her but a few seconds to get into action. When the Moore's captain, Cdr. John Blackburn, saw that his ship was under fire, he kicked his ship into high gear, too, started maneuvering about at a high speed, and commenced making a smoke screen. He also opened fire on the shore batteries almost immediately and knew exactly where they were located. All 6 of her 5 inch guns were firing at a rapid rate. The ship looked like it was continuously exploding with great billows of smoke surrounding the guns after every shot. Those 5 inch guns were shooting at the fastest rate that I have ever seen. It was an awesome sight to watch. However, in spite of all the shells raining down on her, the Moore never retreated a yard. She just maneuvered around at high speed in a relatively small area and just shot it out with the enemy gunners on the mainland until they just suddenly quit firing – for whatever reason. The skirmish lasted about 10 minutes.

According to the Moore's log book, she observed gun flashes at enemy position U339751 at 1629 and soon thereafter saw 2 shell bursts on the surface of the water about 600 yards off her bow. At 1630 she commenced firing back at the enemy gun position. At 1633 another enemy position, CU346796, opened up on the Moore. The Moore knocked out the CU339751 gun position and then started concentrating her fire on the new threat, gun position CU346796. At 1639 that shore battery stopped firing. Maybe it was destroyed, too.

It was estimated that the shore batteries fired a total of 60 rounds of 76 to 90mm shells at the Moore. The Moore, in turn, fired 44 rounds of 5 inch high capacity shells at the shore batteries. There weren't any casualties on the Moore. The Moore did suffer one near miss at frame 90, starboard side, 3 feet above the water line that badly dented the hull but it was not punctured. Minor damage was also inflicted to the towing gear and life raft on the fantail that was caused by shrapnel. The Moore escaped this incident without serious damage, by some miracle, but she experienced many near misses. I feel she was a very lucky ship during this encounter with the shore batteries.

The things I wonder about is – why did the enemy gunners fire all their shells at the Moore and none at us? We were right there with her. It was like we were invisible to the North Korean gunners. I'm not complaining, of course, just wondering. It was just a coincidence that the Brush and Moore were operating close together at that particular time. I also wonder – if the Moore hadn't been there, would we have been the target. Would they have rained shells down on us like they did on the Moore? I guess I'll never know the answers to those questions for sure, but it's something I've always wondered about. After the shelling incident, the Brush and Moore continued on with their respective patrols.

After nightfall on, 8 May, we started patrolling in Tin Pan Alley to give GFS to the minesweeper, Chatterer. However, at 2146 we ceased doing that and proceeded out of the harbor to rendezvous with the USS Comstock(LSD19). At 2238 we made our rendezvous with the Comstock and commenced lying to near her. The Comstock sent her small boat over to us and it stayed alongside for nearly an hour. I don't remember now what the purpose of it all was, but it must have been important to do it in the middle of the night. At 2344 the small boat returned to the Comstock; the Brush got underway and proceeded back into the harbor to the Tin Pan Alley patrol area. Upon arriving at the station, the Brush stopped all engines and commenced lying to for the next 4 hours. However, at 0430 she got underway and patrolled around in the area at various courses and speeds until 1244 Saturday afternoon at which time we left the harbor again to rendezvous with the tanker, USS Mispillion(AO105), to take on fuel. And that is the way it was, we left the harbor everyday for something, but it usually was for the purpose of rendezvousing with another ship for one reason or another. We were steadily going, doing something, all the time. During the process of refueling, 3 seamen were sent over by highline and were received aboard for duty. After refueling from the tanker, the Brush returned to the harbor and resumed her patrolling.

I had the 0800 to 1200 watch the next morning, 9 May, and when I went up to the bridge to relieve the watch, I immediately noticed that we were operating in a dense fog and the visibility was essentially zero. You couldn't see much further than the bow. All the navigating was done by radar, as I remember. Thick fog was present in the harbor all the time for the next 5 days and concealed us from the enemy gunners. However, out of the harbor and away from land, the visibility was better and was even clear sometimes. I think the presence of dense fog in the harbor was a very lucky break for us.

Saturday night the Brush gave GFS to the Curlew while she conducted minesweeping operations in the East Muffler patrol area.

Sunday, 10 May, was a rather quiet, uneventful day. The Brush just slowly steamed around in the harbor all day, in the fog, and into the evening without anything memorable happening. However, Sunday night, starting at 2230, the Brush commenced firing star shells at irregular intervals as directed by a shore fire control spotter. She ceased firing at 0300 and during that time expended a total of 22 rounds of illumination shells. After that, the Brush gave GFS to the ROKN(AMS502) for a couple of hours.

Monday, 11 May, we left the harbor twice, once in the morning and once in the evening. In the morning part of the day, we left the harbor to rendezvous with the cruiser, USS St. Paul(CA73), so that the commodore could have a conference with the commander of TG 95.2 who was aboard the St. Paul. The commodore left the Brush at 0948 by motor whaleboat for the cruiser. He stayed aboard her for approximately 2 hours. During the meantime, the ship just laid to near the cruiser while the commodore had his conference. The commodore came back aboard at 1147 and we went back into the harbor and resumed our patrolling.

That night, around 2000, the Brush left the harbor again to rendezvous with the destroyer, USS Rowan(DD782), at Buoy H at the harbor entrance. We arrived at the buoy at 2037 and commenced lying to. Our motor whaleboat was sent over to the Rowan to pick up a medical officer, Lt(jg) Bennallock, who was to temporarily become part of the commodore's staff. Upon receiving him aboard, we returned to the harbor and proceeded to the Muffler areas to patrol. During the night we gave GFS to the Firecrest for awhile. Also, during the night, we fired 3 rounds of 5 inch star shells as directed by a fire control spotter on Mo Do Island. In the early morning hours the Brush started patrolling in the Lake and Acre areas.

On Tuesday morning, 12 May, at 0939, we proceeded out of the harbor to rendezvous with the destroyer, USS Cowell(DD547), at Buoy H for a personnel transfer. At 1005 the Brush stopped all engines and commenced lying to 100 yards from the Cowell. The Cowell's small boat came alongside with the Cowell's captain and some of his officers embarked who came aboard the Brush for a conference with the commodore. After the Cowell's officers were safely aboard, we returned to the harbor and steamed around in the Lake patrol area for a couple of hours. At noon we proceeded out of the harbor again to rendezvous with the Cowell to return her officers. The Cowell's officers returned to their ship in their small boat. Upon their departure, the Brush went back into the harbor and patrolled in areas Lake and Acre. The fog got very thick at this point and the visibility decreased to about 300 yards.

## A Lost Boat

A little after nightfall the ship became engaged in trying to find a lost small boat, LB14 , from Yo Do Island that apparently had gotten lost in the thick fog outside the harbor. At 1925 we began blowing the ship's whistle and firing a Very pistol. However, the boat never showed up. Later, we began sounding our foghorn. That didn't get any results either. Then, we fired 3 rounds of 5 inch star shells, but still no LB14. I don't know what happened to the boat and her crew, or if it ever showed up. We never heard whether it did or didn't. We gave up on trying to find the boat around 2200, went back into the harbor, and started patrolling in Tin Pan Alley.

At 2216 the Brush received a fire mission to commence firing illumination shells at irregular intervals as directed by a spotter somewhere. At 0340 the ship ceased her fire mission having expended 29 rounds of 5 inch star shells during the time from 2216 to 0340.

Early Wednesday morning, 13 May, the ship proceeded to Buoy E off Yo Do Island for a personnel transfer. At 0647 a boat from the island came alongside and the commodore departed the ship to proceed to the USS St. Paul via Yo Do Island. We went back to patrolling in Tin Pan Alley.

A few minutes after 0800, however, we proceeded out of the harbor to rendezvous with the tanker, USS Cimarron(A022), for refueling. We were alongside the tanker at 1010 and completed refueling at 1054. The ship set a course to return to the harbor. However, en route to Wonsan, we rendezvoused with the St. Paul to receive the commodore back aboard. We went alongside the St Paul at 1220 and the commodore came back aboard by way of highline. With that done, the Brush continued on to Wonsan. Upon arriving there, the Brush patrolled around in the Lake and Acre areas until 2010 that night, then she went to the Muffler patrol area.

## A Pilot Bails Out Over Yo Do Island

Something happened late in the day on, 13 May, that I will always remember. At 1825 the bridge personnel observed the pilot of a U.S. Navy jet (F9F) bail out of his plane over Yo Do Island. In fact, as I remember it, he announced on some radio frequency of his intentions. Apparently, his plane had flown as far as it was going to and he had to leave it. But he was able to fly it back to friendly forces and safety – he thought. However, he didn't land on the island like he intended to. Instead, he landed in the ocean. Actually, before he landed in the water, the Brush was speeding toward him as was the Moore that was just entering the harbor after being at sea for refueling. Almost immediately after the pilot landed in the water, a helicopter from the LST 1138 was hovering over him and was attempting to pull him out of the water. At this point, the commodore directed the Moore to assist the helicopter in the rescue effort since she was a little closer to the splash site than we were. So, the Brush backed off from the rescue effort. However, for some reason, the helicopter crew couldn't pull the pilot out of the water. In fact, so the story goes, the pilot was still hooked to his parachute, his life jacket wasn't inflated, and he was underwater. The parachute was complicating his rescue somehow. Apparently, his life jacket wasn't inflated either because he wasn't able to inflate it or it wouldn't inflate. Therefore, he sank beneath the waves. It took the Moore several minutes to reach the splash site, and when they did, they immediately pulled the pilot out of the water, but it was too late; he had already drowned. The pilot's name was R.C. Clinite Lt(jg), according to the Moore's log.

Upon retrieving the pilot, the Moore proceeded to LST 1138 which was close by. At 1906 she commenced lying to near the LST and a Lt(jg) H.C. Lee (M.C.) came aboard the Moore to inspect the body. Mr. Lee verified that the cause of death was by drowning. The body of Lt(jg) Clinite was sent over to the LST by way of the LST's small boat accompanied by Mr. Lee.

I've always thought the death of that pilot was such a sad thing; because, I'm sure the pilot must have mustered all his flying skills to nurse his plane back to the coast and Yo Do Island so he could bail out over friendly territory and avoid being captured by communist troops on the mainland. I'm sure he was thinking about what a relief it was to be floating down over Yo Do Island and safety. Somehow, things went terribly wrong for him. First, He missed landing on the island and things got worse for him from there. He must have been unconscious when he hit the water, because he never unhooked from his parachute or inflated his life jacket. That is just speculation, of course.

Wednesday night, 13 May, was a rather quiet, uneventful night. We patrolled around in the Muffler area most of the night, which was in the western part of the harbor. However, we also provided GFS for a couple of minesweepers while we were patrolling and they were sweeping. We first provided GFS for the Curlew for a couple of hours, and then, a little later for the ROKN(AMS502) for another couple of hours.

## A Ringside Seat

I've always thought that Thursday, 14 May, was an interesting day. We stayed in the harbor all day steaming around in various patrol areas. However, what made the day so interesting and memorable to me was the fact that the day was a beautiful, clear, spring day. The fog was totally gone after 6 straight days of mostly foggy, gloomy weather. In addition, and the most important reason was that we watched planes, Skyraiders, fire rockets at gun positions and other targets on the mainland all day long. In a sense, we had a ringside seat to the action going on and we weren't a participant in it. Skyraiders are rather slow, or could be, propeller-driven planes that were used a lot in Korea for close support of ground troops and for knocking out enemy positions of all kinds. They were doing their work right close to us, whatever it was; although, I think they were firing their rockets at gun positions in caves.

We also did a little firing on the 14th ourselves. In the afternoon around 1300 one of our guns opened up on a truck and a bunker that was spotted on Ho Do Pando. We fired 5 rounds of 5 inch HC ammunition and 3 rounds of 5 inch HC white phosphorous shells. The truck got away.

In the early evening the Brush fired at gun positions on the mainland south of Hwang To Do Island. This time, we fired 4 rounds of 5 inch HC ammunition but the results were not known. We also provided GFS for 2 different minesweepers during the night – these were the Heron and the Firecrest.

## The Brush Under Fire – An Unforgettable Day

Friday, 15 May, 1953, turned out to be a very memorable day for the crew of the Brush, and the action that took place on this day is the reason why everyone was so apprehensive about being in Wonsan Harbor for 10 days. However, we were fortunate in one respect in that dense fog concealed us most of the time for 6 days. And the airplanes kept the enemy shore batteries in their caves on the 7th day. Friday, 15 May, was different, however. The fog was gone. The planes were gone. And it was another beautiful spring day. The enemy gunners must have decided that it was a good day to do some shooting because that is what they started doing.

The day started with the Brush patrolling in the southern part of the harbor. At 0927 the bridge personnel began hearing gunfire on the mainland southeast of Hwang To Do. At 0928 explosions were observed on Yo Do Island and in the water about 1000 yards off our port beam. So, they were shooting at us, too. Ensign Robbins was at the conn and he promptly increased speed to 25 knots. In a few seconds Captain Quigley took the conn and began maneuvering the ship on various courses (zigzagging) toward the harbor entrance to get out of range of the enemy guns. He also ordered a smoke screen to be created from the smoke generator on the fantail and from the smoke stacks. However, in a few seconds it was noticed that there didn't seem to be any more enemy shells coming in our direction since no more splashes were observed in the water. Consequently, at 0933 the captain slowed the ship down to 15 knots, stopped making smoke, and resumed patrolling in the southern section of the harbor.

At 0935 the bridge personnel again observed gun flashes coming from several caves on the mainland southeast of Hwang To Do. The captain again increased speed to 25 knots, began zigzagging, making smoke, and heading toward the harbor entrance as before. However, none of the enemy shells came in our direction so the captain slowed the ship down, ceased making smoke, and resumed patrolling in the southern part of the harbor. The communist gunners were apparently more interested in firing on Yo Do Island than at us at this point.

The story goes that it was about this time that the commodore decided it would be a good idea to attempt to destroy some of the communist shore batteries since they were out of their caves, and that is what the Brush started doing. At 1007 the Brush commenced firing one of her main batteries, Mount 51, at the enemy gun positions that had previously been observed firing. The communist shore batteries continued to fire sporadically on Yo Do Island as indicated by gun flashes on the mainland and explosions on the island. The Brush steamed around at 20 knots and fired her 5 inch guns rather steadily for the next 30 minutes, and over that time fired a total of 25 rounds of high capacity (HC) shells at the enemy gun positions.

The communist gunners apparently objected to the hostilities displayed toward them by the Brush and turned all their attention to her. Shells began to fall in the water around the Brush. The enemy guns found the range and at 1037 the ship came under intense fire.

Captain Quigley quickly increased the ship's speed to 27 knots and started radically maneuvering (zigzagging) her toward the harbor entrance again – trying to get out of range of the enemy guns. He also attempted to make another smoke screen to hide behind. Black smoke poured from the smoke stacks, but this time the smoke generator failed to work. My friend, Dave Prado MM3/C, was manning the smoke generator on the fantail. He told me that when it failed to work, he left it and dropped down into the after crew's quarters to get some protection from the shells that were falling all around the ship.

In spite of all the evasive action taken, at 1040 the Brush received a direct hit on the starboard side of Mount 51 in which there were 10 gunners. Mount 51 was knocked out of commission by the hit and so were the gunners in it. I'm sure there was a great deal of uncertainty experienced by the captain and the other officers on the bridge immediately after the hit concerning the extent of the damage to the ship and the fate of the men in the mount. But I'm sure it didn't look good to them, especially the condition of the men in the mount. And I imagine it took the captain 2 or 3 anxious minutes to gather enough information to assess the situation and to determine what kind of action to take. The damage control party arrived on the scene in a relatively short time and, I suppose, they are the ones that began to get him informed about the situation at the mount and in the magazine. I know at one point he thought he was going to have to flood the forward magazine based on the information he was receiving. He learned that there was fire in the forward magazine handling room which was a very dangerous situation. He knew that the ship could blow up if it wasn't quickly extinguished. Fortunately, it was.

In a few minutes the captain also began to learn about the condition of the gunners in Mount 51. It turned out that none of them were killed, but 9 of the 10 men in the mount were wounded – 4 of them seriously. The shelling incident was bad enough that day, but it could have been much worse as I will reveal a little later on in my writing.

## Shell Damage

**Emile A. Mouton SN**
**Looking at Shell Hole**

## My Experience On That Day

Where was I and what was I doing on this beautiful spring morning as things began to happen in the harbor? I had had the midwatch (00–04) the night before and wouldn't go back on watch again until 1200. As I've previously mentioned, nobody was supposed to be topside when we were in Wonsan Harbor unless they were on watch or had something important to do up there. So I was below deck where I was supposed to be, but I was also sound asleep in my rack where I wasn't supposed to be at that time of day. However, my sleeping-in certainly wasn't intentional.

I hit my rack around 0400 after coming off watch. Reveille was at its usual time of 0600, but I didn't hear reveille on this particular morning and get up. How did that happen? What was so unusual about my sleeping-in was that I had always been easy to wake up, but on this morning, I didn't wake up. This was the only time in my navy career that I didn't wake up at reveille and get up at reveille, regardless of how sleepy I was or how little sleep I had gotten during the night. Apparently, I was in a deep sleep, an unusually deep sleep for me, and one like I had never experienced before and have never experienced since. Was my sleeping-in just an unusual coincidence? I don't think so. I have reason to believe that it was more than just a coincidence.

So there I lay, sound asleep in my rack, late into the morning as hostilities began to take place in the harbor. I began to wake up after Mount 51 started firing at 1007. I woke up slowly even then. When I became semi-awake, before I opened my eyes, I sensed that something wasn't right concerning my surroundings and finally decided that the compartment was simply too quiet. I opened my eyes, raised my head up a little, and looked around. I quickly observed that there wasn't anyone in the compartment except me. Furthermore, I didn't hear any voices anywhere, either. I thought, "Something is not right here." I looked at my watch to see what time it was. E-gads! It was 1015. I thought to myself, "How did this happen – my sleeping-in?" I hurriedly got out of my rack and put on my shoes. I didn't have to dress because I had slept with my clothes on, which I almost always did when we were operating off North Korea. It was the most practical thing to do, I thought, because if we had to go to battle stations or if I needed to get up to the bridge in a hurry, there really wasn't time to dress. So, I usually slept with my clothes on.

I went up to the head (bathroom) to brush my teeth, shave, and to do whatever else I had to do. All the time I was in the head doing my morning chores, I had a strong feeling of uneasiness, of apprehension, perhaps, which I really didn't understand at the time. I did later, however.

I was hearing a sound below deck that morning that I had never heard before, or at least had never noticed before. One of the 5 inch guns in Mount 51 would fire and the explosion was immediately followed by a loud "clang", which was the spent brass powder canister hitting the main deck. The gunners would drop the spent powder canisters down a chute at the bottom of the mount that ended up on the main deck. The chute was a way to get the spent canisters out of the mount to keep them from cluttering up the place. It also served as an emergency exit for the gunners in case they had to get out of the mount in a hurry. Anyway, I had never noticed that particular "clang" sound before even though I must have heard it many times before by then.

Actually, at the time, I didn't know which mount was firing, never gave it much thought, or cared. It was just a gun firing which wasn't anything new or unusual. However, in addition to the gun, or guns, firing, I could tell the ship was doing a lot of maneuvering around at a relatively fast speed.

While I was in the head doing my morning chores, I developed a strong urge to sneak up to the bridge and find out what was going on – what kind of action the ship was engaged in. By now, I had been up for 15 minutes or so and still had not seen anybody. Not seeing anybody and not hearing any voices made me feel like I was the only one on the ship. I thought, where is everybody? I finished my morning activities in the head as quickly as I could and went back down into the sleeping compartment to store my shaving gear and toothbrush. I was anxious to get up to the bridge and find out what was going on, whether I was supposed to be up there or not. I climbed the ladder (stairs) out of the compartment and started walking across the mess deck to the hatch going into the chow serving line compartment, and then on up to the bridge. I took about 4 steps across the mess deck and saw my friend, Ed Geffert, coming into the mess deck from the chow serving line compartment – where I was headed. He was the first person that I had seen. We met in the middle of the mess deck and mutually decided to sit down on a bench at the nearest mess table. Ed totally distracted me from going on up to the bridge. Instead, I sat in the mess deck and talked to him – but not for long because of the way events developed.

Ed was also very curious and concerned about what was going on topside with all the firing and fast maneuvering going on. But he wasn't on watch so he knew he wasn't supposed to be on the bridge either. We had only been sitting there in the mess deck a couple of minutes when the ship's Master-at-Arms walked in and joined us, but he never sat down. He was actually a 3rd class boatswain's mate, an older fellow (late 20's, probably) and a career sailor. Unfortunately, I can't remember his name now. Anyway, he joined in on the mess deck conversation and also wondered about what the ship was involved in. There was nobody else around which was rather strange and unusual. There weren't even any mess cooks roaming around doing something in the mess deck. It was just me, Ed, and the Master-at-Arms.

It was now 1037 and the Brush came under intense fire from the communist shore batteries. Enemy shells commenced raining down on the ship, but we, the 3 of us, didn't have any way of knowing that was happening, because we didn't hear a thing down below that would give us a clue. Blower noises were probably drowning out the sound of shells passing over us.

Around 1043 something was announced over the P.A. system, but I couldn't understand a word of what was said. I looked at the Master-at-Arms and asked him, "What did he say?" The Master-at-Arms said, "He said, standby to flood magazines." That puzzled me and I asked him another question, "Why would the captain do that?" The Master-at-Arms didn't say anything for a few seconds but then he said, "We've been hit." He looked very concerned. I looked at Ed; he looked very concerned too, and I could see the color draining out of his face. He didn't say anything. I began to get concerned myself. But I was still puzzled to some extent. How did the Master-at-Arms know that we had been hit? I hadn't heard or felt anything to indicate that. I hadn't heard an explosion, other than the ship's guns firing followed by the sound of the metal powder canisters hitting the deck. And I hadn't felt a shudder of any kind either. But I really didn't question what the Master-at-Arms said because he was on old veteran and I figured he knew what he was talking about. He certainly knew more than I did.

I quickly added things up in my mind after I heard the words, "Standby to flood magazines" and the words, "We've been hit." I knew that, if the captain thought it was necessary to flood the magazines, then the situation on the ship was very serious, in fact, critical. The only reason he would order that done is because he had reason to believe that one of the magazines was in danger of blowing up. He knew, I knew, and everybody else knew, that if the magazines, or a magazine blew up, the ship would sink in seconds and there would be few, if any, survivors. I had seen movies and pictures of ships blowing up and after the smoke settled, there usually wasn't any ship to be seen. It was gone and so were all the people that were on it.

It began to occur to me that I might be dying here in just a few seconds, and there would be absolutely nothing left of me, because I was directly above one of the forward magazines. I began to experience the sensation of all the energy draining out of my body. This peculiar feeling started at the top of my head and progressed slowly down through my body to my feet. I remember looking around at the mess deck bulkhead and thinking that this could be my last look at anything on this earth, because I could die at any second. I kind of resigned myself to the fact that my life was over. I also knew the end would come in an instant. Then, I seemed to have gotten a little irritated about the whole matter and mentally verbalized, "This is not fair – to die before I really have ever had the chance to live." I'm not sure whether I was talking to God or to myself. Anyway, God, or his angel, had already taken care of the situation but I just didn't know it yet.

Five seconds went by, 10 seconds went by, 20 seconds went by, more seconds went by, and I could tell I was still alive. After a relatively brief time went by, and I can't remember exactly how long, maybe a minute or two, word was passed over the P.A. system to, "Secure from flooding magazine." I knew the crisis was over, whatever it was, and I was going to live after all. I looked around me after I came back to my senses and discovered that Ed and the Master-at-Arms were gone. I don't know when they left the mess deck. I wasn't aware of them leaving.

It is my firm conviction that somebody didn't want me on the bridge that morning, 15 May, 1953, because it was going to be a dangerous place to be. In addition to my being in an unnatural deep sleep until late in the morning, I was distracted in the mess deck on my way up to the bridge and never made it up there. If I had continued on up to the bridge like I intended to do, I would have arrived up there just about the time the enemy shells started falling around the ship. I have reason to believe that a supernatural, or heavenly being, was looking out for me and trying to keep me out of harm's way as much as they could. I will explain why I make that statement a little later on in the book.

I got up, left the mess deck, and went up to the charthouse. However, curiosity about what happened to the ship got the best of me, and after about 3 minutes or so, I went on up to the bridge. I found that we were out of the harbor and lying to near the LST 1138 and out of range of the enemy guns. The men on the signal bridge were still in a state of excitement. They were excitably talking about the recent event of shells loudly shrieking over their heads, falling about the ship, and with no place to take shelter from them. It apparently was a harrowing experience for them, and I'm sure it was something that they will never forget. I believe it was Tommy, Billy, and Beason that were on the signal bridge at the time we were being shelled. So, I began to learn a little about the action that the ship had been engaged in, at least what they knew at the moment. We all learned more about the incident as the day went by.

## What Happened That Day

Basically, what happened that day, 15 May, 1953, is that an enemy 76mm shell hit the forward 5″/38 mount, Mount 51, in the upper left-hand corner of the starboard shield. It made a hole in the shield that was large enough for a big man to crawl through. There were 10 men in the mount that had been busily engaged for the previous 30 minutes firing at enemy gun positions on the mainland. The shell wounded 9 of them. One didn't get a scratch; that must have been his lucky day. The names of the sailors that were wounded on that day are: Arnold A. Crete GM1/C, William P. (Willie) Nash GM3/C, Joseph J. Valentine GM3/C, Lloyd M. McCord GMSN, Ronald P. Erwin GMSN, Billy W. Melson SN, Harold V. Ballard SN, Ronald R. Wooten SN, and Donald D. Norskog SN. Crete, Nash, Valentine, and McCord were the most seriously wounded.

However, there is a whole lot more to the story, and there was also a great deal about the shelling incident that I never knew until many years later when I had the opportunity to talk to some of my old shipmates at some of the Brush reunions that I attended in the early 1990's. Two of the men I talked to were in the mount when it was hit, Willie Nash and Joe Valentine. I also talked to Sammie Baker GM3/C and Henry Garner RM2/C who also gave me some interesting information; and even more years later, I talked to Lloyd McCord GMSN over the phone who was also in the mount that day. There were things that I always wondered about concerning the hit by the enemy shell, but I never bothered to ask anybody that might have been able to have set my mind straight about them. Why? I don't know why I didn't ask questions at the time about things that puzzled me, unless it was because I knew that we all had such a close call with death that I just didn't want to talk about it. In fact, the shelling incident was never discussed by anybody, or even mentioned much after the day it happened that I was ever aware of. It was certainly never a major topic of conversation amongst the crew for whatever reason. So, I lived in almost total ignorance of much of what happened on that day for many years. And I imagine that much of the Brush's crew has had the same experience whether they know it or not. Hopefully, this tale of the shelling incident will get them better informed about it if that is the case.

One thing that I wondered about for years was – why weren't all the men in Mount 51 killed when the shell fell in their midst? I posed that question to Henry Garner at a Brush Reunion in Baton Rouge one day. He told me, "I can tell you exactly why they weren't all killed when the shell hit the mount. The shell was a dud. It didn't explode. The shell penetrated the mount shield and disintegrated against the heavy metal breech of the right gun; shrapnel flew all around inside of the mount and injured the men." I had never thought about that possibility before but it made sense to me. Because, I believe, that if a 76mm shell actually exploded in the midst of a group of men, like in the mount, it would most likely badly mangle and kill them all. In addition, both Nash and Valentine said that they did not hear an explosion when the shell hit the mount. They had already told me this before I ever talked to Garner, which had kind of puzzled me. Likewise, I didn't hear anything that sounded like an explosion from my vantage point in the mess deck, other that the ship's guns firing, followed by the loud "clang" of the powder canister hitting the deck. Henry seemed to know with certainty that the shell was a dud. So, based on the information I gathered from these shipmates and what I experienced myself, I believe Garner is right. The shell was a dud and that is the reason why all the men in the mount weren't blown apart and killed and why the ship didn't blow up. I know everyone may not agree with the idea that the shell was a dud, but it seems likely to me that it was, which was a very lucky break for us; or, was it just luck involved there?

## A Heroic Act

An interesting thing also took place in the forward magazine handling room. After the shell hit, sparks from the burning powder canister was spilling down into the handling room around all the gun powder that was stored there. For the ammunition handlers, it was a very frightening and potential explosive situation to be in. In fact, it was so frightening to them that they fled the scene – so I was told years later. Fortunately, a gunner's mate soon arrived on the scene, quickly realized the danger the ship was in, entered the magazine handling room, and extinguished the fire with a fire extinguisher that was there. His quick, brave action may have just saved the day for all of us. The fellow that performed this heroic deed was J.W. Calvert GM1. He was presented with the commendation ribbon a few months later for his action. I've always felt that he certainly deserved that much recognition, because it took a very brave man to enter a magazine that could be exploding at any second. And actually his quick action may have just saved the ship. Calvert also made chief petty officer a few months later and was transferred off the ship to other duties.

At 1048 the ship proceeded out of the harbor to the vicinity of LST 1138. Upon arriving there, she commenced lying to. In a few minutes a boat from the LST came alongside with a doctor that came aboard to assist in giving medical aid to the more seriously wounded men. After receiving the doctor aboard, the ship then proceeded to the USS Comstock(LSD19) that was also nearby. At 1121 the Brush commenced lying to near the Comstock and the 5 less injured men were transported to the LSD by an M boat. Erwin, Ballard, Melson, Wooten, and Norskog were the ones that were sent over to the LSD. They would remain on this ship for 3 days while the Brush continued to operate elsewhere up the coast.

## The Wounded Men Being Transported Over to the USS Comstock

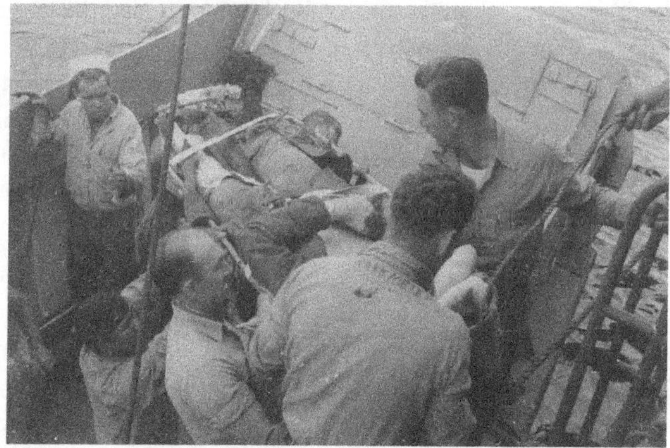

**Harold V. Ballard on stretcher**

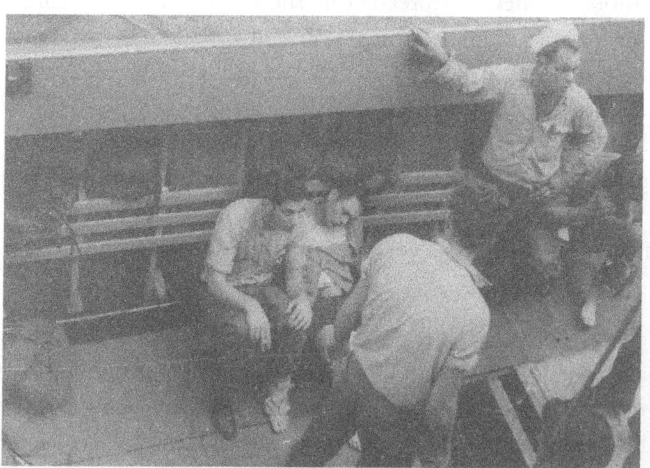

**Ronald R. Wooten & Billy W. Melson**

After the personnel transfer was completed to the LSD, the Brush got underway to rendezvous with the cruiser, St. Paul(CA73), that was some miles away to transfer the 4 most seriously wounded men to her. At 1228 the Brush was alongside the St. Paul and started sending the casualties over to her by highline. The men were strapped in stretchers for the transfer over to the cruiser. Fortunately, the sea was relatively calm and nobody got wet in the process – like they do sometimes. The wounded men that were sent over to the St. Paul were Crete GM1, Nash GM3, Valentine GM3, and McCord GMSN. The cruiser transported them to the naval hospital in Yokosuka. I imagine the cruiser's medical staff gave them more medical attention on the way there.

## Transporting the Wounded to USS St. Paul

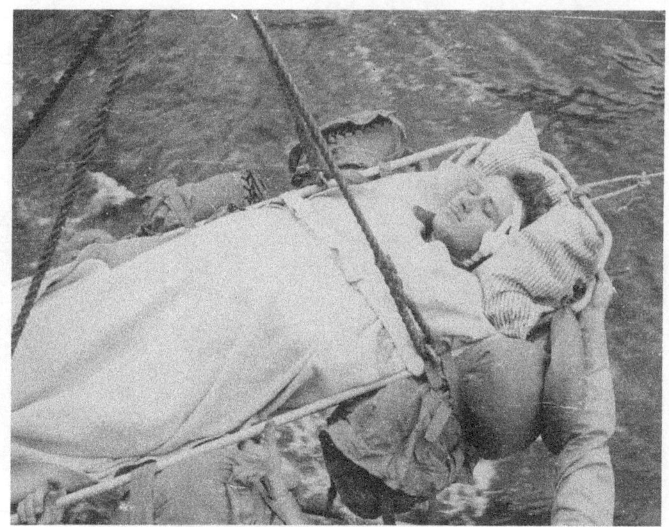

Lloyd McCord

Willie Nash

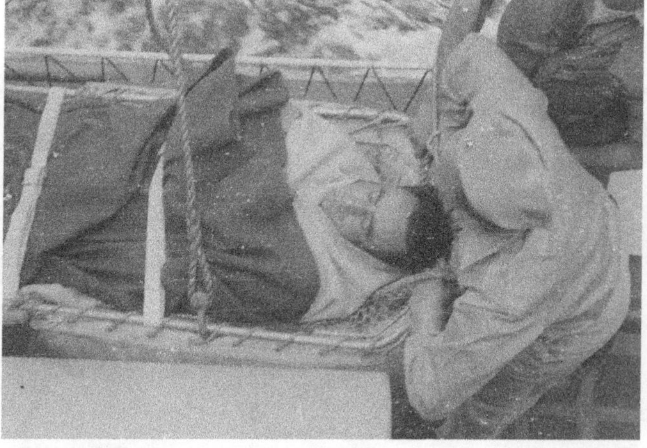

Arnold Crete

After the transfer of the wounded to the St. Paul was completed, the Brush returned to the entrance of Wonsan Harbor and commenced lying to in the vicinity of LST 1138. In a few minutes a small boat from the LST came alongside and retrieved their doctor. With that done, the Brush proceeded to Buoy H to await the arrival of another destroyer, the USS Rowan(DD783). At 1737 the Rowan arrived, a "guard mail" transfer was made, and the Rowan then went on her way to parts unknown.

**USS St. Paul Firing Off the East Coast of North Korea (U.S. Navy Photograph)**

**Official Photograph U.S. Navy**

## What Some of the Gunners Experienced

Each sailor in Mount 51 had his own personal experience about what he saw and heard when it was hit by the communist shell. The following pages are the experiences that some of the gunners had that day.

### Willie Nash's Recollection

Willie said that he didn't hear any noise like an explosion when the shell hit the mount. He heard a noise that sounded somewhat like breaking glass. The electric lights were knocked out. Mainly what he saw was the light from a burning powder canister. Its top had been sheared off by shrapnel and it was burning similar to the way Roman candles burn. Sparks from the burning canister were spewing out and falling down into the ammunition handling room. Willie grabbed a fire extinguisher off the mount's shield and put out the flame. The burning powder was the only light in the mount and it gave off an eerie kind of light. The burning powder was also filling the mount with smoke.

Everyone got out of the mount by sliding down the spent shell chute at the bottom of the mount. Willie said he was the last one to leave the mount. He also knew that Crete GM1/C, the mount captain, had his leg blown off when he slid down the chute. When Willie got to the bottom of the chute, to the main deck, he saw Crete sitting on the deck tying a shoestring around the stump to slow down the bleeding.

Willie didn't realize he was wounded when he left the mount. He headed for sickbay to get a stretcher for Crete. On the way to the sickbay, he encountered some sailors of the damage control party. He told them to get a stretcher for Crete. One of them told him to get the stretcher himself. He continued on to sickbay to do just that.

Willie never realized that he was badly wounded in the legs, both upper and lower legs, until he got to sickbay and happened to look down and saw blood all over his clothes. When he first saw all the blood on the upper part of his pants, he was afraid for a few seconds that he had lost the family jewels and other necessities. He reached down inside his pants for an on-hands inspection and found that everything was intact, much to his relief. However, it wasn't long after that that he passed out from loss of blood while he was waiting to be treated.

Willie was put on a stretcher a little later and sent over to the St. Paul(CA73) for further treatment and to be transported to a hospital in Japan. He stayed in the naval hospital in Yokosuka for several weeks. Then, he was flown to a naval hospital in Great Lakes, Illinois. He was hospitalized for a total of 5 months but recovered enough to remain in the navy for several more years, then got unhappy with the navy and joined the air force to finish out his 20 years.

Willie also told me about his experience being transported back to the States from Japan, weeks later, which I thought was quite interesting, too. He was on a military plane loaded with convalescing wounded servicemen – an ambulance type sort of airplane. The nurse that was tending to them was a young, pretty thing and he couldn't keep his eyes off of her. But she had a problem, he could tell, because she kept scratching her privates. Willie figured she had a good dose of crabs. He was the only one of the wounded men that was awake and she was aware that he kept looking at her. Finally, she came over to him and gave him a shot of something that quickly and completely knocked him out. He figured she did it because she wanted to scratch in private. Those crabs were driving her crazy.

## Joe Valentine's Recollection

Joe was the first one out of the mount after it was hit by the shell. He said Crete GM1/C, the mount captain, told them to get out of the mount – to which he quickly complied by sliding down the empty shell chute. He was followed by Crete. Everybody was out of the mount in a few seconds because they all thought the mount might blow up. The only light in the mount was from the burning powder canister. The powder canister's top had been sheared off and it caught fire. The burning powder put out an eerie light in the darkened mount and was filling it with smoke. Many years later, Joe said he can still see that powder canister burning.

Valentine also said that he never heard any noise that sounded like the mount had been hit, or an explosion. (Of course, the reason that he didn't hear anything was because there wasn't an explosion. The shell was a dud.)

When Crete hit the main deck, he realized his leg was gone, a little below the knee, and he exclaimed something about, "My leg is gone" and then he started tying a shoestring around the stump to stop the bleeding.

Joe also went to sickbay to get a stretcher to carry Crete back to the sickbay, or actually to the officers' wardroom, which became the aid station for the wounded during combat.

However, when Joe got to sickbay the corpsman didn't want him to leave and kept telling him to come in. Valentine kept telling him not to touch him, that he was alright. The corpsman could look at him and tell that he was far from being alright. However, Joe was mainly telling him not to touch him because he wasn't sure about his sexual orientation, so to speak. Finally, he looked down and saw blood all over his clothes – lots of it. At first, he thought it was Crete's blood, but on closer examination of himself, he found that he had been hit in the chest and had also had the right side of his cheek split open. In addition, there was a big gob of Crete's leg on his face near his wound. Later in the day Valentine was put on a stretcher and transferred over to the St. Paul by highline.

Valentine said that, at the hospital, Crete took the loss of his leg and the end of his naval career very casually. He didn't seem to worry a great deal about it. However, he did try to persuade the navy to let him stay in with an artificial leg but they wouldn't let him.

## Lloyd McCord's Recollection

McCord was the left gun captain in Mount 51. He said he clearly remembers the burning powder canister that was spewing sparks all over the mount and creating a lot of smoke. The electric lights had been knocked out and the burning powder was the only light in the mount.

McCord said he was looking straight at Valentine when the shell hit. Valentine was standing in front of him and he saw his cheek split open by shrapnel. Valentine was laughing and was rather amused by the inability of the shore batteries to hit the radically maneuvering ship – up to that point. He had just made a negative remark about their failure to do so.

Lloyd was hit by shrapnel in several places on his left side. He was hit in his temple, which caused nerve damage in his left eye. He was also hit in the left side and in the left foot. McCord could tell at a glance that his left foot was badly injured by the flying shrapnel, because the top of his shoe was blown off and he could see that his foot was bloody and badly mangled. However, he didn't know the full extent of his injuries until a little later after he arrived at the aid station. He was, although, able to limp to the aid station without any help.

A few seconds after the mount was hit, the mount captain, John Crete GM1/C, gave the order, "Get out of the mount; it's on fire!" McCord didn't hesitate; he was one of the first ones out of the mount.

Crete was also known by the gunner's mates as "Honest John Crete". He was highly thought of by the other gunner's mates. Crete had one of his legs blown off below the knee at the incident. Crete was carried to the aid station by one of the torpedomen, according to McCord.

Lloyd also mentioned that the 76mm shell that hit the mount only missed a white phosphorus shell and a star shell by about 18 inches. They were setting in a rack on the starboard shield.

McCord was met at the aid station by his buddy and fellow gunner's mate, Sammie Baker GM3. Sammie had come up from Mount 53 to assist the gunners of Mount 51 in any way he could. Sammie could tell that McCord's foot was badly hurt because blood was oozing out of his shoe, the top of his shoe was gone, and he could see his bloody foot. He took McCord's shoe off to determine how bad his foot was injured. When Sammie took off his shoe, the front half of his foot stayed in the shoe. A piece of shrapnel had completely severed his foot. The medical personnel gave McCord first aid and did what they could for him, but a couple of hours later he was also transferred over to the cruiser, St. Paul, on a stretcher.

McCord was a short-timer on the ship and was to be released from the ship for discharge as soon as the ship got back in port, which was less than a week from the time the ship was hit and he lost his foot. Actually, McCord's enlistment was up 1 ½ years previously, but his time in the navy had been extended for 1 year because of the Korean War. But he re-enlisted for 2 years, instead of one, so he could take his wife-to-be home to meet his folks. I don't quite understand why that had to be done that way but it was.

Interestingly, the captain had called McCord into his cabin a few weeks before the ship was hit on, 15 May, and told him that he would release him from the ship the next time we were in port, which would be around 20 May. But he wanted him to remain on the ship for just one more trip up the coast of North Korea because he was so good with the 40mm guns. The captain thought that the ship might need his skill with these guns this one more time.

It does seem like a very unfortunate break for him to lose his foot during his last few days aboard ship, especially after his enlistment in the navy had been extended for 2 years. However, it could have been worse – he could have been killed. I suppose a person needs to be thankful for the blessings that he does receive, in this case – his life.

I used to stand a lot of pilothouse watches with McCord during the early months of my time aboard ship. As I remember him, he was a real nice fellow, blonde, medium height, rather good-looking, married, and was from the great state of Alabama. But when he left the ship on a stretcher, I never saw him again or ever heard anything about him – until 55 years later when I talked with him on the phone in 2008.

## Russell Maxwell's Experience That Day

Russell Maxwell BT3/C was in the forward fire room at the time of the shell hit but not on watch. He was the "Oil King" and was there testing the boiler water. While there, he felt a slight shudder and commented to one of the boiler tenders on watch, "We've been hit." His shipmate replied, "Naw, we ain't been hit." His shipmate didn't believe him because he hadn't felt or heard anything to suggest that that had happened. Nevertheless, in a minute or so the bridge called away the "damage control party" and passed the word to, "Standby to flood magazines."

Maxwell was a member of the damage control party, and it was his job to shut off a fuel valve to the forward boiler room if there was a danger of the forward boiler blowing up, which there seemed to be at that moment. If a forward magazine was to blow up, the forward boiler probably would, too. The fuel valve was located topside on the main deck, starboard side. He quickly proceeded topside to close that fuel valve if he was ordered to do so.

Maxwell came out of a hatch on the main deck that opened up in the inside passageway just aft of the amidships passageway. He started walking forward up the inside passageway. He was just passing the "sick bay" compartment when a corpsman forward of him, outside the officer's wardroom, spotted him and told him to go into sick bay, get a bottle of oxygen, and bring it up to the wardroom, which was the aid station during combat. Maxwell proceeded to do what he was told to do. When he got up to the wardroom, he expected them to take the oxygen bottle and send him on his way. Instead of that, they put him to work. Apparently, the medical personnel needed some help because they had a room full of wounded men that needed some medical attention. They gave him the job of administering oxygen to Crete while the doctor, and whoever else, worked on the stump of his right leg. Maxwell performed his job by holding an air mask to his face. This wasn't exactly part of Maxwell's job description, and he wasn't used to seeing so much blood all at one time, but he managed to get through it and without fainting, too.

An interesting thing was taking place all the time the medical personnel were working on Crete's right leg. Crete was complaining about the severe pain in his left leg, his good leg, and he couldn't understand why they couldn't give him something to relieve the pain. Apparently, they were all thinking that Crete was confused about which leg was hurting. It was later learned that Crete was right about which leg was hurting him – his good leg. Crete's left leg was hurting him because he had taken a hard fall on that leg when he slid down the chute getting out of the mount. He didn't realize the lower part of his right leg was gone when he slid down the chute, and, somehow, that missing leg caused him to land hard on the deck on his left knee. He also injured that leg in some way, but there is no record of how that leg was injured and why it was causing him so much pain. I'm sure the doctors finally got it figured out and corrected his injury to that leg, too. Anyway, Maxwell was glad when they relieved him from his corpsman duties. The boiler room was more to his liking.

## Cleaning Up and Repairing Mount 51

The starboard shield of Mount 51 had a big, jagged hole in the upper left-hand corner of it. It was big enough for a large man to crawl through. However, before nightfall there was no evidence that the hole was ever there. The shipfitters cut out the damaged area with a welding torch and welded a new piece of metal in its place. Then, they smoothed out the welding lines and painted it the same battleship grey color. When the paint dried, you couldn't tell it had ever been damaged. Some of the shrapnel from the disintegrating shell had also put some smaller holes in the deck, which was also patched up. As I understood it, the shrapnel went down into the chief's quarters and did some minor damage, but nobody was in the chief's quarters at the time to get hurt.

Also, somebody had to clean up the inside of the mount. As I understood it, there were pieces of flesh splattered around in the mount. I imagine someone just took a water hose and hosed down the inside of the mount. I never even went down to the mount to look at the damage myself, and I don't know why I didn't now. But I saw pictures of the damage that were taken by someone that did. In fact, one of my shipmates gave me a copy of a picture he had taken, which I still have.

Although, the outside of the mount was repaired rather quickly, the guns were out of commission and would be until we got to port. The hydraulic system of the guns was damaged to the extent that it couldn't be repaired aboard ship. The repair of the hydraulic system would have to be done by technicians aboard a repair ship when we got to port. Consequently, the Brush would moor alongside the Ajax(AR6) when we got to Yokosuka a few days later.

The following is a series of messages sent by various entities concerning the action on, 15 May, 1953, involving the Brush.

USS Brush DD745, May 15, 1953, Wonsan, Korea

I take great pride in extending sincere appreciation to every member of the BRUSH crew for their splendid performance during the action against enemy guns and taking care of the personnel and material casualties suffered when ship was hit. To every member of the crew "WELL DONE!"

Following dispatches are quoted for your information.

FM: CTU 95.2.1

TO: CTG 95.2

Brush putting very destructive fire in caves TWIKOTCHWI when 76's opened up on 20 rounds received with one hit starboard shield mount. One penetrating gun chamber x Nine casualties* four serious x BRUSH full operative except power driven Mt. one. And ready for duty x BRUSH did best job on caves I have seen putting two out of commission but didn't have time to get the western ones.

FM: 95.2.1

TO: 95.2

INFO: CTF. 95/Com7th Flt/COMNAVFE/BRUSH

BRUSH received one hit Mount One shield starboard side penetrating gun chamber and disabling hydraulic system x Total 20 rounds very accurate estimated 76MM fired at ship maneuvering radically at high speed x BRUSH had previously put highly destructive fire in RPT in caves x Casualties sustained four serious five minor x BRUSH ready for duty except power drive Mount One and on station Wonsan.

FM: COMDESDIV 92

TO: BRUSH

By your competent destructive effort and splendid performance under extremely accurate enemy fire you have joined the fighting Ninety Two team x Well done x My sympathies for your casualties x Signed x BOWEN

FM: COMCRUDIV 1

TO: BRUSH

COMCRUDIV 1 is proud of the gallant crew of the BRUSH x

## A Close Call

How close did the ship come to blowing up with probably the loss of all hands? In one respect, it seems to have been very close because of 3 things. The shell was apparently a dud, but if it had actually exploded in the mount, it would have undoubtedly caused the powder canisters in the powder hoist to explode. There would have been a big explosion that would have most likely caused all the powder in the magazine to explode and probably all the shells, too. It would have been an awfully big BOOM. In addition, there was a considerable amount of sparks falling down into the magazine handling room and around a lot of powder, which could have ignited the powder also, but didn't. Furthermore, if the shell had hit one or more of the shells in the rack on the starboard shield, even as a dud, it would have most likely caused it to explode and thus explode the powder canisters in the hoist, which would have caused the powder in the magazine to explode. Of course, if one shell in the rack had exploded, it would have probably caused the rest of them to detonate as well. So, it appears that the ship came mighty close to blowing up. It is unlikely, though, that there would have been anyone left to write about it. However, I have reason to believe that things simply weren't supposed to have happened that way, and the ship may not have been in any real danger of blowing up. I will explain my reasoning behind that statement in the following paragraphs.

## A Reassuring Voice

I have good reason to believe that an angel was present and looking out for us. Twice, while we were operating off the coast of North Korea, I had a supernatural experience which I have never revealed to anybody until now. Naturally, being in a combat zone, I was sometimes concerned about my well-being, because I had no interest in dying for my country and never met anybody on my ship that was. I was only 19 years old at the time and I felt like that I was much too young to be dying for any reason. If I had died in Korea that would have meant that somebody took my life; I didn't willingly give it for my country. And I think that is probably the way it was with all of us because everybody I knew wanted to live.

Anyway, twice, a few weeks apart, right out of the blue, a voice said to me, "Don't be too concerned about being in this place, but you will need to be concerned about being in Southeast Asia." Those were the words the best I can remember. I was alone both times this voice spoke to me. I can remember exactly where I was the second time he spoke to me. I was on the signal bridge standing between the 2 flagbags and just forward of the mast. I can no longer remember where I was the first time I heard it, but I believe I was on the inside of the ship somewhere. This voice that I heard was not audible, however; but it was a strong, authoritative sounding voice and was just as real as if it had been audible. It spoke to me both times right out of the blue with the same message, the same words. I would like to emphasize here that this message given to me was not just a thought that passed through my mind. I know that some people think that every thought that passes through their mind is put there by God as a message from him. Maybe so, who am I to say? But I'm not talking about that kind of thing. This voice and message that I heard was just as clear and real as if it had been audible. And it was meant only for me to hear. Maybe other men on the ship heard supernatural voices and got messages, too. How would I know? I can only speak for myself. In addition, I had no reason to be thinking about Southeast Asia in the first place. The second time I received the message, I remember thinking, "Why did I have to be concerned about Southeast Asia because I hadn't heard of any American ships going down that way?" But, I thought, maybe I'll be going down there someday. I also took the message to mean that I would survive Korea. For that to happen, though, that shell simply couldn't explode because I was right above one of the forward magazines.

At the time I heard the message, I wasn't quite sure who was doing the speaking – God, Jesus, or an angel. But after giving it much thought through the years, I decided it must have been an angel sent by God to watch over me, to keep me from getting hurt, and to reassure me. I reasoned that God and Jesus had more important things to do than to follow around after me. They sent an angel to look after me instead. However, I could be wrong. It could have been Jesus that gave me the message. I'll have to ask Him one day who it was for sure. But I can say one thing for certain – it wasn't Allah.

I would also like to give some recognition to my mother's "Ladies Prayer Group" at the Ocklawaha Bridge Baptist Church in the Ocala National Forest for regularly praying to God, Jehovah, for my protection. He undoubtedly heard their prayers. In addition, I probably had some other people praying for me, too. So, from what I know about the shelling incident, it appears to me like we all survived the enemy shell hit by the grace of God and we shouldn't forget it. We should all be thankful that we were allowed to live a little longer and not have spent all these years at the bottom of Wonsan Harbor.

I might add that it is rather humbling to know that God and his angels were giving me and us some special attention and protection in Korea. However, in my case, at least, their attention did not end there. It followed me throughout the rest of my naval career and afterwards, too. Actually, this angel still makes his presence known from time to time – even to this day.

## A Message to the Doubters

I know that some of the people that read this book will question whether a supernatural being spoke to me because of a number of reasons. Some people will question it because I belong to a Christian denomination that is different than theirs, and God, Jesus, or an angel couldn't possibly have spoken to someone that is not a member of their particular group, because they have, in their opinion, the only true religion, are the only ones that have God's ear, and the only ones that have a chance of going to Heaven. Well, the only thing I will say to them is, "Non-Sense," and you need to rethink and adjust your beliefs to something more realistic. Chances are you don't have the only true path to salvation, Heaven, or an earthly paradise. Neither are you the only ones that God cares about or listens to, so you might as well get used to the idea.

Then, there are those people that don't believe there is a God in the first place. Therefore, no heavenly being could have spoken to me. Those "voices" that I heard was just a figment of my imagination. Well, for those people, I can assure you that there is a God because I have encountered him, or one of his representatives, too many times in my life to doubt it. There is one God and his name is Jehovah, or Lord. He also has a son and his name is Jesus. And the only way you can gain entrance into Heaven and see God is through his son Jesus Christ. If you don't believe that now, you will in time. And I would say that it would be a very good idea to get acquainted with him while you are here on earth. Otherwise, your eternal destination may not be to your liking and eternity is a very long time.

Then, there are other religions in the world that worship other gods. The only thing I'm going to say about that is, there are going to be a lot of surprised people when they get to their final destination. And there is one thing that you can be sure of; there is not going to be a horde of young virgins waiting on any man for any reason. Instead, it is more likely that there will be a horde of demons waiting on him to punish him for the despicable acts that he committed on Earth. And their job would be to torment him for the rest of eternity. That is something that some people need to think about.

The Brush spent the night of, 15 May, slowly cruising around the Wonsan Harbor entrance. However, around daylight on, 16 May, the ship started lying to in the vicinity of Buoy H to rendezvous with the Moore for a personnel transfer. Saturday, 16 May, turned out to be a day filled with rendezvousing with other ships and having conferences.

The Moore arrived at Buoy H at 0615 and the captain, executive officer, CIC officer, and communications officer left the ship and went over to the Moore by motor whaleboat for a conference. In addition, at 0710 the commodore shifted his flag to the Moore and he and his staff left the Brush and transferred over to the Moore. At 0717 the captain and the other officers returned to the Brush. The ship got underway and slowly steamed around the harbor entrance until early afternoon when the USS Eversole(DD789) arrived on the scene for the purpose of relieving the Brush at Wonsan. The Eversole commenced lying to for a transfer of files and to have a conference. At 1341 Captain Quigley and some of his officers went over to the Eversole by motor whaleboat for the conference. They returned to the ship at 1422. At this time the Brush was officially relieved of the Wonsan patrol – forever. We never went back into Wonsan Harbor again.

The Brush got underway again to rendezvous with another destroyer, the USS Henderson(DD785), which was some miles away and in the vicinity of Nan Do Island. We rendezvoused with the Henderson at 1530 and commenced lying to again so that the captain and some of his officers could go aboard the Henderson for another conference. They left the ship by motor whaleboat at 1549 and returned to the ship at 1646. However, when the ship's officers returned to the Brush, they were accompanied by a Major Perry USMC and army liaison officer and who was also an officer from the Nan Do Island garrison. However, we didn't get underway this time. Instead, we dropped anchor and stayed put for several hours, because we were going to take part in a covert operation that night with some ROK Marines from the Nan Do garrison. The USS Henderson departed the area, however.

## COVERT OPERATIONS

The night of, 16 May, and the following night, the Brush participated in a couple of interesting covert operations with a group of ROK Marines that were led by a U.S. Army sergeant.

### Covert Operation #1

At 2053 the Brush weighed anchor, got underway, and proceeded to escort the landing barges LB 14 and LB 16 that were transporting these marines on the first covert mission. At 2135 we arrived offshore from the landing site and the 2 landing craft headed for the beach. The ROK Marines mission was to destroy either a gun position or a radar site, but I've forgotten which one it was – if I ever knew. The Brush's mission was to provide gunfire support for the raiding party when they called for it. While waiting for the call to start firing, the ship just steamed around very slowly in the dark about 3000 yards off the beach. Of course, we were in a darkened ship condition.

At 2246 the Brush got the word to commence firing their 5 inch guns as directed by the sergeant. The Marine Corps officer that came aboard played a part in this operation somehow but I never knew what it was. However, I imagine he was the one on the ship that was communicating with the sergeant by radio. Anyway, the ROK Marines had accomplished their mission and were now trying to escape back to their boats. We commenced firing and over the next hour and fifteen minutes the Brush fired 40 rounds of 5 inch shells, including 18 rounds of high capacity shells and 22 rounds of white phosphorus shells. Exploding white phosphorus shells at night is an awesome sight. The burning phosphorus must shoot at least 50 feet up in the air. And when several W.P. shells are exploding at about the same time, it is a spectacular sight. It is the ultimate fireworks display. The normal fireworks display at the city park on the 4th of July doesn't come close to matching it – regardless of how good the display may be. On this particular night, it must have been a fiery hell to the enemy troops on the beach.

The raiding party in their LB's came back out to the ship around midnight, and we escorted them back to Nan Do Island. We never heard what they accomplished on the operation, but apparently all the ROK Marines got back safely because none of them were brought aboard for medical treatment. The captain might have been informed about what took place on the mission, but if he was, he never shared that information with the crew.

Upon arriving at the island around 0052, the ship stopped all engines and commenced lying to about 1000 yards off the island for what turned out to be a food stores transfer to the island garrison. A sampan came alongside the ship and the stores were put in it for transport to the island. Apparently, the island was running short of food.

The Brush left Nan Do around 0115 and proceeded to the Bombline; we steamed around off of it for the rest of the night. However, we weren't called on to do any firing at enemy positions on the mainland on this occasion. The spotters on the beach may not have known we were out there in the dark and was available to do it. Or, maybe he was asleep. Who knows?

Early the next morning, Sunday, 17 May, the Brush departed the Bombline and proceeded to rendezvous with a couple of replenishment ships – a tanker and a supply ship. At 0752 we went alongside the USS Virgo(AKA20) to take on ammunition and some provisions. Over the next 30 minutes the ship received by highline 130 rounds of 5 inch shells of various kinds and 130 canisters of gun powder. Then, at 0852 the ship went alongside the USS Platte(A024) to take on fuel oil and received 89,364 gallons over the next 45 minutes. The Brush went back to the Bombline after refueling. At 1124 the Brush commenced firing on enemy positions on the mainland as directed by a spotter that was positioned somewhere on a mountainside. She ceased firing at 1515 after expending a total of 57 rounds of 5 inch high capacity shells. That was a different way to spend a Sunday afternoon. Around 1630 the ship departed the Bombline and proceeded back to Nan Do Island. We arrived there around 1900, dropped anchor, and waited for night and the departure time for the second covert operation.

## Covert Operation #2

The Brush weighed anchor at 2234 and got underway to play her part in the upcoming mission – to escort the ROK Marines to their landing site and to give them GFS. The ROK's were transported this time in 2 boats called Yaks to their landing site. I don't know what they looked like because it was dark and I couldn't see them. I think 15 to 20 ROK Marines were taking part in these operations. However, I don't know if this was the same bunch of marines that conducted the operation the night before or if it was a different bunch. We escorted the 2 Yaks full of marines to their departure point at a speed of 5 knots. That slow speed was probably necessary to keep the boats and the ship from getting separated in the dark. We arrived at the departure point a little after midnight and the boats headed for the beach. The Brush stopped all engines and commenced lying to. Again, we were about 3,000 yards offshore and were to just lie to in the dark until we got the word from the raiding party to give them gunfire support and where we were to put the shells. We had a little help from another ship on this operation. The USS James E. Kyes(DD787) arrived on the scene and was also lying to about 2,000 yards from us. She was to give the ROK Marines GFS, too.

The ROK Marines and their U.S. Army sergeant leader landed on the beach at 0035 without being detected. It was a very dark night and I don't know how they were able to see enough to do anything.

I spent a lot of time out on the bridge looking toward land to see if I could see any action going on but I never saw anything. I thought I might see some tracer bullets flying around or the flash from an explosion but I never did.

The ROK Marines were on the mainland about 2 hours. The story was that their mission on this night was to sneak into a little village and either capture a fellow there or to liberate him, but I'm not sure which way it was. However, they never accomplished their mission because they were spotted by an enemy sentry just as they entered the little village, and a machinegun opened-up on them and wounded some of them. So, there wasn't going to be a surprise raid that night. The marines retreated and after that they were simply attempting to escape back to their boat with the enemy in hot pursuit. We got the call at 0247 to open fire on the enemy troops that were pursuing the raiding party. We opened fire with one of our 5 inch guns and were laying high capacity shells on the pursuing enemy troops. We fired one round per minute as directed by the sergeant and did so for 20 minutes until the marines got back to their boats and headed out to sea.

The Kyes also opened fire on the enemy troops at the same time that we did, but they fired white phosphorus shells. They fired about the same amount of rounds as we did. Again, the exploding white phosphorus shells were an awesome sight.

Anyway, the raiding party got back into their boats and escaped; at least most of them did. However, they did pay a price for their little expedition. They had some casualties. Four wounded ROK Marines were brought aboard the Brush around 0350. Three of them were on stretchers. The wounded marines were taken into the officer's wardroom to receive first aid. I was standing on a ladder just outside the wardroom and watched other ROK Marines carry them in there. As I remember, all the ROK's were conscious as they were carried by me, but their facial expressions indicated that they were in considerable pain. We also heard the next day that they left one of their casualties in the boat because he didn't have any need for medical attention.

When the boats got back out to the ship that night, some of the crew was down on the main deck to help bring the wounded ROK Marines aboard to be given first aid by the corpsmen. The Brush didn't have a real doctor aboard, but she could take them to one pretty quick. Lt. Jack Easterling went down to the main deck from CIC to see if he could help them in some way. It was now drizzling rain and the deck was wet and slippery. Mr. Easterling assisted in pulling one of the fellows aboard that was seriously wounded. He had been hit in the mid-section by a 50 caliber machinegun bullet, was in bad shape, and all doped-up with morphine. In the process of pulling him up on deck, Mr. Easterling slipped and fell back on the deck with the wounded ROK just about on top of him. Mr. Easterling sat up and the poor fellow's head ended up in his lap. So, Mr. Easterling just sat there on the wet deck and covered the man's head with his raincoat to keep the rain from falling in his face. And there is where the fellow died a few seconds later. So, some of the other ROK's just put him back in one of their boats. That ROK Marine had been on his last raid.

We were also informed the next day by the army sergeant that the ships were putting their shells on the enemy troops just where they were needed. That was good to know. Maybe that was the reason they were able to escape.

As soon as the wounded were brought aboard, the Brush got underway to rendezvous with the cruiser, USS Bremerton(CA130), in the vicinity of the Bombline to transfer the wounded ROK's to her. At 0600 we went alongside the cruiser for a highline transfer of the wounded. This was accomplished in a very few minutes. Three of the wounded went over on stretchers and one in a boatswain's chair.

## THE BRUSH IS RELIEVED OF PATROL DUTY

After transferring the wounded to the Bremerton, the Brush returned to the Bombline and commenced steaming around at 3 knots. Actually, I think we were mainly just waiting around for another destroyer to arrive to relieve us. It was now Monday, 18 May. Around 0900 the USS Duncan(DD874) arrived at the Bombline, but they didn't relieve us right away. At 0908 the captain of the Duncan and 6 of his officers came aboard the Brush for a conference. However, at 1012 we received a fire mission and the Brush commenced firing on enemy positions as directed by a spotter onshore. At 1108 the Brush ceased firing having expended 34 rounds of 5 inch high capacity shells. Our fire mission probably delayed the Duncan officers from returning to their ship, but their motor whaleboat finally came alongside again and carried them back to their ship at 1136; at that time the Brush was officially relieved by the Duncan.

However, we weren't going back to Japan just yet. The Brush now set a course for Wonsan to retrieve her 5 wounded men from the Comstock (LSD19). We arrived in the vicinity of the Comstock at 1450, stopped all engines, and commenced lying to. In a few minutes the Comstock's small boat came alongside with our 5 crewmembers and they came aboard. We also had to transfer some supplies to the Comstock. They were apparently running short on some things, too.

The Brush now set a course to rendezvous with the Maddox for a guard mail transfer. With that completed, the Brush set a course to rendezvous with the Firecrest(AMS10) for a personnel transfer

– to transport someone back to Yokosuka, Japan with us. Finally at 1725 the Brush was free to head for Japan and that is what we did. The Brush soon joined up with the Moore, fell in astern of her, and together the 2 ships headed for Japan via Shimonoseki Strait. The ships increased speed to 25 knots and stayed at that speed all night which was kind of unusual. They called it an "economy run exercise", but I personally think that the captain of the Moore was just anxious to get to port so he could go on liberty. I could understand that. I think everybody else was anxious, too, but the enlisted men would say it just the way it was. They, or many of them, just wanted to go ashore and get drunk, among other things.

As we got into South Korean waters, and later, Japanese waters, fishing boats were everywhere, and we had to do a lot of maneuvering to get around them. It was night by now and we couldn't see too much of them visually. We had to rely on radar to keep clear of them. Sometimes we encountered fleets of fishing boats that we would have to maneuver around at 25 knots. We did turn on our navigational lights at 2132, the first time in several weeks.

At 0917 Tuesday, 19 May, the Brush entered Shimonoseki Strait and the captain took the conn. The navigator was on the bridge and Holly was at the wheel – with Tommy looking over his shoulder. This was my first time on the wheel as the special sea detail helmsman. I was still in training, however, I didn't experience any difficulties, but it was comforting to have Tommy standing behind me to take over in case I encountered something I wasn't experienced enough to handle. We got through the strait at 1120 and the officer-of-the-deck took the conn and a regular helmsman took the wheel.

At 1149 the ship experienced a steering casualty. That is, the ship lost steering control on the bridge due to the rudder jamming at right full. That is something that just happens every now and then. Losing steering control of the ship can be very hazardous, depending on where the ship is, and it's something every conning officer dreads. In this case, the conning officer acted quickly and proficiently. He stopped the starboard engine with the port engine at back full. Then, he stopped all engines. However, steering control was regained at 1155 from the after-steering control station, which is always manned when the ship is underway for just such an occasion. At 1157 the ship assumed its regular course and speed and was being steered from after-steering. At 1222 the steering casualty was restored and the steering of the ship was resumed on the bridge.

At 1800 the Brush and the Moore joined up with the Maddox and the 3 ships formed up into a column formation with the Maddox in the lead and the Brush in station 3. They continued on their way to Yokosuka together. At 1440 Wednesday, 20 May, the Brush set the special sea detail to enter Tokyo Bay. At 1454 we passed through the submarine net at the entrance to Tokyo Bay and commenced maneuvering at various courses and speeds to conform to the channel. At 1512 the Brush entered Yokosuka Harbor and commenced maneuvering to go alongside the USS Ajax(AR6) at buoy B-3. At 1532 we were moored starboard side to the Ajax. At 1550 the ship secured the special sea detail and set the regular inport watch. Everybody was glad to be back in port, and Japan, for a few days of rest and recreation.

# TOKYO BAY

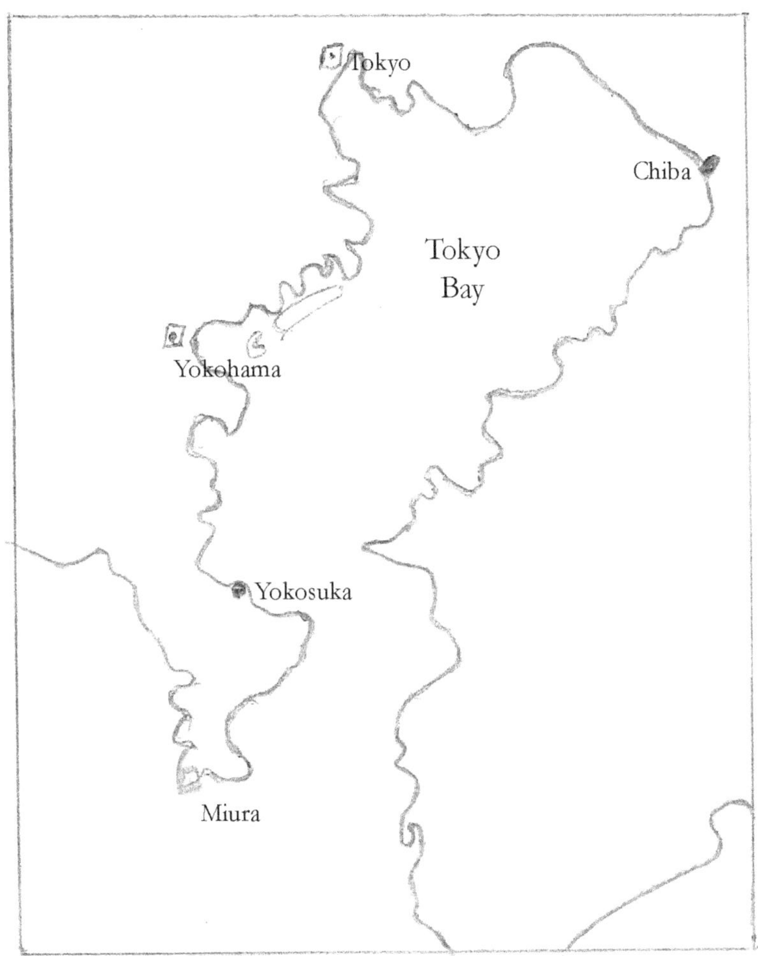

## A WALL OF BLUE

Something interesting happened the afternoon of, 20 May, as the ship made her approach to go alongside the Ajax in Yokosuka Harbor. We had to pass close by the cruiser, USS St. Paul(CA73), which was already moored and probably had been for a couple of days. We passed by the cruiser very slowly, maybe at a speed of 2 or 3 knots. I was standing on the port side of the signal bridge and was not doing anything in particular except watching the scenery go by. As we slowly passed by the starboard side of the cruiser, I saw a "wall of blue". This "wall of blue" was sailors dressed in undress blue uniforms, mostly – their uniform-of-the-day in port, I suppose. This "wall of blue" extended from the bow of the ship to the stern and as far up on the superstructure as a person could get and stand. There were hundreds of sailors in blue uniforms just standing there watching us go by. Their numbers suggested that it was most of the crew. At first, I didn't pay any attention to them. I saw them with my eyes but I really didn't see them. Then, this "wall of blue" registered in my mind, and I asked myself the question, "Why are all those sailors out on deck looking in our direction?" I was even more puzzled by the looks and demeanor of this crowd of sailors. They were just standing there, mostly at the rail, staring at us without any kind of expression on their faces. Their faces looked like they had been carved out of stone. In addition, they were standing there as still as statues and were totally silent. I thought the whole situation was rather strange.

Then, all of a sudden it hit me. I realized what all those sailors on the St. Paul were doing and it made my scalp crawl, and I felt a flushed feeling sweep over me. They were there on deck to watch the Brush come in port. I was touched that they would feel like we rated that much attention, but I really didn't think we had done anything to deserve it; but apparently they thought so, otherwise, they wouldn't have all been out there on deck watching us go by. Why were they so interested in us? I don't know for sure, but maybe they had heard about our encounter with the enemy in Wonsan Harbor and were just curious about us. Or, maybe they were hoping to get a look at the big shell hole in Mount 51. Regardless of the reason for them being out there, though, I'm sure every one of those sailors was on deck because they wanted to be. It is unlikely that their captain or anyone else made them do it. However, the time of our arrival in port must have been announced over the P.A. system, because they were all out there waiting for us to pass by them. And it must have taken a few minutes for that many sailors to gather on the deck and superstructure.

Later, after having time to think about the incident, I thought it was kind of odd, under the circumstances, that nobody smiled, nobody waved at us, nobody saluted us, and nobody cheered us. So, it didn't seem like they were there on deck to necessarily honor us. If that had been their purpose, they would have done something. Instead, they just stared at us in stony silence. What were they thinking? To me, they acted like we were a long lost ghost ship that was finally arriving in port. Perhaps they had heard about how close the Brush came to blowing up in Wonsan Harbor as a consequence of being hit by the enemy shell. They realized how lucky the men on the Brush were to be alive, and they just wanted to take a look at us – men that could have just have easily been dead. So perhaps that was the reason for their strange behavior.

I've often thought about that "wall of blue" through the years. I don't know if anybody else on the Brush even noticed what I did that day. I kind of doubt it because I never saw any indication that they did and nobody ever mentioned it later on. I almost missed it myself because I only saw them for a few seconds just before we went alongside the Ajax and out of sight. But I can still see that "wall of blue" in my mind just as clearly as if the incident happened last week. Some things I remember that happened over 50 years ago and some things I don't; the "wall of blue" happens to be one of the things that I remember clearly.

The Brush stayed around Japan 12 days, but we didn't stay in port all that time; we had to go to sea one day to operate with the aircraft carrier, USS Point Cruz(CVE119), while she conducted flight operations. We went to sea early Tuesday morning, 26 May, and came back in port early Wednesday morning. Then, we went out 2 days to conduct antisubmarine warfare (ASW) exercises with a submarine, the USS Sabalo(SS302). We went out of port Saturday morning, 30 May, and came back into Yokosuka Harbor late Sunday afternoon, 31 May.

The Brush played with the submarine Saturday until 2100 and then proceeded to an anchorage in Miyata Wan some miles away. At 2240 the Brush dropped anchor in 22 fathoms of water, sandy bottom, with 90 fathoms of chain to the port anchor. It was a short night, however. The Brush weighed anchor and got underway again at 0500. She proceeded to rendezvous with the submarine and conducted ASW exercises with her all day Sunday. We went back in port around 1800.

In one sense, 31 May, was a special day for me. It was my birthday and I turned 20 years old. I was no longer a teenager and was now a veteran besides. It wasn't exactly a fun day, though, and no celebrating took place.

**USS Brush**

## JAPAN

I found the country of Japan to be a fascinating place because everything was so different there – the landscape, the buildings, the boats, the customs of the people, the looks of the people, the dress, and the special oriental charms of the young ladies. There were a tremendous number of servicemen that visited Japan during the Korean War era, and I think that most of them that spent much time around Japan would agree that the girls could be very charming.

The sailors spent most of their time in Japan around the seaport towns of Yokosuka and Sasebo, because that is the only places that the ships visited during the Korean War. After the war, however, the ships occasionally visited other ports. The seaport towns of Yokosuka and Sasebo didn't appear to be too prosperous during the early 1950's in spite of the fact that the sailors and other servicemen spent a large amount of money in those towns during that time. As I remember it, most of the streets weren't paved in either town; however, the main street in Yokosuka was paved. The streets tended to be muddy much of the time because it rained so frequently in Japan. The buff-colored mud didn't look too good on black shoes. The fleet landing (the place where sailors came ashore) at Yokosuka was on the main street, and it was just a short walk for the sailors to be in the business district and with their shoes still black at this point.

As previously mentioned, the business section of Sasebo was about one mile from the fleet landing. The bicycle rickshaw operators would meet the sailors as they came ashore and solicit them for a ride into town. The price the rickshaw drivers charged was rather inexpensive, as I remember. In fact, just about everything in Japan was cheap back then. However, we didn't always ride into town in a bicycle rickshaw. Sometimes, especially if it was a pretty day, and early in the day, we would walk into town just for the walk. In addition to unpaved, muddy streets, the buildings were all one or two story, were wooden, and were just plain drab looking.

Furthermore, generally speaking, many of the people in either place didn't appear to be too prosperous, especially the working class of men; because they usually wore shabby, loose-fitting type clothes, were skinny, and looked undernourished. The older women usually wore plain-looking type kimonos – not the real expensive, colorful ones like the Geisha girls wore or worn by well-to-do women on special occasions. The shopkeepers and the younger women usually wore western type clothes and looked more prosperous, however.

We could always spot the school children as far as we could see them because of the uniforms they wore. The girl's uniforms looked like sailor outfits. They wore a navy blue skirt, a white blouse that had a light blue sailor-type collar in the back, and a black neckerchief just like the American sailors wore. From a sailor's point of view, they looked sharp. The boys wore black pants, a white shirt, black boots, and a little black cap. It could have been a type of sailor outfit, too. I would say that the Japanese people as a whole are closely associated with the sea and get a lot of their food from it.

### Fish Markets

I thought the outdoor fish markets in Japan were interesting places to visit. If it lives in the ocean, I think the Japanese people eat it. The fish markets that I saw were all open to the street, and I liked to just browse around in them and look at the great variety of sea creatures. I saw a lot of things that I was familiar with, but I also saw a lot of things I had never seen before or since. I could smell a fish market a block away, but it really wasn't a bad smell. They just smelled of the sea. It might have been seaweed that I was smelling because they sold that in the fish markets, too.

# Street Scenes of Yokosuka

## The Custom of Removing One's Shoes

There were a number of Japanese customs that the sailors and other servicemen had to adjust to that was very different than those of the western world. But the custom that the sailors had to adjust to the quickest was the Japanese custom of removing one's shoes before entering a house or a place of business in some cases. A fellow just hated to lose sight of his shoes, because he was afraid that if he pulled them off and left them at the door, they might not be there when he went back to retrieve them. Besides that, how would a sailor know which pair of shoes was his if there were several pair of black shoes left at the same entrance and all of them were about the same size. It was a puzzle sometimes. However, the American sailors usually didn't have to worry about Japanese men stealing their shoes, because the American's usually wore shoes that were several sizes larger than what the Japanese did. I never heard of a sailor losing his shoes, but it was always a great concern of his that he might lose them.

## Money

We used yen and military scrip for money when we were around Japan. The exchange rate for yen was 360 yen per 1 dollar and stayed at that rate the entire 3 years I was in that part of the world. As I remember, we were paid in military scrip and converted it into yen when we went ashore. However, I believe we used military scrip when we bought anything on a navy base, which, I believe, was only at Yokosuka in Japan. I don't remember Sasebo as having a naval base, but I can't be sure about that.

## Souvenir Shops

There was a multitude of souvenir shops in both Yokosuka and Sasebo that catered to the thousands of servicemen that were coming and going. Everything imaginable was sold in these shops. Sometimes entire streets were reserved for small shops and stalls and no automobile traffic was allowed. Most of these shops did a thriving business, I believe. It was a good business arrangement for both parties – the merchants and the sailors. The shopkeepers were anxious to get all the money they could from the sailors, and the sailors were anxious to give it to them or somebody. Somebody in town was going to get all the money the sailors had. Most of the sailors were going to be flat broke when their ship left port. Oh well, another payday was just a few days away, and they were going to be at sea where they couldn't spend any money for awhile.

I will always remember those streets that were devoted to souvenirs because of the smell of rice straw and mud. The streets were dirt, it rained a lot in Japan, and many of the souvenirs were packed in straw. I will always remember that smell of rice straw and mud. Over a 3 year period, I bought and sent or took home a lot of interesting things, and it all was made in Japan – not China.

## Japanese Cars

The cars in Japan were rather junkie in the 1950's. They rattled a lot and they seemed to smoke a lot. Most of the cars I saw were taxis. Very few people owned an automobile, but the sailors rode in the taxis a great deal even if they did rattle and smoke a lot. It certainly beat walking long distances. The Japanese have come a long way in making automobiles. They are now some of the best in the world in every respect. They must have learned a lot from Detroit about how to make automobiles.

**Street Scenes of Yokosuka**

**Japanese School Boys & Girls**

Japanese Homes

Japanese homes were very unique and added greatly to the fascination of the country. All the Japanese houses that I saw were quite small and made out of wood, or at least the exterior walls were. In addition, they were on very small lots with little space between houses. The interior of the homes is what made them so unique and so vastly different than the typical American or Western home. The interior walls were very thin and were largely made out of opaque rice paper, I believe; and there weren't any hinged doors in the interior of the houses either; they were all sliding doors. Of course, the sliding doors were made of rice paper, too, and light wood.

I suppose the floors were wood of some kind, however, they were always covered with mats, or a tatami, as they were called. I believe they were made out of thin bamboo strips, and they were never to be walked on with shoes, only in your bare feet or with socks on. It was a big no-no to forget and walk on the tatamis with your street shoes on. The Japanese would get real excited about that and call it to your attention real fast. Walking on the tatami with your street shoes on would dirty it up and wear it out quickly also. I could understand their concern about dirty street shoes.

Japanese homes had very little furniture in them. Typically, the homes would have a small table with short legs that looked similar to a Western coffee table. It might have a small dresser or two to store some of their personal stuff. There were not any chairs, beds, stoves, washing machines, clothes dryers, or dish washers.

The Japanese cooked in, on, over, or whatever they did, a hibachi which burned charcoal. The hibachi was also their source of heat in cold weather. The sailors usually called a hibachi a hibachi pot. It looked like a pot to them. I'm not sure what the hibachis were made of but I believe they were porcelain.

Of course, the Japanese people sat on the floor in their homes since they didn't have any chairs. Dragging chairs across the tatami would wear it out quickly, too. So the Japanese sat on the floor around the low table to eat their meals. Actually, they sat on the floor for everything unless they needed to stand up for some reason.

The Japanese also slept on the floor. At night they would drag out a thin mattress or mat from a closet to sleep on and store it away again the next morning. So, that is somewhat the way the Japanese people lived. It certainly was different than the way people lived in the Western world.

## Getas

Sometimes the Japanese people wore an unusual type of shoe that we Americans had never seen before and that we found interesting. They were called getas. Getas were mostly a wooden sole that had 1 ½ to 2 inch ridges on both the front and rear of the bottom side of the shoe that kept the feet dry and up out of the mud. The shoes were a solid piece of wood and, of course, didn't bend. The getas were kept on one's feet by means of a strap similar to that found on modern day flip flops. In addition, when a person was wearing these getas, they usually wore a special kind of short sock that had split toes that the toe strap fit into.

This type of shoe, these getas, was quite practical for Japan's rainy climate and muddy streets and paths. I think the Japanese people had been wearing them for many generations. I doubt that they are wearing them as much today in modern Japan because of more paved streets and all. However, when people were walking in them on a hard surface they made a terrible racket. The getas made a clopping noise and you could hear people coming for some distance when they were wearing them. In addition, people had a peculiar walk when they were wearing getas. They tended to walk fast to keep them on their feet or something.

## Japanese Girls

There were a lot of charming things about Japan, but I believe most of the servicemen that visited there during the Korean War would consider the most charming thing about Japan was the Japanese girls. I personally didn't appreciate them that much on my first Far Eastern tour of duty, as much as most sailors, probably, but they grew on me as the years went by.

The Japanese girls had a special kind of charm that most sailors found hard to resist, especially if they were pretty. Like everywhere, some of the girls were pretty and some of them weren't so pretty. Most of them that we saw tended to be highly westernized in their dress, hair styles, and makeup. Most of them could speak a little English, in a fashion. Sometimes the way they expressed themselves in English was rather amusing and added to their charm. For instance, some of the expressions that were heard frequently were, "How much you speak?" or "Why you speak?" or "You all time speak." Another thing they would say sometimes when they were talking about a previous boyfriend, that had gone back to the states, maybe, was the term "Before boyfriend".

## Sailors Speaking Japanese

Of course, the sailors would pick up a few words of the Japanese language, too – like arigato (thank you), sayonara (goodbye), ichi ban (number 1), and takusan (much). And, in addition to that, they would sometimes corrupt an English word and call it speaking Japanese – like the English word "change". They would say the words "changee changee" instead of just the word "change" during a conversation with a Japanese person and even amongst themselves sometime. They were kind of fooling themselves.

## The San Custom

The Japanese have a custom of putting the word "san" at the end of a person's name and maybe a title, too. Consequently, an older Japanese man was always referred to as "Papa san", and an older Japanese woman was referred to as "Mama san". At least, that is what American sailors called older men and women and the Japanese people did, too; however, I think they adopted that way of referring to older people from the Americans. "Mama san" and "Papa san" don't sound like Japanese words to me.

Sometimes the young Japanese women would be called "Baby san", particularly if she happened to be a fellow's special girlfriend. However, "Baby san" is the term that best describes a pretty, charming Japanese young lady. At least, a young fellow that has been there understands what the term means, and he may have a few memories to associate with the term.

## Unwanted Babies

On one of my earlier visits to Tokyo Bay and Yokosuka, I was enlightened by one of my veteran shipmates that Japanese doctors in Tokyo simply flushed unwanted, newborn babies out into Tokyo Bay. Whether this was actually done or not, I can't say for sure, but it was common knowledge amongst the sailors on the ship that it was done as a routine practice. I don't know how they gained that information, but they believed it and I assumed it was so.

I thought that flushing unwanted, newborn babies out into the bay was a very inhumane and barbaric thing to do. It was difficult for me to imagine that there was a nation of people anywhere in the world that was so heartless and could put so little value on human life, especially little, helpless babies. It made me proud to be an American, a nation of people that would never consider doing such a thing to little babies, maybe to unwanted dogs and cats but not to human babies.

However, in recent years, as a nation, we have become much more "progressive" in our thinking concerning unwanted babies. Now doctors just shove a pair of scissors through their little skulls and suck their brains out. How we have "advanced" in our thinking as a nation, at least, according to some people's estimation.

In all our steaming around in Tokyo Bay, though, I never spotted a little baby floating around on the surface of the water; but I was always keeping an eye out for one. Maybe we were too far away from the place they were flushed into the bay; or maybe they had already sunk to the bottom or something had eaten them. Anyway, I never saw one over the 3 years that I was in and out of Tokyo Bay. I also wondered if the Japanese medical personnel had a big garbage disposal type gadget that ground the babies up first, like so much garbage, before they flushed them out into Tokyo Bay. If so, that would explain why I never saw a dead, bloated baby floating around in the bay. Anyway, if they did, it would make it easier for the crabs to eat them. I wonder if our "enlightened" abortion doctors or radical pro-choice feminist ever thought about getting rid of unwanted babies that way. Maybe I should call it to their attention. I bet they would love the idea.

## Visiting Japan in 1982

I've had the unique experience of visiting Japan in the latter days of "old Japan" during the 1950's and "modern Japan" in the early 1980's – actually 29 years after I was first there in the spring of 1953. I spent 3 weeks in Japan in the spring of 1982 during cherry blossom time and that was something to see. Actually, I found Japan to be a totally different place in 1982 than it was in the early 1950's. It was hard to imagine that a country could have changed so much in such a short period of time. In a sense, the country advanced from rags to riches in a very short period of time simply by adopting the capitalist economic system and a democratic form of government similar to that of the United States. From what I know about it, General Douglas McArthur has to be considered the father of modern Japan. Also, from what I understand, General McArthur is held in very high regard by most of the Japanese people, even though he played a big part in defeating them in war. He saw to it that they adopted capitalism and a democratic form of government. In addition, it turned out that the Japanese were a highly intelligent and industrious race of people once they had a chance to do something with their lives.

Just think, there are probably a lot of other poor, third world countries that could become prosperous nations, too, if they would only do what Japan did – just adopt the American form of government. But they won't and consequently they will most likely remain poor third world countries. It is not the United States fault that they are poor countries like so many politically correct, mentally challenged college professors and teachers in the United States like to claim and teach their students. So, my solution to the problem is to just let them remain poor countries. It is not our problem. If they don't have the intelligence to follow our example and make the changes necessary to help themselves, then why fool with them?

Japan is now a very prosperous nation, and one of the things that I especially noticed was the size of the people. In 1953 the people were rather small. The height of the men generally ranged from 5 feet and 2 inches tall to 5 feet and 6 inches. In addition, they were scrawny looking. The women tended to be a little smaller and were generally from 5 feet to 5 feet and 3 inches tall. Furthermore, I didn't see any fat people in Japan in the 1950's.

In 1982 the population as a whole was probably 4 inches taller than they were in 1953. In addition, most of the people were well dressed and looked well fed. In fact, I saw some men that had a little too much padding on them, and I saw Japanese women that were down right pudgy. However, most of the women that I saw that were overweight were either going into or coming out of a pastry shop. However, I didn't see any grossly overweight people in Japan like you see so many of in the United States these days.

Other things that I noticed in 1982 were that most of the buildings were constructed of something other than wood, and most of the streets were paved, too. In addition, a lot of people now have cars, probably too many. They also have the money to eat out a lot in restaurants, to have fun with, and to put in savings accounts.

In 1982 I traveled around Japan a great deal and discovered that Japan is a very mountainous country. It reminded me very much of the Appalachian Mountains region in the Southern United States. As I understand it, all of Japan was created by volcanic activity millions of years ago.

## Liberty in Yokosuka 1953

What did the ship's crew do on liberty in Yokosuka? There really wasn't much sight-seeing going on because there wasn't much to see. All of the sailors probably visited a restaurant somewhere. Some of them went souvenir hunting around the shops and stalls. However, I would say the main attraction and the greatest source of entertainment for the sailors were the cabarets, because that is where the beer and the girls were. Many, or most, of the cabarets had live entertainment of some kind, although, the girls were the main attraction. They were there to entertain the sailors and get their money, and they were usually successful at doing so. In addition, sometimes the girls would make a little money on the side.

The live entertainment usually consisted of Japanese men playing and singing familiar American songs. As I remember, all the songs played or sung were country and western. The country songs sung were usually tearjerkers and the western songs were the old fashioned cowboy songs that you seldom hear anymore. Of course, rock music had never been heard of at that time. There were some very good musical groups. However, it was somewhat amusing to see little Japanese men all dressed up in American cowboy outfits that were able to play and sing almost any country or western song that you would want to hear. The story was, though, that they didn't understand a word of what they were singing. They just memorized dozens of American songs without actually understanding the words. I thought that was quite a feat for them to be able to do that. I always wished that I had a memory as good as theirs.

There were just dozens of these cabarets because lots of navy ships went in and out of Yokosuka Harbor during the Korean War. Also, a good number of British, Canadian, and Australian Navy ships pulled into Yokosuka, as well as Sasebo. Consequently, there were just thousands of sailors walking the streets everyday looking for something to do and spend their money on. The cabaret people and the souvenir shopkeepers were anxious to help them out.

For the sailors, the cabaret entertainment was great, the cold Japanese beer was good, but, of course, the main attraction in the cabarets were the girls, or hostesses, as they were called. Essentially, every time a sailor walked in the door of a cabaret, he would be greeted by at least one, and maybe two or three, hostesses. Their job was to make conversation with the sailors, get them another beer or mixed drink when they began to run low, and to get the sailors to buy them drinks, which I'm sure were mostly colored water. They could drink all day and never show any signs of intoxication; it looked mighty suspicious to me. A hostess would normally concentrate all her attention to one sailor at a time. That would be his girl for the afternoon, evening, or for as long as he was there. The aim of the management was to get as much money out of the sailors as they could and as fast as they could.

There would also, usually, be a photographer circulating around in the cabarets trying to take a picture of the sailors and "their" girl. And they took a lot of them. Many of the sailors had a picture taken with their "girlfriend" to impress the fellows back home. The pictures gave the implication that they were really making out with those Japanese girls like a real sailor – trying to live up to their reputation, you know. Of course, the hope of many of the sailors was that he would rate high enough with his "lady friend" that she would let him go home with her after her work hours. Chances are that if he treated her nice, bought her enough drinks, and had enough yen, he would get that chance. However, during the Korean War, liberty was usually over at 2400 and the sailors had to be back to the ship at that time or be AWOL. A lot of them chose to be AWOL and didn't come back to the ship until 0700 or 0800 the next morning. After the war, however, during our next cruises to the Far East, things got easier for the sailors because they could stay out all night; liberty lasted until 0700 or 0800 the next morning which reduced the AWOL problem in Japan to some extent.

There were also other houses of entertainment for the sailors – dozens of them. A Mama san, an older woman, would have a group of young women at her house that stayed with her for the purpose of entertaining the troops and to give them special and individualized attention. When a fellow showed up at her door, the Mama san would bring out her girls for him to choose from. He would select one and she would be his companion for the afternoon, night, or whenever it was. There was always a fee involved, of course. I suppose the arrangement between the Mama san and the client could be considered somewhat like that of a dating service. Whatever it was, it tended to make everybody happy.

Japanese girls had their special charms and it is easy to understand why so many young servicemen that were stationed in Japan took one home with him to meet the folks. However, the destroyer sailors never really had the opportunity to meet one of the keeper types. They were always in and out of port too quickly to really get to know a Japanese girl that well. Although, I've known incidences of young sailors falling madly in love with the cabaret girls. The girls would introduce them to the finer things of life and they would "fall in love", apparently. They would have taken them home to mama if they could have, but luckily for them, they didn't get the chance.

## What I Did on Liberty

What did I personally do on liberty in Yokosuka? I usually went to a restaurant first and got myself a good meal. However, there weren't Japanese restaurants there like we see in America today. There were restaurants in Japan that cooked American style food the best they knew how – food like American servicemen were accustomed to. And really there wasn't that big of a variety, as I remember. I usually got a small steak, 6 ounces, because that is the only size they served. I also got fried potatoes – Japanese style. Other than that, I can't remember what I had. However, I know I didn't eat any salads or leafy vegetables, because we were informed that that was a bad thing to do; because if you did, you would have to stay close to the head for days afterwards. All the vegetables were fertilized with "night soil" and the American digestive system wasn't accustomed to it. We didn't drink the water either for the same reason. You either drank beer, bottled coke, or nothing. I never saw any bottled water.

I would usually spend some time looking at souvenirs. The shopkeepers always had their prices jacked up in the hope that young, inexperienced sailors would drop in and pay their price. However, an experienced shopper learned to haggle with them. You never paid the marked price. If a person was sucker enough to pay it, though, the shopkeeper was always glad to take their money. He usually came off his asking price when you told him that his prices were too high and you started to walk off; that was his cue to blurt out a lower price. Most of them couldn't speak very good English – just enough to communicate with their American customers in a fashion. Oh well, haggling was something to do.

I spent some time in the cabarets, occasionally. I usually went on liberty by myself, but sometimes I would go ashore with a couple of my shipmates or would meet up with them somewhere while ashore. My usual practice was to drink a beer and, of course, buy my hostess a few drinks of colored water. If I stayed in the cabaret very long, my second drink would be a coke. And if I stayed a little longer, my third drink would be another beer. But that was it, two beers in an afternoon, or an evening, was my limit. I had no intentions of getting drunk.

One thing I always wondered about, and never asked, is where did the officers and chief petty officers go on liberty? I don't remember ever seeing them hanging out in the places the white hats went.

# JAPAN AND KOREA TO FORMOSA

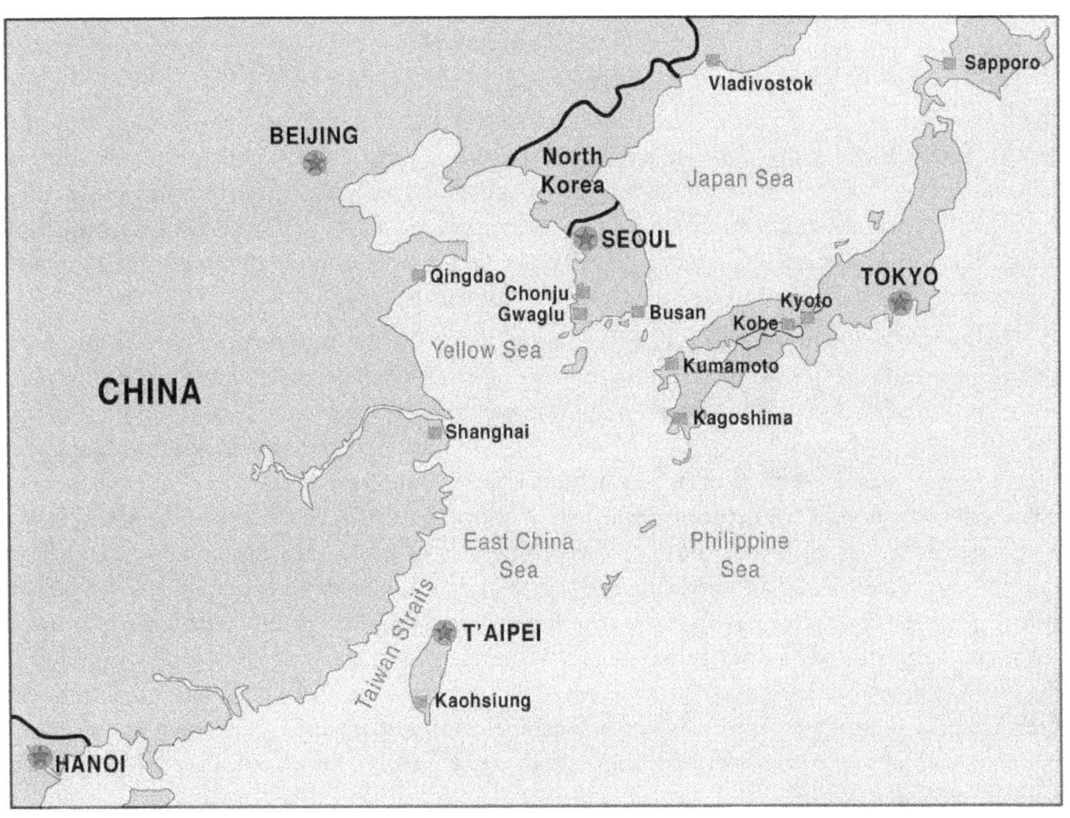


Terry Miller map, TCS

While the Brush was in port, 8 new sailors reported aboard for duty. Also, 3 of the wounded men, Ballard, Melson, and Wooten were transferred to the Naval Hospital in Yokosuka for further treatment. In addition, 3 men and 1 officer were transferred off the ship. And that is the way it was the entire time I was on the ship. Some of the old crew members were leaving the ship and new men were coming aboard. Consequently, the crew members on the ship were always slowly changing.

The ships of Destroyer Division 92 departed Yokosuka and all its pleasures, Tuesday, 2 June, 1953, en route to Buckner Bay, Okinawa. However, it wasn't a fun trip. After leaving Tokyo Bay, we joined up with 4 other ships and formed a small convoy which included the carrier, Point Cruz, and 3 ships of destroyer Division 51 – the USS Henderson(DD785), the USS Rowan(DD782), and the USS Southerland(DDR743). There were also 2 submarines that were operating with the surface ships – the USS Remora(SS487) and the USS Sabalo(SS302). However, we didn't see much of the submarines because they stayed underwater most of the time, at least during the day.

The journey from Tokyo Bay to Okinawa normally takes 1 or 2 days, but it took the convoy 7 days to reach Buckner Bay because we played around so much. The entire trip was filled with training exercises of various kinds, including flight operations with the carrier, lots of antisubmarine warfare (ASW) with the submarines, and on-going convoy exercises. The exercises went on almost continuously both day and night. Actually, it all got rather tiresome, in my opinion. But, I suppose it was all necessary for training purposes. At least, the navy thought so.

The destroyers spent a great deal of time practicing changing screening stations in the convoy. That was something that CIC and the radarmen were especially involved with. For instance, the convoy would be steaming along at 15 knots with each destroyer being in a designated screening station around the carrier – all 7 of them in this case. The object of it all was to protect the carrier from a submarine attack. Anyway, the officer in tactical command (OTC) would give the destroyers a signal to change screening stations around the carrier. Each destroyer would be assigned a new station, and it would be the responsibility of CIC and the radarmen to figure out how their ship could reach their new station without colliding with another ship. The destroyers would be dashing around all over the ocean proceeding to their new station. It was especially scary at night when all of the destroyers were scurrying about in the dark without any navigational lights on. The conning officer could only hope that CIC gave him the correct information so he could get to his new station without colliding with another ship. There wasn't any room for a mistake and seldom was. However, there have been a number of collisions involving naval ships that were operating under these conditions. In my opinion, the CIC bunch had a tough job and a critical job.

The ships finally arrived at Buckner Bay, Okinawa, Tuesday morning, 9 June, around 1000. We soon went alongside the USS Navasota(AO106) for refueling. After refueling, the Brush proceeded to anchorage B-176 and dropped anchor in 10 fathoms of water with mud and shale bottom. At 1635 the Brush weighed anchor and proceeded to go alongside the USS Faribault(AK179) to take on provisions, or foodstuff. She completed that task at 1919 and went back to her anchorage, dropped anchor, and quietly spent the night there.

## THE FORMOSA PATROL

Early the next morning, Wednesday, 10 June, the ships of Destroyer Division 92 got underway, departed Buckner Bay, and left the rest of the ships behind. We were en route to the Pescadores Islands that were located a few miles off the southeast coast of China and west of Formosa, or Taiwan, as it is called today. We were going down there to take part in what was called the "Formosa Patrol". The American Navy constantly patrolled the Formosa Strait, the strip of ocean between southeast China and Formosa, back in the 1950's to discourage the Communist Chinese from invading Formosa. The task of patrolling the Formosa Strait and protecting Formosa was largely assigned to U.S. Navy destroyers. Other types of navy ships passed through this strait frequently, too, usually on their way to Hong Kong, B.C.

**THE FORMOSA STRAIT**

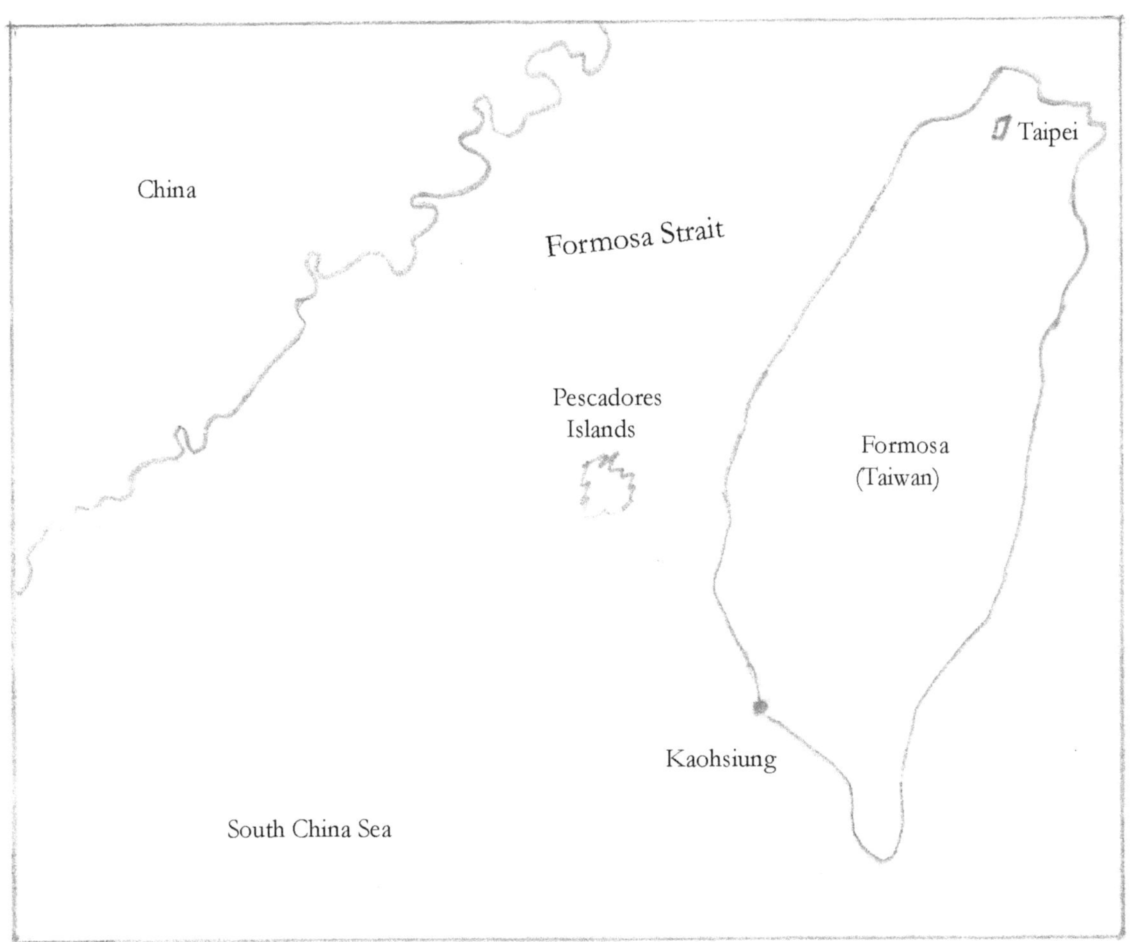

## Visiting the Pescadores Islands

DesDiv 92 arrived in Boko Ko, Pescadores Islands late Thursday afternoon, 11 June. We dropped anchor in the harbor at 1819 in seven fathoms of water with mud and sand bottom. The Brush set the regular inport watch at 1832 and here is where we spent the night. There wasn't anywhere to go. I believe there was a garrison of Nationalist Chinese troops on the island. In addition, there were some natives on the island, too, because they came out to the ship in small rowboat type craft and tried to peddle all kinds of stuff to the sailors – things that they had made. Most of what they were selling was clay vases and other objects covered in small sea shells. A lot of work went into their crafts and they sold them for very little. I'm sure that what little they got for their stuff was a lot more than they had. They looked like a very poor bunch of men to me. They tended to be very aggressive and would climb aboard the ship in a desperate effort to sell something. However, they were kept off the ship by the threat of a water hose, as I remember. Also, there were sailors stationed on the fantail with loaded rifles to help keep them off the ship. Loaded rifles are usually a pretty good deterrent.

Another item that the boat peddlers had that was quite popular with the sailors was cane bottom chairs. A number of sailors bought themselves one and used them daily until we got back to the States. A person could buy anything he wanted to from these boat people, but they couldn't take any of it back to the U.S. Whatever a sailor bought from the Pescadores Islands had to be thrown overboard before we arrived back in the States. I think it was a customs or a health issue that prohibited the sailors from bringing anything they bought there back to the continental U.S.A.

I don't remember buying anything from the boat people because I knew I couldn't keep it. We were there a number of times over the years. I wish now that I had bought something from them to just help them out because they sure needed some financial help.

Early the next morning, Friday, 12 June, the USS Navasota(AO106) arrived in the harbor and dropped anchor. The Brush almost immediately commenced making preparations for getting underway to go alongside her to refuel. The Brush went alongside her and took on 42,752 gallons of fuel oil.

Around noon, the Brush received orders from the commodore to proceed independently to the Northern Formosa Patrol area, which we did. At 1700 the Brush arrived at the northern patrol area and rendezvoused with USS Taussig(DD746), the ship that we were to relieve. At 1737 the Brush officially relieved the Taussig and she departed the area. The Brush assumed the patrol.

On the Formosa Patrol the Brush steamed up and down a few miles off the coast of China at a speed of 9 to 12 knots. We would steer a northerly course for awhile and then a southerly course for awhile. However, occasionally, we would have to depart from the regular patrol course and go and investigate a surface contact somewhere, usually at night. We also patrolled without our running lights on and in a darkened ship condition. Generally, it was rather uneventful duty which was great for a change. We saw a number of merchant ships passing by on this patrol. Some of them were British ships which were going to or coming from Hong Kong. At night there seemed to be quite a few small Chinese fishing boats in these waters.

## Sailing Down a Moonbeam

One calm, moonlit night when we were on the Formosa Patrol, we had a rather unusual experience that I've always remembered. We were steaming along rather slowly and came upon a fleet of small fishing floats, or rafts, on which there was one man. The rafts looked to be about the size of a large house door. There were dozens of these little rafts floating around on the water with one man on each one of them. The ship was among them before the OOD realized that they were there. The rafts were so low in the water that they didn't show up on radar. The sea just happened to be as smooth as glass on this particular night, otherwise these little rafts couldn't have been out there – miles from land. I don't remember seeing a light of any kind on these rafts; the moonlight was the only source of light for the fishermen. There must have been a mother ship out there somewhere, but we didn't see it or see it on radar either, as I remember.

We passed some of these little rafts very close – like 20 or 30 feet or so. Anyway, the OOD slowed the ship down to 2 or 3 knots and weaved his way through this fleet of little rafts by looking down the moonbeam. That was the only way he could see them. I always thought that was an interesting little experience we had that night. I suppose the raft men thought it was interesting, too, having that big ship among them. It would have been interesting to know what they were fishing for and if they were having any luck.

The Brush patrolled in the Formosa Strait for 3 days. Then, late in the afternoon of Monday, 15 June, we departed the northern patrol area and proceeded to rendezvous with the USS Manchester(CL83) that was steaming down from the north. Around 2000 the Brush joined up with the cruiser and assumed our usual screening station 2000 yards ahead of her. Together, the 2 ships continued on a course for Hong Kong, Victoria Island, the destination of the cruiser. We steamed all night at 24 knots. I think somebody was anxious to get there. The captain of the Manchester probably wanted to get there as soon as possible the next day in order to give his crew more time to go on liberty. Hong Kong was generally considered to be one of the best liberty ports in the Far East.

## HONG KONG

The ships arrived at the entrance to Hong Kong Harbor early in the afternoon the next day, Tuesday, 16 June. At 1252 the Brush set the special sea detail and commenced maneuvering at various courses and speeds to enter the harbor. At 1300 we passed Channel Rock Light abeam to starboard at 200 yards. At 1327 the Brush was moored to buoy B-4 in Hong Kong Harbor. The ship secured the special sea detail and set the regular inport watch at the quarterdeck. Liberty call commenced almost immediately. I didn't go ashore the first afternoon there, but I did go on liberty the following 2 days and half the nights.

### Hong Kong Titles

Hong Kong had several titles. Sometimes it was referred to as the "Pearl of the Orient" and it probably was. It was also considered to be the "Gateway to China", and another way it was referred to was that it was the "Crossroads of the World". I wouldn't disagree with any of those titles.

### Junks and Boats

I found Hong Kong harbor and the surrounding ocean to be a most interesting place. As we approached Victoria Island from seaward, we began to encounter these strange looking Chinese junks of all sizes. I had seen pictures of them but actually seeing them made me appreciate their uniqueness even more. I'm not sure you can call them beautiful, but they certainly looked different than the vessels that we normally see in the Western World. The bigger junks are seagoing vessels that have somewhat square canvas sails that were spread by battens (narrow strips of wood) that were slanted upward. They also had high sterns and a flat bottom, usually. I don't think they are seen anywhere in the world except off the coast of China. They certainly were exotic looking.

As soon as the ship got moored, we were swarmed by dozens of small, open peddler boats. The occupants of the boats had all kinds of crafts, mostly junk, that they were trying to sell us and desperate to do so it seemed. Many of them were met by a strong stream of water from a fire hose. However, they didn't seem to mind getting hosed down with water. Apparently, they were used to it. The boatmen would just retreat away from the ship until they were out of the range of the water that was directed toward them – all the while just grinning and jabbering. I'm sure they attempted to come aboard every smaller naval ship that came into the harbor. Maybe they were sometimes successful at climbing aboard and sometimes they weren't, but it was all in a day's work with them. They knew that a person can't succeed at something unless he tries. However, the Brush had been to Hong Kong a number of times before, and the older hands knew what to expect out of the peddlers and were ready for them. I'm sure some of the peddler boat people were able to sell some things to the crew later on when the situation settled down and they used a less aggressive approach in their attempt. However, I don't remember buying anything from them myself.

These little peddler boats that descended on us were about normal rowboat size but were different in shape than the boats I was accustomed to seeing back home. These Chinese boats were about 15 feet long, and the bow was pointed and curved upward to where it was 1 to 2 feet higher than the gunwales. Sometimes the stern was square and sometimes it was pointed and curved upward, too, but not quite as much as the bow. The boats were propelled by a long single scull at the stern and the operator had to stand up to use it. These boats we saw in Hong Kong Harbor were very similar to the boats we saw in the Pescadores.

## Hong Kong Harbor Scenes

# Hong Kong Harbor Scenes

## Women Painters

No sooner had the ship got moored good than a boat load of Chinese women came alongside and negotiated a deal with somebody to paint the hull of the ship. The deal was that these women would paint the sides of the ship in exchange for the ship's garbage for as long as we were in port. This business arrangement wasn't something new, however, because this practice had been going on for some years, as I understood it. This same woman and her girls had painted the hull of the Brush before on previous visits to Hong Kong, and they also did it on our next 2 visits to the harbor in the following years. I think most American ships, destroyers at least, allowed them to paint the hull of their ship for the garbage. This woman needed the garbage for something and I imagine it was to feed some hungry people somewhere. Why not let them have it? The ships were going to dump it anyway. Actually, the head painter came aboard ship at chow times and took each sailor's tray as he passed through the scullery and dumped the uneaten food into a clean garbage can. I'm not sure what she did with it after that. But, I believe these women painters ate their share of the garbage because I noticed that they were fleshed-out pretty good for Chinese women.

It is just hard to imagine that some people in the world have to resort to such measures in order to stay alive. It's a reality that the depth of poverty in many parts of the world is much deeper than what is normally found in the United States, and it has been that way for centuries. And their poverty is not the fault of the United States like so many mentally challenged people in the U. S. like to believe.

## Rickshaws

The Brush stayed in Hong Kong for two and one-half days, and I went ashore 2 of those days – Wednesday and Thursday. Our trip to Hong Kong was strictly for recreational purposes. Consequently, liberty would commence in the mornings around 1000. I found Hong Kong to be a most fascinating place, and I had a very interesting and enjoyable time ashore both days. The first day I went ashore alone, as usual, and looked over the downtown business sections and did a lot of shopping.

However, the first thing that a sailor encounters upon reaching the landing to come ashore is the old fashioned, man-drawn Chinese rickshaws. When you step on shore, the rickshaw coolies clamor for your business – to take you to the downtown business district, or wherever else you might want to go. I'm sure everybody has seen pictures of these Chinese rickshaws. They are light, high-wheeled vehicles with 2 smooth, solid, narrow tires that are about the size of bicycle tires. Two poles extend out from the body of the rickshaw between which the coolie stands and holds on to when he pulls the rickshaw. The rickshaws also have a flimsy cover that provides the passengers with some shade and a little protection from rain. As I remember, the rickshaws were only big enough to hold one person.

The coolies that pulled the rickshaws were always barefooted and pulled their passengers at a run. They also wore knee length britches that exposed the calves of their legs, which I noticed were always muscular.

The coolie-powered rickshaws were a part of old China and were probably way out of date and unnecessary even back in the 1950's, but people rode in them anyway, mainly for the novelty of it, I think. I know I did. However, I saw them all over the city with people riding in them. Maybe it was just a tradition in Hong Kong. However, I found the rickshaw coolies tended to be a little dishonest, because they always wanted to charge me more at the end of the ride than what they quoted me before the ride. I quit riding in them because of that practice. In my opinion, they were just taking advantage of anybody they could. I'm sure most Americans would just go ahead and pay them the additional amount that they demanded, and the coolies had learned that about Americans. I'm also sure that the English and Australians would have just told the coolies what they could do with themselves. They understood the culture and knew how to deal with them. The coolies had probably learned that, too, and didn't mess with them.

## Child Beggars

In addition to the rickshaw coolies, another thing the sailors encountered when they came ashore were the child beggars. If a person decided to walk downtown, instead of riding in a rickshaw or a taxi, he would be besieged by child beggars – 4, 5, and 6 year old children. My instructions about how to handle the situation was to just keep walking – don't stop. Dozens of small children would come running up to you begging for money. If you stopped and gave a few of them a few coins, that would increase the numbers around you quickly. They came running toward you from all directions. It reminded me of feeding seagulls on the beach and how they start gathering around you when you start feeding them. Some of the beggars were little girls under 6 years old that had little brothers strapped to their backs. All of them seemed desperate for you to give them something. What is a person to do under such circumstances? I kept walking like I was told to do and gave a little something to a few of them as I walked along and walked away. That was a bigger problem than I could handle. I never saw any adult beggars, however, as I remember.

## Roaming Around Hong Kong

I found Hong Kong to be a very modern city in many respects, especially in regards to its buildings, streets, utilities, stores, restaurants and the quality of life of the British people that lived there. Some of the Chinese people lived well and some of them not so well. However, the average Chinese probably lived far better in Hong Kong than any place on mainland China. There was a Chinese section of town, but I didn't venture into it because I wasn't sure it was a safe place for an American sailor to be. I could stand at the edge of it and look down the streets. Most of the Chinese, I believe, lived in apartment buildings on narrow streets – too narrow for cars to go down. I saw a lot of people walking around on the streets, a lot of Chinese signs, and a lot of laundry hanging out to dry on poles that extended out from windows.

Some other things that I noticed as I walked around the city were, for one, the meat markets. I saw a lot of dressed hogs, chickens, and ducks hanging around in the butcher shops. The chickens and ducks always had their feet and heads still attached to their bodies. The heads and necks weren't cleaned that well either and always had plenty of pin feathers on them. I don't know what the purpose was for leaving them on the head and neck. All these carcasses were just hanging around in the hot air. Around in back of the meat markets were cages, or coops, full of live chickens and ducks awaiting their fate. Another thing that caught my attention in back of the butcher shops was entrails. The entrails of fowl were stretched and hung out to dry in the hot sun. Apparently, they didn't discard anything; everything of an animal was eaten.

Another thing that caught my eye as I walked along the streets was pressed ducks that were hanging out in front of food stores. A flat duck, if you can imagine. I think they were called jelled flat ducks. I don't know what the advantage was of flattening them, but there must have had a reason. They must have been cured in some way, too, that kept them from spoiling. They didn't look too appetizing to me and they still had the pin feathers on their heads.

## Street Scenes of Hong Kong

## Shopping

Hong Kong was regarded by American sailors, and by world travelers in the know, as the place to buy things at bargain prices – like 25 to 50% of what you would pay in the States. I spent $60 in those 2 days which is like $800 in today's money, and the value of the things I bought would be somewhat more than $800 in today's money. Hong Kong dollars was the kind of money that was used in Hong Kong. When we got ashore we had to exchange American dollars for Hong Kong dollars. I've forgotten the exchange rate. I can't remember everything that I bought on my first trip to Hong Kong, but I do remember some of the things. I bought a Persian rug for one thing and several Persian rug type things that you throw around on furniture or hang on walls; I don't know what you call them, but I thought they were pretty. They are still in the family. I also bought a number of pillow cases that I thought were very pretty and foreign looking. In addition, I bought a large table cloth and several smaller ones, some cloth napkins, a bathrobe, and 4 shirts for myself. I bought all of those things at unbelievably cheap prices.

However, I might mention that in order to get the low prices, you had to stand around and haggle with the merchants. It was only when you started to turn and walk away without buying that they came down on their prices. They meant to sell you something.

## Tailor Shops

Long before we visited Hong Kong, some of my shipmates enlightened me to the fact that Hong Kong was the place to buy great tailor-made clothes at very low prices – like about one-fourth to one-half of what you would have to pay in the States. I decided I would certainly take advantage of that opportunity, but I would wait to do that on my last trip to Hong Kong before being released from the navy. I knew I wouldn't have much opportunity to wear civilian clothes until I got out of the navy so why bother to have them. As I walked around town, though, I did notice that there were dozens of tailor shops. However, they just had to wait awhile longer before getting my business.

## Old Colonial Hotels

Hong Kong had a lot of modern, well constructed buildings, but the buildings that attracted me the most in the city were the old colonial hotels. They were constructed in a style that was ideal for a tropical climate. The buildings were painted white both outside and inside. All the rooms had high ceilings and overhead fans that kept the air moving. However, they could depend on ocean breezes to keep the rooms cool much of the time. All the rooms were clean and neat, too, and they had a lot of cheap and dependable labor to keep them looking that way.

Most, if not all, the old hotels had restaurants in them, and that is where I ate most of my meals ashore. I especially liked the tropical atmosphere in these old hotel restaurants and they reminded me of days gone by. I thought the food and service was exceptionally good also. I remember having lamb chops a couple of meals because I liked lamb; I knew the British ate a lot of it and I wanted to see how they served it. I also drank hot tea with my meals just like they did to see how their tea was. It was pretty good. I was having a new experience and was enjoying it. The old colonial hotels helped me to imagine what it must have been like to be an important person of the ruling class. I liked the feeling. Somehow, I think I missed my calling. I could have comfortably fit right in with that class.

## Hong Kong Women

It was my observation that the younger Chinese women in Hong Kong were generally quite attractive in an oriental sort of way. They all seemed to have pretty faces, perfect complexions, long black hair, and well shaped, slender bodies. And, in addition, they dressed real sharp. I would like to clarify something here. When I say Hong Kong women, I'm referring to the women that lived in the city and worked in the stores, restaurants, hotels and other places. I'm not referring to the boat people or the coolie class. There was a huge difference in the appearance of these people and what I think of as "Hong Kong" women. I think anybody that has been there will understand what I mean.

I've often wondered why the "Hong Kong" women were so attractive as compared to most of the other Chinese women that I've seen. Personally, I suspect that it had something to do with the diet of a generation or two before them. The British came to Victoria Island, built a modern city, and brought a significant amount of prosperity to the area as compared to mainland China; consequently, the Chinese people that lived there got more to eat and a more varied diet. As a result, they evolved into a more attractive people. Anyway, that is my assessment of the situation. Something certainly brought about a better looking bunch of women.

## Hong Kong Dresses

The Hong Kong Women wore dresses that were different than any other place in the world, and they were known as "Hong Kong dresses", at least that is what the sailors called them. I will try to describe them. Hong Kong dresses had high collars that were stiffened with a strip of clear plastic. The dresses could be a print or a solid color. They might have been made of silk, too, but I'm not sure about that. The dresses clung to their slender bodies and showed every curve of it, which was usually great. The dresses extended about 6 inches below the knee but were slit about 12 inches up each side which showed some of the thigh as they walked along and also when they were sitting. The dresses looked like they weren't completely sewn up on the sides. So, that is generally how they were – as I described them. However, you would actually have to see them to fully appreciate their attractiveness. I think most people would agree, men at least, that they were real sexy looking dresses and the women wore them well. I've never seen those type dresses anywhere else in my travels. I don't think they would be as attractive on Western women anyway unless they looked similar to the Hong Kong women. I wonder if very many English men took one of those attractive Chinese women back home to meet the folks. I bet they did.

## British Men in Hong Kong

I could always spot the British men as far as I could see them because they always wore white clothes. They always wore a white shirt and white short pants that were about knee length. They also wore white knee-length stockings and white shoes. The British Naval officers also wore about the same type of white clothes, as I remember. However, the British Army officers wore darker clothes that were also short pants; I believe they were kind of a greenish khaki color. The British men were always neatly dressed and always walked like they had somewhere to go and something important to do. Any time I saw a man with a suit on, and maybe a brief case, I knew he was from somewhere else.

## Weather in Hong Kong

The weather in Hong Kong was very hot and it rained a lot; however, the rains weren't of a long duration. It would rain frequently both day and night. The weather would be clear and hot and suddenly it would rain hard for a few minutes. Then the rain would stop, the sun would come out again, and it would be hot and steamy. In a few minutes, or an hour or two, it would rain hard again for a few minutes and stop. The sun would shine again and it would be hot and steamy again. It kept this up all the time we were there. That is just the way the weather was in that part of the world.

## Sampan Homes

The harbor was home to hundreds, and maybe thousands, of small sampans and boat people. The sampans were about the same size and shape of the peddler boats but were maybe a little wider, and they had a little shelter over the boat at the midsection. This shelter over the middle of the boat was a mat of some kind that provided some shade and protection from rain. The sampans also had a long pole for a mast and a sail. The sails weren't canvas, however. I believe they were split bamboo and were raised if they had the need to travel very far. Most of the time, though, they moved themselves around with a scull at the stern.

People lived on the sampans full time and raised families on these boats, so we were told. This was their home and they did not have any other place to go. The story was that most of the boat people were escapees from Communist China. Apparently, these people decided they would rather live in a small boat for the rest of their lives, as free people, than live under communism – the workers paradise. That doesn't say too much for communism does it? A lot of our well-fed communistic-leaning college professors and intellectuals in the United States today could learn a lesson from the boat people if they had mind enough to learn anything.

A lot of these sampans hung around the ship and I could easily see how the boat people lived. I know that some of the people that lived on the sampans found work of some kind ashore, but the story goes that there weren't nearly enough jobs on the island for all of them. I'm sure it was quite a chore for the boat people to find a way to survive. According to what I was told, they weren't helped by the British government in any way – no welfare of any kind. After all, they weren't actually citizens of Hong Kong, and the British didn't want them there in the first place – so why feed them? It would have just encouraged more of them to come. Consequently, the boat people had to make it on their own the best way they could. The British government did tolerate them living in the harbor, however. There really wasn't much else they could do.

I know the boat people got some of their food from the harbor waters, as polluted as it was, because I saw them throw small nets in the water and bring up small fish and shell fish of some kind. They ate whatever they brought up in their nets. The fish didn't get too small for them to eat either.

I noticed the boat people ate a lot of rice that they got somehow. The women cooked it on a little portable stove. Sometimes they cooked under the shelter and sometimes in the stern of the boat – the place depended upon their notion at the moment. It's rather hard for us in the Western World to imagine that people would spend most of their lives on a small boat and struggle everyday to get enough food to survive another day. And in addition to that, these same people had been doing it for thousands of years. And some people in the United States think that they've got it tough, because their welfare check is not big enough, the TV is on the blink, the roof on their subsidized housing is leaking, and their car won't start. The poor in most countries would envy the "poor" in the United States because they have so much more than what they've got.

One of the things I noticed about poor people in foreign countries was how skinny they were. In America, on the other hand, I've noticed that a big majority of the poor people seem to be fat, especially those on welfare of some kind. I wonder why there is such a difference in the appearance of poor people between the U.S. and other places.

## Eating Rice

I noticed that many of the common Chinese people had a unique way of eating rice. I had never seen it eaten that way before. They would take their bowl of rice in one hand and put their chopsticks in the other hand; thus far, that is sort of the normal practice. Then, though, they would bring the bowl of rice up to their mouth, open their mouth, and just rake it in with quick motions of their wrist using their chopsticks. I didn't see much chewing or swallowing either. They kept their mouths open, raked the rice in it, and somehow it went down their throats without any chewing or swallowing that I could see. It was a mystery to me how they could do that. They would empty their bowls in that fashion and never close their mouths.

## Coolies

One thing that fascinated me in Hong Kong, usually near the Chinese business section, were coolies that wore black pajama-type clothes and a cone-shaped straw hat. They wore their shirts loose on them and their breeches were knee length. The men and women wore the same type clothes and were hard to tell apart at a distance. The black pajama clad coolies that I saw always had a long pole across their shoulders with a heavy load of something at each end of it. They carried this load at a fast walk, or at what I would call a "jig". They would go jigging along at a fast pace. That way of carrying something was definitely a part of old China.

## The British

Hong Kong was a British colony, of course, and had been for many years. They built the city and brought the modern world and prosperity to the area. It, undoubtedly, was the most modern city in China in the 1950's and by far the most prosperous. The Chinese people that were lucky enough to live in Hong Kong got to share and enjoy some of that prosperity, too, and as a whole were probably the most affluent people in China. Some of them were even rich. However, most of the Chinese people that I talked to didn't like the British for a couple of reasons that I am aware of. One of the reasons why the Chinese there didn't like the British was the fact that the British were foreigners on Chinese soil and they just resented them being there; even though, the British presence provided many of them with a standard of living that they never could have obtained on mainland China, especially after the communist took over. In my opinion, they really didn't appreciate what they had, and they should have been thankful that the British were there; otherwise, they would be living like their cousins on mainland China – dirt poor and starving.

Another reason that the Hong Kong Chinese didn't like the British was because they tended to be a little uppity toward them as a people and were very class and race conscious. However, the British didn't just single out the Chinese people to feel superior to; they felt themselves to be a little superior to the people in all their colonies that they controlled, according to what I have heard. However, I think that kind of attitude is just part of being the ruling class. From what I know, all the European countries that had colonies acted in much the same manner toward their subjects. In fact, from what I hear, many of the French people today consider themselves to be much superior to the people in the United States, although, I can't think of a single reason why they should feel that way. The United States accomplishments have greatly exceeded theirs in every respect, and we are a very young country compared to them.

The British, on the other hand, maybe had a reason for feeling good about themselves because they did rule over much of the world at one time and for a long time. In my opinion, if you can judge the worth of a group of people by what they have accomplished in this world, you have to give the British people a superior rating whether you like them or not. Americans haven't done so badly either as compared to the rest of the world. Personally, I like the British. The ones I have encountered in life have always treated me great.

## Victoria Peak

The second day of liberty I went ashore with the idea of just looking around some more and taking pictures. Once ashore, I ran across a couple of my shipmates and I teamed up with them. We looked around downtown some, shopped a little bit, ate dinner (lunch), and then went up to Victoria Peak, the highest point on the island. We got up to the Peak by means of a taxi. There were some spectacular views on the Peak and that is the reason we wanted to go up there. We had heard about them and wanted to see them for ourselves. On one side of the mountain there was an excellent view of the harbor and the city. There were a lot of ships in the harbor that day, and they looked mighty small from the height we were. It was worth the trip up there to be able to look down on the harbor and city. However, in the opposite direction, on the other side of the mountain, there was even a more beautiful view, in my opinion. This view looked down on a bay – Repulse Bay is what it was called, I believe. I thought the scene was indescribably beautiful.

To begin with, it was a beautiful clear day. It didn't rain while we were on the mountain. The sky was a deep blue. The green mountainside, covered in grass, sloped down to the bay way below. The water of the bay was a greenish blue and relatively calm it appeared to me from where I was. A green peninsula jutted out into the bay, and the bay was dotted with several small islands. Several junks, with their high sails, silently floated around on the bay, fishing, I suppose. Then, beyond the bay and the peninsula was the vast open ocean as far as you could see with towering thunderheads way in the distance. It was a beautiful picture that will be in my mind forever.

There was a little ivy-covered refreshment cottage on the Peak in a garden setting – a garden of grass, flowers, and shrubs, a very beautiful and quiet place. It was a hot day and my party went into the cottage to get some cold refreshments. I got an "orange squash", as it was called; I called it lemonade. In the cottage my party met up with another shipmate; he joined us and we became a foursome for the rest of the day. What do you make of salty sailors drinking lemonade? That is about like dusty cowboys drinking a glass of milk in a bar, isn't it?

In the cottage we met a middle-aged English school teacher on vacation. We struck up a conversation with the teacher, and she kind of took a liking to us young American sailors, and as a result, we all went outside to a patio table and sat around and chatted for a couple of hours. She was a very likeable, witty, and entertaining lady. She also spoke with a limey accent which made her even more interesting. Really, I think we entertained each other. She seemed to enjoy our company and attention. She referred to us as being "nice, young, American boys".

## On Victoria Peak

## On Victoria Peak

## On Victoria Peak

**The Foursome**

**The English School Teacher**
**and**
**My Three Shipmates –Names Forgotten**

She even wanted to buy us all a round of drinks, which we allowed her to do. I got another "orange squash". I don't remember what my shipmates got, but it didn't cost too much whatever it was. She told me I looked like her nephew back in England. I wonder if we were distantly related.

It was a very enjoyable couple of hours, I thought, and I think everyone else felt the same way. I went back up to the Peak twice more in the following 2 years, but it wasn't the same and I didn't stay on the Peak very long either time. The later visits back to the Peak tended to be a little sad for me. I was looking for something that wasn't there anymore. I could never relive that pleasant afternoon that I spent on Victoria Peak with my shipmates and that nice English school teacher. I didn't realize it at the time, but that time on Victoria Peak became one of the special moments of my life.

## The Priest

After a couple of enjoyable hours on Victoria Peak, my shipmates and I went back down into the city. We decided to go into the Seamen's Center, which was a place where seamen were encouraged to go and hangout. I think it was primarily there for the benefit of British merchant seamen; however, seamen from anywhere were welcome to go there. The place was actually called "Sailors Home and Seamen's Mission". We, the 4 of us, were just sitting around this table making conversation when an American Catholic priest walked up and started visiting with us. After a few minutes of getting acquainted, he proposed the idea of him touring us around the city in his car and insisted on it. We saw no reason to not take him up on his offer and agreed to it. His name was George N. Gillingan – thus Father Gillingan. It developed that he had been in China for 14 years and could speak the language fluently. Anyway, he was a real nice older fellow. He must have been in his 50's. We had a great time touring around the island with him, and I think he enjoyed touring us around as much as we enjoyed being toured. He told us that he wanted to show us around the island to keep us out of trouble. Actually, what he meant was – to keep us out of the bars and away from willing women. It worked. One of the places that Father Gillingan took us to was a place called Tiger Balm Gardens. It was a most unusual place. As I remember, this garden was full of strange looking Chinese statues. The garden was built by a rich Hong Kong Chinese. But I think a person had to be raised in China to understand the meaning of those wild-looking statues.

Right at dark, the Priest took us back to the Seamen's Mission and we had supper there. After supper we all went out on the veranda that overlooked the harbor, sat around in white wicker chairs, and talked for a couple more hours. Around 2300, I decided it was time for me to go back to the ship, and did, and left my shipmates there. It had been a good day and a very enjoyable liberty.

The Priest wrote my mother a letter and told her what a good son she had. I read the letter many years later; however, I don't know what happened to the letter. It has been put away somewhere. Maybe somebody will find it again one day.

## FORMOSA PATROL CONTINUED

At 0945, Friday, 19 June, the Brush got underway and proceeded out of Hong Kong Harbor en route to Boko Ko, Pescadores Islands. We cruised all day and night at a speed of 16 knots and on a course of around 073° until we arrived at the Pescadores. We arrived at Boko Ko around 0545 Saturday morning, 20 June, 1953. We went alongside the USS Navasota(A0106) to take on fuel. As soon as the Brush completed refueling at 0730, she proceeded out of the harbor and headed toward the northern patrol area in the Formosa Strait. At 1358 the Brush arrived on station and commenced patrolling. She patrolled at a speed of around 12 knots most of the time. On this patrol, the Brush also patrolled the southern section some of the time. I guess we were the only destroyer present in the strait during this patrol. According to the ship's log, we were steaming off the east coast of China in the Formosa Strait in defense of the island of Formosa and the Pescadores Islands. We always patrolled in a darkened ship condition at night and without the navigational lights on. We investigated every ship and boat that we sighted both day and night. However, we never saw anything that was from mainland China, unless it was small fishing boats which we didn't bother with. A number of British merchant ships passed us on the way to Hong Kong, which I always found interesting because I knew that they traveled all over the world like I wanted to do.

At 0047, 24 June, the Thomas relieved the Brush of the southern patrol, and we assumed the northern patrol for a few hours. At 0530, however, we left our Formosa Patrol station and proceeded to Kaohsiung. The Brush had patrolled in the strait for around 5 days on this occasion, all alone, I believe. The Brush arrived in Kaohsiung that afternoon at 1500. The first thing we did upon reaching Kaohsiung was to go alongside the Navasota again for refueling. It seemed like the tanker was waiting on us everywhere we went. She was Destroyer Division 92's gas station for this particular time in our tour. The tanker wasn't the only thing waiting on us when we came into Kaohsiung; several men were there also. While we were refueling alongside the tanker, 7 men reported aboard for duty, including 3 officers: Ensigns Jordon, Cates, and Hart. I became pretty good friends with Ensign Cates over time, at least, as much as an officer and an enlisted man can be. In addition, 2 officers and 3 enlisted men came aboard for temporary duty a little later after we completed refueling and had moved to our berth. At 1742 we moored to buoy 10. Liberty was granted that evening in Kaohsiung but not very many men went ashore because there really wasn't much to see or do except drink beer. A few of those inclined to do that went ashore, but most of those that did didn't care to go ashore. In addition to that, women were scarce and not too cooperative, so the scuttlebutt was. Furthermore, the risk of bringing home something you didn't want from the women that were available was very high, according to some of the old salts. All in all, Kaohsiung was not a good liberty port, and I never went ashore there on this cruise.

The Brush wasn't sent to Kaohsiung for recreational purposes anyway. She was sent there to give some on-hands training to some Nationalist Chinese Naval personnel – both officers and enlisted men. Consequently, the next morning at 0600, Thursday, 25 June, 8 officers and 30 enlisted men came aboard for training in gunnery, CIC, and damage control.

The Brush got underway at 0825 and proceeded out of the harbor for a day of training at sea. We also rendezvoused with a couple of Nationalist Chinese destroyer escorts and conducted a flaghoist drill with them for 30 minutes or so. It was an intense day of training for the Chinese sailors. The Brush went back into Kaohsiung Harbor late that afternoon and moored at buoy 10 again. The Chinese sailors disembarked.

The next morning at 0830 the same 38 Nationalist Chinese Naval personnel came aboard; the Brush got underway and proceeded out to sea for a morning of gunnery practice and aircraft tracking exercises. At 0930 an aircraft towing a sleeve showed up, and the ship went to general quarters for the gunnery practice. At 0935 the gunnery practice commenced and lasted for about 2 hours with the Chinese sailors doing some of the shooting. During the gunnery practice the Brush expended 68 rounds of 5"/38 AA shells and 112 rounds of 40mm shells. Gunnery training was completed at 1143 and the Brush returned to Kaohsiung. At 1445 the Brush was moored to buoy 10 and there she spent the night.

The next morning, 27 June, the Nationalist Chinese sailors came aboard again for training, but the Brush never left the harbor this time. At 1115 the Chinese sailors left the ship; their training was completed. The ship spent the rest of the day idle in port.

Around 1100, Sunday, 28 June, the Brush got underway, departed Kaohsiung Harbor and set a course for Boko Ko, Pescadores Islands. She arrived there that afternoon around 1630. At 1637 the Brush dropped anchor in Boko Ko in 7.5 fathoms of water with muddy bottom. Here we spent a quiet night.

At 0547 Monday morning, 29 June, 3 ships of Destroyer Division 52 stood into the harbor and dropped anchor. These were the ships that were going to relieve Destroyer Division 92 from the Formosa Patrol. These ships were the USS Brinkley Bass(DD887), USS Bradford(DD545), and USS Taylor(DD468). At 0635 the USS Maddox stood into the harbor and dropped anchor. Around noon the Brush and the Maddox got underway and proceeded out of the harbor en route to Sasebo, Japan. The Brush took station 500 yards astern of the Maddox. They steamed toward Japan at a speed of 18 knots and on a base course of 047°(t). At night, they increased the distance between them to 1000 yards. En route to Sasebo there was not any drills or practicing of any kind. We just steadily steamed toward Japan which was rather enjoyable.

## SASEBO – JULY

We made landfall Wednesday morning, 1 July, at 0919 when we sighted Ohiki Jima bearing 020° (t) at a distance of 9 miles. Then, we began to sight other things as we got closer to our destination. At 0930 we sighted Odate Shima light at a distance of 14 miles. At 0946 we sighted Mitoko Shima at a distance of 10 miles. We sighted a number of other navigational objects as we steamed along the coast of Japan toward Sasebo. At 1051 we commenced maneuvering at various courses and speeds to enter the harbor. At 1108 we entered Sasebo Harbor but commenced lying to to await berthing instructions. We had to wait awhile, but finally the Brush received instructions to go alongside the USS Hector(AR7) at buoy 16. The Brush proceeded to do that, and at 1231 we moored port side to the Moore that was moored to the USS Henrico(PA45) that was moored to the Hector. So, we were in a nest of ships. A little later in the day the Maddox and the Thomas came in port and moored in the same nest, as did the USS McGinty(DE365). Berthing places must have been scarce on that day to berth us all at buoy 16. Liberty started around 1500.

The Brush stayed in port for ten and a half days which was somewhat longer than usual. We didn't leave port until 12 July. Liberty started in the late morning or early afternoon every day. Of course, it was over at 2300, as usual, and everybody was expected to be back on the ship by that time and were in trouble if they weren't. It was just a fact of navy life, though, that some of the crew would be late coming back aboard almost every liberty. Consequently, they would have to go before the man for punishment. A sailor that comes in late off of liberty very much doesn't stand much chance of getting promoted to a petty officer. And if a petty officer comes in late a time or two he can expect to be demoted. On this occasion in port, 3 first class petty officers went AWOL together for approximately one day. Upon coming back aboard a day late, they were all immediately demoted to second class petty officers. That was a big price to pay for their indiscretion. I don't know what they were thinking about; they should have known better.

It seemed the main focus of our stay in port was just to allow the men to go on liberty. We didn't do much else other than that. However, there were a few other things that took place. One day, Thursday, 9 July, a rear admiral Olsen came aboard and presented purple hearts to 3 of our crew members – R.P. Erwin GM3, C.E. Wentworth SN, and R.R. Wooten SK3. Also, the captain conducted a lower decks inspection one afternoon, and the next morning he held a personnel inspection. Everybody usually passed inspection and made a special effort to do so. You were probably in trouble if you didn't pass inspection for some reason. So, the reasoning of the crew was– why make life difficult for yourself?

Sunday, 12 July, at 0415 the Brush commenced making preparations for getting underway. At 0520 the crew was mustered on station, and it was determined that there weren't any absentees. At 0630 the ship got underway and proceeded out of the harbor at various courses and speeds to conform to the channel. At 0659 we passed through the submarine net into the open ocean en route to operating area Sugar off the east coast of Korea. Soon after departing Sasebo Harbor the Brush joined up with the Maddox and fell in 1000 yards astern of her. At 0810 the Moore joined the formation and fell in 1000 yards astern of the Brush. The 3 ships steamed toward North Korea at a speed of 18 knots and generally maintained that speed until they arrived on station.

## OPERATING WITH TASK FORCE 77

The ships of DesDiv 92 were going to be operating with Task Force 77 this time out off North Korea. Task Force 77 usually consisted of 2 to 4 aircraft carriers and 5 to 10 destroyers. Other types of ships were also present sometimes, including replenishment ships like tankers and ammunition ships.

At 0642, 13 July, we sighted the task force at a distance of 15 miles, and at 0845 we caught up with it and joined them. The task force at that particular time consisted of the carriers, USS Princeton(CVA37) and the USS Boxer(CVA21), and 4 destroyers, the USS Bronson(DD668), the USS O'Bannon(DDE450), the USS Fletcher(DDE445), and the USS Carpenter(DDE825). Of course, the ships of DesDiv 92 increased the number of destroyers to 7. However, the Maddox immediately left the task force to go on some kind of "special mission". But the Thomas joined the task force on 15 July. The task force steamed up and down the coast about 20 miles offshore and conducted flight operations against communist positions and installations on the mainland.

Operating with Task Force 77 was a very busy time. The carriers launched and retrieved planes off and on all day long and at night some, too; thus, the task force was steaming at a speed of 25 to 27 knots much of the time as they were launching and landing aircraft. At night, Task Force 77 slowed down to a speed of 10 to 15 knots except when they were conducting flight operations. Of course, the destroyers formed a protective screen around the carriers and other large ships that might be present in the task force. However, the destroyers didn't assume a screening station and stay there; instead, they were constantly changing stations in the screen. Consequently, the destroyers were dashing around all over the ocean in the process of reaching their new stations. It's a wonder they didn't run into each other, especially in the dark.

**The Brush on plane guard station astern the Princeton**

In addition to all that dashing about, destroyers were frequently leaving the formation for what they called "detached duty" somewhere else. Also, different destroyers were constantly joining the formation for a day or several days. Some of the destroyers that joined up with the task force while we were a part of it were the USS Cotton(DD669), USS Blue(DD744), USS McKean(DDR784), USS Frank E Evans(DD754), USS Smalley(DD565), USS Alfred A Cunningham(DD752), and the John A. Bole(DD755).

In addition to the destroyers joining the task force, some carriers did, too. Monday night at 2245, 13 July, the USS Lake Champlain(CVA39) joined the task force and the next day assumed tactical command. Later, on Friday, 17 July, the Philippine Sea(CVA47) joined the task force. So, from then until the end of the conflict there were 4 aircraft carriers and all their planes operating off the east coast of Korea; all together, they must have carried over 300 aircraft. As I remember it, there were 3 kinds of winged aircraft aboard the carriers. They were the Banshee and the F9F Panther jet planes and 1 propeller-driven plane – the Skyraider. The Skyraiders were very good ground support planes because they were somewhat slower than the jets.

A weather thing that the task force had to contend with sometimes was fog. For several days we were going in and out of fog banks where the visibility would be reduced to 100 to 500 yards. Occasionally, flight operations would have to be delayed until the visibility improved. It was a strange thing. We would be in dense fog for awhile, then all of a sudden the task force would break out of it and the visibility would abruptly increase to 5 to 10 miles or more.

On one day we had some pretty rough seas, but most of the time strong winds and rough seas didn't present a problem while we were with the task force. In fact, most of the time the wind speeds were from 5 to 15 mph and the seas just had a light chop.

Operating with Task Force 77 was very breezy duty because aircraft were constantly either taking off or landing all day and half the night. As I've previously mentioned, the carriers usually conducted flight operations at a speed of around 25 knots and were always headed into the wind when doing so, if there was any. Consequently, the men on the bridge and deck, too, had to face a wind of 35 to 40 knots much of the time; that was certainly enough wind to mess up your hairdo.

The Brush certainly spent her full share of time in "plane guard station" 1000 yards behind one of the carriers.

We only witnessed one serious incident involving aircraft during our tour with the carriers. On Monday, 20 July, at 1458 three of the carriers – the Princeton, Boxer, and Philippine Sea – commenced launching aircraft. We were steaming along about 1000 yards off the starboard beam of the Philippine Sea. I was standing on the port side of the signal bridge just watching the planes take off; that is what we did for entertainment during the times that we didn't have anything better to do. At 1504 this F9F Panther jet took off from the Philippine Sea, but instead of gradually gaining altitude like they normally did, it gradually lost altitude until it went into the drink and sank immediately. However, the pilot was able to get out of the plane and didn't go down with it. The plane disappeared in the water so fast, though, that I didn't think the pilot had a chance of getting out of it, but he did. Although, the plane was probably under water before he was able to free himself from it. The Brush commenced maneuvering around to reach the site of the crash in a rescue effort, but the plane guard helicopter was hovering over the pilot in a matter of seconds after the plane hit the water and pulled him up to safety. The pilot was probably in the water for less than a minute. I thought that was quick action on the part of the helicopter crew and they were to be commended.

The task force was racing up and down the coast so much at 25 to 27 knots that the ships were using a lot of fuel oil and needed to be replenished frequently. Consequently, the ships had to rendezvous with a tanker about every other day and take on fuel. In addition, the carriers had to be re-supplied with ammunition for the planes – rockets, and maybe bombs, too; I'm not sure what they took on, but they went alongside ammunition ships frequently. The tankers that came out to bring the ships fuel oil were the USS Cimarron(A022), USS Passumpsic(A0107), USS Caliente(A053), USS Chikaskia(A054), and the USS Navasota(A0106). The ships that re-supplied the carriers with ordnance were the USS Firedrake(AE14), USS Mt Katmai(AE16), USS Vesuvius(AE15), and the USS Mt Baker(AE4). A supply ship also came out a couple of times to provide the ships with fresh and frozen provision; this ship was the Grafias(AF29). The first time the Brush went alongside her, she received 3500 pounds of provisions, the second time, 29,777 pounds. The ships were replenished with fuel oil, ammo, and provisions at night about half of the time. This replenishment business was a big task because there were so many ships involved.

There was an all hands working party every time provisions were brought aboard, and everybody that wasn't on watch, or sick, had to participate in it. The crew formed a line from the main deck down to the reefers, or wherever the provisions were going to be stored. There was one thing for sure, if there was any fresh fruit among the provisions, all of it didn't get to the reefers. Because we didn't get much fresh fruit and everybody was starved for it. A box would be broken into early in the line and everybody that handled the box would help himself to one or two pieces when it went by him. I'm sure some of the boxes arrived at the reefers empty. So, the commissary personnel knew that this petty thievery was going on and the officers, too, but what could they do about it? They did the only sensible thing they could do; they turned a blind eye to the practice. From the crew's perspective, we got the fruit and ate it as fast as we could so as not be caught with it in our pockets. There wasn't any thought given to washing it to get the germs and pesticides off it either. After all, we were just trying to prevent ourselves from getting scurvy, you know. The kinds of fresh fruit that I remember us receiving aboard from time to time were oranges, pears, plums, and apples. These types of fruit tended to keep well. It was probably all California grown and they tasted mighty good.

## Detached Duty with the Battleship New Jersey

On Wednesday, 22 July, the Brush received her "detached duty" orders. At 0400 the Brush was detached from Task Force 77 to proceed to the USS New Jersey(BB62) and assume the duty as her screening ship for the next 5 days. It so happened that the commander of the 7th Fleet was embarked in the battleship – a real big shot. I imagine the accommodations for an admiral was pretty good on a battleship, too. We were now part of Task Group 70.1.

At 0730 we sighted the battleship at a distance of 4 miles, and at 0745 the Brush was on station 3000 yards ahead of her. When we were operating with the New Jersey, we were usually 3000 yards ahead of her when we were steaming along the coast. Or, if the battleship was just lying to, the Brush stayed 3000 yards to seaward of her – sometimes slowly steaming back and forth or lying to herself. The battleship was usually lying to when she was engaged in shore bombardment.

Upon rendezvousing, the 2 ships proceeded to close the coast in the vicinity of the Bombline. At 1500 the New Jersey reached a position about 6000 yards off the beach and commenced lying to. Soon thereafter, she commenced firing her big 16 inch guns at targets miles inland. It is my understanding that the battleship could shoot their huge 16 inch shells 15 miles or more.

The New Jersey fired her big guns for about 3 hours on this occasion. While the battleship was involved with firing her guns, the Brush took a position 3000 yards to seaward of her and slowly steamed around some of the time and was also lying to some of the time.

The battleship's big 16 inch guns are awesome things. Every time she blasted out a salvo, which was every few minutes, our ship would shudder at 3000 yards away because the concussion was so great. Also, there would be a tremendous cloud of smoke every time their guns fired. I think they always fired all three guns in the mount at the same time. Around 1800 the New Jersey ceased firing and got underway. The Brush again assumed her screening station 3000 yards ahead of her. The 2 ships started patrolling along the coast on north and south courses. At 2247 the Brush left her screening station and proceeded to rendezvous with the USS Whetstone(LSD27) to affect a mail transfer. At 2324 the Brush rendezvoused with the LSD and commenced lying to to receive the LSD alongside for the mail transfer. At 2342 the mail transfer was completed. We received 43 bags of U.S. mail aboard for further transfer to the New Jersey. Upon completion of the mail transfer, we returned to the battleship and assumed our screening station 3000 yards to seaward of her. We rejoined the New Jersey at 0020. The battleship was again back in the vicinity of the Bombline and was conducting a fire mission.

Around 0300 the battleship ceased firing, got underway, and we steamed down the coast. Early the next morning, 23 July, the Brush delivered the 43 bags of mail to the New Jersey by small boat. I'm sure it made a lot of sailors happy. We didn't get any. After all, we were just a destroyer and not too important compared to the battleship.

Most of Thursday, 23 July, wasn't too eventful. The battleship did do a little firing during the morning part of the day, but we mainly just steamed up and down the coast. In the afternoon we did conduct a man overboard drill and a steering casualty drill – I think for something to do. However, at 2030 that evening we were detached from the New Jersey and proceeded to take station for harassing and interdiction firing at targets around the Bombline. We commenced firing our main battery at 2112 and fired until 0252. During the night the Brush expended 60 rounds of 5″/38 high capacity shells. While the Brush was engaged in her firing, she was slowly steaming around at 7 knots. We didn't know it at the time, but that was the last firing that the Brush would do during the Korean War. The war was about over.

Upon completion of the fire mission the Brush rejoined the battleship. At 0800 the New Jersey started firing at enemy positions north of the Bombline. At 0950 the Brush was detached from CTG 70.1 to proceed to rendezvous with the tanker, USS Chikaskia(A054), for refueling. Around 1100 the Brush had completed refueling and proceeded to rejoin the New Jersey. Nothing of any consequence happened the rest of the day. Later in the day the New Jersey set a course for Hungnam with the Brush leading the way. Task Group 70.1 arrived off the coast of Hungnam around 0830 Saturday, 25 July, and the New Jersey soon thereafter commenced the bombardment of Hungnam. As usual, the Brush was screening the battleship 3000 yards to seaward at a speed of 5 knots.

At 1118 the Brush was alerted that there was going to be a plane crash in the vicinity. The New Jersey ceased her firing at 1130, and the ships headed in the direction of the plane crash at a speed of 25 knots. At 1207 the Brush was detached from the battleship to proceed independently to the crash site as indicated by an emergency IFF. The Brush increased speed to 27 knots. At 1400 we sighted the USS Cocopa(ATF101) bearing 055°(t) at a distance of 12 miles. The Cocopa reported to the Brush that they had the body of the pilot on board. There was nothing else we could do about the plane crash incident, so the Brush turned around and headed back toward the battleship.

It turned out that the Cocopa was also informed about the plane crash and proceeded toward it. They were closer to the plane crash site than the Brush was so they reached it first. The Cocopa arrived at the crash site at 1336 and found the parachute floating in the water with the pilot still attached to it. The pilot apparently had bailed out of his plane. The Cocopa hoisted the pilot and parachute on board as quickly as they could but the pilot was dead. His name was Jack William Ingram, Jr., Lt(jg) The tug was instructed to take the pilot's body to the New Jersey and that is what she did. The tug rendezvoused with the battleship and transferred the body to her around 1500.

Ingram sure picked a poor time to die because the war was going to be over in just another day or two. He was probably the last navy pilot to die during the Korean War, certainly one of the very last. He was a F9F pilot, but we never knew the reason for the crash, or which carrier he came from.

We rejoined the battleship at 1415 which was trailing us during the rescue attempt and wasn't too far behind us.

Late Saturday afternoon at 1710 the New Jersey did some more firing of her 16 inch guns at installations on the mainland around Hungnam, I believe. However, the formation was steaming along at 10 knots on this firing session. She usually was lying to when she was engaged in firing her 16 inch guns.

Saturday night at 2230 the New Jersey commenced lying to offshore from a place called Kiammi-Tachon, lowered her motor whaleboat into the water and sent it toward the beach. Of course, the Brush was screening her to seaward. I'm not sure why they sent the small boat closer to shore unless it was to observe the shoreline in an effort to spot a train. In some places the North Korean railroad tracks were right close to the ocean and the trains were vulnerable in these places. It was difficult to see the trains, especially at night, at the distance the battleship stayed offshore. The battleship did fire a few shots toward the railroad tracks, but apparently she was unsuccessful at hitting a train because we didn't see any evidence that she did such as fires, an explosion, and such.

Around 0130, Sunday, 26 July, Task Group 70.1 got underway and headed south toward Wonsan and arrived there at 0830. At 0835 the New Jersey commenced firing her main batteries at enemy installations around Wonsan Harbor. The last shots the New Jersey fired during the Korean War was here at Wonsan on this day. In fact, Sunday, 26 July, was the last shooting day of the war, as far as I know. The battleship shot for an hour or so, left the harbor, and we went out to sea.

The rest of the day was spent rendezvousing with other ships for some purpose, such as receiving new crewmen aboard or refueling. First, we rendezvoused with the USS Uvalde(AKA88) and both the Brush and the New Jersey received some new personnel aboard. At 1338 the Uvalde's LCM came alongside the Brush and delivered 6 new crewmen to us, all seamen apprentice (SA) and firemen apprentice (FA). They barely made it to the Korean War.

Next, Task Group 70.1 headed south to the Bombline to rendezvous with the USS Bremerton(CA130) to receive some more personnel aboard. The Brush received 5 more new seamen from the cruiser and 3 more men that were returning aboard for duty, including Ballard SN, who was one of the wounded. I thought it was interesting that we got 11 new men aboard on the last day of the shooting war in Korea. The Bremerton transferred these 8 men to us by way of a highline. Next, we went alongside the New Jersey to transfer 2 seamen to her via highline. With that task completed, around 1900, Task Group 70.1 set a course to return to Task Force 77. We rendezvoused with the task force at around 2030 and the Brush was assigned a screening station around the formation. At this time our operating with the battleship was over and the war was essentially over, too.

## The War Ends

Monday, 27 July, 1953, was the day that a cease fire was declared in the Korean War. I was glad at the time, but I didn't know enough about world affairs at that point in my life to know whether it was a good thing or a bad thing. The only thing I knew for sure was that I wasn't too interested in dying for my country in Korea and didn't know anybody that was. In fact, I contend that normally men in combat don't give their lives for their country anyway – it is taken from them against their will.

The sailors on destroyers got very little news about anything that was happening in the world unless they got some information in a letter from home. We lived in our own little world on the ship and it was a little world. However, knowing what I know now, and the way things have turned out in regards to North Korea, I fully agree with General Douglas MacArthur that there is no substitute for victory. We should have finished the job while we were there. In my opinion, it is absolutely criminal for politicians to send young men into war and not allow them to win it. If it isn't worth winning – then don't send them to fight it. There needs to be a victory, short of that, everyone that dies in the conflict, dies for nothing. They gave their lives for nothing, in my opinion. In other words, limited war sucks. It only enables a weaker foe to win. And, in my opinion, any of our leaders – politicians, generals, or whoever – that send young men to fight limited wars, without being allowed to win it, suck, too.

In addition, if it becomes necessary to do some negotiating with an enemy country, we should be kicking ass while we are negotiating in order to put them in a little more receptive frame of mind. It has been my observation over the years that the United States is the world's worst negotiator. Her only approach to it seems to be to give away the farm and to believe anything our opponents say they will do, which they never plan to do. It seems like our politicians and leaders never learn.

## Task Force 77 After the War

Anyway, as far as activity in Task Force 77 was concerned, there seemed to be just about as much of it on the 27th as any other day. Flight operations were being conducted from the carriers, and destroyers were dashing about changing stations in the screen as much as ever. However, I assume, though, that the planes weren't attacking anything. That may have been the only difference.

Early in the morning of the 27th, 4 destroyers left the formation and late in the day the New Jersey left the formation. On the next day, 28 July, the carriers, Lake Champlain and the Philippine Sea, were detached from the task force to proceed to Japan. Then, a little later in the day the USS Jupiter(AVS8) was detached from the formation to proceed to Japan also. There were relatively few flight operations conducted on the 28th; nor did the destroyers have to do much dashing about changing screening stations either.

We were part of Task Force 77 for an additional 14 days. The war was over and the grueling activities of the task force slowed down to some extent. There were fewer flights after the 27th. The task force really didn't have anything important to do. To occupy us a little, we began to have anti aircraft gunnery practice in the afternoons of about half the days. An airplane towing a sleeve at the end of a long cable would fly over and the gunners would shoot at it either with the 5″/38's or the 40mm rapid fire guns. The Brush's gunners were pretty good at hitting or knocking down the sleeves. However, those towing planes were much slower than a fast jet; with those, I don't think they could have done as well. On Wednesday, 29 July, the Brush expended 17 rounds of 5″/38 AA common shells. On the 30th, the Brush expended 12 rounds of 5″/38 AA common and 270 rounds of 40mm shells. On the 31st, the ship expended 29 rounds of 5″/38 AA common shells. On the 3rd of August, the ship expended 54 rounds of 5″/38 AA Common shells. On the 4th, the ship expended 54 rounds of 5″/38 AA common shells. And on the 7th, she expended 40 rounds of 5″/38 AA common shells. Oh well, it was something to do to occupy our time.

There must have been a change of mind by someone concerning the carriers because early in the morning of, 1 August, the Lake Champlain returned to the formation and the Princeton left. She was gone just about enough time to get to Yokosuka and turn around and come back. I bet that was a bunch of disappointed sailors on the Lake Champlain.

Task Force 77 continued to cruise up and down the coast as they did before, but the war was over and they launched much fewer planes. Of course, it was necessary for the ships to refuel every 2 or 3 days and that took up some time. However, nothing of real significance happened the rest of the time we spent with the task force. Some of the destroyers left the formation and others came in and took their place. Also, the cruiser, Quincy(CA71), joined the task force, 5 August, probably from lack of anything better to do. In addition, the carrier, USS Kearsarge(CVA33), joined the formation, Saturday, 8 August, and the Boxer departed the task force for Japan.

Finally, it came Destroyer Division 92's time to leave, and early on Monday morning, 10 August, we were detached from Task Force 77 along with the cruiser, Quincy (CA71). We headed for Yokosuka, Japan by way of Shimonoseki Strait. The Quincy was OTC. However, at 0748 the formation rendezvoused with the Bremerton(CA130), and she also accompanied us to Japan and as OTC. We passed through the strait around the middle of the afternoon on our way to Yokosuka. Most of the time the 6 ships were steaming in a column formation with the Bremerton in the lead and the Brush bringing up the rear. There were 1000 yards between ships. The formation was traveling at a speed of 15 knots.

The ships of DesDiv 92 arrived in Yokosuka early Wednesday morning, 12 August, and moored at buoy B-7. The Brush moored port side to the Maddox at 0644, and the Moore moored to our starboard side at 0700. At 0718 the regular inport watch was set.

At 1415 that afternoon 5 firemen apprentice reported aboard for duty. How unfortunate for them; the cruise was over and they had just missed out on all the fun and excitement. That was sure bad timing.

DesDiv 92 only stayed in port 2 days this time in. However, that gave the crews enough time to buy a few souvenirs for the wives, girlfriends, and the folks back home. In addition, I think everybody made a point of behaving themselves and coming back to the ship from liberty on time, because the ships were headed back to the States and nobody wanted to be left behind. When muster was taken on the morning of departure, there were not any absentees.

At 1010 Thursday morning, 13 August, there was a ceremony held on board for the presentation of awards to some of the officers and enlisted men. The commander of Destroyer Division 92 came aboard and awarded the bronze star to the captain, Cdr. D.F. Quigley. He presented the commendation ribbon to Lt. H.E. Childers, Lt. A.N. Beaty, J.W. Calvert GM1, G.C. Leiby SK3, R.P. Erwin GM3, and D.C. Straley SN. The presentations of awards were the only significant thing that happened while we were in port. I missed the ceremony. I must have been on liberty at the time it took place. Somehow, I didn't get the word that it was going to take place. If I had known about it, I would have stayed on board long enough to witness it.

**Captain Quigley Being Awarded the Bronze Star**

## HOMEWARD BOUND

Early Friday morning, 14 August, DesDiv 92 departed Yokosuka Harbor en route to Pearl Harbor, Hawaii via Midway Island. At 0817 we stood out to sea from Tokyo Bay. The ships joined up into a column formation with the Maddox in the lead and the Brush bringing up the rear as usual. They were cruising at a speed of 16 knots. However, around 1500 the ships changed formation into a line abreast at 1500 yards apart. So for the next 5 days DesDiv 92 steamed toward Midway at 16 knots in a line abreast and at 1000 to 1500 yards apart. There was essentially no maneuvering or drilling of any kind. It seemed the commodore was just content for his ships to steam east toward home. Nothing eventful took place which was wonderful for a change. I would say everybody was tired and worn out after 6 months of constantly going with little rest.

We did encounter one thing that was interesting to me on the way to Midway. We passed by the Coast Guard ship, USCG Finch(WDC428), that was patrolling a weather station, Weather Station Victor, which was hundreds of miles from the nearest land – that being Midway to the east and Japan to the west. She was just steaming around in a relatively small area out there in that big ocean all by herself and probably did so for weeks at a time. It looked like boring duty to me. In addition to that, they had to face the weather, I'm sure, regardless of how bad it may get. However, the ocean was relatively calm the day we passed her. It appeared to me like it would be quiet, un-stressful duty most of the time – but boring.

We made landfall on Midway Island around 0730 Wednesday, 19 August, when we sighted the lighthouse on the island. The ship set the special detail at 0847 and commenced maneuvering to conform to the channel that led into the lagoon where we would dock. At 0925 we entered the lagoon and went alongside the Moore at pier 2 to receive fuel oil. At 0953 the ship secured the special sea detail and set the inport watch. At 1012 the ship commenced receiving fuel. The ship completed refueling at 1400 and had received 97,623 gallons. The ships of DesDiv 92 got underway around 1400 and proceeded out of the lagoon to continue on to Pearl Harbor.

### Midway Island

Midway Island is a speck of sand out in the middle of the Pacific Ocean that is located about 1000 miles northwest of Pearl Harbor. It is actually part of the Hawaiian chain of islands. The island is barely out of the sea. The highest point on it is probably only 10 to 15 feet above sea level. It's about 1 square mile in size and there are also 2 or 3 smaller islands around it. The only trees I saw on the island were young, medium-size Australian pines that had been planted a few years previously.

I believe Midway was used by the U.S. Navy primarily as a refueling station for smaller naval vessels and for airplanes, too, since there is an airstrip there. The fueling docks were located in a small lagoon on the east side of the island and the ships had to go through a narrow channel between 2 islands to get to them. Midway was probably a weather station also since it is so far from anywhere else. Midway Island is also a major nesting place for Albatrosses, a large sea bird. But I will write more about that later.

On Thursday, 20 August, the ships conducted what they call a "full power run" during which the ships gradually increased their speed to 32 knots. The Brush commenced her "full power run" at 0530. She achieved that speed at 0704 and maintained it for 5 hours. Just before completing the "full power run", she tested her rudder to see if it would respond properly at that speed. It did. The captain started slowly decreasing the speed over the next hour until it reached 18 knots – the formation speed at the time. The ships now formed-up into a line abreast for the rest of the day. The trip between Midway and Hawaii was filled with ship exercises of various kinds after Wednesday. No more just steaming along. However, it only took around two and a half days to get to Hawaii.

## Pearl Harbor

The ships of DesDiv 92 arrived at Pearl Harbor late Saturday morning, 22 August, 1953. We sighted the island of Oahu at 0508 bearing 073°(t) at a distance of 53 miles. At 0725 the ships shifted into a column formation at a standard distance of 500 yards between ships. At 0805 we sighted Barber's Point light bearing 055°(t) at a distance of 10.5 miles. We sighted Koko Head bearing 082°(t) at a distance of 29 miles at 0816. At 0829 we sighted Diamond Head light at a distance of 19 miles. At 0844 we passed Barber's Point light abeam to port at a distance of 5 miles. At 0910 the Brush was detached from the formation to proceed independently into port. We began maneuvering at various courses and speeds to conform to the Pearl Harbor entrance channel. At 1018 the Brush was moored starboard side to berth M-3, Pearl Harbor, Hawaii. At 1036 the ship secured the special sea detail and set the regular inport watch. At 1110 we received inspectors on board from the customs, agriculture, and Public Health Departments. They all granted the ship clearance.

Liberty was granted to the crew both days in port, but I didn't go ashore either day because I didn't have any money due to a crazy situation as follows. Before we left the states, an insurance salesman came aboard one day and talked to some of us about signing up for a savings plan with his company. He said the navy would take the proper amount out of our pay each month and it would accumulate over time. It sounded like a good idea so I did it. However, months went by without any money being taken out of my pay. After awhile, I assumed something got fouled up and that arrangement fell through somehow. The arrangement was all but forgotten by me. However, we had a payday just before getting to Pearl, but I didn't get anything. The money that was supposed to have been taken out of my pay each month was all taken out at one time – just before arriving in Pearl. I was so disgusted with what took place that I cancelled the whole thing and just lost what they had taken out of my pay. After that, I arranged for my own savings plan with the navy and had a nice sum when I got out. Anyway, that is why I didn't have any money when I got to Pearl Harbor.

A number of my shipmates got in trouble Saturday night while on liberty and were brought back to the ship by the shore patrol. There were 6 of them that were making a nuisance of themselves somehow. I'm sure it all involved getting drunk and being obnoxious. In addition, another sailor that never was too successful at staying out of trouble attempted to leave the ship while he was in a restricted status. He was put under restraint at 2220. At 2232 the captain held an impromptu non-judicial punishment session, or captain's mast, especially for him and awarded him a special court martial. Apparently, this fellow had already been before the captain several times and he was tired of fooling with him.

Late Sunday afternoon the Yorktown(CVA10) stood into port and moored at berth B-26.

Late Monday morning, 24 August, the ships of DesDiv 92 departed Pearl Harbor en route to Long Beach, California. It took 6 days for us to make the crossing. The ships generally just steamed along in a line abreast at 16 to 17 knots and didn't do much of anything else.

On Wednesday morning the commanding officer held a captain's mast for several of the wayward sailors and awarded various amounts of punishment to them.

On Friday afternoon at 1400 the commanding officer held an inspection of the lower decks. Then on Saturday morning, from 0900 to 1030, the captain held a personnel and weather deck inspection. In addition, on Saturday evening a summary court martial was convened for the benefit of a misbehaving crewmember.

At 2009 Saturday night the ships shifted to a column formation with the Maddox in the lead and with the Brush in no. 2 position. The ships were steaming along with a distance of 500 yards between them.

## HOMECOMING 1953

Early Sunday morning at 0732, 30 August, 1953, we sighted the Long Beach Harbor Light bearing 063°(t) at a distance of 9.5 miles – our first glimpse of the continental USA. The ship set the special sea detail at 0810 to enter port. We passed through the outer breakwater at 0825. At 0845 we passed through the inner breakwater, and at 0909, 30 August, 1953, the Brush was moored port side to Net Pier, Long Beach Naval Station. Of course, when we docked there was a crowd of people on the pier that had come to meet their special person – husband, son, friend, or whatever. It was a great homecoming for some of the crew, but there wasn't anybody on the dock for most of us. Our families lived too far away from the West Coast for them to come. However, we got a certain amount of pleasure out of watching those men that did have a great homecoming. Of course, there was a lot of hugging, kissing, and laughing going on. I was glad for them that they had somebody to meet them. There were quite a few that were going home on leave as soon as they stepped off the ship. I was happy for them, too, but it would be another 2½ months before I would get to go home on leave, because I wanted to be home for either Thanksgiving or Christmas.

The navy band was on the pier playing "Anchors Aweigh" as we were docking. That was great, too. It kind of livened things up and added something to the homecoming. It was a happy occasion.

A little later in the day 3 members of the crew had a very special homecoming experience; they were transferred to the Long Beach Naval Station brig under guard. All 3 of them misbehaved the entire time they were aboard ship. I don't think they liked being in the navy or being on the ship either.

On Monday, the captain went on a 10 day leave. The Brush would stay in port for 5 weeks and most of the crew went on leave during this time. A lot of liberty was granted for those that were left on the ship. We also ate a little better on the ship and even got a whole cup of fresh milk for breakfast each morning, at least for the first 2 weeks in port. After that, we got our usual half cup a day. The chief commissaryman didn't want to take the risk of fattening up any of us. At least, that is my thought on the situation.

**Homecoming Crowd**

# 7

# SECOND STATESIDE DUTY – 1953 & 1954

## VISITING THE RANDALL FAMILY SEPTEMBER AND OCTOBER 1953

I went to visit my hometown friends, the Merwin Randall family, a week or so after getting back to the States. However, while I was overseas they had bought a house in Hawthorne, California, had moved there, and that is where I went to visit them. Mrs. Randall had written me and informed me of this move, and, I guess, what city buses to take to get to their house on Menlo Avenue.

However, what I didn't know was that Mr. & Mrs. Randall's youngest son, Jerry, was no longer living with them, but their older son, Beuford, and his wife, Eluoise, were. So, I got acquainted with them. Beuford had just gotten out of the army but was still in the active reserve and had to attend meetings on weekends every so often. He and Eluoise were just a few years older than I was. Beuford was a rather tall, slim fellow with coal black hair, and Eluoise was a tall, slim, attractive woman with black hair.

Beuford had a motorcycle and that is how he, and we, got about when I went to visit them. However, we also used the public transportation system some, too. Beuford and I did a lot of sightseeing on his motorcycle when I came around. I don't remember everywhere we went but I do remember going to a few places. And I was only around Long Beach for 6 weeks after coming back to the States before my ship left for an extended stay in the San Francisco area.

I remember us going to downtown Los Angeles a couple of times to see what we could see. One time we went to an interesting city park; I believe it was called McCauther Park. It had a small lake in it on which wild ducks were swimming around that didn't seem to be afraid of people. They would swim right up to you hoping, of course, that you would feed them something. Apparently a lot of people did but I didn't have anything to feed them. I wonder if they would have shown me as much friendliness as they did if they had known that I had killed so many of their relatives back home.

Another thing I remember about downtown Los Angeles was seeing a number of characters standing around on street corners spouting off about something. They were usually expounding on something pertaining to religion or politics that was way off in left field somewhere. I noticed that a few people would stand around and listen to what they had to say for a few minutes and then move on. I think most of the people figured out pretty quick that they were flakes of some kind. I don't believe any of them got too many followers unless they were flakes, too.

California is a great state in many respects, but it was my observation then and my observation now that California seems to attract more than its share of nutty people. Some of them even get into politics and are elected to office.

Another place I remember us visiting one Sunday afternoon was the old San Juan Capistrano Mission, a place where swallows visit at certain seasons. However, there weren't any birds there that day. I believe, at least Eluoise went with us on this excursion.

One Sunday afternoon we rode to the mountains on the motorcycle. The mountain road was very curvy and there was only a narrow strip of dirt, 4 to 5 feet wide, between the paved road and a cliff of several hundred feet. We met a car going around a sharp curve and the car was on our side of the road. Beuford didn't have any choice but to leave the road or get hit and didn't have long to think about it. He managed to get onto the dirt strip and stop the motorcycle. We looked over the side of the cliff. It was a long drop down to the bottom. That could have been the day that he decided to get a car, but I can't say for sure.

Thursday morning, 8 October, 1953, the Brush and the Moore got underway and departed Long Beach Harbor en route to Mare Island Naval Shipyard, Vallejo, California, which was in the San Francisco Bay area. The ships were going into the shipyard for several months for a general overhaul.

However, early in the afternoon, not long out of port, the Brush and the Moore conducted a Y-17-AW exercise which consisted of dropping some depth charges off the fantail to test for structural weakness in the ship. The Brush dropped 11 depth charges off the fantail that were set to explode at a relatively shallow depth. When the depth charges exploded the ship experienced a terrific jolt. As a result of the explosions, the engineers discovered a serious leak in the port shaft alley at frame 148. The water had to be continuously pumped out to keep the space from flooding. The leak was corrected when we got to the shipyard.

Fog was a big problem Thursday night and the ships had to resort to making fog signals for safety sake for much of the night.

## MARE ISLAND NAVAL SHIPYARD – SAN FRANCISCO BAY

We arrived off the entrance to San Francisco Bay, Friday morning, 9 October. At 0939 the Brush was detached from the Moore to proceed independently into the bay. At 1037 we passed beneath the Golden Gate Bridge. I was at the wheel.

I was now the ship's "special sea detail" helmsman and would have this position for the next 2 years that I was on the ship. I was the helmsman that usually took the wheel whenever the ship went into or out of port, when we went alongside ships at sea – for whatever reason, and when we went to battle stations. Although, as I remember, Billy Tomlinson QM3/C steered occasionally and also relieved me sometimes if I had to be at the wheel too long – like over an hour or so.

At 1052 the Brush passed Alcatraz Island abeam to starboard at a distance of 1000 yards. Fog was still a problem off and on in the bay. At 1241 the Brush dropped anchor in anchorage 21, U.S. Naval Ammunition Depot at Mare Island. The ship had to remove all of her ammunition before going into the shipyard. At 1325 a harbor pilot came aboard, and at 1330 a tugboat came alongside to starboard to assist the pilot in moving the ship alongside pier 35 at the depot. At 1348 the pilot and the tug had the ship alongside and moored to pier 35. An all-hands working party soon followed the docking to off-load all the ammunition. It took nearly 4 hours to unload all of it. At 1803 a harbor pilot came back aboard and with the assistance of 2 navy tugs moved the ship to pier 21 at the Mare Island Naval Shipyard. The Brush would stay in the shipyard for nearly 4 months. Upon docking, the ship immediately went into "cold iron status" and started receiving all of her needed services from the shore –like electrical, telephone, steam, and water.

The Brush was going to have a lot of work done to her in the shipyard. For one thing, the ship's 40mm guns were going to be replaced with 3 inch guns. The navy thought the 3 inch guns were better than the 40mm's for some reason, but that was out of my realm of knowledge and I didn't have an opinion about it, or care. Also, as I remember, a lot of work was going to be done in the boiler room – like replacing the fire bricks. In addition, the ship would go into dry-dock for a few weeks to have her bottom inspected, scraped, and painted. There were workmen all over the ship doing something for all those months. It was kind of inconvenient at times but we managed. However, at least some of the crew slept in a barracks ashore and ate their meals in a mess hall, but I don't have any recollection about those things.

I don't remember too much about what the quartermasters did to occupy their time while we were in the yards. I know we chipped paint and painted the entire bridge area, and shined brass, but I know that didn't take up all our time. That is a blank spot in my memory. However, I did go on leave for 3 weeks; I do remember that.

At 2000, October 9, soon after we docked, Lt. Cdr. Bennie W. Jones came aboard. He was going to be our new executive officer and was relieving Lt. Herbert Childers in that capacity. Lt. Childers was also our navigator, and Lt. R.W. Bryan came aboard a day or so later to assume that role. I didn't have any idea that Lt. Childers was leaving the ship at that time. There was never a word said aboard ship about him leaving. Although, I suppose the officers knew about it. I was rather sorry to see him leave. I had served under him for over a year and had greatly respected him as a naval officer. He seemed to be a very capable and dedicated career officer. He was also a mustang officer; or, in other words, he started his naval career as an enlisted man.

Lt. Bryan was also a very capable naval officer and navigator, too, and I quickly learned to like and respect him as well. Although, they seemed to have totally different type personalities. Lt. Childers was a rather intense person. Lt. Bryan seemed to be much more relaxed and laid back for one thing. I served under Lt. Bryan for a year and a half or so before he moved on. I hated to see him depart, too, when he left.

Early Wednesday morning, 25 November, the Brush was moved from pier 21 to dry dock 2 by means of 2 tugboats and a harbor pilot. The Maddox was also moved into the same dry dock just ahead of the Brush. However, I wasn't there to witness this event. I was home on leave. The Brush stayed in dry dock about 3 weeks and was then moved to pier 19.

## THANKSGIVING LEAVE 1953

Like I previously mentioned, I waited to go home on leave so I could be there during one of the holidays – Thanksgiving or Christmas. I ended up deciding on Thanksgiving because it was sooner, and I was anxious to get home to see someone that was very special to me. It had been nearly a year since I had been home by then, and I had seen a lot of water pass under the keel during that time.

Around the middle of November, the 18th to be exact, I boarded a Greyhound bus in San Francisco and headed home. It was going to be another 3 day and 3 night trip without a chance to stretch out, bathe, or change clothes. It's hard to sleep sitting up in a Greyhound bus but I certainly gave it a try.

The bus headed a little northeast for the first day or so because we went through Salt Lake City, Utah. My impression of Utah was that it was a dry, barren land with few trees and a lot of uninhabited spaces. I could understand why so few people lived in the state; there was so little water and so little of anything that was green that I saw.

The only other thing that I remember about the trip home was going through a little town in Arkansas on a Saturday afternoon. The reason I remember this day so well is because of all the mules, horses, and wagons that I saw parked around the courthouse square. I had never seen so many wagons in one place before. It was like going back in time to before the days of the automobile. I saw few, if any, cars parked around the square that afternoon. Also, most of the people that I saw were black. Back in those days most of the rural people in the South went to town on Saturdays to do their shopping and also do some socializing with friends and acquaintances around the courthouse square. And that is what many of the people seemed to be doing that day. I noticed that many of them appeared to be having a great social time standing around the square engaged in a lot of friendly talking and laughing.

I had a 21 day leave at Thanksgiving, but I actually was only home 15 days because 6 days of my leave was spent traveling. I arrived home Sunday night, 22 November. During my leave, I went hunting a few times; I visited some of my friends and relatives; I went to Ocala a few times to shop a little, but I mainly wanted to just walk around the square and visit with people that I knew. After Thanksgiving, many people were Christmas shopping around the square, and, of course, the Christmas decorations were up by then to liven up the town and to get the shoppers in a Christmas spirit and in a mood to buy things.

I also attended church services 2 or 3 times at my home church, the Ocklawaha Bridge Baptist Church, where I also got to see a lot of my old friends.

On this leave, I ran with a young cousin of mine some, Otis Randall. He was only 13 years old at the time, but he was already driving his daddy's pickup truck on the local country roads. They were all dirt roads at that time, and the law didn't patrol these back roads too much back then so he could get by with it. Otis and I were essentially the same size on this leave. Then, after my leave was over, I didn't see him again for 2 years. And what a shock I got when I did see him again.

Early one morning right after I got back home and out of the navy, Otis came to see me. I was still in bed the morning that he came to visit me. My mother came to my bedroom door and informed me that I had a visitor. She didn't say who it was. I sat up in bed and told her to send them in. It was Otis, but not the Otis that I once knew. Otis walked through the door and essentially filled it up. I could hardly believe my eyes that a boy could grow so much in just 2 years. My young cousin had grown at least 6 inches in height in my absence and had obtained the size of a big, grown man. I'll always remember how shocked I was to see him. There are a lot of big people in his background on both sides of his family. So, he must have inherited a full dose of bigness. Otis and I share a lot of the same genes, but I think he inherited all the bigness ones.

Of course, my mother served up a wonderful Thanksgiving dinner and a lot of other great home-cooked meals besides. She was good at that sort of thing. In fact, she did everything she could to make my brief stay at home pleasant. She was glad to have her young, seafaring son home for a few days. I certainly enjoyed my visit home in most respects, but in other respects, my leave was far less than what I had hoped for. I didn't leave home with any special, fond memories this time.

My leave was over in a flash, it seemed, and I was faced with the 3 day journey back to the West Coast and 2 more years of sea duty. One year of sea duty on a destroyer as a quartermaster had made me physically and mentally exhausted. I didn't know how I was going to be able to endure another 2 years of it. I did, of course, but it wasn't easy.

My last day at home was a Thursday and it was a rather cold, cloudy, damp day. There was a fire burning in the fireplace all day, and I spent the day sitting in front of it looking at the flames dancing around in it and thinking. I thought about some of the things I had experienced the previous year. I thought about my disappointing leave. And I thought about what fate had planned for me in the coming year, because I had already been given a clue as to where I would be going when I was off Korea.

As I previously mentioned, my last day at home was a Thursday, and in order to get back to my ship on time, without being AWOL, I had to leave late that afternoon. However, I could also leave early Friday morning and be 12 hours late getting back off leave and be AWOL. I decided to be AWOL, which might have lessened my chances of being promoted to a petty officer, but I wasn't in any frame of mind to care at the time. And, in addition to deciding to go AWOL, I also made the decision not to come home again until I was out of the navy.

So, I slept in my own bed one more night. The next morning someone took me to the bus station in Ocala and dropped me off. I can't remember now who that person was, but whoever it was, he had to go to work and couldn't wait around to see me off. I was there alone and in very low spirits. This occasion was certainly one of the low points of my life.

However, just before I got on the bus my uncle Flint Holly walks up. He had walked over from his furniture store downtown to the bus station to see me off. I never thought to ask him, but I've often wondered how he knew when I was leaving town. I never told him when I was leaving and there wasn't any phone service in rural areas back then to call the house. In fact, I didn't know when I was leaving myself until late Thursday afternoon when I decided to go AWOL. Anyway, I've always thought it was thoughtful of him to come see me off. He actually didn't say much to me, but he had tears in his eyes when I got on the bus. I probably did, too.

I had a very lucky break on my trip back to San Francisco, however. My bus went to El Paso, Texas for some reason, and there I had a layover for several hours. Then, it was announced over the loud speaker that a special bus was going to be put in service for servicemen returning to the West Coast. I immediately went to the ticket counter and arranged to get on that bus. The bus soon left and was loaded with servicemen, mostly sailors and marines, and was going straight through to San Francisco without any stops except for restroom and meal stops.

The bus got to the San Francisco bus station real early in the morning; I believe it was a Monday morning. Upon arriving at the station, I realized that there was a possibility that I could get a taxi and get back to my ship on time. And that is what I did. I reported in from leave 20 minutes before the deadline and I wasn't AWOL after all. I thought that was a remarkably good break to travel 3 days and 3 nights, 3000 miles or more, across country, planning on being 12 hours late, and reported aboard with 20 minutes to spare. I considered myself very lucky on that occasion. Or, was someone looking out for me and arranged for all that to happen? I wonder. Anyway, my military record remained clean and stayed clean.

## CHRISTMAS 1953

I spent Christmas of 1953 with the Dent and Vera Snider family that lived in Scott's Valley near Santa Cruz, which was down the coast aways from San Francisco. Their home was in the mountains and in a very beautiful rural area. I had been in touch with them and Vera knew my ship was going to be in the San Francisco area over Christmas. She wrote me a note and invited me to their home for Christmas. I gratefully accepted the invitation. In fact, I spent several days at their place. I believe it was 4 days and I had a very enjoyable time.

They knew I was a hunter back home so Dent loaned me a shotgun and let me do some quail hunting in a big, undeveloped valley behind their home. So, I spent Christmas Eve morning hunting valley quail in this valley. I soon learned, though, that valley quail didn't act the same way as bobwhite quail. Bobwhite quail, the kind I was used to, would squat and you could walk up on them. Valley quail, however, wouldn't squat; they would just keep running from you. Thus, it was hard to get close enough to a covey to get a shot. Also, they just about wouldn't fly either. I encountered several big coveys that morning but they always kept running from me and stayed just out of range of my shotgun. I finally was able to kill 3 or 4 of them after much effort. We ate them for supper that night. It was a wonderful hunting experience in a beautiful place even if I didn't have too much success. It was a very beautiful, sunny day to be out hunting, too.

Vera is one of the world's best Southern cooks and Christmas dinner was all that you could hope it to be – Southern style. I can't remember whether Santa Claus left me a present under the tree or not, but he probably did. Some things I remember after 55 years and some things I don't.

The day after Christmas Vera made a dish out of the leftover turkey that has haunted me ever since. She made something called "scraffle". I had never eaten any before or even heard of it. It is a Pennsylvania Dutch dish. As I remember, it is turkey scraps and corn meal cooked together and seasoned a certain way that only Vera knows. The cooked mixture is poured into a pan, it jells, and forms a cake after it cools. Then you slice a piece off the cake to eat it. It was some great tasting stuff. Unfortunately, I've never seen any since.

My little "fwiend", Vera Marie, was 10 years old at this time. We were still buddies and it was good to see her, too. It was easy to see that she was going to be a pretty young lady one day and was as time went by.

I believe Dent and Vera drove me back to San Francisco when the time came for me to go back to my ship. I don't know how I was able to get 4 days off over Christmas but I did somehow. Maybe it was because we didn't have anything important to do on the ship since it was in the yards. I had a wonderful Christmas with the Snider family and will always remember it and be grateful to them for the invitation.

## SEASICK SAILORS

Early Wednesday morning, 20 January, 1954, the Brush got underway and went outside San Francisco Bay to test her main engines and her new 3″/50 guns. The seas were quite rough that day. At 0944 the ship commenced steaming at various speeds to test her engines and got up to speeds of 30 knots in this rough water. It was a wild ride for several hours. I was at the wheel most, if not all, of that time, so I actually didn't witness what I am about to write about. As I understood it, we had 17 new seamen aboard that had never been to sea. They all came aboard while the ship was in the shipyard. They all had a terrible experience that day. To the man, they got violently seasick and were lying around all over the deck unable to move. All they were able to do was raise their heads enough to vomit and then lay back in it. Some of them weren't even able to raise their heads; they just puked. I'm sure none of them will ever forget their first day at sea off San Francisco. Of course, their plight was terribly funny to the older hands that actually saw them lying around puking. The old hands never showed any sympathy toward them whatsoever. They were too busy laughing at them. Besides, there wasn't anything you could do for them anyway.

## FINAL DAY IN SAN FRANCISCO

Our time in the shipyard and in the San Francisco Bay area was drawing to a close at the end of January, 1954. The overhaul was over and everything had been tested satisfactorily. But before we could leave the bay, we had to replenish the ship with ammunition. That was the only thing left to do. Early Thursday morning, 28 January, the Brush got underway from pier 19, Mare Island Naval Shipyard and proceeded to Port Chicago Naval Magazine to take on ammunition. At 1020 the Brush moored starboard side to pier 2 at the magazine. At 1120 the ship commenced loading ammunition and did so for the next several hours. After completing loading ammunition, the Brush stayed there and spent the night at pier 2.

Early the next morning, Friday, 29 January, the Brush got underway and proceeded out of San Francisco Bay en route to Long Beach. Our extended stay in the San Francisco Bay area was over. We arrived at the entrance to Long Beach Harbor early Saturday morning in a dense fog, and it took the ship most of the day to get into port and moored. We finally moored to Net Pier around 1700.

### Making Memories

We had a special passenger aboard on the way down from San Francisco. This was Dennis Quigley, Captain Quigley's young son. Below, in his own words, is Dennis' recollection of that trip – 55 years later.

"While I have a number of memories related to the Brush, one that sticks foremost in my mind is my sailing on her from the San Francisco Bay area to Long Beach. I believe this trip was made in late 1953 or right at the beginning of 1954. I believe our family, which at that time consisted of my Dad, Mom (Max), my older sister Dianne and younger sisters Pat & Judi, had been living in temp quarters (Quonset huts) on Mare Island late in 1953 while the Brush was undergoing some repair/retrofitting. When these were accomplished and we had to relocate to the Long Beach area in So Cal, my Dad decided it would be educational for me to experience shipboard life firsthand by sailing her down. I have no idea whether this was strictly legal or not, but nevertheless we embarked one fine sunny morning for what I believe turned out to be a trip of one day.

I must have been only about 7 years old but can clearly remember standing on her bow as we powered out of the Bay under the Golden Gate Bridge heading into the heavier seas. I was being held secure on the bow by some unnamed seaman who kept a strong hold on me as we bobbed and rocked, up and down, back and forth, with a stiff wind and sea spray blowing in our faces. The sailor told me to keep facing into the wind taking deep breaths and to try and get a feel for the ship's motion. It was at first exhilarating and exciting to this small lad, but I must confess it took no time at all before I observed some other sailors apparently getting sick over the side and I, too, was soon overtaken by my first encounter with sea sickness. While I did not actually lose my lunch, I was extremely nauseous and dizzy. Being unable to stay my post, I was led down to my Dad's quarters to lay in his bunk where I continued to experience the ship's disorienting movements from the inside, accentuated by watching and hearing the drawers in his stateroom opening and closing to the steady "to and fro" rhythm of the ship. I don't know how long I felt ill but it seemed like hours and maybe even for the entire trip as I really don't remember much more about the journey except that which I've recounted here. Fifty five years later these memories of my Dad, the Brush and the sea are still fresh and heartwarming to me."

## OPERATING OFF THE COAST OF CALIFORNIA – SPRING 1954

The ships of DesDiv 92 only had 3 months of stateside duty left after leaving San Francisco before heading back to the Far East. And I would say we had relatively easy duty during this 3 months period compared to our previous stateside tour of duty during the fall and winter of 1952 and 1953. We spent about half the time in port either in Long Beach or San Diego during these 3 months. In addition, we came back in port at night much of the time when we did spend the day at sea. Also, we operated relatively little with the other ships of DesDiv 92. Instead, we operated by ourselves most of the time conducting various shipboard drills and exercises like: engineering casualty drills, steering casualty drills, man overboard drills, general quarters exercises, radar tracking exercises, and aircraft tracking exercises. The ship also conducted gunnery practice on several occasions including: surface targets, anti-aircraft, and shore bombardment. In addition, the Brush operated with an aircraft carrier one day while she conducted flight operations, and we conducted antisubmarine warfare (ASW) exercises for several days on a couple of occasions.

The Brush spent a lot of time around San Diego during the months of February and March – both in port and operating out of there during the day. Most of the men didn't care, I'm sure, but I imagine it was rather inconvenient for the married men aboard. Much of our time at sea was spent around San Clemente Island and we spent several nights anchored there in one of its coves.

Monday morning, 1 February, the Brush departed Long Beach Harbor en route to San Clemente Island. We left port in a dense fog and had to resort to making fog signals. However, the visibility improved somewhat a few miles out at sea. The captain exercised the crew at general quarters on the way to the island. Around 1600 the ship arrived at the island and dropped anchor in Pyramid Cove. Here we spent an uneventful night.

Early Tuesday morning, 2 February, the Brush got underway and steamed around in the San Clemente Island operating area and conducted some engineering casualty drills, radar tracking drills, general quarters exercises; and early in the afternoon, we conducted a surface firing exercise and expended 77 rounds of 5 inch AAC shells. With the completion of gunnery practice, the ship proceeded to Wilson Cove, San Clemente Island and dropped anchor in anchorage 3 at 1710. Here we spent a quiet night again.

Early Wednesday morning, 3 February, the Brush departed Wilson Cove and proceeded to operating area MM 16. Here we conducted an AA firing exercise. An airplane came over pulling a sleeve behind it. The Brush expended 25 rounds of 5 inch ACC shells and 22 rounds of 3 inch shells during the exercise. Later on, in the afternoon, the Brush conducted some more engineering casualty drills and an aircraft tracking exercise. Around 2030 the Brush rendezvoused with the Maddox and the Moore and the ships conducted tactical maneuvers all night. At 0551 Thursday morning, 4 February, division tactics were completed and the Brush was detached from the division to proceed to rendezvous with the USS Manatee(A058) to refuel. At 0811 the Brush was alongside the Manatee. The ship was rigged to receive fuel both fore and aft. At 0824 the ship commenced taking on NSFO. Baker was broke at the truck. At 0845 the ship secured from taking on fuel and Baker was hauled down. Baker is a red signal flag that means a ship is taking on fuel.

Later in the morning the ship conducted some more engineering casualty drills and in the early afternoon we conducted some more gunnery practice. At 1307 the ship commenced an anti-aircraft firing exercise with the 3 inch batteries. However, there is no record of how many shells were expended. At 1436 the ship set a course for Wilson Cove, San Clemente Island. She arrived there around 1600 and soon thereafter dropped anchor in anchorage no. 3; here, we spent another quiet night.

A very dense fog developed Thursday night and the visibility was decreased to 100 yards. However, the ship got underway anyway and proceeded out of the anchorage en route to operating area MM 19. The visibility improved around 0730 after we got away from the island.

The Brush spent the morning and early afternoon of Friday, 5 February, conducting various shipboard drills. However, around 1445 she rendezvoused with the Maddox and the Moore and those ships transferred 14 observers over to us by small boat. They were from the Fleet Training Base in San Diego. I suppose the Maddox and Moore were headed to Long Beach. Anyway, we arrived at San Diego around 1700 and the observers disembarked into a small boat from the base. Upon the observers disembarking, the Brush proceeded to pier 2 at the naval station. On this occasion, we had the assistance of a harbor pilot and a tug to get us there. We were moored to pier 2 at 1810. The watch shifted to the quarterdeck. At 2020 the ship commenced receiving electrical power from the dock. At 2026 the engineers let fires die out under boilers 1 and 3. And at 2050 the ship started receiving fresh water from the dock. The Brush was going to be moored at the naval station for the next 9 days. I believe we were there at the San Diego Naval Base because something was wrong with the ship and we went there to get the problem corrected. I believe the naval base was also called the San Diego Destroyer Base.

## Fabulous Chow

During the process of getting the problem corrected on the ship, the crew had to eat some of their meals at the destroyer base chow hall – probably for 3 or 4 days. I remember a petty officer would march a group of us to the mess hall at the noon meal. I don't remember how we got there at breakfast and supper.

We discovered that the food at the destroyer base mess hall was fabulous, and I don't see how anybody could have had any complaints about it. It was without question the best chow that I had in the navy, and it was infinitely better than what we had on the Brush. The navy has the reputation of having great chow and the cooks and bakers at that facility helped contribute to that reputation I'm sure.

We had a choice of 2 or 3 entrees at every meal and you could have as much as you wanted of everything. And everything was skillfully prepared and tasted good, too. I felt like I was eating buffet meals in a big, fancy hotel restaurant somewhere. In addition, the chow hall had drink dispensers at the head of the serving line, and a person could get all the fresh milk, orange juice, coffee, and iced tea he wanted at every meal. Also, around the drink dispensers there was a big table covered in ice where you could help yourself to chilled oranges, apples, plums, bananas, and maybe other kinds of fruit, too; this was at every meal and that was quite a luxury, too. So, we were greatly impressed by the quality and quantity of the food served there. It was a far cry from what we were used to getting aboard ship. In fact, it was almost more than we could imagine because destroyer sailors simply weren't accustomed to much luxury.

After eating at the Destroyer Base chow hall, I can understand how the navy gained the reputation for having great chow. However, and unfortunately, not all navy chow was as good as what we had at the San Diego Destroyer Base. Maybe good chow on shore bases explains why most of the sailors that were transferred to the Brush from shore bases planned to stay in the navy and make it a career. However, most of them changed their minds after 6 months, or less, on the ship and got out. There was certainly a world of difference between shore duty and destroyer duty.

Monday morning, 15 February, we went to sea again and returned to the San Clemente Island operating areas. Here we steamed around all day and conducted various shipboard drills. We also steamed around all night in the same area but we didn't conduct any drills. It was a very quiet night for the signalmen because we were operating alone.

Tuesday, 16 February, the captain conducted some more shipboard drills. However, around 1600 we rendezvoused with the carrier, Philippine Sea(CVA47), and assumed plane guard station no. 2; she was already being escorted by another destroyer. We didn't stay with the carrier too long because at 2200 that night, we were detached from the carrier to proceed to San Diego. So we set a course for San Diego. However, en route there the ship received new orders to rendezvous with the carrier, USS Boxer(CVA21), which was north of us aways. So we changed to a northerly course to meet her. We rendezvoused with the Boxer around 0600, 17 February. We followed her around all day while she conducted flight operations off and on. However, at 1526 the USS Leonard F. Mason(DD852) arrived on the scene to relieve us. A little later, at 1755, the Brush was released from plane guard duty and proceeded to San Diego. We sighted Los Coronado's light at 2150, 20 miles. At 2225 we sighted Point Loma Light at a distance of 16 miles. We arrived at the entrance to the harbor around midnight and soon thereafter anchored in anchorage 211 in 6 fathoms of water with sand and shell bottom and with 45 fathoms of chain on deck.

Around 0700 the next morning, Thursday, 18 February, a boat from the Fleet Sonar School brought 10 men, 3 officers and 7 enlisted men, out to the ship to spend a couple of days on board to observe how the ship carried out certain activities pertaining to sonar and radar. We immediately got underway after the observers came aboard and proceeded to nearby Coronado Roads to conduct a shore fire support exercise. At 0815 we arrived at Coronado Roads and steamed around in the area to conduct the gunnery exercise. At 0837 the ship sounded the general alarm. The ship also conducted engineering casualty drills at the same time as she did the shore fire support exercises.

At 1120 the ship secured from conducting exercises in Coronado Roads and headed for the off-shore operating areas. Upon arriving there, the ship conducted some more exercises. However, around 1600 the Brush went alongside the tanker, USS Platte, to refuel, which she completed at 1655. However, the ship didn't depart from the tanker. Instead, the Platte, the Brush, and the Hanson(DDR832) formed a small task unit and steamed around together for a couple of hours conducting screening drills and steering sinuous courses. At 2042 the Brush was detached from the formation and proceeded to area II 2 for night steaming. And that is what we did Thursday night; we just steamed around all night on various courses at 8 knots. It was another quiet night on the bridge.

Friday morning, 19 February, the Brush went back to Coronado Roads and conducted some more shore fire support drills. However, at 1124 the Brush secured from those drills and set a course for the offshore operating areas. She arrived at area MM 18 at 1305 and a few minutes later rendezvoused with the Hanson(DDR832). Together, the Brush and the Hanson conducted some exercises for an hour or so. However, around 1430 the ship stopped all engines, and the Brush's motor whaleboat transferred all the Fleet Sonar School observers over to the Hanson who took them back to San Diego. The Brush now headed for Long Beach. We hadn't seen Long Beach in nearly 3 weeks.

The captain must have been anxious to get there because he conducted a full power run much of the way there at speeds of 30 to 32 knots. We arrived at the entrance to Long Beach Harbor at 1739, and at 1835 we were moored starboard side to the USS O'Brien(DD725) at buoys 9 and 9A. We would stay in port 9 days.

Monday morning, 1 March, the Brush got underway and proceeded to the outer harbor. She arrived there at 0743 and commenced lying to to wait on a boat to arrive from Seal Beach to bring us some depth charges. At 0854 an "M" boat arrived and delivered 11 mark 6 depth charges to the ship. When the transfer was completed, the Brush departed the harbor and set a course for an operating area off San Diego.

At 1324 the ship's crew was called to general quarters and the ship commenced conducting a Shore Fire Control Communications exercise in operating area YY 4 off Coronado Roads. At 1527 the ship ceased the exercise and proceeded to enter San Diego Harbor. At 1623 the Brush dropped anchor in berth 211. At 1627 the ship secured the special sea detail and set the inport watch. Liberty call soon followed after dropping the anchor.

The Brush operated out of San Diego for the next 17 days and never went near Long Beach. We spent 2 consecutive weekends in San Diego. I'm sure the married men on the ship would have preferred that our operating schedule would have included Long Beach in it some of the time. However, the single men probably didn't care. We went to sea every day but we came back in port late in the day.

Tuesday, Wednesday, and Thursday we went to sea and operated with the USS Tilefish(SS307) and conducted antisubmarine warfare (ASW). On Wednesday and Thursday the USS George A. Johnson(DE583) participated in the ASW exercises with us.

Friday, 5 March, the ship engaged in some surface gunnery practice during the morning. She fired at a sled that was being towed by a vessel of some kind, a tug probably. At 0900 the ship commenced the firing exercise and completed it at 1037. The ship expended 54 rounds of 5"/38 AA common shells and 23 rounds of 3 inch AP shells during the gunnery practice.

At 1119 the Brush commenced a torpedo rehearsal exercise with the USS Saur (ARH-1) as the target. However, the ship didn't actually fire a torpedo on this occasion. The exercise was completed at 1206. The rest of the afternoon was spent conducting shipboard drills like man overboard, abandon ship, and general quarters. We went back to San Diego around 1600 and moored to buoy 13 for the weekend.

We left San Diego early Monday morning, 8 March, for another week at sea without coming into port at night. We left port in a fog and had to sound fog signals. However, the fog cleared after we got away from land. We were en route to San Clemente Island again. We arrived at Wilson Cove at 1145 and commenced lying to to put a shore fire control party ashore under the command of Lt(jg) Bailey. That done, the Brush left the cove and steamed around in the San Clemente operating areas south of the island. We didn't do much during the afternoon, except the captain exercised the crew at general quarters for awhile and conducted a steering casualty drill. I think we were mainly killing time until night when we would conduct some illumination firing on a sled towed by a tug. At 1800 the crew was called to general quarters, and at 1809 the ship commenced her night firing exercise. At 1914 she ceased firing and during that hour or so of firing expended 36 rounds of 5″/38 illumination projectiles and 24 rounds of 5″/38 AAC shells. At 1926 we secured from general quarters after the gunnery practice was completed.

The Brush steamed around in the vicinity of San Clemente Island for the rest of the night. However, early Tuesday morning, 9 March, the ship went into Pyramid Cove to conduct a gunfire support exercise. At 0700 the ship went to general quarters and commenced maneuvering at various courses and speeds while conducting the exercise. She commenced firing at 0800 and ceased firing at 1150. The ship expended 48 rounds of 5″/38 AAC shells and 16 rounds of 3 inch shells during the exercise. At 1207 the ship resumed firing her 5 inch guns and ceased firing at 1357. She expended 30 rounds of 5″/38 AAC shells during this shoot. At 1409 the ship secured from general quarters and set the regular steaming watch.

That night, commencing at 1828, the ship conducted another night illumination firing exercise. She completed the exercise at 1905 and had expended 33 rounds of 5″/38 star shells and 4 rounds of 5″/38 AAC shells. We anchored in Pyramid Cove around 2000 and spent the night there.

Early Wednesday morning, 10 March, the Brush got underway, departed Pyramid Cove, and went around to Wilson Cove to pick up the fire control party she had put ashore the previous Monday afternoon. We arrived at Wilson Cove at 0813, stopped all engines, and commenced lying to. The motor whaleboat left the ship to pickup the fire control party. The boat returned to the ship at 0835. The ship departed the cove, went out to sea, and rendezvoused with the USS Platte(A024) to take on fuel oil. The Brush went alongside her around 1030 and commenced taking on fuel. Refueling was completed at 1107.

The Brush then proceeded to rendezvous with another ship, the USS Jason(ARH-1). We rendezvoused with her at 1330 and operated with her the rest of the day. They conducted a radar calibration exercise, at least some of the time when they were operating together. In addition, the captain exercised the crew at general quarters and conducted an atomic attack drill. The 2 ships parted company at 1800 and we proceeded to operating area MM 19, which was about 20 miles west of San Diego. We arrived there at 2000 and steamed around in that area most of the night at 10 knots. However, at 0410 the ship proceeded to operating area MM 17 to rendezvous with another ship, the USS General Randall(ATP115).

At 0818 the captain exercised the crew at general quarters and soon thereafter started conducting a torpedo rehearsal exercise with the USS General Randall as the target ship. The Brush completed that exercise around 1000 and then proceeded to area KK 28. She arrived there around 1300, and at 1309 the ship sounded the general alarm again for the purpose of conducting an anti-aircraft firing exercise. The ship commenced the firing exercise at 1320 when the plane came over towing a sleeve. The exercise was completed at 1535. The ship expended 48 rounds of 5″/38 AA common shells and 60 rounds of 3″/50 VT ammunition during the gunnery exercise. At 1545 we secured from general quarters and departed operating area KK 28 en route to operating area MM 18. We arrived there around 1900 and just steamed around all night at 10 knots waiting for the new day. It was very quiet on the bridge.

Friday morning, 12 March, the ship rendezvoused with the USS Epping Forrest(LSD4) to conduct another torpedo rehearsal exercise. At 0900 the ship commenced maneuvering at various courses and speeds to conduct the exercise. The torpedo exercises were completed around 1130 and the ships parted company. The Brush headed for San Diego, but en route she conducted various exercises and drills including man overboard drill, steering casualty drill, general quarters exercise, atomic attack exercise, and passing through a minefield drill. We arrived off San Diego Bay around 1400. At 1435 the Brush passed Point Loma Light abeam to port at 1500 yards and stationed the special sea detail. At 1519 we were moored to buoy 13 in San Diego Bay. Liberty call began at 1700.

We spend the weekend in port but nothing of any consequence happened while we were there. I have no recollection of what I did on the beach, but on the ship, I always spent some time watching the seaplanes take off and land in the bay, which was taking place constantly in those days.

Monday morning, 15 March, the Brush went to sea again and conducted various kinds of drills and exercises like she had been doing the previous week. The ship first conducted a steering casualty drill at 1121. At 1243 the captain exercised the crew at general quarters for the purpose of conducting an anti-aircraft firing exercise. However, no plane ever came over towing a sleeve so no firing was actually done. We secured from general quarters at 1441.

At 1552 the commanding officer held a captain's mast and awarded various punishments to 9 sailors. One of the sailors was awarded a special court martial. Two petty officers, both boilertenders 2nd class, were awarded reduction to next inferior rate, probably for being AWOL.

The Brush really didn't do much the first day back to sea but just steam around. However, late in the day, about dark, the Brush went alongside the USS Caliente(A053) for refueling. Refueling was completed at 1843 with the ship taking on 34,202 gallons of Navy Standard Fuel Oil forward and aft. The Brush departed from the tanker and headed toward her night steaming area KK 28, which was a little south of San Clemente Island. She arrived in that area at 2015 and steamed around on various courses all night. It was another quiet night on the bridge.

On Tuesday morning, 16 March, the ship conducted a steering casualty drill and some engineering casualty drills. The ship went to general quarters at 1000 in preparation for some gunnery practice. However, the airplane towing the sleeve developed engine trouble and had to return to its base without the ship ever firing a shot. However, at 1245 the ship commenced an antiaircraft drone firing exercise. She completed the firing exercise at 1416 having expended 100 rounds of 3 inch non-fragment VT shells. Then, the Brush rendezvoused with the USS St. Paul(CA73), which was nearby, for a torpedo rehearsal exercise. At 1616 the ship commenced maneuvering to conduct a simulated torpedo attack on the St. Paul. The simulated torpedo attack was completed at 1635 without the ship actually firing one.

The Brush and the St. Paul then spent the next 2 and 1/2 hours conducting tactical maneuvers together. At 1902 the Brush departed the St. Paul and proceeded to her night steaming area – areas II 1 and MM 16. We spent another quiet night just steaming around in the ocean off Southern California.

Wednesday morning, 17 March, the Brush spent part of the morning at general quarters conducting a battle problem of some kind, and in the afternoon the Brush conducted a torpedo attack on the USS General Breckenridge(ATP176). At 1353 the ship commenced maneuvering to make the attack on the ship. At 1415 the Brush fired the torpedo at the Breckenridge at a range of 5850 yards. Then the Brush proceeded to recover her torpedo and did so at 1450. Next, at 1524, the ship commenced an anti-aircraft drone firing exercise and completed it at 1605. The ship fired 49 rounds of 5″/38 shells and 39 rounds of 3″/50 shells during the gunnery exercise.

At 1705 the Brush headed for San Diego on course 096°(t) at a speed of 15 knots. She arrived at the entrance to San Diego Bay at 1815 and dropped anchor in anchorage 206 at 1838.

Thursday, 18 March, the Brush got underway at 0850 and commenced maneuvering to pick up some observers from the Fleet Sonar School. At 0908 we received the observer party aboard plus the commander of DesDiv 92, who temporarily shifted his flag to the Brush. The Brush left the bay and went out in the ocean aways where she conducted some battle problems for the observers benefit. At 0934 the crew went to general quarters. At 1139 the ship opened fire with a main battery on a sleeve target towed by an airplane and fired 3 rounds. Next, at 1147, she commenced maneuvering to simulate an attack on a simulated sonar contact. At 1210 the Brush secured from battle problems and set a course for San Diego Bay. She arrived there around 1400 and proceeded to anchorage 206. She dropped anchor there at 1423. However, she didn't stay anchored there too long. She weighed anchor at 1555 and proceeded out of the bay en route to Long Beach. The Brush entered Long Beach Harbor at 2019 and at 2107 was moored to a nest of ships at buoys 6 and 7. The next morning, though, the ship got underway and shifted her position in the nest to go along the port side of the tender, USS Frontier(AD25). We stayed in port for 10 days.

Early Monday morning, 29 March, the Brush went to sea in company with the Maddox and the Moore. These ships of DesDiv 92 operated together for the next 4 days and conducted a lot of tactical maneuvering both day and night. However, they did spend one night at anchor in Pyramid Cove, San Clemente Island. We went to general quarters a couple of times every day most of which was for the purpose of conducting gunnery practice. The ship was always firing at a sleeve being towed by an airplane. The ships also engaged in a number of radar calibration exercises and radar tracking exercises during the week.

Monday, the ship went to general quarters at 1420 and commenced a firing exercise at 1440. During that exercise the ship's guns fired 12 rounds of 5 inch shells and 24 rounds of 3 inch shells.

Tuesday, 30 March, the ship went to general quarters at 1251 and commenced a firing exercise, firing at a sleeve, and expended 30 rounds of 3 inch shells on this occasion. The ships spent Tuesday night anchored in Pyramid Cove.

Wednesday afternoon we had 2 gunnery practice sessions. One was at 1310 where the gunners expended 26 rounds of 5 inch shells and 23 rounds of 3 inch shells. The second practice was at 1533 and during this session the ship expended 24 rounds of 5 inch shells.

Thursday, 1 April, the ships conducted division tactics for much of the day, but the Brush was also involved in some other things, too, like some sonar exercises called Y20 and 21 AW(PAC), which I don't know anything about myself. But this exercise involved putting some kind of underwater gadget in the water for the sonarmen to ping on, I think, and thus improve their skills at detecting submarines. In addition, we went alongside the cruiser, St. Paul, in the middle of the afternoon to refuel, but I think this was mostly for practice for somebody's benefit because we really didn't take on very much fuel. The ship was also involved in some more radar calibration exercises with the Moore. However, the most interesting thing we did all day from my point of view was to just go back in port, into Long Beach, late in the day. At 2048 the ship entered Long Beach Harbor. At 2125 we were moored port side to the Maddox at Net Pier. So, we were going to have a long weekend in Long Beach.

The next day, Friday, 2 April, we had a captain's personnel inspection starting at 1330. After the personnel inspection, the captain inspected the lower decks, topside, and living spaces. Everything must have been satisfactory because he didn't cancel liberty for that day or that weekend. Nothing of any consequence happened over the weekend.

Early Monday morning, 5 April, the Brush went to sea again for a week of intense training in which the ships of DesDiv 92 conducted almost continuous ASW exercises with the submarine, USS Charr(SS328) – both day and night. We operated in the San Diego operating areas and in operating areas off Baja, California during the week. The ships of DesDiv 92, plus other ships that were present from time to time, also conducted tactical maneuvers and screen re-orientation exercises during the week. I'm sure the submarine, underwater, was engaged in trying to figure out ways to attack the surface ship formation without being detected and attacked herself.

Sometimes the Brush was detached from the formation to conduct ASW exercises independently, or to conduct radar tracking exercises, or to conduct aerial gunnery practice. On Tuesday morning the Brush was detached to conduct gunnery practice. The ship went to general quarters at 0825 and commenced firing at a sleeve towed by an airplane at 0900. She completed the gunnery exercise at 1120, but there is no record of how many shells she expended.

The cruiser, USS Helena(CA133), operated with us for much of the day Wednesday.

Thursday, 8 April, around 1800, the Brush and the Moore went alongside the USS Navasota(A0106) to refuel both fore and aft. The refueling was completed at 1843 with the Brush taking on 48,980 gallons of fuel oil.

Friday, 9 April, the submarine, USS Pomfret(SS391), started operating with us. The Charr apparently had left the area. Friday night around 2200 the ASW exercises were completed. DesDiv 92, less the Thomas, then formed up into a column formation at 500 yards intervals and headed for Long Beach. DesDiv 92 arrived off Long Beach Harbor entrance Saturday morning, 10 April, and the crew shifted into the uniform of the day, which was undress blues. At 0515 the special sea detail was set. At 0554 we passed the Long Beach Sea Buoy abeam to starboard at 400 yards and commenced maneuvering independently to enter port. The executive officer was at the conn. At 0733 the Brush was moored starboard side to the Moore that was moored to Net Pier.

At 0945 one of our seamen departed the ship under guard for the U.S. Naval Brig at Long Beach. He had been a bad boy.

The Brush stayed in port Saturday and Sunday.

Early Monday morning, 12 April, the Brush left port and proceeded to the operating areas west of San Diego to conduct some more ASW exercises. We arrived at the operating area around 1300 and rendezvoused with the USS Renville(APA227) and the USS Rock(SSR274). The Brush conducted ASW exercises with them for 3 hours or so. After completing the ASW exercises, she proceeded independently back toward San Diego. At 1932 the ship anchored in Coronado Roads in berth 117 in 8 fathoms of water with sandy bottom. Here, we spent a relatively quiet night. However, something did happen on the ship during the night that caused a little concern among some of the crew for awhile.

## Some Unexpected Visitors Steal Aboard

The Brush had some unexpected and uninvited visitors steal aboard ship Monday night while she was anchored in Coronado Roads. It so happened that a crewmember discovered a large, wet footprint up forward on the main deck, port side, around 2200. It was much larger then a human footprint and wasn't shaped like one either. The sailor reported the finding to the OOD at the quarterdeck. I suppose the OOD looked at the footprint, too, as did some of the other crewmembers. Nobody had a clue as to what kind of track it was. Naturally, it caused some genuine concern among the people that saw it. Word got around the ship that there appeared to be some kind of unknown creature from the deep aboard the ship.

I was on signal watch on the bridge. Somehow, I heard about the find and decided that I would go down and investigate it myself. There weren't any other ships in sight so there wasn't likely to be any signaling going on. So I left the signal bridge and went forward on the main deck to the area where the wet footprint was found. I found it and immediately observed that the footprint was much larger than a human foot and wasn't the shape of a human foot either. It appeared to look more like a frog track to me but a big frog track. At the time, I couldn't imagine what the footprint belonged to. I wondered – had a monster from the deep climbed aboard our ship in the middle of the night? And if so, to do what?

The visitor was finally spotted by somebody and the mystery was solved. It turned out that the footprint belonged to a navy frogman that had climbed aboard our ship to just see if he could without being spotted. He did. In fact, there were actually 4 frogmen that stole aboard, but only one of them left a footprint on the deck. Of course, the frog-like track was one of the fins of the frogmen. The other 3 frogmen must have pulled off their fins as soon as they got aboard and consequently didn't leave any fin prints behind.

I saw them, all 4 of them, in the galley around midnight drinking coffee with some of the cooks. They all had black wetsuits on. I noticed that they were a strong, husky looking bunch. I suppose they slid back into the water sometime during the night. I went on to bed myself, which was more to my liking.

The Brush departed Coronado Roads early the next morning, Tuesday, 13 April, and proceeded to operating area SS 1 to conduct some more ASW exercises. We rendezvoused with the USS Rock(SSR274) at 0834. The Rock soon submerged to play her part in the exercises. However, before we got started good with the exercises, the Brush stopped all engines and received AVR-1 alongside to deliver to us some ComSubFlot San Diego staff observers. The AVR-1 fell in astern of us.

The Brush maneuvered around on various courses and speeds searching for the submarine. At 1011 the Brush received a torpedo hit below the waterline, starboard side, aft. There was apparently no damage to the ship. Of course, it was a practice torpedo; otherwise, we would have been blown out of the water. The USS Rock surfaced astern of us and recovered the torpedo. That completed the ASW exercises for that day and the Brush proceeded back to San Diego. It was a short day at sea because the ASW exercises were completed at 1035. At 1231 we were moored to buoy 19 in San Diego Harbor.

Wednesday morning, 14 April, we got underway relatively early to go back to sea to the same operating area, SS 1, that we operated in the previous day. The special sea detail was set at 0630 and we were underway at 0645. We departed the bay at 0728 and set a course of 240°(t) to reach the SS 1 operating area. We arrived there at 0845 and rendezvoused with the USS Rock around 0900. She submerged and the ASW exercises commenced.

The Brush also rendezvoused with the USS Renville(APA227) and assumed screening station on her as part of the exercises. However, it was another relatively short day at sea. The ASW exercises were completed at 1535 and the Brush proceeded back to San Diego. We moored at buoy 19 at 1709.

Thursday, 15 April, the Brush went back to sea again to the same operating area and operated with the USS Renville for several hours. The Brush took a screening station 1500 yards ahead of her and they practiced steaming along on zigzag courses. It makes it harder for submarines to intercept ships to fire their torpedoes when they are steaming on zigzag courses. As I remember it, some kind of gadget was installed on the compass that enabled the ships in a convoy or formation to zig and zag at the same time. And there were several different gadgets with different zigzagging patterns that the ships could use. It was the duty of the chief quartermaster to install the proper gadget on the compass. I never got into that part of the quartermastering trade and didn't know that much about it. I think the chief was the only one on the ship that did.

We operated with the Renville until 1430 and then headed for Long Beach at 22 knots. Our training was over before heading back overseas. The Brush arrived at Long Beach Harbor at 1830. At 1925 we moored at buoys 9 and 9A in a nest of 5 destroyers that were alongside the USS Frontier(AD25), a destroyer tender. We would receive all our services from the tender. We would remain in port for the next 17 days until we went overseas.

Saturday, 17 April, all the ships in the nest were moved to buoys 6 and 7 for some reason. The most important thing that happened while we were in port from my perspective was that R.G. Emerson QMC reported aboard for duty. He was replacing Eugene Cote QMC who had just been transferred off the ship, although, I didn't know he was leaving and he had never said a word about leaving. So, Emerson was going to be my chief petty officer for the rest of my navy career and he was a good chief. Although, it developed that we had some personality problems working together in the beginning, we worked things out, and the last year we served together on the Brush we had a great relationship and I enjoyed serving with him.

Tuesday morning, 27 April, a harbor pilot came aboard; a couple of tugboats came alongside and moved the Brush, Maddox, and Thomas in a nest to the ammunition anchorage in the outer harbor. At 0815 we anchored at the ammunition berth with an anchor from the Maddox. At 0830 the Thomas stood out from the nest. At 0900 we commenced receiving ammunition. At 1000 we completed receiving ammunition. At 1215 the tugs took us back to buoys 6 and 6A, alongside the Frontier, and we commenced receiving our steam and electrical power from her again. Here we stayed until 4 May, 1954.

## Crabbing

Saturday morning, 24 April, I went to visit the Randall family and spent the weekend with them. It was the last time that I would see them before going back overseas.

Saturday afternoon, Beuford, Merwin, and I went crabbing on the San Pedro Harbor breakwater. The breakwater extended several hundred yards out into the ocean. We did most of our crabbing on the harbor side of the breakwater. As I remember, there was very little wind that afternoon, and the harbor was as calm as a lake on a still day. In addition, the weather was a good day to be around the seashore and a perfect day to catch crabs. We would walk along on the big rocks that formed the breakwater and look for crabs that were lying on the rocks underneath the water. The water was real clear so the crabs could be easily seen. Our crab catching device was a long pole with a scoop net on the end of it. When we saw a big crab laying on a rock, one of us would slowly bring the net down on top of him. When the crab tried to swim away, it would swim into the net, and then we would just lift it up out of the water. It was a rather easy way to catch crabs and a lot of fun. I think we were catching Dungeness Crabs; although, I didn't know what they were called at the time. To me, they were just crabs, but big ones.

We saw and caught 11 big Dungeness crabs in a couple of hours. I thought that was a rather successful fishing trip. Besides, that was the first time that Beuford and myself had ever been crabbing in California or anywhere else. We took the crabs home, cleaned them, and had a feast of boiled crab that night. They certainly tasted good. I learned to like crab on that occasion. I never had liked them before, although, I had tried to develop a taste for them in the past because so many people I knew thought they were so good to eat. I have loved eating crabs ever since that occasion. For some reason we never went crabbing again. Why? I can't imagine why we didn't now. Maybe we just didn't ever get around to it.

**A Nest of Ships in San Diego Harbor (National Archives Photograph)**

**USS Dixie AD14**
**A Destroyer Escort**
**USS Brush DD745**
**USS Taussig DD746**
**USS Maddox DD731**

# 8

# LIFE ABOARD SHIP

## Reveille

Normally, reveille was at 0600 and every morning at this time the boatswain's mate-of- the-watch would get on the P.A. system, either in the pilothouse or on the quarterdeck, blow his boatswain's pipe and announce, "Reveille, reveille, reveille, everybody heave out and trice up. All hands have a clean sweep down fore and aft." What this meant was, everybody was to get out of their racks and shorten the chains that held up their racks, so they couldn't get back in them and which would also provide a little more space in the compartments, too.

Immediately after getting up, everybody was supposed to clean up their work spaces, which included a sweep down and a swab down, too, in some cases. The boatswain's mates were in charge of the deck force and from the bridge we could look down and see the deck force sweeping and swabbing down the main deck. However, all that work was suspended if the weather was bad and the seas were rough.

The signalmen on the bridge that had the 0400 to 0800 watch would, just after daybreak, get a bucket of water and some rags and wipe down the outside of the pilothouse and the captain's cabin to get the salt off the bulkheads, which were frequently coated with salt. Occasionally, a rain shower would save us the trouble of having to do that. The signalmen would also sometimes swab down the bridge deck to get rid of the salt.

It was always amazing to me how much dirt people could collect during the sweep down when we were at sea. There wasn't any dirt or dust at sea so it was always puzzling to me where all the dirt came from. I never did figure it out.

## Standing Watches

Standing watches is just part of life for many of the sailors serving aboard ships, especially at sea. Some rates don't normally stand watches, though, at sea or in port. I don't know how they were able to swing such a deal.

Most of the crew that stood watches stood what was called 3 section watches – that meant the sailors were on watch (duty) 1 watch and off 2 watches. There were normally 7 watches during a 24 hour period and most of the watches were for 4 hours. However, there were two 2 hour watches in the evening between 1600 and 2000 instead of one 4 hour watch, which caused the watches to rotate, and it also provided an opportunity for everyone to get to evening chow, too. It was preferred by all the watch standers that the watches rotate so that the same people wouldn't be standing the same watches all the time, especially the mid-watch (00–04). However, occasionally, for some reason the watch routine would be changed to 6 or 12 hour shifts and people had to stand an all day or an all night watch; at least the signalmen would do this from time to time, especially in port. I stood some of them myself, both in the daytime and at night. At night, it made for a very long night and sometimes I had to just keep walking to keep from falling asleep on my feet.

Underway, the watch standers got relatively little sleep compared to civilian standards. The most sleep a fellow could expect to get at night would be 6 hours. Some nights you only got 4 hours of sleep and some nights you might only get 2 hours. Bear in mind, reveille was normally at 0600 and that is when everybody got up, regardless of how little sleep they may have gotten the night before or the night before that. There was no sleeping-in during the day on destroyers. I don't know what the practice was on other type ships. So, the watch standers, the quartermasters at least, suffered from serious sleep deprivation all the time we were underway and consequently felt sleepy most of the time. I'm assuming all the rest of the watch standers felt the same way; although, I'm not sure about that, but I think we all had the same deal about standing 3 section watches. We usually were able to catch up on our sleep when the ship came into port and stayed a few days, but not always; because sometimes the signalmen had to stand signal watches in port, too.

I confess, though, that I did go into the charthouse a few times and shut and lock the door behind me because I was so sleepy that I could hardly function. I would sit on the deck (floor) and put my head on my arms that were folded on my knees and tried to get just a few minutes of sleep. I figured that nobody could catch me sleeping with the door locked. I knew that if someone tried to get in, I would wake up, hopefully, and have to get up and unlock the door to let them in. I'm not sure that I would have been in trouble if I had been caught sleeping during the day, during duty hours, but I didn't want to take that chance or put some officer on the spot. I felt like I had some officer friends that looked out for me to some extent, but I didn't want to strain that relationship because of a little untimely sleeping.

## The Bridge Watch

A regular underway steaming watch on the bridge of a destroyer usually consisted of 12 men. The officer-of-the-deck (OOD) and the JOOD stood their watches at the forward part of the bridge, or the conning station as it was called. The forward part of the bridge was covered with a piece of canvas and it also had a plastic windshield. The canvas cover and the windshield together went a long ways toward protecting the OOD and the JOOD from the weather and keeping them dry. I mention this because the OOD's and JOOD's didn't have this luxury on earlier destroyers; they were just exposed to the weather – wind, sun, rain, and waves breaking over the bow during rough seas. Just the addition of these two features made sea duty much more tolerable for destroyer conning officers.

There was also a phone talker and two lookouts on the forward part of the bridge – one on the starboard side and one on the port side. The lookouts were constantly scanning the ocean with a pair of binoculars. It was their duty to report to the OOD anything that they saw that he needed to know about. They were totally exposed to the weather and had to endure whatever it happened to be. The lookouts were newer men on the deck force and probably seaman apprentices. It was an important job, however.

Two signalmen, quartermasters, stood watch on the after part of the bridge that was called the signal bridge. The signal bridge was just forward of the mast. There was usually a 2nd or 3rd class petty officer and a striker on watch. However, much of the time during the day, particularly if it was a good day, there would be other quartermasters there, too, just hanging out because they really didn't have any other place to go. The signalmen were totally exposed to the weather and sometimes it got to be very tiresome. Sometimes, though, during rainy weather or real rough seas, with waves breaking over the bow and drenching the bridge, the signalmen could step into the pilothouse for a few minutes to get out of the weather if there weren't any other ships around.

Underway, there were five sailors in the pilothouse. There was a helmsman, an engine-order-telegraph operator, a boatswain's mate, a messenger, and a quartermaster.

Of course, the captain would be on the bridge some of the time, and he was there anytime his presence was needed or his career was at stake.

The bridge of a destroyer was a very busy and hectic place much of the time during the day and early part of the night if we were operating with other ships, which we were much of the time. I've always thought that the OOD of a destroyer probably had the most stressful job in the navy, and the quartermasters weren't too far behind them.

The radarmen also had a very critical job at times, too, because they had to tell the OOD what course he had to steer to get to a new screening station when we were operating with a task group. They had to be right too, otherwise, a collision could occur. I greatly respected their abilities in that regard.

The midwatch, from 0000 to 0400 hours, was usually, but not always, a quiet time in the pilothouse when we were underway. Normally, the activities of the day were over and we were just steaming along. It was a time for telling sea stories, tall-tales, and lies in the pilothouse; all kinds of topics were discussed. However, it was a great opportunity for sailors to enlighten their shipmates about their sexual prowess with girls and their ability to drink large quantities of strong drink. It made me feel totally inexperienced and inadequate to hear some of the old salts expound on their exploits. Although, I questioned sometimes if all the claims they made were entirely true.

The deck force supplied most of the sailors for the bridge watches. There were a lot of different men that stood these watches on the bridge, and I've forgotten most of their names. However, I do remember three of the men I stood pilothouse watches with in the earlier days of my navy career, and they all happened to be gunner's mates. These three men that I remember standing watches with are Sammie Baker (GM3/C), Willie Nash (GM3/C), and Lloyd McCord (GMSN). They all stood helmsman watches in the pilothouse and were great sailors in my estimation.

## Pilothouse

The pilothouse was a space about 20 feet wide at the after part of it and 15 feet wide at the forward part of it. And it was from 12 to 15 feet deep fore and aft. In the pilothouse was located the ship's wheel, the engine-order- telegraph, a gyro compass, a magnetic compass, a radar scope, a sonar scope, a navigator's table, the captain's chair, and the Quartermasters' Desk. The wheel, compasses, and engine-order- telegraph stood in the middle of the pilothouse. On the rounded bulkhead at the after part of the pilothouse was a P. A. system, the general quarters alarm, the collision alarm, the fog horn, an inclinometer, a short wave radio, and the navigational lights switch, at least, those are the things I remember; there may have been some more things. In addition, the pilothouse had portholes, a dozen or so of them, and one of the two places on the ship that did have them. It was very necessary for the officers, especially, to be able to see into and out of the pilothouse at times. Also, there was a little square wooden box that was mounted on the outside starboard bulkhead of the pilothouse that housed a dry-bulb and a wet-bulb thermometer, and a barometer. At times, keeping track of the atmospheric pressure was pretty important.

## Signal Bridge

The signalmen communicated with other ships and shore stations by means of signal lights, flaghoist, and semaphore. However, semaphore was rarely ever used to send messages, and when it was, it was when the ships were real close together.

There were two signal lights on the signal bridge, one on each side of the ship. They were about 1 foot in diameter and had a handle on each side of them that operated a shutter on the front of the light that enabled the signalmen to send Morse code messages, dots and dashes, to other ships. These signal lights were the primary way in which the ships communicated by light. However, there were a couple of other ways to communicate by light also, but they were seldom used and then only at night. There were two small lights rather high upon the mast at each end of the yardarm. They were operated by a key that was similar to a telegraph key. These yardarm lights were used at night so that a formation of ships could execute a course change, a speed change, a formation station change, or something at the same time. An infra-red light lantern was another way that light signals were sent. These infra-red light signals couldn't be seen with the naked eye; they could only be read by looking through a special kind of scope that enabled the signalman to see the light and read the messages. These messages were always sent at night at pre-arranged times so that the receiving signalman would be expecting them and have his scope in hand at the designated time.

Flaghoist – the brightly colored signal flags were about 3 foot square in size and had about a 6 foot length of rope sewed into them at the back end. This rope had a clip attached to it at the top end and a ring at the bottom end so that the flags could be hooked together and hoisted into the air by means of a halyard that was attached to the yardarm rather high up on the mast. The signal flags were stored in something called a "flagbag" when they weren't in use. There was a flagbag on each side of the signal bridge. These storage bags, flagbags, were about 6 feet long and 4 ½ to 5 feet deep. The signal flags were hung in the flagbags in their designated places in alphabetical order and in numerical order for the numbered flags. An experienced signalman could grab the correct flags out of the flagbags very quickly – almost without having to look at the letters. Navy ships always hoisted their "call sign" when they were entering or leaving port. I think it was a matter of formality more than anything else. The Brush's "call sign" was NKMX. I will never forget it.

Essentially all communications between ships in sight of each other was done by either signal lights or flaghoist in the early 1950's. There was a short wave radio in the pilothouse but it was rarely ever used. And, I might add, there was usually a lot of communication going on between ships. Consequently, the signalman usually stayed busy when we were operating with other ships. The modern navy may do things differently today, however. The flagbags also had another good use other than for storing signal flags. It was a good place to sleep off a drunk. But I'll write more about that later.

Heavy duty 10x50 binoculars were another important piece of equipment on the bridge that the signalmen used daily to help them read signals. We always had several pairs of them handy and in good working order. They were indispensable at reading long distance signals, both light and flaghoist. We could hardly perform our signaling duties without them.

In addition to the hand held 10x50 binoculars, there was also a big and very powerful mounted pair of binoculars that was 127 power and must have weighed 50 pounds. There was a mount for it on each side of the bridge, and it was carried back and forth as needed, which wasn't too often. We used it mostly for "long glass liberties."

Other things on the signal bridge that were used occasionally, and that were generally stored in the signalman's desk, was a pair of semaphore flags, an infra-red signal light and scope, a hand-held signal light, and a signal book. The signalman's desk was located on the port side of the signal bridge up against the captain's cabin. It was in a rather sheltered location and on this desk is where the signalmen kept the most important items – the coffee pot and hot plate. We had to make our own coffee and hot coffee was available to the men on watch most of the time. It tasted especially good in the middle of the night when standing watch. The sailors that stood watches drank a lot of coffee, especially at night.

## Captain's Cabin

The captain's cabin was on the bridge right behind the pilothouse. This is where the captain slept when the ship was underway. And it was just a few steps away from the forward part of the bridge where the conning station was and where the OOD stood when the ship was underway. The captain's cabin was a very small space with only enough room for a small bunk, a commode, and a tiny wash basin. The captain hung his uniforms on a rod at the foot of the bunk, as I remember, and he stored his smaller clothing items in a drawer built into the bottom of the bunk. I don't know for sure, but I suspect he always slept with his clothes on, because he would always get to the forward part of the bridge in a matter of seconds when he was summoned; and he was always fully dressed when he arrived. I'm sure it would have been considered undignified for the captain to show up on the bridge in just his underwear. In an emergency he couldn't take the time to dress. However, in port the captain slept and lived in the commodore's quarters, which were the only decent size living space on the ship. These quarters were the most forward compartment on the main deck, and I believe it even had some portholes. The captain also hung out in these quarters during the day, too, when the ship was underway and when he wasn't on the bridge. The commodore seldom stayed on our ship so the captain had the use of it most of the time.

## Fire Control Compartment/5 Inch Guns

The fire control officer usually did the aiming and firing of the 5 inch guns. He did this from a little compartment that was located above and just aft of the pilothouse. A fire control petty officer was always there with the officer. I have no idea what either one of them actually did. I do know that they received a lot of help electronically. For instance, the fire control officer could lock onto a target with radar and the guns would automatically stay locked on the target regardless of how the ship maneuvered about. I don't understand how all that was done. It's the job of the fire control officer and the fire controlman to know about such things. I only understood that if the 5 inch guns were fired and the shells hit the target, they could claim credit for a job well done. Likewise, if the shells missed the target, they had to claim credit for that, too.

The fire control officer was always in constant communications with the gunners in the mounts and directed their activities in regards to loading the guns and the kind of shells to load. The gunner's mates could fire the 5 inch guns in the mounts but the fire control officer decides when they would. The gunner's mate's job was primarily to maintain and load the 5 inch guns as I understood it. Of course, they had a lot of other duties to perform, too, in regards to the other guns, small arms, K guns, hedge-hogs, and magazines to name some of them.

## After-Steering

After-steering was a small, stuffy compartment back aft near the stern. A seaman was on duty there whenever the ship was underway. He was in this space to take over the steering of the ship in case there was a steering casualty on the bridge, or in other words, if the ship couldn't be steered from the bridge for some reason. This situation happened occasionally but never while I was at the wheel. Duty in after-steering was a bad job as far as I was concerned, because you were in this small, cramped space way below deck and a very undesirable place to be if the ship started going down. In addition, in after-steering the ship had to be steered manually and it was hard to do. Someone from the deck force was assigned this duty during regular steaming watches and was always quick to assume the steering when the bridge lost steering control.

I was only in the after-steering compartment a couple of times myself, but a quartermaster was assigned that job at general quarters and when the special sea detail was set. Thankfully, I never was assigned that job.

## Charthouse

An inside ladder from the 01 deck, on the port side, led up to the pilothouse. At the bottom of this ladder on the 01 deck was located the charthouse. It was an interior space about 10 x 12 feet in size that was beneath but just aft of the pilothouse. The charthouse was considered my space and here is where I spent a lot of my time correcting navigational charts and doing other things pertaining to navigation.

There were several pieces of equipment in the charthouse including a big navigator's desk with several drawers in it in which the charts were stored. In addition, there was a fathometer, the loran gear, the chronometer, a sextant, and an electric eraser. There were also several book shelves on which the navigational books and publications were stored. The book shelves had a bar across the front of them to keep the books from falling out during rough seas.

The chronometer was located in a sunken space on the left side of the desk and was covered by a thick sheet of glass. The chronometer was the official navigational time piece and was very accurate. It was set to Greenwich Time in England, but it would develop an error in it over time, and we, or I, had to keep track of the amount of that error. And I did that by getting a radio signal every few days that told me the exact time, the exact Greenwich Time to the second. The exact time was important when we were celestial navigating and this error had to be taken into consideration when calculating our position.

The fathometer was a good piece of equipment to have on board, but I never saw it used by the navigator because the ship never had the occasion to venture into unknown shallow water. The depth of the water was shown on the navigational charts and that is all the information he normally needed. However, I used the fathometer for my own pleasure sometime just to see what the depth of the water was under us. I also turned on the fathometer sometimes when we were in real deep water – like out in the mid-Pacific where the water was miles deep. I would turn it on the deep depth setting and listen to the sound waves just go on and on and on. Sometimes the sound waves would never reach bottom that I could hear. It was an eerie sound and gave you quite an uncomfortable feeling to know that the water beneath the ship was 6, 7, or 8 miles deep. It seemed to me like it would be awful wet, cold, and dark down there at the bottom of the ocean. I would just visualize the sound waves going on and on through that dark and cold depth. And I also thought how horrible it would be to be trapped in a sinking ship going to the bottom in that depth. What a horrible death that must be. There have been a lot of seamen that have experienced it through the years, though. However, to think about it, I suppose it would be a horrible situation to be trapped in a sinking ship at any depth.

The loran gear was a navigational piece of equipment that received a special kind of radio signal, as I remember. There were loran stations scattered around the world in coastal areas that transmitted these signals for the benefit of ships at sea and maybe airplanes, too, but I'm not sure about that. Anyway, if you could get signals from three different loran stations you could get a rough navigational fix. We only used the loran when we were way out at sea and when the sky was overcast and maybe had been for days. It was a very primitive piece of equipment compared to modern day loran gear. I doubt that what we used is around anymore because other things have replaced it that are much better.

One of my biggest jobs in the charthouse was to keep the necessary navigational charts on hand and up to date. Every month or so the ship would receive a publication from the U.S. Hydrographic Office that was full of information about changes to navigational charts of waters all over the world. However, I was only interested in the changes to the charts that covered the areas of the Pacific Ocean that the Brush operated in, which included the west coast of the United States, the waters around the Hawaiian Islands, Japan, Korea, and the entire east coast of Asia as far south as Formosa and Hong Kong. However, in the summer of 1954, I also had to correct, or bring up to date, the charts of the waters around the Philippine Islands and French Indochina.

The changes to the navigational charts included such things as the emplacement of new buoys, new lighthouses or lights erected, new sunken ships, new rocks or reefs located, new breakwaters, etc. All these things had a symbol. So that is how I spent a lot of time – keeping these charts up to date. In addition, I had to order, or go get, new charts occasionally as we wore them out with use. However, I might mention that everything that took place in the charthouse was the responsibility of the chief quartermaster. I was just the one that did the work for him. Of course, the navigator himself was over us and was the one that we had to keep happy – and did.

## Celestial Navigation

Another one of my charthouse duties was to determine which 3 stars we would "shoot", or the 3 best stars we would "shoot" in the evening, just at dusk, when we knew we had to determine our position by means of celestial navigation. I had a navigational book that I referred to to help me in this respect. I would jot down the names and general location of these stars in the sky in the navigator's notebook. The navigator was the one that normally used the sextant to shoot the stars, and he was always assisted by the chief quartermaster who was recording the exact time of the shots with a stopwatch. Although, sometimes the navigator would be tied up with other duties at the correct time to shoot the stars, so at those times the chief quartermaster and I would do it. Sometimes the chief would use the sextant and sometimes he would let me do it. Chief Emerson is the one that I worked with the most in celestial navigation.

After shooting the stars, the navigator and chief would then go down to the charthouse and do some calculations to actually determine our position. Again, if the navigator was tied up with other duties, the chief and I would do it.

## General Quarters

The term "general quarters" means "battle stations". Every man on the ship had a battle station somewhere. Of course, mine and the other quartermasters were on the bridge, except for the one in after-steering.

When the general quarters alarm is sounded, every man on the ship rushes to his battle station. The entire crew is expected to be at their stations in a couple of minutes or so. The captain would exercise the crew at general quarters occasionally to just give them practice at getting there in a hurry. Actually, in combat situations the survival of the ship and the crew could depend on them getting to their stations in seconds. The crew was fully aware of this and made a special effort to get to their stations in a hurry, even the slackards, because they all were interested in surviving, if possible.

Traffic was supposed to flow in a certain way when the men were proceeding to their battle stations. Men that were going forward on the ship ran up the starboard side of the ship, and the men that were going aft ran down the port side. In my case, I usually just went straight up.

When the time came for the ship to go to battle stations, the boatswain's mate-of-the-watch would get on the P. A. system, blow his boatswain's pipe a certain way and say, "General quarters, general quarters, all hands man your battle stations." He would then activate the general quarters alarm, which made a loud dong, dong, dong, dong sound and everybody on the ship was going to hear it. There was no sleeping through that sound.

## Special Sea Detail

The "special sea detail" was set when the ship was either leaving or entering port. It takes a lot of sailors with many different skills to man a naval vessel, even a smaller one like a destroyer. But many of the ship's crew weren't exactly involved with the business of operating the ship; they had other essential duties to perform. However, when the word was passed over the P. A. system to "set the special sea detail", the sailors involved with the operation of the ship went to their duty stations. The men that are largely involved with this duty are the boatswain's mates and other men on the deck force, the quartermasters, and the engineers below deck in the engine rooms and boiler rooms – like the boiler tenders and the machinist mates and maybe others. I'm not very knowledgeable about all the things that went on below deck in the engine room.

However, I am very familiar with what went on on the bridge when the special sea detail was set. The officers that were always on the bridge at this time included the captain, the executive officer, the navigator, the officer-of-the-deck (OOD) and the junior officer-of-the-deck (JOOD). The captain almost always took the conn when we were going in and out of port, but occasionally he would let the executive officer take the conn for a little while – for him to get a little experience, I suppose. The navigator, of course, advised the captain about what courses to steer to get the ship in or out of port. The officer-of-the-deck (OOD) and the junior officer-of-the-deck (JOOD) assisted the captain in anyway they could, or if there wasn't anything for them to do, they just stood back out of the way. Also, at the forward part of the bridge was a telephone talker that enabled the captain to communicate with other parts of the ship. In addition, there were two lookouts – one on the starboard side and one on the port side. These three men, boys actually, were sent up from the deck force.

All of the quartermasters, but one, would be on the bridge. Three of the QM's would be in the pilothouse – one would be at the wheel, one would be on the engine-order- telegraph, and one kept the quartermaster's notebook from which the official ship's log was written. The rest of the QM's would be on the signal bridge. However, the chief would sometimes be on the signal bridge and sometimes he would assist the navigator by taking bearings on navigational objects.

In my earlier days aboard ship, I sometimes kept the QM notebook and sometimes I was on the signal bridge. Later on, I became the special sea detail helmsman and took the wheel. The one QM that wasn't on the bridge was in "after-steering".

One of my duties as the charthouse quartermaster was to have the proper navigational charts on the navigator's desk in the pilothouse when we were underway or planning to get underway. The charts were usually stored in the navigator's desk in the charthouse, and I would bring the proper ones up to the pilothouse when the ship set the special sea detail. However, if we were only going to be in port for a day or so, I might just store them in the desk in the pilothouse. I kept close track of those navigational charts, because it would have been a very serious matter if the ship didn't have the proper charts on hand when they were needed. Someone would have been in big trouble if those charts had come up missing when the navigator needed them, and it probably would have been me and maybe the chief quartermaster, too. I certainly didn't want to be in that kind of predicament and never was.

## Special Sea Detail Helmsman

One of the duties of an experienced quartermaster is to be a skilled helmsman, and the "special sea detail helmsman" is always a quartermaster. He takes the wheel when the ship is going in and out of port, going alongside ships at sea, going through narrow or tricky channels, and when the ship goes to general quarters, or battle stations.

I remember the first time I received helmsman training. Tommy was my instructor. Before Tommy actually started giving me steering lessons, he took time to give me some revealing insight into the perils of being a special sea detail helmsman. Tommy told me to remember that, if anything unpleasant ever happened to the ship in the way of an accident, a collision, or a disaster of any kind, it was always going to the helmsman's fault. The captain was always going to blame the helmsman for not obeying a steering order correctly, or something; it was never going to be the captain's fault – his career was at stake. The helmsman had to sacrifice his career for the captain's sake if possible. That was a sobering revelation and I'm sure he was telling me the truth to the best of his knowledge. Nevertheless, I still was anxious to learn how to steer the ship because that was part of being a quartermaster. Fortunately, there was never a mishap of any kind during my navy experience, so I never got to know for sure if what he told me was true or not. I did become an expert helmsman over time and became the ship's special sea detail helmsman for the last two years I was in the navy. I don't remember any of the other quartermasters ever taking the wheel during that time except Billy Tomlinson who relieved me a few times after I had been on the wheel for an hour or more alongside another ship. I also remember relieving him a couple of times after he had been at the wheel for an hour or so alongside another ship. Going alongside other ships during rough seas was probably the most challenging steering situations we had to face. You really had to pay close attention to your steering and try to anticipate what the ship was going to do and try to correct any wayward movements of the ship before they happened.

The quartermasters only steered the ship when the special sea detail was set and when the ship was at battle stations or general quarters. Someone from the deck force always steered the ship when we where at sea under regular steaming watches. Steering the ship under normal steaming conditions really wasn't too difficult of a job. However, where the problems came in are when the ship was in a tight situation and the captain was barking out orders to the helmsman fast and furious. Many times the captain would give the helmsman a new order before he was able to get the last one completed, and sometimes this same situation would go on for several minutes. Of course, the helmsman had to repeat it and start working on the new order. I know many times I got quite a workout spinning that wheel around. The most important thing was to just follow the captain's last order. Apparently, some people could handle those very stressful steering conditions and some couldn't. I could and was one of the best to just state a fact.

I witnessed an experienced, regular steaming watch helmsman get rattled one time and just froze up on the wheel and couldn't do anything. The captain quickly realized the helmsman was confused and was just standing there at the wheel unable to do anything and hollered into the pilothouse to put another man on the wheel. So another sailor took the wheel; I think it was the boatswain's mate that did. The original helmsman was terribly embarrassed for freezing up at the wheel. He just was not used to receiving so many helm orders so fast. He was actually a good helmsman, normally.

I would think that steering a big ship was probably a little different experience than steering a destroyer. I don't believe that the demands on the helmsman of a big ship are anything as great as those on a destroyer, because the big ships just go plodding along on a set course and don't have to do all the maneuvering and dashing about that a destroyer does, and also they aren't affected nearly as much by wind and wave action either. In addition to that, I believe the bigger ships always had assistance from tugs and maybe harbor pilots, too, when they came into port. Occasionally, we were also assisted by tugs and pilots when we came into port. I'm not sure why they were needed though.

## Sleeping Compartments

There were 4 main sleeping compartments for the enlisted men. There were 2 forward on the ship and 2 back toward the fantail. They all had pretty much the same sleeping arrangement, but the forward sleeping compartments were 2 decks down from the main deck instead of one deck like the after sleeping quarters were. The operations department sleeping quarters, and where I slept for 3 years and 2 months, was below the mess deck and rather deep in the ship. And there weren't any portholes to look out of or to let light and air in. Fresh air was pumped into the compartment by means of blowers. The air pumped in was the same temperature as that on the outside, whatever that happened to be, hot or cold. There wasn't any attempt made by the ship to heat it or cool it in any way. The size of our sleeping space was about 30 feet wide, the width of the ship at this location, and from 15 to 25 feet long fore and aft. The compartment was actually about the size of a large living room in a house. With the exception of the chief petty officers, all the operations department personnel slept here, which included the quartermasters, radiomen, radarmen, and sonarmen; in all, there were a total of about 40 sailors that slept here.

The chief petty officers had their own little compartment in the bow, the roughest riding place on the ship. It was not a good place to be in my opinion. However, during my time aboard the Brush, there was only one chief in the operations department and that was the chief quartermaster.

In the compartment the sailors slept on what was called racks; they could hardly be called a bed, bunk, or cot because of what they were. The racks consisted of long pieces of one inch aluminum tubing that was bent into a rectangular shape that was approximately six and a half feet long and two and a half feet wide. A piece of heavy canvas-type material was stretched across this space created by the metal tubing. Then, a thin mattress, about one and a half inches thick, was laid on top of the canvas. That was our bed, so to speak. Sometimes, a wire mesh thing was used instead of canvas. The racks were stacked three high in tiers with about two feet between them. You could barely turn over when someone was in the rack above you. When I first came aboard, I was assigned a bottom rack-the forward most rack on the starboard side and which was located on top of a row of three deck (floor) lockers, one of which was going to be mine. It was one of the few racks that was unoccupied at the time. This rack was undoubtedly one of the least desirable ones to have, because it laid on top of this row of deck lockers. And anytime someone wanted to get into one of them when I was in my rack trying to sleep, I had to roll over toward the bulkhead (wall or hull) so he could lift my rack up enough to get into his locker. It was kind of a nuisance situation for both of us, but what else could a fellow do if he needed to get into his locker? They always apologized to me for having to disturb me. My rack was also located right at the waterline and I could hear a lot of swishing of water outside the ship when we were underway. The hull of destroyers is a sheet of metal only ¼ inch thick. Therefore, destroyers didn't have any armor on their sides like some of the bigger ships. However, I was very thankful of that thin sheet of metal that was between me and the big, deep waters of the Pacific Ocean. A few months later on, however, I got a much better located rack and an upright locker, too, when one of my shipmates left the ship. In fact, it was one of the best ones in the compartment; it was amidships and right at the bottom of the ladder that led down into the compartment.

The sonar shack was also located in the operations department sleeping compartment – right behind the ladder that led down into the compartment. It was a relatively small space where a sonarman, maybe two sometimes, stood watches looking at their sonar scope when we were underway. They were listening for submarines, of course. For some reason, I never once looked into the sonar shack to see what was going on. Looking back, I don't know why I wasn't more curious than that. However, there also was a sonar scope in the pilothouse that the bridge personnel could turn on and listen to the pings if they wanted to or needed to.

One interesting feature about our sleeping compartment was that one of the ship's magazines was directly beneath us and was usually full of powder canisters and five inch shells. We didn't think about it too much, but it was something we were aware of and all hoped that the magazine wouldn't explode one day for some reason and blow us all to kingdom come. Fortunately, that never quite happened.

## Forward Head

The forward head (bathroom) was located just forward of the mess deck on the port side. The size of the head was about 15 feet by 20 feet and was divided into 2 parts, somewhat. In the after part and the part we walked into were located 6 or 7 wash basins and mirrors and a small shower. In the other part of the head, just forward of the wash basins and separated by a partition, were 2 urinals and a 3-holer toilet. There weren't any commodes like most people are accustomed to. Our toilet was a stainless steel trough about 5 feet long with sea water continuously running through it. A sailor could answer the "call of nature" and get washed off at the same time. Wasn't that convenient and thoughtful of the navy to provide us with such an accommodation? There were enough toilet seats to accommodate 3 sailors at one time, too. Wasn't that a cozy situation? We got to know our shipmates quite well over the months and years as we went to the toilet together. Many times we got to enjoy a bowel movement together and had a nice chat while we were waiting for things to happen. That is how you can develop some real camaraderie.

The operations department personnel weren't the only ones that used this forward head either. About 40 men of the deck force also used it. The deck force's forward sleeping quarters was just forward of ours and just forward of the mess deck. So, in all, around 70 to 75 men used this head, and sometimes things got real crowded when half these men were trying to get ready to go on liberty at the same time. The rest of the time, though, the head really wasn't too crowded like you might think it would be.

Most sailors showered everyday and accomplishing that was sometimes rather challenging with this one shower for 70 to 75 men. However, it was only when we were in port and everybody was trying to get ready to go on liberty at the same time that the showering situation became trying. The rest of the time the showering situation was livable, according to ship sailor standards, but not necessarily according to civilian standards. However, in order to speed up the showering process we usually showered with a buddy. The small shower was rather crowded with 2 people in it, naked at that, but we managed. Showering aboard ship was a rather short operation anyway; it consisted of wetting down, soaping down, and rinsing off and was usually accomplished in 2 or 3 minutes. There wasn't any lingering in the shower because some of your shipmates were usually standing there waiting for you to get out. It was quite a luxury for me, on those few occasions that I was able to do it, to shower alone and to spend 5 minutes doing it instead of the usual 2 or 3 minutes with someone.

Many times there was a little good-natured arguing going on between showering buddies during the busy showering sessions. They would be arguing over whose turn it was to drop the soap. It was all a joke, of course, and a way for them to be gross. Some sailors loved to talk gross and did it at every opportunity.

## Uniform of the Day

Dungarees and a chambray shirt was normally the uniform of the day aboard destroyers. We were also sometimes referred to as the dungaree navy. These uniforms were washed aboard ship and were never ironed, and consequently they were always worn wrinkled. Of course, nobody cared because everybody was dressed the same way. Dungarees were worn both at sea and in port.

However, a few times, as I remember, we had to change into undress blues or undress whites when we were entering port. I suppose that was to look sharp for some admiral that happened to be in port. I believe some of the bigger ships, like cruisers and battleships, may have required their crew to wear undress blues or undress whites all the time when they were aboard ship. Of course, all sailors wore dress uniforms when they went on liberty. Dress whites were the same as undress whites except for the black neckerchief.

Sailors had to buy their clothes and I noticed that some of my shipmates let their daily uniforms get mighty tattered and faded before they spent their money on some new ones; these were always members of the deck force or the men that worked below deck. The men in the operations department had to dress a little sharper.

## Galley and Serving Line

The galley was located on the main deck a little forward of amidships. A port hatch opened into the inside passageway and a starboard hatch opened onto the main deck. The serving line was several feet forward of the galley, up the interior passageway and down a ladder to the next deck. Whoever designed that arrangement didn't put much thought into it from a practical standpoint and certainly had never spent any time aboard a destroyer to know how rough they rode. The mess cooks had to carry heavy pots and pans of hot food down a steep ladder (stairs) to the serving line. That was a risky chore even in calm seas, but it was especially difficult in rough seas or even moderately rough seas if the ship was involved in a lot of maneuvering. Many times I saw the mess cooks get halfway down the ladder with a heavy pot or pan of food in their hands trying to keep their balance on a rolling and pitching ship. Keeping your balance in rough seas could be a difficult job even without having anything heavy in your hands. The poor mess cooks would just have to stand there on the ladder, swaying with the ship, until the ship's movements would stabilize enough for them to take another step down. It was quite a feat for them to keep from falling off the ladder with the heavy load of food in their hands. However, in spite of the difficult job the mess cooks had in this respect, I never heard of any of them falling off the ladder and spilling dinner.

## Chow Time

The ship served chow 3 times a day – morning, noon, and evening at certain times and that was it. If you failed to eat at those times, you just missed out. You would just have to wait till the next meal and go hungry. The chow line formed on the port side of the main deck at the ladder that went down into the serving line compartment. You usually had to stand in line for awhile unless you were coming off watch and was one of the last ones to eat. At the serving line we would pick up our metal tray and eating utensils, if there were any, and go through the serving line. The cooks would put the various food items that were being served on our tray. There was always one entrée; I think the cooks made a point not to overfeed the crew. I feel like the men were served mighty skimpy portions most of the time and as a result the men felt hungry much of the time. I would rate the quality of our food as poor the entire 3 years and 2 months that I was on the ship, and I believe most of the crew would agree with me on this point.

I had the opportunity to eat chow on 2 different carriers during my navy career and both times the chow servers gave the men all they wanted; if you wanted more, all you had to do was ask for it. However, the carrier chow wasn't exactly on par with home cooking either.

I also lived on another destroyer for 3 weeks during the latter days of my shipboard life and for 2 weeks on a destroyer escort after that. The food on both these ships was far superior to what we had on the Brush. On both these ships the cooks served man-sized portions and the food even tasted good. I was impressed with the quality of the food on these 2 ships. So, I know the chow on the Brush could have been much better. I will admit, though, that the menus that were posted in the interior passageway looked pretty good most of the time, but what we got wasn't all that great. I will, however, give the cooks credit for making good bread. I would rate their ship-made bread as excellent.

Anyway, after the men were served their food, they went into the mess deck and took a seat at one of the tables. However, eating their food wasn't always a simple matter either. In port, and in calm seas with little maneuvering of the ship, the sailors could eat their food more or less like normal people.

However, during rough seas the task of eating got a little more complicated. The sailors learned that they had to crook an arm around their tray to keep it from sliding all over the table or onto the deck. Sometimes the men had to forego their eating and just hold on to their trays because the ship would be pitching and rolling so violently. Furthermore, if there were any soupy items on the tray, it would spill out onto the table. The mess deck got to be a real mess during rough seas. Food would be all over the tables and deck, too. Some mess boy had a big job cleaning it up.

What did we have to eat? I've forgotten some of it, but I clearly remember some of the things we had.

Breakfast. Sometimes we would have dry cereal or oatmeal with milk. That was fine when we were in the States where the ship could get fresh milk. However, overseas the ships used powdered milk that was always warm and lumpy. I found it very unappetizing and didn't use it on my cereal. I ate my cereal dry. The enlisted men always drank out of mugs. We never saw a glass. We got fresh milk in the states, but our ration was ½ cup per day at breakfast. Sometimes we were served scrambled eggs and bacon, or Canadian bacon, which was fine most of the time. However, there were times the bacon wasn't so great. The cooks cooked the bacon in a big pan in the oven and I suppose they stirred it some, but on some occasions the bacon that I was served wasn't edible. By that I mean, one half of the strips of bacon I got would be totally burnt to a crisp, and the other half would be totally raw. So I actually didn't get any bacon for breakfast that I could eat. Another thing we had occasionally for breakfast was chipped beef on toast. I liked that and it was one of my favorite breakfasts. However, the shipboard name for that item was "foreskins on toast". Another thing that was frequently served for breakfast and that a lot of the crew liked, although, I didn't care much for it myself, was something called "shit-on-a-shingle". Actually, it was hamburger, tomatoes, and tomato sauce that was cooked together and put on toast. In my opinion, it was just barely edible. We also had canned corn beef hash and French toast occasionally, too. That's all I can remember about breakfast.

For the noon and evening meals we had kind of run-of-the-mill stuff, with one exception, we never had a thing that could be considered Southern. The meats served were usually good but not a large enough portion. We had steak occasionally but it was only about 4 to 6 ounces in size. We also had pork chops, hamburger steak, Salisbury steak, boiled beef, and baked chicken. We had chicken fricassee occasionally, too, which was always good and was one of my favorite meals. As I remember, we always had fish on Friday. It was always filet of sole, fillet of halibut, salmon steaks, or canned salmon made into patties. I don't remember having any other kind of seafood. We also had beef stew sometimes, which could be quite good if you were at the head of the line. However, if the cooks misjudged how much to make to feed the crew, they would start adding water to it toward the end of the meal. I've eaten it when it didn't have any flavor at all. It tasted just like water and was more of a thin soup. The only fresh vegetables I remember seeing aboard ship were Irish potatoes and cabbage. However, overseas the green cabbage had usually turned yellow by the time we ever received it aboard from a supply ship. Needless to say, the cabbage wasn't exactly fresh by any standard. And the potatoes, I normally like potatoes cooked any way, but for some reason the potatoes we got aboard ship never had a good flavor and I can't imagine why. They were barely edible in my opinion. Some of the other vegetables they served us from time to time were canned sweet potatoes, tomatoes, creamed corn, and asparagus; we also had frozen English peas, cauliflower, broccoli, and brussel sprouts. We also had navy beans occasionally and they were usually good and made a hearty meal. We ate a lot of rice, too. I believe that one of the crew's favorite meals was chili-on-rice.

One of the things that I purely hated was canned asparagus. It was soft, mushy, and had a terrible flavor in my opinion. That was my first introduction to asparagus. That is what I thought asparagus was, and I wouldn't touch it for 20 years after getting out of the navy. However, somewhere along the line, someone persuaded me to try some of their fresh, lightly cooked asparagus and I found it to be quite good. Consequently, I love fresh asparagus today and eat it at every opportunity.

## Big Kettle

There was a big stainless steel kettle at the end of the serving line. It must have held 30 or 40 gallons. It was used for various things. The cooks make coffee in it some mornings. They would fill the kettle full of hot water and then put a big bag of coffee in it which they pushed around with a big stick until the water turned brown. The bag of coffee must have weighed 3 or 4 pounds. Other times, always overseas, the cooks would use the kettle for making "milk" from powdered milk. We were supposed to put the milk on dry cereal or oatmeal for breakfast. It was some gross stuff. It was always warm and lumpy. I tried to use it but I decided I would much rather eat my cereal without any "milk" on it. I believe they made stew in it sometimes, too. The stew was always pretty good if you were one of the earlier ones to eat. However, if you happened to be one of the latter ones to eat, you would probably get the watered down version. It was probably used for other things, too, but that is all that I can remember.

## Scullery

After the sailors finished their meals, they took their metal trays and eating utensils to the scullery. The scullery was a small compartment just aft of the mess deck on the starboard side. Here is where the garbage was collected and the trays and eating utensils were cleaned. Inside the scullery the sailors scraped off the scraps from their trays into a garbage can, dipped them into a small drum of water, and scrubbed off the remaining food with a small, short-handed mop. Then, the trays were placed on a ledge in reach of the scullery boy. He would do the final cleaning of the utensils with some cleaning equipment and a lot of hot water. The sailors would exit the scullery by climbing a ladder at the rear of the compartment that led up to the main deck. This was the procedure that was followed by everybody after every meal. So, as you can gather, we didn't exactly have very classy dining accommodations.

The scullery boy had a bad job it appeared to me. It certainly was a hot and nasty place to work. A person would get a steam bath if he stayed in there very long. The scullery duty was probably the least desirable job aboard ship and was usually assigned to a new seaman apprentice. I don't know how they were selected for the job, but some of them would have the job for several months before they were relieved of it. I doubt if any of those sailors ever re-enlisted in the navy.

## Officer's Mess

I imagine the officers pretty much ate the same food as the enlisted men did, but it was probably prepared better and served in a more dignified manner. The officers had stewards to prepare their food for them, and if it wasn't up to par, I'm sure the head steward would be notified of that fact in short order. The steward mates were usually Filipinos on the Brush, but the personnel would change from time to time, and sometimes there would be a black one. As I remember, there were usually 3 of them on board at any given time. Their sole purpose on board was to serve the officers, and they didn't have any other duties to perform as far as I could tell. However, I suppose they had a battle station to man like everyone else, although, I never knew what it was; maybe it was to man the coffee pot. Who knows? Just a thought. I noticed the Filipinos just tended to mind their own business. I never saw one talking to or socializing with any other member of the crew. They were an unfriendly bunch it seemed to me. Maybe it was because they served the officers exclusively and somehow felt themselves superior to or at a higher social level than the common sailor.

As I previously stated, the officers ate in a more dignified and gentlemanly manner than the crew. They sat around a long table, in chairs, in the officer's wardroom. The table had a green tablecloth on it, too, as I remember. The officers ate off of China plates, drank out of China cups and nice glasses. In addition, they always had eating utensils available to them. I believe all the officers ate at the same time as much as possible. Of course, the officers on watch couldn't be there. I suppose they ate together after getting off watch. The officers didn't have to stand in line and go through a chow line either to get their meals. The steward mates served it to them – and on plates, too, mind you. The officers had a big advantage in rough weather also. A wooden form was placed over the table that had spaces in it to set the plates, glasses, and cups that prevented them from sliding around. That was a wonderful feature at their dining table and a smart idea on somebody's part.

I don't know for sure, since I never ate in the officer's wardroom, but I imagine the mood at the table was set by the captain. If the captain was happy, I would imagine there was a lot of pleasant chatter going on, but if the captain was in a foul mood for some reason, I would imagine the occasion was rather strained with very little verbal exchange going on between the officers. It was not a good thing to get on the captain's bad side and was to be avoided if at all possible.

I couldn't help but notice that there were a lot of advantages being an officer, and I think it had a lot of influence on my future thinking. They had a somewhat better life on the ship than the enlisted men, and I liked their accommodations much better. Most of the officers had college degrees and were a little older then most of the sailors.

## Officer's Country

Main Officer's Country, or the main officer's living quarters, was located on the main deck, starboard side, and somewhat forward of amidships. They had rather Spartan living conditions, too, it appeared to me, and wasn't anything to get excited about. Fourteen or so officers were housed in 4 relatively small compartments around 12 x 12 feet in size. The executive officer and one other officer, a lieutenant, were housed in one of them. They had the best accommodations since there were only 2 of them. The other officers, ensigns and Lt(jg)'s, were housed in the other 3 compartments, 4 to 6 men to each compartment; however, their racks were only 2 high. And there was a small desk or 2 in each compartment. There was also some closet space for them to hang their uniforms in. There weren't any portholes in Officer's Country either to let in the light and fresh air, which made it rather stuffy, I thought. However, the compartments were topside which might have helped some in hot climates. They had a common head but I never was in it, so I don't know what it was like. I had to go to Officer's Country occasionally to set the ship's clocks that were there to the correct time. However I never did see an officer in there while I was taking care of my business. Officer's Country was generally off limits to enlisted men, as you can imagine. There was also a small officer's quarters back aft where 2, 3 or 4 officers were berthed, but I was never in that one.

## Recreation Aboard Ship/Movies

There was a movie aboard ship almost every night, both at sea and in port. The movies were shown either on the fantail or in the mess deck. However, they may not have always been shown during the times we were operating off North Korea. If they were shown, they were shown in the mess deck. The movies were mainly for the enlisted men. I don't believe the officers attended them very much, if at all. However, I rarely ever attended one myself because I was always trying to get a little sleep when I had the opportunity. The quartermasters, along with some of the other watch standing rates, never got a good night's sleep when we were underway, which was much of the time. Consequently, we felt sleepy all the time and slept if we got the chance.

However, going to the movies usually wasn't that great of an event anyway, because after a new sailor had been on board for 6 months, he had already seen the same movies several times. There couldn't have been over 25 to 30 different movies shown. These same 25 to 30 movies were kept circulating around through the different destroyers we operated with. Every now and then we would go alongside another destroyer for something and she would send us over some movies, or the ships would swap some movies, but it was always the same movies over and over. Some of the men had seen the same movies so many times that they just about had the scripts memorized. I don't know why they kept going back to watch the same movies time after time. I guess they were bored and didn't have anything better to do.

A short film of the singer Theresa Brewer was attached to one of the movies that circulated around. It was always ahead of the main feature, whatever that was. She sang 3 songs on this little film. They were very lively songs and some that she made quite popular during her heyday. I can't remember the names now but would recognize them if I heard them. Her songs were quite pleasant to listen to for the first 8 to 10 times you heard them. However, after awhile when that little film of Theresa showed up, the sailors would whoop and holler, stomp their feet, whistle, and shout obscene things just like she was there in person and it was the first time they had ever heard her sing. Really, I believe their actions were more of an expression of frustrations than anything else.

Going to the movies was the only kind of approved recreation we ever had aboard ship. However, there were crap games (dice) every now and then, according to the scuttlebutt circulating around. I think it was always played in the after-sleeping quarters by some of the deck force or engineers. I never witnessed any of the gambling myself, and dice were never rolled in the operation's compartment that I ever saw or heard about. After weeks at sea and the same ole things day after day, it is no wonder that sailors tended to get a little rowdy sometimes when they went ashore.

The closest thing to gambling that the bridge gang ever did was play poker for one cent a game. There was a period of time that we played poker frequently when we were in port and when we had all our work caught up – work such as cleaning up, painting, and shining brass. I would win a game occasionally, but I always ended up losing by the end of the day. I think the most I ever lost in one day was 10 cents. Maybe that wasn't too big of a sin or a loss. It certainly was a good way to relieve boredom.

## Phosphoric Lights

One thing that I did occasionally on dark nights was to lean on the ship's rail and watch the millions of little lights in the water go by. I always stood on the port side and about 50 feet or so forward of amidship to observe these lights. These little lights were caused by tiny particles of phosphorous in the ocean water, so the story goes. I'm sure many in the crew indulged in this same pastime from time to time to observe this phenomenon. I never did quite understand why these little lights appeared as the ship cut through the water. But for some reason, the disturbing of the water would activate these tiny particles of phosphorous and cause them to show a bright flash of light. Each flash of light probably didn't last over a half second, but there were thousands, or millions, of them depending on how long a fellow stood at the rail and looked at the water passing by. These little flashes of light reminded me of "lightening bugs" on land. This pastime could only be participated in under certain sea and steaming conditions. First of all, it had to be a dark night; then the sea had to be relatively calm with the ship just steaming along at a modest speed, otherwise, a person was subject to getting wet.

## No Lounge Area

A major shortcoming of an American destroyer was that there wasn't any kind of lounging area for a sailor to go hang out, read, write letters, socialize, or do whatever else he wanted to do when he wasn't on duty. It created quite a problem in regards to relieving boredom. Everything aboard ship got tiresome after awhile. The Brush, and most of the other destroyers in use in the Pacific during the 1950's, were built during World War II, and there apparently wasn't much thought given to living conditions for the crew. The navy probably thought that most of the destroyers wouldn't survive the war so why worry about such trivial things as living accommodations for the crew. The World War II destroyers were built to fight in, not to live on with any degree of comfort. But sailors still had to live on them in the early 1950s, 5 and 10 years after WWII and even for years after that. The sleeping compartments were rather off limits during the day; besides, there really wasn't any room to do much there anyway. There wasn't any space to put a table or chair or anything else. Nor was there a place that you could even sit down.

The mess deck was a nice, big area, but it was only utilized for eating. No one was supposed to be loitering around in the mess deck in the way of the mess cooks. However, movies were occasionally shown in the mess deck at night during foul weather. And at those times, it was always wall to wall people and pretty stuffy.

The commodore's cabin was the only other space on the ship of any size, but the captain claimed that space, except when the commodore was aboard; so that space wasn't available either.

So where did the men go when they were off duty? Sometimes you would see them sitting around on the main deck or at the rail just watching the water go by. However, I suppose most of the sailors just hung out at their normal duty station even though they weren't on watch. I know the QM's tended to hang out on the signal bridge during good weather. I don't know where they were during foul weather. I hung out up there sometimes myself; however, most of the time during the day I was in the charthouse when I wasn't on watch. I usually had plenty to do in there. I don't remember any of the other QM's ever hanging out in the charthouse. Every now and then one would come in for a short visit. I don't know why but most of the time they avoided the place. Maybe they were afraid I might find something for them to do. The charthouse was considered my space and I liked it there myself.

Late in my navy career, I had the opportunity to spend a day aboard a British destroyer and found that the crew had unbelievably better living conditions than what we had on the Brush, and I'm sure all the rest of the American destroyers, too. I'll write more about that later.

## Privacy or the Lack Of

This thing called privacy just about didn't exist aboard ship, at least aboard a destroyer. Of course, that is the only kind of ship that I ever lived on so that is all I know about. The average civilian couldn't imagine living under the kind of conditions we lived under, and I don't think very many people would do it by choice. However, ship sailors didn't have a choice; cramped living conditions and no privacy was just part of shipboard life in the old navy. Things may be different in the modern navy.

The young sailors adjusted to their crowded living conditions amazingly well, I thought, as I look back on my seafaring days. And the crew got along surprisingly well according to what I witnessed. I never saw any of the crew fighting each other much. I think we all realized that we all lived in the same unpleasant living conditions, and we had to get along and endure it together as best we could. Consequently, we all, or most of the time, exercised a great deal of patience with each other. However, I think our living conditions affected some of the crewmembers more then others, because a few of our shipmates went AWOL a lot and stayed in trouble all the time. Of course, they got drunk at every opportunity, too. Apparently, they hated being aboard ship and in the navy in general. It was about more than they could stand.

## Medical Care

Medical care on the ship was kind of a joke. I think we had sick call just about everyday, but it didn't amount to much. The joke was – no matter what your ailment was – a stomach ache, a tooth ache, a toe ache, fever, runny bowels, or whatever, all you ever got at sickbay was All Purpose Capsules (APC's). The corpsmen had a very easy job it seemed to me and didn't have much to remember. They didn't have to stand watches and apparently they only had one kind of capsule to dispense, which shouldn't have been too much to remember. I suppose if you got hurt in some way, they could patch you up until you could see a doctor on a bigger ship. However, if a sailor got seriously ill or hurt in someway, my ship and every other ship in the navy would make every effort to see to it that he would get medical attention somewhere as soon as possible.

I only needed some medical attention twice while I was aboard ship and that was due to my trying to cut a wisdom tooth both times. There wasn't enough room in my jaw for the teeth to come out, and it caused some severe pain for several days before I could get to a dentist. The only kind of pain killer I got was APC's from the corpsmen to put on the teeth. It helped some but not enough. I was taken off watch duty for 2 or 3 days both times, however, and it was a miserable 2 or 3 days before I could get them extracted. I was at sea both times when they started giving me pain and it was several days before we got back in port.

There was one other ailment that the corpsmen could treat, and did treat occasionally, and that was the clap. I'm not sure how they treated this affliction, but I think they gave the poor fellows a shot of penicillin, or maybe it was a series of shots, I'm not sure. However, from my observations, it was a very painful condition when a fellow tried to urinate when he had it. I also know that when a fellow got the clap, he was looking for the corpsmen. The corpsmen didn't have to look for him. I believe the afflicted had to carry around a tin can for a day or two for some reason. The clap (gonorrhea) is the only kind of venereal disease that I ever heard of any of my shipmates having. However, there were some real bad ones out there, so we were informed, especially overseas.

## Flagbag Drunks

Over time, I learned that the flagbags served another purpose other than storing signal flags. The flagbags, usually the port one, is where some of the operations department's personnel went to sleep off a drunk. These drunken sailors would usually climb into one of the flagbags after coming in late from liberty. They knew that the ship was going to be getting underway early the next morning, and they also knew that they were going to be too drunk to participate in it. So they climbed into the flagbag to sleep off their drunk. They knew nobody would disturb them there; whereas, if they were in the sleeping compartment, somebody would be trying to get them up at reveille.

Occasionally, one of the operations department's personnel would come up missing as the ship was preparing to get underway. Before declaring him AWOL, someone would go and check the flagbags. Sure enough, they would usually find the missing sailor lying at the bottom of a flagbag in no condition to do anything but sleep. They would leave him there and declare him present. I have found them down there myself. The drunken sailor would usually make his appearance sometime during late morning or early afternoon. The ship would have been at sea for hours by this time. All of a sudden you would see this head poke up out of the flagbag. It would look so out of place. This head with red blood-shot eyes is all you would see of him for several minutes. They always looked pretty rough. They always just stood there in the flagbag with just their heads showing for a good 10 to 15 minutes before they would venture on out. Then, they would just wander off without saying a word to anybody. I never knew of anybody ever getting into trouble for falling out in the flagbags and not being able to perform their duties, stand their watch, or whatever. Somebody would just perform their duties for him and not say a word about it. Who knows, they might be the one passed out in the bottom of the flagbag the next time.

## The Laundry

The laundry was located on the main deck, starboard side, and about midship. The laundryman didn't do anything else but wash clothes. That was his job. I suppose he was a seaman from the deck force because there isn't a laundryman rate, or wasn't then. He had a full time job washing clothes and didn't stand watches. Although, he had a battle station somewhere, I know. The same fellow washed the clothes most of the time that I was on the ship. He must have liked the job because he didn't try to strike for anything else. Maybe he was learning a trade.

## Sorting Laundry

Everybody has to wash their clothes regardless of who they are, where they are, or what they are doing and sailors are no exception. Sailors have to stay clean and they usually changed their clothes every day. So there had to be some means of washing their clothes. There was a big laundry bag in every living compartment in which the sailors put their dirty clothes and on a certain day of the week, the laundry bag of dirty clothes was taken up to the laundry and was washed. After being washed, the laundry bag, now full of clean clothes, was brought back down to the compartment. Now the problem was getting the clean clothes back to the owners. A method was developed to accomplish that and it was called "sorting laundry". Three men usually were assigned the job of sorting laundry. One fellow would stand by the bag in the middle of the compartment and get the pieces of clothes out of it. The other 2 men would take a position on each side of the compartment. Everyone in the compartment knew where everybody else slept so the fellow getting the pieces of clothes out of the bag would toss it to one fellow or the other, depending on where the fellow's rack was. Everybody's clean clothes would be piled on their rack. Of course, the fellow manning the laundry bag would put the clean laundry on racks near him. In addition, every article of clothing was labeled so there wasn't any guessing going on. So that was the system used aboard my ship to distribute clean laundry. Nobody particularly liked the sorting laundry chore but everybody had to do it from time to time. It really wasn't too bad of a job. It was just part of shipboard life.

## Inside Passageway

One very interesting feature about the ship was the inside passageway on the main deck that enabled sailors to go from the fantail of the ship to the forward part of the ship without having to be exposed to the weather and waves. This feature saved a many a sailor from getting wet from rain and waves during rough seas. The Sumner class destroyers were the first American destroyers to have this wonderful feature. Prior classes of destroyers did not have this feature, and during rough weather, sailors trying to go from one end of the ship to the other were exposed to rain and waves crashing over the bow and the sides of the ship, thus, were most likely to get soaking wet. In addition, they had to hold on to a lifeline (rope) that was strung along the deck so that the waves wouldn't wash them overboard. Living closely with the elements was part of being a destroyer sailor because there wasn't any way to avoid it. However, some of the ship's crew was exposed to the weather more so than others. The quartermasters were some of the ones that had to face the weather the most, because they stood their watches on the open signal bridge. They were there in both good and bad weather. During beautiful weather the bridge was a good place to be; however, during bad weather it was a terrible place to be. The lookouts on the bridge were always exposed to the weather, too.

## Shore Patrol Duty

When a U.S. Navy ship went into port and liberty was granted to the crew, the ship was usually required to send 2, 3, or 4 members of the crew ashore as shore patrolmen. These crewmembers were always petty officers of some kind, but occasionally a junior officer was assigned shore patrol duty, too. These men with shore patrol duty had to report to the permanent shore patrol station on the beach, if there was one, for instructions. Their jobs were mainly to walk the streets where the sailors hung out and make sure that the sailors weren't making too big of a nuisance of themselves. Of course, sometimes a sailor, or a few sailors, would get out of line and have to be escorted back to their ship. The over consumption of alcoholic beverages was usually the reason some sailors got obnoxious and troublesome. I never was assigned shore patrol duty after I made 3rd class petty officer, but I didn't miss it because I didn't want to go anyway.

## Ship's Party

Every year the Brush had a ship's party. It was always held in the States at some big hotel, or convention center, or something. It was a place that could seat 300 people or so including most of the ship's crew and their guests. However, not all the crew could attend because some of the crew had to stay aboard and man the ship.

The ship's party always included a big banquet. I know I always had a big steak, although, there might have been other choices for the meal. I don't remember how all this was paid for, but I don't believe it was with taxpayer's money. Anyway, the banquet part of the party was always enjoyable enough, I thought.

The party part started after the banquet and was always a dance with a live band. Of course, this is when the earnest drinking started. Some of the shipmates brought their wives and girlfriends to it; however, most of us didn't have any such thing. I didn't get much pleasure out of watching other people dance or acting lovey-dovey, so I always left the party when that started.

As I remember, the party was always supposed to last until 12 midnight, but it never did according to what I was told; because sometime prior to 12:00 o'clock, the fighting started. Shipmates fighting each other, can you imagine that? I never was present at the end of the party, but according to what I was told, the fighting started after the liquor started taking affect and the men started fighting over the women. Apparently, some of the sailors would object to one of his buddies holding his wife or girlfriend a little too close while they were dancing. Or, he thought one of his buddies was paying a little too much attention to his woman in general. Anyway, one or more of the drinking sailors would get terribly offended when they imagined that somebody was trying to move in on his woman. So the fighting started; a fellow has got to defend his honor, you know.

## Brown Baggers

The married men on board ship usually went ashore at every opportunity. You could usually tell who the married men were because they always went ashore in Long Beach carrying their little shaving kits, which were usually brown in color for some reason. Consequently, the married men were given the name "brown baggers".

## Distance at Sea

The concept of distance at sea is very deceptive. On a clear day a person can look across the open ocean to the horizon, a distance of 15 to 20 miles. You can see an object as big as a ship for 12 to 15 miles. Of course, when you do sight a ship on the horizon, you always see the mast first, and then as the distance decreases, the ship itself comes in view.

When destroyers are operating together, they usually keep a distance of 500 to 1000 yards between them. Five hundred and 1000 yards, that's 1500 and 3000 feet, which seems like a long ways on land; but at sea, 500 yards looks relatively close and that is the closest distance between ships that I have ever seen destroyers operate together. I would say that a ship traveling at a speed of 16 knots, that is following another ship at a distance of 500 yards, is similar to that of a car on a highway that is traveling at a speed of 60 miles per hour 100 feet behind another car. A ship is a big object and it takes a considerable distance to stop the forward momentum of one and even to turn it.

# 9

# SECOND CRUISE TO THE FAR EAST – 1954

## LONG BEACH TO PEARL HARBOR

Tuesday morning, 4 May, 1954, the ships of DesDiv 92 got underway from Long Beach en route to Pearl Harbor, Hawaii. However, we weren't going alone. The cruisers, USS Bremerton(CA130) and USS St. Paul(CA73), left the harbor at the same time and we were to escort them overseas. So after all the ships got outside the harbor, the destroyers took screening stations around the cruisers. The formation steamed southwest at a speed of 17 knots.

Around 2200 DesDiv 51 came up from San Diego, joined our formation, and also took screening stations around the cruisers. The formation of ships was now designated Task Unit 52.3.7. The ships of DesDiv 51 consisted of the USS Rowan(DD782), USS Southerland(DDR743), USS Henderson(DD785), and the USS Gurke(DD783).

Of course, the formation of ships engaged in some maneuvering exercises as they steamed along, but they didn't continually do it all the time as they sometimes did. Also, the ships engaged in various on-board drills and exercises. Thursday, 6 May, was an especially big day of drills and exercises for the crew of the Brush. At 0830 the general alarm was sounded and the crew was exercised at general quarters for an hour or so. At 0905 there was an abandon ship drill. At 1000 the ship conducted a fire drill. At 1255 the bridge shifted steering control to after-steering. At 1532 the Brush conducted another fire drill. And at 1815 the ship commenced a steering casualty drill. That was all the drills for that day but it was enough for one day.

Saturday, 8 May, at 0830 the ship held a fire and rescue party drill on the port quarterdeck. The captain commenced a lower deck and living space inspection at 0930. At 1300 the captain exercised the crew at collision drill.

Sunday morning, 9 May, the ship went alongside the St. Paul for refueling. A member of the fueling detail was pretty seriously hurt during this operation. The crew was also exercised at general quarters at 1600.

The formation of ships arrived at Pearl Harbor, Monday morning, 10 May. However, just before the Brush proceeded into the harbor, she had a change of command ceremony. At 0845 word was passed over the P.A. system for all the crew and officers not on watch to assemble on the fantail for a change of command ceremony. At 0850 Commander Arlie G. Capps relieved Commander Donald F. Quigley as our commanding officer. I must have been on watch because I don't remember attending it.

## HAWAII

At 0900 the Brush was detached from the formation to proceed independently into Pearl Harbor. The special sea detail was set at 1000. At 1044 our new captain took the conn and brought the ship into the harbor. At 1056 the Brush was moored starboard side to the USS Maddox at berth K-8. The OOD shifted his watch to the quarterdeck and set the inport watch.

### Hawaiian Dancers

I went ashore Monday night but I only went to the enlisted men's club on the base. It served the purpose of getting me off the ship for a little while. I had a reasonably good meal there, looked around the club a little bit, and around 2000 headed back toward the ship. I was walking down this long pier toward my ship when I passed this cruiser; I believe it was the St. Paul that was moored on this same pier but not as far down on it as the Brush. As I was walking by, I noticed that some kind of entertainment was in progress on the fantail that looked rather interesting from what little I could see and hear of it from the dock. I decided I needed to get a little closer look at what was going on so I went aboard the cruiser, went back to the fantail, and, by some miracle, found a ringside location to stand and watch the performance. I witnessed one of the most awesome sights of my life. I saw 6 of the prettiest little brown skinned women that you could lay your eyes on. They all seemed to be a mixture of Polynesian and an Asian race, maybe Chinese. They all had long black hair that came down to their waist, slightly Oriental brown eyes, beautiful complexion, perfect little bodies, and beautiful smiles. They were smiling all the time. They were all small, young women about 5 feet and 2 to 4 inches tall. The entertainers were wearing grass skirts and coconut halters and were dancing to Polynesian music, which is much faster and different than Hawaiian music. Hawaiian hula dancing is interesting, but South Sea Islands dancing is more interesting. It was an awesome performance and lasted for an hour or so after I started watching it.

It was absolutely amazing to me how fast those little women could shake their hips. Those grass skirts that they were wearing were just just awiggling. There wasn't anything indecent about the dancing. It was just exotic – for lack of a better word to describe it. The dancers seemed to be enjoying their performance as much as the sailors were, too. Those little brown women knew that their entertaining efforts were being appreciated, and I would venture a guess that they all had a good self image. The dancing was over much too soon to suit me. I could have watched them all night. I've never seen anything like it since but I keep hoping.

Tuesday morning, 11 May, DesDiv 92 went back to sea and operated with the light carrier, USS Point Cruz(CVL119), and a submarine. We would operate in Hawaiian waters for the next 3 days engaged in ASW exercises with the submarine and screening the carrier. The carrier would also conduct flight operations occasionally. DesDiv 92 went back into Pearl Harbor late Thursday afternoon and the Brush moored alongside the Thomas at berth B-23.

### My Favorite Restaurant on Waikiki Beach

Late Friday afternoon, 14 May, I went on liberty and went to Honolulu & Waikiki Beach. I went to a little patio type restaurant on Waikiki Beach called the "Wagon Wheel Restaurant" and had a sea turtle steak dinner. I had been there before and kind of liked the place. It was a little different type restaurant. The place had a roof but no walls much. It was located in a garden type setting and the smell of flowers (Plumeria) was heavy in the night air. A breeze was always coming in off the ocean cooling the place and rustling the coconut palms. There weren't any mosquitoes either which made it even nicer. I thought it was a very special place and went there every time I was in Hawaii.

**Marvin (left) & Russell Maxwell BT3 (right)**
**Russell & his younger brother Marvin coming into Pearl Harbor**
**May 1954 and all ready for liberty**

## Island Tour

I went on liberty again around 10:00 o'clock Sunday morning, 16 May, with the intentions of going back to Waikiki Beach. But upon approaching the taxi stand, my plans were abruptly changed. There were 4 of us servicemen at the taxi stand that was located just outside the Pearl Harbor Naval Base. We all just happened to be standing there together, waiting to get a taxi, when this cab driver approached us and made us an interesting proposal. He told us that he would give us a tour of the island for a certain price which was rather modest. I believe it was around $4 or $5 each for a 6 hour tour. We were all strangers. We looked at each other, and after talking back and forth for a minute or two, we all decided that we would like to take the tour. The little group consisted of 3 sailors and a marine. We got in the cab and off we went. Somehow, I ended up in the front seat – the best seat.

We all had a most enjoyable day. Part of the time we were on a road that weaved around the side of a mountain overlooking the Pacific Ocean. It was a very scenic drive. He also drove us down to the shoreline several times to show us a blowhole in the rocks, which we watched for a few minutes, and to show us 2 or 3 small secluded beaches. We dropped in on an old, rustic Polynesian bar that was kind of interesting, but nobody in our party seemed to be interested in having a drink so we didn't stay there long.

Our tour guide also took us inland to a pineapple farm. We all went to the field and the farmer cut a couple of ripe pineapples and gave us all a big hunk of fresh, ripe pineapple. That was a very enjoyable eating experience. I think everybody especially enjoyed that experience. It is easy to understand why the early explorers called it "The fruit of the gods" when they discovered the fruit in the West Indies, as I remember. The rich volcanic soil of the Hawaiian Islands seems to be specially suited for growing tasty pineapples. The warm climate, however, makes it possible to grow them there because they are very sensitive to cold temperatures.

Somewhere during the tour, our guide took us to a large Mormon Church and we got a short lecture on the Mormon religion. However, I don't think anyone converted to Mormonism that day.

The taxi driver ended our tour on the top of Diamond Head. There is certainly a beautiful view of the Pacific Ocean from up there.

Those are the places I remember the taxi driver taking us to, but there might have been more. I know we had lunch in some unusual place, but I don't remember a thing about that. Anyway, it was a very special day and I thoroughly enjoyed it. And I know the rest of my party did, too.

## STEAMING WEST TOWARD JAPAN

Task Unit 52.3.7, less the Moore, departed Pearl Harbor Monday morning, 17 May, en route to Yokosuka, Japan. The Moore stayed behind a few more hours to complete some engineering repairs. However, she caught up with the TU a couple days later. The TU steamed west at a cruising speed of 17 knots or so. As usual, the ships engaged in numerous maneuvering exercises as they steamed along toward Japan. Early Wednesday morning DesDiv 92 was detached from the formation to proceed to Midway Island to refuel. We arrived at Midway early Thursday morning, 20 May. But before entering the channel that led into the lagoon and the fueling docks, a harbor pilot came aboard at 0716 and took the conn. Holly was at the wheel. At 0720 the ship commenced maneuvering at various courses and speeds to enter the lagoon. At 0739 the Brush was moored starboard side to the Maddox at pier 2.

I was a little uptight about steering the ship into the lagoon. Tommy had cautioned me to watch my compass heading real close, because the channel was narrow and the current could be swift and tricky. I felt like I could handle the task, but I had never done it before and I just wasn't sure of my steering ability in this particular kind of situation. Tommy stood close by just in case I got in trouble. However, I didn't have a moment's trouble steering the ship through the narrow and tricky channel. I was pleased with myself and gained a little more confidence in my steering skill.

The ships had completed refueling by 1100, got underway, and proceeded out of the lagoon. The Brush set the regular steaming watch at 1200. In a few hours the ships of DesDiv 92 rendezvoused with the other ships of TU 52.3.7, and the TU just steamed west at 17 knots and didn't do much of anything else for several days. We crossed the International Date Line around 1900 Thursday, 20 May, and advanced the time ahead one day.

## STEAMING SOUTH TOWARD SUBIC BAY

I went up to the bridge early Thursday morning, 25 May, and found out that there had been a change of plans for us and we weren't going to Japan after all. The TU was now 2 days out of Japan. The story was that the ships of DesDiv 92 had received secret orders during the night that directed them to proceed elsewhere. The ships of DesDiv 92 were ordered to take on fuel from the cruisers and to head south instead of west and that is what the ships were in the process of doing when I got to the bridge. The Brush soon went alongside the Bremerton and took on fuel oil. However, we continued to cruise along with the TU until 1400 at which time DesDiv 92 departed from the formation and commenced steering a southwardly course of 210°(t), at least for a time. Actually, the ships were headed for Subic Bay, Philippine Islands via Bashi Channel. However, the crew, for some reason, wasn't informed about what our new destination was until we got there, or nearly so, nor were we told what our purpose was for going south. In fact, I don't think the captain himself even knew at that point. The ships of DesDiv 92 just steamed south for the next 5 days and didn't do much of anything else.

I knew that we were going to Southeast Asia, or French Indochina, before we left the States. However, I never knew when it was going to be during our cruise to the Far East, but I should have known it was going to be early in our cruise, because the navigator, Lt. Bryan, had me taken off the watch list so I could bring the navigational charts of that area up to date. That was a big job and he wanted me to work on it full time. Consequently, I worked on those charts for 10 to 12 hours a day all the time we were crossing the Pacific Ocean, except the time I spent on liberty in Hawaii. I don't remember when I finished the project, but it must have been about the time we arrived in Subic Bay. Then, I had to go back to standing watches.

We had relatively pleasant weather and calm seas all the way to Subic Bay. Sunday, 30 May, we were steaming down the west coast of Luzon and could see the tropical shoreline some distance away. The crew had the day off, except for the men on watch, and was lying around on the decks taking in some sunshine. I think it was one of the best cruising days I had in the navy.

I wrote about the day in a letter to my mother dated May 30, 1954. Part of it reads as follows:

"It's a very peaceful and beautiful Sunday morning where we are today. The sky is blue and clear with only wisps of clouds high up. There is just a light breeze and the ocean is no rougher than a lake, not even a swell on the water. Almost everybody is out sitting or lying around on the open decks soaking up the sunshine and trying to lose their pallor color. I was out there soaking it up, too, but noticed how quiet and peaceful it was and decided it was a good time to write a letter. With the pale skin I have, I can't stay out in the sun but a few minutes at a time anyway.

Another thing that is pretty this morning are the little flying fish. Every few seconds one goes flying out from the side of the ship. They jump in the air and go sailing along like some bird. It's interesting to watch them."

## SOUTH CHINA SEA

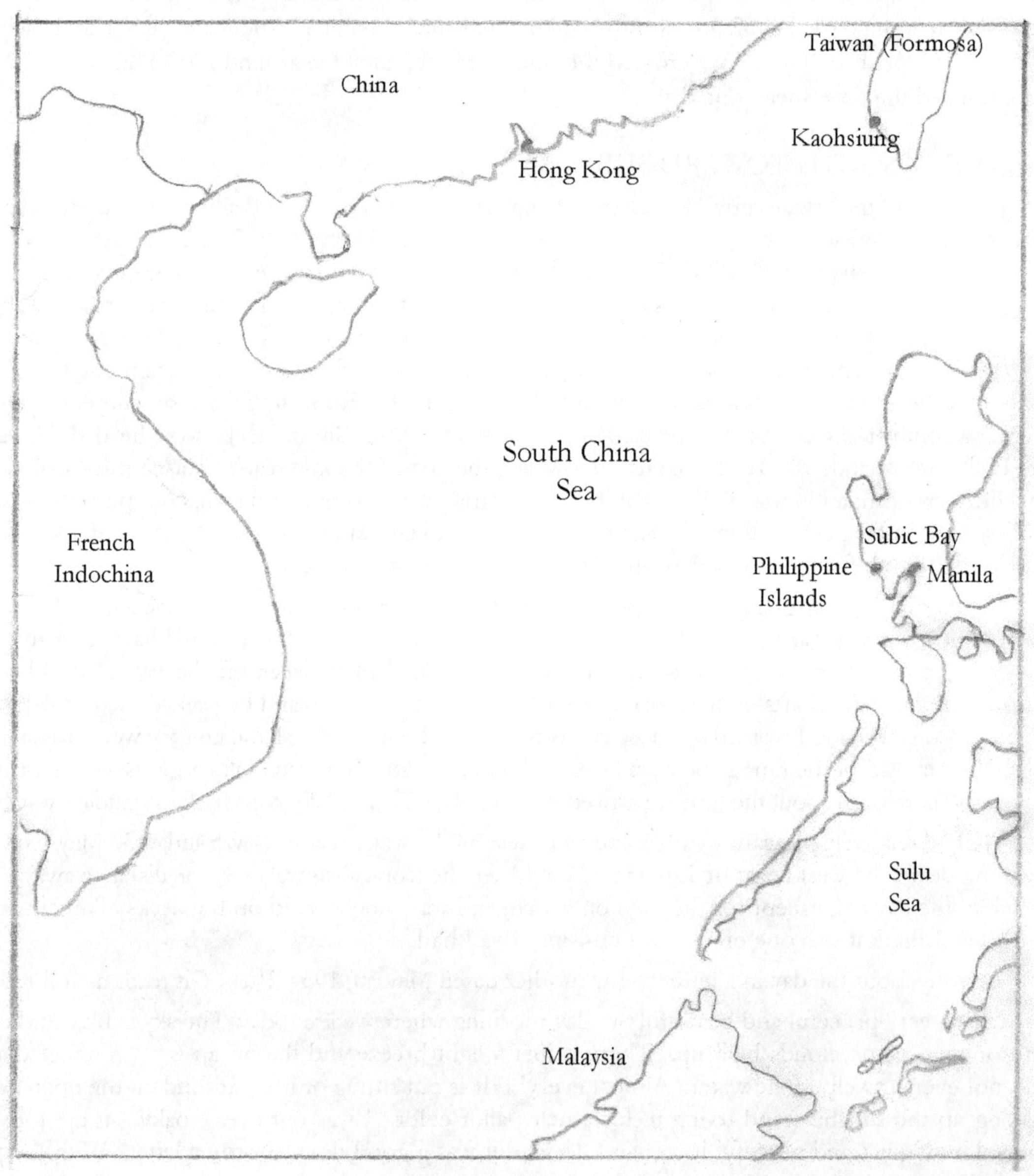

## SUBIC BAY

We arrived in Subic Bay, Philippine Islands late Sunday afternoon and moored to buoy 20. Subic Bay is located a little north of Manila on the island of Luzon. There was a relatively small naval station there. There were several ships present in the harbor when we arrived. The ships present in the harbor included the USS Virgo(AKA20), USS Manatee(A058), USS Delta(ARH-9), USS Montrose(APA212), and DesDiv 31, which consisted of the USS Kyes(DD787), USS Higbee(DDR805), USS Eversole(DD789), and the USS Shelton(DD790). In addition, DesDiv 111, with ComDesRon 11 embarked in the USS Wiltsie(DD716), stood into the bay early Thursday morning, 3 June. However, early Friday morning DesDiv 111 got underway and stood out of the bay. There seemed to be a big buildup of American warships in the region and more were coming.

**Lt(jg) William (Robbie) Robbins**

The day after we arrived at Subic Bay, Monday, 31 May, was my 21st birthday, but I don't remember doing anything to celebrate it. Actually, liberty opportunities were rather slim in Subic Bay. There probably was an enlisted men's club on the base where sailors could go and drink beer but I never went to it. Also, there was a small Filipino town right outside the base. It had a reputation of being a rather worthless liberty town. At least, that was the opinion of some of the older hands that had been there some time in the past. But they thought it might be something a fellow would want to do just one time for the experience. So that is what I did. I went on liberty in this little town of Olongapo late one afternoon while we were in Subic Bay. I went just so I could say I had been there. After all, it was a new experience and my first time ashore in the Philippines.

## Liberty in Olongapo

The town was long and narrow. It was one building wide and about a quarter of a mile long, as I remember. I walked the entire length of it to see what I could see. However, I didn't see much. There were a number of bars along the one street and I went into a couple of them because I saw evidence of some fighting going on – like broken glass and such. Apparently, there was an unusual amount of fighting going on that afternoon. There were hundreds of sailors in the little town and there wasn't a female in sight. The story was that all the bar girls had left the town because they knew that there was going to be a multitude of ship sailors in town that day and that meant big trouble. They were used to just a few peace-loving sailors and marines from the naval base being in town. Anyway, the ship sailors took out their frustration on each other. I only stayed in the town an hour or two, left, and went back to the ship where it was much safer. I was told that the shore patrol brought rowdy sailors back to fleet landing by the bus load that night. Even the officers got a little wild – so I was told.

The thing I enjoyed the most about my first time ashore in the Philippines was standing at the fleet landing at dusk waiting for a boat to take me back out to the ship. I was just standing there feeling the cool tropical breezes blowing in my face and listening to the wind rustle the coconut palms. A person can get a certain amount of pleasure of simple things like that. Anyway, I now had the experience of going on liberty in Olongapo, which led me to agree with the old timers that going on liberty in Olongapo wasn't worth the effort to get there.

The scuttlebutt on the ship was that the ships of DesDiv 92 would only be staying in Subic Bay for 3 days when we first got there, but we ended up staying 7 days. I believe our departure from the harbor was postponed a couple of times during the week. It's pretty certain that the navy sent us down to that part of the world to take part in a special mission of some kind. However, there seemed to be a lot of uncertainty about when this mission was to take place. I'm pretty certain that the political leaders in Washington and the U.S. Navy had a big operation planned for us to take part in around French Indochina, or Vietnam, as it is called today. My assumption is derived partially because of all the urgency put on my getting all the navigational charts of that region corrected and brought up to date. In addition, there was this big buildup of U.S. warships in this region and all the secrecy involved with the ships' movements.

The French Army was in the process of being defeated by the communist forces in Vietnam and, in addition, the communists were causing a lot of trouble in Cambodia, too. I've always felt that we were going down there to assist the French in some way. However, it seems to me like the "Powers That Be" in Washington couldn't make up their minds about what action to take, when to take it, or if to take it. This indecision seemed to have lasted for several months.

It was quite hot in Subic Bay and the ship (and probably ships) went to something called "tropical hours". Reveille was at 0500 and the crew worked to 1200 and then had the rest of the day off. However, there really wasn't much to do during that time off.

In a letter I wrote to my mother dated June 7, 1954, I mentioned the kind of weather we were experiencing in the Philippines.

"The weather over here gets to be kinda routine. It's sunny everyday, but almost as sure as night comes, it rains, thunders and lightning. I kinda enjoy seeing lightning once more for a change. First time I've seen any since I left Florida. It's not the streaked kind – just big balls of light.

Almost everyone sleeps topside under the stars every night till they get rained on. It's nice and cool out in the open, but down below, it's so hot it's miserable. To most people, the way we sleep wouldn't be comfortable but sailors don't mind. We just throw a blanket down on the steel deck and go to sleep. It's not very soft as you can imagine."

Actually, our sleeping efforts would usually get interrupted 2 or 3 times during the night by rain showers. However, the showers wouldn't last more than a few minutes but it forced us inside every time. The quartermasters did their sleeping on the bridge.

Saturday morning, 5 June, the captain had a personnel and upper decks inspection. And a little later in the morning, he held a non-judicial punishment session where he dealt out varying amounts of punishment to 9 wayward sailors.

## SOUTH CHINA SEA – JUNE

All the destroyers in the harbor got underway Monday morning, 7 June, and went to sea, mainly to just get us out of port and doing something, I believe. All the destroyers scattered to engage in various assignments or exercises. The Brush and the Moore stayed together and rendezvoused with the submarine, USS Stickleback(SS415). These navy vessels conducted ASW exercises for the next couple of days, just for something to do, I'm sure. The ships were operating a few miles off the entrance to Manila Bay.

### Task Group 70.2

At 2130 Tuesday evening, 8 June, the Brush and the Moore were directed to secure from the ASW exercises and proceed to rendezvous with a task group steaming down from the north. So the ships commenced steaming north on a course of 005°(t) and at a speed of 16 knots. At 0257 they changed course to 300°(t) to accomplish the rendezvous with the TG. At 0515 one of the bridge lookouts sighted the navigational lights of the task group at a distance of 10 miles. At 0549 the ship observed sunrise and turned off the navigational lights. At 0625 the Brush and the Moore rendezvoused with Task Group 70.2 and the Brush commenced maneuvering to take station 6 in a 6 station screen around the task group.

The ships in TG 70.2 included the aircraft carriers USS Essex(CVA9), USS Tarawa(CVA40), and the USS Philippine Sea(CVA47). They were being escorted by the ships of Destroyer Division 51, which consisted of the destroyers USS Rowan(DD782), USS Southerland(DD743), USS Gurke(DD783), and the USS Henderson(DD785); these were the same destroyers DesDiv 92 crossed the Pacific with. With the arrival of 3 aircraft carriers on the scene, it would suggest that some kind of serious action was about to take place, somewhere. The Maddox and the Thomas also joined the formation at 2335 Wednesday night, 9 June, and took screening stations around the task group.

Task Group 70.2 steamed around in the South China Sea for the next 9 days without doing anything of any significance that I am aware of. In addition, the carriers launched relatively few planes during those 9 days. They did launch some planes Thursday afternoon, 10 June, and one of the planes from the Philippine Sea crashed into the sea. I don't know what the fate of the pilot was. We did a lot of steaming around those 9 days we were out there, but I don't believe we accomplished a whole lot. Some of the destroyers left the formation from time to time to go off and do something on their own. The Brush did, too. We conducted anti-aircraft gunnery practice on a couple of days. The first day, the Brush expended 30 rounds of 5 inch AA shells, and on the second day, she expended 39 rounds of 5 inch AA shells.

The tankers, USS Chikaskia(AO54) and USS Caliente(AO53), came out to refuel us, the TG, a couple of times. Also, the supply ship, USS Regulus(AF57), came out one time to replenish the ships in the TG with provisions.

Sunday, 14 June, 2 ships from DesDiv 51 were detached from the formation and Monday the other 2 ships were detached from the TG. Those ship departures were a pretty good indicator that the TG wasn't going to do anything that would make the headlines. However, Monday afternoon the ships of Destroyer Division 31 joined the TG, which included the USS James E. Kyes(DD787) with ComDesRon 3 embarked.

## INTERESTING SIGHTS OBSERVED IN THE SOUTH CHINA SEA

The weather was hot and the sea was relatively calm the entire 9 days we were out in the South China Sea. I observed a few things during this time out there that made a lasting impression on my memory.

### Giant Jellyfish

Sometimes the sea was as smooth as glass without a ripple on it. At these times I could look down into the water and see giant jellyfish floating around. They seemed to be just hanging there in the water at a depth of about 30 feet. You could easily see them because the water was crystal clear. The jellyfish appeared to be about 10 feet across and looked much like an open umbrella in shape. I believe they were bluish in color. They had long tentacles that hung down about 20 feet. Hundreds of small fish were hanging around the tentacles of each jellyfish. I suppose they were waiting for a meal, somehow. There seemed to be thousands of these giant jellyfish, because I would stand at the ship's rail and watch them go by for 15 to 20 minutes and they would continue to float by. This field of them seemed to be endless. Eventually, I would get tired of looking at them and go do something else.

### Sea Snake

One day I saw a sea snake. It was a very calm day and he was swimming along on the surface of the water just as big as day. It had to be a sea snake because we were probably a hundred miles from land.

### Clouds

Another thing that was plentiful in the South China Sea were big, towering cloud formations from way in the distance to close up. They were always fascinating to look at. Of course, when we passed under one, we would get rained on.

### Quaint Little Merchant Ships

Occasionally, we would pass unusual looking little merchant ships. These little ships looked similar to regular merchant ships but were only about half their size. They also seemed to be wider in proportion to their length than a regular size merchant ship. In addition, their bows were rounded instead of pointed and tapered like most ships. I think you could describe them as being "quaint" looking little ships. I don't remember ever seeing a flag flying on them that identified their nationality.

### Mirage

I saw a mirage of a merchant ship one day when the ship was out operating alone in the South China Sea. It was a partially cloudy day and somewhat hazy. All of a sudden, this mirage of a merchant ship appeared about 6,000 yards off our port quarter. It was lying out there on the surface of the water just like it was real. However, we knew it was a mirage instantly because the ship was upside down. I never knew before that they ever appeared that way. It would have been interesting to know just how far away that the real ship was that it was an image of. The horizon was completely empty of ships in every direction at the time. All of a sudden it just faded away. That was the only mirage I remember seeing during my years at sea.

## LIBERTY IN MANILA

At 0926 Thursday, 17 June, the Brush was detached from TG 70.2 to proceed independently into Manila Bay via the North Channel. At 1431 the ship set the special sea detail to enter the bay. The captain was at the conn. Holly was at the wheel. Upon entering Manila Bay, I was amazed at the number of sunken ships I saw. The masts of sunken ships were sticking up out of the water all over the place. That bay had experienced some terrible times in the past. However, I wasn't able to view the sights in the bay as much as I would have liked to, because I had to mind my helm so close. The captain was continuously giving me helm orders. Consequently, I could only steal a glance at things from time to time.

At 1510 the Brush was moored port side to the Moore at pier 5 in Manila Bay. At 1530 the ship secured the special sea detail and set the regular inport watch. The Maddox and the Thomas were also in port as were the 3 aircraft carriers. So, there was a bunch of sailors roaming around Manila on that weekend.

In a letter that I wrote to my mother dated June 19, 1954, I mentioned some of the things that I observed in Manila.

"Thursday night I went ashore and looked the town over a little. A lot of sign still remains from the last war (WWII) – bombed buildings and such like.

One thing that catches everyone's eye is the number of sunken ships with masts and sometimes bows sticking up out of the water in Manila Harbor. There are dozens of them. A lot of them are big ships.

Manila is a pretty modern place. The people seem to be pretty prosperous, too. People dress just about like Americans. The streets, though, are like just about every other place over here – narrow and crowded."

I enjoyed my visit to Manila. I did a lot of walking around and looking. I went ashore at least a couple of days and bought a number of souvenirs, as I remember.

**MANILA BAY**

Terry Miller map, TCS

## Petty Thief

I had an interesting and unusual experience Sunday morning. I was just walking around looking and shopping when I met a friendly Filipino that wanted to sell me a watch and talk. The inside of his coat was lined with watches of all kinds. However, I wasn't interested in buying one because I already had a good watch. That was fine with him. He didn't get his feelings hurt; he just wanted to make conversation with me, it seemed, because I was an American. We probably carried on a conversation for 15 minutes or so and then he decided it was time for him to move on. He wanted to shake my hand before he left and somehow ended up shaking my left hand. I wore my watch on my left arm and I had a strap watchband. He looked me in the eye like I was his best friend and started shaking my left hand. But he made quick little motions while shaking my hand like he was putting a lot of feeling into it. All of a sudden I realized something didn't feel quite right with my arm. I looked down and saw that he was trying to steal the watch right off my wrist. My band was rather tight on my arm and he was having a little trouble getting it unbuckled. His weird way of shaking my hand somehow covered up the other feelings on my hand and wrist. He was an expert at stealing watches, I'm sure, and he almost got mine. But, like I say, I felt something that wasn't right under the circumstances. However, it hadn't crossed my mind that this friendly fellow was in the process of stealing my watch. Anyway, I looked down at my hand and saw instantly what he was attempting to do. I gasped. He knew that he had been caught so he just turned and walked off. I just stood there a few minutes trying to get over the shock of catching someone trying to steal my watch right off my arm and by someone that pretended to be so friendly. He was just a petty thief plying his trade.

## A Great Meal in Manila

We were warned not to drink the water or eat any vegetables when we were ashore in Manila, because, if we did, it would give us much gastrointestinal discomfort. I believed it. So, if you got thirsty, you just about had to drink beer whether you liked it or not. San Miguel beer was the only kind of beer sold in the Philippines and it was made there. The Philippine government wouldn't allow any other kind in the country – so the story went. And I certainly never saw any other kind there.

I don't remember eating but one meal ashore in Manila and it was on Sunday, our last day there. I went into this very nice Chinese restaurant with the intentions of having something safe to eat. I knew I didn't want to take a chance on eating any raw vegetables. But I did order a Chinese dish that had some cooked vegetables in it. The dish looked very appetizing and it was well cooked. I thought to myself that surely it would be safe to eat the meal since it was well cooked. All the germs would be killed in the process of cooking it; so I decided I would take a chance on it. The dish certainly tasted good and I ate all of it. But I did pay the price later on just like I was told I would. To put it politely, it did cause me much gastrointestinal discomfort and inconvenience for several days afterwards. I learned the hard way that you couldn't eat any vegetables in the Philippines without paying a price.

The ships of DesDiv 92 departed Manila early Monday morning, 21 June, en route to Subic Bay. They arrived at Subic Bay around noon on Monday and proceeded to moor at buoy 11. DesDiv 92 would spend the night there. At 1310 the paymaster departed the ship with $3,913. At 1436 he returned to the ship with $21,000. I suppose that is why we stopped there – to pick up some money to cover payday for the crew.

Tuesday, around noon, the ships departed Subic Bay en route to Sasebo, Japan. Around 1400 they rendezvoused with the carrier, Essex, and took screening stations around her. The formation steamed north toward Sasebo.

## SASEBO, JAPAN – JUNE/JULY

The formation arrived at Sasebo early Saturday morning, 26 June. The ships of DesDiv 92 moored in a nest alongside the USS Ajax(AR6) at buoy 16. The Brush was the outside ship in the nest. We finally got to Japan, a month late, but I don't think very many of the crew was able to go ashore to enjoy the pleasures of Sasebo when we first arrived, because almost everybody was broke including me. We had spent all our money during those 4 days that the ship had been in Manila. We got paid twice a month and payday was still a few days away. However, DesDiv 92 stayed in Sasebo 11 days and the sailors had another payday while there, so the merchants and mama sans of the town had time to get most of that money before they left port.

There was a big change in the weather around Japan when compared to that in the Philippines. In a letter to my mother dated June 26, 1954, I wrote about the difference in weather here.

"Arrived in Sasebo this morning. It's the rainy season over here now, and it has been raining on us steady for the last three days – since we got in the region. It will probably keep it up for several weeks yet. The rain is really just a hard drizzle....This cool weather around Japan feels mighty nice after sweating ourselves to death down around the Philippines. In fact, the atmosphere feels just like Smokey Mountain weather during dog days."

Our 11 days in port at Sasebo was rather peaceful and uneventful. On Tuesday, 6 July, the ship did take on water, ammunition, and provisions. The ship received 540 pounds of butter, 600 dozen eggs, 1,728 pounds of fresh fruit, 8,355 pounds of fresh vegetables, 423 pounds of frozen vegetables, and 4,566 pounds of fresh meat. I'm sure there was an all hands "working party" involved here to get it all to the proper storage spaces. The next day, Wednesday, the ship took on 58,937 gallons of fuel oil from a harbor fuel barge.

## YOKOSUKA, JAPAN – JULY

Thursday, 8 July, the ships of DesDiv 92 departed Sasebo en route to Yokosuka. It was a relatively short trip down there, but the ships engaged in tactical maneuvers continuously and it took 2 days to arrive there instead of one. The ships entered Tokyo Bay around 0542 Saturday morning, 10 July, and at 0715 the ship was moored starboard side to the Samuel N. Moore at buoy 5, Yokosuka Harbor.

In a letter to my mother, dated July 10, 1954, I mentioned again the kind of weather we were experiencing around Japan.

"We arrived at Yokosuka early this morning and leave in the morning.

We left Sasebo Thursday and had a rather uneventful two days trip. Nothing happened to get excited over. It rained on us a little. This morning it turned off pretty cold. A cold, damp wind made everybody shiver till morning. We haven't access to any coats; we had to turn them all in for the summer. We sure needed them this morning."

Sunday morning, 11 July, The Brush departed the harbor and Tokyo Bay to rendezvous with the submarine, USS Charr(SS328), and the USS Henderson(DD743) to conduct antisubmarine warfare exercises for 3 days. Other ships from DesDiv 92 and DesDiv 51 joined us in the exercises some of the time. The ships anchored every night in Sagami Wan.

Wednesday morning, 14 July, the Brush got underway from her anchorage and returned to Yokosuka. At 0912 she was moored to buoy D-1. Late in the day the Moore moored alongside to starboard. We only stayed in port 2 days.

## TASK GROUP 96.7 – KOBE

Friday morning, 16 July, the ships of DesDiv 92 got underway and departed Yokosuka and Tokyo Bay. Upon reaching the open ocean, DesDiv 92 joined up with the ships of DesDiv 51 and the aircraft carrier, USS Point Cruz(CVE119). This formation of ships was designated as Task Group 96.7 and was also known as a Hunter Killer unit. The Task Group wandered around in the ocean for the next 5 days and conducted ASW exercises with several submarines. I thought it was a rather tiresome time, but I suppose the sonarmen and the guys in CIC got a lot out of it. I guess I should have been a merchant mariner because I got tired of playing war games. I liked going places myself and didn't get any pleasure out of just wandering around out in the ocean.

Wednesday morning, 21 July, the ships of TG 96.7 went into the port of Kobe, Japan. That was a new port of call for us. At 1036 we moored at pier 6 alongside the Maddox. However, we only spent one day and night there. I went ashore Wednesday afternoon for a few hours, but I don't remember anything about the liberty or the place. Apparently, I didn't do anything or see anything that made a lasting impression in my mind, except a fight between two shipmates from a ship that was part of DesDiv 51. These two fellows wanted to hurt each other–bad. They were fighting on the pier where their ship was moored. I learned the fight was over a girl back in the States. I believe alcohol was playing a part in their aggression toward each other, too.

## En Route Formosa/A Gigantic Wave

DesDiv 92 departed Kobe, Japan Thursday afternoon en route to Kaohsiung, Formosa. This time out we just steamed along toward Formosa without conducting any exercises. The seas were probably too rough to do any unnecessary maneuvering. The trip took approximately 2 ½ days.

The trip was rather uneventful, although, the men on the bridge did have a rather frightening moment during the midwatch(00-04) Friday night, 23 July. The ships were steaming along in a diamond formation at a distance of 500 yards apart, which was quite close under the circumstances. The seas were rather rough much of the way down to Formosa due to a typhoon in the region somewhere. On this night, the ship encountered a gigantic wave. It was a dark night but there was still enough light to see this wave coming. Lt(jg) George T. Bailey was the officer-of-the-deck on this watch. He said he saw the wave coming toward the ship and it looked to be 50 to 60 feet high. Fortunately, we were going to meet it head-on. Mr. Bailey thought, "This thing is big enough to turn us over." Just before the wave hit the ship, he wrapped his arms around the forward voice tube – for dear life. The JOOD just happened to be in the pilothouse where it was a little safer, maybe. I'm sure everyone in the pilothouse was hanging onto something. The 2 lookouts on the port and starboard wings of the bridge were hanging onto the compass repeaters – for dear life, too. The wave hit us and knocked the ship off course about 20 degrees and keeled the ship over 45 to 50 degrees. For a few seconds the ship was just hanging there on the side of this huge wave.

Mr. Bailey hollered in to the helmsman to put the rudder over to right full – in an effort to get the ship pointed back in the right direction. The helmsman hollered back and informed Mr. Bailey that the rudder was already at right full but the ship wasn't responding. The wave simply had the ship in its grip, so to speak. However, the wave soon passed under the ship, and the ship righted itself and started responding to the rudder, too. In a few seconds we were back on course and the danger of capsizing was over. The whole incident was just another experience in the life of a destroyer sailor.

## KAOHSIUNG, FORMOSA

At 0654 Sunday morning, 25 July, the Brush entered Kaohsiung Harbor and moored alongside the USS Chevalier(DDR805) at buoys 9 and 10. However, at 1150 the Chevalier got underway and stood out of the harbor. The ship got underway briefly during the afternoon and went alongside the tanker, USS Mispillion(AO105), and took on fuel. Upon completion of refueling, the Brush went back to buoys 9 and 10.

The Brush stayed in Kaohsiung 5 days. The rest of DesDiv 92 was elsewhere. The tanker, USS Mispillion, was the only other American ship in the harbor with us. Other destroyers would come into the harbor from time to time to get refueled and then leave again. Hanging out in Kaohsiung Harbor wasn't very pleasant duty because it was so hot. There were very little breezes blowing and I don't remember it raining on us. The metal of the ship would get so hot you couldn't touch it without blistering yourself. The place was interesting in some respects, I suppose. We were in Chinese country and Chinese music played over loud speakers all day. There was a loudspeaker set up on a little cliff at the entrance to the harbor and that is where we first started hearing it. This unusual sounding Chinese music played all day every day. I don't think they played it at night, however.

There were 2 Chinese merchant ships moored in the harbor and were there in the same place the entire 3 years we visited there. I know seamen lived on the ship because we saw them going about their business every day we were there. The story was that they had escaped from the communist takeover of mainland China. I suppose the owner of them wasn't in a position to tell the seamen what to do or where to go to haul something, so they just stayed moored in the harbor.

Kaohsiung wasn't much of a liberty port, or a town either for that matter. There wasn't much to see or do. Consequently, relatively few of the crew ever bothered to go ashore there. The only thing to do in town was to drink beer in a few rustic bars and that wasn't done very much. The sailors just saved their money for better liberty opportunities, which usually weren't long in coming.

## A SHORTAGE OF EATING UTENSILS

The crew developed an eating problem soon after we arrived overseas. We didn't have half enough eating utensils to accommodate the crew at mealtimes. We had plenty when we left the States but something happened to them. About half of them disappeared. I don't know what happened to them but I bet somebody did.

Ideally, there would be a fork, a knife, and a spoon for each person that went through the chow line. Although, they might have to be washed a time or two during each meal. However, when we went through the chow line, we might find a fork, or a spoon, or a knife, or sometimes, nothing. You just ate with what you had, if anything. And if you didn't have a tool to eat with, you just ate with your hands. However, hands aren't too good at picking up soupy stuff. It's also kind of hard to keep English peas on a knife, too, especially in rough seas.

I also noticed that some of my shipmates weren't as polished and cultured as maybe they could be and they handled the shortage of eating utensils in their own special sort of way which seemed to suit them. For instance, sometimes, or frequently, a fellow would enter the mess deck without anything to eat with, and he would see a buddy across the mess deck that had finished eating or was about to be. He would holler out, "Hey, Joe, can I have your fork, spoon, or whatever when you get through eating?" Joe would always say, "Sure." So, Joe would finish up and throw his utensil across the mess deck to his buddy. But his buddy seldom ever caught it. Instead, the utensil would go bouncing around on the mess deck, but the fellow would finally run it down, pick it up, swipe it across his dirty dungarees a couple of times, and start eating with it. The practice didn't look too sanitary to me but they never gave it a thought. I doubt if cleanliness was anything that some of my shipmates gave much thought to. Of course, the freshly used eating utensil wouldn't always go bouncing around over the mess deck, because sometimes a fellow could just conveniently hand his utensil to his buddy. The buddy could then just swipe the used utensil across his dirty dungarees a couple of times and go to eating with it. As you can see, that was much easier than chasing after the utensil.

## LIBERTY IN HONG KONG

Late Saturday morning, 31 July, the Brush got underway and departed Kaohsiung Harbor en route to Hong Kong, B.C. the Pearl of the Orient. We steamed all afternoon and all night on a course of 237°(t) and at a speed of 18 to 20 knots. We arrived at Hong Kong early Sunday morning and moored to buoy B-3 in the harbor. Liberty commenced at 1000 and I went ashore soon thereafter.

Again, as on the previous visit, the ship was besieged by boat peddlers and had to be driven back with a water hose. The boat peddlers seemed desperate to sell something, and a mob of them would climb aboard the ship if they weren't forced back with a water hose. In addition, an armed sentry had to be stationed on the fantail to discourage boarders later on.

The painter women also came alongside and negotiated their usual deal to paint the sides of the ship in exchange for the ship's garbage as long as we were in port. The boss of the women painters had a name she was known by, but I can't remember what it was now for sure, although, I believe it was Mary something. Anyway, some of the older hands had been seeing her for years and were practically on a first name basis with her. She was allowed to come aboard and collect the garbage in the scullery. Each sailor would hand her his tray as he passed through and she would sort the uneaten food to suit herself. I'm sure it was all fed to somebody and they were probably glad to get it.

Also, as usual, there were a multitude of Chinese junks and sampans of all sizes scurrying about in the harbor. A fellow could spend a good deal of his time in Hong Kong just observing all the activities taking place in the harbor. There was no mistaking it, you knew you were in China.

The boat people were still there in great numbers, and some of them would park their sampans right beside the ship and you could easily see what they were doing and how they were living.

At night the ship was well lit up with a lot of extra lights to discourage people from trying to sneak aboard to steal what they could. Many of the people in the harbor were struggling to survive and would do anything to help accomplish that. Of course, millions of people in China were struggling to survive and had been doing so for centuries. It was just a way of life for them.

## An Interesting Proposition

I went on liberty in Hong Kong Sunday morning around 1000 and stayed until it was just about dark or 2030. I didn't want to be roaming around the streets of Hong Kong all by myself after nightfall. It probably wasn't a safe thing to do. Anyway, I had a very pleasant and enjoyable day and took a lot of pictures.

I went to the "Sailor's Home and Seaman's Mission" soon after I got ashore to see if I could run across my Catholic priest friend, Father Gillingan, that I had met on my previous visit to Hong Kong. However, he wasn't there; he was conducting services on some ship out in the harbor. Although, I did see him briefly later in the day.

I didn't eat breakfast on the ship that morning. I was hungry so I decided I would eat an early dinner (lunch) at the mission. I was busy eating my dinner of lamb chops, vegetables, and hot tea when this big stout Englishman walked up to my table and started making conversation and asking me questions about how much of Hong Kong and the surrounding islands I had seen. This friendly fellow was attired in typical tropical dress of white shirt, white short breeches, long white socks that came to the knees, and white shoes. My answers didn't seem to please him so he started talking about taking me on this extensive tour around the area, loan me some civilian clothes, and furnish his yacht, too. I was overwhelmed. I didn't know what to say, him being a total stranger and all. I turned his offer down. I made an excuse of some kind why I couldn't go or shouldn't go. We talked a little more, and when he started to leave, he told me he was the chaplain there and if I wanted him any time just ask somebody where he was. If I had known he was the chaplain before I turned him down, I might have accepted his generous offer. But I missed out on a grand tour of the place, I'm sure. Anyway, I went on about my business and did what I had planned to do.

**Moored in Hong Kong Harbor**

## Victoria Peak

The first place I went was up to Victoria Peak to enjoy the view. I stayed on the Peak for an hour or so, drank "orange squash" (lemonade), looked over the harbor for awhile, and then spent some time looking down on Repulse Bay. I was rather lonesome up there without my shipmates and my English school teacher friend that I had met and socialized with on my previous visit in June, 1953. The scenic views I saw up there on Victoria Peak will forever be imprinted on my mind.

**Views from Victoria Peak**

I left the Peak after an hour or so and went back down into the city and did some shopping. I bought several Persian pillow covers and rugs. I really liked that kind of stuff and they were very cheap in Hong Kong – most things were. I bought several other things including a nice tablecloth that I really liked. Although, we didn't have a table at home that it would fit on. I guess we got another table just for it.

## Chapel Services

Late in the day I went back to the mission and had supper, and after that, I went to a church service at the mission. In a letter to my mother dated August 2, 1954, I wrote about going to that church service.

"Just as I was finishing my supper, the church bells started ringing in the building. I decided I might as well attend church, so I went into the chapel. The preacher was the same fellow that I had met earlier in the day. Brown was his name. There weren't but about 3 dozen people there. They were mostly young merchant seamen it looked like. It was an Episcopal service with a lot of formality. I didn't know what to do so I just followed the crowd. It was a lot different than any service I had ever attended before. There wasn't any sermon. The preacher would read things out of some kind of Episcopalian book, sing songs, and do a lot of praying. They also had kneeling pads. As I first walked in, I noticed those little pads on the floor, and I couldn't figure out why they were there but I soon figured it out.

One thing that struck me as kind of amusing was the way the preacher was dressed. He had on a long white robe and underneath the robe you could see the shorts and long socks he had on that morning when I saw him in the dining room. It was kind of a different garb than what I've seen most preachers wear in the pulpit."

They sang a hymn in the chapel that evening that I had never heard before and that really moved me. It's the hymn of seafarers almost everywhere, so I was told. The name of the hymn was "Eternal Father, Strong to Save". I really liked the song and I could really relate to it at that time in my life. This song is also known as the Navy Hymn. On the following page are the words to the first verse of the song.

# Eternal Father, Strong to Save

Eternal Father, strong to save,
Whose arm hath bound the restless wave,
Who biddest the mighty ocean deep
Its own appointed limits keep;
Oh, hear us when we cry to Thee,
For those in peril on the sea!

O Christ! Whose voice the waters heard
And hushed their raging at Thy Word,
Who walked on the foaming deep,
And calm amidst its rage didst sleep;
Oh, hear us when we cry to Thee,
For those in peril on the sea!

Most Holy Spirit! Who didst brood
Upon the chaos dark and rude,
And bid its angry tumult cease,
And give, for wild confusion, peace;
Oh, hear us when we cry to Thee,
For those in peril on the sea!

O Trinity of love and power!
Our family shield in danger's hour;
From rock and tempest, fire and foe,
Protect us wheresoever we go;
Thus evermore shall rise to Thee
Glad hymns of praise from land and sea.

I went ashore again Tuesday, August 3, but I know I didn't have much money left to spend so I must have just looked around. There are a lot of interesting sights to see in Hong Kong that doesn't cost anything. I do remember visiting with some of my shipmates in the place they told me they would be. However, I didn't stay with them too long because I didn't want to participate in their activities. I had more interesting things to do. But they seemed to be enjoying themselves.

## A Friendly Chinese Lady

I remember having an interesting experience in a nice restaurant while I was having dinner. I had a friendly conversation with an attractive, well dressed Chinese woman that was sitting close by me at an adjoining table. However, as our conversation progressed, I became suspicious that I was talking to a "business" woman, and before I finished my dinner, I knew I was. However, we didn't consummate any business deals because I wasn't interested in being one of her "clients". We parted company on friendly terms even though I turned her down. I'm sure she didn't have any trouble finding someone more agreeable than I was.

I was a little disappointed with my friendly encounter with the Chinese woman, because I was thinking, at first, that it was my good looks and irresistible charm that made her want to be friendly and talk to me. Finally, I had to come to the realization that she had other things in mind concerning our relationship – and my money was her primary interest. Oh well, I should have known better than to think that an attractive, classy looking Chinese woman would be interested in an American sailor unless it was for monetary reasons.

## Kowloon 1954

The City of Kowloon is across the harbor from Hong Kong. It is on the mainland of China but it was also under the control of the British. I decided I would like to go there and see what it looked like. In a letter to my mother, I wrote about my excursion over to the city of Kowloon.

"The last day ashore I went over to Kowloon that is across the harbor from Hong Kong on the mainland of China. The only way to go from either city to the other is by ferry or a boat of some kind.

It's about a mile trip across the harbor. It normally costs 20 Hong Kong cents, or about 3 ½ cents in American money, to ride the ferry across to the other side. However, a serviceman's ticket is 10 cents Hong Kong money. That's mighty cheap riding, isn't it?

I believe I like Kowloon even better than Hong Kong because the city is prettier and the prices are much cheaper."

My sister Fay was married while I was in Hong Kong. She married my main boyhood chum, John Rogers, that I ran with when I was growing up in the Forest. Of course, I was anxious to get a letter from home to find out all the details about the event

**The Ship's Officers – Hong Kong 1954**

Front Row from left, Frank Sala, Pat O'Meara, Bennie Jones, Capt. Arlie Capps, Dick Bryan, John Koett and Ted Johnston – Back Row from left, Cal Parkhurst, Joe Lochridge, George Bailey, Larry Cates, Pat King, William (Robbie) Robbins, Joe Jordan, Ted Calbeaux, Dean Abrahamson, Ron Hurst and Dick Hart.

**Brush Officers – Hong Kong 1954**

Showing off their new Hong Kong tailor made sport coats and ties.

From left to right, they are:

Cdr. Arlie Capps, Captain
Lt(jg) Frank Sala, 1st Lt.
Ens. Dean Abrahamson, Eng.
Lt(jg) Larry Cates, Elect. Off.
Ens. Cal Parkhurst, Eng.
Ens. Dick Hart, Comm.
Lt(jg) William Robbins, Gun Off.
Lt. Dick Bryan, Navigator
Lt(jg) George Bailey, ASW Off.
Lt(jg) Ted Johnson, Supply Off.
Lt(jg) Joe Jordan, 1st Div. Off.
Ens. Joe Lochridge, Eng.

**The Ship's Crew – Hong Kong 1954**

## FORMOSA PATROL

The Brush departed Hong Kong late Wednesday afternoon, 4 August, after 4 short days there and returned to Kaohsiung. We arrived there early in the afternoon of the next day – Thursday. However, we didn't stay in Kaohsiung very long, just long enough to refuel from the USS Manatee(AO58) and to take on some provisions from her, too. The Brush left Kaohsiung at 1620 en route to the Southern Formosa Patrol station. She arrived on station around noon, 6 August, and commenced patrolling in the strait off the coast of China. The Brush spent 11 days patrolling the Formosa Strait without any major incidents. However, she went back to Kaohsiung 3 times during this time to refuel. One time when the Brush went into the harbor to refuel, Sunday, 8 August, she didn't go straight back to her southern patrolling station; instead, she went to the Pescadores Islands for some reason before going back to her patrolling station.

### An Enraged Boatman

The Brush went into the Pescadores around 1730, 8 August, and dropped anchor; she was going to stay in the islands about 1½ hours. Of course, when American Navy ships come into Boko-ko Harbor, actually more of an anchorage, they are greeted by a fleet of native peddler boats selling all kinds of homemade stuff. However, most of it was flower vases and other objects made from clay and covered with little seashells. It was interesting stuff but we couldn't take any of it back to the States. The ship was anchored and I was standing on the signal bridge looking back toward the fantail where all the peddler boats had gathered a few feet off our starboard quarter. I noticed that 2 of my shipmates from the deck force, I believe, were very amused about something. One of them had a bucket of water in his hand but he set it down on the deck. Those 2 fellows were the only people on the fantail. These fellows were laughing and talking about something. I could tell they were up to something, and when one of them motioned for one of the boats to come in, I knew what it was. There were 2 men in the boat; the one in the stern was handling the boat and the one in the front was doing the selling. The boat came in close to the ship, and when it did, one of the fellows grabbed the bucket of water off the deck and dumped it on the peddler's head. The boat quickly backed away 20 feet or so. Needless to say, the 2 sailors thought that was the funniest thing they had ever seen and just bent over laughing about their joke. They howled.

The peddler didn't think it was so funny, however. He stood up in the bow of the boat, shook his fist at those fellows, and shrieked at them at the top of his voice. He was literally trembling with rage. He was shrieking in Chinese, of course, and I couldn't understand what he was saying, but you can be sure it wasn't anything nice or complimentary. I believe he was the maddest human being that I've ever seen. I'm sure that little incident didn't improve Chinese and American relations any. I believe that Chinese fellow would have shot those fellows if he had had a gun. He was mad.

## THE TACHEN ISLANDS OPERATION

Early Monday morning, 16 August, the Brush went back into Kaohsiung Harbor to refuel. This time she refueled from the USS Tolovana(AO64), which had relieved the Manatee(AO58). The ship refueled and departed the harbor around 1130 in company with the Moore and the Thomas that had come into the harbor to refuel, too. The ships of DesDiv 92 were scheduled to depart for Sasebo, Japan upon leaving the harbor, but again, they received secret orders to proceed elsewhere. Instead of heading north to Japan, the ships headed south to rendezvous with a group of ships coming up from the south. The ships of DesDiv 92 rendezvoused with Task Group 70.2 at 0715 the next morning, Tuesday, 17 August. The task group consisted of the aircraft carriers, USS Boxer(CVA21) and the USS Philippine Sea(CVA47), and the Destroyer Divisions 52 and 71. When the 3 ships of DesDiv 92 joined up with the TG, it then consisted of 2 carriers and 11 destroyers. The Maddox and the cruiser, St Paul(CA73), also joined the TG the next morning. That should have been enough ships to accomplish something.

According to my understanding of the matter, the task group was formed to conduct a military operation against Communist Chinese forces on mainland China opposite the Tachen Islands. The Tachen Islands were a group of small islands just a few miles off the coast of China and within range of communist artillery. The islands were also occupied by a few Nationalist Chinese troops and Communist China didn't like it.

The story was, as I understood it, that the communist forces on the mainland harassed the troops on the islands almost daily with artillery fire or air strikes. Apparently, the Nationalist Chinese troops wanted some relief from it. Thus, the TG was assigned the job of providing them with that relief. I think the objective of the TG was to, at least, destroy the communist guns on the mainland that was causing all the trouble. According to the plan of action, as I remember it, the carrier planes would actually do the job of destroying the communist guns. However, the carrier planes would need an excuse to do it and that is where the ships of DesDiv 92 would enter the picture. The ships of DesDiv 92 would play a prominent part in the overall scheme of things. We would be the bait, or the tied goat, so to speak. We would be the excuse for the planes attacking the communist guns. The carriers and their planes would remain out of sight way over the horizon while the destroyers of DesDiv 92 would go into the islands and, hopefully, be attacked by the communist in some way – either by artillery fire or by airplanes. As soon as we came under attack, the carrier planes would come to our rescue and do whatever they had to do. That was the plan, as I understood it at the time. However, the operation was delayed for a couple of days because of stormy weather and fairly rough seas. The TG had to ride out the tail end of a typhoon that was passing to the north of us.

At 0424 Thursday morning, 19 August, 1954, the ships of DesDiv 92 were detached from the formation to proceed to the Tachen Islands to play their part in the operation. They arrived at the islands around 0800. At 0820 the Brush proceeded into the island group and dropped anchor off Shangtachen Shan – the main island, I believe. The ship was at "general quarters" and had been since 0600. Our sister ships anchored at other locations around the islands.

Immediately after anchoring, the Brush put a "liberty party" ashore. After all, this was just a friendly visit to the islands by some American destroyers, you know. In fact, I believe this was the first time that any American warships had ever visited the Tachen Islands. The "liberty party" consisted of 3 men and all of them were old-timers and first or second class petty officers. Tomlinson QM2/C was one of them, but I don't remember who the other 2 were for sure. The other ships may have sent a small liberty party ashore, too, but I don't know and never knew. However, if the islands were attacked in any way with the liberty party ashore, that would have been reason enough for the American planes to attack and destroy the communist airplanes or guns on the mainland.

We stayed in the islands for about 6 hours, anchored, and with all the guns manned. As I remember, it was a rather tense time. I don't think the crew worried too much about the risky situation they were in, even though they knew they were subject to being attacked at any moment by airplanes or artillery shells. It was all in a day's work. All the guns were manned and ready for whatever. The cooks brought us up a sandwich at noon, which was greatly appreciated, but I really wasn't expecting anything. In fact, the crew probably wasn't thinking too much about food at the time. I wasn't, I know, even though we didn't have any breakfast that morning because we went to general quarters so early.

Around 1430 the liberty party came back aboard ship. The ship then weighed anchor and proceeded out of the islands. In very brief words, the mission was a flop. The hoped for attack on us, or the islands, never came for some reason. Actually, nothing eventful happened that day but it could have. Things could have happened that day that would have made the headlines in all the papers, but they didn't. The Chinese communist on the mainland simply didn't play their part in the scheme – for whatever reason. Knowing what I know now, I suspect the operation fizzled because the Chinese were alerted to the planned operation against their forces; and they just laid low that day and never gave the U.S. Navy the excuse they needed to attack and destroy their guns or planes. I'm sure that an operation of that significance had to have been approved by someone at the highest level of government in Washington. If that is the case, then a number of people in Washington would have had to known about the plan. If that is also the case, then it is my opinion that a soviet spy got wind of the planned operation and notified his soviet bosses, who, in turn, notified the Chinese. Consequently, nothing happened. However, I suppose I should be thankful that nothing did happen. It was much safer for us that way. After all, I'm more inclined to be a lover than a fighter anyway.

## Tachen Islands Liberty Party

What did the "liberty party" do during their 6 hour stay on the island? According to their story, they went into a cave that served as the enlisted men's club, sat around, and drank warm Chinese beer. It must have been some good and potent stuff because Tommy Tomlinson QM2/C consumed a little too much and had great difficulty walking when the group left the cave. Consequently, he had to receive a great deal of assistance getting back to the ship. Some of his shipmates helped him get into his rack, which was right above mine, and he wasn't good for a thing until the next morning. He did have a very restful sleep during the rest of the afternoon and night, though; he probably needed it because he hadn't been getting much. That was the only time I ever saw Tommy in that condition. He actually was an old veteran drinker and could usually handle his adult beverages quite well. So, Tommy was the only casualty the ship suffered during the Tachen Island operation, but it really wasn't due to enemy action. It was due to free, friendly beer – not fire.

Oh yes, I think the beer was on the house. Actually, it was a rather small price to pay for the services of 2 aircraft carriers, a cruiser, and 12 destroyers for a day. I believe the Nationalist Chinese got the best end of that deal.

The other ships of DesDiv 92 also got underway about the same time as the Brush did and proceeded out of the islands, too. The ships didn't return to the task group, however. The Tachen Island operation was over.

At 1505 the ships of DesDiv 92 formed up into a column formation and headed northeast toward Sasebo, Japan. The Brush, however, was soon detached from the division to proceed independently to Buckner Bay, Okinawa to pick up a couple of ROK Naval officers. The Brush arrived at Buckner Bay the next afternoon around 1500, which was Friday, 20 August, and anchored briefly. The ROKN officers soon reported aboard and the ship weighed anchor and departed the bay at 1640. The ship then set a course for Sasebo again.

We had a very uneventful trip up to Sasebo and arrived there about 1700 Saturday afternoon, 21 August. We moored alongside the Maddox at buoy X-3 in a nest of 4 ships – the ships of DesDiv 92. In one sense, arriving in Sasebo was a happy occasion for everybody, I believe, because there were 20 bags of mail waiting on us and there was something for everybody. That was a lot more mail than we ordinarily received at one time. Of course, we were several weeks behind in getting our mail, too. The ship usually got 2, 3, or 4 bags at a time. I got 3 letters from my mother and one from my Uncle Flint. Unfortunately, there was none from a sweetie and wouldn't be. One letter gave me the details of my sister's wedding that took place on August 3, 1954, when we were in Hong Kong.

## KOREAN PATROL

The Brush only stayed one night in Sasebo. Early Sunday afternoon the Brush and the Maddox got underway and departed the harbor en route to the east coast of Korea to participate in the Korean Patrol. We were going there by way of the Shimonoseki Strait. The ships arrived at the strait around 2200 and dropped anchor in Aishima Ko. The ships anchored there to have a turnover conference with the captains of the ships that they were relieving – the USS Hamner(DD718) and the USS Wiltsie(DD716). The captains had a long conference in the middle of the night. There was never any word on what they discussed or what they decided. However, the Brush and the Maddox finally got underway again around 0200 and went on through the strait.

At 0918 Monday morning, 23 August, the Brush was detached from the Maddox and proceeded to Pusan, Korea to disembark the 2 Korean naval officers that she picked up in Buckner Bay. The ship arrived at the harbor entrance at 0955 and commenced lying to. At 1021 a ROK patrol craft came alongside to port to receive the ROK officers. That accomplished, we got underway and proceeded on to our patrol station up the coast aways. The Brush arrived at her patrol station, station 3, around 1600 and commenced patrolling. We would have the Korean Patrol duty for 3 weeks and some of it would be rather pleasant duty; mainly, because we were operating alone and didn't have to get involved in anything too stressful, except for one day.

**THE SEA OF JAPAN**

## Ensnared in a Fish Net Cable

The ship did have an unfortunate incident happen to her early on our second day of patrol, Tuesday, 24 August. The ship was in the process of going into this rather large cove, P'ohang Hang, to anchor around 0900 in the morning. The anchor detail had already been set. However, at 0912 the captain realized that something was wrong with the screws and stopped all engines. At 0925 he dropped the anchor in 11 fathoms of water and sent a couple of divers over the side to find out what the trouble was. The divers found out that we had gotten tangled up in a fishing net and a large steel cable had wrapped around the starboard screw about 15 times. Consequently, we weren't going anywhere for awhile.

According to a letter that I wrote to my mother in which I told her about the incident, it took 12 hours for 10 divers taking turns working at it to get the ship free from it. I suppose they used underwater torches to cut the cable from the screw. The fish net cable was finally cut free from the starboard screw at 0935 Wednesday morning.

During the meantime, the Maddox stood into the cove at 0750 Wednesday morning and dropped anchor 1000 yards from us. Also, at 0835 the Columbian frigate, Captain Tono (F12), showed up and anchored nearby, too. So, we had plenty of company to sympathize with us during our plight. I suppose they showed up to assist us if they could and to give us moral support.

The Brush finally got underway at 1241 and the captain put the ship through some speed trials to try and assess the damage if there was any. Apparently, there was some damage to the screw but not enough to quit the patrol and go into port. However, the ship went into dry-dock the next time she went into Sasebo and had the damage repaired. During the meantime, the Brush continued on with her patrolling off the South Korean coast.

The Brush went into some small coves and stayed at anchor all day for 5 days out of the 3 weeks we were on this patrol. These little coves we dropped anchor in were called Sopcho Ri and P'ohang Hang. The ship went into them a number of other times, too, for some reason, but didn't stay very long.

The Brush refueled 4 times from tankers while she was on the Korean Patrol. She refueled twice from the USS Manatee(AO58) and once from the Cimarron(AO22) and the Passumpsic(AO107).

The ship also conducted gunnery practice twice while we were out there. The first gunnery practice she expended 5 rounds of 5″AAC shells and 18 rounds of illumination shells. The second practice session, on Friday, 10 September, the ship fired 123 rounds of 5 inch shells and 167 rounds of 3 inch shells.

On Thursday, 26 August, the Brush and the Maddox made a run down to Pusan for something. We entered Pusan Harbor around 1540 and moored alongside the Maddox at pier 1. We stayed in the harbor for 2 hours.

In a letter to my mother dated August 29, 1954, I described what I saw in Pusan Harbor.

"Thursday, we went into Pusan Harbor for a couple of hours on some kind of business. The harbor entrance is rather pretty, but inside, it's not so pretty. That's a poverty stricken looking city. I didn't go ashore but I could see a good bit of it from where I was. I saw, I guess, thousands of shacks that looked worse than any chicken house you've ever seen. I imagine they were refugee shacks."

## Big Steaks

The crew of the Brush experienced a sight at a noon meal one day in the early days of the Korean Patrol that made their eyes bug out. They went through the serving line and their eyes fell upon a big pile of huge steaks. They must have been 16 to 20 ounce steaks. The crew was going to be served a grilled, man-size steak. They were the first and only ones that they ever saw on the Brush. The sight of those big steaks brought a gleam to their eyes because it was so far out of the norm. Their mouths started watering and they couldn't wait to start in on theirs. Every crewman went into the mess deck with the intentions of having himself a feast on his big steak. Each fellow got his knife, or a knife, and started cutting on his steak. Everybody at the table was looking at him, although, he hadn't noticed it yet because he was concentrating on his steak. But each fellow soon realized he wasn't making any headway toward cutting himself off a bit of steak to chew on. He would cut and saw but to no avail. His shipmates would start laughing at him about now, because they had already experienced the same frustration and they knew he wasn't going to have any success cutting himself a bite of meat off his steak. Those steaks were so tough that you couldn't even cut them with a sharp knife. Most of the deck force carried a sharp sheath knife because they used them frequently for cutting line (rope).

Some of the fellows, that could, would linger at their meal longer than usual just so they could laugh at the new arrivals trying to cut themselves a bite-size piece of steak. The meal was a total disappointment for everybody. The big steaks seemed too good to be true and they were.

A favorite joke that some of the mates played on their buddies when they came into the mess deck with their big steaks was to ask them if they would like to have the rest of their steak, because they couldn't eat it all. The new fellow would always say, "Yes" and the generous shipmate would pile his steak on top of his buddy's steak. However, the new fellow would soon find out that he couldn't eat either one of them and that is why his shipmate was so generous. Of course, a big laugh would follow the joke. All those big steaks got dumped in the garbage can – whole.

As I remember it, the scuttlebutt was that the commissary department had bought these steaks, and some other "beef", too, in the Philippines at a bargain price. Actually, if that was the case, it got unloaded on them. Anyway, their intentions were good. I don't believe any meat that tough could have come from the United States. I believe the meat had to have come from an old, worn out water buffalo from the Philippines. The scuttlebutt was, too, that there was more of that same meat in the reefers, and the cooks just dumped it overboard to get to rid of it. That meat was so tough that it is doubtful that the sharks could have even eaten it.

## Up to Siberia

The highlight of the Korean Patrol occurred on Sunday, 5 September, 1954. The Brush and the Maddox were sent on a search and rescue mission. Actually, the rescue attempt commenced the evening before. Around 2230 Saturday evening the Brush received a message informing us that an American patrol plane with 10 men aboard had been shot down off the east coast of Siberia near the Russian port city of Vladivostok. All 10 men had survived the crash and were in the water. The crash was close to 350 miles north of us, but apparently we were the only American or allied ships in that part of the world and thus the ones closest to them. Consequently, we, the Brush and the Maddox, were assigned the job of rescuing the 10 airmen. So around 2230 Saturday evening, the 2 ships headed toward Siberia as hard as they could go.

The commodore just happened to be aboard the Brush. He had shifted his flag to the Brush for a few days that afternoon. Thus, the Brush was the lead ship.

The seas were quite rough that night and the next day, too. The wind was blowing from the north at probably 25 to 30 knots. The ships steamed north all night and all Sunday morning at a speed of 25 to 33 knots and were going into a headwind of 25 to 30 knots. It was one wild ride. The ships were trying to get to the crash site as quickly as they could, but it was still going to take them 13 ½ hours to get there. The ships were ploughing into the waves at high speeds and tons of water would come spilling back over the bow time after time. It was one of those situations where you could feel the ship go into the waves and literally be buried by the salt water. You could feel the ship struggling to come up out from under all that water with each of those waves. She did it dozens and dozens of times during the night when it was black dark and you couldn't see anything much outside the pilothouse. One could only hope and pray that the ship would come up out of the water and not continue on down into the depths of the ocean. Damaged and water-logged ships have done just that with the loss of all hands. No sooner than the ship would shake free of one wave than she would be buried by another one. It was a ride that I'll never forget.

The Russians had shot down the plane because it had intruded into their air space, and we were going into their territorial waters to look for these fellows. There was a big question about how the Russians would react to us being there. Would they attack us too? We were a long way from any help in the event that took place. We were on our own and surviving would be entirely up to us and God. It was one of those situations where you prepared for the worst but hoped for something better.

I'm sure if we had been attacked and sunk, our government would have quickly sent a "strong protest" to the Kremlin. I'm sure that would have been a big comfort to the parents and wives of all the lost sailors. However, an attempt to save those airmen had to be made by somebody and apparently that somebody was us, because there weren't any other ships in the area to do it.

It was a rather sleepless night for some of the Operations Department's personnel and some of the officers. I think all of their activity involved communicating with somebody in regards to those downed airmen. I only had 1 hour of sleep myself because I had been on the midwatch (0000–0400). It was also a short night for the entire crew because the captain exercised the crew at general quarters at 0500 – way before daylight. I'm sure the captain was very apprehensive about what could happen during the coming day. The ship also went to general quarters again at 0948 because of an unidentified radar contact at a distance of 22 miles. However, it was secured 10 minutes later after the contact was identified as a friendly aircraft – a search plane.

The ships arrived in the vicinity of the crash site at 1215 Sunday afternoon and commenced searching. It developed that a seaplane had found and rescued 9 of the 10 airmen at 0730 that morning but couldn't locate the 10th one. It was amazing to me how a seaplane could have landed and taken off again in those rough seas but it did. So it ended up that we were just looking for that one airman. Of course, the wind and the waves weren't cooperating too much with our search, and he probably had drifted miles from the crash site by the time we arrived there. It was kind of like looking for a needle in a haystack, as they say.

The ship went to general quarters again at 1227 because of another unidentified radar contact at 19 miles. In a few minutes it also was identified as a friendly aircraft and GQ was secured.

One time a search plane reported a possible life raft in the water approximately 10 miles from where we were at the time. We proceeded to the area and looked for it but we never were able to locate it.

At 1740 GQ was sounded again, but it also was determined to be an American search plane.

The ships searched for that one airman until 1900, which was almost dark, but we never found him. In fact, we never saw anything of any consequence all day. We didn't see a plane, a boat, debris or anything. We didn't even see as much as a seagull. I think that everything that could get there was on shore. It was a nasty day to be at sea. We left the poor fellow out there, and, I suppose, he's still there unless the Russians picked him up – never to be seen again.

At 1831 the ship observed sunset and lighted all navigational lights. At 1904 the ships set a course of 229°(t) and headed back south. The search was over without a good conclusion. At 2000 the ships changed speed to 12 knots and maintained that same slow speed all night because the ships were getting low on fuel. The ships had burnt a lot of fuel on their high speed run up to Siberia.

Around 0700 the next morning the Brush and the Maddox rendezvoused with the tanker, USS Passumpsic(AO107), to take on fuel. I believe the tanker was sent out especially for us to replenish us with fuel before we ran completely out. The Brush received 92,615 gallons of fuel oil from the tanker. After refueling, the Brush and the Maddox escorted the tanker back south for 100 miles or so and then the ships had to go their separate ways. The destroyers went back to their patrol stations.

Tuesday, 7 September, the Brush spent most of the day at anchor in P'ohang Hang, probably to rest up.

Sunday, 12 September, the Brush and the Maddox were relieved of the Korean Patrol by the destroyers, USS Rowan (DD782) and the USS Gurke (DD783). The turnover took place in P'ohang Hang Cove. The Brush and the Maddox headed for Sasebo upon being relieved.

## SASEBO – SEPTEMBER 1954

The seas were running rather high on the run down to Sasebo because there was a typhoon headed our way. The ships arrived in Sasebo Harbor right at daylight, Monday, 13 September. The Brush was moored to buoy 61 at 0650. Typhoon condition 1 was set in the harbor when we arrived, which meant the harbor was going to experience some strong winds.

In a letter to my mother dated September 13, 1954, I wrote about arriving in Sasebo and the situations we found there.

"We're back in Sasebo after three weeks on patrol. And it was a long three weeks, too. It was rather quiet duty but somewhat boring. Most all duty gets boring after awhile. As I say, we're back in port but we're not getting any recreation. In the first place, a typhoon is passing over Japan tonight and tomorrow. A pretty good size blow they say. We got in early this morning. Out at sea the ocean was rather rough, but inside the harbor there is pretty good shelter. Sasebo Harbor is pretty well protected by high mountains so the water doesn't get too rough. There's been a wind of around thirty knots blowing all day, and there is the usual cloudy and rainy weather that goes along with a typhoon. Around midnight the winds are expected to be 85 knots, a nice breeze, but in here, we should be in no danger.

Even if there wasn't a storm, we still wouldn't be getting any liberty. The Japanese are on a strike again, and when that takes place, no one gets to go ashore. The navy is afraid some sailor will get himself hurt. When the Japanese go on a strike they have a regular riot and a lot of people get hurt sometimes. We're supposed to be here for 10 days so maybe they'll quieten off before we leave. I hope so. I would like to go ashore. We've only had 6 liberties in the last 2 months and 4 of those were in Hong Kong all at one occasion. We've been in several ports alright but none of them were what you would call liberty ports."

Tuesday morning, 14 September, the Brush got underway and proceeded to go alongside the USS Piedmont(AD17) at buoy 1 in a nest with the Moore, Thomas, and the Maddox.

Thursday morning, 16 September, the Brush was moved to dry dock 1 by shipyard tugs to have her damaged starboard screw repaired. She stayed in dry-dock for 3 days to accomplish this.

## Japanese Tavern

As I remember, the dry dock was located in an out-of-the-way part of the harbor. A gangplank connected the ship to the shore so we could get off the ship. There was a dirt road that ran past the dry dock and up a hill.

The ship finally allowed the crew to go on liberty Friday, 17 September. Apparently, the Japanese workers' strike was over. Friday night some of my shipmates discovered a quaint little Japanese tavern about a quarter of a mile up the road from the dry dock. They thought it was a nice, cozy little place so Saturday night I decided I would check it out. I didn't have anything better to do.

Saturday evening, just at dusk, I walked up the road to this little tavern that was located on the side of this hill. It was a rather steep climb up to the place. The tavern looked like a typical Japanese building on the outside, and on the inside, it was typical Japanese also with low tables. There were 15 to 20 Brush sailors in the place. Of course, we all had to leave our shoes at the door. I don't remember how we were able to identify our shoes when we left the place since we all had black shoes that looked just alike.

We all sat on the floor around these low tables. It was a long evening so I had my 2 beers with several rounds of coke in between them. It was a great social time. I didn't see anybody get drunk or loud-mouthed. Everybody just had a good time talking and socializing. Some of my shipmates were drinking Japanese sake as well as beer. Sake is a potent rice wine. I had heard sailors talking about it, but I had never seen any or ever had the opportunity to drink any. So, I decided the time had come for me to try it. I knew it was a favorite Japanese beverage and it normally was drunk hot or at least warm. It is always served in real tiny cups that hold 2 to 3 ounces. So, I ordered some sake. It tasted okay. I sipped it slowly, as was the custom. An hour or so later I ordered another cup of it and sipped it slowly, too. I couldn't tell it had any effect on me at all.

It was a very enjoyable evening, but all good times have to come to an end. Liberty was over around 2300 and we all had to get back to the ship. I walked back down the road to the ship, went aboard, and as soon as I could undress, climbed into my rack. However, I found out I couldn't stay there, because when I laid my head on my pillow, the world started spinning around. I would rise up and the spinning would stop. But every time I laid my head down, the compartment started spinning and it would get faster and faster. I soon decided the best thing to do was to get up for awhile and that is what I did. I went up to the mess deck and visited with some of the night owls. I stayed up an hour and tried lying down again. I was normal then. My world didn't spin anymore. The sake didn't affect me in any other way that I could tell, however. That was the only sake I drank while I was in the navy. I drank a little in later years, however, without it affecting me in any way.

Sunday morning, 19 September, 2 Japanese tugs moved the Brush back to buoy 1 alongside the Piedmont and the other ships of DesDiv 92. We would stay in port another 6 days. However, nothing happened during that time that gave me any additional memories of that time in port.

## SOUTH CHINA SEA – SEPTEMBER AND OCTOBER 1954

Early Saturday morning, 25 September, the ships of DesDiv 92 got underway and departed Sasebo en route to Subic Bay. We mainly just steamed along toward our destination and the journey was rather uneventful. The trip took 3 ½ days.

We arrived at Subic Bay early in the afternoon of Tuesday, 28 September. We first refueled from the USS Passumpsic(AO107) and then proceeded to buoy 14 and moored. However, we only spent one night in Subic Bay. Around 1000 the next morning the Brush, Maddox, and Thomas got underway and left the harbor en route to rendezvous with a carrier task group in the South China Sea. We left the Moore behind for some reason. However, she joined the task group a few days later.

DesDiv 92 (less the Moore) rendezvoused with Task Group 70.2 at 1645 Wednesday afternoon, 29 September. The task group consisted of the aircraft carriers, USS Philippine Sea(CVA47) and the USS Hornet (CVA12), and they were being escorted by destroyer divisions 131 and 132. The ships of DesDiv 92 spent most of the month of October in the South China Sea operating with the task group. However, the composition of the T.G. would change some from time to time with some ships leaving the group and other ships joining it. The task group was using a lot of fuel oil with all their steaming around and tankers came out to refuel the ships every three or four days. And we also were replenished with provisions a couple of times. The escorting destroyers were detached from the formation sometimes to go off and conduct individual or division exercises of various kinds – mainly to give them something different to do, I believe. The Brush went off and conducted gunnery practice a couple of times and shot up a lot of ammunition. We also went into port three times during the month of October – twice in Subic Bay and once in Manila.

**USS Moore alongside Philippine Sea (U.S. Navy Photograph)**

**USS Moore pulling away from a carrier (U.S. Navy Photograph)**

**USS Maddox & Philippine Sea (U.S. Navy Photograph)**

## MANILA – OCTOBER 1954

The most exciting thing that happened during the month of October was when the task group went into Manila for 3 days and 4 nights for rest and recreation (R & R).

The Brush was detached from the task group early Monday afternoon, 4 October, to proceed independently into Manila Harbor. We were moored starboard side to pier 3 in Manila Harbor at 1515. The Thomas came into the harbor and moored to our port side. The Maddox came into the harbor a little later and moored to the port side of the Thomas. Thus, we were moored in a nest of 3 ships. I don't know where the Moore was.

The rest of the ships of the task group were moored at various places around the harbor, but I never knew where they were – but didn't care either. As far as I was concerned, the Brush had the choice berthing place in the harbor. We were moored to the pier and were within a block or so of downtown. I don't know how we got such a spot. Somebody must have made a mistake, or got confused, or something, to assign us such a good berthing place. I went ashore at least 2 of the days that we were there and left port with some great memories.

There just happened to be a beautiful merchant ship moored across the pier from us that really attracted my attention. In fact, I invited myself aboard her to get a closer look. I walked around all over the main deck and the bridge area. I never saw anybody while I was roaming around over her. I was surprised that the ship didn't have somebody on duty to keep curious people like me from coming aboard uninvited. The ship looked like it was well maintained. The name of the ship was the SS Gibbes Lykes. I believe I would have enjoyed taking a trip on her.

## An Interesting Day at a Coconut Plantation

Early Thursday morning, 7 October, the communications officer came up to the bridge and asked me if I would like to visit a coconut plantation an hour or two inland from Manila; and it would be an all day trip. The excursion sounded to me like it would be something interesting and different to do so I said, "Yes, I would like to go." It turned out to be one of the most interesting days of my navy career.

In a letter to my mother dated October 10th, I wrote about the things I saw and experienced that day.

"My trip to Manila proved to be quite educational as well as entertaining. Twenty-two of us were invited, through the USO, to spend last Thursday at a coconut plantation down in San Pablo, which is about 60 miles from Manila. Actually, there were about 5 American families living there, and all of them were connected with the Baker Coconut Company. They ran a big coconut mill in San Pablo. It was supposed to be the largest one in the world.

Anyway, we left the ship at 9:30 A.M. and got back around 9:30 P.M. As I said, it was sixty miles across country and along the way we saw how the average people lived and what they grew. We saw miles and miles of rice paddies in all stages of growth, from just planted to being harvested. We saw how the farmers worked their crops following along after an old water buffalo pulling an ancient wooden plow and in mud half way up their knees. They cut the rice straw with a sickle, gathered up a hand full, and beat it against a wire screen of some sort to shake the rice loose from the straw. Then they gathered up the rice grains in a large wooden bowl, held it over their heads, and let it slowly fall back to the ground. While falling, the wind blows the impurities out. Some of the farmers, though, have thought of a different and easier way to get the straw and stuff out of their rice. They spread it out alongside the road on a canvas. As the cars go by, the wind caused by the cars going by cleans the rice for them. The farmer just sits down in the shade close by and watches his work being done for him. A lazy lot they are, huh?

Other than rice, we saw gobs of coconut groves and several cane fields. Also, we saw lots of banana trees, but they looked like they just belonged to the land or the jungle.

The homes were something to wonder at, too. Practically all I observed were one-room straw or leaf shacks up on high stilts; you might call them platform houses. There were some wooden ones of the same style but very few. I didn't see what kept the mosquitoes from carrying the people away. There were no windows or screens to be seen.

We had a dinner of two barbequed pigs, rice & gravy, rice muffins, bananas, tangerines, and some other kind of fruit belonging to the grape family but native only to the Philippines. They were pretty good, too. For dessert, we had ice cream and coconut cookies. To drink, we had a choice of coffee, soft drinks, or beer. A fine feast we had. It had been a long time since I had eaten so much.

After eating, we either played tennis, bowled, went swimming, or just sat around and talked. I must be getting old; I just sat around and talked.

After lounging around for a couple of hours, most of us were taken to the coconut factory and given a guided tour through the factory by a couple of our hosts. We started at the peeling end and went through the finished product – all very interesting. I ate so much coconut going through the plant I could hardly stand to look at it. Talk about working. Those people in that factory put out; I'm not kidding you. I don't see how they could work as hard as they did all day. The next time you see a can of "Baker's Coconut", you can figure I saw it when it was still in the shell. After leaving the factory, we went back to the recreation hall kind of doing as we pleased until time to leave.

One of our hosts and entertainers was an old retired chief petty officer. His name was Stalker from Greensboro, N.C. He had been around the Philippine Islands for twenty-five years. He sat around telling us sea stories of things that happened to him and about the Japanese taking Bataan and Corregidor. He was a prisoner for three years, etc. He just enjoyed talking. Just before we left, though, he began to feel kind of merry and started singing songs. He had been drinking beer all day and it was beginning to make him happy. Thus, a pleasant day ended. I guess it was about the most enjoyable day I've ever spent overseas."

I didn't mention it in the letter, but I might add that the old chief was about 45 to 50 years old and was married to a young Filipino woman. They had 2 or 3 relatively young children. He was our main host and lived in one of the nice homes there. His wife lived like a queen compared to how most of the native Filipino women lived. I would say all the Americans that worked for the Baker Coconut Company had a very high standard of living.

I think the old chief enjoyed being together with a bunch of young American sailors – like he once was himself many years before. He was probably the one that instigated the whole affair and probably did it again later on. It was a very enjoyable day and I'm sure I enjoyed it as much as the old chief did.

There were a lot of American Navy ships in the harbor that day, and it is a mystery to me why the Brush was the ship chosen to provide the sailors to go on the excursion. I'm glad we were, of course, because no one in the fleet could have been more interested in going than I was. I'm also glad that I was one of the ones from the ship invited to go. I know everybody that went on the trip enjoyed the day. I'm sure the officers selected members of the crew, too, that could be depended on to behave themselves and everybody did. I noticed, though, that a couple of them started talking a little loud toward the end of the evening.

Another thing that I saw on the trip that I thought was interesting, very scenic, and beautiful in a unique sort of way, were the terraced mountainsides where the natives were growing rice. I saw a number of them and they looked just like pages out of a geography book.

**Sam Smith QMSN**
Swabbing the top of the pilothouse in Manila

## SOUTH CHINA SEA – OCTOBER 1954

Early Friday morning, 8 October, the ships of Task Group 70.2 left Manila and went back out into the South China Sea and steamed around some more, doing what task groups do. Only now, the 2 carriers were the Philippine Sea and the USS Wasp(CVA18). The Hornet had departed for parts unknown. The ships went out into fairly rough seas when they left Manila and it got worse over the next couple of days, because we were on the fringes of another typhoon that was passing to the north of us. It was rather unpleasant living conditions for a couple of days.

The fifteenth of October the ships went into Subic Bay for a couple of days but I'm not sure why we did. Subic Bay wasn't considered a liberty port because few people ever went ashore there.

Monday, 18 October, we left Subic Bay and rejoined the task group. However, now, the only carrier in the TG was the Wasp. The Philippine Sea had departed for parts unknown, too. In addition, for several days it was just the Wasp and the destroyers of DesDiv 92 steaming around out there. The other destroyers had also departed for parts unknown. However, on Saturday, 24 October, the carrier, Yorktown(CVA10), and the destroyers, Fletcher and Carpenter, joined the formation. The TG continued to steam around in the South China Sea but actually nothing of any significance was taking place. We were just there.

I'll always remember the time I spent in the South China Sea, although, I really can't consider it one of the better times of my life. It really wasn't much fun, mainly because the weather was so miserably hot.

The 3 main things that I remember about the place were the great lightning- filled thunderheads at night, the terrible sleeping conditions, and the multitude of giant jellyfish that I saw down in the water. I will describe 2 of these things on the following pages. I wrote about the giant jellyfish earlier in the book when we were operating with the task group the first time back in June. The jellyfish were still there in October, too, but you could only see them down in the water on calm days.

### Hot Compartment

The weather in the South China Sea was very hot during the day. The metal of the ships would get so hot you couldn't touch it without burning yourself. We could endure the heat during the day well enough, topside, because there was always a good breeze blowing – because of the movement of the ship if nothing else. And the night temperatures were pleasant enough, but the fact that the ship absorbed so much heat during the day made the sleeping compartments miserably hot at night. Everybody suffered – the crew, the officers, and the captain, too, I'm sure. Cooler night air was continuously being blown into the compartments but it didn't cool the spaces down. The only way that I could sleep down there at all was to put a wet towel over me. I could barely tolerate being down there even then.

In addition, it was difficult to wake people up to relieve the watch. Normally, all you had to do was just touch someone, tell them that it was time to relieve the watch, and they would answer you and immediately get up without any further encouragement. However, when we were operating in the South China Sea, it wasn't that easy to wake people. Sometime you would have to shake them, and even then you would have to stand by their rack to make sure that they got up. Furthermore, a couple of times they even threaten me with bodily harm for waking them up. Normally, everybody was very pleasant about getting up, because relieving the watch on time was very important and was something all watch-standers had a practice of doing, regardless of how sleepy they were. In addition, there must have been something wrong with the air in the compartments, too, because everybody's eyes were terribly bloodshot after a few hours of sleeping in the hot compartments. And I don't think the officers had any better sleeping conditions than the enlisted men either. It was miserable living conditions for everybody.

A good many of the sailors tried to sleep topside out under the stars, including myself, even though it was against regulations. However, trying to sleep topside wasn't too satisfactory either, because the ship would steam into a rain shower every so often and force you to seek shelter. Consequently, your sleep was constantly being interrupted and you would end up with even less sleep than usual, which was never enough at best.

## Thunderheads

One thing I got a certain amount of pleasure in watching at night when I was on watch was the lightning displays in big, towering thunderheads. I could stand on the bridge and observe 2, 3, or 4 big thunderheads off in the distance being continuously lit up with great flashes of lightning. This would go on for as long as I cared to stand there and watch them. I don't remember ever seeing any bolts of lightning, however. And I don't remember hearing any thunder either, although, we might have been too far away to hear it most of the time.

You can imagine what it must have been like standing there on the bridge, in the dark, with a light breeze blowing in your face, looking out across the open ocean at those towering thunderheads in the distance that were continuously being lit up with great flashes of lightning every few seconds. It was an awesome display of nature. You can only witness that sort of thing in certain parts of the world, and even then you would have to be out on the open ocean or in a big, open space somewhere. I happened to be a young seaman down in the South China Sea witnessing this sort of phenomena. And, in addition, I just happened to be inclined to notice such things – some people aren't. I knew I was observing something very unusual, and I have never witnessed that type of natural display of light again, at least to the extent I saw it there. I'm sure many of my shipmates would have rather seen a flashing neon sign, especially if it had read "cold beer and spirits".

DesDiv 92 was detached from the TG early Thursday afternoon, 21 October, to proceed into Subic Bay again. This time, however, we wouldn't be rejoining the TG. We would spend a couple of days in Subic Bay and then depart for Japan. In fact, my second tour in the Far East was quickly coming to a close.

Our time of operating around the Philippines and in the South China Sea was over, and I had somewhat mixed feelings over our departure from the region. I had spent many hours correcting and bringing the navigational charts of the entire Indochina region up to date and not one of them was ever used. So I was very disappointed in that respect. It would have been very interesting to me for the ships to have navigated some around the coastal waters of Indochina, especially Vietnam, but we never even came in sight of those countries – by a couple of hundred miles. But, maybe that was a good thing and best for all of us.

I was also relieved that we never had to engage the enemy – the communist in Southeast Asia, because I still remembered what the "Voice" had told me when we were operating off the coast of North Korea a year earlier. That is, "I needed to be concerned about being in Southeast Asia." As I understood the message, my future was going to be uncertain when I went to that part of the world.

I'm sure Washington had something important in mind for the navy to do when they sent all those ships down to operate in the South China Sea – 3 aircraft carriers, at least 12 destroyers, and all the auxiliary ships to supply them. I'm sure the action they had planned for us would have made the headlines in all the newspapers if we had actually executed them. Apparently, for some reason, the "Powers That Be" changed their minds at the last minute about us going into action. The task group spent several months steaming around in the South China Sea, but I believe it was the first 2 weeks out there in June with the 3 carriers that was the critical time for us. After that, I believe the navy was just out there killing time and they knew it. So, I guess I'm grateful that they changed their minds about us going into action.

DesDiv 92 departed Subic Bay early Sunday morning, 31 October, en route to Sasebo, Japan. At 0735 we passed Point Suente light abeam to starboard at 1500 yards for the last time. I would never be in the Philippines again.

It would be another 3½ day trip to Sasebo, cruising along at 16 to 18 knots. We just steamed along toward our destination without doing anything in the way of ship exercises or maneuvers; mainly, because the weather wasn't conducive to doing anything else other than steaming along. In a letter to my mother dated November 7, 1954, I described our voyage up to Sasebo.

"We're in Sasebo today. We arrived here last Wednesday, I believe. We had a rather rough trip up. We were in a tropical storm nearly all the way from Subic Bay to Sasebo – high winds and rough water all the way. We left the Philippines just in time because a bad typhoon was headed in our direction when we pulled out. We've been mighty lucky keeping out of those things."

## SASEBO – NOVEMBER 1954

DesDiv 92 arrived in Sasebo around noon on Wednesday, 3 November, and moored alongside the USS Hector(AR7) that was moored to buoy 16. The engineering plant was put on cold iron and the ship(s) commenced receiving steam and electrical services from the Hector. In other words, the ships and their crews were going to be given a rest for a few days or at least as much as they could be. We would stay in port 8 days. That was more than enough time for us to spend all our money. A lot of it would be spent on souvenirs this time in port, because we would soon be headed back to the States.

In this same letter dated November 7, I wrote some more about our stay in Sasebo.

"I've been on the beach a couple of times since we've been in. I got myself a steak dinner both times. Last night I got one so big I just could eat it all. It only cost $1.50. A sailor doesn't think anything at all about paying that much for a meal after he had been at sea for a few weeks. After a few days of sea rations everyone begins to crave something as satisfying as a big, thick steak.

I'm almost down to the same weight I was when I came in the navy. It's been a long, hot, undernourished summer. Hollows are in my cheeks again, and I'm about 27 inches in the waist now. I was 29 inches. My clothes don't fit so well anymore.

We're wearing blues now. It feels kind of good to get back in them. The nights here are pretty cool, around 50 °, but the days are still warm.

I went to church this morning aboard a big ship that we're tied up next to. It was a good service."

Thursday morning, Lt. Cdr. B.W. Jones, was detached from duty as the executive officer and departed the ship. He was headed for shore duty in Washington, D.C.

Saturday morning, 6 November, the captain held a personnel inspection and also an inspection of the upper deck and living quarters.

I thought it was kind of interesting that no one was going AWOL or coming in late off liberty this time in port. Everybody was behaving themselves because we were going back to the States very soon and no one wanted to take a chance on being left behind.

We left Sasebo early Friday morning, 12 November. The crew was mustered on station at 0530 and there were no absentees. The special sea detail was set at 0540 and the ship was underway at 0618. The captain was at the conn. At 0648 we passed Kogo Sake light abeam to starboard at a distance of one mile. We observed sunrise at 0650 and turned off the navigational lights. At 0657 we passed Shira Se light abeam to port at a distance of 500 yards. At 0700 the ships reached the open ocean and formed up into a column formation. However, a little later the ships went into a diamond formation and proceeded most of the way to Yokosuka in that fashion. It took the ships 2 days to reach that port.

In a letter to my mother dated November 14, I wrote about our trip down from Sasebo. "The trip down from Sasebo was uneventful. The first day and night out from Sasebo was what I call ideal sailing weather. The ocean was as calm as a lake early in the morning–almost like a mirror. There was a full moon at night too, to light up things. That kind of weather makes a guy not mind being out on the ocean so much."

## YOKOSUKA – NOVEMBER. 1954

We arrived in Yokosuka around 0600 Sunday morning, 14 November. It was before daylight. We moored to berth 8 at the U.S. Naval Base. The Brush was assigned a berth alongside the pier at the naval base because we had a leak in one of our fuel tanks that needed to be repaired. We would stay in Yokosuka for 5 days.

I bought quite a few souvenirs and gifts in Sasebo and Yokosuka. I sent a big box full of Christmas gifts home to my folks, sister, and to an aunt and uncle. I heard later that everybody had a big time opening up the box that came from the Orient. It was amazing the amount of stuff the crew took back to the States. Sailors hid their purchases in various spaces around the ship. I stashed my stuff in various little spaces in the charthouse.

## Promoted to Third Class Petty Officer

Right after we arrived in Yokosuka, I was notified by the navy that I had been promoted to 3rd class petty officer, which made me very happy. The promotion gave me substantial more prestige and a pay increase. I was now going to make around $150 per month, as I remember. Wow.

That doesn't seem like very much money today, but when you look at that amount of money in terms of buying power, it's similar to making $1500 per month in today's money. And the best part, the money I made was all throw away money – when I got the chance to spend it. However, in my case, I didn't throw it all away because I had $50 per month deducted from my pay by the navy, which was sent home and put into a savings account. But, usually, I still had enough money to do whatever I wanted to do, or buy, when I was in port, except when we were in a place like Hong Kong; I could have spent a lot of money there.

I was glad to get the promotion, but I felt like I should have received it at least 6 months earlier. However, the navy did promote me to 2nd class petty officer just before I got out of the navy, which, I believe, was an enticement to get me to re-enlist but it didn't work. I had had enough of sea duty and life on a destroyer. I can feel proud of the fact, however, that I did make 2nd class during my first enlistment, because that is something that relatively few quartermasters achieved, at least, during that period of time in history.

Immediately upon learning that I had been promoted, I went ashore to a tailor shop and had a 3rd class petty officer's insignia sewed on my uniform. Then, I went to a photography shop and had a picture taken of myself with the new stripes on my sleeve. It actually was the best picture I had taken of myself while I was in the navy. And I believe it was the only one I ever had taken in a photography shop.

## Aussies

I had some interesting experiences during the last two days I was in Japan. I went aboard an Australian ship, met, and made friends with a number of Australian sailors. Plus, I went on liberty with some of them.

In a letter to my mother I wrote about how I got acquainted with these Aussie sailors and what I did with them.

"An Australian aircraft carrier, the HMAS Vengeance, came into port and tied up to a pier down from us. I've wondered for a long time what kind of fellows the Australians were and what kind of navy they had. So, around 2:00 pm the day they arrived, I went aboard her, went up to the bridge, and got acquainted with their signal gang. There were about a dozen of them on the bridge and I visited with them for about an hour or so. They seemed to be the nicest bunch of guys I've ever met and seemed to enjoy my visit.

At tea time, 3:00 pm, they invited me down to their mess for tea. That is an everyday occurrence with them. I drank a cup of hot tea and ate a butter and blackberry jam sandwich; both were mighty good. It was the first hot tea I ever drank that I really liked. After tea, they took me down into their compartment and showed me pictures of their girlfriends, or "honeys", as they called them and gave me a pocket full of Australian coins. Those Australian women showed me plenty. Those guys almost persuaded me to go home with them. Who knows, I might get down there yet.

That night ashore I ate supper at the same table with an Aussie chief petty officer and we struck up a conversation and a friendship. The chief and I and a couple of his shipmates finished out the night together – until 12:00 o'clock midnight anyways, when liberty was up.

The chief invited me over for tea the next morning at 10:00 o'clock. So the next morning I went over for tea"……

I liked their tea, and I also tried their coffee, which I thought was very strange looking stuff and tasted strange, too. It was very different from what I was accustomed to. It was a real light colored beverage and looked to me like it was half milk, but it didn't taste like "milky coffee". I drank a mug of it but I can't say that I really liked it. Although, I said I did. I lied just a little bit because I didn't want to offend them and ruin a new friendship. Back to the letter.

"Afterwards, he showed me around his ship and introduced me to a lot of his shipmates. Then I ate dinner with them. I thought it was a pretty good dinner. We had kidney – vegetable soup, mutton roast and gravy, baked potatoes, boiled cabbage, bread, custard-peach pie, and tea. They were complaining about the chow but I thought it was pretty good myself.

That afternoon I went ashore with the chief and a couple of the signalmen and had a jolly good time. I enjoyed being around them, the Aussies, they were really a likeable bunch of boys.

The next day we left. The Aussies have a funny way of saying a lot of things, but most of them you can understand alright. I learned a lot of new words from them and a lot about Australia."

I didn't mention it in my letter, but the last night we were in Yokosuka, my Australian buddies and I ended up in the Enlisted Men's Club on the naval base. There were a lot of other Australian sailors there, too. I sat around with my new friends for several hours socializing and drinking beer, that is, my 2 beers with several cokes downed in between them.

I had a great time talking and socializing with the Aussie sailors. And I also got introduced to the popular Australian song, Waltzing Matilda. I thought it was one of the prettiest songs that I had ever heard and was certainly sung the prettiest and with the most gusto that I have ever heard it sung. A large group of Aussie sailors spontaneously decided to sing the song and at the top of their voices. I believe they sang every verse of it from memory because it took awhile for them to get it all sung. They were really into singing it and they sounded as good as any men's choir that I've ever heard. They all seemed to be very happy, and some of them felt like it was necessary to stand on the chairs to do their singing and put a lot of arm and body motion into it. I felt like they couldn't have done a better job of singing the song than if they had rehearsed it all week.

I liked the song, Waltzing Matilda, so much that I asked one of my Aussie friends to write the words down for me on a piece of paper. He was glad to oblige me, but the only piece of paper we could find was a small, brown paper bag, and he wrote one verse of the song on the little bag. I still have the little bag among my mementoes. The song eventually got to the United States a few years later and, of course, became quite popular there, too, for a time. But I'll always remember the night I first heard the song when it was sung by a bunch of happy, beer drinking Australian sailors in Japan.

There were some things in particular that I noticed about the Australian sailors. Most of them that I met were reasonably good-looking, well-built, and healthy looking. They all seemed to be good-natured and friendly, at least, the ones I met. Furthermore, they used little, if any, foul language, which I thought was kind of unusual for sailors. They may have used foul language amongst themselves, but they never used any while I was with them. In addition, I never saw any of them drink beer to excess and get mouthy, obnoxious, and want to fight. I thought that was remarkable, too.

The name of the Australian chief that I made friends with was G.H. (Geoff) Judd. I've forgotten what his duties were on his ship. We corresponded occasionally for the next year or so, or until I got out of the navy. However, I saw him one other time while I was in the navy. He also gave a pretty Australian girl my address and persuaded her to write me. I wrote to her occasionally, too. Her name was Wendy Harper and she was a good friend of his girlfriend back in Australia. Unfortunately, I never got to Australia to meet her.

## HOMEWARD BOUND

DesDiv 92 departed Yokosuka, Japan early Friday morning, 19 November, 1954, en route to CONUS Via Midway and Pearl Harbor, Hawaii. I think everybody was glad to be going back to the U.S. for awhile. But I believe most of the crew had a certain amount of affection for Japan, too, because it was sort of our "home away from home". It was just a different world and a place that kind of grew on you.

Upon departing Tokyo Bay, the ships set a course for Midway Island and generally cruised along at 16 knots or so. The ships didn't do anything except steam east for 5 days. I believe the sea was too rough to try and conduct exercises and drills of any kind. However, on Wednesday, 6 November, the sea was much smoother and the ships conducted a little gunnery practice. We were nearing Midway by then and the weather had greatly improved.

I was now standing signal watches. I had stood signal watches on the bridge from time to time since I had been on the ship, but now I would be standing signal watches all the time when I was on watch and as the supervisor of the watch. My career as a signalman got off to a bad start, however. In a letter to my mother dated November 21, 1954, I wrote about our first few days out of Japan, headed toward Midway, and how my new career as a signalman got off to a bad start.

"We are 3 days out of Japan and are about a thousand miles from the nearest land and almost halfway to Midway Island. It has been miserable weather so far. It has been cloudy, windy, and rainy. The first day out was very rough. I had to face the weather all day and was cold and wet all the time. Water was coming over the bridge and hitting me like somebody was throwing buckets of water on me. Thus, now I have a bad cold. The last 2 days haven't been so rough, but it has been raining a lot, which isn't helping my cold any."

It was times like those mentioned above which made me sometimes question whether I should have been a quartermaster in the first place. The signalmen had to face stormy weather too often for my liking. But I had to face a lot of stormy weather during the following year that I stood watches as a signalman. Personally, I liked working in the charthouse and pilothouse much better. I was out of the wind, rain, and waves there.

The ships arrived at Midway Island at midmorning on Wednesday, 24 November. The Brush proceeded independently through the channel and into the lagoon. At 1100 the Brush was moored starboard side to the Thomas at pier 2 to take on fuel. The ship completed refueling at 1550 and had received 96,053 gallons of fuel oil. At 1714 we got underway and proceeded back out of the lagoon. At 1730 the Brush had completed passage of the channel and had joined back up with the other ships of DesDiv 92. The ships now set a course for Pearl Harbor. At 1753 the ship observed sunset and turned on the running lights.

Thursday, 25 November, was Thanksgiving Day and the ship observed holiday routine as much as possible. The ships steamed along at a speed of 20 knots and on a course of 108°(t) all day en route to Pearl Harbor. I'll give the cooks credit for preparing a good Thanksgiving dinner. I think everybody had all they wanted to eat. It might not have been as good as home cooking but it was good enough.

The next day, Friday, 26 November, the ships separated somewhat and conducted what they call a full-power economy run. At 0645 the ship gradually increased speed to 32 knots and maintained that speed for nearly 6 hours. The ocean was relatively calm now and the ship was churning up a long, white trail of foam. At 1232 the captain started reducing the speed every few minutes until it reached 18 knots and then he maintained that speed, more or less, until we arrived at Pearl Harbor. Also on Friday afternoon the ship conducted an atomic defense drill. However, I don't remember now what all that amounted to. Thankfully, we never had to use any of that training.

## Hawaii

Early Saturday morning, 27 November, various navigational lights on the Hawaiian Islands began to come in sight. At 0527 we passed Barber's Point light abeam to port at 3½ miles. At 0532 the ship commenced maneuvering at various courses and speeds to enter Pearl Harbor. At 0654 we observed sunrise and turned off the running lights. At 0744 the Brush was moored starboard side to the Thomas at berth B-24.

DesDiv 92 stayed in port 2 days over the weekend. I went ashore one of those days and went to my favorite restaurant on Waikiki Beach, the Wagon Wheel Restaurant, and had a supper of sea turtle steak, my usual meal there. I liked to go there because of its tropical garden setting, the smell of flowers, and the gentle ocean breezes that cooled the night air and rustled the coconut palms. I knew that I was in an exotic, tropical place.

We left Pearl Harbor early Monday morning, 29 November, bound for Long Beach, California. The voyage would take 6 days. We just steamed along toward Long Beach at a speed of 17 knots and didn't do much of anything else. Apparently, the commodore was played out like the rest of us. The trip was uneventful.

We first began to sight the navigational lights on the offshore islands at 2243 Saturday night when we sighted San Nicholas Light at a distance of 39 miles. We soon began to sight other lights on other islands as we got closer to the mainland.

## HOMECOMING – 1954

The ship passed through the outer breakwater of Long Beach Harbor at 0838 Sunday morning, 5 December. At 0927 the Brush was moored to the port side of the Thomas at Net Pier. The pier was full of people that had come to see the ships come in and to greet their husbands, sons, boyfriends, friends, or whatever. Homecoming was a great and exciting time for both the sailors and the visitors. The navy band was there and was playing "Anchors Aweigh" as we came in to dock, which added a great deal to the occasion. I couldn't take in too much of the festivities myself until we got docked, because I was steering the ship and was having to "mind my helm" too close to spend much time looking around. However, when I did get time to look the crowd over, I discovered that there was someone on the pier to meet me, which was a very pleasant surprise because I wasn't expecting anybody. Beuford and Elouise Randall were on the pier to meet me. I left the ship and visited with them for awhile and made plans to visit them at their home a few days later. I had brought back a few Christmas gifts for the Randall family, but I waited another week or so before giving them the presents.

Also, since Beuford and Elouise were there on the dock, I thought it would be a good idea to show him the ship even though it wasn't a visitor's day; and that is what I did, but I'm sure nobody noticed or cared. However, we left Elouise on the dock because we couldn't be sure what we would encounter along the way. The sailors weren't expecting any women aboard so there is no telling what she might see or hear. We thought it might be simply too much for her delicate nature to take a chance.

Anyway, I gave Beuford a grand tour of the ship, from bow to stern, and even took him to places that visitors normally don't go. I think Beuford enjoyed looking over the ship, and I got a lot of pleasure out of showing it to him. He got to see where I lived while I was in the navy – the only person from back home that ever did.

**USS Brush DD745**

## A Sailor and His Family Reuniting After a Long Deployment

This statue is part of the U.S. Navy Memorial in Washington, D.C., which depicts the reuniting of a sailor and his family after a long deployment.

## Stuffy Nose

I had an interesting experience coming into the harbor that homecoming day. It seems that the air around Long Beach never agreed with me too much, because all the time I was around Long Beach, my nose stayed stopped up. And there wasn't anything that I knew about that would open it up like there is today. Consequently, I went around with a stuffy nose all the time. On this morning, I had been gone from Long Beach for 7 months and my nose had been open all that time except when I had a cold, which wasn't much. As we came into the harbor that morning, I wondered if my nose would stop up again as before. It had been a great pleasure and relief to be able to breathe normally for all those months. I didn't have long to wonder because my nose was all stopped up before we even got docked. So much for Long Beach's smoggy air – at that time. Hopefully, their air is better and cleaner today.

The ships of DesDiv 92 would stay in port for 4 weeks or until after New Years. Much of the crew went home on leave during this time in port, but I wouldn't be one of them. Although, I certainly needed one because it had been a year since I had been home, and I had been at sea most of that time, too, without the proper rest, sleep, and nourishment. However, I chose not to go home on leave for a number of reasons including all the traveling time and expense involved in taking one – to mention a couple.

On Wednesday, 8 December, the ships of DesDiv 92 were moved by tugboats from Net Pier to alongside the USS Hamul(AD20) at buoys 6 and 7.

Our rations improved somewhat after we got back in Long Beach. I wrote to my mother about these improvements in our chow.

"The food aboard ship has improved quite a bit since we've been back. We're getting all the milk we want, plenty of fresh fruit, fresh eggs once in awhile, and bakery sweets of one kind and another. We also get fresh salad vegetables occasionally. We didn't get any of those things overseas."

## My 1954 Christmas Leave

My "leave" in 1954 consisted of a phone call home just before Christmas, and I had to make some special arrangements to accomplish that. Rural areas, where my folks lived, didn't have telephone service back then and actually didn't have any for a good many years afterwards. A neighborhood store, however, did have a phone, and I wrote and told my folks to be at that country store on a certain day at a specific time to receive my call. The store owner was in on the plans and it was perfectly agreeable with him. My folks were at the store at the pre-arranged time and I talked to them for 10 or 15 minutes. I called them from a pay phone at the YMCA in Long Beach and talked to them until my quarters ran out. As I recall, I had $8.00 worth of quarters and I kept plugging them in the phone when I was instructed to by the operator. We had a nice conversation; however, they wouldn't hear my voice again for another year, not until I was released from active duty and had arrived home.

## Christmas 1954

I spent Christmas weekend with the Randall family. Christmas was on Saturday that year – 1954. I arrived at their house early Friday afternoon and stayed until Sunday evening. I wrote about my Christmas in a letter to my mother dated December 27, 1954.

"Christmas is over now and I reckon I'm glad of it. Although, I had a right nice, enjoyable Christmas weekend, I never did get what you would call the Christmas spirit. It seemed like any other ordinary time for me with no special feelings much. Maybe a person has got to be home to have it.

I spent almost 3 days at the Randalls' home and had a very enjoyable time. I never got to go hunting but I went fishing instead.

First of all, we got up early Christmas morning and gathered around the tree. Their little girl, Marcelle, naturally, got the biggest kick out of it. She got a bunch of stuff.....Santa Claus brought me a few things, too.....I also had a very good Christmas dinner of turkey and all the trimmings. It was probably the same thing you all had. It was really a good dinner anyway – Southern style.

I gave the Randalls their Christmas gifts before Christmas, actually the first weekend after arriving back in Long Beach. However, I did bring in a big bag of nuts, fruit, candy, and such like Christmas Eve. I brought the whole family an 8-place set of China that I got in Japan. I gave Elouise a pair of Jade earrings that I bought in China, I believe. I brought Beuford and Merwin ocean fishing rods from Japan and they seemed pleased to get them, especially Beuford. They are very pretty rods that are made of split bamboo; they are varnished nice, trimmed in bright colors, and can be taken apart to make a different length rod. I bought a rod for myself too that is just like theirs. I bought the rods pretty cheap in Japan, but they are quite expensive in the States. I've forgotten what I gave Mrs. Randall.

Beuford and I gave our rods a workout the day after Christmas. We went surf fishing early the next morning at Arredondo Beach for about 5 ½ hours and caught 22 ocean perch. They look a whole lot like large bream and taste as good as any fish I've ever eaten. We caught 11 fish each. That was not bad considering neither one of us had ever surf fished before or used that kind of fishing gear before. We felt right proud of ourselves, not only for catching that many fish, but because there were probably two dozen people fishing along the beach on both sides of us, and we caught twice as many fish as the whole lot of them put together. I guess it was beginner's luck. The rest of the weekend was spent sitting around the house talking, drinking coffee, watching TV, and stuff like that. It was a nice, quiet time. That is what I did Christmas weekend 1954."

**Ted Holly, Marcelle & Beuford Randall holding a string of fish**

I also spent the New Year's weekend, 1955, with the Randall family. New Year's Day was on Saturday that year. However, it rained all day Saturday and we couldn't do much outside. Sunday was a beautiful, clear day, though. Just being off the ship for a little while was entertainment enough for me.

**Nest of Ships in San Diego Harbor**
**(U.S. Navy Photograph)**

**USS Piedmont AD17**
**USS Maddox DD731**
**USS Herbert J. Thomas DDR833**
**USS Samuel N. Moore DD747**
**USS Spangler DE696**
**USS George DE697**

# 10

## THIRD STATESIDE DUTY – 1955

### OPERATING OFF THE COAST OF CALIFORNIA

The Brush stayed in port for nearly a month after getting back from overseas. This third tour of stateside duty was relatively easy compared to the first one I had in the latter part of 1952. It was easier, mainly, because we spent a great deal of time in port. Also, those weeks that we did go to sea were usually 4 day weeks. We would usually go to sea Monday morning and come back in port sometime Thursday afternoon or night. However, some of the weeks that we did go to sea were real rough ones, especially when we were operating with the other ships of DesDiv 92. At these times the ships engaged in division tactics a great deal.

In addition, we spent nearly all of our time in port in Long Beach, which, I suppose, made all the married men happy. We did spend one weekend in San Francisco and a few nights in San Diego, but the rest of the time in port was in Long Beach.

I don't know why the navy high command allowed us to stay in port so much, unless it was now peace time and they didn't feel the need to train us all the time. Or, maybe they were trying to improve the re-enlistment rate because it was dismal with the ships of DesDiv 92. I don't know anything about what the re-enlistment rate was in other destroyer divisions or on other ships, however.

During the days we spent at sea the Brush was conducting either antisubmarine warfare (ASW), gunnery practice, operating with aircraft carriers, torpedo practice, or division tactics. In addition, the ship engaged in a lot of shipboard drills like: general quarters, steering casualty, engineering casualty, fire, abandon ship, man overboard, and atomic defense.

All these naval activities are quite interesting to people that have never seen them before, or maybe new men coming aboard, but after a person has participated in these activities dozens of times, they all got rather tiresome and boring. However, I suppose all this training was mainly for the benefit of the new men coming aboard, both officers and enlisted men. The purpose of all this training was to train the men to the point that they could perform their duties almost without having to think about it. The petty officers and some of the more experienced non-petty officers probably had already reached that point, and it probably wasn't as necessary to subject them to all this training, but they got it anyway.

### Sunday Brunch

Early in this tour of stateside duty the cooks started serving brunch on Sunday mornings when we were in port, which was every Sunday in the States. I don't know whose idea it was to do this but the crew seemed to like it. The ship didn't have reveille on Sunday mornings and the men could sleep in as late as they wanted to, which was noon in some cases. Of course, the men that had watches had to get up at the regular time.

Brunch was served until around 1400, as I remember. The cooking was mostly done in the mess serving compartment on some kind of portable stove or grill. I believe they gave you a choice of several things or all of them if you wanted them. Most of the men wanted eggs in some fashion, and the cooks would cook them any way you wanted them and as many as you wanted. We all thought it was a pretty good arrangement and it probably added something to the morale of the troops.

It was a strange thing about those eggs, though. I always ordered 4 eggs for breakfast because that was the number that seem to satisfy me. However, most of my life one or two eggs were all that I ever wanted. Most of the guys ate more eggs at brunch than I did. I was told that some of my shipmates would eat a dozen eggs for breakfast, because that is what it took to satisfy them. The only reason that I can think of for this increase in egg consumption by the men was the age of the eggs they were being fed. The story was that they had been on cold storage for several years. I can't say for sure whether this was true or not, but that was the story. In other words, the eggs weren't exactly fresh, although, they were still in the shell – as opposed to powdered eggs out of a box. Yuck! There were some things that I didn't eat and powdered eggs were one of them. Warm, lumpy, powered milk was another thing that I didn't eat. I preferred to go hungry.

On, 3 January, 1955, the Brush got underway and departed Long Beach Harbor all by herself. The other ships of DesDiv 92 must have gone in a different direction. We headed south toward the San Diego operating areas to engage in ASW with a troop ship. We rendezvoused with the USS Menard(APA201) at 1249 and assumed screening station 2000 yards ahead of her. The USS Redfish(SS395) was the submarine that was operating with us. The submarine's role in the operation was to try to get in a position to fire a torpedo at the APA. The ships started steering courses according to a zig-zag plan to confuse the submarine. However, some time during the exercise the submarine fired a practice torpedo at the Menard, but the ship's log doesn't say whether the sub was successful at hitting her or not. Another naval craft present, AVR-2, recovered the torpedo and returned it to the Redfish.

The ships conducted ASW all afternoon until 1841. At that time the Brush ceased operating with the Menard, changed course, and started proceeding to area MM 1 where she steamed around all night on various courses alone. It was a quiet night on the bridge.

However, around 0700 the next morning the Brush rendezvoused with the Menard again and started conducting some more ASW exercises. The Redfish was also operating with them. At 1135 the ships completed the ASW exercises and the Brush proceeded to San Diego. At 1309 the Brush set the special sea detail to enter port, and at 1352 the ship was moored to buoy 18. We spent the night there.

Early the next morning, 5 January, the Brush departed the harbor and proceeded to operating area VV 1 to rendezvous with the USS Redfish to conduct some more ASW. On the way there, the ship conducted some fire and abandon ship drills. At 1007 the Brush arrived at the operating area and started conducting ASW with the sub. The Brush and the sub ceased the ASW exercises around 1700 that afternoon. The Brush just steamed around independently all night in op area VV 1.

Early the next morning, Thursday, 6 January, the Brush and the Redfish started conducting ASW exercises again. However, the ship and the sub ceased conducting ASW exercises at 1114 and the Brush set a course for San Diego. At 1327 we were moored to buoy 13. We spent another night in San Diego. Liberty was granted but I don't remember whether I went ashore or not. If I did, I didn't do anything exciting enough to remember it.

The Brush got underway around 0800 Friday morning, 7 January, departed the harbor, and proceeded to operating area MM 11 up toward Long Beach to rendezvous with another submarine, the USS Razorback(SS394), to conduct some more ASW exercises. The Brush arrived at the area at 0930 and commenced ASW with the submarine. A little later, the sub fired a practice torpedo at the Brush, but there is not any record of whether she hit us or not. Around 1320 the ship's motor whaleboat recovered the torpedo and returned it to the Razorback.

Around 1434 the Razorback fired another torpedo at the Brush, but, again, there is not any record of whether she hit us or not. The ship's motor whaleboat recovered the torpedo and returned it to the sub. The ASW exercises were over at 1512 and the Brush set a course for Long Beach. We arrived there just before dark and moored to buoys 8 and 10 alongside the Thomas. We would stay in port for the next 9 days or until 17 January.

The next morning we were to have a personnel inspection, so I went ashore Friday night in an effort to better prepare myself for it, which included getting a haircut, getting my dress blues cleaned, and getting my shoes shined.

## I Meet Up with a High School Classmate – Billy Williams

An interesting thing happened to me on the way back to the ship Friday night. I rounded a corner and almost ran into Billy Williams, one of my old Haines City classmates. He was still aboard the DeHaven(DD727), but I hadn't seen him for 15 months because most of the time we were on opposite sides of the ocean. We stood around and talked a few minutes about our old classmates and their whereabouts. He was the only source of information I had about my Haines City friends and acquaintances.

It so happened that he had met and married a California girl since I last saw him. They, or she, mostly, lived in an apartment somewhere around Long Beach. Of course, he stayed there as much as he could. He invited me to come see him, which I happily agreed to do. So, the next day in the early afternoon, Billy picked me up at Fleet Landing and took me to his apartment. I met his wife, of course, and she seemed like a nice little woman to me. He seemed to like her anyway. I spent both Saturday and Sunday afternoon with him. We didn't do much except talk and loaf around. I enjoyed talking to him and he caught me up on all the Haines City news, including which girl classmates of ours had gotten married. There were some mighty nice girls around Haines City, and some lucky fellows took advantage of that fact and married them while I wasn't paying attention.

I also visited Billy the following week-end, and we went on a little excursion to the mountains and did a little snow sleighing. I believe I spent the night with him on this occasion. In a letter to my mother dated January 16, 1955, I wrote about going snow sleighing the day before with my old schoolmate, Billy Williams.

"Saturday morning I got up at 4:30 a.m. and went up in the mountains with Billy Williams, his wife, and her brother to do a little sleigh riding in the snow. Where we went was a very pretty place with big pine trees and nice little hills to slide down. We took a few pictures and if they are good, I'll send you some. The snow was about a foot and a half feet deep and real soft. It must have snowed the night before. It was the first time that I ever played around in the snow. I'm not very good on a sleigh. I wouldn't get very far down the hill before I would get thrown off and my feet liked to have frozen off. I had on rubber boots but the only thing they did was to keep out the snow. They didn't keep out the cold. I had a very different and good time, though."

I believe that is the last time I ever saw Billy Williams. He soon went back overseas and then got out of the navy. I lost track of him and our paths have never crossed since, although, in recent years I've talked to him over the phone a couple of times.

## I Ran into Another High School Classmate – Bobby Claywell

I had another interesting encounter on the beach this time in port. I accidentally Ran into Another Haines City classmate that was in the navy, Bobby Claywell. He was stationed at a naval base in Oxnard, California, which was only a short distance from Long Beach. Apparently, when he got stationed there his mother and father moved out there, too, and Bobby lived off-base with them. He invited me to spend the week-end with him the first chance I got and I did a few weeks later.

The only thing of any significance that happened aboard ship those 9 days in port was that Commander W.B. Whitehurst reported aboard for duty. He was going to be our new commanding officer.

A little minor incident happened aboard ship around noon on Saturday, 15 January. Yard oiler (YO219) came alongside to deliver us a little fuel oil. Somehow, approximately 2 barrels of fuel oil was spilled in the water on the port side forward. The oil was contained between YO219 and the Brush with fire hoses. At 1406 an oil skimmer barge came alongside and cleaned up the oil spill. Consequently, no harm was done to the harbor waters. It was great that the navy was fully prepared for such emergencies. I'm sure that wasn't the first time that oil had been spilled in the harbor and cleaned up.

Monday morning at 0800, 17 January, the Brush and the Maddox got underway and departed Long Beach Harbor. However, they parted company around 1000 and both ships proceeded to conduct a 15 knot economy run. The Brush steered a northwestwardly course most of the day at 15 knots. The Brush and the Maddox planned to rendezvous with the carrier, Oriskany(CVA34), up around San Francisco the next day. The Brush and the Maddox joined back up late in the day and steamed along together most of the night.The 2 destroyers rendezvoused with the Oriskany at 0625 the next morning and formed a column on her at 1000 yard intervals with the Brush in station 1. The Brush and the Maddox operated with the carrier for the next 3 days while she conducted flight operations and other exercises.

Sometime Thursday night, 20 January, the Brush was detached from the formation to proceed independently into San Francisco Bay. At 0819 Friday, 21 January, the Brush passed under the Golden Gate Bridge. At 0833 we passed Alcatraz light abeam to port at 500 yards. At 0834 the ship set the special sea detail and the captain assumed the conn. At 0923 the Brush was moored starboard side to pier 17 at the U.S. Naval Station, Treasure Island, San Francisco Bay.

At 0940 Cdr. A.G. Capps was relieved of command as captain by Cdr. W.B. Whitehurst. Cdr. Capps soon departed the ship never to be seen again. I would say that Cdr. Capps was a very good captain. I learned years later that he retired from the navy upon leaving the Brush.

We stayed in port 3 days over the weekend, but I have no recollection of what I did while I was ashore.

Monday morning, 24 January, the ships departed San Francisco Bay and proceeded to an operating area off Monterey Bay. The carrier, escorted by the Brush and Maddox, operated in this area for the next 4 days conducting flight operations and various radar tracking exercises. The ships did a lot of steaming and maneuvering during these 4 days at sea but nothing of any great significance took place. Although, one day, Wednesday, two junior carrier officers came aboard by helicopter to observe destroyer operations and 2 personnel from the Brush, Ens. J.C. Lochridge and R.G. Emerson QMC, went over to the Oriskany by helicopter to observe carrier operations.

At 0040 Friday, 28 January, the Brush and the Maddox were detached from plane guard duty with the carrier to proceed to Long Beach and that is what they did. They arrived at Long Beach during the middle of the afternoon and moored to buoys 8 and 10 alongside the Moore. The Thomas stood into the harbor at noon the next day and moored alongside to port. We would stay in port 9 days.

Around 0820, 7 February, the Brush and the Maddox got underway, departed the harbor, and proceeded to the San Diego operating area. The Brush was sent there to rendezvous with the carrier, USS Philippine Sea(CVA47). The Maddox was sent elsewhere. We were to escort the carrier around for the next 4 days while she conducted flight operations off and on. Of course, we were in plane guard station 2000 yards astern of her when she was conducting flight operations and 2000 yards ahead of her much of the time when she wasn't conducting flight operations. In addition, the 2 ships conducted some tracking exercises from time to time. The Philippine Sea didn't launch any planes at night so the nights were rather quiet. The 2 ships would just steam along at 10 knots or so on various courses and waited for day to arrive. The Brush was also detached from the carrier from time to time to go off and conduct various shipboard drills.

At 1502 Thursday, 10 February, the Brush was released from plane guard duty and we set a course for Long Beach. However, on the way in we encountered some dense fog and had to commence fog signals at 1815. At 1852 the ship set the special sea detail to enter Long Beach Harbor. At 1940 the Brush was moored to buoy 3. We spent the weekend in port.

Not much happened over the weekend while we were in port. The captain did have a personnel and upper decks inspection Friday afternoon. And, on Saturday, the commodore shifted his flag from the Maddox to the Brush for a few days.

I spent the weekend at the Randalls but I don't remember what we did on this particular visit.

At 0752 Monday morning, 14 February, the Brush got underway and departed the harbor. At 0825 the Brush assumed a course of 215°(t) and a speed of 15 knots. At 0855 the ship ran into a fog bank and commenced making international fog signals. Then, for the next hour or so the ship conducted various shipboard drills including a fire drill, fire and rescue drill, collision drill, and abandon ship drill. I suppose the captain was conducting these drills for the benefit of the commodore. At 0901 the ship changed speed to 10 knots because of the presence of heavy fog. At 0951 the ship ran out of the fog and secured from making fog signals.

During the early afternoon the ship conducted some more drills; at 1312 the ship conducted a man overboard drill, and at 1400 she commenced an engineering casualty drill. At 1500 the ship secured from those drills and set a course for San Clemente Island to conduct a gunnery exercise. We arrived at San Clemente Island at 1550. At 1600 the ship commenced a shore bombardment exercise, although, the ship didn't actually fire her guns. The ship secured from the shore bombardment exercise at 1700. Then, the Brush left San Clemente and proceeded to San Diego operating area MM 14. She steamed around in this area all night by herself. Consequently, the signalmen had little to do during the night except drink coffee and talk. We never saw another ship all night.

Late in the afternoon, Tuesday, the Brush rendezvoused with the USS Philippine Sea(CVA47) and the USS Shields(DD596). The Brush relieved the Shields of plane guard duty with the carrier. We stayed with the carrier a few hours while she conducted flight operations during the early evening. However, the carrier secured from flight operations at 2050. Around midnight we were detached from the carrier. The Brush then slowly steamed around all night in the San Diego operating area. We didn't see any other ships, so it was another quiet night for the watch standers on the bridge.

The next morning, 16 February, the Brush engaged in some gunnery practice. At 0950 the crew was called to general quarters for the practice session. At 0953 an airplane flew over towing a sleeve and the firing commenced. The gunnery practice lasted for approximately an hour during which time the ship expended 46 rounds of 5 inch AAC shells and 59 rounds of 3 inch shells.

After our gunnery practice, the ship proceeded to Long Beach. At 1530 the ship entered Long Beach Harbor and was moored to buoys 9 and 10 at 1614. We only spent the night in port.

The Brush got underway at 0814 Thursday morning, 17 February, and commenced steaming very slowly out of the harbor because there was a dense fog present. It took an hour for the ship to exit the harbor. Fog was still a problem outside the harbor and the Brush steamed along at 5 knots. The visibility would improve a little from time to time and we would increase speed to 10 knots for a time. I don't know what our purpose was for going to sea that day, but I believe the fog interfered with the captain's and/or the commodore's plans because we didn't do much except sound fog signals. Although, some engineering casualty drills were conducted below deck. The visibility increased to 10 miles at 1453, but around 1500 the captain or commodore decided to go back to Long Beach. We didn't have too far to go because at 1552 the ship passed through the outer breakwater. At 1643 the Brush was moored to the starboard side of the Moore at buoys 8 and 10.

The next morning, Friday, 18 February, 2 harbor tugs moved the Brush and the Moore alongside the destroyer tender, USS Frontier(AD25), at buoys 6 and 7. The Maddox and Thomas were also moved to this nest of ships a little later in the morning. The Brush was the inner most ship and was moored to the Frontier's starboard side. The ships of DesDiv 92 would remain in port alongside the tender for 17 days and then were switched to other buoys or left the harbor. On Monday morning, 7 March, the Brush was moved to buoys 8 and 10 and was moored alongside the USS Knudson(APD101). The Knudson got underway the next morning, though, and kept the harbor. The Brush stayed in port a few more days than planned. In fact, we stayed in port this time a total of 20 days.

Thursday morning, 10 March, the Brush got underway and proceeded to the outer harbor to take on ammunition. In the outer harbor the Brush anchored in explosive anchorage M-5 and waited on the ammunition barge. The ship commenced receiving ammunition at 1010 and completed the project at 1025. The ship then weighed anchor and proceeded on to San Diego. We arrived there around 1430 and moored to buoy 27 in the harbor. We spent the night there. Early the next morning at 0620 the ship received on board 56 enlisted men and 5 officers from the gunnery school to observe gunnery practice on a ship. We got underway at 0705 and departed the harbor en route to area II 3 to conduct gunnery school exercises. The ship went to general quarters at 0945 in preparation for the gunnery exercise. A plane soon flew over towing a sleeve and the firing exercise commenced. The ship ceased firing at 1100 and secured from general quarters. There is no entry in the ship's log as to how many rounds were expended. We steamed around for another couple of hours and then went back into San Diego Harbor to drop off the gunnery students. That task was completed at 1521 and the Brush commenced maneuvering to clear the harbor and return to Long Beach. We arrived at Long Beach around 1900 and moored to buoys 9 and 9A alongside 3 other destroyers – the Thomas, Owen, and Cushing. We spent Saturday and Sunday in port.

## I Spend the Weekend with Bobby Claywell

Saturday, 12 March, I traveled to Oxnard, California and spent the week-end with Bobby Claywell and his father and mother. I had a great time with Bobby over the weekend. We did a lot of riding around with him showing me local things and introducing me to some of his local friends. He seemed to know a lot of people around Oxnard, especially pretty girls. I guess that is the advantage of having shore duty, you get to meet a lot of pretty girls.

I actually spent another weekend with Bobby a little later on but I don't remember when it was or what we did together. Also, I don't have an old letter that I wrote to my mother to tell me. But I'm sure part of our activity was running around the town of Oxnard talking to pretty, young girls. That can be a pretty enjoyable pastime, you know.

Monday morning, 14 March, DesDiv 92 (less the Maddox) went to sea for 4 days of intense training, much of which was division tactics. The commodore was aboard the Thomas. The Maddox had gone to parts unknown and was gone for several weeks. Maybe she was in the shipyard for some kind of repair or change to the ship.

During division tactics, the ships were constantly changing course, speeds, and stations in the formation. All the days were pretty much alike. Most, if not all of these formation changes were communicated by visual signaling, either by flaghoist or flashing light. Consequently, this was a very busy week for the signalmen. This was also a very busy week for some of the crew in addition to the signalmen, especially those men in CIC. This week made up somewhat for those weeks that weren't especially hectic. The division activities slowed down somewhat at night. The ships operated in areas south of San Clemente Island. The ships spent Tuesday night anchored in Pyramid Cove at San Clemente Island. I had an interesting experience this night that we were anchored in Pyramid Cove.

## My Secret Midnight Snack

My mother had sent me a quart jar of fried chicken at my request and I had received it over the previous weekend. Now, I was waiting for the right opportunity to eat it. None of my buddies knew I had it and I didn't plan to tell them because I wanted to eat it all myself. I had the mid-watch (00–04) the night we anchored in Pyramid Cove at San Clemente Island. I was on watch by myself because there was not likely going to be any communicating between ships at that time of night, at that place, unless it was an unlikely dire emergency. So, I figured that night would be a good time to eat my home-cooked, Southern fried chicken. So I did. I ate the whole thing, the whole chicken. Maybe it was a small chicken. Anyway, it tasted mighty good and I thoroughly enjoyed my secret mid-night snack. It wasn't as good as freshly cooked fried chicken, and kind of greasy, too, but I thoroughly enjoyed it.

The other quartermasters didn't know anything about Southern fried chicken, so they didn't know what they were missing, and I wasn't ready to educate them with my precious jar of home-cooked chicken. I liked them all but not enough to share my chicken with them.

The ships got underway at sunrise, or 0605, Wednesday morning, 16 March, went back to the operating areas south of San Clemente Island and continued on with division tactics and other exercises. However, on this day some gunnery practice was added to the operational schedule. The ship went to GQ at 1223. We commenced firing our 3 inch guns at 1415 and did so sporadically until 1735. During this period of time the gunners fired a total of 27 rounds of 3 inch VT non-frag shells.

The ships spent the night south of the island just steaming around at 10 knots.

Thursday morning, 17 March, the training activities started right at sunrise, or 0600, and the ships spent most of the day conducting more division tactics. Around 1400, though, the ships headed in the general direction of long Beach and continued with division tactics all the way in. At 1642 the Brush set the special sea detail to enter Long Beach Harbor. At 1751 we were moored starboard side to the Moore at Net Pier. At 1800 the ship observed sunset and turned on the anchor lights. We spent the week-end in port.

In a letter to my mother dated March 19, 1955, I wrote and told her about this particular week.

"We had a very rough week at sea this past week. I don't mean rough water, but busy, long, tiring days. The division commodore gave his ships a real workout, about 18 hours a day worth, and I, or we (the signalmen), had to be on the bridge practically all that time going just as hard as we could go communicating with visual means–like flaghoist and flashing light. It reminded me of the citrus packinghouse days (in Dundee)…. It was one of the most drudgerous weeks I've ever seen. We're going to be doing the same stuff next week. I'm not sure what I'll do this week-end for entertainment, but I'm sure that I'm getting off this vessel for awhile."

The 3 ships of DesDiv 92 got underway again early Monday morning, 21 March, and went to sea for another very busy week of intense training of various kinds. This week there was a little gunnery practice, too. Of course, division tactics were almost ongoing, both day and night, especially during Monday and Tuesday. We also went to GQ a great deal. Monday afternoon the Brush left the formation for awhile and conducted some gunnery practice during which she expended 78 rounds of 5"/38 AAC shells. Tuesday morning the ships conducted some hedgehog calibration firing runs and they used some sort of sonar buoy to conduct these runs. Tuesday afternoon the ship engaged in torpedo practice and actually fired one at 1644. At 1710 the ship recovered her torpedo. There was no record of how well the ship did during this practice firing. After recovering the torpedo, the Brush rejoined the formation and engaged in some more division tactics.

Wednesday afternoon at 1610 the ships went into Wilson Cove, San Clemente Island to practice anchoring–of all things. The more senior boatswain's mates had already done it for real hundreds of times. I didn't see the necessity for practicing that. Anyway, they did. They dropped the port anchor in Wilson Cove in 80 fathoms of water with rocky bottom. This was at 1818 or at dusk. At 1830 the ship weighed anchor, departed Wilson Cove, and went around to Pyramid Cove. At 2200 we dropped anchor in Pyramid Cove in anchorage D-3. Here we spent the rest of the night. I wonder why they didn't just drop anchor here the first time.

The next day, Thursday, 24 March, started early. At 0532 the ship observed sunrise and turned off the anchor lights. At 0558 the ship weighed anchor and with the other ships departed the cove. The ship spent much of the day engaged in various kinds of gunnery exercises and some were the firing kind and some were the non-firing kind. During the afternoon the ship conducted some of the firing kind of gunnery practice and fired her guns off and on for nearly an hour, but the ship's log doesn't state how many shells were expended or of what kind. The ships continued to conduct division tactics during the early part of the evening, but somewhere along the line they started heading in the general direction of Long Beach. The ships arrived at the entrance to the harbor around 2200. At 2324 we moored to the starboard side of the Thomas at buoys 8 and 10. We stayed in port 6 days.

Early Thursday morning, 31 March, the ships of DesDiv 92 got underway and departed the harbor en route to a point off San Diego to rendezvous with some troop transports. We were to escort them part of the way to Hawaii. I think the object of it all was to screen and conduct ASW with them. DesDiv 92 rendezvoused with the transports around 1200 and formed a screen around them. The ships were headed in a southwest direction and were using various zig-zag steering plans in an attempt to evade a submarine that was operating with us. Although, I don't know the name of it and we never saw it. I know there was a submarine with us because it made a simulated attack on one of the ships. The names of the ships that we were escorting were the USS Calvert(APA32), USS Weiss(APA135) and the USS Diachenko(APA123).

The ships of DesDiv 92 were detached from escort duty around 1600 Friday afternoon, 1 April, and reversed course to return to Long Beach. They steamed toward Long Beach on a course of 060°(t) and at a speed of 20 knots. They maintained that same course and speed almost all the way to Long Beach. The ships arrived at Long Beach Harbor at 0914 Saturday morning, 2 April. At 0955 we were moored to the starboard side of USS McKean(DD784) at buoys 8 and 10. The Moore and Thomas stood in and moored to the same buoys. We would stay in port 9 days. Nothing of any significance happened those 9 days we were in port, although, we did have a personnel inspection Saturday morning, 9 April.

Monday morning, 11 April, the Brush departed the harbor with the Moore and Thomas. They went to sea to conducted ASW exercises and division tactics for 4 days, generally, both day and night. We went to general quarters everyday to keep us in practice. We operated with the submarine, USS Baya(SS318), this time. It was a very busy 4 days for much of the crew including the signalmen. Late Thursday afternoon, 14 April, the ships went back into Long Beach. At 1926 the Brush was moored starboard side to the USS Passumpsic(AO107) at buoys 4 and 5. We would stay in port 10 days. Friday afternoon we took on fuel from the tanker and received 80,011 gallons. We also received 9 tons of commissary stores.

Saturday morning, 16 April, the captain conducted a personnel inspection.

Seven new crewmembers reported aboard for duty over the weekend. They were all new seaman apprentices.

Monday morning, 18 April, the nest, consisting of the Brush, Thomas and Moore, was moved by tug from alongside the Passumpsic to alongside the USS Frontier (AD25).

Wednesday, 20 April, a new quartermaster came aboard for duty, Neubern W. Garrett, Jr. QM3. He was coming from shore duty and was going to replace some of the QM's that were leaving the ship for discharge. I believe that this was his first sea duty.

At 2155, 20 April, two of the Brush's crewmembers were transferred over to the Frontier to spend some time in her brig.

On Thursday, 21 April, another crewmember was sent to the Long Beach Naval station brig for 45 days confinement.

On Friday, 22 April, one more of our crewmembers were sent to the Long Beach Naval Station brig for 7 days of confinement.

It seems like the Brush was plagued with crewmembers going AWOL all of 1955 that I was aboard her. The captain stayed pretty busy just holding non-judicial punishment sessions and awarding punishments. There were a lot of court-martials handed out, too, and a number of men were sent to the brig at one place or another. I'm not sure what the trouble was, but many of the young seamen simply couldn't stay out of trouble. They just made life more difficult for themselves when they did things that they knew would get them in trouble. I guess their life aboard ship was just more than they could mentally handle. I can understand that to some extent. Everybody pretty much had the same deal, but most of the crew never did anything that would get them in serious trouble.

Early Monday morning, 25 April, the Brush, Thomas, and Moore went to sea again to conduct some more ASW exercises, division tactics, and gunnery practice around San Clemente Island. ComDesDiv 92 was embarked in the Thomas and ComDesFlot 3 was embarked in the Moore. On Monday and Tuesday the ships conducted ASW exercises and division tactics both day and night. The submarine, USS Razorback(SS284), was involved in the ASW exercises, at least some of the time. And we went to general quarters everyday for practice.

On Wednesday morning the ships arrived off San Clemente , conducted some gunnery exercises and fired their 5 inch guns. Over the course of the day the Brush fired a total of 55 rounds of 5 inch shells. The ship secured from gunnery practice around 2300. Around 2330 the Brush anchored in berth D-4 in Pyramid Cove, San Clemente Island. It was a short night, however. The ship weighed anchor at 0510–way before daylight. At 0640 Thursday morning the ship sounded general quarters and commenced maneuvering at various courses and speeds to take station for firing exercises. At 0726 the ship commenced firing. It was going to be another long day of conducting gunnery exercises and firing of the 5 inch guns. They would be conducted all day and much of the night, too. The ship fired a total of 62 rounds of 5 inch shells during the day and half the night. The ships ceased gunnery exercise around midnight and headed toward Long Beach Harbor.

At 0619 Friday morning, 29 April, the ships arrived at and commenced lying to off the outer breakwater at Long Beach Harbor. At 0700 the ships commenced maneuvering at various courses and speeds while conducting runs through a dummy minefield. They secured from the minefield maneuvering at 0819 and proceeded on into the harbor. At 0931 we were moored to buoys 8 and 10 alongside the Moore. We were in a nest of 4 ships. At 1510 another one of our crewmembers was transferred, under guard, to the Long Beach Naval Station brig. The Brush stayed in port over the weekend.

Early Monday morning, 2 May, the 3 ships of DesDiv 92 departed the Long Beach Harbor en route to San Diego operating area. But they didn't waste any time on the way there; they conducted various drills and exercises including division tactics, torpedo exercises, and ship-board drills. However, before departing the harbor that morning, 4 observers (1 officer and 3 petty officers) came aboard the Brush to observe how she and the other ships conducted these exercises and drills. They were transferred over to the other ships from time to time during the 4 days we were out operating. I don't know whether they graded the ships' performances or not. At 1340 the Brush went to general quarters and commenced conducting a torpedo exercise during which she fired 2 torpedoes. Afterwards, at 1520, the ship commenced searching for the 2 torpedoes. At 1555 the ship found and recovered one of her torpedoes. She searched for the other one for a couple of hours but never could find it and had to give up the search. It must have sunk to the bottom. The Brush then rejoined the other ships. Around 1900 the Brush went to GQ and conducted atomic defense drills for an hour or so. During the early evening hours the ship also conducted a gunnery exercise without doing any firing. The ship spent Monday night steaming around independently in the San Diego operating areas. I suppose the other ships did the same thing but somewhere else.

Tuesday, 3 May, was another busy day starting at 0800 and ending at 2200 that night. At 0950 the ship went to GQ, commenced a gunnery exercise, and fired 34 rounds of 5″/38 AAC shells. At 0950 the commodore transferred his flag to the Brush and he and his staff came over to the ship via the motor whaleboat. At 1330 the ship went to GQ again and commenced another gunnery exercise but without doing any firing. At 1525 the Brush commenced a battle problem given by the Thomas. At 1640 the ship secured from the battle problem and from GQ. At 1645 the Brush sent alongside the tanker, USS Caliente(A053), for a refueling exercise and took on 7881 gallons of NSFO. Then the Brush rendezvoused with the Thomas for the purpose of transferring ComDesDiv 92, his staff, and the observers back to the Thomas via the ship's motor whaleboat. At 2058 the Brush went alongside the USS Pinola(AFT206) for a guard mail transfer.

At 2119 the ship went to GQ again in preparation for some night gunnery practice with the Pinola. I believe the Pinola was towing a sled at this point. At 2145 the Brush took station 7,000 yards off the starboard quarter of the ATF on a base course of 000°(t) and at a speed of 10 knots. At 2152 the ship commenced firing and fired about 10 minutes. During those 10 minutes the Brush expended 14 rounds of 5″/38 AAC shells and 15 rounds of 5″/38 illuminating shells. The gunnery exercise was completed around 2200. The ship spent the rest of the night steaming around independently in the San Diego operating areas.

Early Wednesday morning, 4 May, the Brush started conducting an ASW exercise with the Thomas and the submarine, USS Redfish. She engaged in this until 1330 when the ASW exercise was secured. At 1354 the ship set a course for Coronado Roads, San Diego. At 1544 the Brush let go the port anchor in anchorage 158 in Coronado Roads in 5 ½ fathoms of water. At 2000 the Brush posted 8 sentries around the main deck in preparation for a sneak attack exercise on the Brush by navy frogmen. The frogmen failed in their effort to attack us because at 2135 a sentry sighted 2 men in a canoe 500 yards astern of us. At 2142 the ship went to GQ to put the entire ship on full alert. At 2144 2 frogmen were captured, and at 2323 two lungmen were captured and that ended the sneak attack exercise by the frogmen. However, it probably would have been a different story if we hadn't known that they were going to attempt to make an attack and were looking for them. Those frogmen can be mighty sneaky people. The rest of the night went by without any incidents. However, the night was short.

At 0500 Thursday, 5 May, the Brush set the anchor detail and the ship weighed anchor at 0511. The ship commenced maneuvering at various courses and speeds to clear the anchorage. The ship set a westerly course to return to the San Diego operating areas. At 0602 we observed sunrise and turned off the running lights. Thursday was another day filled with drills and exercises of various kinds. Also, the observers were transferred to the different ships from time to time by motor whaleboat. The ships were just lying to with all engines stopped during these transfers. At 1430 the Brush and the Moore conducted a gunnery exercise. The Brush was stationed 3000 yards astern of the Moore. The exercise was completed at 1500. The Brush expended 48 rounds of 5 inch shells during the practice. At 1815 the ships ceased all drills and exercises and set a course for Long Beach. The ships arrived at Long Beach around 2100 and moored to buoys 8 and 10 at 2205. We would stay in port for 17 days. However, the next afternoon, Friday, 6 May, the 3 ships, in a nest, were moved by tugs from the buoys to alongside the USS Frontier(AD25) that was docked alongside Net Pier at the naval station.

Three more men were sent to the brig while we were in port this time. Two of them were sent to the Long Beach Naval Station brig for an unspecified length of time. And one of them was sent to the brig on the Frontier for 3 days. This sailor was given 3 days confinement on bread and water.

The Brush left port early Monday morning, 23 May, with the Moore and the Thomas. The cruisers, USS Toledo(CA133) and USS Pittsburg(CA72), left port just before we did and the destroyers operated with them for a couple of hours conducting some sort of ASW exercise. However, around 1100 the ships secured from the ASW exercises and the destroyers were detached from the cruisers. At this time the ships of DesDiv 92 went their separate ways. The Brush proceeded to rendezvous with the carrier, Shangri-La (CVA38). We would spend 5 days at sea this week and much of the time we operated with the carrier while she conducted flight operations from time to time. Although, we would also depart from her sometimes to conduct our own exercises. On Monday, however, we rendezvoused with the Shangri-La around 1300 and assumed plane guard station. The Brush followed the carrier around all afternoon. At 1600 she conducted flight operations for awhile. The Brush was detached from the carrier at 1915 and steamed around independently in air op area all night. It was a quiet night on the bridge.

At 0640 Tuesday morning, 24 May, the Brush again rendezvoused with the Shangri-La. The Brush accompanied the carrier all day and took plane guard station in case she conducted flight operations. Although, she didn't conduct flight operations on this day. At 1655 the Brush was released from plane guard duty. She steamed around independently all night and the next morning, too, in one of the operating areas.

Wednesday, 25 May, around noon, the Brush rendezvoused with the Shangri-La again and assumed plane guard station. However, the carrier didn't conduct any flight operations until 1740 that afternoon. At 1835 the Brush was detached from the carrier. The ship proceeded to Pyramid Cove, San Clemente Island to spend the night. At 2015 the ship dropped anchor in anchorage D-4 in 22 fathoms of water with rocky bottom. We spent a very quiet night in Pyramid Cove. However, we got underway early the next morning, Thursday, 26 May. We departed the cove to rendezvous with the Shangri-La. The Brush followed her around again most of the day, but she didn't conduct any flight operations. However, around 1830 we did go alongside the carrier to take on fuel. We received 23,500 gallons NSFO forward and 33,222 gallons aft. At 2010 we were detached from plane guard duty. The Brush steamed around independently all night north and east of San Clemente Island.

Around 0800 Friday, 27 May, the Brush once more rendezvoused with the Shangri-La and followed her around most of the morning. At 1045 the carrier informed the Brush that they had a man overboard and the Brush commenced searching for the man. However, at 1130 we got another message from the Shangri-La informing us that there might not be a man overboard after all. Of course, we ceased the search. Also, at 1130 the Brush was released from the carrier. Consequently, the Brush changed speed to 25 knots and set a course for Long Beach. On the way in, the captain had a personnel inspection. The Brush arrived at Long Beach around 1500 and moored alongside the Moore at buoys 9 and 9A. We would stay in port 5 days, but nothing of any significance happened during that time.

Around 0800 Tuesday morning, 31 May, the Maddox and Moore got underway and stood out of the harbor. The Brush also got underway and proceeded out into the outer harbor to explosive anchorage M-7 and dropped anchor. An ammunition barge came alongside at 1410 and the Brush took on a considerable amount of ammunition of various kinds. I suppose the navy was getting us loaded up prior to going overseas. At 1621 all the ammunition on the barge had been brought aboard and a tug boat moved the barge away. The Brush returned to the inner harbor and moored alongside the Thomas at buoys 9 and 9A.

This day, 31 May, was my birthday, but there wasn't any opportunity for me to do any celebrating. I was now 22 years old and covered in salt.

The Brush and the Thomas got underway early Wednesday morning, left the harbor, and proceeded to the San Diego operating area to rendezvous with the Maddox. The Brush and Thomas made the rendezvous with the Maddox during the early afternoon. The ships conducted ASW exercises with the USS Remora(SS487) all afternoon and into the early evening. At 2125 the Brush and the Moore were detached from the Maddox and proceeded to San Diego to spend the night. At 2318 we moored to buoy 19. The Thomas came in the harbor a little later and moored to buoy 19, too.

Around 1030 Thursday morning, 2 June, the ships got underway, departed the harbor, and returned to the San Diego operating area. The ships of DesDiv 92 conducted division tactics most of the afternoon, but late in the day they set a course for Long Beach. Around 1945 the Brush moored alongside the Moore at Net Pier at the Long Beach Naval Station. And here is where we would stay until we left to go back to the Far East, 14 June.

I don't think anything of any consequence happened those last few days before going overseas. Of course, the ship took on a lot of provisions during this time and all the ship's departments made sure they were prepared to go overseas in every way. The crew was also given a lot of liberty and some of the real short-timers departed the ship to be released from active duty just before we left port. I believe some of the old time quartermasters left the ship at this time, although there is no record of it in the ship's log. As for myself, I'm sure I spent a couple of weekends with the Randall family; although, I don't remember what we did to entertain ourselves, but we usually found something interesting to do.

## VISITING WITH THE RANDALL FAMILY

During my third and last period of stateside duty, mostly in early 1955, the Brush spent most of her weekends in Long Beach. I spent a number of those weekends with the Randall family. I probably spent 8 to 10 weekends with them over the 6 months or so that we were in the States.

Beuford and I were the ones doing most of the running around, but not always. Some of the other members of the family went with us some of the time. I also remember going on some excursions with Mr. Randall, Merwin. We always found something interesting to do. I probably can't remember all the things we did, but I can write about the things I do remember.

I know I spent Christmas weekend 1954 and New Year's weekend 1955 with them, but I wrote about those things earlier. The following tales are some of the things we did during the first half of 1955 that I haven't written about. I'm putting all these activities in one section because I don't remember when they took place or in what order they took place; it has been too long ago to remember those details, and I don't have any old letters from that period to refresh my memory.

### Deep Sea Fishing

Beuford and I went deep sea fishing one Saturday on a party fishing boat. The boat must have been 50 feet long and there was a pretty good crowd of people on it. We took the boat out of Arredondo Beach early one morning and we must have fished for half a day; at least, I did. Beuford got seasick right after leaving the dock and didn't feel like doing too much fishing. We were fishing for Rock Cod and I caught several of them. I can't remember whether Beuford caught any or not. However, fishing on the boat wasn't that great of an experience because there simply were too many people on the boat throwing lines in the water. Consequently, people spent about half their time trying to get their lines untangled from those of their neighbors. I noticed that some of the more experienced party boat fishermen, like 3 or 4 of them, got a position at the rear of the boat and didn't seem to get their lines tangled up as much. And I also noticed that they were continuously reeling in fish. Every time I looked back at them they were busy pulling up a fish. So, they caught more than their share, it looked to me. I decided right there, if I ever went deep sea fishing again, I was going to claim a place at the rear of the boat. Anyway, I enjoyed the outing and did catch some fish, but Beuford probably didn't enjoy the fishing trip as much as I did. The ocean was a little rough that day and an excellent day for a landlubber to get seasick. We had a fish fry that evening at the Randalls' house, which was enjoyed by all.

### Gathering Abalone

One afternoon Beuford and I was riding up the coastal highway north of San Pedro. We came upon the prettiest little cove you ever saw. The tide was out and there were dozens and dozens of rocks exposed just above the surface of the water. There was a parking area at the cove but there wasn't anybody there. It was such a pretty place that we decided to stop and look around.

We stopped the car, got out, and decided to venture out on those rocks in the cove. The tide was out and we could step or jump from rock to rock and went out quite a distance into the water. The water was crystal clear and smooth, and we began to notice an abundance of abalone attached to the sides of the rocks. There were abalone of all sizes from small to large. It must have been the ideal spot for abalone because there was so many of them there. We began to play with them. We found that we could pull them away from the rocks if we grabbed them quickly, but we couldn't detach them at all if we alerted them to the fact that we were there.

We knew that people in California ate abalone and we decided that maybe we should harvest some and try them ourselves. We gathered all the big abalone we could carry and started back to shore with them. About that time another car stopped; a fellow got out and started walking out on the rocks, too. We met him and he seemed like a nice fellow. He mentioned to us that he thought it was out of season for harvesting abalone, although, he wasn't sure about it. It didn't occur to us that there was a season on abalone, but that probably explained to us why there was so many abalone there and no people there gathering them. It was out of season. Anyway, we put our abalone back into the water. We didn't want to take a chance on being caught by a game warden and having to pay a big fine. We might have needed a license, too, for all I know.

We never did have the opportunity to go back and gather abalone there. Beuford and I went back at a later time with the intentions of getting some, but the tide was in and the rocks were covered with water. However, I think Beuford gathered a few at some time when I wasn't with him. So I never got in on the fun or the feast.

## Hunting Gemstones on Arredondo Beach

Mr. Randall, Merwin, was a rock hound and liked to look for gemstones. Apparently, he found boxes of them during the few years he lived in Southern California. Sometimes when I was staying with the Randalls over the weekend, he would want to take me gemstone hunting with him. I loved to go with him and it was a different experience. We always went to Arredondo Beach to do our rock hunting. He also liked to get up early and be at the beach at daybreak and that is what we would do. We would start walking up the beach at daylight. He wanted to start early and be the first one on the beach in case someone else was there looking for gemstones, too. It was a pleasant time of day and quite cool that early in the morning, and it was always a clear California sky the mornings we went to the beach. I think Mr. Randall kept track of the weather, maybe the tides too, and knew when it was a good time to go to the beach to look for gemstones. He said that the waves were continuously washing the stones upon the beach. An especially good time to look for gemstones was after a storm when there had been a lot of big waves.

I believe we always found some gemstones on these early morning walks on Arredondo Beach. As I remember, it was mainly moonstones and agates that he was finding. He knew what to look for and I learned that there wasn't anything pretty about them in their unpolished state. But I also learned that they could be quite pretty after they had been polished.

Another thing I noticed as we walked along was the smell of the seashore. There was a strong saltwater smell. I suppose it was caused mainly by washed up seaweed, kelp maybe, and also seaweed growing on wet rocks by the water's edge that was producing the seashore smell. Anyway, it was very noticeable. I also realized that Florida beaches have very little smell when you compare them with California beaches.

I always enjoyed those walks on the beach with Mr. Randall. We would probably walk a couple of miles along the water's edge before turning back. I know that I went with him at least twice on these early morning walks along the beach, but there might have been 1 or 2 more times; I can't remember for sure.

## Army Reserve Meeting and Smog Creators

Beuford was in the army reserve and had to attend meetings ever so often on weekends. I went with him to one of those reserve meetings one time and sat in on a class with him that lasted several hours. I was probably out of place because I was the only sailor there. But we were all on the same side and nobody objected to me being there. I've forgotten what the instructor talked about, but I'm sure it didn't pertain to any of the army's top secrets. It was kind of an interesting day, but I didn't bother to take notes.

The Army Reserve Center was located on top of a hill that overlooked the city of Los Angeles. At the time there was a big debate in the area as to what was causing a real serious smog problem in the region, especially around Long Beach and San Pedro. As I looked out over the city from this high point, it became obvious to me what was a big contributing factor to the problem. Right before my eyes I saw a multitude of smoke stacks spewing out smoke all over the city and that, I realized, was one of the main causes of the smog problem. The smoke, in conjunction with certain atmospheric conditions that occurred from time to time, like fog coming in off the ocean, in my opinion were the causes of the smog. I came to this conclusion at a glance because a similar type thing occurred occasionally in the Ocala National Forest where I largely grew up. In the forest, we would have forest fires occasionally, and when fog would develop during the night, we would have a visibility problem. When the smoke mixed with the fog it would cause smog just like in Long Beach. Sometimes in the forest the visibility would be reduced to 10 feet at night and during the early morning hours. I saw smog so bad in Long Beach a number of times that you could barely see across the street and the city would turn on the street lights during the middle of the day. Still, the visibility would be so poor that you could hardly find your way around. I've often wondered if the Long Beach officials ever got the smog problem figured out as to what was causing it. Surely they did.

Being at the Randall home was the next thing to being at home, and I'll always be grateful to them for the hospitality they showed me during that period of time in my life.

# 11

# THIRD CRUISE TO THE FAR EAST – 1955

Late Tuesday morning, 14 June, 1955, DesDiv 92 departed Long Beach Harbor en route to Yokosuka, Japan via Hawaii and Midway Island. It would take the ships 6 days to reach Pearl Harbor. It wasn't a pleasant, leisurely, fun-filled voyage to Hawaii, however, because the ships conducted division tactics, various exercises, and ship-board drills every day all day. It wasn't a fun trip in any sense. In my opinion, we were drilled too much and all the old-timers got tired of the whole thing.

## HAWAII

DesDiv 92 arrived at Pearl Harbor, Hawaii during the middle of the morning, Tuesday, 21 June. Around 1000 the Brush was moored at berth B-25 at the Pearl Harbor Naval Station. Liberty commenced soon after our arrival in Pearl, but I don't have any recollection of going ashore. Anyway, we were in Hawaii and that was something by itself. We didn't stay in port very long, however, because the next morning the ships left the harbor and went to sea to conduct their usual exercises around Hawaii–like operating with a carrier, gunnery practice, and engaging in ASW.

### Swim Call Off Diamond Head

The only thing I remember about operating around Hawaii this visit was the morning we had "swim call" about 2 miles at sea directly off Diamond Head. The ship simply stopped her engines and commenced lying to for the occasion. I had the signal watch at the time and couldn't participate, but I didn't want to go swimming out there anyway. That water looked mighty deep to me at that spot – 2 miles off Diamond Head. Besides, I never cared too much about swimming with sharks, or even when there was a possibility of there being some. However, Captain Whitehurst did take some precautions in this respect and posted a sailor with a rifle to shoot the sharks if any showed up. Fortunately, no sharks made their appearance.

There must have been 20 or 30 men that took advantage of the swim call. All the swimmers swam near the fantail where it was easier to climb back aboard ship – and in a hurry if necessary. Of course, they jumped off the fantail to get into the water. The swimmers acted like they were enjoying themselves – good for them. Swim call must have lasted for an hour or so. It was a beautiful Hawaiian day, too, as I remember.

### Sharks

Speaking of sharks. Sharks are the dread of all shipwrecked seaman, but I can truthfully say that I never saw a shark during the 3 years that I spent at sea. You would have thought that I would have seen some by accident, occasionally, but I didn't. Of course, I was never shipwrecked and in the water floating around to attract them. If I had found myself in that unfortunate situation, I probably would have seen a lot of them, because sharks seem to love to eat people that are floating around in the ocean. Sharks, undoubtedly, have satisfied their hunger with the flesh of sailors many thousands of times over the centuries.

**Diamond Head**

Porpoises

On the other hand, I saw a lot of porpoises. They seemed to be plentiful around coastal areas, especially off the coast of California. I have a very special, friendly feeling toward porpoises because of my numerous contacts with them during my seafaring years. Many times they would swim alongside the ship as we were entering or leaving port and steaming rather slowly. They almost always swam alongside the ship abeam the signal bridge. We would be standing on the signal bridge looking down at them and they seem to be looking back at us. To me, they acted like they would like to be friends with us. They would always swim alongside the ship at the same speed as the ship. And they would usually swim alongside of the ship for 15 to 20 minutes. Sometimes there would be just one of them and other times there would be 4 or 5 of them swimming along together. After awhile, though, they would get tired of playing that game, go underwater, and streak away from the ship. Other times, they would find it fun to swim under the ship. They appeared to be highly intelligent creatures and acted to me like they were humans in a fish-like body. I've always felt that it would be a shame for anyone to catch or hurt them in anyway, because they are so intelligent and so friendly toward humans.

The Brush went back into Pearl Harbor Thursday afternoon, 23 June, and spent the week-end there. I know I went ashore a couple of those days and went to Waikiki Beach at least once to the Wagon Wheel Restaurant in the early evening, but my mind is totally blank about any of the other things that I did on this occasion in Hawaii.

Monday morning, 27 June, DesDiv 92 departed Pearl Harbor en route to Yokosuka, Japan via Midway Island. Again, the ships stayed busy conducting all kinds of drills and exercises all the way to Midway.

MIDWAY ISLAND

The ships arrived at Midway early Thursday morning, 30 June, and went into the lagoon to take on fuel oil. We went alongside the refueling pier around 0630.

**Ted Holly at Midway Island**

Gooney Birds on Midway Island

The ships were going to be in the lagoon for 3 or 4 hours and some of us were permitted to go ashore to look around and to go swimming if we wanted to. I did. I went ashore and went swimming at one of the designated beaches for a few minutes, but I mainly wanted to look at the Gooney Birds. I had been hearing about Gooney Birds on Midway Island ever since I had been on the ship. Gooney Birds are actually Albatrosses, which are sea birds that look similar to seagulls but are much larger. Pacific Ocean sailors had been calling the Albatrosses on Midway Island "Gooney Birds" for many years. Midway Island was a nesting place for Albatrosses and they came to the island by the thousands every year for that purpose.

The Gooney Birds on Midway were accustomed to sailors walking among them and didn't seem to mind their presence too much, if at all, unless they got too close. You could get within 10 feet of them most of the time without any problem, but if you got any closer than that, they would usually just walk away from you or fly off. A lot of the birds were nesting at the time we were there. I suppose it was the female birds that were sitting on the nest. The "nest" wasn't really much of nest; it was just a spot on the ground or a slight indentation in the ground. The chicks were in all stages of development from just hatched out to about ready to fly. The mama birds would start fussing at you if you got any closer than 10 feet of them. The sailors were usually very careful not to harass the birds or intentionally cause them any stress. In fact, the navy did not allow anybody to harass or molest these birds in any way. A sailor would be in big trouble if he did, but I'm sure that seldom ever happened if at all.

## The Gooney Birds

Most people found it amusing to watch the birds as they went about their normal activities. The sailors called them Gooney Birds because of all their antics, especially in the way they communicated with one another and the way they landed. They were very clumsy on land. When the big birds came in to land they would just go tumbling head over heels, so to speak. And when they tried to take off from the ground, they would have to get a running start. They reminded me of a big bomber taking off. The Gooney Birds communicate with one another by a lot of squawking, but they also did a lot of bobbing and weaving of their heads. I guess all their antics meant something to them, but it was hard for me to understand this bird talk. We occasionally saw an Albatross at sea – miles and miles from land. It was always one by itself. They were graceful birds in the air. They looked to have a wing span of about 4 feet. The ones I saw were always flying close to the water and were usually just gliding on the air currents and seldom flapped their wings. It was hard for me to understand how they could defy the law of gravity to the extent they did.

Seagulls

There was usually an abundance of seagulls in coastal areas and in harbors. And many times, going in and out of port, we had seagulls come to visit us on the signal bridge, which was about 30 feet above the water. They may have been hoping we would feed them something, but I don't know. Anyway, 1 to 3 or 4 gulls would fly alongside the ship about 20 feet away at eye level to us. They would always fly at the same speed that the ship was traveling and stayed in exactly the same spot all the time they were flying alongside us. They appeared to be looking us over real close all the time they were maintaining their eye-level position alongside the ship. They didn't seem to have any fear of us at the distance they were keeping. I wish I had had some food to throw their way. Although, come to think of it, if I had had any, I probably would have eaten it myself. I did try to talk to them, though, but they never said anything in return that I could detect. They would just look at me, no squawking or anything. They would usually fly alongside of us for 10 to 15 minutes, but then, all of a sudden, they would go sailing off in another direction. I wonder what they were thinking about us – maybe it was how stingy we were since we didn't feed them anything.

The ships departed the lagoon at Midway around 1300 all fueled-up. The ships formed back up into a line abreast formation with the Thomas in station 1 as the guide. The ships spent the rest of the day just steaming along toward Japan. After Thursday, however, the ships engaged in various drills and exercises during the day most of the way from Midway to Yokosuka, which took us 5 days. Much of this activity was division tactics and radar tracking exercises. We went to general quarters every day at least once, except Monday, when we steamed 8 miles astern of the formation participating in some kind of tracking exercise. The ships also engaged in highline transfers, mainly for practice, I believe. They also conducted gunnery practice a couple times one day, Tuesday, 5 July, one time during the afternoon and one time after dark when the ship fired 15 rounds of illumination shells.

Wednesday, 6 July, at 1705 the ships formed a scouting line in order to search for survivors of a downed aircraft. The ships searched for survivors of the crash for 5 hours on a heading of 258°(t). However, the Brush had to cut her searching efforts short because at 2210 she was detached from the formation to proceed to Yokosuka for treatment of a probable appendicitis case. The Brush steamed toward Yokosuka on a course of 283°(t) and at a speed of 25 knots. I never heard whether any survivors of the plane crash were ever found or not, but I don't think they were by DesDiv 92, if they were.

We were now nearing Japan. At 0145 Thursday, 7 July, 1955, the Brush made contact with land by radar at the distance of 40 miles. Around 0330 we entered Tokyo Bay. At 0358 the ship commenced maneuvering on various courses and speeds to enter Yokosuka Harbor. At 0532 the ship set the special sea detail. At 0635 the Brush was moored starboard side to the USS Frontier(AD25) at buoy D-4. I suppose the medical patient was taken to the Yokosuka Naval Base for medical treatment, although, there is no record of it in the ship's log.

## YOKOSUKA

At 0925 one of our crewmembers was sent over to the Frontier for special treatment. He was sent over to the tender to serve 3 days of confinement in her brig on diminished rations. He was sent to the brig for direct disobedience to a petty officer.

The rest of the ships of DesDiv 92 came into port around 1230. We would stay in port for 18 days or until 20 July. A lot of liberty in Yokosuka was enjoyed by all. The crew went on liberty as much as they could those 18 days in port, at least as much as their money would allow them to. Liberty was usually over at 0730 in the morning, so the sailors could spend the night ashore if they wanted to and many of them did.

Not much happened aboard the ship during our stay in port that was of any consequence. But a few minor things took place.

Thursday, 8 July, the captain conducted an inspection of the lower decks. The supply officer brought aboard 1,800,000 yen (Japanese currency). There were 360 yen to the dollar at the time. The ship took on fuel oil from a yard oiler and received 106,617 gallons of NSFO. The ship also took on 11,860 gallons of fresh water from a water barge.

On Tuesday, 12 July, another crewmember was sent over to the Frontier to serve 3 days in the brig on diminished rations for being AWOL too many times. I think diminished rations means bread and water.

At 1545 Wednesday, 13 July, a garbage scow came alongside and picked up our garbage from the fantail. At sea, the mess cooks just simply dumped it overboard off the fantail.

At 1445 Thursday, 14 July, the supply officer returned aboard with $37,000 U.S. and M.P.C. currency.

At 2330 Thursday night, one of the firemen returned aboard ship in a dazed condition with a gash over his right eye. He was sent to the tender for medical treatment. I suspect he had a little disagreement with someone in a bar and he lost the argument.

## EN ROUTE FORMOSA

Early Wednesday morning, 20 July, the ships of DesDiv 92 departed Yokosuka and headed south for Kaohsiung, Formosa, which is located at the southern tip of Formosa. It took them 4 days to make the trip. It was rough seas the whole way, but the ships engaged in division tactics and other exercises anyway for the first 3 days of the trip. However, the 4$^{th}$ day, Saturday, the ships just steamed along and didn't do much of anything else. I imagine that it was just too rough to do anything but I don't remember for sure.

The ship conducted some gunnery practice on Wednesday afternoon for 30 minutes or so and shot 54 rounds of 5"/38 AAC shells.

I didn't have a pleasant trip down to Formosa for a number of reasons, but mainly because I was sick with a fever and felt pretty bad. In a letter to my mother dated, July 24, 1955, I wrote about my illness and the trip down to Kaohsiung.

"We left Yokosuka last Wednesday with 3 storms between us and Formosa. Somehow we managed to miss the worst of all 3 of them. Of course, it was pretty rough all the way down. Although, it really wasn't too bad with the exception of one night when we had on full speed. Bouncing across those swells at full speed roughed things up a bit causing tons of water to wash back over the ship. The water caused considerable minor damage to gear about the ship, breaking it up, bending it up, washing things away and such like. What got me, though, was that last Monday night I got a good case of tonsillitis. For 2 days I was a pretty sick boy. I stayed in my pad most of the time taking aspirin and drinking water – that was my treatment. I was still sick enough Thursday and Friday to not have to stand watches. My fever was around 103 all this time. Friday night the corpsman checked my temperature and found it to be almost normal, so I stood a signal watch from 6:00 p.m. to 12:00 p.m. during all this salt water wash down. I stayed a little damp the whole watch, but most of the time I could stand in the pilothouse and keep the water from hitting me.

About 10:30 p.m. we suddenly started having electrical fires around the bridge and I was obliged to grab a $CO_2$ bottle and put them out as they started. Water was shorting-out some wires and making them create some serious glows, sparks flying about, and so on. You know how electrical fires look.

I surely got drenched several times. So much water would hit me that it would almost knock me down. I just knew that staying wet so long and in about a 20 knot wind would make me have a relapse, but it didn't seem to hurt me at all."

## Kaohsiung, Formosa

The Kaohsiung light was sighted about 0450 Sunday morning, 24 July. At 0553 the ship set the special sea detail and soon thereafter commenced maneuvering at various courses and speeds to enter the harbor. At 0650 we observed sunrise and turned off the running lights. At 0734 the ship was moored to buoys 10 and 11. The Brush and the Maddox stayed in port for 3 days. The Moore and the Thomas refueled from the tanker, USS Mispillion(AO105), and left the harbor to go on patrol in the Formosa Strait. However, the Brush was placed on one hour standby to get underway. In the letter to my mother dated July 24, 1955, I wrote about our arrival in Kaohsiung and my opinion of that little port.

"We arrived in Kaohsiung at the break of day this morning. Today is Sunday, but there is absolutely no hint of it being so. Most of the day was spent in mooring and unmooring to and from the buoys and going alongside a number of different ships for one reason or another. All 4 ships of DesDiv 92 went alongside a tanker and took on fuel. After refueling, 2 of them left to go on patrol. The Brush and another destroyer stayed in port. We're to leave here to go out on patrol in a day or so, though. I think it suits everybody better to be at sea on patrol around here instead of sitting around Kaohsiung anyway for this is one of the hottest little ports I have seen anywhere. It is miserably hot. I think I have told you that same thing in previous years, haven't I?"

## FORMOSA PATROL

Early Wednesday morning, 27 July, the Brush left the harbor to go on patrol in the Formosa Strait off the coast of China. We went out to relieve the Thomas. Immediately upon leaving the harbor, the Brush set condition 3 watches on the ship with the main battery directory and Mount 52 manned all the time. The ships were also in material condition "Baker". The Brush rendezvoused with the Thomas around noon and relieved her of the northern patrol. However, the Thomas was on the way into port and we were still some distance from our patrol station. We proceeded north toward our patrol area and arrived there at 1635.

The Brush generally steamed around at 15 knots unless she was investigating something. The Brush would patrol in the northern patrol area for 4 days this time out. The Brush investigated a number of surface contacts while she was on this patrol – both day and night. At 2255 Wednesday night the Brush had an unidentified radar contact. She proceeded to investigate it and closed to within 1500 yards of it. The Brush asked her to identify herself. She did. It turned out that she was the British freighter, South Breeze. She was allowed to go on her way, of course.

Thursday morning the ship investigated a fishing boat. She was friendly. At 1620 the Brush investigated another contact. It was identified as Chinese Nationalist LSM250. At 2330 the Brush went to investigate a merchant ship. It was identified as a British merchant ship, Lyng Heim, which was en route to Hong Kong.

At 0143 Friday morning, 29 July, the ship proceeded to investigate a contact bearing 197°(t) at a distance of 12 miles. It also proved to be friendly. At 1147 Friday morning the Brush commenced maneuvering to investigate and avoid 10 fishing boats. At 1607 the Brush had a sonar contact bearing 327°(t) at a range of 1500 yards. The ship sounded general quarters. At 1630 the sonar contact was evaluated as fish and the Brush secured from general quarters and continued with her patrol.

Late Saturday afternoon the Brush secured from patrolling in the Formosa Strait and commenced proceeding to Kaohsiung. At 2125 the Brush was relieved of patrol by the Maddox. At 2220 we passed the Maddox abeam to starboard on her way to the northern patrol station. We continued on to Kaohsiung.

At 0550 Sunday morning, 31 July, the Brush arrived at Kaohsiung Harbor. At 0638 she moored to the USS Platte(AO24) to take on fuel. The ship completed taking on fuel at 0837 and soon commenced making preparations to get underway. At 1000 the ship was underway from alongside the tanker and proceeding out of the harbor to return to the duty of patrolling in the Formosa Strait. Lt. C.A. Albright, the executive officer, was at the conn leaving port. At 1113 the Brush relieved the USS Samuel N. Moore of duty in the northern patrol area. At 1645 the Brush changed course to avoid a bunch of Chinese junks. We arrived on patrol station S-6 at 1745 and started patrolling. The Brush patrolled in the S-6 area Sunday night, Monday, and Monday night with nothing eventful happening. But early Tuesday morning, 2 August, the Brush headed back to Kaohsiung to take on provisions from the USS Zelima(AF49). We arrived at Kaohsiung around 1430 and soon went alongside the Zelima. We took on provisions for about an hour and then went alongside the Platte(AO24) to take on fuel oil – since we were there. We received 38,000 gallons of fuel oil from her. We then departed the harbor en route to the Southern Formosa Patrol area. We arrived on station around 0100 Wednesday morning, 3 August, and commenced patrolling. Wednesday morning we had one visual contact that turned out to be a Chinese Nationalist craft, YP-741. Wednesday noon the Brush went alongside a ship that finally identified herself as the HMS Hupeh, of 2,000 tons, that was en route from Hong Kong to Shanghai. She, too, was allowed to go her own way but the ship took a picture of her.

At 1410 Wednesday afternoon the Brush was relieved of patrol duty by the Maddox and the Brush returned to Kaohsiung. We arrived there around 1830 and moored alongside the Moore at buoy 11. However, the Brush only stayed overnight in the harbor. At 1013 the next morning the Brush got underway and went alongside the Platte(AO24) to take on fuel oil again. After refueling, the Brush departed the harbor en route to Hong Kong. We steamed all afternoon and all night toward Hong Kong and arrived there early the next morning, Friday, 5 August, 1955. At 0645 the Brush commenced maneuvering to enter Hong Kong Harbor. At 0645 the ship observed sunrise and turned off the running lights. At 0802 the ship was moored to buoy 6 in Hong Kong Harbor.

## HONG KONG – 1955

The Brush would stay in Hong Kong for 4 days and the sole purpose of the visit was for rest and recreation. The opportunity to do this was certainly taken advantage of by everyone. A lot of things could be bought at bargain prices. Plus, it was just an exotic place. I believe liberty commenced at 1000 and lasted until 2400. As usual, Hong Kong Harbor was a very busy place with lots of water craft, junks mostly, of all sizes that were acoming and agoing. Of course, the Chinese painter women immediately came alongside and negotiated their usual deal of painting the sides of the ships for the ship's garbage. Ashore, everything was pretty much the same. The Chinese rickshaw drivers were still there soliciting business as the sailors came ashore. And the child beggars were still there begging for money from everyone that walked down the street. In addition, the boat people were living in the harbor in as great of numbers as in previous years. I couldn't tell that anything had changed from the first time that I was in Hong Kong.

### Tailor-Made Clothes

One of my main objectives this time in Hong Kong was to buy myself some tailor-made clothes. Some of my more experienced shipmates had informed me on my first trip there that Hong Kong was the place to buy tailor-made clothes, and I had planned to have some made on my last trip there before being released from the navy and going back into civilian life. I wouldn't have any need for tailor-made suits and coats and such like until then. I had never had any tailor-made clothes before. I wanted some and I wanted to take advantage of the cheap prices. Tailor-made clothes in Hong Kong cost from about one-third to one-half of what they would cost in the United States.There were dozens of Chinese tailor shops in Hong Kong to choose from. I'm sure all of them were capable of good work. However, the hard part was to find one that had the reputation of being honest. Many of the tailors had a practice of showing their customers a good quality of cloth and then made their clothes out of a cheaper quality of cloth. The tailors got by with this kind of deception most of the time because foreigners, especially naive Americans, expected the tailor to do what they agreed to do and didn't check their new clothes too close when they picked them up. They just assumed that they were getting what they had ordered – like they did in the States. And it was only later, maybe when they got back home and far away, that the customer realized that they had been taken.

Anyway, somehow, I got steered in the right direction and found myself a good, honest tailor. The name of the tailor was Peter Woo and he owned the Flying Angel Tailor Shop. I remember having a tan cashmere sport coat made, a light blue sharkskin suit, and 3 pairs of pants. Those are the things that I remember. There might have been more things. I ordered them in the late morning and picked them up in late afternoon. The tailor was able to make them that fast because he had several people working for him. As far as I know, I got what I ordered. They looked great to me. I shipped them home the next day or so and they arrived home safely. I wore the clothes for several years after I got back home and until I gained so much weight that they didn't fit anymore. Then, I either gave them away or threw them away. I also remember buying myself a couple of beautiful shirts and a green sleeveless sweater that looked very British. I had a great time shopping because everything was at such bargain prices.

In addition to all my shopping, I spent some time on Victoria Peak looking at the beautiful views up there and drinking orange squash (lemonade). And I know I spent some time at the Seaman's Mission and in some of the old colonial hotel restaurants. The second day in Hong Kong I took a taxi tour around the island with a couple of my shipmates. We saw some very beautiful scenery on the other side of the island away from the city. Hong Kong is certainly a great place to visit. I regret that I didn't have the chance to spend more time there during my life.

In a letter to my mother dated August 13, 1955, I told her a little about my trip to Hong Kong. "We've already been in Hong Kong and out. I had a most enjoyable time there as usual. The only thing about going there is that we never stay long enough, and I never have enough money. I had two and a-half days of liberty. I spent all my money the first two days and I had quite a wad, too. I got several nice things, but I'll have to admit that I spent most of it on myself – mostly clothes, including a beautiful light blue tailor-made sharkskin suit. I paid $36 for it, and it would have cost me probably $80 in the States. I got some other things, too, mostly tailor-made clothes, but I'm not going to write about them. I'm going to send all of it home and you can see for yourself. I also got a couple of linen tablecloths. I wanted to get a lot of other stuff but just didn't have the money."

The Brush departed Hong Kong late in the afternoon of Monday, 8 August, 1955, en route to the Northern Formosa Patrol area. Regretfully, that was the last time in my life that I was ever in Hong Kong.

## BACK ON THE FORMOSA PATROL

We steamed all Monday night and most of the day Tuesday at 20 knots toward our patrol station. However, Tuesday morning around 1100 the Brush rendezvoused with the USS Platte(AO24) out in the strait to take on fuel. That completed, we continued on toward the northern patrol station. However, en route there, Tuesday night, we challenged a couple of contacts. One was identified as a Chinese Nationalist fishing boat. The other one was identified as the British merchantman, Westway, which was bound from Foo Chow to Hong Kong.

The Brush relieved the Moore of the northern patrol station S-4 at 0340 Wednesday morning, 10 August. At 0908 Wednesday morning the ship had a surface contact. We proceeded to close it. It turned out to be the British merchant ship, Chun Sang. We passed her 500 yards abeam to port. We had a couple more surface contacts during the day and night that proved to be Chinese Nationalist fishing boats.

At 0050 Wednesday night the Brush picked up a radar contact bearing 357°(t) at 9 miles. We changed course to close it. It was identified as the Chinese Nationalist DE-25 that was bound for Matsu. We didn't have any contacts to investigate either Thursday or Friday. We had the strait all to ourselves.

However, Saturday morning around 0400 the Brush departed the northern patrol station and headed back to Kaohsiung. The Thomas was to relieve us. The Brush arrived at Kaohsiung Harbor at 0600 and immediately went alongside the USS Cimarron(A022) to refuel. She received 66,146 gallons. After refueling, the Brush moored to buoys 9 and 10. We stayed in port 4 days and I finally went on liberty in Kaohsiung two of those days that we were in port–the first time ever.

### Liberties in Kaohsiung

One day I went to a ship sponsored beach party at some little, out of the way, nothing-type beach. We rode a bus of some kind to the party. It may have been a navy bus. I didn't stay very long at the party because it was terribly hot, there was little shade, the water looked nasty, and the 2 beers that they gave the attendees were hot. It didn't look like a fun time to me. So, a few of us rode back into town and went into one of the local, rustic bars for our entertainment. The bar was also rather warm, but they did serve cold Chinese beer and had some rather attractive female hostesses to socialize with us and that could speak a little English. So I drank beer and coke with the boys for a couple of hours and then went back to the ship cold sober.

One of the things that I noticed as I rode through this little Chinese town was all the naked little boys, maybe those under 4 or 5 years old. Their mothers apparently didn't think it was necessary to put clothes on little boys that young. I'm sure it was cooler for them in that hot climate. Although, some of the little boys did wear clothes, mostly short pants.

Another thing I couldn't help noticing was all the young mothers nursing their babies with their breasts totally exposed. They didn't seem to think anything about that sort of thing. I didn't think too much about it either, but I couldn't help noticing the practice and thinking about the difference between there and the western world.

I went ashore the next afternoon with some of my shipmates and we went into a bar that was owned by an American. This time we sat outside at a table under a small shelter. It was hot but the beer was cold. The American bar owner had apparently gone native, as we called it, because he had married a Chinese woman and they had several small children. They ate their supper late in the evening at a table next to us. I hope he was happy with his situation. But it seemed to me that he was a long way from home and was living in a vastly different culture than where he grew up. He didn't show any signs of being especially happy, but if he was, I was happy for him.

## Street Scenes of Kaohsiung

Little Children in Kaohsiung

## A Sailor Goes Berserk On Bad Whiskey

One of the radiomen came in off liberty one night in a crazy state of mind after being on liberty in Kaohsiung. He didn't know any of his shipmates and everybody was trying to get him. He was hostile to everybody he met and he looked crazy out of the eyes. His condition was something more than simply being drunk. In his mind, he was fighting for his life. He had to have drunk some bad whiskey somewhere while he was on the beach. Finally, some of the quarterdeck personnel, and probably some more people, had to physically subdue him. He was fighting for his life all the time. A corpsman was able to put a shot of something in him that knocked him out. The next morning when he woke up he was in a normal state of mind and probably didn't remember a thing about the night before. Nevertheless, he got into some trouble over the incident and had to see the man; in other words, he had to go to captain's mast. He was charged with disobeying a direct order and disrespect to a petty officer. His punishment was extra duty that was to be performed for a period of 10 days. That was bad enough punishment, but I believe they could have sent him to the brig. However, I think the captain took all the circumstances into consideration and gave him the lighter punishment. Actually, he was a pretty good fellow and normally he didn't get into trouble or cause any. He was just crazy that one night because of some bad whiskey. That is the story as I remember it.

Late Wednesday afternoon, 17 August, the ship once again departed Kaohsiung Harbor and proceeded independently to the southern patrol area to relieve the Moore. At 0105 the Brush relieved the Moore and commenced searching, hopefully, for the survivor of a downed aircraft. However, it's rather hard to see anything out on the ocean in the middle of the night. To make the search even harder, nobody knew exactly where the plane went down. But we looked.

Around noon, Thursday, 18 August, the sighting of a yellow dye marker was reported to us by a search aircraft. The Brush proceeded to the yellow dye marker location some miles away. We passed through the location of the dye marker at 1345 and commenced maneuvering on various courses at 15 knots while conducting an expanding square search for the downed pilot. We searched for the pilot until 1700 at which time the Brush discontinued the search and set a course for the southern patrol area S-6. We arrived at the patrol area at 2024 and commenced patrolling.

Friday, 19 August, was a rather dull day; we didn't see anything much to challenge and investigate. On Friday the captain held mast and dealt out some punishment to four sailors for various offenses. We went to general quarters in the early afternoon, but that wasn't anything unusual because we went to general quarters just about every day at least once. Apparently Captain Whitehurst wanted to keep us on our toes, so to speak. The ship also conducted some engineering casualty and damage control drills Friday afternoon. The ship did challenge one ship Friday night. She was identified as the Panamanian ship, Pollux.

Saturday, 20 August, was another uneventful day. We only exchanged challenges with 2 Nationalist Chinese Navy boats, the PC-116 and the PG-105. They were operating together. Sometime Saturday afternoon the Brush secured from the Southern Formosa Patrol and headed back to Kaohsiung. She arrived at Kaohsiung Harbor around 0700 and moored alongside the USS Cimarron(AO22) at 0750 to take on fuel oil. However, just as soon as she refueled, the Brush departed the harbor and headed for the northern patrol area. On the way to the northern patrol area, the Brush sighted a merchant ship bearing 060°(t) 15 miles away. She commenced challenging her but got no response. At 0710 the Brush changed course to close her. At 1720 four Chinese Nationalist jets made passes at the merchant ship. At 1730 the ship finally identified herself as the British ship, Ettrickean, en route to Japan from Hong Kong. I don't know why she was so slow about responding to our challenge. She should have known that was something she had to do if she wanted to pass through those waters. At 1815, Sunday, 21 August, we arrived on patrol station S-4 and started patrolling.

The Brush patrolled all day Monday without sighting anything. We didn't see any boats or ships to challenge on Tuesday either. At 2025 Tuesday night the Brush was relieved of the patrol by the Maddox. The Brush proceeded back to Kaohsiung. On the way back in, the Brush investigated a contact that was 11 miles away. It was identified as the British merchant ship, Westways. The Brush had another radar contact at 2250 Tuesday night and changed course to investigate it. That ship identified herself as the British ship, Bumboat Bay. We continued on in the direction of Kaohsiung but we never got there because we had to change course at 0234 to avoid a typhoon, Typhoon Iris, that was headed toward Kaohsiung. Instead, the tanker, Cimarron, came out of the harbor to rendezvous with us – to refuel us. At 1433 we sighted the Cimarron at a distance of 7 miles. At 1441 the Brush commenced her approach to go alongside the tanker on her port side. By this time the seas were getting pretty rough. Lines from the tanker were thrown over to the Brush in an attempt to refuel. However, at 1520 all lines were returned to the tanker due to the seas making refueling impractical. Then, the Brush commenced maneuvering to clear the tanker and to go alongside her starboard side. At 1605 we were alongside the starboard side of the Cimarron on a fueling course of 010°(t) and at a speed of 12 knots. Apparently, the Brush achieved some protection from the wind and the waves on the starboard side of the tanker. At 1615 a highline was rigged amidships for the transfer of mail and turnover files. And at 1621 the first fueling hose was across and the ship soon commenced taking on fuel. The Brush secured from taking on fuel at 1709 and all lines were soon clear of the two ships. Upon completing refueling, the Brush set a course to return to patrol area S-4.

I would say the biggest challenge that a special sea detail helmsman has is trying to steer a ship alongside another ship in rough seas – that is, without colliding. It is also a big challenge for the captain, too, and his career is at stake. The helmsman's career is probably at stake, too, but the captain has a much bigger career. So, both the captain and the helmsman have to do a few things right under these circumstances.

We arrived on patrol station at 0230 Thursday morning, 25 August, and started patrolling. We didn't patrol too long, however, because at 0940 the next morning we departed patrol area S-4 and proceeded to rendezvous with the USS John A. Bole(DD755) at a certain latitude and longitude in the strait, which was some miles away. The Bole had some overdue mail for us. We made the rendezvous with the Bole late in the afternoon at 1730, and she transferred our mail over to us by highline. With the mail transfer completed, the Brush set a course for Kaohsiung. The Formosa Patrol was over for us.

We arrived at Kaohsiung around 0700 Friday morning, 26 August. On the way in, the Brush had met up with the Moore and the two ships went into the harbor together. Upon arriving at the harbor, the two ships went alongside the Cimarron to refuel. Refueling for us was completed at 0907.

The Maddox and the Thomas were already in the harbor when we arrived and upon completion of refueling of the Brush and Moore, the ships of DesDiv 92 departed the harbor en route to Buckner Bay, Okinawa. I would never see Kaohsiung Harbor again.

After reaching the open sea, the ships of DesDiv 92 went into a column formation and steamed most of the way to Okinawa in this manner. The ships did engage in some general drills and division tactics, though, on Saturday, 27 August.

In a letter dated August 27, 1955, I wrote my mother about our trip up to Okinawa from Formosa. "We've at last left the Formosa area. Tonight we're en route to Okinawa, arriving there early tomorrow (Sunday) morning. We're to stay there all day, take on fuel, and go back to sea for at least five days before going back into Buckner Bay, Okinawa to refuel. It seems like the only reason we ever go into port is to take on fuel so we can stay at sea some more. Next week we're to play a few games with some submarines.

For two or three days around the first of the week we had kind of an uneasy time. A typhoon passed us going north about 200 miles eastward of us. We thought we were directly in its path for awhile, but it changed course and went up the east coast of Formosa. We got considerable wind from it and naturally some fairly rough water, but it was nothing to get too excited about. I've seen it a lot worse. All week now it has been raining on us. For the last two days since leaving Formosa we've been hitting one rain squall right after another. It rains like heck for a few minutes, we'll steam out of it, and in a few minutes we hit another one."

The ships arrived at Buckner Bay around 0630 Sunday morning, 28 August. The Brush anchored in moorage B-126 at 0745. However, during the afternoon the Brush got underway briefly and went alongside fueling pier B at White Beach. She secured from taking on fuel at 1845 and then proceeded to anchorage B-185 and dropped anchor.

Other ships present in the bay included the USS Epperson(DDE719), USS Nicholas(DDE449), USS Philip(DDE498), USS Renshaw(DDE499), USS Kenneth Whiting(AV14), and the USS Raton(SSR270). The destroyers were all there to conduct ASW together for several days. Other ships would join us in the operation, too, including the submarine, USS Pickerel(SS524), and 3 British destroyers.

## ASW OFF OKINAWA

The Brush, Maddox, and Thomas got underway Monday afternoon, 29 August, and left Buckner Bay to commence the ASW exercises. They would be operating with the Pickerel(SS524). The sonarmen and the CIC personnel are always busy during ASW exercises. The signalmen are usually not so busy at those times. The Moore joined us the next day. Three British ships also joined in on the fun some time Monday afternoon or night because they were present Tuesday morning. The British ships were the HMS Cockade(D34), HMS Comus(D20), and the HMS Arunta(D130). I noticed that the British destroyers were constructed somewhat differently than American destroyers. So, the 11 destroyers and the one submarine conducted ASW exercises essentially day and night for the next 4 days. It was a very busy time for some of the crew.

## My Day Aboard a British Destroyer

Thursday, 1 September, 1955, was a most interesting day for me because I got to spend much of the day aboard a British ship, the destroyer, HMS Cockade(D34). I saw how sailors lived in the British Navy and made some great English friends. This greatly different day came about because the commander of the task group that we were operating with decided that it would be a great idea for the ships of different nationalities, or different types, to exchange personnel for a few hours to observe how they lived and conducted ASW operations. The submarine got in on the exchange, too, with the surface ships because she was a vastly different type of warship than the destroyers.

So, at the given time, around 1000, the ships of the task group stopped all engines and commenced lying to out in the middle of the ocean to accomplish the exchange of personnel. There were motor whaleboats running around all over the ocean for an hour or so transporting sailors to the various vessels. Fortunately, the ocean was quite calm that day, except for the usual Pacific Ocean swells, otherwise, they couldn't have pulled it off. I don't know if all the ships participated in this exchange or not, but I know that the Brush did because of entries in the ship's log, a letter to my mother, and my recollections of being a part of that exchange.

The Brush exchanged personnel with the submarine, Pickerel, and the British destroyer, Cockade. Four men from the Brush went aboard the submarine, and 4 men from the submarine came aboard the Brush also. Three sailors from the Brush, including myself, went aboard the Cockade, and a like number of British sailors came aboard the Brush, I believe. The ship's log doesn't mention it though. The 3 sailors that went aboard the Cockade were Sweeney, P.A. IC3, Sotkiewicz, J.J. RD3, and Holly, O.T. QM3.

We arrived alongside the Cockade around 1100 and climbed up a ladder to the main deck where we were met by a couple of sailors who took us in tow and led us to their messing compartment. In reality this compartment was where a group of sailors lived, in that they slept there, they ate there, and they lounged there when they were off duty. In other words, that was their living quarters and, as I remember, it was topside on the main deck and the compartment had portholes. Apparently, this particular mess was assigned the chore of taking charge of us and entertaining us. Nobody could have done a better job than they did in that respect. This mess happened to have housed a group of engineers who normally performed duties below deck somewhere; I believe at least some of them worked in the engine room.

I wrote about this special day in a letter to my mother dated September 4, 1955. "Last week the Brush and 10 other destroyers played around with submarines off Okinawa aways. Last Thursday our commodore gave the ships the opportunity to send a couple or three men to ships of a different nationality.

I volunteered to go and had a most interesting afternoon aboard the British destroyer, Cockade. Three men from my ship got in the ship's motor whaleboat and we went across two miles of ocean to the Cockade. This was my first boat ride out on the ocean. Our boat then picked up some Englishmen and took them to our ship and some of the other ships. During the afternoon I learned a lot about the ship and the British Navy. And, I must say, it is much superior to ours in some respects. In fact, the British Navy seems to be more like what I thought the navy would be like when I joined it.

Anyway, when we got aboard the Cockade, we were taken to a messing compartment, as they called them, where six or seven men lived, and at night slung their hammocks and made a sleeping compartment out of it. As we entered the mess, a sailor was mixing the British daily tradition of forenoon rum. We all sat around the mess table, the rum was passed out, and we commenced to get acquainted. They all seemed pleased to have us aboard."....

The English sailors had a unique way of serving the rum ration. The leading petty officer in the mess compartment at the time the rum was to be served did the measuring of the rum. I suppose it was so much for each sailor present. Anyway, this petty officer put the proper amount of rum in this tall glass and then added enough water to fill the glass, as I remember. The glass was passed around and everybody took a swig out of the same glass. The glass should have been empty after everybody had their swig. I'm sure each British sailor knew how big a swig to take. I took my swig along with the rest of them, but in a few minutes I was dizzy and light-headed as I could be, although, I didn't let them know that I wasn't man enough to handle the stuff. They had their forenoon rum ration everyday and their bodies were used to it, mine wasn't.

I had another problem. For the first hour or two that I was with these English fellows, I couldn't understand half of what they said. However, after a couple of hours, I could understand most of what they said. I never could understand why I had the problem of understanding them. They were speaking English alright, but they were apparently putting a little twist to it that I wasn't used to hearing.

**HMS Cockade(D34)**

Back to the letter. "After about thirty minutes, a mess boy came in, broke out the plates, dealt out the dinner, and set it before us. This was very different than the way American sailors are fed. We had a dinner of roast beef, mashed potatoes and gravy, boiled carrots, pineapple, and bread. I thought it was a pretty good dinner.

About 1:00 p.m. we were taken about the ship to show us what she looked like. We got through in time for 2:30 tea; and after tea, we went out on the open deck and sat around and talked. At 4:00 o'clock we went down to tea again. This time we also had Australian cheese sandwiches, and they were very good. After that, we went back on deck and shot the breeze some more until time to leave – about 5:30 p.m. It was a very enjoyable day and I learned a lot about the British Navy. I have a lot of respect for those English sailors."

At 1730 the ships of TG 70.4 temporarily ceased the ASW exercises, stopped engines, and commenced lying to again to await the transfer of personnel back to their respective ships. Around 1840 the ships got underway and resumed their ASW exercises.

We went aboard the British ship, supposedly, to observe how they conducted ASW exercises, but we didn't observe anything in that respect. Engineers, who happened to be our hosts, aren't involved too much in ASW anyway. They certainly knew how to treat guests, though. They wined us, dined us, entertained us, and treated us like royalty. If they were trying to impress us – they did. And in the process of being entertained, we gained a knowledge of how well the British sailors lived on their ship compared to how we lived on ours. There was a huge difference and in the British sailors favor.

The British sailors that I associated with were a great group of guys and were great hosts. I've always hoped that the American sailors that day treated their British guests as well as we were treated. But I imagine they had a harder time entertaining their British guests because they really didn't have any way to entertain them – certainly not the way we were entertained. I will always remember the day, Thursday, 1 September, 1955, as one of the highlights of my naval career and actually as one of the special days of my life. But now, that day and event seems so long ago and so far away – when I was a young man. I will always remember that special day in my life.

## What I Learned About the British Navy

There were a number of things that I learned about the British Navy and living on British ships which greatly impressed me. For one thing, it seems that most of the young men that join the British Navy intend to make it a career. And their navy treats them well enough that they want to. I believe their initial enlistment is for 6 years. I suspect, too, that the British Navy is somewhat selective about who they allow to serve in the navy. All the British sailors that I've ever seen, from the Cockade and on liberty in various ports, looked like high quality young men to me. I can't make that statement about all the American sailors, both in their appearance and in their conduct. Although, there are a lot of top-notch American sailors, too, I might add, but not all of them. Maybe things have changed in the modern American Navy and all of them are great seaman. How would I know?

Also, it appeared to me like the British ships were built for men to live on with some degree of comfort. Maybe that is one of the reasons why the British Navy has such a high re-enlistment rate. I know from personal experience that American destroyers weren't built with the comfort of the crew in mind. In fact, most of the men I knew wanted to get off of them the first minute they could and re-enlisting in the navy was not a consideration. Furthermore, from what I saw, the British enlisted men had far better living conditions than the officers did on my ship and other American destroyers that I know about. For one thing, the living compartments were top-side on the British destroyers and not way below deck like ours were. Consequently, the compartments were generally cool because of the ocean breezes or due to the movement of the ship. The compartments had portholes, too, that they could open when they wanted to. Fresh air was no problem topside. In addition, the British sailors had an area that they could go to and lounge around, or whatever, when they were off duty. Also, there weren't any long chow lines to stand in at meal times. The sailors ate in their messing compartment in a dignified manner. Their meals were served to them on plates just like the officers were in the wardroom in the American Navy. They also drank out of glasses, too, and not just mugs. In reality, the messing compartments were actually living areas during the day and sleeping compartments at night, and rather large ones at that. Each one was about the size of a wardroom on an American destroyer. At night, of course, they broke out their hammocks to sleep in. That might not have been an ideal sleeping arrangement, but I'm sure it was as good as our racks.

I also noticed how much more stable the British destroyer was than the American destroyers were. The Brush and other destroyers of that time period were constantly pitching and rolling when they were at sea, even on a calm day. The Cockade didn't pitch and roll nearly as much as I was accustomed to and I couldn't help but notice it. In fact, riding on the Cockade had a totally different feeling than what I was accustomed to. It was a much smoother ride.

The ships of Task Group 70.4 went back into Buckner Bay early Friday afternoon, 2 September. At 1250 the Brush was anchored in anchorage B-185 in 8 fathoms of water. We would stay in port over the week-end, or until late Sunday afternoon, when we went to sea again.

## BUCKNER BAY, OKINAWA

Late Friday afternoon I went ashore with the intent of riding around the island for awhile on a military bus to see what the place looked like. I had been to Okinawa a number of times during my hitch in the navy, but I had never had the opportunity to look around or even go ashore. But I did it that afternoon for 2 or 3 hours. However, I never saw anything to get excited about and my curiosity about the place was satisfied. And I could fully understand why it wasn't considered much of a liberty port or a place to be stationed. In a letter to my mother dated September 4, 1955, I wrote a little about my excursion ashore that day.

"We're spending the week-end in Buckner bay, Okinawa Island. There are no towns here to amount to anything, but there is a small enlisted men's club here that we can go to and entertain ourselves, if for no other reason that to just get off the ship for awhile. Friday afternoon I went ashore and went to a couple of little towns to see what they looked like, but I saw nothing very appealing. They were more of a village than a town. They reminded me of the Philippines a lot because most of the houses had thatched roofs and were very flimsily built."

## A Spectacular Sunrise at Buckner Bay

I saw the most spectacular sunrise that I've ever seen in my life at Buckner Bay on Sunday morning, September 4, 1955. I had the signal watch on the bridge from 0500 to 0800 that morning. We really weren't expecting any visual signals at that time of the day in port, and on a Sunday morning too, and I was up there alone. The only other men on the ship that were awake that morning and topside early enough to witness daybreak were the 3 or 4 men on watch at the quarterdeck. I don't know what they saw, if anything, or if they would have paid any attention to a beautiful sunrise if they had seen it.

The atmosphere was real clear that morning without any haze to speak of. In addition, there wasn't any wind at dawn and consequently the sea was as smooth as glass.

There were at least 14 naval vessels anchored in the bay, but there wasn't any activity on the water that Sunday morning at dawn except for a few sea birds that were busy flying around over the water searching for their breakfast. In other words, it was as quiet and peaceful an ocean scene as you would want to see. In a sense, I had the ship all to myself at dawn, but I probably wasn't appreciating the beauty of a new day as much as I should have. I had other things on my mind. I was sitting in the captain's chair that was at the forward part of the bridge on the starboard side and facing toward the rising sun that hadn't showed up yet. I wasn't in a good frame of mind at all on this particular morning and was somewhat depressed. I had been at sea on the Brush for 3 years by now, and I felt totally burnt out and used up. Besides that, I was sleepy and homesick. I had only been at home for 15 days in the past 3 years or so and that short visit had been nearly 2 years ago. I was ready to go home.

Anyway, while I was sitting there in the captain's chair at the break of dawn feeling sorry for myself, there developed before my eyes the most spectacular sunrise that I had ever seen in my life. There weren't any low clouds that morning, but there was an abundance of small, high clouds in all kinds of arrangements. I suppose you would call them either cirrus or cirrocumulus clouds. I'm sure there were both kinds of them up there. As dawn broke and it became lighter, there developed before me the most glorious display of colors that you can imagine on those high clouds. I cannot adequately describe what I saw that morning, but I can only compare it to what you might imagine the sky and clouds would look like upon the second coming of Christ. I believe I looked closely for Him in the sky that morning but, of course, I didn't see Him. Maybe the Lord simply created that glorious, spectacular sunrise especially for me. Maybe he created it in an effort to improve my spirits, to give me hope that a new life would soon be dawning for me, and to let me know that he was still up there in heaven and still in charge. However, this exceedingly beautiful display of colors in the sky only lasted for 10 to 15 minutes, and then the colors just slowly faded away as the sky became lighter. There was no doubt in my mind that I had just witnessed something very special. I have seen a number of very beautiful sunrises and sunsets in my life, but I have never yet seen anything that would compare to that one. In a letter to my mother dated September 4, 1955, I told her a little bit about this particular morning.

"I just witnessed one of the most beautiful sunrises that I have ever observed…But this morning, having the 5:00 to 8:00 o'clock watch, I happened to be up and at about sunrise, I got to see a very beautiful one. I won't try to describe it. You know what they look like, and besides, I can't find the words to describe it."

## A Walk Along Buckner Bay

I went ashore around 1000 on Sunday morning, 4 September, 1955, and had a different kind of liberty. I felt the need to walk along the bayshore. It was a beautiful, still morning with a clear atmosphere and an abundance of white cottony clouds floating along in the blue sky. The weather was rather warm, of course, and got hotter as the day progressed. Small waves were gently lapping on the beach for there was very little wind.

As I walked along the bayshore, I began to notice a lot of pretty, odd-looking seashells at the shoreline and I began to pick them up. Soon, I had an arm load and all that I could carry. Then, I found a plastic bag floating in the water. I retrieved it, put my shells in it, and collected more of them as I walked along. I wasn't in any hurry to go any place particularly, and I was just enjoying myself walking along the bayshore on that beautiful morning picking up seashells. I walked up the beach for a mile, at least, I imagine, and didn't see anybody else along the way. I was the only one on the beach. As I walked along, I also did some thinking. I thought about the big battle that had taken place there 10 years previously and what a terrible experience that must have been for the men involved in it. But on this morning there wasn't any sign of the battle remaining. All the wreckage and debris of war had been removed. At least, I did not see any. The beach was now just a clean, quiet, and peaceful sea scene. I also thought about home and some of the people back there that I cared about. I had been gone from home for nearly 4 years by now and home seemed so far away and living there seemed so long ago. Years tend to be very long when people are young but they tend to seem shorter as the years go by. At this time in my life, I felt like I had been gone from home 10 years. And this place called home was some vague place that I had read about somewhere.

After walking about an hour or so, and maybe a mile or more up the beach, I came to a pavilion-type structure and a little building that was located about a hundred feet or so up from the water's edge. It seemed so out of place to me. I decided to investigate it and see what it was. As I climbed up the bank close to the water's edge, I also saw some sailors up there, but I couldn't tell what kind of sailors they were. I walked up to the pavilion and, lo and behold, if it wasn't 3 or 4 of my British sailor friends from the Cockade sitting under the pavilion, in the shade, drinking beer. The little building was actually a small concession stand, as I remember. I was glad, but surprised, to see my English friends again and they seemed glad to see me. So I joined them. We sat down there in the shade, overlooking the bay, socializing, and drinking beverages for the next couple of hours.

I showed them the seashells that I had collected, and they thought the shells were pretty and unusual, too, but they didn't feel the need to collect any of them for themselves. I suppose real, hard-core seamen don't do such a thing anyway. I've still got those seashells that I picked up that morning.

After talking for a couple of hours, we all walked back to the fleet landing. I stayed with the Englishmen most of the afternoon, but I don't remember a thing about what we did. Although, in a letter to my mother dated September 11, 1955, I mentioned that we ate dinner on an army base and rode around the island in a taxi to see what we could see. However, like I say, I don't have any recollection of doing those things at all.

I probably got back to the ship around 1700 because she was going to be getting underway around 1900. I didn't want to miss movement of ship at that late date in my navy career.

## TASK GROUP 70.4

At 1840 Sunday, 4 September , the ship set the special sea detail and soon thereafter stood out of Buckner Bay to rendezvous with the light carrier, USS Badoeng Straits(CVE116). The Brush steamed due south all night at a speed of mostly 8 knots. Apparently, we weren't in any hurry to get anywhere. At 0540, Monday morning, 5 September, the Brush reported for duty to the Badoeng Strait. We escorted her around while she conducted flight operations off and on all day and way into the night. Sometimes we were in front of the carrier and sometimes we were following along astern of her. The carrier also conducted some 40mm gunnery practice during the middle of the afternoon. At 2235 the Brush was detached from plane guard duty and proceeded to steam independently for the rest of the night and to steam no closer than 5 miles from the carrier. I don't know what that was all about.

Early the next morning all the other ships of TG 70.4 arrived on the scene, which were the same bunch of ships that we had operated with the previous week. The Badoeng Straits was still present, too. The task group now commenced conducting ASW exercises primarily. The carrier was now in on the exercises, too, and would launch planes from time to time. As usual, the destroyers formed a screen around the carrier. The submarine was now the USS Tiru(SS416). Also, the TG was steaming in the general direction of Japan. The ships conducted ASW and TG tactics both day and night nearly all the way to Yokosuka.

## A Little Tired Brown Bird

One day when we were operating in the Okinawa area, a little brown land bird landed on the Brush. We were probably a hundred miles from the nearest land, that being Okinawa and I think it lit on the ship because she was tired. It didn't seem to be too afraid of us because we could get within 6 feet of her. She didn't show any fear of us at all as long as we didn't get any closer than 6 feet. If we did, she would just put a little more distance between us. I tried to be friends with her. I talked to her and offered her my index finger to set on, but she declined the offer. She sat around in the rigging most of the time just out of our reach. She was probably hungry, too, but we didn't have a thing to offer her. I don't know what she normally ate, bugs and seeds probably, but we didn't have any of either one of those things out there on the ocean. She hung around on the ship for 3 or 4 hours and seemed to be enjoying herself. I suppose she was resting up for awhile before continuing on with her flight to somewhere. But all of a sudden she was gone. I hope she made it to wherever she was going. Maybe she encountered another ship to land and rest on for awhile if she got too tired.

The little bird was about the size of a sparrow but more fluffy. I wonder how many little birds like that get tired on a long flight and fall into the ocean. I referred to the little bird in the feminine sense because it seemed like such a sweet little bird so it must have been a female. Right?

## My Box of Cookies From Home

I put in an order for some home-made cookies with my mother probably around the first of July, 1955. My mother made them, boxed them up, and mailed them to me. However, it took about 2 months for them to catch up with me. I noticed that the cardboard box was rather beat up when it finally arrived. I opened the box and there was not a cookie to be seen, or anything that looked like it might have been a cookie at one time. The box was full of small stale crumbs. Oh well, I was willing to settle for stale crumbs if I had to since my mother went to the trouble of making them. I tasted them and immediately came to the conclusion that the stale crumbs simply weren't worth eating, so I pitched the box and crumbs over the side, or maybe I should say I presented them to King Neptune. That was a big disappointment. I sure was looking forward to getting those cookies because it was something from home.

## A Humiliating Inspection

One day during the latter months of my naval career, a medical officer came aboard ship for a very specific purpose. He was there to inspect buttholes of the young enlisted men. I doubt if he inspected those of the officers, or the chief's either, although, I don't know that for sure. I believe he was mainly interested in inspecting the 18 to 22 year olds. The doctor made his inspection at a ladder in a compartment somewhere in the forward part of the ship, but I can't remember exactly where it was. He spent most of the afternoon making this inspection and he must have looked at 250 rear ends. I believe the different divisions were inspected at the same time as much as possible. Everything had to be done in an orderly manner you know. Anyway, the young sailors formed a line in a passageway at the top of this ladder that led down into the compartment where the doctor was standing at the bottom of the ladder. The sailors had to step down this ladder a few steps to get inspected. The ship's Master-at-Arms, or somebody, was there to give instructions and to keep everybody moving along. And somebody was there to check off names as the men got inspected; a corpsman probably had that job.

Anyway, when the time came for a fellow to get his bottom inspected, he would go down the ladder a few steps to where his rear end was at about eye level with the doctor. The Master-at-Arms, or whoever it was, would give each fellow specific instructions as to how to expose his rear end so that the doctor could observe it. Of course, he always spoke with great authority. The instructions were, "Turn around, drop your pants and shorts, and bend over and spread your cheeks." Get the picture? Everybody did exactly as they were instructed to do, and the body part that was to be inspected was always just at eye-level with the doctor. The doctor would take a quick glance at the butthole that was presented to him for inspection, and then make a little wave of his hand, which meant – next. The inspected fellow would then pull up his pants, continued on down the ladder, and get his name checked off. The Master-at-Arms would take the cue and order, "NEXT", and the line would move down one more fellow. The line kept moving this way until everyone was inspected.

I'm sure the doctor was glad when the inspection was completed. I know the men were; they weren't interested in having it done in the first place. The expression on the doctor's face pretty much told me his side of the story, too, as far as I was concerned. The look on his face told me that he didn't want to be there doing that any more than we did. But it was something that he had to do for one reason or another. I was always convinced that he was sent there to perform that task because a superior officer ordered him to conduct that inspection for reasons other than for health concerns of the men. I believe he was ordered to make that inspection for some kind of initiation practice, or for punishment of some kind, or as a sick joke, or just because some superior officer could make him do it because he had the power.

I can't imagine the doctor found anybody with a defective butthole. At their young age, I don't think you would expect very many men to have defective ones. Besides, if a fellow did have one, the doctors would have discovered it when he was getting his physical examination to enter the navy.

Anyway, we got through the inspection, humiliated somewhat, but we got through it. Most of the people that I know would prefer it to be their idea to have someone alooking and aprobing around back there, but we didn't have a choice about the matter. Also, if it had to be done, I believe most people would prefer that it be done in private and not have a bunch of onlookers present.

## Dear John Letters

Getting a "Dear John" letter was something that occurred from time to time for some of the young sailors on the Brush. It could be pretty accurately predicted who would get one. It was quite easy to predict who would be the unfortunate fellows. Those guys that had a special girlfriend back home when they joined the navy got one. And those guys who didn't have a girlfriend back home when they joined the navy didn't get one. It was just about that simple to predict who would get one.

Several times during the last 2 years of my service aboard the Brush, I had young sailors corner me and talk to me at length about this beautiful girl back home who they planned to marry, etc. They always had several pictures to show me, too. I was always a good listener and would get enthused right along with them. I never once suggested to them that their future might not be as bright as they were envisioning it to be. I would let them talk themselves out without hearing any negative comments from me. They would always leave me feeling real good about their future with that wonderful girl back home.

But, in my heart, I knew he was going to be in for a big letdown; because one of these days he was going to get a "Dear John" letter, and he would be in absolutely no position to do anything about it. He was simply going to have to adjust to living his life without the girl of his dreams. And how long would it be before he got this letter? It depended mostly on how long he had been away from her. Usually, a year would be the longest a pretty, young girl would be faithful and loyal to her far-away boyfriend. After all, she was attractive and other young men were steadily hitting on her. She would probably resist their advances for awhile, but after a few months, maybe even weeks, she would get lonesome and have romantic needs, and a letter from a far-away boyfriend just didn't hack it anymore. So, she would start going out with one of her suitors, and before long she begins to have affection for her new boyfriend, and he is there to satisfy her romantic needs, whatever they might be. Her old boyfriend is far away, will be for a long time, and he won't be able to do her any good for a long time. Two or 3 years is a long, long time for a young person, and most of them aren't going to wait that long for anybody. Thus, the pretty young girl writes a "Dear John" letter to her old far-away boyfriend.

The young sailors usually didn't tell anybody when they received this "Dear John" letter, but you could look at their face and eyes and tell when they did. They always looked wild-eyed, maybe like a trapped animal would, and you could tell they were hurting, bad. They also sometimes had a dazed look on their face. They would never mention their girlfriend to you again either. It was an awful emotional experience for those poor fellows, and it would probably affect them the rest of their lives whether they were aware of it or not. But romantic hurts will usually heal over time and these young sailors would someday find someone else to love, marry, and live happily ever after with. In a quiet moment, though, he might sometimes think about what "might have been" with him and his first love.

There is one angle to this love thing that I've sometimes wondered about, and that is, soldiers and marines that exhibit extraordinary bravery in the thick of battle. They don't seem to care whether they live or die. The question that comes to my mind is, did these men get a "Dear John" letter just before going into combat or had they been severely hurt by a special female friend some time in their past from which they had never recovered? A soldier that doesn't have anything to live for, in their mind, is much more likely to take risks than someone who thinks he's got a lot to live for. The love of a woman, and for a woman, and maybe children, too, makes a fellow much more reluctant to risk his life. He is not interested in dying and being a dead hero. He wants to live and spend his life with the woman he loves.

Personally, I can truthfully say that I never had to go through the agony of getting a "Dear John" letter. I just never got a letter.

In my opinion, it is far better for a young fellow to not have any strong romantic attachment to anyone when he goes into military service, or anything else where he has no control over his life and maybe is to be gone for a long time. It is much easier to get through that period of his life if there isn't anyone back home for him to think about or long to be with.

If a fellow does have a very special girlfriend at this time in his life, one he really, really wants and can't live without her – he thinks; then, my advice is to just go ahead and marry her, if that is at all possible, so that he can have her for a short time, at least. She might not be there for him when he gets back home, but at least he had her for a short time. I believe that having her for a short time would be better than never having her at all. That is my opinion on the subject anyway.

Finally, Saturday afternoon, 10 September, TG 70.4 secured from the ASW exercises, and the destroyers were detached from the carrier to proceed independently to Yokosuka, Japan. DesDiv 92 formed up into a column formation, as did the other American destroyer division and the 3 British destroyers. The columns of ships were 1000 yards apart. The ships of DesDiv 92 were the middle column. All the ships were steaming along together in 3 columns at 15 knots. It must have been a pretty sight from the air if anybody happened to be watching. Then at 0435 Sunday morning the 11 destroyers changed into a single column formation to enter Tokyo Bay and Yokosuka Harbor. The Brush was bringing up the rear in station #10. At 0540 the ship set the special sea detail to enter Yokosuka Harbor. At 0640 we were moored to pier 10 at the Yokosuka Naval Shipyard.

## YOKOSUKA – SEPTEMBER 1955

At 0800 one of our crewmembers was transferred to Fleet Activities, Yokosuka, Japan to be confined at hard labor for 3 months. This fellow was a radarman and was a good, likeable fellow most of the time, but he just couldn't seem to stay out of trouble. He had a bad drinking problem and he got in trouble this time for bringing liquor on board and being drunk on duty. I never saw him again because I was gone before he got back to the ship – hopefully a changed man. I believe he was from the great state of Florida, too. In a letter to my mother dated September 11, 1955, I wrote a little about our arrival in Yokosuka.

"We arrived in Yokosuka early this morning. Everybody seemed to be glad to hit port once again. I volunteered for duty today but intend to go ashore early tomorrow. We're to stay here 2 days and then go up to Sasebo for 19 days, or until the 4th of October…. As you can imagine, the crew is pretty liberty happy after being at sea for 7 weeks without hardly any shore leave at all, and a good deal of that time being under a strenuous operational schedule."

## An Aborted Sleep-In

I went ashore in Yokosuka sometime on Monday, 12 September, I don't remember exactly what I did on liberty, but there was an interesting thing that happened rather late Monday night. I ran into one of my English friends from the Cockade during the early part of the evening. He was roaming around Yokosuka by himself, too, just like I was, so we palled around together for awhile, shopping around and looking at stuff, as I remember. And it seemed like we could always find something interesting to talk about. This fellow's name was Leslie Briggs, petty officer. But rather late in the evening he informed me that he would like to spend the night aboard an American ship, my ship to be specific, and he wanted to know if I thought I could arrange for him to do that. I told him that I thought I could if that is what he wanted to do. He thought he did. Okay. So rather late in the evening we walked back to the Brush that was moored at pier 10 at the naval base. I knew we had some empty racks in the O division compartment, so finding him a rack to sleep in wouldn't be a problem. I checked in with the OOD at the quarterdeck and told him what we wanted to do – the British sailor wanted to spend the night aboard the Brush. The OOD didn't have a problem with the idea, so I led the British sailor down to the O division's sleeping compartment. My English friend seemed to be real excited about the prospect of spending the night aboard my ship. We got to the mess deck; I went down the ladder into the sleeping compartment, and I intended to lead him down the ladder into the compartment. However, he only came about halfway down the ladder. He looked around inside the compartment – where I had slept for the past 3 years. He didn't say anything for a little while. I stood at the bottom of the ladder and waited for him to come on down. Finally, he said, "Jesus Christ, how do you stand it?" I'll always remember those words. I didn't get insulted or defensive because I knew exactly what he meant and why he felt that way. I knew because I had been aboard his ship and saw how he lived, and he knew at that moment that his living accommodations on the Cockade were far superior to ours, and, in fact, even far superior to that of our officers. I found it very interesting that he would not even spend one night in a place that I had slept in for 3 years. Yes, there was a vast difference between the way he lived on his ship and the way we lived on ours.

Whoever designed those U.S. World War II destroyers didn't have the comfort and welfare of the crew in mind when they designed them. Maybe the designers thought the sailors wouldn't be living on them long enough that it would matter much. There was a bunch of them that got sunk during WWII. But the war ended and American sailors had to live on them for 3, 4, and 5 years sometimes. Actually, it was a very unpleasant existence in relation to modern living. Consequently, there was very little re-enlisting taking place on those ships. And, as a result, the navy lost a tremendous number of highly trained and experienced petty officers.

Anyway, my English sailor friend never reached the bottom of the ladder. After he made his profound statement about, "How do you stand it?" he then said, "I don't want to spend the night here," and he went back up the ladder and seemed anxious to leave the ship; so I walked him back to the gangplank and the pier. He seemed to be in a state of shock about how we had to live. We talked briefly on the pier, and I'm sure I must have apologized to him for not having better sleeping accommodations to offer. After our brief chat at the gangplank, he walked on down the pier. I stood on the pier at the gangplank and watched him disappear into the night. I never saw him again, mainly, because I soon left the navy and our paths never had a chance to cross again. Although, we did exchange letters a few times over the next few months. But I soon got involved in going to college and neglected my letter writing. And I suppose that in effect ended that friendship. I still have fond memories of our relatively brief association together, though, after 50 something years. He was a good, likeable fellow. I've always regretted that we never had a chance to associate again.

## EN ROUTE SASEBO

At 0700, Tuesday, 13 September, the ship commenced making preparations for getting underway. The Brush was underway from alongside pier 10 at 0835 and commenced maneuvering at various courses and speeds to depart Yokosuka Harbor. At 0835 we passed through the outer breakwater and soon thereafter secured the special sea detail. We were now steaming down Tokyo Bay with Mount Fuji in plain view. What a beautiful sight.

### Mount Fuji

When the ship was steaming down Tokyo Bay, we always got a good view of Mount Fuji if the weather was clear at all. It is a magnificent mountain. According to my recollection, we got our best observations of it when we were steaming out of the bay on a clear morning when there weren't any clouds yet. The mountain totally dominated the countryside and always had snow covering its peak and for some distance down its side. On these clear mornings the mountain was so beautiful you could hardly take your eyes off of it. It is easy to understand why the Japanese people hold it in such high esteem and sacred.

Nearly 30 years after my first glimpse of it, I had the pleasure of traveling to the top of Mount Fuji, at least as far as a vehicle can take you. I wasn't quite at the peak, but I was fairly close and was in a lot of snow. This was in April 1982.

Below the snow line, the sides of Mount Fuji are covered in large, ancient trees of the hemlock type, it appeared to me. However, lots of them are now dying just like the same type of trees are in the Smoky Mountains in the United States. Nobody seems to know why they are dying in either place. However, personally, I believe it is caused by too much gasoline fumes for some reason, or too much of something in the gas fumes. Because, as I understand it, the trees on Mount Fuji started dying a few years after the road was built up the side of the mountain to near the peak. Now thousands of cars travel up to the top of Mount Fuji every year and they put out a lot of fumes. Just a theory.

At 1030 the ships of DesDiv 92 departed Tokyo Bay and set a course for Sasebo. Upon departing the bay, the ships went into a column formation. The ships steamed all afternoon and most of the night without doing anything else. I imagine the seas were too rough to conduct any training exercises or division tactics, otherwise, they would have.

## A Rouge Wave

One night during this trip to Sasebo, I decided I would attend the nightly movie that was being shown on the fantail. I don't remember why I made the decision to do that, because it had been a long time since I had watched one, and I knew it was going to be one that I had already seen several times before. Anyway, I went.

Everybody had to take their own chair, or whatever, to the movies to sit on. I got one from the charthouse and took it back to the fantail. All the choice spaces in front of the screen were taken by the time I got there, but I found a space right up against the stanchion on the port side. The ocean was a little on the rough side that night but not too bad, otherwise, they would have shown the movie in the mess deck. The wind wasn't too bad either on the fantail because we were largely steaming with the wind and not into it. The waves were coming from the starboard quarter. Everybody was ready to see the movie and be entertained. The movie flicked on and who would it be but Theresa Brewer one more time. The sailors started going through their usual routine of whooping and hollering, whistling, stomping their feet, etc., just like she was on stage in person and it was the first time that they had ever seen her. But then, all of sudden, by complete surprise, a wave came aboard and totally engulfed the fantail to a depth of about waist high to the men seated in their chairs. At the same time, all the chairs were washed over, en masse, to the port side and piled up against the port stanchion and me. The whole incident happened so suddenly, and so unexpectedly, and shocked everybody so completely that we weren't sure what our fate was going to be for a few seconds.

When the wave washed over us, the whooping, hollering, and whistling abruptly stopped, and the voices suddenly changed to that of panic with a few curses and obscenities thrown in. A few men, that could, jumped up, highly confused, and exclaimed a few choice words. However, after 4 or 5 seconds the water drained away and the sailors realized that they weren't going to be washed overboard to drown in the dark after all. Now, some of them started laughing hysterically. I confess it was a huge relief to know that I wasn't going to be washed overboard in the dark of night. Although I didn't make a sound, I was greatly concerned about my safety those few seconds, and I was also thankful that the rope stanchion that I was pressed up against didn't break.

Anyway, everything got settled back down after a few minutes and the movie was started over. The sailors just sat there in their wet clothes and watched the movie without saying much. They seemed to be totally subdued with all the play and horsing around taken out of them. It must have been a warm night for us to have been able to endure those wet clothes while watching that movie one more time.

## SASEBO – SEPTEMBER 1955

The ships of DesDiv 92 arrived at Sasebo early Thursday morning, 15 September. At 0720 the Brush was moored alongside the USS Piedmont (AD17) at buoy 1. The Moore moored alongside to port and the Maddox moored alongside the Moore. We would stay in port for 19 days, or until 4 October.

At 1600 another one of our seamen left the ship in protective custody for transfer to the U.S. Naval FLTACTs Brig pursuant to CO USS Brush(DD745) orders, dated 15 September, 1955. He wouldn't behave.

I know I went on liberty a lot in Sasebo, but I don't remember too many of the specifics. I know I did a considerable amount of shopping because I was now a short-timer for sure. I know I shipped home most of what I bought, because I wouldn't be able to carry much around with me as I was in the process of being released from the navy.

At 1240 Friday, 16 September, the ship commenced taking on provisions and took on 12 tons during the next hour and a half.

At 0915 Saturday, 17 September, there was a captain's inspection of personnel and the upper decks. Also, Saturday afternoon at 1700 a harbor pilot came aboard and with the help of a couple of tugs moved the ship from alongside the tender to a position outboard of the nest. At 1745 the Brush was moored to the port side of the Maddox and the pilot left the ship. There is an advantage to being the outboard ship in a nest, because the outboard ship is the ship that sailors leave to go on liberty and return to coming back from liberty. The sailors from the other ships in the nest have to cross over to the outboard ship to go on liberty.

However, we weren't the outboard ship for long, because during the night or early morning the next day, a destroyer escort, the USS Wiseman(DE667), came alongside our port side and she then became the outboard ship. So, the sailors going on liberty had to catch the liberty boats on the outboard ship; thus, the sailors on the Brush and other destroyers on the port side of the tender had to cross over to the Wiseman to go on liberty, which created a little incident in my case. None of us on the bridge had ever seen or heard of the Wiseman before, but we were in a good position on the bridge to observe what went on on the Wiseman, especially in regards to the treatment of the enlisted men by the officers. We noticed that the enlisted men on the ship were treated by the officers about like you would expect new recruits in a marine boot camp to be treated. We could see that the enlisted men had a bad deal on the Wiseman. For instance, when an enlisted man had to speak to an officer about something, he would have to come to attention, and maybe salute, too, although I'm not sure about that now. The junior officers on the ship were lording it over the enlisted men like you can't imagine. This particular ship was the only time in the navy that I ever witnessed anything like this. I bet their re-enlistment rate was very low. We felt sorry for those guys because we could tell that the officers seemed to take great pleasure in making life miserable for those poor fellows. And this was a DE of all things.

However, I'm sure the attitude of the officers was simply a reflection of that of the captain's. Otherwise, he wouldn't have allowed his officers to treat his men the way they did. I don't know who the captain of the Wiseman was, and I never saw him, but I know, whoever he was, that he would probably fit into the category of a JERK and most of his officers, too, from what I saw. That is just my opinion, of course, but based on my observation of what I saw going on on the Wiseman.

**A Nest of Ships in Sasebo Harbor**
**(U.S. Navy Photograph – NARA)**

## My Confrontation with an OOD

I decided to go on liberty Monday evening just before dark. I crossed the gangplank connecting the two ships. It was after sunset and the colors on the fantail had been taken down as is the normal practice on navy ships that are in port. Consequently, I saluted the quarterdeck as I crossed over to the Wiseman, but I didn't salute in the direction of the fantail because the flag wasn't flying. It had already been taken down. In all my 3 years of sea duty, I had never seen anybody salute the fantail after sunset and I didn't either on this particular evening.

Anyway, this young ensign with shiny gold bars, the OOD, I believe, came dashing up to me and wanted to know why I didn't salute the flag on the fantail when coming aboard his ship, or words to that effect. In his mind, he had caught someone breaking a serious rule of some kind, and this was a big deal with him – I could tell. I noticed he was also checking over my uniform real close and made a comment to the effect that I had been around long enough that I should know the proper things to do concerning navy rules and regulations. He could easily tell that I was a navy veteran with lots of experience. And if the truth was known, he probably was envious of my navy service and experience as revealed by my uniform –rate, hash mark, and ribbons.

I explained to him that navy personnel normally don't salute the fantail in the evening after the colors (flag) have been taken down. He informed me that they did on his ship and that I needed to do the same thing. As I remember, he also said something about the fact that they did everything on his ship properly and exactly according to navy regulations. He probably said some other things, too, but I can't remember them all now. In spite of his efforts, he didn't put any fear into me in the least. I had been beaten up pretty bad by this time in my naval career and was as hard as nails, just didn't care, and was a short-timer besides.

I looked him in the eye and told him that we had been looking over at his ship all day and had been observing all the things that had been going on on his ship, and we had come to the conclusion that this ship (his ship) was the most chicken shit ship that we had ever seen. I think that was an insult. He looked stunned at hearing that remark about his beloved ship and didn't seem to know quite what to say in response to it. However, somebody came to his rescue and maybe mine, too. Another young ensign came up to him and needed to talk to him about something that seemed to be urgent. So he turned his back to me to some extent and commenced to talk to this other officer. I stood there in my tracks for a few seconds waiting for him to turn back around and devote his attention back to me and our situation. However, after a few seconds I distinctly sensed that he would rather that I just go on, because he didn't quite know what to say to me or how to handle me. I didn't respond the same way as the men did on his ship. So I decided not to press my luck and walked off. I caught a liberty boat and went on the beach.

I have always been proud of myself for having the presence of mind to make that remark to that officer because somebody on that ship needed to hear it. We stayed alongside the Wiseman for several days, and I crossed over her several times to catch a liberty boat, but I never saw that officer again. I hope he thought about what I told him and changed his ways.

## My Trip to Nagasaki

The navy got a little more generous with its liberty hours this cruise in 1955, because sometimes we were allowed to stay ashore over the weekend. Although, I only remember taking advantage of that perk one time, and that was the time that we stayed in Sasebo for 19 days near the end of my enlistment in the navy. I spent a Saturday night and Sunday in Nagasaki. In a letter to my mother dated September 19, 1955, I wrote about my trip to Nagasaki.

"Saturday afternoon, having liberty over the weekend, I caught a train to Nagasaki, which is about 40 miles south of Sasebo. Nagasaki, if you remember, is one of the cities where an atomic bomb was dropped. I got into Nagasaki about 9:30 p.m. and checked in at a very nice western style hotel. And then, not having supper yet, I had the desk clerk at the hotel call me a cab and direct the driver to take me to a restaurant. So the taxi took me to a small but very nice and clean place. I believe it was the only restaurant in the city that served western food as well as Japanese. The structure of the building and interior looked more French than Japanese. In fact, I believe it used to belong to a European of some kind. For supper, I had a very tasty steak. These Japanese sure know how to cook a steak. You can always depend on them being good. I sat around in the restaurant for a little while just to watch the world go by. Then, I walked the streets a little bit to see what I could see and then went back to the hotel and went to bed.

Sunday morning I went to the train station to meet a shipmate that was supposed to have met me there, but he didn't show up. As I was standing around the station thinking about how I was going to be able to see the sights of Nagasaki, a young Japanese man who looked to be about 20 years old came over and started talking to me. He could speak English a little bit, and by using sign language and what little Japanese I knew, we managed to carry on a conversation. To make a long story short, we stayed together most of the day. He was from up close to Tokyo, was a tourist himself, and was down in Nagasaki sight-seeing. We went on a three hour bus tour and saw, I guess, everything there was to see including the site where the atomic bomb exploded. We also saw temples, various buildings and monuments of one kind and another – all very educational.

There is not much sign left of the atomic blast. Grass is as green as it ever was and all the buildings have been rebuilt. Although, the people in Japan may never forget it or forgive America for doing it. The people in other places in Japan I've been were reasonably friendly considering the situation but not so much in Nagasaki. They don't seem to like Americans so much, particularly the men. The women, though, seem to be friendlier, and the little kids thought I was quite an attraction. Sometimes they just gathered up around me staring in wonderment. And the little girls stood staring and giggling all the time they were gathered around me. My Japanese friend told me that they did that because they thought that I was good-looking, but I don't know about that."

I didn't mention it in my letter, but I remember going to an atomic bomb museum where I saw many pictures that showed the results of the blast including pictures of some of the victims.

I certainly enjoyed my excursion to Nagasaki. It was a very educational trip and certainly one of the highlights of my naval experience. But I don't know how I would have managed to get around and see things if the Japanese fellow hadn't of shown up. Maybe he was sent by God to take me in tow and to keep me out of trouble in that unfamiliar, foreign city. As I remember, it wasn't the friendliest place I visited in Japan. And I didn't see any other Americans all day of any kind – in uniform or out. Anyway, the Japanese fellow and I had a good time together seeing the sights of Nagasaki. He wanted to practice his English on me and I helped him all I could in that respect. However, late in the day I bid him farewell and never saw or heard of him again. He seemed to be a very likeable and friendly fellow. And he didn't seem to have any hard feelings toward Americans.

The 19 days that we spent in Sasebo were mainly for rest and recreation, and that is what the sailors engaged in as much as possible and as much as their money would allow them to. I know I spent all the time I could ashore entertaining myself and did a pretty good job of it, I think. Otherwise, nothing much else happened except for a typhoon that passed over us.

## Typhoon Louise

At 1700 Monday, 26 September, the ship set typhoon condition 3. Typhoon Louise seemed to be headed in the general direction of Sasebo.

At 1815 Tuesday, 27 September, the ship set typhoon condition 2 and commenced securing the ship for heavy weather. At 1830 the ship commenced making preparations for getting underway. At 2015 the Wiseman(DE667) got underway from our port side. At 2100 the ship set the special sea detail. At 2130 the OOD shifted his watch to the bridge. At 2148 we were underway from the port side of the Maddox, and we were being assisted by a tug to move us to another buoy. At 2247 the Brush was moored to buoy 18 in the harbor. At 2250 the ship secured the special sea detail and the OOD shifted his watch back to the quarterdeck. The engineering plant was put on a 4 hour notice. The ship was getting ready for the storm that would soon be over us.

At 1800 Thursday, 30 September, the ship set typhoon condition 1. At 1810 the ship observed sunset and turned on the anchor lights. At 1850 the ship veered the port anchor chain to 60 fathoms. At 1910 the ship set the underway steaming watch and set an anchor watch on the forecastle. I remember having the 2000 to 2400 watch and it was quite windy at that time but not terribly so. Captain Whitehurst was on the bridge and stayed on it all night. At 2322 fires were lighted under #2 boiler. At 2339 the engine room was instructed to stand-by to answer bells.

I was relieved of the watch at midnight, went below, and hit my rack. I didn't worry about a thing all night. There were plenty of people on the bridge to handle things, so I figured I would let them do just that and they did.

The captain's main concern was the ship drifting or an anchor chain breaking, I believe, and he tried to see to it that not too much strain would be put on the anchor chain. And when the wind got to blowing real hard, he would kick the ship in gear just a little and relieve the strain. He must have done a good job because we survived the night intact. However, at 0145, at the height of the storm, the anchor chain did break away from the stopper and was riding on the winch, but someone in the deck force quickly replaced the stopper and all was well again. The ship was fully manned all night and the ship could have gotten underway at a second's notice, but that never became necessary. I think the eye of the storm passed about 30 miles away from us. According to what I heard, the winds in Sasebo were blowing at 70 to 75 m.p.h. The storm was bad enough but it could have been much worse. The weather conditions began to improve the next morning, and at 1350 the ship secured all typhoon conditions of readiness. During the early afternoon of Friday, 30 September, tugs moved the Brush back to buoy 1 where she tied up to the Moore and the Moore was tied up to the Piedmont(AD17).

## A Dangerous Prank

One of the favorite pastimes for a few of my younger shipmates in the Operations Department sleeping compartment was to bring back young, drunk, passed-out shipmates to the ship and let them fall down the ladder into the compartment – thump, thump, thumping all the way down.

Sometimes you would see a couple of drunk, young sailors at the fleet landing late at night waiting for a launch to take them back out to the ship. They would have a drunk, passed-out buddy that they were taking back to the ship. They were taking care of this drunken buddy, you know. And he would be lying on the ground in the mud while they were waiting on the liberty launch, usually an old WWII landing craft. This young 18 or 19 year old buddy had probably only had 2 or 3 beers to get him in that condition. It wasn't necessarily that he had consumed that much, but it was that his young, inexperienced body just couldn't tolerate that much alcohol. Of course, the new men had a tendency to try and keep up with the older guys to prove that they were a real man and a big drinker besides. Many times, I'm sure, the older guys planned to get the younger shipmate drunk when they took him on liberty with them. They thought that that would be very amusing.

Anyway, the liberty launch would finally arrive, and the lesser drunk sailors would gather up their passed-out buddy and lay him in the bottom of the launch for the ride out to the ship. When the launch arrived at the ship, the drunken sailors would have to pull him up a ladder that was hanging over the side of the ship to get him up to the main deck. It was about all they could do to accomplish that feat for themselves in the condition that they were in, but they always managed to get their passed-out buddy on the deck, too. If they had dropped him, he would have undoubtedly drowned. Luckily, a poor mother somewhere didn't know what was taking place with her son at that moment. If she had known, I'm sure she would have had an anxiety attack.

So, with a lot of struggle and effort the 2 drunken sailors would get their buddy up to the main deck. Then they would gather him up again, put him between them, and half carry and half drag him to the sleeping compartment below the mess deck. When they got him to the head of the ladder going down into the compartment, they would stand him up as best they could and let him fall head first down the ladder. He would go thumping all the way down the ladder. Of course, watching him bounce down the ladder was awfully funny and the big laugh was the real reason for all the effort they expended to get him back. Of course, the passed-out fellow didn't feel a thing. Although, they were fortunate they didn't get their necks broke it seemed to me. I'm sure the poor fellow had a lot of bruises all over his body and probably wondered how they got there. These pranks always occurred overseas because this is the only place these young guys could drink alcohol. A person had to be 21 years old to drink in the States, but a 17 year old could drink overseas. Over there, if a person was strong enough to lift a beer bottle and get it up to his mouth, he was old enough to drink. That was the test to see if they were old enough to drink over there.

Saturday, 1 October, one of our shipmates left the Brush to return to the United States. He was under orders to report to the CO, U.S. Naval Retraining Command, Camp Elliot, San Diego, California, for confinement as imposed by a special court martial. Apparently, he couldn't adjust to life on a destroyer.

At 0956 Sunday morning, 2 October, the USS Philippine Sea stood into the harbor.

At 2145 Monday evening, 3 October, typhoon condition 1 was set and the ship set a modified steaming watch to get underway at a moment's notice if necessary. A heavy weather plan was put into effect. However, I was ashore and wasn't aware of all the precautions being taken about a storm. The Brush secured from typhoon condition 1 at 0642 Tuesday morning.

## I Spend the Night Aboard a Carrier

Late Monday night, 3 October, I caught a liberty launch at Fleet Landing to take me back out to the ship in the harbor. Actually, the liberty launch was an old World War II landing craft. A dozen or so other sailors got on the launch, too, to return to their ships way out in the harbor. However, after getting on the craft, we were informed that none of us were going to be taken out to our ships, because the water was too rough for the launch to go out to where the ships were moored. Instead, all of us were going to be taken to the Philippine Sea that was docked in the harbor, and there is where we would be spending the night. So we were taken to the carrier and all of us went aboard her. I was the only one in the group from the Brush.

A chief petty officer took charge of us as we came aboard her. I suppose we gave somebody our names and what ship we were from so that they would have a record of it. Otherwise, we might all be considered AWOL. Anyway, the chief led us to the mess deck, or one of them, whichever, and issued us a plastic poncho to sleep on – on the deck. I suppose there were dozens, maybe hundreds, of sailors that had to spend the night this way, because they couldn't get out to their ships and the navy had to do something with them. Anyway, this is where some of us were going to spend the night.

I decided I better go to the head to relieve myself like most people do before going to bed. But I didn't have a clue where one was located on that big ship. So I approached the CPO and asked him for directions to the nearest head. He told me. He told me to go this way for awhile and down that ladder and down that passageway for awhile. I followed his directions and found it, but it kind of taxed my brain trying to remember all he said.

Anyway, I walked into the head and it was a big head compared to the size of those on destroyers. I didn't think anybody else was in the head when I walked in it. To my left I spotted the urinals up against the bulkhead at one end of the head – a whole row of them. I had a big choice of urinals, but I chose one of them, walked over to it, and commenced preparing to perform the task that I had come there to do. However, I noticed something out of the corner of my eye (peripheral vision I believe they call it) down at the other end of the head, 25 feet or so away. I instinctively looked down that way and unconsciously my mouth dropped open and my hair felt like it stood straight up on my head. What I saw was far more than my innocent country boy eyes and backward way of thinking was accustomed to seeing. Two big, burly sailors were busy making out. I only looked at them at a glance and felt like I had intruded in on something that I wasn't supposed to see. I looked back at the urinal and started concentrating on what I came to do. I finished up my purpose for coming there and prepared to retreat out of the head. However, on the way out of the head, I glanced back at them for another second or so and noticed that one of them seemed to be the aggressor; the other one was backed up against the door of a stall and seemed to be the passive one. The passive one's eyes were glazed over like he was three-fourths drunk or in the throes of ecstasy; I couldn't be sure which it was. Or maybe he was doped up – I'm not sure. Anyway, they hadn't got around to the hard stuff yet, but I could see that the aggressor one was working toward that climactic end as fast as he could. Of course, I didn't hang around to witness the final act because that was more than I wanted to see. I hurriedly got out of that den of iniquity. I don't believe the aggressor one ever knew that I was in the head because he was so focused on what he was doing and the passive one was out of it already.

I found my way back up to the mess deck, spread out my poncho, and laid down on that hard metal deck. I slept very little that night. Besides, it was going to be a short night. Someone came around and got us all up around 0500 in the morning, because the cooks and mess cooks had to get the mess deck ready for breakfast. The ship fed us a big breakfast when they got it ready, but I can't remember what they served us. But I remember that we could have all we wanted, but one serving was all I wanted because it was a big serving.

The worst of the windy weather passed over during the night, and all the stranded sailors were able to return to their ships early the next morning. Thus ended my experience on the carrier, although, I've always remembered that night.

Apparently, there were a few men in the navy even way back then that possessed an unconventional sexual persuasion. However, none were ever aboard the Brush that I was aware of. At least, they never came out of the closet. And it was probably a good thing for them that they didn't because most sailors weren't very tolerant of such behavior back then.

At 1116 Tuesday, 4 October, ComDesDiv 92 broke his flag aboard the Brush. Late in the day, at 2002, the special sea detail was set and the ship commenced to making preparations for getting underway. At 2037 the ship got underway and proceeded out of the harbor. The ships of DesDiv 92 were en route to operating area "Fox" off the coast of Kyushu. The ships operated in area Fox Wednesday and Thursday conducting division tactics most of the time, but the ships also conducted some gunnery practice on Thursday morning. There is no record of what the Brush was firing at, but she expended 78 rounds of 5″/38 shells during the practice. The ships of DesDiv 92 returned to Sasebo early Friday morning, 7 October, and moored to buoy 2 in the harbor. ComDesDiv 92 shifted his flag back to the Maddox. However, we only stayed in port one day.

## TASK FORCE 77

Early Saturday morning, 8 October, DesDiv 92 departed Sasebo Harbor en route to the Okinawa operating area. This was the last time that I would ever steer a ship out of port. My time as the special sea detail helmsman was about over. Although, I would still steer the ship alongside other ships a few times during the next two weeks off Okinawa and Formosa. The ships conducted division tactics most of the day as they steamed toward Okinawa. DesDiv 92 rendezvoused with the Philippine Sea late in the day – around 1730. We would be operating with her most of the time over the next two weeks.

Sunday, 9 October, was a rather stormy day and we were steaming through heavy seas. The ships didn't conduct any division tactics during the day, but the ships did conduct some gunnery practice during the afternoon during which the Brush fired her 3″ guns at a drone.

So, DesDiv 92 and the Philippine Sea steamed around in the Okinawa operating area while the carrier conducted flight operations from time to time. Of course, the destroyers formed a screen around the carrier most of the time, but when she conducted flight operations, one of the destroyers would assume plane guard station behind the carrier. Sometime during the day Thursday, 13 October, the carrier, USS Boxer(CVA21), arrived on the scene and now we were given the designation Task Force 77.

Friday morning, 14 October, the carriers conducted flight operations but didn't launch any more for the rest of the day. We just steamed around in the operating area.

Saturday, 15 October, the carriers didn't launch any planes at all. But the ships did take on fuel from the tanker, Cimarron, during the morning part of the day. And sometime during the day, Task Force 77 headed in a generally southwest direction to rendezvous with the carrier, USS Hornet(CVA12), off the southwest coast of Formosa. We rendezvoused with the Hornet sometime Sunday, but there is no record of exactly when it was. The carriers conducted flight operations off and on during the day and into the evening hours. Task Force 77 was engaged in the same kind of activities all the following week from Monday, 17 October, to Sunday, 23 October. The ships operated off the east coast of Formosa most of the week, but during the latter part of the week the ships drifted back up to the Okinawa operating area, which was actually west of Okinawa. The ships also refueled from a tanker every 2 or 3 days.

Sometime Monday, 18 October, Destroyer Divisions 52 and 71 joined the task force, and also the cruisers, USS Bremerton(CA30), the USS St. Paul(CA73), and the USS Manchester(CL83). Now there were 3 carriers, 3 cruisers, and 12 destroyers in Task Force 77. With all the ships present and all the operations going on, it was a rather busy time for the signalmen.

Sometime Friday, 21 October, DesDiv 72 joined the task force. Now there were 16 destroyers in the T.F.

## My Sudden Departure From the Brush

Around 1100 Sunday morning, 23 October, 1955, word was passed over the P.A. system for, "All hands that are scheduled to be transferred off the ship, 27 October, in Nagoya, to lay down to the main deck in 30 minutes for transfer over to the John A. Bole." I knew that included me and I will never forget those words. That announcement created quite a commotion on the ship and made the men involved to really do some hustling about to get ready to leave the ship on such short notice.

I was on the signal bridge that morning when the announcement was made but not on watch. I immediately dashed down to the compartment, and my locker, and started packing my seabag. I had to leave some of my clothes behind because they were in the laundry bag, but I'm sure somebody my size claimed them and started using them; that was the usual practice after someone left.

After packing my seabag, I went down to the officer's quarters for just a minute to see Lt(jg) L.G. Cates one last time. Enlisted men normally don't spend too much time around officer's quarters. I told him that I was leaving the ship right then, and I had come by to tell him goodbye, and that it was a pleasure serving with him. Mr. Cates was one of the conning officers by this time in his naval career, and we stood a lot of steaming watches together. He was a good man, a good officer, and I liked him. I also felt like it was kind of a mutual feeling, and that is why I went to the trouble to tell him goodbye. He shook my hand even though I was an enlisted man and that is not normally done. However, we both knew that I was soon going to be a civilian and that would make us equal as human beings. He would always be Mr. Cates to me, though. However, I never saw him again or have ever heard anything about him since.

I hurried on down to the main deck to the place where the transfer was to take place, which was directly beneath the bridge and superstructure. Unfortunately, I never had time to go back up to the bridge to tell Chief Emerson, Tommy, and the rest of the quartermasters goodbye. I've always regretted that I didn't have time to do that.

The sailors, with their seabags, gathered on the main deck at the transfer site. We were being sent over to the Bole by highline sitting in a boatswain's chair. It developed that there were 11 of us that was going to be leaving the ship. I imagine the personnel men had a hectic time getting all of the paperwork ready in that short of time, too.

In a letter to my mother dated, 27 October, 1955, I wrote about my sudden departure from the Brush. "….I ran down to my locker and started throwing stuff in my seabag and was ready to go in 30 minutes. A few minutes later they started sending us and our gear across to the Bole by highline. It all took place before any of us could hardly realize it. The whole ship (crew), I think, was lining the rail to see us off. It kind of got them excited to see so many of their long-time shipmates leaving so fast."

The transfer of the men and their seabags was completed at 1107. Upon completion of the transfer, the Brush pulled away from the Bole and went her own way. The sailors from the Brush stood on the deck of the Bole for a minute or two and watched the Brush steam away from them. The sight of her steaming away from us probably made all of us have a strange feeling. Then, the word was passed over the P.A. system for the men from the Brush to lay down to the mess deck. So the sailors turned around as a group and started filing through a nearby hatch into the interior of the ship, and then, on down to the mess deck. I was the last one to go through the hatch. When I got half-way through the hatch, I turned my head to take one last look at the Brush. She was probably 3000 yards or so away from us by this time and was going away from us at an angle but with her port side fully exposed to me. My last glimpse of the Brush will be forever imprinted in my mind. The Brush had been a big part of my young life, for over 3 years, and now she was suddenly going out of my life forever. I never saw her again. I went on through the hatch and down to the mess deck.

We were guests on the Bole, in a sense, and an officer met us in the mess deck to inform us about where we would sleep and what was expected of us in general. We were also informed that the Bole and the other ships of DesRon 7 would soon be departing the task force for Japan. The Bole would stay in Yokosuka for a couple of days and then depart for the United States. However, upon arrival in Yokosuka, the sailors from the Brush would be transferred to the Yokosuka Naval Station. The naval station would then arrange for transportation to get us back to the United States – by some kind of military plane, I imagine.

I never did understand why it was so necessary for us to be transferred over to the Bole in such a hurry, because the Bole didn't depart from the task force until the middle of the next day. Apparently, the Brush was away from most of the task force during this time because she wasn't operating with us. However, according to the logs, the Brush returned to the main body of the task force just as DesRon 7 was leaving it, but I never saw her.

## HOMEWARD BOUND ABOARD THE JOHN A. BOLE

The ships of DesRon 7 were detached from the task force around noon, 24 October, to proceed to Japan. It would take approximately 2 days for the ships to arrive in Yokosuka. However, a short time after we left the TF, a Bole officer met with the Brush sailors again. He informed us that the Bole was way short of men, and they would like for us, or anyone of us that would, to ride back to the States with them as part of the crew. We had to make up our minds whether we wanted to do that or not before the ship arrived in Yokosuka. So, we had a day or so to think about it.

Naturally, I hung around the bridge area a lot because that was what I was accustomed to doing, and the signalmen were the ones that I could best relate to. I noticed that the Bole only had one quartermaster petty officer, a 3rd class by the name of Ken Binkley, as I remember. I don't remember seeing a chief QM either; surely they had one. Anyway, I can't imagine how the navy would allow a ship to get so short of petty officers. I easily saw their plight, felt sorry for the bridge gang, and agreed to ride back to the States with them as part of the crew, and, of course, stand signal watches. I really didn't want to do it because I wanted to be home for Thanksgiving, but I did it anyway and missed out on being home for Thanksgiving. But, I suppose in the whole scheme of life, it didn't make that much difference anyway, because I have had a lot of Thanksgivings at home since then. So, I became part of the Bole's crew for approximately 3 weeks – that is, until we arrived in San Diego, the home port of DesRon 7. The most interesting thing about my decision to stay with the Bole for 3 weeks is that I was the only one out of the 11 Brush sailors that agreed to stay with them. They didn't have to stay and they didn't. Apparently, they were all anxious to leave the navy and get home; they had had enough.

DesRon 7 arrived in Yokosuka around 1630 Wednesday afternoon, 25 October, and the Bole moored to buoy D-4 alongside the Lofberg(DD759) at 1657. We would only stay in Yokosuka for 1 day and 2 nights. Upon arriving in port, all my old shipmates left the ship.

### Haggling for a Music Box

I imagine I went on liberty both evenings that we were in Yokosuka, but I only remember some things that I did on my last evening there. For one thing, I had a most enjoyable, chance encounter with an old friend, my old Aussie friend, Chief Geoff H. Judd. I mainly went ashore that evening to buy a beautiful music box that I had previously seen. I was on my way to buy it when I ran into Chief Judd. I told him that I was on my way to a little shop to buy a music box, and that I was on my way back to the States to be released from active duty. Chief Judd wanted to go with me to the shop and help me buy the music box. Of course, I welcomed his help because I knew there was going to be some haggling involved over the price of the box and I wasn't that good at that sort of thing.

We got to the little shop and I picked out the music box that I wanted. It had an asking price on it that I would have paid if I had had to, but here is where the chief came to the forefront and took over the haggling on my behalf. It was unreal to me how he was able to take over the price negotiations.

Apparently, he had a lot of experience doing that sort of thing. The shop-keeper didn't have a chance. It ended up that I bought the music box for about half the asking price plus 2 American cigarettes, which the chief had on him. The chief saved me several dollars on the transaction.

I enjoyed my liberty with Chief Judd my last night in Japan. He was a great fellow and a great friend. Unfortunately, I never saw him again after that last liberty in Yokosuka.

I gave the music box to my mother 2 or 3 years after I got back home. That wasn't exactly what I planned to do with it, but that is what I did. Then, after my mother died years later, I gave it to my daughter, Lauren. She still has it and it is now over 50 years old. It is now beginning to show its age, though. Where have the years gone? They went by so fast.

The Bole and the other ships of DesRon 7 departed Yokosuka early Friday morning, 28 October, en route to San Diego via Midway Island and Pearl Harbor. I got my last look at Mt. Fuji as we were steaming out of Tokyo Bay. I wouldn't see it again for many years. I was now part of the crew, was standing signal watches, and would stand them all the way across the Pacific Ocean. The ships just steamed along toward Midway Island at 17 knots and didn't do much of anything else. It took us 6 days to get to Midway.

## Promoted to 2nd Class Petty Officer

I received an interesting message from Captain Whitehurst of the Brush on, 29 October, 1955, 2 days out of Japan. The message informed me that I had been promoted to Quartermaster 2nd Class, effective, 10 November. He also congratulated me on the promotion. I was happy to receive the message even though I was only going to be 2nd Class for a few days before being released from active duty. However, I still had 4 years of naval reserve to serve before actually being discharged from the navy. And I served one of those years in the active reserve as quartermaster 2nd class. I found that 2nd class petty officer has a certain amount of prestige attached to it, as well as somewhat more money. I had some 2nd class stripes sewed on my sleeve when I got to San Diego. But I wish I had had a picture taken of myself in a photography shop, too, with my new stripes, but I didn't think about doing that. Captain Whitehurst had tried hard to get me to re-enlist in the navy but that was to no avail. I had had enough of the navy and destroyer duty.

I had an interesting encounter with an old acquaintance on the Bole when we were crossing the Pacific. I met a fellow I went through boot camp with who was also riding the Bole back to the States to be released from the navy. This was a fellow by the name of Harry Pearce. He was from South Georgia and we were inducted into the navy together in Jacksonville, Florida. He was glad to be going home, too.

The ships arrived at Midway around 0730 Wednesday morning, 2 November. The Bole moored starboard side to pier 1 at 0805. At 0910 she commenced receiving fuel and at 1137 she completed refueling. She received on board 103,540 gallons of Navy Standard Fuel Oil. After refueling, the ships left the lagoon. Upon reaching the open ocean, the ships got back into formation and proceeded on to Pearl Harbor, which would take about 2 days. Again, the ships just steamed along without doing much of anything in the way of drills and exercises. Although, they did conduct a full power run for about

4 hours Thursday morning. And Friday morning they conducted a 15 knot economy run for about 6 hours. But most of the crew wasn't involved in any of that.

DesRon 7 arrived at Pearl Harbor Saturday morning, 5 November. The Bole moored port side to berth M-2 at 0828. We stayed in Pearl Harbor for 2 days. The only thing I remember about going ashore this time in Hawaii was having supper Sunday evening at the Wagon Wheel Restaurant on Waikiki Beach. I had my sunset dinner and came back to the ship. I suppose I was more excited about going home than anything else, and I didn't stay on the beach very long. When I got back to the ship that night, around 2000, I never dreamed that I would never see Hawaii again. I thought I would be going back there occasionally throughout my life but it never happened that way. It has been my observation that Hawaii has a special charm of its own, and I doubt if there is another place in the world quite like it. Although, I know that there are other places in the world with their own special charms.

## Serving on the John A. Bole

I found that duty on the Bole was somewhat different than that on the Brush in some respects. For one thing, duty was much less stressful on the Bole. The Bole and the other ships of the squadron didn't feel like it was necessary to conduct tactical maneuvers, various exercises, and shipboard drills every time they got underway, which was usually done in DesDiv 92. In my opinion, those things were just overdone in DesDiv 92.

In addition, there wasn't nearly as much visual signaling taking place in DesRon 7. Instead, the shortwave radio in the pilothouse was used a great deal to convey messages between ships instead of using flashing light and flaghoist all the time as was done in DesDiv 92. I only remember seeing the shortwave radio on the Brush used once or twice during the 3 years I was aboard her. I learned on the Bole that communicating between ships by means of a shortwave radio was a much easier and faster way than using flashing light and flaghoist all the time. DesRon 7 crossed the Pacific Ocean, homeward bound, without conducting any tactical maneuvers, exercises, or shipboard drills according to the ship's log. That kind of cruising was seldom done for any length of time in DesDiv 92 unless it was simply too rough to do anything else.

In addition, in my opinion, the food served on the Bole was much better than that served on the Brush for the entire 3 years and 2 months that I was aboard her. I hate to criticize my old ship, the Brush, but that is just the way it was. As I remember, the Bole always had 2 entrees at each meal and they served man-size portions, too. Consequently, I don't believe anyone could have ever gone hungry based on what I experienced. The Bole even served fried shrimp at one noon meal. I never once saw any of those on the Brush. They even served hominy one time, which, I believe, is supposed to be a Southern dish, although, I had never seen any or eaten any before. Anyway, that was the closest thing to Southern food that I saw in the navy. I don't remember ever hearing anyone complaining about the food on the Bole. I don't believe I would have complained about it either if I had served on the ship. In fact, I was rather impressed with the quality of it, and I thought the chow was as good as could be expected on a small ship that stayed at sea most of the time.

I got to be friends with some of the Bole's crew, although, I've forgotten most of their names. One of the fellows that I do remember, though, was Ken Binkley QM3/C. He was from North Carolina. I planned to go see him after he got out of the navy, but I never did because I got too busy with my own life and never had time to go see him or anybody else much.

I also got to be good friends with one of the Bole's officers, and we even went on liberty together one night after we got to San Diego. We had one big thing in common – the desire to get out of the navy. I was in the process of getting out and he soon would be. He was the Bole's communications officer, and I had a few conversations with him on the ship from time to time. His name was E.J. Robrecht, Jr. Lt(jg). He was from New Jersey. We even exchanged letters after I got out of the navy. He soon got out of the navy, too, and got a job with a company that sent him to the heart of Africa because he could speak French. The letters quit coming while he was down there during a time of great turmoil in the region. I've always thought he must have met with great misfortune down there, because he was concerned about his safety somewhat in one of the last letters that I got from him.

## Search and Rescue Mission

The ships of DesRon 7 departed Pearl Harbor Monday morning, 7 November, en route to San Diego. The ships steamed toward San Diego for 3 days without doing anything else and without any incidents. But around 2000, Wednesday, 9 November, the ships received word that an airplane, a C-119 U.S. Air Force plane, had crashed in the ocean some 300 miles behind us, and DesRon 7 was given orders to go back to the crash site and look for survivors. Five men had bailed out of the plane and were in the water. Apparently, we were the closest ships to the crash. The ships steamed all night at 27 knots back toward the crash site. We arrived at the search area around 0800 Thursday morning, 10 November. However, sometime before we arrived on the scene, 4 of the airmen had been found and rescued, I suppose by a seaplane, but one of the men couldn't be located. So that is what we had to do – look for that one man. At 0835 the ships reduced speed and formed a scouting line to search for that one man. Two merchant ships and another naval vessel joined us in the search. The ships searched all day Thursday and half the day Friday for that one man but never found him. Nor did any of the ships find anything, like debris, that could have come from the plane. We didn't find any parachutes either. Maybe the sharks got him.

At 1236 Friday, 11 November, the ships reversed course and steamed back toward San Diego. The search and rescue mission put us 2 days behind schedule getting to port. Consequently, the ships arrived in San Diego Tuesday morning instead of Sunday morning. The ships steamed toward San Diego for the next 3 ½ days without any more incidents and without doing anything else. The ships arrived at San Diego around 0930 Tuesday, 15 November. At 1014 the Bole was moored port side to the South Broadway Pier. A little later in the morning I was transferred over to the San Diego Naval Receiving Center to be processed out of the navy. My seafaring days were over.

# 12

# BACK IN THE STATES

It took 7 days for the receiving center to process me out of the navy. To occupy our time while we were there, the center assigned us, those who were being released from active duty, little piddling projects to do, things you would normally expect a seaman apprentice to do. But nobody cared particularly because we were very short-timers. Actually, we had relatively short work hours – like until early afternoon. Then, we were allowed to go on liberty. I know we were assigned a bunk in the barracks, which was nice enough, but I don't remember a thing about the chow hall or the chow they fed us; that has totally left my mind.

I got on a bus Friday afternoon and I went up to Hawthorne, California and spend the week-end with the Randall family. When I arrived at their place, I got a very pleasant surprise. Beuford and Elouise were going on vacation to Florida, and they scheduled their vacation so that they could take me home when I got out of the navy. Wasn't that great and thoughtful of them to do that? That is what you call a real friend, and I will always be indebted to them for doing that and the many other things they did for me while I was in California.

I was released from active duty in the U.S. Navy, Tuesday morning, November 22, 1955. I went back up to the Randall family home and arrived there sometime in the early afternoon, and a few hours later, in the late afternoon, we left for Florida. Beuford did all the driving and he drove both day and night for 3 days and 4 nights except for one relatively brief stop for 6 hours, maybe, so that he could get some rest and a little sleep. I don't know how a person could drive that long without any sleep to speak of, but it didn't seem to bother him or affect his alertness and driving ability. Thanksgiving day we were in central Texas somewhere. Thanksgiving dinner for me was a turkey sandwich in a restaurant. We did very little stopping except to eat and go to the restrooms. We did stop alongside the road a few times when we were going through the desert when we saw some exceptionally pretty scenery. And I took a few pictures when we stopped at those places.

## ARRIVING HOME

My mother and father knew that I was coming home, but they just didn't know exactly when it would be. I didn't know either, but we finally arrived in the front yard of my old home place around 5:30 a.m., Saturday morning, November 26, 1955. It was still dark. My home had a big, old fashion front porch. I went up on the porch and roused my folks out of bed, and just as soon as they could get dressed, they came to the front door to let me in. However, Beuford and Elouise went to the door with me to meet them and to claim credit for delivering me safely back home. They chatted a minute or two with my folks, but they soon left and went down the road a couple of miles to his Uncle Oliver Randall's house which was their destination. I suppose that they got their relatives up at an early hour, too.

My parents and I didn't go into the house immediately, however. Before actually making a motion in that direction, my mother asked me, "Do you want to come in the house, or would you rather stay out here on the porch for awhile?" I said, "I believe I would like to stay out here for awhile," and we did. I don't know why she suggested such a thing, but it seemed like a good idea to me after she brought it up. Anyway, they sat down in some rocking chairs that were there. But, for some reason, I decided that I didn't want to sit in a chair. Instead, I sat on the edge of the porch with my legs hanging off and with my back toward them somewhat. I don't know why I wanted to sit there that way. I've never felt the need to do that again. It was still dark, although, there was enough light coming from inside the house that enabled us to faintly see each other. Nothing much was said by anybody, as I remember. They might have said something to me to which I didn't respond so they didn't try to talk to me anymore. They also must have sensed that I was going through some kind of mental thing, because I seemed to be deep in thought and my mind seemed to be far away. So, we sat there in the semi-darkness, in silence, for several minutes. I know that I was thinking about at least 2 things. I was trying to adjust to the idea and reality of being back home. And, I also was thinking about my ship, the Brush, the ship that had been my home for over 3 years. I knew it was steaming around somewhere in the Far East without me. I wondered where she was and what she was doing at that moment. The Brush had been my little world for over 3 years, but now, I was no longer on her and my seafaring days were over. I also knew that I would probably never see her again. That was kind of a strange feeling. I think I was experiencing both gladness and sadness at the same time. I was wondering who would assume my duties on the signal bridge, in the charthouse, and at the wheel. Who would be the ship's "special sea detail helmsman"? The navy would certainly find someone to assume my duties; that was something I didn't have to worry about.

After a few minutes my mother interrupted my thoughts by asking me, "Would you like to have a cup of coffee?" I answered her, "Yes, I believe I would." She got up out of her chair and went into the house to make the coffee. I continued to sit there on the edge of the porch in the dark. My father never tried to make any conversation with me but remained silent and let me continue with my thoughts. My thoughts were interrupted from time to time by a cricket nearby that was attempting to serenade me. That was a sound that I hadn't heard for a long time and it was rather pleasant to hear once again.

In a few minutes my mother returned with my coffee, handed it to me, and then sat back down in her chair. They remained silent. I sat there on the edge of the porch and sipped my coffee. A feeling of relaxation began to come over me. It felt like a great weight was being lifted from my shoulders. I had lived a very stressful life for over 3 years, like most people can't even imagine, and now, I fully began to realize that part of my life was over; I was returning to the real world and my nerves began to relax for the first time in years. However, at the time I didn't realize that it was going to take months, and maybe even years, for me to adjust to civilian life. Over the next few months, especially, I experienced a lot of "the shakes" and a lot of "knots" in my stomach. However, I suffered in silence. I never told anybody what I was going through, and I don't think anyone suspected that I was except my mother. She knew to some extent but there was nothing she could do to help me. It was something I had to handle all by myself. In addition, I really didn't know how to act in a civilized society. Looking back on that period of time in my life, and my interactions with people, I realize now, and have for a long time, that I made a lot of social blunders. And if I had the chance to do things over, I would handle a number of situations differently. But, of course, I know that can never happen. I will just have to live with the mistakes I made back then. I know a lot of my decisions and actions were influenced by the fact that I felt like I had totally missed out on much of my youth, in fact, the very heart of it. At the time in life that most young men are highly engaged in romantic endeavors and the pursuit of happiness, I was totally out of circulation – for 4 years. Uncle Sam had more important things for me to do far from home and hearth. Time goes by rather slowly when a person is young. I feel like those 3 years at sea was equal to 10 years in today's time.

Back to the porch: Some birds nearby began to chirp, stir, and announce the arrival of a new day. I sat there on the edge of the porch, sipped my coffee, and watched the night turn into day. The dawn developed into a beautiful, clear morning and without a breath of air stirring like so many are in Florida in the fall of the year.

A little after the break of dawn, my mother got up and announced that she was going into the kitchen to fix breakfast – bacon and eggs, I'm sure it was. In a few minutes she came back to the front door and let us know that breakfast was ready, and to come in and get it. I got up and went into the house to have my breakfast – at home. The adventure was over and I was glad and relieved. It was good to be back home.

**Ted Holly**
Arriving Home as QM2/C

# EPILOGUE

I want to end my story with a poem that was written by a Mr. Frank L. Johnson who is from the great state of Ohio. Mr. Johnson served on the Brush during 1945-1946. He left the Brush and the navy when the war was over and assumed the life of a civilian, a landlubber's life, if you will, and never was on the ocean for many years. But in April, 1996, Mr. Johnson did go to sea again on a Russian cruise ship. While he was on this cruise, and I believe it was on an Easter Sunday, he got the inspiration to write a poem that reflected his thoughts and feelings about his seafaring days many years before when he was a young man. The words that he jotted down that day probably express the same thoughts and feelings of many other sailors that served on the Brush, other destroyers, and perhaps other ships, too. So, on the following page, I thought it fitting to end my story with the words of Mr. Frank L. Johnson – an old sailor.

**The Lone Sailor**

**On An Ocean I Have Trod**

by Frank Johnson,
13 April, 1996
Salaverry Port, Peru

I've had my chance to sail again
Aboard a mighty ship,
To feel the deck beneath my feet
And sense the sway and dip,
To watch the waves o'er long bow break
And know again the fantail wake,
To brace my legs and hold on tight
As mighty waves impede her flight
To think of those who went before,
Of those who sank to ocean's floor,
They slipped beneath a spangled sheet,
Cast o'erboard with weighted feet,
Mid battles booming and cannon roar,
With kamikazes, flames and more.
Now peaceful, tranquil, quiet sea
With bird and sun and God and me,
I pledge allegiance to all of these
And to all the creatures of the seas;
To dolphins rising in the air,
To soaring birds from everywhere.
I've watched again the sun come up
At quiet break of day,
The lazy calming of the sea
Where flying fishes play.
And, oh, the stars, those brilliant stars
Who guide the sailor's plight
And, oh, the moon with shimmering rays
Cast on a starless night.
How small is man in all of this?
I stand in awe, in total bliss,
Again on ocean I have trod;
This Holy Day, I thank you God.

# ABOUT THE AUTHOR: OTIS TED HOLLY, MAg, BSA, BS

The author went to college after leaving the navy. He first attended Stetson University in DeLand, Florida for 3 semesters, but he then transferred to the University of Florida in order to major in Geology. He thought it would be interesting to roam around remote areas of the world hunting valuable mineral deposits. He graduated from the University of Florida in January, 1960, with a Bachelor of Science Degree in Geology. However, after graduating from college, he soon realized that his dream in the field of Geology was never going to take place because there wasn't a job to be had in the entire world. Consequently, he went back to college and majored in a different field. He graduated from the University of Florida again in August, 1963, with a Bachelor of Science Degree in Agriculture with a major in Soil Science. And, in August, 1964, he graduated with a Master of Agriculture Degree in Soil Science. Thus, he finished his formal education with 2 bachelor degrees and a master's degree.

In the early 1960's the author worked 2 ½ years for the U.S. Geological Survey in the field of surface water resources, mainly measuring stream flows and determining watershed areas in Central and North Florida.

Also, in the early 1960's he worked 2 years in South Florida for the U.S.D.A. Soil Conservation Service as a Soil Surveyor, which entailed identifying soil types in the field and making soil maps for land use purposes.

In June, 1966, the author took a sales job with Wilson & Toomer Fertilizer Company out of Jacksonville, Florida recommending and selling fertilizer and pesticides to citrus growers and other farmers in the Central Florida area, but primarily in Volusia and Putnam counties. He lived in DeLand, Florida and worked out of his house. Wilson and Toomer was a great company, but they were bought by another company in 1970. However, the author stayed with the fertilizer business and worked with 3 other fertilizer companies over the years including Kerr-McGee Chemical Corporation, Florida Favorite Fertilizer Company, and Diamond-R Fertilizer Company. The fertilizer business was a great way to make a living in many ways including a lot of freedom to do as you pleased on a daily basis. However, severe freezes in December, 1983, and January, 1985, essentially wiped out the long standing citrus industry in North and Central Florida and all of the fertilizer and pesticide business that was associated with it. So much for global warming. Consequently, the author had to find another occupation. In 1986, he went into the agricultural consulting business specializing in the areas of soil fertility, plant nutrition, and fertilizer. He then worked with other crops in Central Florida but mainly with ornamental ferns. He has been involved in that occupation ever since. He is essentially retired now, though, and lives in the old family home in Marion County, Florida.

The author married a wonderful woman in 1961, had 3 children, and now has 4 grandchildren to brag about.

CPSIA information can be obtained
at www.ICGtesting.com
Printed in the USA
BVHW021235250123
657012BV00008B/494